PAUL
The Apostle

PAUL
The Apostle

BY

GIUSEPPE RICCIOTTI

(TRANSLATED BY ALBA I. ZIZZAMIA)

THE BRUCE PUBLISHING COMPANY
MILWAUKEE

NIHIL OBSTAT:

    REV. PASCHAL PARENTE
    Censor deputatus

IMPRIMATUR:

    ✠ HENRY J. O'BRIEN, D.D.
    Bishop of Hartford

June 18, 1952

Author's Preface

It is said that during the famous Sack of Rome in 1527, the celebrated Cardinal Cajetan remained unperturbed at home and calmly continued to write his theological treatises. Outside, the lansquenets were killing, plundering, and burning, faithful to the traditions of their ancestors, the Goths of Alaric and the Vandals of Genseric, who in their time had performed a similar service for Rome. His attitude, however, was not due to any lack of feeling or sensitivity, but was rather a reaction and a protest. The Cardinal could accomplish nothing against the halberds and harquebuses of the German mercenaries. He understood very well, however, that those barbarians, in addition to some atavistic instinct, were motivated by certain racial and religious concepts. Unable to fight against their halberds, he fought against their ideas, and so continued his writings until he was taken prisoner.

This book in large measure was written in similar circumstances, that is, during the new Sack of Rome carried out by the Nazis from September, 1943, to June, 1944. . . . During this time my house was filled with Jewish and other refugees from death. For them and still others hidden elsewhere it was necessary to provide food. We were watched and trailed with every likelihood of ending up in one of the scientific torture chambers the Nazis had set up in the city. But all went well and we were not discovered. Nevertheless, after this small effort on behalf of the persecuted it seemed something should be done for the unhappy persecutors by fighting the ideas which inspired them and which were quite the same as those of the lansquenets of Cardinal Cajetan's time. . . .

And so I imitated the good Cardinal by setting to work on St. Paul. If at that time Hitler could have laid hands on Paul, he would have beheaded him all over again both because he was a Jew and because he had dared to declare that before God a Jew was as good as a German or any other Aryan. This *furor teutonicus* of Hitler was good reason to set against it the compelling serenity of St. Paul. If the world was to rise from its ruins it would have to turn to the tenets of Paul, certainly not to those of Hitler.

At the beginning of World War II, I had published the *Life of Christ*, and the extraordinary success it encountered in Italy and abroad indicated I was on the right road. It seemed I should continue for the disciple the work I had done on the Master. Thus I would bring to a close the series that had evolved, although without a pre-established plan, that is, the *History of Israel*[1] together with the translation of *Flavius Josephus* with a commentary, then the *Life of Christ*, and now finally *Paul the Apostle*.

The criteria for this book are the same as those I outlined in the preface to the *Life of Christ*. For the sake of brevity, I have referred the reader to the *History of Israel* and the *Life of Christ*[2] where necessary to avoid repeating the same material.

It has been my intention to write a critical biography. While it is naturally impossible to discuss St. Paul without discussing his thought, since his life is nothing but his thought in action, I have not tried to present a "systematic" exposition of St. Paul's thought, which would in fact have required another volume. For this, the reader may wish to refer to *Il pensiero di S. Paolo* by L. Fondelli, Milan, 1928, and to F. Prat's *La Theologie de S. Paul*, Volume 2.

G. R.

Rome, 1946

---

[1] English translation in preparation.
[2] Page references are to the unabridged edition [Trans.].

Author's Acknowledgments

The author gratefully expresses his appreciation to Prof. Arnaldo Malpiere for the sketch of St. Paul on the jacket of the original, the general theme of which was adopted on the jacket of the present English Edition, and to Prof. Centini for the maps and diagrams he prepared. The author's thanks are due to the Very Rev. Mariano Cordovani, *Magister S. Palatii*, for reading the manuscript and for the improvements he kindly suggested; for other suggestions the author is indebted to his colleague Rev. Angelo Penna, who has himself recently published a book on St. Paul.

G. R.

Translator's Note

The present translation has been edited and all quotations from Hebrew, Greek, and other texts have been checked by the Rev. Patrick Skehan, Professor of Semitic Languages, Catholic University of America, Washington, D. C., to whom the translator is deeply grateful.

ALBA ZIZZAMIA

Hartford, Conn.
October 4, 1952

Acknowledgments

Most of the New Testament quotations in this book are from *The New Testament of Our Lord and Savior Jesus Christ — a Revision of the Challoner-Rheims Version,* by license of The Confraternity of Christian Doctrine, owner of the copyright.

The texts of Acts 27:39–40; Hebrews 12:2; 2 Tim. 4:6; 2 Cor. 12:10; and Ephes. 3:4–9 are from *The New Testament,* by Rev. F. A. Spencer, O.P. (1937). By permission of the Macmillan Co., publishers.

Contents

Introduction

I

Geographical Background

TARSUS

1. The great peninsula of Asia Minor looks, on the map, like the upper part of a human arm raised horizontally and pointing toward the west. Close to the armpit — or at the angle where the peninsula joins the continent — lies Tarsus, the fatherland of Paul the Apostle and the ancient capital of Cilicia.[1]

Today those coming by sea arrive in the very commonplace port of Mersina and, after a journey through some 20 miles of almost desert country, reach Tarsus. It is a dismal little Turkish town of about 22,000 inhabitants, with no hotel and no European conveniences. The hill on which it rises tacks on to the last foothills of the Taurus Mountains. The river Cydnus, which flows by at a short distance from the city, has piled up so much silt through the centuries that it has cut Tarsus off from its ancient seaport, whose place today is supplied by Mersina.

2. The origin of Tarsus is as ancient as it is obscure. It goes back perhaps to the time of the decadence of the Hittite empire. Its name appears for the first time on the Black Obelisk of Salmanassar III, about the middle of the ninth century B.C., and from then on its history, despite wide gaps here and there, can be traced down to modern times. The various dominations which succeeded one another in this commercial center of Asia Minor each left its mark upon it. The Aryan Persians followed the Semitic Assyrians, who were followed in turn by the Greeks and then the Romans. The Greeks happily wove the origin of Tarsus into one of their own legends, linking it with the mythical heroes of the Homeric poems. Coins of the time of Caracalla confirm the legend handed down by Strabo (XIV, 5, 12), which speaks of the ancient Argive companions of Tryptolemus as the founders of the city. Lucan (*Pharsalia*, III, 225) associates it with the myth of Perseus.

Xenophon, who marched through Tarsus with Cyrus the Younger, called it "a great and happy city" (*Anabasis*, 1, 2, 23). But the troops of the Persian prince sacked it because it held the palace of Xiennes,

---

[1] For this whole chapter see map at the end of the book.

3

Tarsus Today

sovereign of Cilicia, faithful to the king of kings of Persia. With his victory over the pirates (67 B.C.), Pompey the Great added Cilicia and its capital Tarsus definitively to the Roman Empire. Tarsus remained constant in its fidelity to Julius Caesar, receiving as a consequence the name *Juliopolis,* and it stayed on the side of the imperial party even when the republicans Brutus and Cassius were triumphing in Syria. Mark Antony, who met Cleopatra for the first time on the banks of the Cydnus, granted the city autonomy, and Augustus later increased its privileges. In Apollonia he had been a friend of Athenodorus, an outstanding citizen of Tarsus.

3. Trade brought people from all parts of the world to Tarsus. From its ample harbor, called Rhegma or Rhegmoi, small galleys climbed the gentle current of the Cydnus, past docks and warehouses to the center of the city, for the river flowed through Tarsus until the time of Justinian. The tenacious labor of its citizens kept even the skirt of land

The Falls of the River Cydnus Near Tarsus

between the sea and the city fertile. Today, greatly widened in area, it is a desolate stretch of miasmic swamplands.

Within the city all races of people jostled and mingled, filling the air with their strange tongues. There were the mountaineers from Western or "Rugged" Cilicia (*Tracheia*), Lycaonia, and Cappodocia, who crossed the Taurus Mountains through the Cilician Gates to bring to Tarsus their rough textiles woven of goat's hair, and the peasants of Syria and Mesopotamia who came along the various caravan routes and from the ports of the Mediterranean to barter.

A View of the Taurus Mountains

4. Tarsus, however, was not merely a great market place but also a cultural center which, in certain aspects, surpassed Athens and Alexandria. Her scholars were to be found in many parts of the world. "Rome is full of Tarsians and Alexandrians," said Strabo (XIV, 5, 13, 15), and among those listed by the geographer, we are particularly interested in Athenodorus and Nestor, both Stoic philosophers. The former, son of Sandon, not to be confused with Athenodorus Cordylion, the friend of Cato Uticensis, acquired a certain reputation as a philosopher. Cicero studied his writings in composing the *De Officiis,* and Seneca quoted with warm praise certain of his maxims, which would seem to have been written by a Christian moralist (*De tranquillitate animi,* 3; *Ad Lucilium,* 1, 10, 5). Augustus, as a mark of esteem and a reward, sent Athenodorus to Tarsus at the beginning of the Christian Era to reform the corrupt government of Boethus, "a bad poet and a bad citizen" (Strabo, XIV, 5, 14), and the emperor's envoy fulfilled the hopes placed in him. The other Stoic philosopher, Nestor, was also called to the imperial court to act as tutor to the young Marcellus, for whom Virgil wrote his oracular verses (*Aeneid,* VI, 869 ff.).

But the praises addressed to Tarsus by Strabo, Dion Chrysostom, and Ammianus Marcellinus, must be balanced by the criticisms, however exaggerated, of Philostratus, who in his romantic biography of Apollonius of Tyana (1, 7) censures the ostentatious luxury and sloth of the Tarsians.

5. The cosmopolitan character of Tarsus was reflected also in its religion. Indigenous, Assyrian, Persian, and Greek elements were often superimposed one on the other or blended in not always harmonious fashion. A very ancient divinity, perhaps the Anatolian Tarku, figures in it as the supreme lord of Tarsus (*Ba'al Tarz*). Beside him there appears the young energetic god, Sandon, who soon became identified with the Greek Heracles. Every year, as Dion Chrysostom relates (*Tarsica prior*, XXXIII, 47), a huge pyre, on which had been placed the statue of the god, was burned with great solemnity in Tarsus. The first part of the ceremony was funereal in character, but before long the resurrection of the god was celebrated amid uncontrolled frenzies. The ceremony represented the death of plant life under the scorching arrows of the sun and its resurrection to new life.

The Greek *polis*, although it accelerated the process of Hellenization in Tarsus, especially at the time of Antiochus IV Epiphanes, never effaced its original oriental character, and oriental customs still prevailed at the time of St. Paul. When he admonished the women of Corinth to wear veils on their heads in attending religious gatherings (1 Cor. 11:5 ff.), he was probably thinking of the custom in Tarsus, for which we also have the testimony of Dion Chrysostom. The latter, for instance, describes the Tarsian women as walking with modest composure and covered with ample veils (*Tarsica prior*, XXXIII, 48). The *palestra* and *gymnasium*, mentioned by Strabo, helped accentuate the Hellenic influence, but many, and perhaps most of the population remained restive to such innovations and were unmoved by the ideal of Hellenic beauty. Religion in Tarsus, although permeated with elements from the Greek Olympus, was still oriented around the primitive divinities of Anatolia. From the political viewpoint, the city had distinguished itself, it is true, by its attachment to the imperial cause, but it should not be forgotten that Cicero, one of its first governors, treated it with cold neglect. He mentions Tarsus barely a couple of times, although it was the principal city of the region and the headquarters of the *koinon*. Cassius speaks with rancor of the Tarsians as very bad allies (*pessimi socii* — Cicero, *Ad familiares*, XII, 13, 4).

6. The local Jewish community, which must have been quite large, also helped not a little to preserve the basically oriental character of the city. The presence of the Jews in Tarsus is connected with the vast movement of the Diaspora,[2] of which the capital of Cilicia must have been an important center because of its extremely active trade. If we agree with Ramsay[3] that the greatest increase in the Jewish colony of Tarsus occurred under Antiochus IV Epiphanes, we must conclude that it was composed for the most part of Jews with Hellenic sympathies,

---

[2] Cf. *Storia d'Israele*, Vol. II, p. 203 ff. (§ 180 ff.).
[3] W. Ramsay, *The Cities of St. Paul*, London, 1907, p. 173 ff.

given the well-known sentiments of the king. When he re-established order in Tarsus (2 Mach. 4:30 ff.), we may suppose he also recognized the Jews as a distinct "tribe" in the polity since a Jew of the strict observance could not consider himself a member of a pagan tribe. And finally, the Romans granted the individual members the right of Roman citizenship. Therefore the "kinsmen" (συγγενεῖς) of Paul, who appear in *Romans* (16:7, 11, 21), would be members of such a tribe. Other explanations of Paul's citizenship have been offered, however.

In short, Tarsus, with its world trade, its oriental traditions, its learned Hellenists, its Roman functionaries, and its Stoic and Cynic philosophers, who lingered in its busy agora or along the banks of the silent Cydnus in erudite discussion, was a true cosmopolitan city in the best period of the Roman Empire.

CILICIA

7. Tarsus was the principal city of the region of Cilicia. This was divided geologically into two districts: the Cilician Plain (Πεδιάς, *Campestris*) which extended toward the east between the Taurus Mountains and the sea as far as Mount Amanus and toward the west as far as the city of Soli (famous in antiquity for the *solecisms* or ungrammatical vagaries of its dialect), and "Rugged" Cilicia (Τραχεῖα, *Aspera*), which stretched from Soli in a westerly direction toward Pamphylia.

A Pass in the Taurus Mountains

Substantially Cilicia comprised about one half the southern coast of Asia Minor from the angle where the latter projects westward from the continent.

The eastern part of Cilicia, crossed by the rivers Sarus (modern *Seyhan Irmac*) and Pyramus (*Jihun Nehri*), was in close contact with nearby Syria, which was reached through two passes in the Amanus Mountains, one above Antioch called the Syrian Gates (Σύριαι Πύλαι), and the other farther north called the Amanus

Gates. Crossing the Taurus Mountains presented much greater difficulties. This long and compact mountain range, rising not far from the coast which faces the island of Cyprus, marks a clean-cut division between the coastal strip and the interior of Asia Minor. Only toward the east, where the height of the mountains decreases somewhat as they slope toward the Antitaurus is there a pass, called in ancient times the Cilician Gates (Κιλίκιαι Πύλαι). It is the modern Gülek Bogaz, about 3570 feet above sea level. This was the principal means of communication with the northern and eastern regions of Cilicia. But either because of the wildness of the place or the nasty reputation of the thieves nesting in the mountain caves of the region, the pass was usually practicable only in the summertime when there was no snow, as Cicero tells us in one of his letters (*Ad Atticum*, V, 21, 14).

8. The alluvial lands which form the greater part of the Cilician Plain are suitable for almost all types of Mediterranean cultivation. In ancient times, when there were wide stretches of woodland around the Amanus, the cultivable area was undoubtedly more extensive than it is today, surrounded as it is by broad steppes. Adana, in addition to Tarsus, was an important commercial center in ancient times.

Rugged Cilicia, which shared an indefinite frontier with Isauria and Pamphylia, has always been less populated than the Cilician Plain because of its impassable mountains and steep ravines. In the north, tower the Taurus Mountains of Cilicia, which with the peak of the Bulgar Dagh reach a height of 11,570 feet above sea level. The wild, bleak aspect of the region is accentuated by the solitude and the higher one goes the rarer the vegetation becomes until it finally disappears altogether. In the more accessible areas, however, there are stretches of forest and of the famous Lebanon cedars. The region is poor in water. Only the Gök Su, ancient Calycadnus, where Frederick Barbarossa met his death, forms a good water basin, and the vegetation is luxuriant in certain of the coastal areas. The climate varies greatly with the seasons and from one area to another.

9. The population is also heterogeneous. There was a constant fusion of the different races and cultures from the time of the Assyrian Kings, whose inscriptions boast that they had carried their conquests as far as distant *Kilakku* (Cilicia). The indigenous Anatolians were blended successively with the Semite Assyrians, the Aryan Persians, then to a much larger extent with the Greeks and finally with the Romans. Notwithstanding previous contacts with the Greek world, it is only after Alexander the Great that one may speak of an effective Hellenization of the region, and this became more pronounced under the various successors of the Macedonian conqueror. They were replaced by the Romans, who, however, did not bring the influence of their own culture to bear until later.

Rome began to take a direct interest in these regions toward the end of the second century B.C. when the death of King Attalus III of Pergamum (133 B.C.) made her mistress of most of Asia Minor. The pirates constantly plagued Rome's growing sea power, provoking repeated interventions on her part especially in Rugged Cilicia, where these sea plunderers had their lair. The best Roman generals like Metellus, Sulla, Servilius Vatia, who was given by decree the epithet Isauricus, down to the more fortunate Pompey, who ended the persistent struggle, worked hard to drive the pirates from their impenetrable fastnesses. Cicero was one of the first administrators of the new Roman province, which he held as proconsul in 51–50 B.C. but with little satisfaction. After various other alternatives, Cilicia, it seems, was joined by Augustus to the province of Syria. This juridical status remained unchanged, generally speaking, during the first century A.D. but at the same time the autonomy of several principalities, like that of Olba in the Taurus Mountains north of Soli, was recognized. For a short time, Rugged Cilicia was subject to the king of Cappadocia, Archelaus, and then to the ruler of Commagene.

PAMPHYLIA-LYCIA

10. The regions to the north and west of Cilicia form the rest of the great peninsula of Asia Minor, also called Anatolia from the tenth century A.D. This vast tableland, with its many mountain ranges and extremely irregular western coastline, measures about 400,000 square miles. It is over 900 miles long and from 400 to 550 miles wide. In general, it has greatly deteriorated from what it was in ancient times, and under the Turkish domination the area of swampy and unwholesome waste-

Adalia: The Harbor

land has greatly increased. We shall here review briefly the regions most closely associated with our subject.

On the southern coast immediately west of Cilicia lies Pamphylia, bounded on the north by Pisidia and on the west by Lycia. Marshes and swamplands cover part of the coastal area and render it quite unhealthy. Part of the year a few nomad shepherds are to be found wandering across the bogs, where malaria rages during the summer. In certain places at the westernmost end of the Pamphylian coast and in the inland region among the mountains opposite Pisidia, the climate is healthier, and good vegetation, fruit orchards, cultivated fields, and little villages are to be found there. Along the shore line, the only pretty view is offered by the bay of Adalia, with its luxuriant groves of citrus trees. This charming little city was in Roman times, as it is today, the only important center in a half-empty region.

We have very ancient data for Pamphylia, as for the other regions of Asia Minor. It, too, underwent various successive dominations through the centuries and, after the death of Attalus, king of Pergamum, it came under Roman rule. The Romans added it at first to the province of Cilicia, then to that of Syria, and finally the emperor Claudius formed the province of Lycia-Pamphylia, uniting these two contiguous regions. In the first century A.D. the principal cities of Pamphylia were Side, considered perhaps the metropolis, Perge, famous for its temple of Diana Pergea, and finally Adalia, which supplied the only harbor in the region. Today Adalia is the capital of the *vilâyet* of Antalya, which extends into part of ancient Lycia.

11. The tiny region of Lycia, bounded by Pamphylia, Pisidia, Caria, and the sea, consists of a rocky tableland crossed by deep valleys and stretches of savanna. It has practically no roads and its scanty population is scattered through small towns, none of which have any importance. In the first century A.D. Lycia still preserved traces of a very ancient pre-Hellenic culture with its own language, a few inscriptions of which are still extant. Under the Roman Empire it suffered severely in the struggles that followed the death of Caesar, but then Augustus showed it favor because of its fidelity to the cause of the dictator. In A.D. 43 Claudius, as we noted, merged Lycia and Pamphylia into one province, which underwent a number of changes until Vespasian reconstituted it an imperial province. Tacitus mentions as governor of the Lycians in the time of Nero a certain Eprius Marcellus, whose subjects filed a complaint against him before the emperor (*Annal.*, XIII, 33).

In ancient times, ships sailing from the Phoenician or Egyptian shores often docked in the port of Myra for shelter against the storms whipped up by the winds from the west. Situated at the mouth of the river Andriace (today *Andraki*), Myra was the capital and the best harbor in the region. A little farther west, Patara, opposite the islet of Castlerosso and near the mouth of the Xanthus, was another little refuge for sailors along the tall, steep coasts of Lycia.

THE PROVINCE OF ASIA

12. At the beginning of the first century A.D., the western part of Asia Minor, which extended north from Lycia and Pisidia, formed the Roman province of Asia Minor. It was bounded on the south by the Indus River, which separated it from Lycia, and on the north by the Propontis and an irregular frontier extending from Cyzicus to Dorylaeum, north of which lay the province of Bithynia. Even more uncertain and wavering was its eastern boundary, which separated the province of Asia from Galatia, properly so called, and Lycaonia.

This broad territory could be considered unified administratively and also by a wide and more profound Hellenization than had taken place in adjacent regions. But even then the various ethnic groups living in the province were clearly distinguishable, many of whom could boast a very ancient and glorious history.

In the southernmost part, between the Indus (today *Dalaman*) and the Great Meander (*Mendere*), lay Caria. Its unhealthy climate and lack of roads have made it an almost deserted region. In ancient times its coastal areas, today swampy and unwholesome, bore towns and villages which flourished through trade and the cultivation of the surrounding valleys. Conspicuous among them was Miletus, which the muddy waters of the Meander later cut off from the sea thus causing its rapid decline, and Halicarnassus, the ancient Doric colony opposite the Island of Cos. The former, according to Pliny (*Nat. Hist.*, V, 31 al. 29), was the capital of Ionia and had colonies scattered a little everywhere as far as the Black Sea and the Sea of Marmara. While Greeks, particularly of Ionian origin, had predominated for centuries along the coast and the adjacent islands, in the interior the descendants of the ancient Carii, famous for the warlike character which made them good mercenary soldiers, were still to be found at the time of the Roman Empire. Only a few traces remain of the indigenous language they spoke before Greek took its place. It was quite like the Lycian, and pre-Indo-European. Homer described the Carii as "a people of barbarous speech" (βαρβαρόφων ι, *Iliad*, II, 867).

13. On the other hand, Lydia, the region lying between Caria, Mysia, and Phrygia, with uncertain and frequently changing boundaries, had been almost completely Hellenized even before the time of Alexander. This rich region, which held the basins of the Cayster and the Hermus (today the *Kuchuk Mendere* and the *Gediz Chai*), owed its importance to the fact that it formed the natural passage between the European continent and Asia. In ancient times a very brisk trade was carried on through the coastal cities of Lydia, almost all of them old Greek colonies. The most famous were Ephesus, Colophon, Clazomenae, Smyrna, and Magnesia, the modern Manisa, at the base of the Sipylus, near which the Romans won their famous victory over Antiochus III the Great of Syria (190 B.C.). In the interior, Sardis, on the slopes of Mount Tmolus, had been the capital of the Lydian kingdom, but it had lost its pre-eminence as the neighboring cities became more flourishing, especially Ephesus and Pergamum.

The wonders which classical writers recount of Ephesus have been verified in part by the recent excavations made in the region, which is today quite desolate and at some distance from the sea because of the sand piled up by the Cayster. Among other discoveries, we have the monumental ruins of the theater built against the western slope of Mount Pion at the end of the main street of the city (named *Via Arcadiana* at the time of Emperor Arcadius). In this spacious theater, which could hold approximately 23,000 persons, an incident occurred fraught with danger for the Apostle Paul (§ 468 ff.). Many other edifices adorned the capital of the province of Asia: a Greek agora to the south of the theater with a great clock which was probably hydraulic, another Roman agora with porticoes and vestibules, several gymnasia, a stadium, and other magnificent structures.

After a long period of wars and other misfortunes, Ephesus again enjoyed a beneficent peace in the reign of Augustus. This emperor's favors almost re-created the time of Lysimachus, the diadochus who greatly contributed to the growth of the city on the Cayster, surround-

Sardis: Ruins

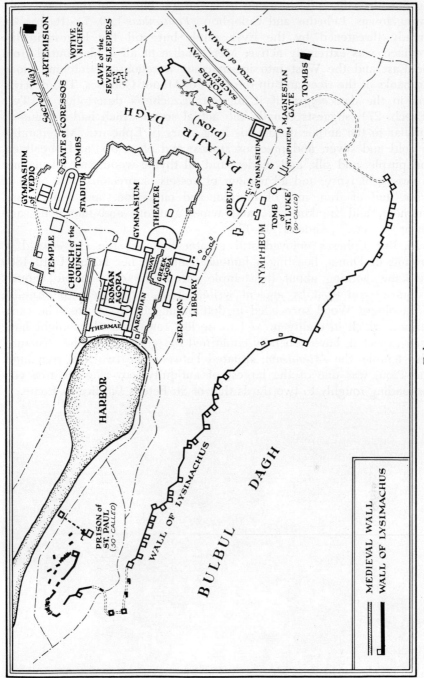

Ephesus

ing it with walls and attracting to it the inhabitants of the two neighboring towns, Lebedus and Colophon (*Pausanias,* 1, 9, 7). Its harbor,
already threatened by the river sands but still the largest in the
province, was extremely active. Merchandise of all kinds poured from
the East and the West into its spacious warehouses stretching along
the banks of the river and up the sides of Mount Coressos. The description in the *Apocalypse,* if it suggests Ezechiel's description of Tyre
(Ezech. 27), suggests equally the actual scene which had become so
familiar to the author during his long years in Ephesus: "Merchandise
of gold and silver, and precious stones; and of pearls, and fine linen,
and purple, and silk, and scarlet, and all thyine wood, and all manner
of vessels of ivory, and all manner of vessels of precious stone, and of
brass, and of iron, and of marble, and cinnamon, and odours, and
ointment, and frankincense, and wine, and oil, and fine flour, and
wheat . . . etc." (Apoc. 17:12–13).

14. But Ephesus enjoyed still greater fame as the city sacred to
Artemis or Diana, boasting a famous temple in her honor. Until 1869
we knew nothing about the temple except the dithyrambic tributes
of praise paid to it by ancient writers, but in that year the English
archaeologist Wood succeeded in determining its exact site. The excavations, which in reality proved to be less rewarding than might have
been expected, have generally confirmed the grandeur of the structure.
This temple, the *Artemision,* situated between the two hills Aya-Soluk
and Pion, was one of the largest of antiquity, covering an area corresponding roughly to two thirds that of St. Peter's Basilica in Rome.

Ephesus: Ruins of Theater and the Via Arcadiana

Its origins are naturally legendary. When in 559 B.C. Croesus captured Ephesus (*Herodotus*, I, 26) he not only spared the city out of respect for its sacred character, but was responsible for a complete remodeling of the temple, which emerged no less splendid than its successor, described for us by Pliny. In the year 356 B.C., in fact, the sumptuous edifice of Croesus' time burned down on the very night on which the goddess — according to the explanation given by the obliging theologians of the time — was assisting at the birth of Alexander the Great. The subsequent reconstruction proceeded very slowly, but left nothing to be desired from the viewpoint of magnificence. This new temple, according to Pliny (*Nat. Hist.*, XXXVI, 21 al. 14) boasted 127 columns donated by as many kings, each 60 feet high and 36 of them with sculptured bas-reliefs. The best Greek artists, Polycletus, Praxiteles, Scopas, had adorned it with priceless works. The Romans in their turn continued to bestow favors and contributions on the famous temple. Augustus established there an enclosure in honor of Dea Roma and Julius Caesar (Dion Cassius, LI, 20, 6) and little by little the worship of the emperor, practiced with oriental servility, fused with the cult of Diana. Later, cults of foreign divinities like Isis were also introduced.

15. As for the goddess who presided over the temple, Jerome pointed out that she was not the Artemis or Diana of Greek mythology, with the bow and girt tunic of the huntress, but a divinity with multiple breasts (*multimammia*, πολύμαστος). Her distinctive characteristic, "to be the nurse of animals and living things,"[4] could be deduced from her image. This must have been a primitive fetish, which the popular fancy decided had fallen from heaven. The numerous breasts which hung from the chest, as in several reproductions preserved in Rome and elsewhere, recall the Phrygian Magna Mater (§ 68 ff.) or the Phoenician Astarte. She belonged, then, to the group of nature divinities and was a symbol of fertility. Since her function was to produce and conserve life, she was the protectress of animals and the patroness of births. Many feasts were celebrated in her honor throughout the year. In the shrine of Ortygia south of the Coressos range and near Mount Solmissos, special mysteries were celebrated to commemorate the birth of the goddess as Diana. The principal role in these mysteries seems to have been played by the sacred college of *Cureti*. Nocturnal processions held in the spring recalled the birth of the twins, Apollo and Diana, amid great shouting to scare away the envious Juno, who was plotting against their mother, Latona. Certain of the Greek authors, like Strabo, speak of wild orgies taking place on the occasion of this rite.

At the time of Paul, the worship of the goddess was no longer pre-

---

[4] *Bestiarum et viventium esse nutricem* (*Prologus in Epist. ad Ephesios*, in Migne, *Patr. Lat.*, 26, 470).

sided over, as it had been in the past, by a eunuch high priest (called the *Megabyzos*), but was entrusted to priestesses who had to remain virgins through their term of service. This was a purely legal reminder of the "virgin goddess," Diana, and it had no influence whatever on the morality of the cult.

The temple enjoyed the "right of asylum" and there was no dearth of evildoers of all kinds who took refuge in its enclosure to escape justice. When, under Tiberius, there was talk of abolishing this privilege a delegation of Ephesians hurried to defend the rights they had acquired in this regard (Tacitus, *Annales*, III, 60–61). The temple also served as a bank, both for the numerous offerings that poured into it from all regions and for the sums deposited there for safekeeping by various individuals.[5]

16. Mention must be made also of an Ephesian custom associated both with the temple of Diana and the story of Paul, namely the *Ephesia grammata*. These were little combinations of letters of the alphabet, or words, or brief formulae, which were considered to have magic powers in cases of illness, gambling, love, and the like.

---

[5] Valuables were deposited for safekeeping in the Hebrew Temple in Jerusalem also; cf. *Storia d'Israele*, Vol. II, pp. 159, 259 (§§ 144, 225).

Statue of Diana [Artemis]
of Ephesus

Ephesus: Ruins of the Odeon

In the beginning, they were probably imitations of the inarticulate and meaningless sounds given forth by the soothsayers of the temple. Then gradually there grew up a whole industry of these leaflets or little scrolls which, worn on the body, could be helpful in numerous situations in daily life. Clement of Alexandria records a few brief examples.[6] Paul found the industry organized and widespread in Ephesus, where many recent Christians had followed the local custom (Acts 19:19).

After the death of Croesus, the luckless adversary of Cyrus the Great, Lydia shared the fate of the neighboring countries and successively underwent Persian, Greek, and Roman domination. By the time the Romans came, the profound Hellenization which had taken place in the region had already obliterated almost every indigenous characteristic, including the language, only a few traces of which remained.

17. North of Lydia, between the Troas, Phrygia Minor, and the Aegean Sea, lay *Mysia*. The poverty and neglect which characterize it today are in complete contrast to its great wealth and importance in ancient times. Today one rarely comes upon a town that can muster a few thousand inhabitants (Balikesir, capital of the *vilâyet*, population about 26,000). Various rivers, like the Bagir (ancient Caicus) and the Susurluq, favor cereal farming, but it cannot be compared to that which flourished there in antiquity.

Within its territory Mysia numbered several Greek colonies, installed along its fragmented coastline, and several important inland cities. Notable among the latter were Thyatira and Pergamum. The former, famous for its commerce in purple dye, was a colony of Macedonians in the southernmost part of Mysia on the Lydian frontier, and for this reason was often considered part of Lydia. Pergamum was the capital of the kingdom of the same name. The generous kings of the house of Attalus, who had taken over the rule of Phileretus, adorned this city with famous monuments, some of which have been rediscovered in archaeological excavations that testify to the refined Hellenism of the dynasty. Among the harbors of this region mention must be made of Adramyttium in the wide gulf of the same name where the assizes (*conventus*) of the western district of Asia Minor were held.

18. The northwestern tip of the "province of Asia" and of all Asia Minor was occupied by the Troas, a small region bounded by the gulf of Adramyttium and the Hellespont. Across part of it travel the mountain range of the legendary Ida and the no less celebrated rivers, the Scamander and the Simois. In this region, sown with Greek colonies, lay the important Alexandria Troas, which received every kind of privilege from the descendants of the *gens Julia* because of

---

[6] *Stromata*, v, 8, 45, 2 (ed. Stählin, Vol. ii, p. 356).

the Homeric memories associated with the origins of the family, and in his own time Julius Caesar was thinking of making it no less than the capital of the Roman Empire (Seutonius, *Divus Julius,* 79). Augustus made it a Roman colony. The adventuresome and fortunate excavations of Schliemann brought to light the ruins of Troy-Ilium, the city of the Homeric poems, on the hill of Hissarlik. Archaeological research carried on by the University of Cincinnati has enabled us to trace the sequence of successive civilizations on the same site from the most remote era down to Roman times.

Besides the innumerable islands famous in Greek culture, among which the greatest were Rhodes, Samos, Chios, and Lesbos, the province of Asia also included the peninsula of the Thracian Chersonesus, which was part of the European continent, but these places are not related to our subject.

Pergamum: The Theater   Typical Landscape Near Hierapolis

19. To the north and the east of all the other regions (Troas, Mysia, Lydia, Caria) forming the "province of Asia," lay the broad land of Phrygia, which belonged to the same province and in certain periods extended from the Hellespont to the river Halys. On the north Phrygia was bounded by the province of Bithynia, on the east and southeast by Galatia and Lycaonia, and on the south by Pisidia. In reality it embraced the greater part of the western tableland of Asia Minor.

The ancient Greeks mention a very old Phrygian kingdom founded by emigrants from Thrace (Herodotus, VII, 73; Strabo, VII, 3, 2)

before the destruction of Troy (Strabo, XIV, 5, 29), but little is known of this fabled era, or of the primitive civilization of its people. In historical times its fate was that of the adjacent ethnic groups, who passed from one domination to another until Roman times. Even before the Emperor Diocletian subdivided it for administrative purposes into Phrygia *prima* and *secunda*, or *Pacatania* and *Salutaris*, the vast region was considered to be divided into Phrygia Minor, below the Propontis, and Phrygia Major in the center.

20. Among the cities of Phrygia, the three which lie in the Valley of the Lycus, a tributary of the Meander near Caria, are of interest to us, namely Laodicea, Colossae, and Hierapolis.

Pliny says of Laodicea: "It is situated on the river Lycus, at the confluence of the Asopus and the Caprus, called first Diospolis, then Rhoas."[7] It was named Laodicea by its founder, the Seleucid King Antiochus II (261–246 B.C.) in honor of his wife. Strabo (XII, 8, 16) describes it as a very wealthy city because of its brisk commerce, which throve especially on a prosperous livestock trade. When in 60 B.C. it was seriously damaged by an earthquake, it was able to repair its losses from its own resources without outside help (Tacitus, *Annales*, XVI, 27). Today nothing remains but the dull ruins at Eski-Hissar.

The progressive growth of Laodicea caused the slow decline of the neighboring city of Colossae, on the banks of the upper Lycus. Its importance had been due to the fact that it lay on a trade route which joined Sardis with Apamea (Celaenae). Strabo (XII, 8, 13) rightly calls it a little city (πόλισμα), while Pliny (*Nat. Hist.*, V, 41 al. 32), thinking perhaps of its history, lists it among the "most famous towns" (*oppida celeberrima*).

There is even scantier information about Hierapolis, the "holy city," as it was called because of its religious character. It was also famous for its mineral waters, rich in salts and calcium compounds, and for stone very similar to travertine. Wool and dyeing industries were highly developed there, although the principal center for these was Laodicea.

21. By the beginning of the second century B.C. Rome had begun to extend her influence over all these profoundly Hellenized regions, but it was only by virtue of the will of Attalus III, King of Pergamum, that the Roman people inherited the territories of the Attalan dynasty (133 B.C.). After overcoming no little difficulty, chiefly owing to the strong resistance captained by the nationalist Aristonichus, Rome firmly established her dominion over the tableland of Asia Minor and elevated it to the status of province. In his reorganization of the Empire,

---

[7] *Imposita est Lyco flumini, latera adfluentibus Asopo et Capro, appellata primo Diospolis, dein Rhoas* (*Nat. Hist.*, V, 29).

Augustus declared Asia, which had been impoverished as a result of the civil wars, a senatorial province and granted it favors and privileges. It was called *Asia proconsularis* because the post of governor (proconsul), as in the case of the province of Africa, was held by an ex-consul, who had the privilege of the twelve lictoral fasces. The proconsul, on whom devolved all the ordinary functions of a provincial governor, usually resided in Ephesus. At intervals, personally or through deputies, he visited the centers of the various judiciary districts (*conventus*) to hold court. According to a list of Pliny, which is perhaps incomplete (*Nat. Hist.*, V, 29–33 al. 28–30), these judiciary assemblies were held in Laodicea (or in Cibyra), Sinda, Apamea, Alabanda, Sardis, Smyrna, Ephesus, Adramyttium, and Pergamum.

The business of collecting taxes was allotted by contract to tax farmers, who had a crowd of publicans operating under them. Together they bled the province white through abuses and oppressions and we have evidence of this in not a few victims' protests which have come down to us as inscriptions, the oration *Pro Flacco* of Cicero, and in other texts of Roman historians (Tacitus, *Annales*, XII, 63; XIII, 33).

In Asia as elsewhere there existed cities declared "immune"— exempt from the obligation of paying property taxes into the imperial treasury — and "free" — with great autonomy in the election of their own magistrates and the passing of certain laws. The Romans, however, always reserved the right to revoke the privileges of freedom and immunity, and this was often exercised on cities which showed too little submission to Rome.

22. An ancient institution of religious character achieved great development and importance in the time of Augustus, and this was the Asiatic Assembly (κοινόν 'Ασίας). It met, at irregular intervals, to provide for the worship of the Dea Roma, to which oriental adulation, following the example of Pergamum, soon added the worship of the emperor. This assembly, to which every principal city sent delegates, was accompanied by festivals and solemn games. In addition to religious affairs, it could express its opinion on administrative matters, praise or blame a governor, ask to have a law modified or a heavy tribute decreased (cf. *Corpus Inscriptionum Graecarum*, Vol. II, n. 3487). But in reality its power in political or administrative matters was very limited and it rarely succeeded in correcting abuses or reducing oppression, although it served as a useful meeting ground between the governor and his subjects. The president of this assembly had the much sought after title of "Asiarch." On him rested the direction of the festivals and games in honor of the emperor and often the burden of the expense as well. The religious character of the assembly is suggested in the title "high priest of Asia" (ἀρχιερεὺς 'Ασίας) which seems to have been practically synonymous with Asiarch and was sometimes given the president. Since the Asiatics were fond of titles of honor and since the number of cities given the privilege of erecting a temple to the emperor rapidly multiplied, this title, which was retained by everyone who had once held the office, came to be worn by innumerable people. Because of institutions like these, which created an illusion of broad freedom, and also because of the watchful and tolerant policy of the Romans, it may be said that in the first century A.D. the "province of Asia" enjoyed all the benefits of the *pax romana*, which must have been the more appreciated since the province was emerging from an unhappy period of war and spoliation. Not without surprise do we read the praise Augustus bestows on himself in the *Monumentum Ancyranum:* "In the temples of all the cities of the province of Asia, I, the conqueror, replaced the ornaments which he, with whom I had warred, had taken, despoiling the temples."[8] And in reality under the Empire the condition of the people of Asia was excellent in comparison with their experience under previous governments, so that Cicero's words, with some modification, still held true: "Asia is so rich and so fertile, as to surpass without question all other regions in the fertility of her fields, the variety of her cultivations, the extent of her pastures and the multiplicity of her exports."[9]

GALATIA, LYCAONIA, PISIDIA, ISAURIA

23. In Roman times, Galatia was the name given the region in the center of Asia Minor which, with somewhat uncertain frontiers, was bounded on the north by Bithynia, on the east by Cappadocia, and on the west by Phrygia. Even geologically Galatia is a country of transition from the mountainous tableland in the west to the more level expanse in the east. The mountain peaks generally are under 6000 feet above sea level but there are extensive alluvial valleys cut by the rivers, such as the Kizil Irmac (ancient *Halys*), the Delyx, and the Sakaria (the ancient sacred river *Sangarius*), and stretches of savanna and arid, rocky limestone highlands. Herding is the chief occupation, even on the lower slopes and in the valleys where there is also some cereal farming. Today, the principal cities are Ankara (Ancyra, Angora), the capital of the Republic of Turkey, the mining center of Keskin, and a few others.

In the second half of the third century B.C., this region was invaded by Celtic tribes, which having overrun the ancient Balkans under the leadership of Lutharius and Leonnorius, finally came to settle in this,

---

[8] *In templis omnium civitatum provinciae Asiae victor ornamenta reposui, quae spoliatis templis is [Antony] cum quo bellum gesseram privatim possederat (Res gestae divi Augusti,* IV, lin. 49–51).

[9] *Asia vero tam opima est ac fertilis, ut et ubertate agrorum, et varietate fructuum et magnitudine pastionis et multitudine earum rerum, quae exportantur, facile omnibus terris antecellat (De imperio Cn Pompeii,* 6, 14).

to them, utterly new territory. These Celts or Gauls,[10] who spread terror wherever they swarmed, divided the territory among the three tribes which composed the invasion, namely, the Tolistobogi, who settled in the west around Pessinus (Balahissar); the Trocmi in the east with their capital Tavium (Nefezköy); and the Tectosages in the center around Ancyra (Ankara). Warriors by nature, they took part in almost all the conflicts among the petty monarchs of Asia Minor during the second century B.C., for they were much sought after as mercenaries because of their courage. In the second half of the first century B.C., Deiotarus, tetrarch of the Tolistobogi, repulsed the invader Eumachus, the satrap of Pontus, and united under his own rule the three Celtic tribes in the territory, by now called *Galatia*. Pompey recognized the kingship of Deiotarus, who allied himself with the Romans in the Mithridatic War, and enlarged his territory. After the death of the king, in whose service Cicero had used his eloquence (*Oratio pro rege Deiotaro*), his kingdom passed into the hands of his secretary, Aminta. Antony, as triumvir, favored the new king, giving him part of Pisidia (Appian, *Bellum civile*, V, 75, 319), Lycaonia, and Pamphylia (Dion Cassius, XLIX, 32, 3). Subsequently Aminta extended his dominion over Isauria and Rugged Cilicia. Augustus recognized his rights over these possessions, since he had fought on his side at Actium. But after the death of Aminta, in A.D. 25, the emperor detached Cilicia and Pamphylia from his kingdom and formed a Roman province (Strabo, XII, 5, 1; Dion Cassius, LIII, 26, 3).

24. This province, enlarged by the addition of a few districts of Paphlagonia, was composed of Galatia, properly so called, Lycaonia, Pisidia, and Isauria, and so it remained until the time of Vespasian when it underwent certain modifications. The heterogeneous character of the province is attested by the fact that the original names of the different zones were generally used in order to distinguish one from the other. Thus in the inscriptions we find that the governor of the province, instead of being called simply the Legate to Galatia, is clumsily but more accurately referred to as "The Legate of Augustus as praetor of the province of Galatia, Pisidia, Phrygia, Lycaonia, Isauria, Paphlagonia, etc."[11] The term "Galatian region" (Γαλατική χώρα) referred to the territory originally occupied by the Galatians, namely, the northern part of the province. In fact, Phrygia was distinct from this territory (Acts 16:6; 18:23) although they both belonged to the province of Galatia

---

[10] For this double name we have the testimony of Julius Caesar, an expert on the matter: *Gallia est omnis divisa in partes tres, quarum unam incolunt Belgae, aliam Aquitani, tertiam qui ipsorum lingua Celtae, nostra Galli appellantur* (*De bello gallico*, I, 1).

[11] *Legatus Augusti pro praetore provinciae Galatiae, Pisidiae, Phrygiae, Lycaoniae, Isauriae, Paphlagoniae, etc.* (*Corpus Inscr. Lat.*, III, 291, supplem. 6818; cf. 312, 318).

(§ 376). The practice of distinguishing from one another the various regions which formed the province is confirmed by the fact that, at least in the second century A.D., each of them had an assembly or κοινόν of its own. We have documentary evidence that the κοινόν of Lycaonia and that of Galatia, which met in Ancyra or Pessinus, were in existence at the same time.

Galatia harbored a very small Roman population along with a mixture of the Celtic-Gallic invaders and the Phrygians and Greeks who had inhabited the region before them. This mixed population was reflected in the name, commonly used, of *Gallogrecia* (Strabo, XII, 5, 1) or *Grecogallia* (Livy, XXXVIII, 17). Nevertheless we cannot speak of a very thorough Hellenization of the Galatians since in the fourth century Jerome could still say that a particular language was spoken in Galatia which was very like that used at Trier in Gaul (*In Epistulam ad Galatas*, lib. II, *Praefatio*, in Migne, *Patr. Lat.*, 26, 382).

25. To the south of the region of Galatia lay Lycaonia, a tableland averaging about 3000 feet above sea level, in the deep pocket between the mountains of Phrygia and Isauria. It was bounded on the south by the Taurus Mountains and on the northeast by Cappadocia. There are a few large salt lakes like Tuz on this tableland. Recently an irrigation system has been put into effect which uses the waters of the Isaurian lakes, Beyshehir and Soghla, to offset the lack of rainfall over wide areas.

Iconium Today (from Monmarché et Tillion, *Les pays d'Asie*)

In ancient times Lycaonia was ruled by various foreign powers until the Romans incorporated it into the province of Galatia, to which it remained attached at least until the reign of Antoninus Pius. There is no agreement among ancient writers as to whether the important city of Iconium (today *Konia*) belonged to Phrygia or Lycaonia. Xenophon (*Anab.*, I, 2, 19) lists it among the Phrygian cities and so does Pliny (*Nat. Hist.*, V, 41 al. 32) but Cicero (*Ad familiares*, XV, 4, 2) and Strabo (XII, 6, 1) assign it to Lycaonia. Luke seems to consider it a Phrygian city (Acts 14:6). Although of ancient origin and the capital of a tetrarchate, it was only late in its history that Iconium acquired any importance. Hellenistic influence barely penetrated it, and indigenous customs remained predominant. In Paul's time Lycaonian, an ancient Anatolian language, was spoken in the surrounding country (Acts 14:11). The Romans gave Iconium to Polemon, King of Cilicia, but soon it appears united to the province of Galatia. The emperor Claudius, probably without making it a colony, bestowed on it the honorary title of *Claudiconium*. Hadrian made it *Colonia Aelia Hadriana Augusta Iconiensis*.

26. At the base of the Kara Dagh, a majestic extinct volcano, nestles the little town of Lystra, which acquired no particular reputation until the beginning of the Roman Empire. After the death of Aminta, the Romans added it to the province of Galatia, and stationed a military garrison there as a protection against the robbers in the neighboring mountains. All trace of Lystra was lost until 1885, when Sterret identified its ruins near the modern Khatyn Serai. The only archaeological find of any importance is a crude pagan altar stone, with an inscription dedicated to Augustus by the decurions of the Roman colony.

Also in Lycaonia was the small city of Derbe, which Stephen of Byzantium mistakenly describes as the "fortress and harbor of Isauria." At the beginning of the first century A.D. it must have been no more than a village with a military garrison to insure the safety of the neighboring countryside. It was called *Claudioderbe* in honor of Claudius. A little before Paul's visit there, it seems to have been detached for a short time from the province of Galatia, because — according to the most acceptable interpretation of the vague phrase in Dion Cassius (LIX, 8, 2) — it was ceded by Caligula in the year 38 to Antiochus IV, king of Commagene. Soon afterward, however, Antiochus was dethroned by the same Caligula, and later put back on his throne by Claudius in 41 (Dion Cassius, LX, 8, 1). It has been suggested that Derbe is to be identified with the modern Gudelissin, near Zosta, or Losta.

27. North of Pamphylia and Lycia, two other small regions stretched between Lycaonia, Phrygia, and Caria. These were Pisidia in the east and Isauria in the west. They are mountainous regions scattered with numerous lake basins. Among the largest lakes are Kirili-göl (3700 feet above sea level), Bundru-göl (about 3000 feet above sea level), and Egerdir-göl, a fresh-water mountain lake. Isauria was a wild-looking country and its inhabitants had the reputation of singular ferocity.

As they penetrated these regions, the Greeks were careful to establish sentinel posts to defend the most traveled passes. The Romans did the same when, after the death of the vassal king, Aminta (25 B.C.), they resumed direct control. In the first century A.D. Pisidia and Isauria together with Lycaonia formed part of the province of Galatia. However, they all retained, and especially Pisidia, a certain administrative autonomy, emphasized by the presence of numerous Roman colonies established there by Augustus, such as Sagalassus, Olbasa, Comana, Cremna.

Antioch also was commonly listed among the cities of Pisidia, although properly speaking it was situated in Phrygian territory. Its ruins have been found near the Turkish village of Yalowatch, north of Lake Egerdir, on a height facing the mountain range of the Sultan Dagh. The city was founded by Seleucus Nicator about 280 B.C. on the site of a village inhabited by emigrants from Magnesia on the Meander (Strabo, XII, 8, 14). As early as Antiochus the Great, the Romans declared it a free city (189 B.C.) and used it as a frontier post. Augustus established a colony of veterans there and from then on its official name was *Colonia Caesarea Antiochia*, while the Greek authors rightly called it "Antioch toward Pisidia," or "Pisidian Antioch" ('Αντιόχεια πρὸς [τῇ] Πισιδίᾳ, Strabo, XII, 6, 4; 'Αντιόχειαν τὴν Πισιδίαν, Acts 13:14). Antioch acquired special importance for the Romans during the war against the Homonadenses, when the Senator P. Sulpicius Quirinius made it the headquarters of his campaign against those raiders.[12]

Excavations have unearthed vestiges of the ancient cult of the moon god Men — Lunus in Latin — and of other Phrygian deities, especially Cybele. Great gateways and a Roman aqueduct still testify to the importance of the city. Among the records of Emperor Augustus, many fragments of his *Res Gestae* have particular importance for they have made it possible to complete several passages in the *Monumentum Ancyranum*. A spacious Christian basilica still preserves its mosaic floor with an inscription dating from Bishop Optimus (375–381).

28. As for the peoples of Asia Minor in general, there is little to add to what we have already said in this rapid review of its various regions. There were two principal zones: the coastal area, cosmopolitan in character, and the inland region of the tableland, whose geographical structure itself helped preserve the character of the indigenous races or those who had settled there in much earlier migrations. In the smaller towns and villages scattered among the mountains of Phrygia, along the Taurus or across the plains of Galatia the indigenous element always predominated, tenaciously loyal to its ancestral language and traditions despite the constant spread of Greek influence. Along the coast, on the other hand, and generally in the large cities of the immediate interior like Sardis, Pergamum, Philadelphia, Laodicea, Apamea, and others, situated on the principal routes of communication, the prevailing element of the population was the Greek, whose ancestors in far-off times

---

[12] Cf. Ricciotti, *The Life of Christ*, p. 169 ff.; on p. 170 mention is made of an inscription relating to Quirinius found in Antioch.

had laid the foundations of these cities. They were very ancient colonies which had endured the epic struggles against Persia and were still bound to the mother country by their common language and culture, for the oldest Greek literature in almost all its forms had had its beginnings in these same distant colonies. For the most part, they had been founded during the ancient Ionian migrations and consequently the coastal belt nearest the European continent was usually called Ionia; but the Doric and Aeolian elements were also present among them. These circumstances constitute one of the principal reasons for the expansive energy developed by Greek civilization, which, with Alexander the Great, marched triumphantly to first place in Asia Minor.

29. But it is even more important for our purpose to note that the Jewish Diaspora had filtered widely through this heterogeneous population. This "dissemination" of the Jewish nation beyond Palestine formed a tight network which already stretched over the greater part of the ancient world, and therefore over Asia Minor as well. In his journeys, Paul finds Jews almost everywhere, and he always goes to them first before addressing himself to the pagans. The Jewish colony, whether in some lonely village of Lycaonia or Pisidia or in a cosmopolitan center of proconsular Asia, is ordinarily his immediate goal. Paul regularly counted on these separate knots in the spiritual net and he traveled from one to the other along the threads of the net itself, that is, by means of the various contacts established between one center and the other.

We have already examined elsewhere the documents which attest both the extent and the tenacity of the Jewish Diaspora, both the internal structure and the spiritual activity of these Jewish settlements outside of Palestine, and the reader is referred to that study.[13]

SYRIA

30. Syria is also very important in the story of Paul's life. It was bounded on the north by the southern border of Asia Minor (an imaginary line extending from the gulf of Alexandretta to the Euphrates), on the west by the Mediterranean, on the south by Palestine, and on the east by the Arabian desert and the Euphrates. Geologically it is composed of a coastal plain with a few mountain crags and an interior tableland which rises at the most to a height of 3400 feet above sea level. The distinctive feature of the southern part of Syria, above the river Nahr-el-Qasimiye which marks the beginning of Palestine, is a deep geological depression between Lebanon and Anti-Lebanon, called el-Beqa'a. The natural extension of this to the south is Ghor, where the Jordan flows. In the northern part of the territory rise the mountains

---

[13] Cf. Ricciotti, *Storia d'Israele*, Vol. II, pp. 203–247 (§§ 180–214).

which mark the Cilician frontier, such as the Kizil Dagh, the Amanus, and Gavur Dagh. The principal river of Syria is the Orontes, which flows through the depression mentioned above and then widens out near Antioch into a broad alluvial basin.

For thousands of years Syria was the inevitable bridge between Egypt and the Mesopotamian lands, namely, between the two centers of the most ancient human civilizations. The origins of many of its cities, therefore, naturally go back several thousand years B.C., such as Byblos, Tyre, Sidon, Aleppo, etc. In the Greco-Roman era, the most important city of all Syria was Antioch on the Orontes, served by the neighboring port of Seleucia. Other flourishing cities of the time were Apamea, Laodicea, and, farther to the south, Damascus, all of them along the threshold of the Arabian desert. After the period of Persian domination, Syria became the kingdom of the Seleucids until, exhausted by incessant wars and revolutions, it fell under the dominion of Rome. Pompey, while in Asia, took advantage of the general state of anarchy and in 64 B.C. reorganized Syria, making it a Roman province. Its boundaries varied during the first decade of Roman rule, including for a time even parts of Cilicia, Commagene, and Palestine; the latter, however, had its own particular history in the first century A.D.

Syria's natural riches and her frontier position with respect to the Parthians, the traditional enemies of Rome, made this province one of prime importance. In A.D. 20 Augustus made a journey through Syria, bestowing great favors, giving freedom to many cities and introducing various changes in the administration. When he divided the provinces

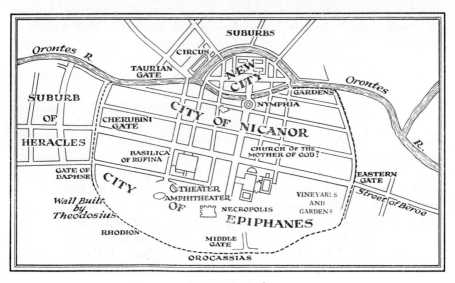

Ancient Antioch

between himself and the Senate, Syria was placed among the imperial provinces. Her governor, *legatus Augusti pro praetore,* had an important contingent of troops under his command to defend the frontiers from the Parthians and the Nabateans, and he was usually chosen from among those of consular rank, at the end of their career.

31. Antioch, the seat of the governor, had very humble origins. At the end of the fourth century B.C., Seleucus Nicator provided the first stimulus to its development and changed its original name, Antigonia, to Antioch in honor of his father Antiochus. Subsequent Seleucid kings rivaled one another in adorning their capital. The broad plain around it (the unhealthy lake there today did not exist then), the majestic foothills of the Amanus and Mons Casius, the verdure of the Silpius, and the abundance of streams and waterfalls formed a natural setting of great beauty. The port of Seleucia, only twenty-eight miles away and easily reached down the navigable Orontes, placed the city in communication with every Mediterranean harbor, while numerous caravan routes linked it with vast regions of the interior, beyond the Euphrates and even as far as mysterious India.

But more than a city of commerce and trade, Antioch was the home of pleasure. About eight miles from the city, beyond a charming succession of villas and gardens, one came to Daphne, a famous center of delights. Amid thick laurel groves (hence the name Daphne), which severe laws forbade cutting, rose the temple of Apollo. Within and around it, where everything invited enjoyment, were performed religious rites of the most refined sensuality, which ended regularly in wild orgies, as even the pagan authors admitted (cf. Libanius, *Oratio,* XLV, 23). Crowds of voluptuaries and courtesans flocked there from Antioch and more distant cities to honor Apollo and Artemis in that temple of license. Like all other temples this too had the right of asylum (§ 15), and that is why — by an ironical twist of fate — even the high priest of Jerusalem, Onias, took refuge there when he fled the assassins of Menelaus (2 Mach. 4:33–34).[14]

Except for Rome and Alexandria and excluding even Athens, already in decline, no city could compete with Antioch in architectural beauty. The charming little island formed by the Orontes at the northern end of the city was covered by the splendid palace which was the residence first of the Seleucid kings and then of the Roman governors. A very long street, "the street of the columns," crossed the entire city from east to west. Many wealthy foreigners had contributed to the embellishment of this magnificent "avenue," among them the king of the Jews, Herod the Great, who had had it paved with marble and lined with porticoes for a distance of twenty stadia (Flavius Josephus, *Antiquities of the*

---

[14] Cf. *ibid.,* Vol. II, pp. 265–266 (§ 233).

Jews, XVI, 148; *Wars of the Jews,* I, 425). It was crossed by another broad avenue, also lined with columns, which extended from north to south. The beautiful structures throughout the city were adorned with masterpieces of Greek art, while in the southern sector and on the slopes of the Silpius were the splendid villas of the rich. A strong wall, built by Antiochus IV Epiphanes, encircled the city and guaranteed its safety. From the ruins of Justinian's wall we are able to determine that it was about twenty-four miles long with huge towers at regular intervals. The myriad fountains bubbling in the nymphaia and a brilliant illumination at night, at least in the time of the rhetorician Libanius, increased the air of enchantment.

The inhabitants of such a city naturally reflected its character. They were frivolous and lightheaded, interested only in festivals and spectacles, according to the testimony of Herodianus (II, 7, 9; III, 1, 3; 4, 1). One particular dance, characteristic of the Antiochenes, is described for us by Lucian (Περὶ ὀρχήσεως, *De saltatione,* 76). In short, they interpreted life as one long entertainment.

32. Damascus, the *esh-Shâm* of the Arabs, rises at the edge of the desert, on a plain flanked on the west by the foothills of the Anti-Lebanon range and on the south by the Gebel el-Aswad. Thanks to a wise system of irrigation, in use even in very ancient times, Damascus is surrounded by luxuriant vegetable and flower gardens spread over the plain of El-Ghutah, which is crossed by the river Barada, the *Chrysorrhoas* of the Greeks. A natural commercial and political center, Damascus has always occupied a position of special importance in the various civilizations which succeeded one another in the course of its history. And this can be traced without a break from modern times straight back to at least the second millennium B.C., its name appearing on Egyptian monuments of the Eighteenth Dynasty (cf. Gen. 14:15). It came under Roman rule in the first century B.C. when Pompey, during his campaign in Armenia, sent Lollius and Metellus to oc-

The Falls of Daphne Near Antioch (Vester)

cupy it in 65 B.C. (*Antiquities of the Jews*, XIV, 29; *Wars of the Jews*, I, 127), and from then on the city became part of the Roman province of Syria. According to Pliny (*Nat. Hist.*, V, 16 al. 18) and Ptolemy (V, 14, 18) Damascus was among the cities in the federation of the Decapolis (cf. Mk. 5:20; 7:31). In Hadrian's reign it bore the title "metropolis," and under Alexander Severus it became a Roman colony. As a free city it had the right to coin its own money, and in fact there are extant coins of Damascus cast in the reigns of Augustus, Tiberius, and Nero. But since there are no coins extant from the time of Caligula, and since the passage in 2 *Corinthians* 11:32, mentions that "the governor under King Aretas was guarding the city of the Damascenes," it has been supposed that for a time Damascus was under Nabatean rule, having been ceded to her neighbors by Caligula. Such an act on the part of the paranoiac emperor is quite possible, although others explain the reference in 2 *Corinthians* differently (§ 152).

33. The population of Syria was no less Hellenized than that of Asia Minor, with this difference that here the Greek element was superimposed on and blended with a background for the most part Semitic. The most ancient cities of Syria, especially in the south, were all of Semitic origin, and the lowest and most populous strata of its society had remained Semitic in language, customs, and religion even after the invasion of Hellenism. The latter had by preference won the upper classes, but not without absorbing even from these a number of Semitic elements.

In such an environment, the Semitic Jews from Palestine felt less strange than in other regions and they consequently settled widely throughout Syria and firmly established themselves there. Their position, especially in the capital Antioch, is summed up in the first century A.D. by Flavius Josephus as follows: "The race of the Jews, which had scattered widely in all the land among the peasants and had mingled with them especially in Syria because of the nearness [of the two regions], was particularly numerous in Antioch, because of the size of the city, but especially because the kings who succeeded to Antiochus had given them there a safe abode. Antiochus Epiphanes, it is true, had plundered Jerusalem and sacked the Temple, but those who succeeded him in the kingdom had restored to the Jews of Antioch all the votive objects made of bronze, having them place them in their synagogue, and granted to them the same rights of citizenship as the Greeks. Favored in similar manner by succeeding kings, they increased in number. . . ." (*Wars of the Jews*, VII, 43–45). The same historian also confirms elsewhere (*Antiquities of the Jews*, XII, 119) that Jews and Greeks in Antioch enjoyed equal civil rights and attributes the granting of these rights to Seleucus Nicator, the founder of the city. The favor shown the Jews by the Seleucid kings was continued by the Roman governors,

Damascus Today

whose protection saved them from the easy reprisals of their enemies, even during the tragic years of the Palestinian revolt (*Wars of the Jews*, VII, 54 ff., 100 ff.).

Much more ancient than the Jewish contacts with Syrian Antioch were those with Damascus. The ancient kingdom of Israel had had multiple relations with the latter city, not all of them friendly. For the first century A.D. we have evidence of the great number of Jews in Damascus not only in the *Acts* (9:2) but also in Flavius Josephus. He narrates that in this city at the beginning of the Jewish war 10,500 Jews were killed for revenge (*Wars of the Jews*, II, 561), and elsewhere he sets the number at 18,000 (*ibid.*, VII, 368). Even allowing for some exaggeration in these figures it is clear that the descendants of Abraham in Damascus were extremely numerous. There was also the fact that Damascene women of other races were almost all "won to the Jewish religion" (*ibid.*, II, 560). Jewish proselytism had encountered a similar success among the Greeks in Antioch also (*ibid.*, VII, 45).

CYPRUS

34. Cyprus, the largest island in the eastern Mediterranean, is a little over fifty miles from the southern coast of Asia Minor, opposite Cilicia. It has an area of about 7500 square miles, its greatest length from east to west being 164 miles. The island is formed by two mountain ranges which extend in almost parallel lines with the broad plain of Messaria between them. Despite its irregular shape, there are scarcely any inlets along the coast which are suitable for harbors. The lack of any large stream and a scanty rainfall account for several desolate areas, which, however, were less extensive in ancient times because of the broad forest lands. Classical writers mention the island's fertility and abundant forests (Strabo, XIV, 6, 5; Ammianus Marcellinus, XIV, 8, 14). Its rich copper mines were another source of wealth. This was a rare and highly prized metal in ancient times, and made its way around the world as *cyprium* or *cuprum*, a name which has come into modern languages, as in our *copper*.

Cyprus became a Roman possession in 58 B.C. After being annexed for a brief period to the province of Cilicia, it became a province in its own right, at first imperial, and then in 22 B.C. senatorial. As an imperial province it was governed by a propraetor (Strabo, XIV, 6, 6; XVII, 3, 25), and as a senatorial province by a proconsul with the rank of praetor (Dion Cassius, LIII, 12, 7; 13, 3; 15; and especially LIV, 4, 1–§ 324).

35. It probably was not very densely populated. Pliny (*Nat. Hist.*, V, 35 al. 31) lists fifteen centers of habitation (*oppida*). In any case the principal towns were to be found in the lower part of the island and were joined by a road. These were Salamina in the bay of Famagusta opposite the shores of Syria, and Citium and Amathus on the southern shore, the former in the bay of Larnaka and the latter in that of Akrotiri. The largest city and harbor was Salamina, but in the ancient world Paphos (today Baffo) near modern Ktima on the western shore of the island was much more famous for religious reasons. It became the residence of the proconsul and was greatly favored by Rome. After its destruction in a violent earthquake, Augustus completely reconstructed it a short distance away from its original site. This was New Paphos, officially called Sebaste (Dion Cassius, LIV, 23, 7). In an inscription of the third century it appears as *Sebaste Claudia Flavia Paphos*, sacred city of the states of Cyprus. In Jerome's time it was a heap of ruins (*Vita Sancti Hilarionis*, 17, in Migne, *Patr. Lat.*, 23, 52). About 60 stadia to the southeast among the ruins of Old Paphos, which had been destroyed by the earthquake, stood the temple of Aphrodite. The origins of this shrine undoubtedly went back to pre-Hellenic times, but in the first century A.D. it was still very famous, and many groups of pagans, even from outside the island, flocked there to celebrate the goddess of reproduction and of love in rites which were often indecent. During the Jewish war, Titus made it a point to visit this temple, "famous among natives and foreigners." Tacitus, who recounts the episode, is perplexed by the fact that the image of the goddess did not have a human form, but was a crudely sculptured stone: "The image of the goddess is not a human figure: it is a round image, wider at first and rising to a narrower top, like a goal post."[15] And with a certain disappoinment he concludes by saying that he does not understand the reason for a puppet of such shape: "But the reason is obscure"[16] (*Histor.*, II, 2, 3).

---

[15] *Simulacrum Deae non effigie humana: continuus orbis latiore initio tenuem in ambitum, metae modo, exsurgens.*

[16] *Sed ratio in obscuro.*

New Paphos: The Harbor

There were great numbers of Jews in all the cities of Cyprus, especially after King Herod the Great leased the copper mines from Augustus (*Antiquities of the Jews*, XVI, 129). At the time of the insurrection under Trajan the Jews are reported to have killed 240,000 pagans in Cyprus and to have razed to the ground the city of Salamina (Eusebius, *Chronicon*, ed. Schöne, Vol. II, p. 164; Migne, *Patr. Gr.*, 19, 558). Dion Cassius (LXVIII, 32) states that, after the ruthless Roman suppression, any Jew who set foot on the island, even if he were shipwrecked, was killed.

MACEDONIA

36. With the victory of Pydna (168 B.C.) Rome extended her influence over the kingdom of Macedonia, but it was only later, in 146 B.C., that the region was made a province, and from then on it became a battleground in one war and invasion after another. In his reorganization of the provinces Augustus assigned it to the Senate and gave it the right to coin its own money (Suetonius, *Claudius*, 25; Dion Cassius, LX, 24, 1). The propraetor, with the title of proconsul, resided in Thessalonica. But the assembly, or κοινόν, met in Beroea, because Thessalonica as a free city, did not participate.

The boundaries of the province changed frequently. In the first century A.D. it included Macedonia, properly so called (bounded on the north by Thracia, Moesia, and Illyria, on the south by Thessaly, and on the west by Epirus), and in addition, Thessaly, Epirus, and the cities of the Adriatic, Apollonia, and Durazzo (*Dyrrachium*), extending as far as the river Drilon (Drin). To facilitate the Romanization of the province, the Romans built roads and established colonies of veterans in various centers. The most important road was the *Via Egnatia,* or Egnatian Way, which crossed the whole territory from Durazzo to Neapolis and the Hellespont, and from it branched the secondary roads of the ancient Balkans. Despite Rome's efforts, however, Macedonia absorbed very little that was Roman, and remained permeated with the Hellenism which had spread through it a long time before.

Macedonia, a hilly and uneven region, had few towns in the interior, and its principal cities were situated along the coast, both on the Aegean and the Adriatic. Among these, Neapolis, Philippi, Thessalonica, and Beroea are of interest to our story.

37. Neapolis was a little city opposite the island of Thasos, on the site of present-day Kavalla. It was situated on a promontory, with the sea on two sides, and its position with reference to Asia Minor gave it a certain importance. A branch of the Egnatian Way connected it with nearby Philippi and, across Macedonia, with Durazzo, opposite Brindisi, which marked the end of the Appian Way. In Neapolis reigned the same mixture of races and dialects to be found in any port of Asia Minor, since this little city was the first point of contact between two continents.

Philippi owed its splendor to the favor of Augustus, who could never forget the place where the star of fortune rose for the Julian *gens.* The city, however, took its origin and its name from King Philip II of Macedon, Alexander's father, who, attracted by the gold of Mount Pangaeus, occupied the locality and built a city there to replace the ancient village of Krenides. On the surrounding plain, along the Gangites, in 42 B.C. died the last Roman dreams of republican freedom. Octavian, in memory of the stubborn battle, founded there a colony of veterans with the honorary title of *Colonia Augusta Julia (Victrix) Philippensium.* The granting of the *jus italicum* exempted the city from taxes and gave it numerous privileges. In addition to a large native population, there grew up a sizable colony of Italians, since after the battle of Actium (31 B.C.) Augustus sent to Philippi many of the former partisans of Antony, whose properties had been confiscated and given to the emperor's veterans (Dion Cassius, LI. 4, 6). The name of ancient Philippi is recalled in its present one, Philibedjik. Archaeological research has uncovered the composite pantheon of this old Roman colony, where along with the Roman deities, Greek, Thracian, and Asian divinities continued to be worshiped as well as the Egyptian Isis and Serapis, whose cults were so widespread at the time of the Empire. The ruins of the acropolis, the theater, and the temples in the upper city, and those of the forum in the lower city, suggest the life lived on this fringe of Macedonia, where Italians brought the Roman language and customs. The magistrates, called *archons* or *strategoi,* were elected by an assembly of citizens and had the right to be preceded by lictors carrying the fasces.

Amphipolis rose on a little peninsula formed by the river Strymon (today Struma), near its exit from Lake Cercinites (Tachynos) and an hour's distance from its entrance into the sea. Since it was surrounded by two arms of the river, it was given the name "City between two [banks]." Although it was a free city (Pliny, *Nat. Hist.*, IV, 17 al. 10) and, in the Diocletian division, capital of *Macedonia Prima* (eastern Macedonia), it had no great importance, being overshadowed by the growing influence of Philippi.

Thessalonica: View of the City and Harbor

38. Thessalonica, on the other hand, was extremely important. It was founded in 315 B.C. by one of the generals of Alexander the Great, Cassander, who gave it the name of his wife, Alexander's sister, modified today to *Salonika*. Situated at the head of the Thermaic Gulf, Thessalonica was a flourishing city in Paul's time. The Egnatian Way linked it in the east to the harbors opposite Ionia and in the west to Durazzo on the Adriatic, while the secondary roads connecting with the Egnatian Way placed it in communication with the heart of Balcania. Ships from all over the Mediterranean docked in its harbor. It was the residence of the governor of the Roman province and a "free city." At the head of its "people's assembly" or δῆμος there were, in Paul's time, five or six "politarchs" according to the exact term used by Luke (Acts 17:6) and confirmed by various inscriptions. The population of Thessalonica was a mosaic of races, but Greeks predominated to a certain extent. The Jews, attracted by its easy opportunities for trade, were very numerous. Their synagogue probably functioned as the religious center for the Jews of Philippi, Amphipolis, Apollonia, and other Macedonian cities.

Beroea lay at a certain distance from the coast. It was a little "out of the way city" as Cicero described it (*In Pisonem*, 36), situated on the left bank of the Haliacmon (today Vistritsa). A little to the south rose the majestic height of Olympus, and before it stretched a broad plain crisscrossed by aqueducts and canals, which breathed an air of tranquil serenity. Nearby, three centuries earlier (289 B.C.) Demetrius I of Macedon had been defeated by Pyrrhus, the enigmatic king of Epirus (Plutarch, *Pyrrhus*, 11). After the Battle of Pydna, Beroea was the first city to open its gates to the Romans (Livy, XLIV, 45), who included it in the third region of Macedonia (Livy, XLV, 29). When Paul came to this city, it was undoubtedly more prosperous than the modern Veroia, which now rises on its site. The very presence of influential Jews suggests it had an active commerce.

ACHAEA - EPIRUS

39. In 146 B.C. with the total destruction of Corinth, the Achaean league collapsed and the whole territory passed to the Romans, who added it to the province of Macedonia. In Augustus' great administrative reform in 27 B.C., Achaea was detached from Macedonia and became a senatorial province (Dion Cassius, LIII, 12, 4). This arrangement lasted until the time of Diocletian, except for two brief periods, the first in the years A.D. 15–44, when Achaea was again joined to Macedonia, and the second in 67–74, when it enjoyed the autonomy granted it by Nero during his histrionic journey through that region (Suetonius, *Nero*, 24; Pliny, *Nat. Hist.*, IV, 10 al. 6).

The boundaries of the province of Achaea varied. For a certain time it included Thessaly and Epirus, but for the most part the jurisdiction of its proconsul was limited to the Peloponnesus and the region below Thessaly in Balcania, together with the numerous islands in the surrounding archipelago. The Romans treated the various cities of this province with special consideration out of deference for their noble history and cultural tradition. Athens was immediately declared a city *foederata*, that is, its liberty was guaranteed by treaty. Several of the cities were "free" and "immune" with broad privileges, while others, like Corinth and Patraxos, were declared Roman colonies (Strabo, VIII, 7, 5; Pausanias, VII, 18, 7). In Epirus the same privilege was granted Actium and Buthrotum (Butrinto) (Pliny, *Nat. Hist.*, IV, 1–2). Many of the local federations or amphictyonies also remained in existence, although they were generally reduced to leagues of a religious nature whose chief purpose was to provide for the worship of the emperor or to decree honors for the individual magistrates of the region. The committees for the traditional national festivals, in charge of the various games, were also continued. In the time of Augustus the Actian games which were held every four years became particularly famous. But in general the Roman occupation marked for Achaea a period of decline. Impoverished economically and artistically, Greece now lived on the memory of her glorious past. One could search in vain among the loquacious "Greeklings" in its fallen cities for a worthy heir to the great thinkers and artists who had flourished in the age of Plato and Pericles. The countryside, devastated by war and its population depleted, was even more desolate.

40. Of the Greek cities, we are concerned only with Athens, the cultural center of the classical world, and Corinth, the capital of the Roman province.

Compared with what it had been five centuries earlier, the Athens of the first century A.D. seemed but a ghost, though it was a luminous enough ghost to attract the attention of the intellectual world of Rome.

Athens: The Parthenon (Alinari)

Its walls enclosed an incomparable museum of artistic beauties, but at the same time the city harbored crowds of petulant and bumptious idlers, who seemed almost the dim shadows of its monuments. The masterpieces of Athens were gathered on the Acropolis, in the famous *agora* and along the magnificent street lined with porticoes which led from the agora to the Dipylon gate. As one studies the interminable lists of works of art which philologists and archaeologists have tried to identify in this section of the city, one seems to be wandering through a labyrinth of architecture and statuary. There the gods most familiar to the Greeks — Zeus, Athena, Apollo, Aphrodite — had their temples. The space between one temple and another was occupied by statues of demigods, eponyms, heroes, down the line to ordinary mortals, both men and women, who had become famous for one reason or another, including their vices. About the time Paul went to Athens, a statue had been erected to Bernice,[17] the Jewish queen before whom the Apostle later appeared in Caesarea, and who was no less famous for her divorces and her amorous and incestuous adventures than she was for her beauty.[18]

---

[17] *Corpus Inscriptionum Graecarum*, Vol. I, n. 361.
[18] Cf. *Storia d'Israele*, Vol. II, pp. 456–457 (§ 402).

The Royal Portico, that of Zeus Eleutherios or Soter, the famous Poikilē of Zeno, were adorned with the statues and paintings of the best artists of classical Greece. As a central milestone stood the altar of the twelve gods (Herodotus, 11, 7), near which the statue of Demosthenes recalled far different times.

But the most holy and majestic part of the city was the Acropolis, which in the first century A.D. still boasted almost all its monuments (to which, however, political servility had added a temple in honor of Rome and of Augustus). The whole ensemble was sacred to the father of the gods, honored as the patron of the city under the title of *Zeus Poliéus*, and to Pallas Athena, as the goddess of the olive, which was the wealth of Attica. In her honor rose the Parthenon, the miracle of beauty enthroned on the Acropolis, with another miracle of beauty inside, the statue of Pallas Athena, which was the masterpiece of Phidias. Close by, the Erechtheum, a little shrine of Pentelican marble housed the olive tree of the

Corinth: Ruins, With the Acrocorinth in the Background

goddess: as a symbol of gratitude, a lamp of purest oil was kept burning continuously in her honor (Plutarch, *Sulla*, 13). From the center of the shrine, the statue of Athena Polias, said to have fallen from heaven, exercised her protection over the city. Just outside the shrine, still another statue, that of Athena Prómachos, recalled the epic adventures of Hellas against Persia. Thus Athens honored the most noble of the pagan divinities, the goddess of wisdom, conceived as a pure virgin (whence the name of the Parthenon), almost as a counterpoise to the licentious cults of Aphrodite and Dionysius. This ideal virgin, endowed with "strength and judgment" (Hesiod, *Theogonia*, 896), represented the most sublime attainment of Greek beauty.

41. After Athens, Paul went to Corinth. The modern city is rightly called *Nea Kòrinthos* (New Corinth) since except for its name it has nothing in common either with the Greek city destroyed in 146 B.C. or the Roman one which succeeded it. The new Corinth, in fact, was built after the earthquake of 1858, which leveled whatever was left of the former city. Its steady development in modern times underlines the importance of its site and explains the power of the ancient city.

At about four miles southwest of the modern city, archaeological research has uncovered the area of the ancient Corinth,

> "Corinth the happy, portal
> of the king of the sea, rejoicing in
> her youths"
> (Pindar, *Olymp.*, 13, 4–5).

Corinth: Airplane View of the Canal Across the Isthmus (from Monmarché, *Les pays d'Europe*)

The level of the Roman reconstruction follows almost exactly that of the Greek city. This was built on two terraces extending north from the Acrocorinth, which was the citadel. On the Acrocorinth stood the temple of Aphrodite, where more than a thousand courtesans exercised the profession of sacred prostitution (Strabo, VIII, 6, 2). Archaeological findings, although meager on the Acrocorinth, permit us to trace almost the entire plan of the lower city. The Doric temple of Apollo (sixth century) rose on one of the terraces, while on the other, to the south and west, stretched the market place, or *agora*. Of this important feature of every Greek city, nothing remains but the ruins of the Roman reconstruction. Excavations have confirmed another characteristic of ancient Corinth mentioned by the classical authors, and that is the abundance of springs. The fountain *Glauke* was discovered among others, and the famous Peirenian Spring on the Acrocorinth (Pliny, *Nat. Hist.*, IV, 5 al. 4), which Herod Atticus adorned with marble and to which he added a nymphaion. Also due to this wealthy patron was the Odeon, which was very similar to the one he had built in Athens.

At the time of Paul nothing remained of the Greek Corinth. Monuments, temples, fountains, everything had been razed to the ground in 146 B.C. Thus had ended the centuries-long history of the city which had been the rival of Athens, Sparta, and Thebes for the hegemony of Greece. But its geographical location did not permit it to lie in ruins for long. When Horace speaks of the "walls of Corinth on two seas" (*bimaris Corinthi moenia — Carmina*, I, 7, 23) he is stating the reason why the city revived. The isthmus on which it lay, with the port of Cenchrae on the east and that of Lecheum on the west, was a point so vital to the ancient world that a field of tumbled ruins could not be tolerated there. Hence the city was rebuilt by decree of Julius Caesar, and was called *Colonia Laus Julia Corinthus*. Italian colonists, freedmen and veterans for the most part, flocked there immediately and from the Orient came merchants of every race, including the Jews. There resulted a hybrid population in which the Greeks formed perhaps the minority (Pausanias, II, 1, 2).

42. The main source of income was derived from the traffic which moved between the two harbors of the city. Many ships, to avoid

Corinth: The Bay With the Snowy Peak of Parnassus in the Background

the long haul around the Peloponnesus, unloaded their cargoes in one of the harbors, and these were then transported by land across the isthmus and reloaded in the opposite port. A passage had been built — the *diolkos* — through which smaller boats could be hauled with their cargo from one harbor to the other (Strabo, VIII, 2, 1). The canal across the isthmus, which had been inaugurated by Nero with great fanfare (Flavius Josephus, *Wars of the Jews*, III, 540; Suetonius, *Nero*, 19; Dion

Cassius, LXVIII, 16) was about a mile and a half long when its construction was stopped (the modern canal, finished in 1893, is 600 miles long).

Of the two harbors, Cenchrae, today Kenkris, on the Aegean Sea toward the east, is related to Paul's story. Now almost deserted, it was, of course, much more important in his time than it is today. Near the harbor stood temples to Aphrodite, Aesculapius, and Isis. It was the cradle of a little Christian community (Rom. 16:1), which was founded certainly by Paul.

43. Epirus, situated between the Ionian Sea and Thessaly, was joined by the Romans first to Macedonia and then to Achaea, and it finally became a province by itself under Trajan. The city of Nicopolis was founded at the behest of Augustus who wished to perpetuate there the memory of his victory over Antony. It became a very important center and its inhabitants numbered people from Aetolia and Acarnania as well as many Roman veterans. Augustus made this city, which marked the very site where he had drawn up his army before the battle of 31 B.C., a Roman colony and granted it many favors and privileges. Pliny calls it a "free city" (*Nat. Hist.*, IV, 2). On the opposite side of the Ambracian Gulf, that is, to the southeast, extends the promontory of Actium which gave its name to the historic battle.

II

Cultural and Intellectual Background

44. So vast and varied is the world traversed by Paul's tireless activity that it is practically impossible to give an adequate summary of its social and cultural aspects. Under the apparent uniformity produced by Hellenism, there persisted many cultural elements proper to the various ethnic groups. Recently discovered papyri and private documents show how one-sided and incomplete are those judgments concerning the moral structure of the Roman Empire which are based solely on the assertions of famous ancient authors, who usually mirror only specific social classes. Much less can any moral homogeneousness be argued from the fact that all of the regions through which Paul journeyed, from wild Lycaonia to Spain, from Palestine to Illyria, formed part of a single empire. Rome, in fact, was prudently content with the recognition of her sovereignty, but she left the subjugated kingdoms a certain degree of autonomy and respected the different local traditions, both social and religious.

The great process of assimilation accomplished by Hellenism is an undeniable fact. But this can be exaggerated if the estimate of the society of the time is based entirely on the great literature that has come down to us. That society certainly was not composed exclusively of wealthy men, of *honestiores*, who could acquire a considerable degree of culture. At their side, and in fact far more numerous than they, lived the great mass of peasants, of *humiliores*, far from the large cities, faithful to their ancestral traditions, and scarcely brushed by this international Hellenistic culture. Paul's missionary efforts were expended, it is true, in large cities, but he in no way neglected these little people, who were more simple and more solid, less educated but also less spoiled. Keeping in mind this danger of too facile generalization, we may note certain elements which cast a little light on the social and cultural conditions in the various parts of the Roman Empire.

45. In Roman society, family life, based on monogamous marriage, was characterized by the absolute authority of the *paterfamilias*. The father, or head of the *family*, was considered the sole proprietor of all the persons composing it, and he exercised very broad power over them. He could expose his own children to die, sell them, or even have them whipped to death. A son could not own anything as long as he stayed in his father's house. All that he acquired became his father's property. The subjection of the wife to her husband was somewhat less severe since she could not ordinarily be sold or put to death. In Rome especially the *materfamilias* enjoyed a position of dignity. She shared with her husband the same human and divine rights.[1] She was charged especially with the education of the children, and exercised the duties of mistress of the whole household, but she worked at domestic tasks along with her handmaidens. According to the testimony of Suetonius (*Divus Augustus,* 64, 2) even the women of Augustus' family spun and wove. The Roman matron took her meals with her husband and frequented public places like the theater (Suetonius, *ibid.,* 44, 2–3). Everyone treated a matron of dignity with respect (Valerius Maximus, V, 2, 1). Woman's freedom increased considerably under the Empire and was reflected even in the new formula for contracting marriage. The ancient religious rites in which the couple swore fidelity to each other before the *Pontifex Maximus* had by now fallen into disuse. Not even was the so-called *coemptio* used very much longer, whereby the father of the bride, in a fictitious sale, handed her over to the *patria potestas* of the groom, which meant that her husband could now exercise the same severe rights over her as he would over a daughter. Instead, in the first century A.D., the formula of free marriage, *sine in manum conventione,* became increasingly widespread. In this form of marriage, the wife remained under the authority of her father and was mistress of her own property. She could easily obtain a separation from her husband, and she retained the rights over her dowry, which she administered as she wished. Under such circumstances, a wife could exercise a certain power over her husband, as Horace wryly noted: "A wife with a dowry rules her husband."[2]

The status of Greek woman was much lower than that of the Roman, and still lower was woman's position in other oriental regions, where she was completely subject to her husband and confined almost exclusively to domestic tasks. The difference, noted by the ancients, is expressed by Cornelius Nepos (*Praefatio,* 6–7) in these terms: "What Roman is ashamed to take his wife with him to a banquet? What mother does not occupy the first position in the household and is not surrounded by respect? These things are very different in Greece. In fact, (the wife) is not admitted to a dinner except among relatives, and she resides only in the inner part of the house, called *gynaeconitis,* where no one may enter except those closely related by blood."

---

[1] *Divini et humani juris communicatio* — *Digest,* XXIII, 2, 1.
[2] *Dotata regit virum . . . coniunx* — *Carmina,* III, 24, 19, 20.

46. As for sexual morality at the time of the Empire, it would be easy to compile a copious and lewd anthology of passages from various authors who narrate revolting obscenities with an impassiveness which, however surprising today, was entirely natural for them. The reason for this was rooted in their environment, which Paul described with blunt objectivity. According to him, the pagans, whose moral conduct did not conform to the natural knowledge of God which they possessed, "became vain in their reasonings, and their senseless minds have been darkened. For while professing to be wise, they have become fools, and they have changed the glory of the incorruptible God for an image made like to corruptible man and to birds and four-footed beasts and creeping things.

"Therefore God has given them up in the lustful desires of their heart to uncleanness, so that they dishonor their own bodies among themselves — they who exchanged the truth of God for a lie and worshipped and served the creature rather than the Creator who is blessed for ever, Amen.

"For this cause God has given them up to shameful lusts; for their women have exchanged the natural use for that which is against nature, and in like manner the men also, having abandoned the natural use of the woman, have burned in their lusts one towards another, men with men doing shameless things and receiving in themselves the fitting recompense of their perversity. And as they have resolved against possessing the knowledge of God, God has given them up to a reprobate sense,[3] so that they do what is not fitting; being filled with all iniquity, malice, immorality, avarice, wickedness; being full of envy, murder, contention, deceit, malignity; being [informers], detractors, hateful to God, irreverent, proud, haughty, plotters of evil; disobedient to parents, foolish, dissolute, without affection, without fidelity, without mercy" (Rom. 1:22–31). Black as it is, the picture is a true one, as anyone knows who has any familiarity with the Greek and Roman classics.

Although today one ordinarily avoids speaking of homosexual relations, which Paul castigates here, in ancient times they were the subject of frank apologias. The island of Lesbos gave its name to the women (λεσβιάζω) while the men found defenders like Socrates and Plutarch. Their relations were commonly considered the prerogative of warriors, politicians, and men of letters and were considered to foster heroic sentiments which commonplace matrimony did not.

47. Marriage had remained monogamous only in theory. In Greece the *hetaerae* had become almost an institution. In Rome, at least at the time of Seneca (*De beneficiis*, III, 16, 2), a contemporary of Paul, matrons in high society considered it witty to count the years not by

---

[3] There is a play on words here in the Greek: οὐκ ἐδοκίμασαν . . . ἀδόκιμον.

the consuls but by their own various husbands. The family of Augustus himself, who tried to revive public morality, was not free from notorious scandals, and he was forced to send his only daughter Julia into exile on the island of Pandataria, so great was her shamelessness, although she had had three husbands and was the mother of five children. During Augustus' efforts to restore morality, Horace declared the decline of the Roman people began with the moral decay of the family:

> "The degeneracy of our times has defiled first
> our marriages, our offspring and our homes.
> Sprung from this source, disaster has overflowed
> our people and our fatherland" (*Carmina*, III, 6, 17–20).[4]

Tacitus, in comparing the dissolute customs of the Romans with the simple mores of the Germans, refers to the obscene spectacles as the principal cause of so much corruption. His praise of the customs of the barbarians testifies against the Roman world of his time: "No one there laughs at vice; nor is corrupting and being corrupted called the vogue" (*Germania*, 19). Seneca is equally frank in denouncing feminine corruption, and he finds reason to praise his mother because she has not subscribed to the common practice of abortion (*Ad Helviam matrem, de consolatione*, 16, 3). He, too, sees an incentive to vice in the spectacles and baths where "often [there is found] voluptuousness which hides itself and seeks the shadows . . . soft, enervated, stuffed with wine and smeared with ointments, pallid or rouged, and already near the tomb" (*De vita beata*, 7, 3–4).

By way of remedy Augustus had proclaimed certain measures, such as the laws for the repression of adultery (*de adulteriis coercendis*) and to regulate marriage (*de maritandis ordinibus*), for example, completed by the basic provision of the *Papias-Poppean* law relative to the famous "right of three children" (*jus trium liberorum*), which granted privileges to large families. Despite their fine aims, however, these measures had very little efficacy, especially since bad examples lived in high places, and as the Messalinas carried on in the families of the Caesars, so did the Trimalchios among the moneyed classes.

48. Not everyone was a Messalina or a Trimalchio, however, and if the dispassionate historian does not soften the shadows, he must also brush in the light, be it much or little. And there was light to be found in these times and among these same classes of people. Even Tacitus, whose portraits of Roman matrons are done in such dark tones, is struck by the faithfulness and heroism of the women who voluntarily

---

[4] *Faecunda culpae saecula nuptias*
primum inquinavere et genus et domos:
hac fonte derivata clades
in patriam populumque fluxit (*Carmina*, III, 6, 17–20).

follow their sons and husbands into exile to share their sufferings (*Histor.*, I, 3). And he takes pleasure in describing the courage of Seneca's wife (*Annales*, XV, 63 ff.) and of other women worthy of the best Roman tradition. The two women who, according to Pliny the Younger, killed themselves with their husbands in order not to be separated in death (*Epist.*, III, 16; VI, 24) are examples of somber stoicism but also of deep human affection.

But in addition to these conspicuous examples, there must have been innumerable families who lived their daily lives in patient fortitude, and who passed unnoticed because they furnished no material for history or satire. If the Roman Empire survived victorious for some centuries longer, overcoming severe difficulties, this certainly was not due to the Messalinas and Trimalchios prancing through the orgies of the capital, but to the many *cives*, the ordinary citizens, who in the army or in public office, at home or in the colonies, preserved more or less deeply their sense of morality and of the family. There is evidence of this in the numerous inscriptions on tombs — the sincerity of which cannot be entirely denied — and the crude graffiti in the temples with which pilgrims recorded their longing for their dear ones far away.[5]

49. Another old wound in ancient society was slavery. Here, too, we must not judge with a modern Christian mentality a social institution condemned at the time by very few. The structure of the ancient world was such that neither public nor private life could do without slaves, whose number was legion. Tacitus states that the more noble-minded among the Romans were concerned over the steady growth of this rabble of unhappy creatures streaming in from every region (*Annales*, IV, 27; XIV, 44), who very often did not even know their own masters. Since the rural areas were literally deserted by free men, farm work was done almost entirely by slaves. Many of them occupied positions of delicate responsibility in the great patrician homes of the city, and were often charged with the care and education of the children.

The legal status of the slaves was most unhappy, since there existed no law to protect them from the caprice of their masters. Some provisions in their favor began to appear, it is true, at the beginning of the Empire, but even these were not particularly effective. The earliest writers speak of slaves as "objects," having no more rights with respect to their owner than the other objects listed in the inventory of his possessions (Varro, *De re rustica*, I, 17, 1). There is the famous episode described by Juvenal, in which a slave's punishment is mockingly decreed: "He has not committed anything wrong, I know. But I will it and thus I command it; let my will stand in place of reason!"[6]

---

[5] Cf. A. J. Festugière, *Le monde greco-romain au temps de Notre-Seigneur*, Paris, 1935, Vol. II, p. 192.

[6] *O demens, ita servus homo? nil fecerit, esto*
Hoc volo, sic iubeo, sit pro ratione voluntas (*Satires*, VI, 222–223).

50. Here, too, however, we do not lack happy examples to the contrary, which testify to affectionate relationships between slaves and masters. Very well known is the friendship between Cicero and Tiro his slave, later his freedman, who merited the writings of his friend and master, who loved him (Cicero, *Ad familiares*, XVI, 4, 3; cf. XVI, 17, 1). Stoicism in particular attempted to introduce the concept of a certain equality among men insofar as they were all part of the universe, identified with the divinity. Seneca's words are famous: "Slaves! Yes, but men. Slaves! Yes, but fellow tenants. Slaves! Yes, but humble friends.... Remember that he whom you call slave was born of the same human race, has smiled beneath the same skies, breathes, lives and dies as you do. You might see him free, and he might see you a slave" (*Ad Lucilium*, V, 6, l. 10). But ideas like these were confined to a few noble minds, while philosophers were not lacking who discussed the question whether the slave had a reasoning soul. In any case, they remained abstract ideas and were almost never translated into concrete fact. Seneca himself — who spoke with so much wisdom — took good care not to emancipate his own numerous slaves.

There is evidence that in Greece and Asia Minor slaves were treated more leniently. They were accepted for initiation in the Eleusinian mysteries, and were thereby accorded a conspicuous testimonial of their common humanity.[7] Slowly the official world of Rome (cf. Suetonius, *Divus Claudius*, 25, 2) formulated laws intended to alleviate the lot of slaves. For instance, Hadrian abolished the terrible house of correction (*ergastula*) and limited the master's freedom to punish his slave (Aelius Spartianus, *Hadrianus*, 18).

It is unnecessary to describe the moral degradation which ultimately overtook these discards of human society, a degradation often reflected in the patrician youths confided to their care. And even when a slave

---

[7] Cf. V. Magnien, *Les Mystères d'Eleusis*, Paris, 1938, pp. 150–151. One of the fragments extant of the comic poet Theophilus (*Fragmenta comicorum graecorum,* ed. Meineke, Vol. III, p. 724) would indicate that once initiated into the mysteries he was no longer considered a slave but a free man who nevertheless remained with his master.

Incidentally, it is opportune to remember that among the Hebrews slavery was a much more humane institution, especially in the case of slaves who were one's compatriots. The latter had the right to be set free every seventh (sabbatical) year (Exod. 21:1 ff.). Note also the advice of Sirach's son:

"If thou hast but one slave, let him be as thine own soul;
  treat him as a brother, though thou has bought him for a price"
                                        (Ecclus. 33:31–32).

This fine counsel, however, is preceded by a harsh recommendation:
"Fodder, and a rod, and a burden are for an ass;
  bread, and correction, and work for a slave" (*ibid.*, 25).

And it is followed by the interesting observation:
"For if thou abuse him so that he runs away,
  where then wilt thou go to recover him?" (*ibid.*, 33.)

was emancipated and became a *libertus,* a freedman, his conduct was judged on principle to be reprehensible. This is the origin of the meaning of *libertine, libertinism.*

It was an inhuman institution, but it was so deeply imbedded in the society of the time and permeated it so completely, that many arguments were advanced for continuing it. And many centuries of Christianity had to pass before it was finally abolished.

51. The cultural picture varied, of course, according to the various social classes. Slaves ordinarily had no access whatever to education. Learned men who fell into slavery usually served in their masters' homes as *grammatici* or *litterati.* The possibilities of getting an education were also very limited to those who were free but *humiliores,* that is, without property, since they lacked both the means and the practical opportunity. The sons of wealthy families, on the other hand, took great pains with their education and generally went to some great city for the final polish. Usually this was Athens which had always been the favorite of students because of its incomparable past. Through its streets and in its squares, which had once echoed to the admonishments of Socrates, there wandered in Paul's time crowds of traffickers in words and sophisms, but even among them there were persons of serious moral intent, as we may gather from the various testimonies dating from the first century A.D.[8]

The ideal of a well-educated Greek was to acquire those virtues which were embodied in the concept of σωφροσύνη, a noble blend of "virtue," "justice," and "rectitude." The upright man dominated his lower instincts with firm justice and prudent fortitude. In his relations with his neighbor his goal was to observe the counsels which had been handed down by the noblest minds and corresponded exactly to the dictates of nature itself speaking in the heart of every man. As for the Divinity, it was deemed prudent to maintain an attitude of reverent homage toward its mysterious decrees, since no mortal, whatever his efforts, could escape his fate if a god was impelling him toward it.

The vicissitudes of life, its alternating joys and sorrows, formed the iron law of the inexorable Fate and an inscrutable Divinity. To strive toward this Being, to seek to be transformed into it through philosophical speculation, had been the dream of the greatest geniuses of Hellas, beginning with Plato. In the contemplation of the Idea, man progressed toward intellectual and moral perfection until he became a participant in the Idea itself. This was his ultimate goal. Man achieved all this himself, redeeming himself through his own spiritual activity. Throughout this process of self-deification no help descended from Olympus to aid man's effort and intention. In direct contrast to this

---

[8] A. J. Festugière, *L'idéal des Grecs et l'Evangile,* Paris, 1932.

philosophico-religious concept were the liturgies of the "mystery religions," which, repeating in the "mystes" the adventures of the god, promised him participation in the god's happiness. In these rituals the human contribution was reduced to a minimum. All depended on the god's gracious concession of his gifts to the initiate (§ 67 ff.).

52. The more prominent philosophers of Paul's time were the followers of Zeno of Cittium and of Epicurus, although both schools had traveled quite far from the principles of their respective founders. Each was completely materialistic, and morally speaking aimed at the attainment of perfect imperturbability (ἀταραξία), but their respective concepts of this differed. Both philosophies also admitted a divine principle but under different aspects.

The god of the Stoics, a material god naturally, was a kind of soul of the world, but a gelid soul which neither loved nor was loved. We read, it is true, "If we have reason, need we do other in public or in private than sing hymns to the divinity, praise it and admire its gifts?" (Epictetus, *Dissertations*, I, 16, 15 ff.), but statements like these, besides being the exception, had a quite different meaning from that which they suggest to Christian minds today. Imprisoned in matter, the Stoic was a pessimist on principle. At death, the elements of man dissolved once more into the great all. The Stoic, ignorant of what awaited him in the beyond, would hasten his own dissolution with suicide.

Because they were very practical the disciples of Zeno won great influence especially among the Romans. The latter were not very much affected by Platonic speculation on the eternal ideas, which they found too vague, and they were left unsatisfied by Aristotle's abstract reasonings on pure act, but they were attracted rather to what seemed a practical solution of the riddle of life. Stoic philosophy seemed a salutary medicine for the soul, a means to free it from all the evils which torment it. This gave rise to the constant effort to reach that imperturbability which lifts the true wise man above the turbulent vicissitudes of life, and which is itself the fruit of repeated victories over one's passions. This was a moral philosophy which in theory seemed almost as sublime as the eternal ideas of Plato, but translated into practice it, too, risked being as unsatisfactory as those ideas. And, in fact, at the end of the second century A.D. Sextus Empiricus, of the Skeptic school, maintained that the truly wise man is an undiscoverable being, who has never really existed (J. Arnim, *Stoicorum veterum fragmenta*, Vol. II, Leipzig, 1923, p. 216, 39) while at about the same time Diogenianus, an Epicurean, conceded that there had been one or, at the most, two such men (*ibid.*, p. 167, 34). Notwithstanding the difficulty of attaining their goal, the Stoics multiplied the lists of various evils to be eliminated and at the same time formulated precepts of very austere and completely autonomous morality. They almost arrived at the *categorical imperative* of Kant, whereby laws are imposed by virtue of themselves alone and not of a higher legislator.

53. The material god of the Stoics resolved into the pantheistic concept of the world, the goodness and perfection of which was recognized as the consequence of a fatality which decrees and sanctions all things. To recognize and reverence this irrevocably fixed order was the duty of the true wise man. Whatever happened, he was undisturbed, because all had been foreordained. In any case, since all things had also an intrinsic value, which determined their place in the scale of preference, the wise man, guided by his virtue, would choose the best while aiming always at a higher degree of *adiaphoria* or indifference. Hence the ethics which guided the wise man in his choice.

While gathering all things within the pantheistic concept, Stoicism affirmed the equality of men, not on the basis of a humanitarian principle, but because all men were considered components of an ideal "city of the world," *civitas mundi,* which transcended social and national differences. In the first century A.D. particularly, after the eclectic movements of Panetius of Rhodes and the encyclopedic Poseidonius of Apamea, Stoicism seemed to return to its original position, approaching again the Cynic concept from which it had derived and with which it shared the negation of desire and exalted an impassive and self-governing freedom. The best exponents of this new current were Athenodorus of Tarsus and Seneca, who were followed by Epictetus, Marcus Aurelius, and others.

Even today, after so many centuries of Christian thought, it is impossible to read the maxims of the "moral Seneca," the *Dissertations* and the *Manual* of Epictetus, and the meditations of the philosopher emperor without being profoundly impressed. Their humanitarian sentiments certainly contributed some betterment to ancient society, especially in mitigating somewhat the laws governing slavery. But on close examination, the whole Stoic structure seems today a castle spun in air, a code of laws that was never promulgated. The castle lacks the foundation of God, the code lacks the divine decree.

Stoicism has frequently been likened to Christianity, principally because of the Christian quality of certain pages in the writings of Epictetus and Seneca. In fact, it was suspected that Paul had exerted a direct influence on his contemporary, Seneca, just as in the second half of the fourth century a whole correspondence between them was manufactured.[9] If we search into the soul of the matter, however, we find beneath the apparent similarity an immeasurable spiritual difference.

54. In their writings and discourses the Stoics used the "diatribe"

---

[9] Cf. W. Barlow, *Epistolae Senecae ad Paulum et Pauli ad Senecam* (*quae vocantur*), in *Papers and Monographs of the American Academy in Rome,* X, 1938.

(διατριβή) a great deal, and since traces of this form are believed to be evident in the writings of Paul,[10] let us examine it briefly.

The διατριβή was not a "diatribe" in the modern sense. It was a particular type of philosophical discussion, part exposition and part dialogue. It was a cross, therefore, between a lecture and a debate. Its origins are to be sought in the question dialogue introduced by Socrates, but it was widely used by the Cynics as well as the Stoics and was raised to a literary form by Bion of Boristhenes at the beginning of the third century B.C. A simple exposition of abstract concepts made little impression on the listeners in the streets and market places to whom these philosophers addressed themselves, but the new form of the "diatribe" fastened their attention. The dialogue passages, in which imaginary persons asked leading questions, gave the exposition a concreteness the listeners enjoyed, and it achieved especial vivacity when caustic invectives and salacious witticisms were woven through the discussion. Horace is referring to this when he speaks of Bion's discourses with their caustic wit.[11]

The use of dialogue made the "diatribe" particularly suitable for the Greek crowds, who were always witty and prompt to argue, while its expository passages answered the purpose of the philosophers. By virtue of this compromise it asserted itself as a new literary form, in itself a compromise between the two forms mentioned above.

But it was a spontaneous compromise since it was the natural answer for two different aspects of the reasoning human spirit, inquiry and affirmation, represented respectively by the dialogue and the exposition. Even after the diatribe had become widely known as a literary form, therefore, it is not at all extraordinary that some later writers who were unfamiliar with it as such should unconsciously adopt some of its features. They did this not because they were imitating some previous literary model but because these elements were to be found in the reasoning processes of the writers themselves. Paul may have been among this number. It is hardly likely that he read the written "diatribes" of Stoic or Cynic philosophers. It is more possible that he heard them use the oral "diatribe" in public discussions. But in any case he may have used features of the "diatribe" simply because he reasoned with his own mind.

55. The other philosophical current of Paul's time with the widest following, after the Stoics, was Epicureanism, the diffusion of which through the Roman world had been especially helped by the philosophical poetry of Lucretius Caro (died perhaps in 51 B.C.). Epicurean thought did not accept any causality transcending the world; all was

---

[10] Cf. R. Bultmann, *Der Stil der Paulinischen Predigt und die kynischstoische Diatribe*, Göttingen, 1910.

[11] *Bioneis sermonibus et sale nigro* (*Epist.*, II, 2, 60).

reduced to pure chance. In morality it preached a prudent moderation of one's needs and a sane seeking after pleasure in order to escape from evil, which was man's supreme goal. Since everything that existed was matter, the gods too — whose existence the Epicureans did not doubt — were also material, although they were ethereal and composed of lighter atoms than man. In man, too, there were heavier and grosser atoms, and these formed the body, while the lighter atoms formed the soul, which, however, was also corporeal. At death the atoms of the soul were scattered through space. The gods did not interfere at all in human affairs and in fact paid them no attention whatever. The "fear of the gods" was the source of the greatest evils and also the proof of consummate ignorance:

> "Oh unhappy race of mankind, to ascribe such things
> to the gods and to add thereto bitter wrath!
> What groanings did they then prepare for themselves,
> what wounds for us, what tears for generations to come!"
>
> (Lucretius Caro, *De Rerum Natura*, V, 1194–1197.)[12]

56. The teachings held by Orphism and Neo-Pythagoreanism were more religious in character than philosophical. The former claimed to be a doctrine of salvation, an asceticism of dualistic inspiration. It promised its adherents a progressive purification until finally the liberation of the divine spark shut within them should be achieved. The Orphic myth centered on Dionysius, identified with Zagreus (§ 71). The concept that the Dionysiac and Titanic elements, namely, good and evil, exist together in man, produced the Orphic morality, the aim of which was to free the luminous, divine element, which composes the soul, from the dark titanic element, the body, considered the prison house of the soul. The liberation was accomplished through a long series of transmigrations and metempsychoses.

Having overcome the first diffidence evoked by its esoteric teachings, Orphism became widely diffused throughout the Roman world, and in the first Christian centuries, particularly the fourth, it inspired an abundant literary production which rivaled the Hermetic.

Neo-Pythagoreanism, which aspired to union with the divinity, was also a philosophico-mystic current. The hero who best achieved this union was Apollonius of Tyana in the first century A.D., about whom the rhetorician Philostratus wrote a romantic biography in the third century. He is supposed to have wandered over almost all the world,

---

[12] *O genus infelix humanum, talia divis
cum tribuit facta atque iras adiunxit acerbas!
Quantos tum gemitus ipsi sibi, quantaque nobis
volnera, quas lacrimas peperere minoribus nostris!*

preaching an austere morality, and — according to Philostratus — performing not a few miracles, which earned him the epithet of wonder-worker. However, Neo-Pythagoreanism, like Stoicism, did not rise to the concept of a personal God. Its "monad" — or elementary being— is identified sometimes with the highest part of the universe, sometimes with the ether, and sometimes with light air. The kinship (συγγένεια) which it claimed existed between the monad and the human soul is merely the capacity of the latter to unite with the monad upon its liberation from the body.

III

Religious Background

57. The Roman Empire in the first century A.D. had achieved great compactness politically, but it had not done so in the field of religion, nor had it tried to do so. The religions peculiar to the various populations gradually gathered into the Empire usually were left undisturbed and continued to live their own life, so that in the end the territory of Rome harbored an endless array of divinities venerated with the most diverse rites and surrounded by innumerable traditions and beliefs. Nevertheless, the new political relationships also produced religious contacts, and these in turn gave rise to "contaminations" and fusions. Early Hellenism had already begun to merge the pantheon of ancient Greece with the various divinities it encountered in its ever widening diffusion. The process was intensified under the Empire and the Greco-Roman pantheon, as it assimilated other local deities, produced numerous syncretist religions in which cults and creeds of the most divergent origin were fused and blended.

This internal process was influenced from without by various currents of philosophic thought. All of the ancient philosophies had inevitably concerned themselves with the concept of the divinity, and we have noted the views of the Stoics and Epicureans (§ 52 ff.). The conclusions of the philosophers were by no means a dead letter but profoundly influenced the practical side of religion wherever their teachings were disseminated. A disciple of the Stoics, convinced of the doctrine of the immutability of Fate (Εἱμαρμένη) could not seriously ask Aesculapius to cure him, nor Mercury to give him success in business. An Epicurean would smile tolerantly at such poetic fancies as Hades and the Elysian Fields. And philosophic thought in general was hostile to the ancient religions, either rejecting them altogether, or interpreting them rationalistically, or undermining them in other ways.

58. But then came the reaction, and this had a mystical character. If this or that religion was to be rejected on philosophical grounds, and if, on the other hand, philosophy itself provided the human spirit with no adequate substitute, then there was nothing to do but abandon the old gods and the old rites and turn to some divinity which really provided "salvation." Even if it had become known only recently, this divinity must represent the unceasing, the eternal, or rather that breath of life which is evident even in physical nature. From such a divinity, "salvation" was to be expected, almost as an infusion of its own perennial life breath. It would be conferred by the divinity itself once the suppliant had accomplished some act which symbolized his implantation in the divinity and at the same time the divinity's acceptance of him. Thus the various "mystery" religions developed, deriving certain elements from the ancient myths but adapting them to the human psyche and infusing into them a new and mystical spirit.

This persistence of religious feeling, despite the largely negative verdict of philosophy, was a fact of particular importance, and seemed a clear-cut answer to that very verdict. By way of reply the philosophers had recourse to an expedient which they have used in all ages. They decamped from the field of doctrine and moved into the pragmatic, admitting that religion might be permitted the ignorant masses since the various beliefs and ritual practices helped to maintain a certain standard of morality (Epictetus, *Dissertations*, II, 20, 32 ff.; Cicero, *De natura deorum*, I, 22, 61), whence the skeptical but utilitarian conclusion of Ovid: "It is expedient that there be gods, and since it is expedient, let us think that they exist" (*Ars Amatoria*, I, 637). In this way, with or without the sanction of philosophy, the religions continued through that evolutionary process, the principal features of which we shall attempt to outline.

59. Throughout the Italian countryside and in the villages (the *pagi*, which later gave their name to *paganism*) the ancient forms of primitive religion were still alive in the first century A.D. They had little mythological embroidery but an abundance of practices designed to capture the divine benevolence. All the events of man's life, whether external or internal, all meteors, plants, animals, illnesses, dreams, etc., were manifestations of the presence of particular deities who presided over these various happenings in the life of the family and the farm, as we may gather from the ancient *Indigitamenta*. The practical mentality of the Latins defined the competence of the individual divinities and the most effective rites to render them benevolent. The relationship between man and the divinity was a bilateral contract, a true *do ut des,* in which these shepherds and farmers obliged themselves to perform certain specific acts of worship and the god to grant their requests. From this resulted the importance assigned to even the smallest acts or gestures that accompanied the rites, and the minute rubrics concerning the different qualities required in the sacrificial victim, and also the calendars which carefully fixed various festival days, most of them agricultural, of the primitive *feriae* of Latium. Several examples of the latter are extant.

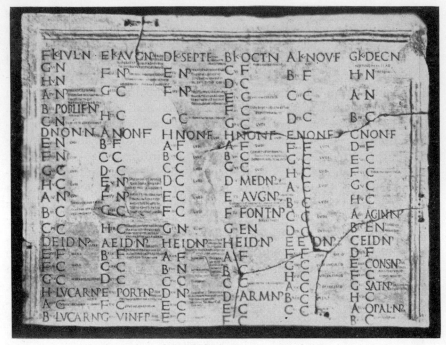

Calendar from Amiternum — First Century A.D.

Christianity came into full contact with this type of nature religion much later, but Paul encountered it during one of his journeys and the episode gives us some idea of its persistence and diffusion in the more out-of-the-way places. Although later in Athens the Apostle does not hesitate to use philosophical expressions in his discourse on the Areopagus, in primitive Lycaonia he adapts himself to the mentality of its untutored people and speaks of the God who bestows "rains from heaven and fruitful seasons" (Acts 14:16). Though a little earlier the narrative mentioned Jupiter and Mercury (*ibid.*, 12) the religious concepts of these mountain people hardly rose above the primitive, nature characteristics reflected in the most ancient religious documents (§ 341 ff.).

60. This primitive religion of Latium, austere and profoundly ethical, was quite rightly deemed one of the principal factors of Rome's greatness. This judgment was expressed in the Senate in 56 B.C. by Cicero, who, after recalling in detail the religious institutions of the ancient Romans, concludes: "However great the love we bear ourselves, O Conscript Fathers, nevertheless (we must acknowledge that) we have not surpassed the Hispani in number, nor the Gauls in bravery, nor the Carthaginians in cunning, nor the Greeks in the arts, nor finally the Italic peoples and the Latins themselves in that shrewdness which is

familiar and congenital to this race and region, but we did surpass all
peoples and nations in piety, in religion, and in this sole wisdom, which
is to recognize that all things are ruled and governed by the providence
of the gods" (*deorum numine — De haruspicum responsis*, 9, 19).
Polybius had expressed the same opinion even earlier: "But the greatest superiority of the Roman commonwealth seems to me to reside in
their attitude of mind toward the gods. What would be blamed among
other peoples, is here, in my opinion, precisely that which sustains Rome,
I mean their great religiousness (δεισιδαιμονία). Religion among them has
acquired such authority over their spirits and so influences their affairs,
both public and private, that there is nothing left to which that influence could be further extended — a fact which may seem surprising to
many. This, as it seems to me, they have brought about with a view to
the common folk" (Polybius, VI, 56, 6–9).

61. The character of Rome's early religion, however, began to be
altered at the time of the Punic Wars when it came into direct contact
with the more evolved Greek pantheon. From then on a kind of indifference for their own gods, a spirit of skepticism nurtured by the
tolerant mythology of Alexandrian origin, began to spread through the
inhabitants of Latium. The complicated Greek myths, into which the
imagination of the poets had projected a few of the bright and many
of the darker human passions, were soon utilized by Latin comedy,
evoking the laughter of the crowds thanks to the irreverence of the
Greek poets. The influence of philosophic theories, like those evolved in
the school of Epicarmus or Euhemerus, increased the sense of religious
malaise among the educated. The populace remained faithful in general
to the ancient gods, but the skeptical attitude of some of the outstanding
representatives of religion could not fail to have some influence on the
plebeian masses too. Augustine is justifiably surprised at the audacious
words of the pontifex Quintus Mucius Scaevola, who said, "Three kinds
of gods have been introduced [among us], some by the poets, others
by the philosophers, and the last by the politicians: the gods of the first
type are fables, for things unworthy of gods are attributed to them;
the second group is not suitable for States, since it includes some things
which are superfluous and others which, if known about, could harm
the people" (*De civitate Dei*, IV, 27; in Migne, *Patr. Lat.*, 41, 133).[1]
On the other hand, the civic and collective character of Roman religion
did not stand up very well upon contact with the Greek religions,
which were more individualistic by nature and could therefore be
extended to persons not included in the *polis*. The cold legal aspect

---

[1] The third type of god is not explicitly mentioned even in the Latin text. But it
is implicit in Scaevola's final sentence: *expedire igitur existimat falli in religione
civitates*. This would be the type of gods which are false, but which must be considered true for practical social and political reasons.

which marked the relationship between man and his deities among the ancient Romans seemed inferior to the exalting enthusiasm which distinguished some of the oriental religions. All of these factors contributed to an increase of syncretism, and at the same time to a sense of bewilderment and skepticism.

62. Augustus, keenly aware of this situation, decided to make the official religion flourish once again. He repaired numerous temples – he claims to have restored eighty-two (*Res gestae divi Augusti,* IV, 20) – and revived many of the ancient customs, which had been abandoned through indifference or because of the influence of the foreign cults. Once the emperor's purpose became clear, various writers resolved to foster the religious renascence. The licentious Ovid evoked the principal religious traditions of the Romans in his monumental *Fasti,* Virgil incarnated in the "pious Aeneas" the feeling of reverence for the native gods, and Horace composed the *Carmen saeculare* for the celebration of the anniversary ordered by Augustus, and pointed out to the Romans their temples abandoned and in ruins (*Carmina,* III, 6, 2 ff.).

But the zeal unfurled by Augustus had a predominantly political purpose. He aimed among other things to cement with religion the heterogeneous structure of the Empire. Consequently one of his chief measures was to spread the worship of Dea Roma, to which the cult of the emperor was later appended.

63. Actually the adulation of the oriental courts, which had deified the Seleucid and Lagid princes, had invented the apotheosis of the sovereign. Later Rome found it a convenient means of binding the various parts of the immense Empire more closely to the center. A temple in honor of Dea Roma had appeared as early as 195 B.C., but this had been in the Orient, in Smyrna (Tacitus, *Annales,* IV, 56), just as in the preceding year Calchis had decreed divine honors for T. Quintius Flamininus, the conqueror of Philip (Plutarch, *Flamininus,* 16). In Rome, however, the first to ascend Olympus was Julius Caesar, for whom divine honors were decreed both during his life and after his death (Suetonius, *Divus Julius,* 76, 1). Augustus was very prudent in this whole matter, on the subject of which the Quirites were highly sensitive. He favored the cult of Dea Roma and Julius Caesar, and he accepted for himself titles which were commonly reserved for the gods as well as the Senate's proposal that the honors of the Lares be offered his "Genius." But he consistently refused to permit temples or altars to be erected in his honor in Rome.[2] He later yielded in the case of cities far from Rome, like Pergamum, Nicodemia (Dion Cassius, LI, 20), and Caesarea in Palestine, which had been completely rebuilt by Herod

---

[2] *In Urbe quidem pertinacissime abstinuit hoc honore* (Suetonius, *Divus Augustus,* 52).

the Great (Flavius Josephus, *Wars of the Jews*, I, 414), but on condition that these temples be dedicated at the same time to Dea Roma.[3] After his death the Senate decreed him various divine honors, which became the concern of a confraternity of priests called the *Sodales Augusti*.

Tiberius was equally reluctant to be worshiped and granted the privilege of building a temple in his honor only to Smyrna, although no less than eleven Asian cities had requested it (Tacitus, *Annales*, IV, 55–56). Under later emperors, and especially Caligula, emperor worship spread throughout the Empire and the cities that were "custodians" of the (imperial) temple, *neōkoroi*,[4] multiplied.

But this cult of the emperor was viewed in practice as nothing more than a political measure, a routine administrative act. It had no effect on the real religious sentiments of the Empire's various populations. Augustus refused the title *dominus* (Suetonius, *Divus Augustus*, 53) more for political than for religious reasons. Tiberius also was opposed to titles of divinity (Suetonius, *Tiberius*, 26). Although their successors accepted them, it is quite evident how little seriousness attached to them, especially after Claudius. At his death, the Senate decreed him the usual apotheosis or "deification," and for the occasion Seneca composed a witty but pitiless satire on the new god, entitling it the *Pumpkinification of Claudius*,[5] in which the emperor's transformation into a pumpkin instead of a god is solemnly described. If the court philosopher could think and write of the event in this fashion, we may be certain the ironical Quirites at home and caustic Greeks abroad showed no greater reverence for the routine deifications of their masters on the Palatine (cf. 1 Cor. 8:5–6). In the truly religious field, emperor worship had no more effect than this.

64. Apart from the emperor worship, however, we must grant that the revival fostered by Augustus did have a certain effect. In the first place, however, this was due exclusively to his own personal power, and in the second, the improvement was a material and external one only — a coat of whitewash on a dilapidated and decaying building. In their hearts there were very few satisfied with the official pantheon. Many of the conservatives and the rural populations disliked it because it was contaminated with foreign deities alien to the Latin spirit. And finally, the majority among the educated, either through philosophical conviction or indifferentism, would have sold all the official gods for an "obol." Juvenal may have exaggerated for the purposes of his satire,

---

[3] *Templa . . . in nulla tamen provincia nisi communi suo Romaeque nomine recepit* (Suetonius, *Divus Augustus*, 52).

[4] Ephesus is given this name in *Acts*, 19:35, because of the temple of Diana.

[5] *Apocolocyntosis divi Claudii;* the title derives from Dion Cassius (LX, 35), and is the best attested. The manuscripts have *Divi Claudii Apotheosis per saturam.*

but what he says of his own time, which followed the Augustan revival, could not have been all sheer invention, namely, that not even the children believed any longer in the existence of the Manes, the underworld, and the river Styx with its ferryboat.[6] And yet, almost all the epitaphs began with the traditional words D(*iis*) M(*anibus*)!

65. So much for the Empire's religious horizons as contemplated from Rome, its political center. There are a few observations to add on Greece, its greatest cultural center.

Vestiges of the primitive forms of nature and animist religions still persisted in Greece, too, in the first century A.D. But profound changes had been introduced in Homeric times and subsequently developed by the mythologists and philosophers, who showed a vague tendency toward monotheism. On the other hand, the restless and fanciful character of the masses, quite different from the cold and traditionalist Romans, was extremely susceptible to syncretism, which was followed, inevitably, by indifference and open negation. Greek atheism antedated the Roman.

In Greece syncretism reached its peak with Alexander and the Diadochi, and nowhere met the diffidence it at first encountered in Rome. Wherever he arrived as conqueror, whether in Egypt or Babylonia, Alexander hastened to be initiated into the local religions, almost as if to seem invested with his power by the respective deities of the localities he subjugated. In contrast to this, Augustus, traveling through Egypt three centuries later, avoided paying a visit to the venerated bull Apis, and praised his nephew because, during his tour of Palestine, he had not paid an act of homage at the Hebrew Temple in Jerusalem (Suetonius, *Divus Augustus*, 93).

66. There entered the Greek pantheon, then, gods of every origin, on an equality of rights with the gods of Hellas. At a certain point the crowding and confusion became so cumbersome that the divinities most resembling each other began to be fused and their rites combined. The Ptolemies of Egypt distinguished themselves particularly in this regard. They had recourse to an even more radical measure, that of proposing a deity which, without banishing his fellow divinities, would be a summation of all of them. The new god was Serapis, who had already entered the Greek pantheon, but was now judged worthy to substitute for all his colleagues. The cult of Serapis quickly became widespread. Even in Italy, at Pozzuoli, a temple to Serapis existed before 105 B.C. But here again the difference in mentality between Latium and Greece was apparent. Rome was at first hostile to this new centralizing deity, and tried to prevent his worship with various decrees of the Senate. But

---

[6] *Esse aliquos manes et subterranea regna*
Et contum et Stygio ranas in gurgite nigras
Atque una transire vadum tot milia cymba,
Nec pueri credunt, nisi qui nondum aere lavantur (*Satires*, II, 149–152).

the hostility was finally forced to yield, the cult found its way into Rome, and the names of Isis and Serapis served to indicate the third region of the Urbs.

But the Hellenism which exported Greek civilization to the Orient imported in exchange certain religious elements of great importance. In the last centuries B.C. they are to be found throughout the Greek religions, from where they naturally penetrated the Latin. These are the mystery religions mentioned previously, which are among the most important of the oriental cults.

67. The originality of the mysteries lies in the mystic inspiration which pervades their rites. It is possible that these go back to some ancient era, to a remote agrarian origin in the nature religions. But it was only in much later times that they assumed a symbolic significance and came to represent the spiritual drama which must take place within the devotee who accepts the mystery in himself. This drama is revealed to him in the initiation rites, but it must be kept hidden from the non-initiated. The devotee must keep his "lips closed" with regard to what he has seen and heard during his initiation, and this obligation of secrecy gave its name to the rite itself: μύω, "I shut (my lips)," whence μυστήριον, the rite of the "mystery," and μύστης, the "mystes," or the one initiated into the rite.

The mystery religions concerned the individual. They do not represent the interests of a group of farmers or shepherds who with incantations invoke fertility for their fields or flocks, as was often the case in the primitive nature cults. Nor do they invoke for the *polis* or the *respublica* the protection of some tutelary deity, to whom these communities have been entrusted, as in the official religions. They concern the individual, apart from all national, political, and social considerations, and they promise him a "salvation," a life beyond death, patterned after that of the god and already begun, symbolically, with his initiation. This symbolic meaning for the individual, however, is historically later in development than the elementary features of the rites themselves. These had an ancient origin in nature worship, while the symbolism is something added later. It answered the needs of those who were dissatisfied with the political religions and had lost their faith in the various mythologies. The individualistic character of the mystery religions, together with their psychological appeal and their essential connection with life after death, marks a truly new period in the development of pagan religion.

68. The particular god venerated and the rites themselves varied from one mystery religion to another. It is possible to trace the primitive features of some of them as far back as the seventh century B.C., but it must be remembered that their symbolism and their diffusion outside their locality of origin belong to a much later period. Cybele from

Anatolia, **Dionysius from Thrace, Osiris** from Egypt, Adonis from Syria, Mithra from Iran began their triumphal progress across the Hellenistic world. The first to reach Rome was the *Magna Mater,* Cybele, in 204 B.C., but official opposition to the mystery religions persisted more or less until the beginning of the Christian Era, when certain of the emperors began to favor one or another cult. They reached their full flowering in the second and third centuries, especially under the Severi, who were of Syrian origin. We may note briefly some of the mysteries which are pertinent to our subject matter.

69. The cult of Cybele, the Great Mother of the Gods, originated in Asia Minor. In a few regions, like the wild and tumbled Anatolian tableland, nature was prodigal in her display of creative force. Wide forests bursting magically into foliage as the last snows melted, broad plains suddenly alive with luxuriant vegetation, suggested to the inhabitants the existence of a mysterious force which rendered woods and valleys fertile. This was the divinity which generated All and to it was given the title of Great Mother. The ordinary mythologies distinguished between the deities of one sex and another, but on the Anatolian tableland the Great Life Principle had no sex, because it contained both sexes within itself. The distinction between the male and the female element implies the idea of mortality, which is overcome

Archigallus with the symbols of Attis (from Turchi, *La religione di Roma antica*)

by the union of the two, while the perfect life rises above this distinction since it is, in itself, continuously self-generating. Attis was already associated with the Great Mother in ancient times. The myth of this young shepherd is to be found in two versions, the Lydian and the Phrygian, but both agree on his emasculation and violent death. The emasculation of Attis, while associated with the idea of the asexuality of the Great Life Principle, was a basic canon in the rites of this mystery. The priests of Cybele, whose mythical prototype was Attis, were castrated and this persisted as a requisite for their priesthood even in later times when the savage rite had been moderated as a result of its diffusion through the West. In ancient times even the devotees of Cybele who were not priests emasculated themselves in the course of frenzied orgies, and by this sacrifice of their virility united themselves with the Great Mother as Attis had done after his death. In the later, mitigated form of the rite, the devotees who were not priests offered instead the sex of the bull killed for the initiation (*taurobolium*). In any case, the offering, whether personal or vicarious, was indispensable, because it constituted the mystic marriage whereby the "mystes" was united with the goddess. Her priests were called *Galli*. They were presided over by an *Archigallus* and assisted by priestesses.

70. The rite originated in Pessinus in Galatia and spread from there to other regions but gradually lost its wild and orgiastic character. Even when it had penetrated Rome and while the threat of Hannibal hung over the city, the Senate remained hostile to it. Citizens were forbidden not only to be initiated into the mystery, but even to assist at any of the ceremonies of the cult. Because of the natural repugnance for emasculation the sacrifice of a bull or a ram was introduced. The blood of the animal was sprinkled on the "mystes" and its male organs served as the vicarious offering mentioned above.

Due to the strict religious secrecy ($\mu\acute{\upsilon}\eta\sigma\iota\varsigma$) binding the initiated, very little specific information has come down to us about the various ceremonies of the rite. We find mention of them in only a few late Christian documents. They occurred in the second half of March, ending on the twenty-fourth, called the day "of blood" (*IX Kal. Apr. Sanguem*), because the emasculation and paroxysmal flagellation of the *Galli* took place on that day. Clement of Alexandria (*Protrepticos*, II, 15: in Migne, *Patr. Gr.*, 8, 76), gives us the formula uttered by the new initiate when the essential part of the ceremony had been accomplished: "I have eaten from the tympanum, I have drunk from the cymbal, I have borne the kernos [the ritual dish], I have lain in the nuptial chamber." This information is confirmed also by Firmicus Maternus (*De errore*, 18, 1). Prudentius (*Peristephanon*, X, 1011 ff.) describes with abundant detail the complicated ritual of the sacrifice of the bull, the chief effect of which was salvation. But its efficacy did not last more than twenty years and so it became necessary to repeat it. When the initiation was over, the devotee ("mystes") was mystically united with the Great Mother and already shared her immortal life.

71. Although we have a greater number of ancient documents in the case of the Dionysian and Orphic mysteries, there is still much we do not know about them. Some scholars consider that the three divinities, Dionysius, Sabazius, and Zagreus, are identical, while others consider them three separate deities with different, although very similar, origins and significance. The wide diffusion of the Dionysian cult in Greece and its minglings with Orphism complicate further the question of its origin and the meaning of certain of its rites.

The riotous Dionysian cult, which originated in savage Thrace, made

The Mysteries of Isis

Above, a priest is holding a vase filled with water from the Nile for the purification. Below, a minister is shaking the sistrum between two groups of devotees.
The National Museum, Naples (from Turchi, *La religione di Roma antica*)

its way through Greece only very slowly and not without open opposition. The Greeks, more balanced by nature, could not comprehend the
orgiastic paroxysm which marked the festivities. With regard to Rome,
we have, in addition to the faithful account in Livy (XXXIX, 14 ff.),
the exact text of a Senate decree which severely forbade the baccha-
nalian rites in the year 186 B.C. (*Corpus Inscriptionum Latinarum*, I,
n. 196). Despite this opposition, the mysteries of Dionysius did
become widely diffused, and evidence of this is to be found also in
the "Villa of the Mysteries" in Pompei. No mystery, with the possible
exception of the Cybelene, carried exaltation to the point of paroxysm
as this one did. The sacred orgies were celebrated at night, for the
most part by women, in the waving light of brandished torches and

amid dizzying dances accompanied by noisy music. The bacchantes, oddly decked in goatskins (*nebridi*) and with horns on their heads, worked themselves up with music, dancing, and fierce gestures, brandishing daggers and wands (the *thyrsi*) until they felt themselves pervaded by the god. Then they threw themselves on the sacrificial animals, tore them to pieces, and ate the still bleeding flesh. This savage rite was later set within the complicated Orphic theology, which attributed a cathartic and eschatological meaning to it. In fact, the Orphics, on the basis of the myth of Zagreus, who was torn to pieces and devoured raw (ὠμοφαγία) by the Titans, presented the eating of raw flesh as a means of attracting the spirit of the god, represented by a kid, and thus of achieving a mystic union with the tutelary deity, which was a guarantee of blessed immortality.

72. Famous among the mystery religions of antiquity were the national Greek mysteries of Eleusis, which still retained very ancient elements of a magic-agrarian character. They were based on the myth of Demeter, representing the fertile and cultivable earth, and the young goddess, Core or Proserpina. Admixtures of the Dionysian myth, however, are evident from early times.

We owe to Apuleius (*Metamorphoses*, XI, 1–30) the ample information we have concerning the mysteries of Osiris and Isis, which spread from Egypt throughout Europe and Asia. They were notorious for their sex orgies, and in A.D. 17, because of a scandal which occurred in the temple of this divinity in Rome, the emperor Tiberius ordered the temple destroyed and the statue of the god thrown into the Tiber (Flavius Josephus, *Antiquities of the Jews*, XVIII, 65 ff.). Juvenal speaks sarcastically of the temples of Isis the procuress (*Satire*, VI, 489).

In the first Christian centuries, the mysteries of Mithra, of Persian origin, were those most widely diffused. They were especially popular among the soldiers, who carried them to the most western regions of the Empire. Although the stars played a predominant part in this particular cult, it never lost its agrarian character, which persisted in the sacrifice of a bull as the symbol of the fertility of nature.

These various mysteries were influenced by one another at different times, and sometimes their respective deities were exchanged for similar ones from the Greco-Roman roster of gods, as the great syncretist movement prevailed again.

73. In general, we may say that in the confusion created by syncretism and the lack of faith engendered by philosophic rationalism, the mysteries seemed to many minds the only means of rising toward a higher world, whence they might control or at least mitigate the iron law of Fate. The mysteries promised to satisfy the anxious yearning that rose from many hearts and which Seneca described in the disconsolate words: "No one is sufficient of himself to lift himself

up; it is necessary for some one to stretch out a hand to him, for some one to draw him upward" (*Ad Lucillium*, LII, 2). The mystery religions pointed out the benevolent divinity which would free man from evil. Hence those who yearned after the good turned to them, all the more so because they appealed to the whole man, composed of body and spirit, and while they consoled the spirit with the promise of the future, they delighted the senses with the emotions produced by the symbols, and the intoxicating effect of the music, dancing, and general festivity which accompanied the ritual.

It was this longing for a "salvation" and an "immortality" on the part of the initiated which kept the mystery religions alive. This indestructible yearning in the human soul is reflected even in the humbler documents of the time. On the tomb of a young man, for example, we find: "Mother, do not weep for me. What would be the good of it? Rather venerate me; I have become the divine star which rises at evening time."[7] No less moving in its intimate religious feeling is the following letter of the third century A.D. found among the papyri at Oxyrhynchus: "Serenus to Diogenes his brother, Greetings. With the help of the gods (our) sister has improved and (our) brother Harpocration is safe and well, for our ancestral gods assist us always, giving us health and salvation (ὑγίαν καὶ σωτηρίαν). . . . I pray always for your health and (that) of your whole family."[8]

---

[7] A. J. Festugière, *L'idéal religieux des Grecs et l'Evangile*, Paris, 1932, p. 150.
[8] B. Grenfell and A. Hunt, *The Oxyrhynchus Papyri*, Vol. VI, London, 1908, p. 302, n. 935.

IV

Jerusalem—Center of Learning

74. We have treated elsewhere the material and moral aspects of the Jerusalem of Paul's time.[1] Here, however, we must examine it more closely as a center of learning.

In the second decade of the Christian Era, Paul went to Jerusalem to complete his education. There, in fact, flowed the purest and richest source of authentic Jewish doctrine, there taught the most venerated masters of the national-religious tradition, whose very presence in the city made it a sacred university. A fervent Jew would no more have chosen to go to some other center of Jewish culture — Alexandria in Egypt, for instance — in preference to Jerusalem than a young Roman patrician of the time would have gone to perfect his Greek education in some Ionian or Peloponnesian city instead of Athens. It would have been the same kind of ignorant mistake.

The great teachers of Jerusalem conducted lessons in private homes, and often also in the courts of the Temple, which were the great meeting places for the entire city.[2] Within the Temple courts and colonnades, the disciples of different schools engaged in friendly dispute, and the followers of a given teacher listened while he explained a passage of the law in the light of "tradition," and resolved an elaborate case problem by way of illustration. The rabbi sat on a stool, while his pupils squatted on the ground around him, their writing tablets on their knees. The visitor to the famous Moslem university in the Mosque of Al-Azhar in Cairo even today will see similar groups of students squatting here and there about their respective teachers, who sit leaning against a column. It was because of this custom that Paul's contemporaries boasted of having been taught in Jerusalem "at the feet of" such and such a rabbi (Acts 22:3).

75. Famous teachers were not scarce in Jerusalem just before and shortly after the beginning of the Christian Era, and Paul arrived to

---

[1] *Storia d'Israele*, II, pp. 417–469 ff. (§§ 364–418); *The Life of Christ*, pp. 17–77 (§§ 13–86).
[2] Cf. *The Life of Christ*, p. 46 (§ 48); p. 263 (§ 262).

Cairo: The Mosque of Al-Azhar. A teacher surrounded by his
students (from *Le Vie del Monde*, 1938)

pursue his studies during a golden age. A few decades before, the
two great masters, Hillel and Shammai, had taught there, and their
light was destined to shine through Judaism for many centuries. The
two different currents or tendencies in the interpretation of the law
which they had initiated were called respectively the "school of
Hillel" and the "school of Shammai."

As a student Paul attended the lessons of Gamaliel, "a teacher of
the Law respected by all the people" (Acts 5:34). In the rabbinical
writings he is called Gamaliel the Elder, or Gamaliel I, to distinguish
him from Gamaliel II, his grandson, who flourished about the year
A.D. 100. The same writings give Gamaliel I the title of *Rabban*, which
carried greater honor than the simple title *Rabbi*. It had never been
attributed to anyone before him, and was given only to four or five
other great teachers who lived shortly afterward. This title, however,
does not prove that he was the president of the Sanhedrin (as some
have maintained although this would clearly be anachronistic), but he
was certainly a member of that body and a very influential one (Acts
5:33–39). A rabbinical maxim says of him: "When Rabban Gamaliel
the Elder died the glory of the Law ceased, and purity and abstinence
died" (*Sotah*, IX, 15). As for his ancestry, it is probable that he was the
son of Hillel, more so than that he was his grandson, that is the son of
Hillel's son, a certain Simeon, whose existence is problematical. However, there is no certain proof in the ancient rabbinical writings that
he was the son of either one of them; neither do these writings always
distinguish between Gamaliel I and Gamaliel II in quoting their sayings.
But even if Gamaliel was not the heir by blood of Hillel, he did inherit
his spirit of gentleness, and this is evident in his defense of the first

Christians before the Sanhedrin (Acts 5:34 ff.).[3] It was a gentleness that characterized his teaching also, for he followed the "school of Hillel," which was almost always more adaptable and kindly than the habitually strict and severe "school of Shammai."

76. In the schools of Jerusalem in Paul's time, the study of the Law (*Torah*) was based on the tenets of the Pharisees. The most fundamental of these, and the one which distinguished them from the Sadducees,[4] was that God had given Moses the Law on Sinai in both written and oral form. The written Law contained only 613 precepts, while the oral Law contained an indefinite but certainly much larger number. The first had been fixed once and for all in writing, but the latter had been handed down through the centuries by "tradition" (παράδοσις), the chief custodians of which were the Scribes and the Doctors of the Law. Although existing in two forms, the Law was one, absolutely, and was infused with the authority of God's revelation. In practice, however, the oral Law as expounded by the Scribes had greater importance than the written Law, so that we find the following maxim: "It is a worse thing to go against the words of the Scribes than the words of the [written] Torah" (*Sanhedrin* XI, 3).

The content of the entire Law was divided into two categories, according to its subject. One division was the *halakah* (the "way"), legal in character since it contained the norms that were to guide the moral pathway of the practicing Jew. The second was called *haggadah* ("narration"), and was mainly historical, for it included all the remaining material which was mostly narrative. The *halakah*, or legal section, had a far greater importance than the other, since rabbinical teaching had an essentially practical aim, namely, to establish an extremely detailed set of rules which were to direct the pious Jew in every action of his religious and civic life. The *haggadah* served as a kind of pedestal to the *halakah*. At the base of the innumerable rabbinical decisions which were to guide the devout Jew were always to be found the historical facts which gave them their legal sanction. The broadest and most general historical fact was that God had spoken in Revelation, the guardians of which the rabbis claimed to be. The specific facts were that God had commanded circumcision, the Sabbath rest, legal purity, and all the other precepts which the rabbis extracted from the written or the oral Law. Every precept, therefore, had to be linked, indirectly at least, with some historical fact which proved its divine origin and by which it was supported as a statue by its pedestal.

77. Naturally no contradiction could exist between the written and the oral Law. In fact, the principal task of the rabbis was to demon-

---

[3] Later Christian legend made Gamaliel a Christian. Cf. *Recognit. Clement.*, I, 65 ff. in Migne, *Patr. Lat.*, 41, 807–818.

[4] Cf. *The Life of Christ*, p. 30 ff. (§ 30 ff.).

strate how the precepts which they derived from the oral Law were more or less implicit in the written Law. The oral Law was rejected by the Sadducees as a human invention devoid of all divine authority. In answer, the Pharisees strove to base the oral Law on the written bolstering the precepts of "tradition" with scriptural texts and with the revered narratives of the *haggadah.*

It is clear, then, that an expert Doctor of the Law had to have a perfect knowledge of the Bible (the written Law). Many legal norms could be deduced from its text by using certain hermeneutic rules, which had been established even before Paul's time.[5] The expert Doctor had to know besides and with equal accuracy the "tradition" (the oral Law), both its legal content (*halakah*) and its narrative content (*haggadah*). As for the former, he had to know the decisions pronounced by the Doctors of the past on each individual concrete case and pass on (*tradere*, "tradition") these decisions to the Doctors of the future. As for the narrative material, he was in no way obliged to worry about profane learning, including the history of foreign peoples (subjects which were never included in rabbinical teaching), but he did have to know as completely as possible that whole collection of stories, beliefs, customs, etc., which was the patrimony of the Jewish people and which, being religious in character, was filled with allusions to the Bible and the history of the nation. Where sporadic elements of profane history and learning may have slipped into this national-religious folklore, they had value only insofar as they were incorporated into the Jewish "tradition" and had consequently become in a certain sense sacred material. The Pharisees, who relied for support chiefly on the populace (in contrast to the Sadducees who belonged to the aristocracy), attached great importance to the historical material, for they quite rightly considered it the genuine product of the whole nation, which was extremely pleasing to the people and at the same time very useful for their task of spiritual edification. Therefore, the expert Doctor had to be able to

---

[5] There were seven hermeneutic rules for deducing a given legal norm from the written Law, and they were attributed to Hillel. Later, Rabbi Ismael, by a series of adaptations and combinations, increased the number to thirteen. I list here only the seven rules of Hillel: (1) "light and heavy" (an argument from the lesser to the greater); (2) "equal norm" (argument *a pari*); (3) "principle from one text" (a norm deduced from a single passage in the Law); (4) "principle from two texts" (a norm drawn from two passages); (5) "general and specific, specific and general" (argument from comparison between two terms); (6) "from something similar in another passage" (a norm arrived at by comparison with a different passage in the Law); (7) "what is learned from circumstances" (a norm deduced from the context of a given passage) (Tosephta, *Sanhedrin*, VII, 11; *Aboth de R. Nathan*, 37). These rules had genuine demonstrative force for the rabbis. If a true demonstration was not achieved by applying them to a given biblical text, the latter might nevertheless contain a "reminiscence" (*zeker*). Note, however, that these rules were valid only for the legal matter of the *halakah*, while other rules were followed in dealing with the content of the *haggadah.*

refer to the *haggadah* and use its material wisely in accordance with certain given rules.[6]

78. How could all this knowledge be acquired by the pious Jew who wished to become a perfect Doctor of the Law? Mastery of the written Law obviously required constant reading and study of the biblical text until he became so familiar with it that he could promptly quote any given passage, and sometimes he knew it all completely by heart. But there were no written texts for the "tradition" in Paul's time. The accurate transmission of its content was still entrusted to the memory of its scholars in accordance with a very ancient custom among Semitic peoples, who always held the memory in the highest esteem.[7] The student of "tradition," therefore, was forced to gather his material here and there wherever he found experts in the subject, then sum up and accurately memorize the material thus gathered, and eventually add to it his own deductions and reflections. This noble labor had been described at the beginning of the second century B.C. by Ben Sira in his portrait of the wise Jew who contemplates the Law of the Most High:

> "The wise man will seek out the wisdom of all the ancients,
>   and will be occupied in the prophets.
> "He will keep the sayings of renowned men,
>   and will enter into the subtilities of parables.
> "He will search out the hidden meanings or proverbs,
>   and will be conversant in the secrets of parables"
>
> (Ecclus. 39:1–3).

The content of "tradition" continued to be transmitted from memory for more than a century after Paul's time, but toward the end of the second century A.D. there did appear a collection in writing (after previous partial attempts to write it down, about which we know very little). This had official approval and began to circulate somewhat timidly. It is our *Mishna,* or "repetition" of the Law, done by Rabbi Juda ha-Nasì, called also Juda the Holy (between approximately A.D. 135 and 220). In it were gathered the decisions of the Doctors who had flourished from the first to the third centuries and were called *Tannaim.*[8]

---

[6] The rules for the interpretation of the *haggadah* were not written down until many centuries after the time of Paul, but they must have been in use long before their appearance in written form. There were four techniques, forming an acrostic on the Hebrew word P R D S ("paradise"); (1) *Peshat:* "simple" (literal interpretation); (2) *Remez:* "allusion" (allegorical interpretation); (3) *Darash:* "search" (an exhortation or homiletic interpretation); (4) *Sod:* "mysterious" (mystical interpretation).

[7] Cf. *Storia d'Israele,* p. 156 ff. (§ 188 ff.); *The Life of Christ,* pp. 130–131 (§§ 150–151).

[8] To the *Mishna* was later added an ample commentary (*Gemara*), which was mostly legal in character. It contained the judgments of the Doctors who flourished between the third and fifth centuries and were called *Amoraim.* The *Mishna* and its commentary form the *Talmud* in its alternative Palestinian and Babylonian editions.

79. The *Mishna* is of precious help in any attempt to picture the schools of learning of Jerusalem in the first century A.D. It is, in fact, an anthology, a distillate, of the rabbinical schools in general and — as we shall see later (§ 89) — the date of its writing does not affect our present purpose.

If we were to give a general estimate of the spirit and mentality of the moral world revealed in the Mishna, we might say that the great teachers of the Law took as the guide for all their activity the longest of the Psalms (119; Vulg., 118), interpreted according to Pharisaic principles. This psalm, in fact, is one long glorification of Divine Law, to which it refers under ten different epithets.[9] In a variety of different ways, its 176 verses express the desire of the perfect Israelite to attain the supreme ideal, namely, to deepen constantly his knowledge of the Divine Law, to observe it in its minutest details and with perfect exactness, consider it the light which illumines his path (v. 105), esteem it greater than infinite riches (v. 72), find it sweeter to the palate than honey (v. 103), and meditate on it every day (v. 97) and every night (v. 148). But the "Law" exalted by this psalm is all of Divine

The Palestinian Talmud. Vatican Codex of the Thirteenth Century

Revelation, contemplated as the support and guide of the faithful Israelite and the principal inspiration of his whole life. The Pharisaic teachers, on the other hand, interpreted it in the legal sense, restricting

---

[9] Cf. A. Robert, *Le sens du mot Loi dous le PS CXIX*, in *Revue Biblique*, 1937, pp. 182–206.

its meaning to the precept and the norm, so that for them the study of the Law consisted in proposing and solving an interminable series of "cases," and they ended up in a veritable sea of casuistry.

80. The perfect Doctor of the Law was required to have a precise and minutely detailed knowledge of the various precepts relating to the purity of foods and objects, the Sabbath rest, the tithe, sacrifices, etc., and above all he had to know how to make the practical application of this knowledge. In other words, he had to be able to solve different concrete "cases" on the basis of the decisions of the most authoritative rabbis and also from his own fund of learning.

It is easy to see that the field was a vast one, and we find it summed up in the six main "orders" or parts into which the Mishna is divided. The first is called Zera'im, "seeds," and discusses the prayers and precepts relating to agriculture; the second, Mo'ed, "set feasts," treats of the Sabbath and the other holy days; the third, Nashim, "women," deals with the legal position of women, especially in relation to marriage; the fourth, Neziqin, "damages," considers various cases of civil and penal law; the fifth, Qodashim, "holy things," gives the liturgy of the sacrifices; the sixth, Tohoroth, "purity," treats the instances of legal purity and impurity. Each "order" is subdivided into treatises, which total sixty-three in all.

In all this vast subject matter, the most frequent "cases" were those posed by the laws on "purity" and the Sabbath rest. We may glance briefly at these here.

81. On the subject of "purity," the perfect Doctor of the Law had to know by heart the long, long lists of receptacles and utensils of all kinds, which varied in material, shape, use, and place for which they were destined, in order to be able to decide whether they were pure or impure, and determine the manner in which they were to be purified. The same was true for other objects of common use both private and public, from benches to shovels and sandals, from baskets to the quills used in writing and musical instruments.[10] But in addition to objects, impurity might attach itself to a whole house, especially if there were a dead person in it. Therefore it was also necessary to know in what instances and to what degree houses incurred contamination, the legal consequences of such contamination, and how it might be remedied.[11] Cases of leprosy were very frequent, and the disease carried with it serious legal-social consequences. The Doctor of the Law, therefore, must be acquainted with it, must know how to recognize the symptoms in order to diagnose it, and be familiar with the legal measures to be taken with reference to it, etc. In addition to human leprosy, there was also

---

[10] An entire treatise is devoted to this subject, entitled Kelim, "utensils." It is the first treatise in the "order" Tohoroth, "purities."

[11] Treatise, Ohaloth, "tents" (houses), the second in the same "order."

a leprosy that attached to objects, and he must know how to deal with this too.[12] He had to know the rite of the "red heifer" (cf. Numbers 19),[13] and he had to have a particularly accurate knowledge of the impurities which lasted until sunset[14] and the requisites for purity which applied to receptacles for water[15] because of the practical importance of these subjects. An extremely difficult and delicate matter was that of menstruation, which gave rise to innumerable and very specific precepts.[16] The matter of liquids which communicated impurities[17] was not to be neglected, nor the subject of sexual emission in men,[18] nor the case of persons who had performed an immersion of purification but were not clean until sunset.[19] But most important of all, from the practical viewpoint, was the purity of the hands.[20] Here the expert legalist had to be able to give precise and definite answers to questions like these: With what water could the hands be purified, and what water could not be used for this purpose? In what utensils must they be washed? Were they to be washed with one water or with two? How far up on the hands must the first water reach, and how far the second? How were they to be dried? etc. Last but not least was the matter of the stems of fruit,[21] which could transmit multiple impurities to be guarded against.

82. As for the observance of the Sabbath, we have already noted conspicuous examples of how the Pharisees who were the contemporaries of Jesus interpreted the precept to rest on the Sabbath day.[22] Here, since we are interested in knowing the mentality of the teachers of Paul's time and of their teaching, let us glance a moment at what they themselves say.

According to the Pharisees, one violated the Sabbath rest by carrying a dried fig.[23] The following passage deals with the Sabbath rest and also indicates certain differences of opinion between the "school of Hillel" and the "school of Shammai" mentioned above (§ 75).

"The tailor shall not go out with his needle near nightfall [Friday evening], for he might forget and go out [carrying the needle on the Sabbath]; thus also, the scrivener [shall not go out then] with his pen.

---

[12] Third treatise, Nega'im, "plagues."
[13] Fourth treatise, Parah, "cow."
[14] Fifth treatise, Tohoroth, "purities."
[15] Sixth treatise, Miqwa'oth, "baths."
[16] Seventh treatise, Niddah, "menstruation." Given the empirical physiology on which these precepts were based, one wonders if they were ever put into practice, or whether they did not remain rather in the field of theory.
[17] Eighth treatise, Makshirin, "what predisposes."
[18] Ninth treatise, Zabin, "flowing."
[19] Tenth treatise, Tebul jom, "immersed during the day."
[20] Eleventh treatise, Yadaim, "hands."
[21] Twelfth treatise, Uqsin, "stems."
[22] Cf. The Life of Christ, pp. 64–65 (§§ 70–71); pp. 313–314 (§§ 308–309).
[23] Cf. ibid., p. 64 (§ 70).

Nor shall a man search his garments for fleas nor read by the light of a lamp.[24] Rightly have [the Doctors] said that the schoolmaster may look where the children shall read [tomorrow, the Sabbath], but he himself may not read. . . .

Shrine for the Scrolls of the Law in the Synagogue

"These are among the rulings which [the Doctors] enjoined while in the upper room of Hananiah, son of Hezekiah, son of Gorion, when they visited him: they counted, and those of the School of Shammai outnumbered those of the School of Hillel. And eighteen things they decided on that day.

"The School of Shammai affirm: Ink, dyestuffs, or vetches may not be put to soak [on a Friday] unless they may be fully soaked the same day; but the School of Hillel permit it.

"The School of Shammai say: Bundles of flax may not be put in an oven [on Friday] unless there is time for them to dry the same day; nor may wool be put into a [dyer's] cauldron unless the color may be absorbed [while it is the same day, Friday]. But the School of Hillel permit it.[25]

"The School of Shammai affirm: Nets may not be spread for wild animals, birds or fishes, unless they may be caught while it is the same day [Friday]; but the School of Hillel permit it.

"The School of Shammai affirm: Naught may be sold to a gentile, nor may he be helped to load [his beast] nor raise [a burden] on his shoulders, unless there is time for him to reach a place near by [the same day, Friday]. But the School of Hillel permit it.

"The School of Shammai say: Hides may not be given to a tanner nor clothes to a gentile launderer unless there is time for the work to be done the same day [Friday]; but all these things the School of Hillel permit so long as the sun is up.

---

[24] Because he might unthinkingly perform some little act to make it burn more brightly.

[25] The difference in opinion in this and the preceding case is based on the principle that according to the School of Shammai, the Sabbath rest is to be extended also to inanimate objects; according to the School of Hillel, it concerns only animate beings. Thus, for Shammai, the dyestuffs in solution or the flax which is drying in the oven violate the Sabbath rest.

"Rabbi Simeon son of Gamaliel[26] said: In my father's house it was the custom to give the white clothes to a gentile launderer three days before the Sabbath.[27] Both [the School of Shammai and the School of Hillel] agree that the olive-press beams and the winepress rollers may be laid down [on Friday evening]"[28] (*Shabbath,* I, 3–9).

83. What garments or personal clothing was one permitted to wear on the Sabbath without violating the prescribed rest? Was it lawful for a woman to go to a public place wearing any ornament she pleased, or were there certain limitations? The following passage answers these and similar questions:

"With what may a woman go out [on the Sabbath] and with what may she not go out? A woman may not go out with bands of wool or with bands of flax or with her headstraps. . . . Nor [may she go out] with forehead band nor side bangles unless they are sewn [on the headdress], nor with a hair net [when she goes] to a public place. Nor [may she go out] with [a tiara shaped like] the golden city, nor with a necklace, nor with nose-rings, nor with a ring that has no seal, nor with a needle that has no eye. Yet if she goes out [wearing such objects], she is not liable to a Sin-offering.

"A man may not go out with sandals shod with nails, nor with a single sandal if he has no wound in his foot, nor with phylacteries, nor with a [health] amulet that has not been prepared by one that was skilled, nor with a breastplate, or helmet, or greaves. But if he goes out [wearing such objects] he is not liable to a Sin-offering.

"A woman may not go out with a needle that has an eye, nor with a ring that bears a seal, nor with a spiral brooch, nor with a perfume-flask, nor with a spice-box; and if she goes out [wearing such objects], she is liable to a Sin-offering. Thus affirms Rabbi Meir. But the Doctors permit the perfume-flask and the spice-box.

"A man may not go out with a sword, or a bow, or a shield, or a club, or a spear; and if he goes out [bearing such objects] he is liable to a Sin-offering. . . .

"A woman may go out with plaits of hair — whether it be her own, or of a friend or of an animal — or with a forehead-band or head-bangles, if these are sewn [on the headdress] or with a hair-net or with false curls [if she remains] within the courtyard [of her own house, but not outside it]; or with wool in her ear, or with wool in her sandal, or with the wool arranged for her menstruation, or with a peppercorn or a grain of salt or aught else that she has put in her mouth, provided

---

[26] This is Gamaliel I, the teacher of Paul.

[27] "Three days before the Sabbath" because the white clothes take longer to be washed, while the colored clothes may be washed in one day (Friday).

[28] Even though the olive press and wine press continue to drip — or to "work" — on the following day, the Sabbath.

she has not first put it there on the Sabbath; and if it falls out she may not put it back. Rabbi permits a false tooth or a gilded tooth, but the Doctors forbid it.

"It is permitted to go out [on the Sabbath] with a coin [that is applied] on a callous [of the foot]; small girls may go out with threads, or even with wood-slivers in their ears [in the holes pierced for earrings]. . . .

"A cripple may go out [on the Sabbath] with his wooden leg, according to the opinion of Rabbi Meir, but Rabbi Josè forbids it. . . ." (*Shabbath*, VI, 1–8.)

84. The divine commandment had ordained that on the Sabbath day the animals of the Israelites should also rest (Exod. 20:10; Deut. 5:14). In what sense was this to be interpreted? That the animals were not to be set to work, or in a stricter sense? The following passage gives the official rabbinical reply:

"With what [burden] may a beast go out [from the stable, on the Sabbath] and with what may it not go out? The camel may go out with its curb, the female with its nose-ring, the Libyan ass with its bridle, the horse with its collar, and all [beasts] which wear a halter may go out with the halter and be led by the halter; these things [to be purified] may be sprinkled and immersed without being removed.

"The ass may go out with its saddle-cloth if this was fastened on before [the Sabbath]. Rams may go out strapped up;[29] and the ewes may go out wearing the strap over or under their tails or wearing the protective cloth; and goats may go out [with their udders] bound up. Rabbi Josè forbids all these things excepting the protective cloth for the ewes. Rabbi Judah says that goats may go out [with their udders] bound up if this is to stop [the milk] but not if this serves to collect the milk.

"And with what may [a beast] not go out [from the stable on the Sabbath]? A camel may not go out with a rag hung to its tail, or with fore and hind legs bound together, or with hoof tied to thigh. So, too, is it with all other beasts. Camels may not be tied one to the other in order to be led, but a man may hold the separate ropes in his hand to lead them provided he does not twist them together.

"The ass may not go out with its saddle-cloth if this was not fastened on before [the Sabbath], nor with a bell even though it is plugged, nor with the ladder-yoke around its neck, nor with its leg-strap. Fowl may not go out with their bands or their straps on their legs. Rams may not go out with their wagon under their tail,[30] nor may ewes go out with the herb to make them sneeze, nor may the calf go out with its rush-

---

[29] This and the following measures were taken to prevent copulation.

[30] These were a breed of fat-tailed sheep; a kind of little wagon was attached beneath the broad, fatty tail to hold it up and protect it from stones and rocks, etc.

yoke,[31] nor the cow with the hedgehog-skin [tied around its udder],[32] nor with the strap between its horns. The cow of Rabbi Eleazar son of Azariah goes out with the strap between its horns, which was not with the approval of the Doctors" (*Shabbath*, V, 1–4).

85. Suppose a house should catch fire on the Sabbath? How should its owner behave? Can he violate the Sabbath to put out the fire? What things may he or may he not carry out of his house? Can he ask Israelites or non-Israelites to help him put out the fire? The answer follows:

"[If fire broke out on the Sabbath] they may save food enough for three meals [for the Sabbath day], for men food that is suited to men and for animals food that is suited for animals. In what way [is this to be understood]? If the fire breaks out on the night preceding the Sabbath, they may save food enough for three meals; if in the morning, they may save enough for two meals; if in the afternoon, enough for one meal. Rabbi Josè says: They may always save food enough for three meals.

"They may save a basketful of loaves even though it is enough for a hundred meals; or a cake of figs or a jar of wine.[33] . . . Rabbi Simeon son of Nanas says: They may spread the hide of a kid over a chest, a box or a cupboard that have caught fire, since it will scorch [but will not burst into flame]; and they may make a partition wall of all the vessels, whether filled [with water] or empty, so that the fire shall not spread. Rabbi Josè forbids new earthenware vessels filled with water since these cannot withstand the fire but burst and put out the fire. If a Gentile comes to put out the fire [the Israelites] may not say to him, 'Put it out,' or 'Do not put it out,' since they are not answerable for his keeping the Sabbath. But if it was a minor [an Israelite] that came to put it out they may not permit him [to do so], since they are answerable for his keeping Sabbath" (*Shabbath*, XVI, 2–6).

86. The case of fire is similar to other cases which are resolved as follows: "If a Gentile lights a lamp [on the Sabbath] an Israelite may make use of the light; but if [he lights it] for the use of the Israelite it is forbidden [to use it]. If [a Gentile] fills [a trough] with water to give his beasts to drink, an Israelite may allow [his own beasts] to drink after him; but if [he did it] for the Israelite, it is forbidden. If [a Gentile] made a gangway by which to come down [from a boat], an Israelite may come down after him; but [if he did it] for the Israelite,

---

[31] A light imitation yoke used to break in the calf.

[32] The prickly hedgehog skin was tied on to keep creeping animals from sucking its milk.

[33] A basket of loaves enough for a hundred meals may be carried because there is only one task involved. This applies also to the cake of figs and the jar of wine, although elsewhere (*Shabbath*, VII, 4), carrying so much as a dried fig is prohibited, except in case of fire.

it is forbidden. There is [in this regard] an episode of Rabban Gamaliel[34] and certain Elders, who arrived by boat and a *goy* ['pagan'] made a gangway by which to come down, and Rabban Gamaliel and the Elders came down by it" (*Shabbath*, XVI, 8).

"If darkness overtakes a man [on the eve of the Sabbath] while he is on his way, he may give his purse to a Gentile, and if there is no Gentile with him he must put it on the ass. When he has reached the outermost courtyard [of the town], he must take off [from the ass] such objects as may be taken off on the Sabbath; and for what may not be taken off on the Sabbath, he must loosen the cords so that the sacks fall down by themselves.

"It is permitted to loosen bundles of hay [tied with two knots] in front of a beast; it is also permitted to shake loose fresh stalks, but not to open bundles [with three knots]" (*Shabbath*, XXIV, 1–2).

87. Suppose a beggar should come to the door on a Sabbath day to ask alms. The householder is within, and would like to give him something. In what manner may he give the alms and the beggar receive it, so that neither violates the Sabbath rest? This is the official answer:

"Thus if a beggar stands outside and the householder is inside [the enclosure], if the beggar stretches his hand inside [the enclosure] and puts anything in the hand of the householder, or takes anything from it and brings it out, the beggar is culpable and the householder is not culpable. If the householder stretches his hand outside [the enclosure] and places anything in the hand of the beggar, or takes anything from it and brings it inside [the enclosure] the householder is culpable and the beggar is not culpable. If the beggar stretches his hand inside [the enclosure] and the householder takes something from it, or places something in it and [the beggar] brings it out, neither is culpable. And if the householder stretches his hand outside and the beggar takes anything from it, or places anything in it and [the householder] brings it inside [the enclosure] neither is culpable" (*Shabbath*, I, 1).

The principle underlying the first instance is that the beggar is guilty because he both takes and carries something on the Sabbath. In the second instance, the householder is guilty because he both takes something and brings it in. In the third and fourth instances, neither is guilty, because neither completes the combined action of taking and bringing out or in.

88. The following passages deal with the differences of opinion between the "school of Hillel" and the "school of Shammai," especially with respect to the Sabbath.

"[If] an egg is laid on a festival-day, the school of Shammai say it

---

[34] It is not clear whether this is Gamaliel I, the teacher of Paul, or his grandson, Gamaliel II.

may be eaten; but the school of Hillel say it may not be eaten.[35] The school of Shammai say: [The quantity of] leaven [which would violate the rules for the Pasch] is the size of an olive, or leavened bread of the size of a date; but the school of Hillel maintain the size of an olive applies in both cases. He who slaughters game or poultry on a festival-day, the school of Shammai say he may dig with a shovel [stuck in the ground the day before] and cover [the blood]; but the school of Hillel say: One may not slaughter unless he has [loose] earth prepared from the day before [the festival]; but they agree that if he has [already slaughtered], he may dig up [earth] with a shovel and cover [the blood], because the ashes of the hearth are considered as having been prepared.

"The school of Shammai say: One may not carry a ladder [on a festival] from one dovecote to another, but he may incline it from one pigeon-hole to another [of the same dovecote]; but the school of Hillel permit [both].

"The school of Shammai say: One must not take pigeons [on a festival day] unless he has stirred them up the day before [the festival]: but the school of Hillel say: [It is enough if] he stands [looking at them without touching them] and says: 'This one or that one will I take.'

"If [the day before the festival] he designated black [doves] but found white [on the festival day], or [designated] white but found black, or [designated] two and found three, they are [all] forbidden; [if he designated] three but found two, they are permitted; [if he designated doves] inside the nest and found them in front of the nest, they are forbidden; but if none except these were there, they are permitted.

"The School of Shammai say: They may not take off cupboard doors on a festival-day. But the School of Hillel even permit them to be put back. The School of Shammai say: They may not lift up a pestle[36] to hack meat; but the School of Hillel permit it. The School of Shammai say: They may not put a hide [of a skinned animal] where it will be trampled on [to prepare it for use], and they may lift one up only if there is an olive's bulk of flesh on it; but the school of Hillel permit it. The School of Shammai say: [On the festival day] they may not carry out a child nor a palm branch nor a scroll of the Law into the public domain; but the School of Hillel permit it. . . .

"The School of Shammai say: [On the festival day] spices may be

---

35 The reference here is to a *festival day* immediately following the Sabbath. If the egg is laid on such a day, then it has been growing inside the chicken the previous day, namely, the Sabbath. Therefore, the chicken had "worked" during the Sabbath rest. This is one of the few instances in which the more rigid school of Shammai is more indulgent than the school of Hillel. This case is the first in a whole treatise of the *Mishna*, to which it gives its name, *Bezah* — "egg."

36 This was the pestle generally used in pounding grain. It was quite heavy and handling it therefore was "labor."

pounded with a wooden pestle and salt in a cruse and with a wooden pot-stirrer. But the School of Hillel say: [On the festival day] spices may be pounded in the usual fashion [as on nonfestival days] with a stone pestle, and salt with a wooden pestle.

"If a man picks pulse on a festival-day, the School of Shammai say he must at once take the edible parts [not the waste] and eat them as he picks them. But the School of Hillel teaches: Let him pick them after his usual fashion into his lap, or into a basket, or into a dish; but not on to a board or into a sifter or sieve. Rabban Gamaliel says: He may even pour water over them, and thus separate [the waste parts, which will float].

"The School of Shammai say: They may send only portions [of prepared food which are to be eaten immediately as gifts on a festival-day]. But the School of Hillel say: They may send cattle, wild animals or birds, whether alive or slaughtered; they may send wine, oil, flour, and legumes, but not grain [which is not milled]. But Rabban Simeon permits grain.

"They may send cloth whether sewn up or not [yet] sewn up, even though it is a mixture [of linen and wool, forbidden for clothing] provided they are to serve [only as tablecloths or coverings] for the Feast; but [they may not send] a nailed sandal nor an unsewn shoe. Rabbi Judah says: [They may not send] even a white shoe, since it requires a craftsman [to blacken it]. This is the general rule: Whatsoever one can [forthwith] make use of may be sent [as a present] on a festival-day" (Besah, I, 1–10).

"If a festival-day falls on the eve of the Sabbath, one may not cook on the festival-day food intended for the Sabbath; but he may cook food intended for the festival-day, and if any is left over, it is left over for the Sabbath. And he may prepare a dish on the eve of the festival-day and depend on it for the Sabbath. The School of Shammai say: [Let him prepare on the eve of the Sabbath] two dishes. But the School of Hillel say: One dish only. But they agree that a fish covered with an egg counts as two dishes. If [the dish intended for the Sabbath] was eaten or lost one may not cook another [for the Sabbath] but if any of it was left, he may depend on that for the Sabbath. . . .

"The School of Shammai say: One may not heat water [to wash] his feet [on a festival day], unless it may also be drunk; but the School of Hillel permit it [as it also permits that] one may make a large fire and warm himself beside it.

"In three things Rabban Gamaliel[37] is more strict, following the School of Shammai, namely, hot food may not be covered up on a festival-day for the Sabbath [the next day]; nor may a candlestick be put to-

---

[37] This is probably Gamaliel I, the teacher of Paul.

gether on a festival-day; nor may bread be baked in large loaves but only in thin cakes [on the festival day]. Rabban Gamaliel said: Never did the household of my father make bread in large loaves but only in thin cakes. But they answered him: What shall we infer from thy father's household, which was strict with themselves, but lenient toward the rest of Israel so that they might permit them to bake large loaves and thick cakes?

"The same authority is lenient in three points [saying]: They may sweep between the couches [of the dining-room], and put spices [on the fire] on the festival-day, and prepare a kid roasted whole on Passover nights. But the Sages forbid [these three things]" (*Besah*, V, 1-7).

89. We have taken the time to quote these documents because they form the moral world in which Paul took his first conscious steps, and they represent the religious and ethical ideas on which he meditated at length during his studies in Jerusalem.

It may be objected that the *Mishna* belongs to a time later than that of Paul and therefore cannot be taken as testimony here. But the objection is not valid. In the first place certain maxims in the *Mishna* either date from Paul's time or antedate it. In the second place, even the more numerous maxims of a later date are relevant here. We are not interested in the separate legal "decisions" handed down by the ancient rabbis, nor the different "cases" they solved. What we are interested in is the general spirit of the rabbinical schools, the characteristic mentality of the teachers and their disciples with whom Paul came in contact. That spirit and that mentality were jealously guarded and remained unchanged not only in the period that transpired between the time of Paul and the *Mishna*, but for many centuries thereafter, and even down to our own day.

To conclude, then, Paul, during his studies in Jerusalem, was striving to become a great teacher in precisely those subjects we have just scanned and the many others we have merely suggested. What a radiant day that would be when he could pronounce with authority on thousands and thousands of "cases" involving this varied content of the Law! On that day, he, Paul, a "Hebrew of the Hebrews according to the Law, a Pharisee" (Phil. 3:5), having attained the highest honor before his compatriots on earth and become greatly pleasing before God in the heavens, might have said that he had indeed gained all things.

Instead he said in the end: "I have suffered the loss of all things, and I count them as dung (σκύβαλα) that I may gain Christ" (§ 170).

V

The Sources for Paul's Biography

90. The sources for the life of Paul are all in the New Testament. Beyond this there is practically nothing, for whatever information is to be found in other ancient documents is as unreliable as it is scanty.[1] These New Testament sources are Paul's *Epistles* and the *Acts of the Apostles.*

There are fourteen letters attributed to Paul in the New Testament and arranged as follows: *Romans, 1* and *2 Corinthians, Galatians, Ephesians, Philippians, Colossians, 1* and *2 Thessalonians, 1* and *2 Timothy, Titus, Philemon, Hebrews.* This arrangement is not chronological, but we shall discuss the epistles in their chronological context. Here it is sufficient to note that allusions or references to Paul's epistles are to be found in the earliest Christian writers, like Clement of Rome (about the year 95), Ignatius of Antioch (a little before 107), and especially

---

[1] These derive principally from the long apocryphal writing, the *Acts of Paul,* which has come down to us in three parts: the *Acts of Paul and Thecla,* the *Martyrdom of Paul,* and the (apocryphal) *Epistles of Paul to the Corinthians and of the Corinthians to Paul.* It is possible that with all its generous flowering of legendary and miraculous detail the story of Paul and Thecla does contain various items of accurate information as some modern scholars have decided (cf. § 188). The exchange of letters between Paul and Seneca is entirely spurious (§ 53). The epistle to the *Laodiceans,* which is still extant, is a medley of passages taken from the Pauline epistles in the New Testament. It seems to be a different writing from the epistles of the same name described as Marcionite in the Muratorian Fragment (ll. 64–65) and was prompted by the passage in *Colossians* 4:16.

Some see an allusion to Paul, almost a *damnatio memoriae,* in the maxim of R. Eleazer of Modin recorded in the *Mishna, Pirqe Aboth,* III, 12 (cf. Strack and Billerbeck, *Kommentar zum N. Test. aus Talmud und Midrasch,* II, p. 754). This is not entirely certain. In any case the passage does not contain any biographical data about Paul but a reproach to rabbinism in his regard. Certainly of Jewish origin is the romantic fable which the Ebionites recounted of Paul. According to them he was not a Jew at all but a Greek born in Tarsus of Greek parents. He fell in love with the daughter of the high priest, and in order to marry her accepted circumcision and Judaism. But when he did not succeed in making her his bride he went over to the opposition and took revenge by writing and acting against circumcision, the Sabbath, and the Law (Epiphanius, *Haer.,* XXX, 16; in Migne, *Patr. Gr.,* 41, 432 ff.). The defamatory and libelous purpose of the story is quite evident; it was invented by Judaism in the same spirit as the rabbinical legends about Jesus (cf. *The Life of Christ,* pp. 79–81, §§ 88–89), and does not merit discussion.

Polycarp of Smyrna (between 107 and 108). The references become more numerous in Justin and in other writers of the second century, which shows that in the first half of that century the Church was already in calm possession of a collection of epistles attributed to Paul, including those to *Timothy* and to *Titus*. Let us look now at the *Acts of the Apostles*.

91. The title for which we find the best testimony in the codices is Πράξεις ἀποστόλων, or *Acts of Apostles*. Less authoritative variants are *Acts of the Apostles* or simply *Acts*. It is a very ancient title and is found in quotations as early as the second century. The term Πράξεις, *Acts*, does not indicate an organic account nor a complete biography, but only the more conspicuous episodes in the life of a given personage. Callisthenes, for instance, the contemporary of Alexander the Great, had written the *Acts* (Πράξεις) *of Alexander*, with this meaning, which was more or less equivalent to the Latin *Res gestae*. The best attested form of the title, *Acts of Apostles* — in preference to the other form, *Acts of the Apostles*, with the definite article — also corresponds best to the content, for the book contains episodes relating not to all the Apostles but only a few,

practically speaking only Peter and Paul, and then its account of them is not complete.

This book comes immediately after the four canonical Gospels in the New Testament and rightly so since its subject matter directly follows the last events narrated in them. The Gospel story closes with the Ascension of Jesus, and the *Acts of Apostles* begins with the same episode and goes on to recount the spread of Christianity first in Palestine, then in Syria and other regions of the Roman Empire. This gradual expansion, which is the general subject of the book, is foretold, so to speak, at the beginning of the words Jesus addressed to His Apostles just before the Ascension: "You shall be witnesses for

Papyrus (Heidelberg) — Coptic Text of the
Acts of Paul

me in Jerusalem and in all Judea and Samaria and even to the very ends of the earth" (Acts 1:8).

92. Since Peter and Paul are the principal persons in the narrative and are presented one after the other, the whole book falls naturally — if not intentionally — into two parts. The protagonist of the first part (Chaps. 1–12) is Peter, of the second (Chaps. 13–28), Paul. But Paul enters the scene toward the end of the first part, and so this becomes a kind of introduction for the second. Here is an outline of both: *First Part* — Prologue: Ascension of Jesus; election of Matthias (Chap. 1). — Pentecost: discourse of Peter; first conversions in Jerusalem (Chap. 2). — The lame man cured; discourse of Peter (Chap. 3). — Peter and John denounced to the Sanhedrin; charity among the faithful (Chap. 4). — Ananias and Saphira; miracles of the Apostles, who are imprisoned and denounced to the Sanhedrin (Chap. 5). — Election of the seven deacons; Stephen is accused (Chap. 6). — Discourse and stoning of Stephen (Chap. 7). — Persecution of the community of Jerusalem, in which Saul (Paul) takes part; conversion of the Samaritans by the deacon Philip, and by Peter and John; conversion of the Ethiopian (Chap. 8). — Conversion of Paul; Paul preaches in Damascus; Paul's flight to Jerusalem; Paul in Tarsus (9:1–30). — Peter cures the paralytic Aeneas in Lydda; Tabitha raised from the dead in Joppe (9:31–43). — The centurion Cornelius; Peter in Jerusalem defends his conduct with respect to Cornelius (10–11:18). — Beginnings of the community in Antioch; Barnabas and Paul; famine and the journey with contributions (11:19–30). — The community of Jerusalem is persecuted by Herod Agrippa I; execution of James the Elder and imprisonment of Peter; miraculous liberation of Peter; death of Herod Agrippa; Barnabas and Paul return to Antioch (Chap. 12).

Second Part. — Paul's first missionary journey (Chaps. 13–14). — Council of the Apostles (15:1–35). — Paul's second missionary journey (15:36–18:22). — Paul's third missionary journey (18:23–21:16). — Paul meets James the Less in Jerusalem; Paul is arrested in the Temple (21:17–40). — Paul's discourse to the people; Paul in prison, and then before the Sanhedrin (Chap. 22). — Discourse of Paul; conspiracy of the Jews against him; Paul in Caesarea (Chap. 23). — Paul before the procurator Felix (Chap. 24). — Paul before the procurator Festus, Agrippa, and Bernice (Chaps. 25–26). — Paul's voyage to Rome; the shipwreck and the winter sojourn in Malta; arrival in Rome and two years' sojourn there (Chaps. 27–28).

The story for the most part is told in the third person (*he . . . they*) as is usual in historical narratives. But the first person plural (*we . . .*) occurs in four passages, as if the narrator had taken part personally in the events in those four instances, which, however, appear suddenly with no warning or explanation for the change of pronoun. The four passages, known as the "we-sections," are the following: 16:10–17; 20:5–15; 21:1–18; 27–28:16.[2] Note that all are to be found in the second part of the book.

93. The earliest writers we know agree in attributing the book of the *Acts* to Luke the physician, whom we discussed in connection with the Third Gospel, which is also attributed to him.[3]

Apart from the allusions or references found in the oldest writings, the explicit testimony for his authorship naturally parallels that for the Third Gospel. In the late second century, the Muratorian Fragment says in its ungrammatical Latin (corrected where necessary for clarity) *Acta autem omnium apostolorum sub uno libro scripta sunt Lucas optimo Theophilo comprehendit quia sub praesentia eius singula gere-bantur* (ll. 34–37). Here the unknown author points out that the facts relating to the Apostles in general are recounted in one book, in contrast to those relating to Jesus which are narrated in the four books of the Gospels. The author of this book is Luke (mentioned earlier by the Fragment in connection with his Gospel) who is writing for the "worthy Theophilus" and describing events at which he himself was present.

The testimony of Irenaeus of Lyons belongs to about the same period. He quotes various passages of the *Acts*, sometimes citing the title, and among other things, he says: "That this Luke was the inseparable companion of Paul and a collaborator with him in the preaching of the Gospel, he himself reveals, not boasting but constrained to do so by the truth itself. In fact, he says, when both Barnabus and John, surnamed Mark, had left Paul and sailed for Cyprus, we came to Troas. . . . Sailing therefore from Troas, we directed the ship toward Samothrace. . . . We spoke with the women (cf. Acts 15:39–16:13). . . . Having been present at all these things Luke put them diligently together in writing. . . . Since he was not only the disciple but also a collaborator with the Apostles, and especially of Paul" (*Adv. Haer.*, III. 14, 1; in Migne, *Patr. Gr.*, 7, 913–914). Also belonging to the late second century are the various Prologues, Coptic, Greek, and Latin[4] at the beginning of different parts of the New Testament and expanded by the later versions of Monarchian Prologues. Even in the earliest Prologues Luke is mentioned as the author of the *Acts*. Usually he is named as the author of the Third Gospel, and then follows the additional information, "afterwards the same Luke wrote the *Acts of the Apostles*."[5]

---

[2] A fifth passage is perhaps 2:27–28; for this see § 317, note.

[3] Cf. *The Life of Christ*, pp. 114–125 (§§ 135–145).

[4] Latin texts in D. de Bruyne, *Les plus anciens prologues latins des Evangiles*, in *Revue bénédictine*, 1928, pp. 193–214; the other texts in M.-J. Lagrange, *Evangile selon Saint Luc*, 3rd edition, Paris, 1927, pp. XIII–XVIII.

[5] . . . *postremo scripsit Lucas Actus apostolorum.*

94. From the second to the third centuries, the testimony becomes increasingly plentiful both among the Latin authors (for example, Tertullian, *De Ieiunio*, 10, in Migne, *Patr. Lat.*, 2, 966 al. 1017) and the Greeks (Clement of Alexandria, *Stromata*, V, 12, 82, in Migne, *Patr. Gr.*, 9, 124; Origen, *C. Celsum*, VI, 11, in Migne, *Patr. Gr.*, 11, 1308, and the quotation in Eusebius, *Hist. Eccl.*, VI, 25, 14). All of these quote the *Acts* as a book of the New Testament and attribute its authorship to Luke.

It is unnecessary to prolong the list of quotations, since all agree that in the third century the *Acts* were accepted both among the canonical writings and as the composition of Luke (cf. Eusebius, *Hist. Eccl.*, II, 22, 1; III, 4, 1–10; III, 25, 1). It is therefore surprising to find in a homily attributed to John Chrysostom the statement that many did not know who the author of the *Acts* was and attributed it to either Clement of Rome, to Barnabas, or to Luke the Evangelist.[6] This is repeated by Photius,[7] but his source is unquestionably the homily, since there is not the slightest evidence in antiquity that the *Acts* were ever attributed to Clement of Rome or Barnabas. As for the homily itself, it is probably a rewrite of one of Chrysostom's other works and not authentic. In any case, whoever the author, he must have confused the *Acts* and the *Epistle to the Hebrews*, which was attributed by some ancient writers to Clement of Rome or to Barnabas (§ 652 ff.).

95. We find much internal evidence in the writing to prove its close relationship with the Third Gospel and confirm Luke's authorship. The prologue to the Third Gospel, which dedicates the book to the "most excellent Theophilus,"[8] has its parallel in the prologue to the *Acts* (1:1–2), which is also addressed to Theophilus and expressly mentions the earlier writing ($\pi\rho\hat{\omega}\tau\sigma\nu$ $\lambda\acute{o}\gamma\varsigma\nu$) sent him, namely, the Third Gospel. It also mentions the final episode of this Gospel, the Ascension, with which the *Acts* resumes the narrative. Hence the connection between the two is quite clear.

96. There is besides a strong kinship between the two writings in language, style, and general method.

We noticed in discussing the Third Gospel that the author likes to present his material in parallel episodes, diptychs so to speak, in which one figure balances another.[9] The same tendency reappears in the *Acts*, and in even greater measure since there is greater opportunity. We find, in fact, that Peter and Paul, the respective protagonists of the two parts of the book, are paralleled in several biographical episodes, particularly those dealing with miracles. For instance, a cripple is cured by Peter

---

[6] *Hom. II in Ascensionem et initium Actorum*, 8, in Migne, *Patr. Gr.*, 52, 780.

[7] Photius, *Quaest. ad Amphilochium*, 123 al. 145, in Migne, *Patr. Gr.*, 101, 716.

[8] Cf. *The Life of Christ*, p. 119 ff. (§ 140 ff.).

[9] *Ibid.*, pp. 221 (§ 227), 247 (§ 251), 459 (§ 455), etc.

(3:2 ff.) and another by Paul (14:8 ff.); Peter raises Tabitha to life
(9:36 ff.) and Paul resuscitates the dead Eutychus (20:9 ff.); Peter
strikes dead Ananias and Saphira (5:1 ff.) and Paul blinds the magician
Elymas (13:8 ff.); Peter's shadow is miraculous (5:15) just as the linen
used by Paul (19:12); the centurion Cornelius adores Peter as a divine
being thereby eliciting his protests (10:25–26), and the Lycaonians
venerate Paul as the god Hermes causing him to make similar protests
(14:11 ff.); both are miraculously freed from prison, one in Jerusalem
(12:7) and the other in Philippi (16:26); one is scourged in Jerusalem
(5:40) and the other in Philippi (16:22), and so on through the other
episodes. This parallel treatment is intentional in the sense that among
the numerous episodes in Paul's life, the author has purposely chosen
those most similar to events in the life of Peter and omitted many
others for which there was no corresponding episode in Peter's activity.
From Paul's letters, in fact, we learn many things which are not recorded
in the *Acts* (cf. 2 Cor. 2:23–27), and which our author was in a position
to know independently from the letters. In this choice and presentation
of his narrative material, his purpose was to demonstrate, among other
things, a secondary thesis which is indicated in Paul's own words:
". . . he who worked in Peter for the apostleship of the circumcised
worked also in me among the Gentiles" (Gal. 2:8). This thesis was
itself a diptych, ready made to the author's own taste. He merely filled
in the two pictures, and the result fell naturally into the two parts
of the book.

97. In language and style the Third Gospel and the *Acts* are unquestionably twin writings. This statement is based on the extremely detailed
vocabulary studies made on both works and the comparative analysis of
these and the other New Testament writings. The point of departure
for these studies were the "we-sections" (§ 92) and rightly so, for once
the characteristic features of style and language peculiar to these passages were established, the next step was to determine whether they
are also to be found in the rest of the *Acts* and in the Third Gospel. If
they are, then we have a confirmation that the author of the we-sections
is also the author of the rest of the narrative in the *Acts* and of the
Third Gospel as well. With this end in view, scholars have drawn up,
with truly admirable patience, long lists of words and grammatical
constructions and special phrases which we cannot quote at length
here.[10] It is to the point, however, to include a very brief summary.

98. The *Acts* are composed of 1007 verses, of which 97 are in the first
person plural (almost a tenth of the book). Excluding proper names

---

[10] In addition to the works of A. von Harnack, cited in § 132, note, cf. also J. C.
Hawkins, *Horae synopticae*, 2nd edition, Oxford, 1909, and E. Jacquier, *Les Actes
des Apôtres*, 2nd edition, Paris, 1926, pp. LX ff., CLXIV ff.

and numbers, Harnack[11] has counted 67 words which appear in the we-sections and also in the remainder of the *Acts* but not in any of the four Gospels; 43 words which occur in these same sections, in the rest of the *Acts* and in the Third Gospel but not in the three other Gospels; twenty words which occur in these sections and in the Third Gospel but not in the rest of the *Acts* or in the other three Gospels. To sum up, there are 63 words used in both the we-sections and in the Third Gospel, and there are 110 words which occur in these passages and in the rest of the *Acts*. In all there are 130 words which form the particular patrimony common in the we-sections, the rest of the *Acts,* and the Third Gospel (and excluding the other three Gospels). The number seems very high when we consider that the entire vocabulary of the *Acts* consists of about 1800–2000 words including the proper names[12] and that of these words 450 are not used in the rest of the New Testament (with the exception of the Third Gospel). These 130 words are like so many links in a chain which binds together the we-sections, the rest of the *Acts*, and the Third Gospel, and at the same time bars the entrance to any other author. The conclusion, therefore, would be that the three groups of texts are the work of one author, who has used in them his usual language equipment, which — as always — is different from that of any other writer.

This conclusion is confirmed by other comparisons and calculations made on the basis of grammatical constructions, syntax, and variations in style, but it is not necessary to go into these here.

99. On the other hand, it has been observed that the we-sections also show great lexical differences in comparison with the other parts of the *Acts.* This is true. The passages contain 111 words which do not appear elsewhere in the same writing. But the reason is clear. These words are used for the most part in the account of Paul's voyage from Caesarea to Rome, and they are nautical terms. Since nowhere else in the *Acts* is there an account of the same kind and length, we do not find the same technical terms. The objection has also been made that the sameness of vocabulary discovered in the we-sections and the other sections of the *Acts* (as well as the Third Gospel) might be due not to the original author writing a first draft but to the skill of a later editor who copied the style of the we-sections in working over the other passages of the *Acts*. In the first place, however, this thesis has to be proved against the opposite alternative, which is unquestionably the

---

[11] *Lukas der Arzt* (quoted § 132, note), p. 111 ff.

[12] The variation is due to the different criteria followed by different scholars in making these calculations (some count in proper names and enclitics, others do not), and also to their choice between variants of the text, and to the additional passages in the "Western" text of the *Acts* (p. 120, note).

more natural. Besides, an imitation so perfect that it cannot be discovered by the most patient modern research was an enterprise extremely difficult in itself and not justified by any special motive (or did the presumed editor perhaps fear that as soon as the book was published it would be subjected to the microscopic scrutiny it has undergone nineteen centuries later?). And finally, the better to conceal his action, this alleged editor would have had to start by eliminating the first person plural from the passages where it occurs since this would compromise him too much, just as he would have had to eliminate certain conspicuous differences in tone which are to be found even today between the first and second parts of the book (§ 111). Such an editor would have been too adroit as a linguist but too clumsy as an imitator.

100. A philological examination of the texts, then, leads to the conclusion that the author of both the we-sections and the rest of the *Acts* (and of the Third Gospel) was one and the same person. And this conclusion is confirmed after all by early tradition, which attributed these writings to no one but to Luke, the physician and disciple of Paul.

As for this description of Luke, we can only repeat briefly what we have said elsewhere.[13] We certainly could not conclude from the *Acts* alone that their author was a doctor, but they do contain good confirmation of this fact (notwithstanding the usual cautious reserve of some scholars). We may interpret as evidence of this kind some more or less technical expressions used in the account of the cure of the cripple (Acts 3:7–8), of Publius in Malta (28:8), and other passages (13:11; 28:3; etc.). Much more evident is the kinship of thought and concept which links the author of the *Acts* with the spiritual world of Paul. It is highly probable that Luke in writing the *Acts* did not know, or at least did not use, the epistles of Paul (§ 113). Nevertheless there are more than a hundred words, phrases, and typical expressions which are found only in the epistles of Paul and the *Acts* and not elsewhere. In addition, the highlights of Paul's teaching, especially the Redemption by Christ, justifying faith, the action of the Holy Spirit, etc., are also to be found in the *Acts*. This is all very clear if we go back to tradition: Luke, the disciple of Paul, has gleaned from his long association with him those ideas and expressions which Paul communicated to others in his letters (§ 566).

101. What was Luke's purpose in writing the *Acts?* The most natural answer is that it was similar to and associated with his purpose in writing the Third Gospel. In the latter, he addressed himself to Theophilus, saying that he was writing "that thou mayest understand the certainty of the words in which thou hast been instructed" (κατηχήθης; Lk. 1:4), an allusion to the apostolic instruction or "catechesis" con-

---

[13] Cf. *The Life of Christ,* pp. 117–118 (§§ 137–138).

cerning the facts and teachings of the Saviour Jesus Christ. Therefore, in the later writing, also addressed to Theophilus, it is probable that Luke wished to recount what had happened to continue Jesus' work after he had left the earth. In fact, as we noted above (§ 91), the general subject of the book is the growth of Christianity first in Palestine, and then in Syria and other regions. Now this account is connected with the narrative of the Third Gospel, because Theophilus was to be instructed also concerning the "certainty of the words" — that is, the reality of the events — relating to the diffusion of Jesus' teachings. While Jesus remained among men, there unfolded the first period of "salvation." When he had gone, the second period began. Theophilus' instruction was to cover both periods.

102. But during this second period, the absent Christ sent a "messenger" to promote the diffusion of his doctrine, the Holy Spirit. In fact, at the very beginning, the narrative in the *Acts* recalls the promise Jesus made his Apostles shortly before the Ascension: "You shall be baptized with the Holy Spirit . . . you shall receive power when the Holy Spirit comes upon you. . . ." and as a consequence of this "baptism" or investiture by the Holy Spirit "you shall be witnesses for me in Jerusalem, and in all Judea and Samaria and even to the very ends of the earth" (Acts 1:5–8). Right after this we have the account of the descent of the Holy Spirit on Pentecost, and then the immediate, and gradually the remote, consequences of that descent. Peter, as soon as he had received the Spirit, spoke to the crowd in Jerusalem and won converts to the teaching of Christ (2:14 ff.), just as shortly afterward, "filled with the Holy Spirit" he spoke before the Sanhedrin (4:8). The seven deacons were to be "full of the (Holy) Spirit," and such a man was Stephen (6:3–5). When the Samaritans began to be converted, Peter and John went to them, and "laid their hands on them and they received the Holy Spirit" (8:17). As soon as Paul was converted Ananias visited him that he might be "filled with the Holy Spirit" (9:17). And as the Church grew "throughout all Judea and Galilee and Samaria . . . it was filled with the consolation of the Holy Spirit" (9:31). The same may be said for the evangelization of the pagans. The conversion of the centurion Cornelius was prepared by the Holy Spirit (10:19) and confirmed by more abundant infusions of the Holy Spirit (10:44–47). Barnabas, who was "full of the Holy Spirit" (11:24) leaves with Paul on his first missionary journey by express command of the Holy Spirit (13:2), so that they were "sent forth by the Holy Spirit" (13:4), and the converts made during that journey were "filled with joy and with the Holy Spirit" (13:52). It is not necessary to continue this enumeration, for the whole narrative is filled with the interventions of the Holy Spirit much more than any other New Testament book. It is evident, then, that in the *Acts* Luke proposed to narrate for Theophilus the story of the spread of Christianity as the work of the Holy Spirit, or rather, to show him how Jesus' work was continued with the help of him whom he had sent.

This purpose was pointed out by the early writers, who with complete historical accuracy and no less perception assert that the "gospels are the story of those things which Christ did and said, while the *Acts* are those things which the other Paraclete said and did."[14]

103. In any case, as we noted in our discussion of the Third Gospel, Luke is not writing for Theophilus alone, but for the many Christians whose spiritual state was more or less the same as his. Behind Theophilus, Luke sees the Christians converted from paganism, who belong for the most part to churches founded by Paul, and especially the converts of Rome (§ 106). To all of these in general, the *Acts* was to demonstrate, in the light of the events they narrated, the validity of a thesis propounded especially by the teacher Paul, namely, that "there is no distinction between Jew and Greek, for there is the same Lord of all" (Rom. 10:12); that before God there is no " 'Gentile and Jew,' 'circumcised and uncircumcised,' 'Barbarian and Scythian,' 'slave and freeman,' but Christ is all things and in all" (Col. 3:11), for "it is the power of God unto salvation to everyone who believes, to Jew first and then to Greek" (Rom. 1:16). This is precisely the thesis of universality demonstrated by the narrative of the *Acts,* which accompanies the expansion of the Church step by step, first among the Jews of Jerusalem and Palestine, then among the heterogeneous Samaritans, and then the Jews of the Diaspora and at the same time the uncircumcised of various regions from the barbarians of Lycaonia and Phrygia in Asia Minor to the Greeks of Ionia and Achaea, and finally to Rome itself, the center of the political power.

104. But the question may arise whether in addition to this theological-historical thesis, which is the essential theme of the *Acts,* Luke had a secondary purpose in mind of a more practical character and with a direct and immediate object in view. There have been various affirmative answers to this question, and some have substituted other theses entirely for the theological-historical one. We shall examine some of these substitutions in a moment. But here we may note a particular theory which completely rejects the thesis mentioned. In 1855 M. Aberle, elaborating on an idea already put forth by others, maintained that the *Acts* had been written as a defense for Paul before Nero's tribunal

---

[14] Thus John Chrysostom, *In Act. hom.,* 1, 5 (in Migne, *Patr. Gr.,* 60, 21). But substantially the same thought is repeated by Oecumenius, *Argumentum in Act. Apost.* (in Migne, *Patr. Gr.,* 118, 29) and later by Theophylact, *Expositio in Act.,* prologue (in Migne, *Patr. Gr.,* 125, 849), which states in its epigrammatic style: "The Gospels show forth the acts of the Son, the *Acts* those of the Most Holy Spirit."

in Rome.[15] Three charges had been made against Paul by Tertullus, the advocate of the Jews, when the Apostle was brought before the court of the Roman procurator, Felix, in Caesarea. The first was that he was a "promoter of seditions among all the Jews throughout the world," the second, that he was a "ringleader ($\pi\rho\omega\tau o\sigma\tau\acute{a}\tau\eta\nu$) of the sedition of the Nazarene sect," and the third, that he tried to desecrate the Hebrew Temple in Jerusalem (Acts 24:5–6). The third accusation could not ruffle Rome's judges very much, although the Romans as a general rule respected and required respect for the religious customs of the peoples they subjected. But the first two accusations were very serious, for that of sedition bespoke a threat to that tranquillity of order the Romans so jealously guarded, and the charge of leading the Nazarene sect capped the first by pointing out the root of the evil: the seditious were the Christians as such and therefore the new religion must be prosecuted as the enemy of public order and a danger to the Roman Empire. Aberle assumes these same accusations were made before the emperor's tribunal in Rome, to which Paul had appealed as a Roman citizen. But Luke, during Paul's two years in Caesarea and the next two in Rome before the trial, is presumed to have gathered documents for the Apostle's defense, demonstrating the charges were baseless. This was the origin of the *Acts*, which were substantially a forensic defense of Paul.

105. This theory is superficially very attractive but in substance quite shallow. It captured the fancy of other scholars, it is true, who advanced it again later, but its weaknesses forced them to modify the general outline in various ways. And then, as usual, the theory began to be specific about certain details: Theophilus was supposedly one of the Christians of "Caesar's household" (Phil. 4:22; cf. 1:13–14); together with Seneca and Burrus, he was one of the members of the imperial council before which Paul's case was brought; in fact, one or the other of these famous personages might well have been hidden under the symbolic name of "Theophilus," and similar flights of fancy. There is no flight of fancy, however, in the argument taken from the *Muratorian Fragment*, which in the fourth line says that Paul took Luke with him *quasi ut iuris studiosum* (almost as an expert in the law). Some have maintained that the reading should be corrected to *itineris sui socium*, or the like, but it must stand as it is[16] and would refer therefore to a kind of semifunction as lawyer which Luke assumed and from which the *Acts* resulted.

The weakness of this hypothesis, however, becomes immediately

---

[15] M. Aberle, *Ueber den Zweck der Apostelgeschichte*, in *Theolog. Quartalschrift*, 1855, pp. 173–236.

[16] Cf. M.-J. Lagrange, *Evangile selon Saint Luc*, 3rd edition, Paris, 1927, XII.

apparent when we examine the actual facts. If the *Acts* was written as a forensic defense of Paul, we cannot explain the presence of at least half of the episodes it narrates. How could the Ascension of Jesus, the descent of the Holy Ghost, the long discourses with their cargo of scriptural quotations, and so many other elements, especially in the first part of the book, possibly matter to the judges in Nero's tribunal? On reading the long succession of miracles recounted therein, they would probably have shaken their heads incredulously muttering something like Horace's "Let the Jew Apella believe these things, not I."[17] No, the *Acts,* given the form in which it was written, could not have been either a brief for the defense or a petition.

106. Nevertheless, there may be some kernel of truth in the theory. It is evident that the *Acts* omits no opportunity to show that Paul was never disturbed by the various Roman magistrates encountered in the course of his journeys, and that rather they protected him from the persecutions of the Jews (13:6 ff.; 16:35 ff.; 18:12 ff.; 19:31 ff.; 23:23 ff.; 25:13 ff.; 27:3 ff.; 28:7, 16, 31). These incidents, almost all of them in the second part of the book, which is devoted especially to Paul, do make it seem a kind of apologia for him. But this is simply the result of the narrative material. It is quite possible, however, that Luke purposely underscored the generally benevolent disposition of the Roman magistrates toward Paul in order to dissipate the malicious rumors spread by the Jews against him, which had reached Rome, and also to help create in that city an atmosphere favorable to Christianity in general.

❊   ❊   ❊

107. In writing a narrative like the *Acts,* it was impossible for Luke not to use information, oral or written, furnished by others.

The book embraces a period of about 32 years, and the first part especially deals with many events at which Luke was not present. Hence he had to gather his material from various sources. In the prologue to his Gospel, Luke tells Theophilus that before writing he has "followed up all things carefully from the very first." We may suppose he undertook the same careful preparation for the *Acts,* which are addressed to the same Theophilus as a continuation of the Third Gospel. This raises the question of the sources, the favorite stamping ground of modern criticism. How many and what were the sources of the *Acts?*

108. Let us begin with the clearest and most certain. For the second part of the book, Luke was his own principal source, since he was an eyewitness of the events. This is indicated by the we-sections (§ 92) mentioned above. These passages require an author who, together with other persons ("we . . ."), participated in the events he is narrating,

---

[17] *Credat Judaeus Apella non ego* (I *Sat.*, V, 100).

namely, the events which occurred from about the middle of Paul's second missionary journey on (Acts 16:10 ff.) although not without interruption. We know only four of Paul's companions on his various voyages, Timothy, Titus, Silas, and Luke, but all of these are to be excluded as possible authors of the we-sections except Luke. Timothy is eliminated by Acts 20:4–6, since he left the group at that point while the narrative continues in the first person plural. Titus was Paul's companion on the journey to the council of Jerusalem (Gal. 2:3), but not on the subsequent journey with which the we-sections begin. Silas is excluded by the fact that he is already in Paul's company while the narrative is still in the third person (Acts 15:40) although it reverts to the first person plural soon afterward (16:10) when the travelers reach Troas, where, therefore, the narrator was. In addition, none of these three — Timothy, Titus, or Silas — accompanied Paul on the voyage to Rome, which is also recounted in the first person plural. This leaves only Luke, and there is excellent confirmation in the fact that Luke is never mentioned in the we-sections and the rest of the *Acts,* but Paul does mention him as his assistant during his first imprisonment in Rome (Col. 4:14; Philemon 24).

109. These precious passages must derive from a kind of travel diary Luke kept for himself. This type of personal diary was not rare in antiquity. Quite apart from the classic illustrations, like Xenophon's *Anabasis* and Julius Caesar's *Commentaries,* we have a very apt example in the Palestinian world of the time. Less than ten years after the *Acts* had been written, a similar diary was kept by Flavius Josephus, who accompanied Titus during the siege of Jerusalem and jotted down notes gathered from his own direct observation or from the Jewish deserters who fled from the beleaguered city (*Contra Apionem,* I, 49; cf. 55). These notes, written in Aramaic, formed the nucleus of the first Aramaic version of the *Wars of the Jews,* and then of the subsequent Greek version.[18] A few years earlier, Luke had done the same thing. The cultured Greek physician, having already in mind perhaps the idea for his future writings (as Flavius Josephus certainly did), kept a careful diary, jotting down the events in the first person plural.

From this diary he then transferred, as they were, the passages in question. This seems strange to us today since the narrative switches from the third to the first person with no transitional explanation. But in ancient times this was not unusual, and we have extant the writings of captains, travelers, governors, and magistrates, where the first and third persons are freely mingled depending on whether the narrator was present or not at the events he is describing.[19]

---

[18] Cf. G. Ricciotti, *Flavio Giuseppe,* Vol. I, Introduction, *Flavio Giuseppe lo storico giudeo-romano,* Turin, 1937, p. 67.

[19] Cf. E. Norden, *Agnostos Theos,* Berlin, 1913, p. 316 ff., which cites, among other

110. For the earlier period, corresponding approximately to the first part of the *Acts*, Luke was able to gather material of all kinds from eyewitnesses. If he was not present at the founding of the first Christian community in Antioch, his native city (11:19 ff.; 13:1–13), he certainly knew its principal members, Barnabas, Simon called Niger, Lucius the Cyrenean, and Manahen. In Caesarea, he knew Philip the evangelist (21:8), who was one of the seven deacons and well informed on the early history of the community in Jerusalem. In Jerusalem itself he was in contact with the "elders" of the mother church, among whom were James the "brother" of the Lord, Mnason an "early disciple" (21:16–18), and others. While in Rome, Luke certainly met Mark, Paul's companion on his first missionary journey and the author of the Second Gospel (Col. 4:10, 14; Philemon 23–24); and Paul's companions on his later journeys, like Timothy, Silas, Aristarchus, etc., were also companions of Luke. From all of these he could obtain basic information on the early years of Christianity in Palestine. And then, of course, there was Paul himself, who was the most important source of information for the events which had taken place since the stoning of Stephen and his own conversion.

111. In addition to these informants, did Luke also have written sources? Generally speaking this would not have been necessary (except for the discourses) but there are certain factors which lead us to think that he did use written documents. A linguistic analysis of the *Acts* does establish the fact that there was one author for the whole book. But this may be one of those instances where a skillful author does not copy his source documents literally but assimilates the content and clothes it in his own style. On the other hand, it is also a fact that the first twelve chapters contain many more Semitic elements than the second half, and the narrative sequence does not proceed so directly or so smoothly. But that is not sufficient to argue that Luke used several written sources, since the Semitisms might derive in part from the subject matter and in part from the conversations with Luke's oral informants, who spoke Aramaic, while the slight fluctuations of the narrative might be explained by the variety of the subjects treated and the number of informants, whose respective contributions did not undergo the same editing process on the part of the author. In any case, although these observations have their importance they are not decisive, and the possibility and probability that Luke had written sources at his disposal still remains.

112. It was from written documents that he undoubtedly took the decree of the apostolic council (Acts 15:23–29) and the letter of the

---

documents, the letters of Cicero, probably rewritten from official reports he had sent to the Senate about his military operations in Cilicia in 51 b.c.

tribune Claudius Lysias (23:26–30). The discourses of Gamaliel (5:35–39), the town clerk of Ephesus (19:35–40), and the lawyer Tertullus (24:2–8) are probably taken from written notes. Then there are many Christian discourses, a long one of Stephen, eight of Peter, ten of Paul, and one of James. Many of these were spoken in Aramaic — as Stephen's for instance — and so their present Greek version must be a translation. They are not recorded verbatim but are in summary form giving only the high lights of the original. Some were given extemporaneously, like Paul's speech in Aramaic to the rioting crowd in the Temple (22:1–21), and therefore could not have been prepared in advance. Hence, at the most, they were noted down afterward from memory.

These summary notes must have circulated among the early Christians, who sought them out and guarded them with veneration, just as they did, on a higher plane, with the "sayings" (λογία) of Jesus,[20] from which, in that same period, the Gospels were evolving. But in the case of these apostolic "sayings," too, there was no slavish literalism, and in the use or translation of the various notes the meaning was preserved intact but not the exact wording.[21] It is not surprising, therefore, to find Luke's imprint even in the discourses. He has, as usual, clothed with his own style the concepts he has taken from the above-mentioned summaries. But it must also be noted that there are certain characteristic expressions which link Peter's discourses to his letters (ἀθέμιτον, found only in the *Acts*, 10:28, and in *1 Peter*, 4:3; πρόγνωσις, only in the *Acts*, 2:23, and in *1 Peter*, 1:2) and there are many more numerous examples of this kind which connect Paul's discourses with his epistles.

113. Several have maintained that Luke used the writings of Flavius Josephus, but this theory is without serious foundation. Quite apart from the fact that, chronologically speaking, Luke's writings could not derive from Josephus,[22] Luke was too careful and accurate a historian to use such a crude and slovenly hack writer as Josephus, in whose works the contradictions are frequent and obvious (§ 542, note).[23] It is almost certain that Luke did not use Paul's epistles, although almost all of them had been written when he composed the *Acts*. The contrary opinion held by some scholars is disproved by the fact that Luke's writing is

---

[20] Cf. *The Life of Christ*, p. 87 ff. (§ 98 ff.) and p. 99 ff. (§ 115 ff.).

[21] This is the rule followed by the Greek translator of the Aramaic text of Matthew also and we find the confirmation of this in the various readings of the Synoptics; cf. *The Life of Christ*, pp. 103–104 (§§ 121–122).

[22] For the chronology of Josephus' various writings, cf. G. Ricciotti, *Flavio Giuseppe*, Vol. I, *cit.*, pp. 46, 97, 157, 171.

[23] Some scholars have supposed instead that Flavius Josephus used Luke as a source (J. Belser, in *Theolog. Quartalschrift*, 1896, p. 78; Th. Zahn, *Die Apostelgeschichte*, 4th ed., II, Leipzig, 1927, pp. 214 ff., 393 ff., 747 ff.). This theory, too, is improbable though less unlikely than the other, but it does not concern us here.

completely independent of the epistles. Not only does the *Acts* never mention Paul's letters, but it makes no reference to certain episodes mentioned in the latter which it would have been very opportune to include, such as Paul's sojourn in Arabia (Gal. 1:17), the three ship- wrecks which occurred before that at Malta (2 Cor. 11:25), and others. Evidently Luke was not concerned with the epistles — even though he knew in general of their existence — because he had their author him- self as a source of information. This independence from the epistles emphasizes even more strongly the historical value of Luke's work, for though it follows a different road it never conflicts with the content of Paul's letters. The *Acts* and the epistles do not know each other, but neither do they deny each other: *nec tecum, nec sine te.*

114. Granting that Luke did use written documents, would it be possible to study these today? Yes, but only in the same way and to the same extent that it is possible today in Palestine to study a Canaanite city, buried three or four thousand years ago under a *tell* (the Arab name for those little hills scattered about everywhere in the Middle East, and which are almost always of archaeological origin). You may climb the *tell*, inspect and measure it in detail, and conclude that the city must have been so many feet wide and so many feet long, and that the piece of pottery sticking out of the ground dates it back to such and such a century before Christ. And that is all. When it comes to describing the plan of the city, its streets and buildings, and the like, the archaeologist gives up unless he can make the necessary excavations to demolish the *tell*, uncover the city, and reconstruct it as far as pos- sible. If the *tell* does not lend itself to excavations nor the city to reconstruction, the archaeologist leaves the description of the buried city to the enterprising novelist.

Modern critics have attempted many excavations in the metaphorical *tells* which bury the probable documents incorporated in the *Acts*, and we shall examine some of them (§ 131). But the descriptions of the cities they uncover, all differing one from the other, leave us with nothing but the well-founded suspicion that they are the work of the enterprising novelists of criticism.

✻   ✻   ✻

115. As for the date of composition, it is obvious that the *Acts* was written after the Third Gospel, to which it refers, and therefore later than the years 62–63, which we assigned as the date of that Gospel.[24] But the interval between the publication of the two writings must have been very short.

In the first place, the fact that the *Acts* contains no allusion, even indirectly, to the destruction of Jerusalem and the catastrophe that

---

[24] Cf. *The Life of Christ*, p. 119 (§ 139).

overtook Judaism in the year 70, suggests that it must have been written before that year. Even more significant is its brief and abrupt ending, which says simply that Paul remained for two years in the house he had rented in Rome, carrying on his ministry in perfect freedom (28:30–31). And with this statement the book comes unexpectedly to a close. What of the trial before the emperor? If Paul had come to Rome expressly for that trial, why did not Luke describe its progress and conclusion, just as he had told the story of the previous trials before the procurator in Caesarea? In fact, the last five chapters of the book (Chaps. 24–28) seem to be leading up to the trial in Rome, both in the accounts of Paul's adventures with the law in Jerusalem and Caesarea and in the description of the journey to Rome itself. Then why do these five chapters lack their logical conclusion, namely, the trial itself and the verdict?

116. Scholars have answered this question in various ways. Some have advanced the theory that Luke wrote a third work, now lost, or that he at least intended to write it and then was unable to do so. In this third writing he presumably would have given us the story of the trial in Rome and the events which followed it.[25] But besides being gratuitous, this theory is belied by the fact that the Third Gospel comes to a logical close, which in turn is referred to and repeated at the beginning of the *Acts*. But the latter lacks any such logical ending. Some have thought that the original manuscript of the *Acts* was accidentally mutilated, the end of it thus being lost, or even that Luke stopped writing abruptly at a certain point because he did not have any more paper; both theories are fantastic or ridiculous. Others have supposed that Luke stopped his narrative to avoid recounting the tragic end of the trial, namely, Paul's conviction and death in 64. But in the first place, Paul was still journeying in the West and the East and writing epistles after the year 64. And even if he had been condemned to death in 64, what possible reason could Luke have had for not narrating a fact that was certainly well known to the Christians of Rome and elsewhere? Would not the death of the apostle have been a worthy close to the story of his life, just as the conviction and death of Jesus brought to a fitting close the story of the Third Gospel? The theory has been recently advanced (K. Lake, *Beginnings*) that Paul's trial did not take

---

[25] The philological argument advanced for this is the expression πρῶτον λόγον with which, at the beginning of the *Acts* (1:1), Luke refers to the Third Gospel. πρῶτος is interpreted as meaning the "first" in a series of three or more, while if a series of only two were indicated the word for "first" would have been πρότερος. The argument is not valid: πρότερος is classical Greek, although we sometimes find πρῶτος used in its stead even by classical writers. In Luke's time, however, πρότερος had fallen into almost complete disuse, as is evidenced by the papyri, and in the New Testament it occurs almost exclusively in its neuter form as an adverb. Therefore πρῶτον λόγον may very well mean the "first" of only two writings.

place at all since the Jews did not appear in Rome to press the charges and so the Apostle was automatically set free. But even granting the possibility that Paul's accusers did not come to Rome (§ 603), the trial could always have been held on the basis of the written report sent by the Roman procurator of Judea. And there would still be the question why Luke did not mention or allude to this unexpected ending of the trial and thus provide his writings with some sort of close.

117. One theory worthy of attention is that the trial was not yet over when Luke finished the *Acts,* and therefore he could not recount its results, but that shortly after the publication of the work, between 63 and 64, the trial did end with Paul's acquittal and freedom. Luke's recently published book helped to bring about this happy result, according to those who maintain it was a kind of brief for Paul's defense (§ 104), and this theory bases one argument precisely on the abrupt ending of the work. But, as we have just pointed out, to consider the *Acts* a forensic defense presents a number of serious difficulties. Here an even greater difficulty is offered by the fact that Paul's Roman imprisonment lasted two years. If Luke wrote the *Acts* in defense of Paul, he should have published it in the first months of his imprisonment in order to exert some influence on the trial, and not when the two years were up and the trial, if not yet ended, had at least progressed to the point where it was possible to foresee the final decision. Two years is a very long time to take to write a book as slight as the *Acts.* Luke, who had already gathered his material, might have written it comfortably in a month or two and published it in the third month of Paul's imprisonment. Instead, according to this theory, he published it twenty-four months later, and without making the least mention of the trial or of the verdict. On the other hand, if we do not hold that the *Acts* was a defense brief, then we may well ask why Luke published it after the two-year period of imprisonment, that is, when everything indicated that the trial would be over very shortly. In that case, would it not have been better for him to wait a few weeks and learn the court's decision, and thus bring the story of the last five chapters, and indeed the whole book to a fitting close? Luke was too polished a writer to leave his work broken off at the end if there were not some serious reason for it.

118. In my opinion this serious reason is to be found in an event which was not only of world importance but had completely catastrophic consequences for Christianity itself, and that was the burning of Rome. If Paul reached Rome in the spring of 61, the end of his two years' imprisonment brings us to the spring of 63. In July of 64 a terrible fire flamed through Rome for nine days destroying ten of the city's fourteen *regiones,* or districts. Immediately afterward there raged a wholesale persecution of Christians, on whom the imperial authorities threw the blame for the conflagration. As a result, the situation is not only changed, it is completely reversed. The idyl between the imperial authorities and Christianity, sketched in rosy and hopeful hues in the *Acts* (§ 106), is finished forever. From now on Rome becomes for the Christians the monstrous Babylon, the great harlot lying on her seven hills, "drunk with the blood of the saints and with the blood of the martyrs of Jesus" (Apoc. 17:6). Now in the months just preceding the fire, Paul was in Rome with the faithful Luke. He was free, because the trial had ended with his acquittal at the beginning of the year 63. It is also highly probable that right afterward, in the period between the middle of 63 and the middle of 64, he made his journey to Spain (§ 636), which lasted only a few months, and that he was back in Rome sometime during the first half of 64. There he found Luke again, who had pub-lished his Gospel shortly before and was now quietly and carefully working over his material for the *Acts*. He had finished the account of the shipwreck at Malta and Paul's arrival in Rome, and he devoted quite a bit of space (15 verses to be exact, 28:14–28) to the first seven or eight days of the Apostle's sojourn in the Urbs. If the same propor-tion was to be kept throughout the narrative, he intended to give a full account of the trial and its ending, and thus round off the whole book.

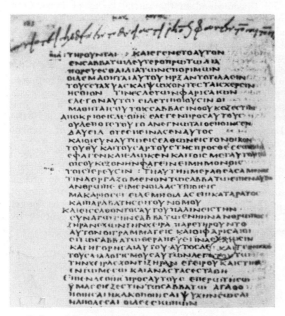

Codex of Beza (Sixth Century — Western text)

119. But suddenly the fire and then the per-secution interrupted his plans. They were inter-rupted physically by the enormous confusion caused by the destruction of three fourths of the city. And they were inter-rupted morally by the antithesis that was now born between the empire of Caesar and the king-dom of Christ. What would have been the use now to continue the detailed narrative which was to show the rectitude of imperial justice in rec-ognizing Paul's innocence? That justice had become supreme injustice, and the recognition of Paul's innocence was atrociously nullified in the "huge multitude" (*multitudo ingens* — Tacitus, *Annal.*, XV, 44) of his colleagues and disciples who were put to death. What Luke had written could remain as true historical testimony of the period just past. But that period was now closed forever, and to continue a narrative that praised the great harlot was inadmissible. It would have meant dissembling the present reality and mocking the "blood of the martyrs of Jesus."

Did Luke, who in the Third Gospel showed himself to be a historian of broad vision, think of this himself, or did Paul suggest these considerations to him? Either is possible, just as it is equally possible that these thoughts occurred to both of them at the same time. In any case, it was decided that the narrative of the *Acts* was not to continue.

And so the detailed account, which had brought Paul to the first days of his sojourn in Rome was finished off with an abrupt ending, which sums up the entire period of two years in about twenty words.

The *Acts* was published in the same year 64. It testifies to a brief day of sunlight that was to be followed by years of storm.[26]

---

[26] I referred briefly to the question of the text of the *Acts,* which it is not possible to treat at length here. It has come down to us in two notably different forms. One is called "Eastern," and is contained in the great uncial codices, the Sinaitic, the Vatican, the Alexandrian, in many minuscule codices, in the Latin Vulgate, and in many early Christian writers (Clement of Alexandria, Origen, etc.). It is a shorter, more condensed form. The other is called "Western" (but incorrectly so, since it also appears in oriental texts) and is contained in the uncial codex of Beza, in a few minuscule Greek codices, in the ancient Latin version (Itala), in the ancient Syriac, in the Coptic-Sahidic, and in various early authors, especially Latin (Irenaeus, Tertullian, Cyprian, Lucifer of Cagliari, Augustine, etc.). It differs from the Eastern text in that it contains numerous additions to the latter text, some passages are transposed or offer variants, and others are omitted. Some scholars suppose a third "mixed" form, which reflects both the others. It is quite difficult to form a complete judgment on each of the two principal versions. One theory (F. Blass) supposes that Luke himself was responsible for both editions of the book, the longer one being destined for the Christian community in Rome (Western form), and the shorter one for Theophilus (Eastern form). Despite other instances of ancient writings which appeared in several editions, this theory is far from being proved. The differences between the two versions must be evaluated singly, but in general the Western text seems a later edition than the Eastern, as if it attempted to clarify the latter and supply additional information. It is quite possible that some of the additional information derives from authoritative sources, since it is very ancient and is attested as early as the middle of the second century. Therefore, the longer or Western version may have been composed at the beginning of that century by some authoritative disciple of the Apostles, either in Syria or Egypt.

VI

History of Criticism

---

120. Who is Paul? The historian's judgment on this question is also his judgment on the sources of Paul's biography.

For those who accept the sources in the light of the guarantees handed down to us by earliest tradition, Paul is a completely unique herald of the Christ Jesus. He is a man suffused with the supernatural and set in a framework of miracles. His first acceptance of Christ, in the act of his conversion, is the first miracle. His progressive knowledge and understanding of Christ is a whole series of supernatural events, for it is the result of special revelations made to him by Christ. His preaching of the doctrines Christ has revealed to him is accompanied by physical and public miracles. Compared to other figures in early Christianity (with the possible exception of John) he seems carved in high relief against a dimly sketched background.

This is without question the impression created by a first reading of the sources. As soon as the reading is finished, therefore, it is natural to ask: But is all that possible? Before asking whether or not this is all fact, one asks if it is all possible. And this is a philosophical rather than a historical question.

Because of this philosophical query, the studies on Paul have followed the very same pattern as those on Christ. The scholars who do not accept a transcendent God and the possibility of the supernatural answer the question negatively, and consequently reject as an absurdity the Paul portrayed for us in the sources. The others, who do accept them, grant that the Paul of the sources is possible, and so proceed to a critical examination of these same sources to determine whether or not they guarantee the figure of Paul presented to us. The former base their judgments on a "lay dogma" which admits no discussion, the latter on a philosophical possibility which must be proved by historical fact.

121. But the "lay dogma" is negative only, that is, it states what is not so, and therefore there still remains the task of positive reconstruction, namely, to determine what is so. First of all, did Paul really exist? If he did, to what extent is the traditional figure false and at what point does it begin to be true? Which characteristics are mythical, which legendary, and which merely tendentious? Through what processes did that traditional figure gradually evolve? Just what type of pruning on the sources will trim the supernatural from this historically absurd figure and make it "rational"? This is the self-imposed task of the "rationalist" scholars.

It is accomplished by a method of "selection," which, as we have seen, was widely used in the biography of Jesus.[1] Each scholar chooses from the sources those elements which according to his particular set of concepts seem the most suitable. He then retouches and rearranges them and so reconstructs the historical Paul. Everything else in the documents not used in this reconstruction is to be rejected as myth or legend or tendentiousness, in short, as historical unreality.

The various portraits of Paul thus arrived at vary from scholar to scholar and from period to period, as paintings do. Just as eighteenth-century painting was quite different from that of the sixteenth, and this in turn from the fourteenth, so the historical figures of Paul portrayed by the Liberal School are a contradiction of those sketched earlier by the Tübingen School; and those produced later by the eschatologists or the school of comparative religions bear no resemblance whatever to any of the earlier portraits. After all — it must be admitted — those who sketched these various reconstructed Pauls make no claim to photographic precision. They aspire only to a greater or lesser degree of verisimilitude. They present their portraits as simple hypotheses.

122. And that is quite as it should be. As we may see from the word itself, a *hypothesis* supposes a *thesis* on which it is based and which it attempts to promote more or less. Now, for these scholars, the indisputable thesis is that the supernatural Paul is an absurdity and to be completely rejected. Once this thesis is assured, they are not so intransigent with regard to their hypotheses. Loisy, one of the most noteworthy and radical of these scholars, begins, with these words, the last chapter, "Conclusions," of the last and most radical book he wrote in his life: "It is not a sheaf of certainties which we shall gather now, but a sheaf of hypotheses which we shall attempt to bind together according to the degree of probability or truth that they contain."[2] In the preceding chapters he had reduced Paul to splinters (and the rest of the New Testament personages for that matter), and scattered the pieces through the first two centuries of Christianity. But for Loisy himself, all this was only a sheaf of *hypotheses*. His real thesis, his only certainty, he set forth and secured in the first chapter of the same book, entitled "The Supernatural

---

[1] Cf. *The Life of Christ,* pp. 179–216 (§§ 194–224), and especially p. 199 ff. (§ 211 ff.).

[2] A. Loisy, *Les origines du Nouveau Testament,* Paris, 1936, Chap. IX, "Conclusions," p. 306.

in the Bible," in which he categorically rejects every true supernatural concept on the pretext that it is a concept of "magic." This dovetails perfectly with what we have said above concerning "lay dogma" and its decisive influences on historical research.

       ✿   ✿   ✿

123. Until the late nineteenth century, there were no particular attacks on the sources of Paul's biography, and they were accepted — when they were accepted — as tradition had handed them down to us. Mention may be made of the view held in the second half of the eighteenth century by J. S. Semler who supposed that the present form of Paul's Epistles does not correspond exactly to their original form, since, in his opinion, they were revised when they were included in the Canon. In 1804, J. E. C. Schmidt expressed some doubt about the authenticity of *1 Timothy,* and the doubt became a certainty for F. Schleiermacher (1807), who rejected its authenticity for "aesthetic" reasons only. Shortly afterward, J. G. Eichhorn (1814) and W. de Wette (1826) rejected all three pastoral letters (*1* and *2 Timothy, Titus*). As for the *Acts,* the first research was directed at discovering the sources used especially in the first part of the book. This was the aim of Königsmann in 1798, who was followed later by Ziegler (1801), Heinrichs (1809), and a few others. They supposed that the material in the first part of the *Acts* derived from an Aramaic narrative of the Acts of Peter, something like the *Kerygma Petrou,* fragments of which have been preserved for us by Clement of Alexandria. A little later, Schleiermacher, although he attributed the *Acts* as a whole to Luke, supposed that the passages in the first person plural were written by Timothy, and there were others of this opinion (Bleek, Ulrich, etc.). Some assigned them instead either to Titus (Horst, Krenkel, etc.) or to Silas (Schwanbeck, von Vloten, etc.).

124. But these were all negligible skirmishes. Meanwhile, systematic attacks on the traditional biography of Jesus were being made first by Reimarus, and then by Paulus and Strauss,[3] who were upturning its very foundations. It was only to be expected that the same fate would befall the biography of Paul. The privilege of launching the first basic attack went to the Tübingen School, which made Paul the principal object of its research on the origins of Christianity.

We have already pointed out that the guiding principle of this school was the conflict in early Christianity between the Jewish-Christian current represented particularly by Peter (*thesis*), and the Hellenistic-Christian current represented by Paul (*antithesis*). From this conflict emerged later the Catholic Church, which tempered and fused both

---

[3] Cf. *The Life of Christ,* pp. 183–186 (§§ 197–199).

currents (*synthesis*).[4] This principle had been inspired by Hegelian philosophy, which was then riding a wave of triumph in Germany. As for historical documents to support this theory, they were made to do so by the usual method of selection, for it was decided that there were irreconcilable differences between the Paul of the *Acts* and the Paul of the epistles, since both sources were the products of tendentious elaborations.

125. In the first place, the majority of the epistles were not authentic. The founder of the school, F. Ch. Baur, first (1835) rejected the authenticity of the pastoral letters, which he judged should be assigned to the end of the second century because they reflected the gnosticism which flourished throughout that century. Later (1845) he rejected the remaining epistles with the exception of *Galatians, Romans,* and *1* and *2 Corinthians.* The reason for this was that these four letters alone reflect Paul's controversy with the Jewish-Christian current. This consideration, in fact, became the touchstone which the school used to evaluate all the other documents and separate the gold from the tinsel. As a consequence, the other epistles were not authentic because they did not reveal Paul as a polemicist, and many passages in the *Acts* were judged to be tendentious or unhistorical because they appeared to conflict with these four polemical letters. To read the *Acts* — said the Tübingen School — one would think that Peter and Paul were in perfect accord and the conflict between them, or rather between the two currents, is almost not apparent at all. Does this perhaps prove that there was no conflict? No. It proves merely that the conflict was made to disappear because the *Acts* defend a certain thesis, that is, their aim is to reconcile the two currents, and for this purpose they paint an artificial picture of Peter and Paul in harmonious agreement. But Paul's four epistles stand to prove that the thesis of the book is false and its narrative plan tendentious.

126. In reality, many episodes mentioned in the Epistles are omitted in the *Acts.* The latter do not tell us anything of Paul's three shipwrecks and very little about his other adventures, which he lists in *2 Corinthians,* 11:23 ff. They say nothing about his quarrel with Peter in Antioch, nor his Judaizing adversaries in Galatia and Corinth. Paul's three journeys to Jerusalem become two in the *Acts.* The Council of Jerusalem in *Acts,* 15, is treated as a private agreement in *Galatians,* 2. Paul, who declares in the Epistles the independence of his apostolate, seems in the *Acts* to receive his investiture from the leaders of the community of Jerusalem. The *Acts* would indicate that Peter and the elders of Jerusalem took the initiative in the evangelization of the Gentiles, while the dispute in Antioch suggests that those same elders could offer nothing but

---

[4] Cf. *ibid.,* pp. 187–188 (§§ 200–201).

obstacles to such evangelization. In addition, the perfect symmetry between the two figures, the fact that every lineament of Peter is paralleled by some feature of Paul (§ 96), points up even more clearly the artificial and conventional structure of both parts of the book, each being devoted to one personage.

In conclusion, the historical Paul is the Paul of the four epistles mentioned above. The Paul of the *Acts* is a portrait made to capture the Jewish Christian, who would admire in him the devoted and subordinate collaborator of Peter in the evangelization of the pagan world. This thesis required that the *Acts* be assigned to the very late second century, because before that time the two currents would not have been ripe for fusion. The other epistles attributed to Paul (except the pastorals) were a little earlier than the *Acts,* and they might be considered attempts to approach the Jewish-Christian current.

127. In this way the Tübingen School managed to reconcile its guiding philosophic concept and the historical documents. The price it paid was the rejection of at least three fourths of the documents, namely, ten of Paul's epistles and the greater part of the *Acts*. But what did that matter? Provided the Hegelian idea of the "thesis-antithesis-synthesis" was saved, any price was well paid.

But there persisted a dangerous possibility. Tomorrow another guiding concept, inspired by another philosophical system, might demand an even greater price — not only three fourths, but all four fourths of the documents. In that case, the disciples of Tübingen would have no right to protest because in reality they would be protesting against their own methods.

And this is what actually happened very soon afterward. The conclusions of the Tübingen School provoked a great deal of opposition among the more or less conservative Protestants, as we shall see in a moment. But here, too, events followed the same curve as the studies on the sources of Jesus' biography,[5] for the most interesting opponents of the Tübingens from the viewpoint of the development of ideas were those who accused the school of stopping halfway and not proceeding to the ultimate logical consequences of their principles. This was done by Bruno Bauer in Germany, and shortly afterward by the much discussed Dutch School.

128. Bauer (1859) found it illogical to keep the four letters spared by the Tübingen School. All the Pauline letters were worked out by Christianity at the end of the second century, and the Epistle to the Galatians, which seemed the most ancient, was later than the *Acts*. As for Paul himself, just as Bauer had denied the historical existence of Jesus, he was more than ready to deny that of Paul. In any case, even

---

[5] Cf. *ibid.*, p. 188 (§ 202).

granting some improbable hypothesis that he ever did exist, he certainly had none of the moral features attributed to him by the *Acts* and the Epistles.

The Dutch School (A. Pierson, S. A. Naber, A. Loman, van Manen, D. Völter, etc.) followed more or less the same trail.[6] The Pauline current, according to them, emerged in the second century as an attempt to spiritualize primitive Christianity as a result of the influence of the Platonizing Judaism of Alexandria. The Pauline letters were a hodgepodge of fragments which could not be separated one from the other and assigned to their respective authors. The traditional Paul was a psychological absurdity, especially since in time he came so soon after the death of Jesus, and whether he had ever existed or not became a secondary matter since conceptually he was to be considered a character analogous to John, the author of the Fourth Gospel. In fact, Van Manen, reversing the verdict of Tübingen, found the Paul portrayed in the *Acts* much more probable than the Paul of the Epistles.

The Dutch School continued its clamor until the beginning of the twentieth century, but the reaction against Tübingen had begun even before the Dutch School was formed. After the first shock produced by the Tübingen conclusions, its opponents began to investigate whether or not the infallible key the school had produced to open all doors — namely, the rivalry between the Petrine and the Pauline currents — really opened them. And they discovered instead that much too often the documents did not fit this preconceived idea, like so many locks which would not take that particular key.

129. In the first place, if the *Acts* had appeared in the late second century, what possible motive could there have been for promoting an accord between the two rival currents? What influence could the Jewish-Christian current have, what threat could it represent to the universalism of Christianity when, at the time supposed for the composition of the *Acts*, Jerusalem and the Hebrew Temple had been destroyed and the Jewish nation dispersed for over half a century? Was the *Acts* really interested in fighting corpses, or was there some fear the latter would come to life? Were the undeniable differences between the *Acts* and the Epistles really contradictions, or were they simple differences in the method of exposition? Did the fact that a given episode was omitted mean that it was thereby automatically denied? When or where could it be deduced from the *Acts* or the Epistles that either of the two writings was intended to furnish a complete biography of Paul? And could not a specific event, like the Council of Jerusalem, be narrated from two different but equally objective points of view? Could not the symmetry noted in the presentation of Peter and Paul in the *Acts* be the

---

[6] Cf. *ibid.*, p. 205 (§ 216).

result of a deliberate method of grouping and presenting historical fact, a method that also characterizes the Third Gospel, which tradition attributes to the author of the *Acts* (§ 96)?

These and many other observations were made in answer to the Tübingen School, and its swollen sails soon collapsed. Vigorously attacked by conservative Protestants, for practical reasons among others, the school rapidly lost ground and after about twenty-five years it dispersed. Its ideas, however, were inherited in condensed form by the above-mentioned Dutch School, and in a much blander form by isolated imitators, who continued their activity for a long time.

130. The reaction against Tübingen invited a study of the documents undertaken with less hostility toward tradition. But naturally, the rationalists and many left-wing Protestants were still carrying the hump of "lay dogma," which excluded any supernatural element. There followed, therefore, a period of compromise — like that already taking place in the studies on the biography of Jesus[7] — which said yes and no at the same time. Tübingen was repudiated, but so were the testimonies of the earliest writers with regard to the *Acts* and the Epistles. Paul had to be definitely a historical figure, and in fact he was proclaimed the true founder of Christianity, on condition, however, that his whole activity be reduced to purely human psychological and cultural phenomena and that the direct action of the transcendent God be excluded from his religious experience. But these prejudgments were left in shadow, while the spotlight was held by research on the sources of the *Acts*.

This was the period when the Old Testament critics could recognize with absolute certainty the five or six documents, fragments of which, fitted together like a mosaic, had been made to form the Pentateuch. They could also discover the six or seven persons who had successively edited those documents to fit them into the mosaic. They could even pick out not only the individual sentences but the separate words in each document to reconstruct the originals, thus reversing the clipping and pasting process accomplished thousands of years before by the group of editors which they, in their wisdom, had uncovered.

Those happy days are now gone forever,[8] but then the word of these

---

[7] Cf. *ibid.*, p. 191 ff. (§ 204 ff.).

[8] As a typical example of the confidence which reigned among them at the time we may cite the American edition of the Hebrew Bible, prepared by a number of experts and edited by P. Haupt, *The Sacred Books of the Old Testament — A critical edition of the Hebrew text printed in colours with notes;* it was published in the United States and Germany from 1893 on. It was popularly called the "Rainbow Bible," since seven or eight different colors were used in the printing of the Hebrew text, each color designating a particular source. Sometimes almost all the colors were used even in a very short sentence, since each word was considered to derive from a different source. Unfortunately, this editorial adventure, so pleasing to the eye, was never finished, the publication being interrupted in 1904 before the proposed work on the text was completed. We should recognize, however, the real

critics was law, and so the same operations had to be accomplished on the *Acts* that was being performed on the Pentateuch. Between the end of the nineteenth and the beginning of the twentieth centuries, therefore, there was a veritable flowering of document theories on the composition of the *Acts*. We have no temptation to list them,[9] it would be like taking a walk through a graveyard. But by way of illustration we may cite one of the "middle" type, neither too complicated nor too simple, namely, the first of the theories presented by C. Clemen.[10]

131. According to this scholar, the *Acts* was compiled from three principal documents. The first was a history of the Hellenist Jews (symbol: *Hellen.*), which narrated their story and in particular the vicissitudes of Stephen and Christianity's penetration of Antioch. The second was a history of Peter (symbol: *Pet.*), which incorporated earlier documents dealing with Christianity in Jerusalem, the institution of the deacons, the episode of Simon Magus, etc. The third was the story of Paul (symbol: *Pa.*), which derived from a fusion of an "Itinerary" of Paul's voyage with the we-sections and various episodes of his missions. This fusion had been accomplished by a first redactor (R-1) toward the end of the first century. Between the years 97–117, a second redactor, with Jewish sympathies (R-j), working particularly on documents *Pet.* and *Pa.*, revised them and stitched them together adding new episodes that redounded to Peter's honor. Between 117–138, the work fell into the hands of still a third redactor, who was anti-Jewish (R-a), and subjected it to a general revision resulting in a more favorable presentation of Paul. He also inserted new information, some of it taken from the Pauline Epistles and some from Flavius Josephus. This was the last step in the composition of the *Acts*, which was, therefore, the product of documents *Hellen., Pet., Pa.* (which had included other earlier documents, in addition to the "Itinerary") and the successive interventions of the writers R-1, R-j, R-a. It was probable but not certain that the author of the we-sections was Luke, to whom later tradition attributed the whole book.

There were several theories similar to this in the above-mentioned period, but today they have all been decently buried. At the same time, a great deal of work was done in the fields of exegesis and biography. The influence of Tübingen is somewhat noticeable, a little before 1870,

---

value of the critical notes on the documents in this edition (they had nothing in common with the rainbow).

[9] Cf. for his time A. Bludau, *Die Quellenscheidung in der Apostelgeschichte*, in *Biblische Zeitschrift*, 1907, pp. 166–189, 258–281. See also, in a more general sense, A. Schweitzer, *Geschichte der paulinischen Forschung*, Tübingen, 1911; A. Wilkenhauser, *Die Apostelgeschichte und ihr Geschichtswert*, Munster i. W., 1921.

[10] *Chronologie der paulinisch. Briefe*, Halle, 1893. In later works (*Paulus, sein Leben und Wirken*, 2 vols., Giessen, 1904; *Die Apostelgeschichte in Lichte der neueren Forschungen*, Giessen, 1905) Clemen practically abandoned his first theory.

in E. Reuss and E. Renan. The former, however, assigned the *Acts* for the most part to Luke and dated it a little later than the year 70, while the latter placed it between 80 and 100. One of the most eminent opponents of the Tübingen School was, toward the end of the century, the Protestant conservative Bernard Weiss, who pointed out the literary consistency of the *Acts* and maintained that Luke had written it about the year 80, using earlier sources in different degree in the two parts of the book.

132. But the most famous representative of the return to tradition was Harnack. The *Acts* was one of his favorite subjects and he returned to it several times.[11] Harnack's arguments were based exclusively on internal criticism, on a highly detailed examination of the vocabulary and style both of the *Acts* and of the Third Gospel. His conclusions were that the two books were the well-connected parts of a single work, the purpose of which was to narrate first the personal ministry of Jesus (Third Gospel) and then the ministry of the Spirit of Jesus through the Apostles (*Acts*). Both parts of the work were authored by Luke, the physician and the disciple of Paul. For the first part of the *Acts*, Luke used written sources, two or three of which came from Jerusalem, one from Antioch, and one from Caesarea. Other information he had obtained from Paul and other eyewitnesses of the various episodes. For the second part of the book, Luke himself was the eyewitness, speaking from his own personal knowledge, but even when he did use written documents, he assimilated them and clothed them with his own customary style. The language study, in fact, demonstrated that the author of the we-sections, which derived from his travel diary, had also written the rest of the *Acts*, both the first and second parts (§ 98). As for the date, Harnack at first assigned the *Acts* to the years between 78–93,[12] then to the period 79–96,[13] and finally he went back to 60–64.[14] In short, the *Acts* was a work of primary historical value composed by an alert and objective writer, Luke, who had witnessed the events described in the second part of the book and for the first part had used excellent oral and written sources of information. On the other hand, there were the miraculous episodes which are scattered through the *Acts*, and Harnack, who also respected the "lay dogma" which did not admit the supernatural, rejected them as distortions of natural facts resulting from the influence of legends. But he observed that such legends form within

---

[11] *Lukas der Arzt, der Verfasser des dritten Evangeliums und der Apostelgeschichte,* Leipzig, 1906; *Die Apostelgeschichte, ibid.,* 1908; *Neue Untersuchungen zur Apostelgeshichte und zur Abfassungszeit der synoptischen Evangelien, ibid.,* 1911; and finally *Mission und Ausbreitung des Christentums,* 1, 4th ed., *ibid.,* 1924, pp. 89–107.

[12] *Die Chronologie der Altchristlich, Literatur,* 1, Leipzig, 1897, pp. 246–249.

[13] *Apostelgeschichte,* p. 221.

[14] *Neue Untersuchungen zur Apostelgeschichte,* pp. 63–81.

a few years and in recording them Luke had merely reported objectively the current opinions.

133. Harnack's conclusions seemed almost scandalous to the rationalist scholars, especially since they had been arrived at by one of the most celebrated adherents of the "lay dogma." It is true that he had tacked on the reservation regarding the miracles. But this reservation was ridiculous if the author of the episodes was an eyewitness who had the support of other witnesses besides. Could tradition, banished *a priori* by the "lay dogma," be right by any chance? Not at all! If Harnack's demonstration was correct, then his reservation was condemned beforehand. It was as if a king banished from his kingdom a certain political party and at the same time secretly furnished it every kind of help.

There were very many who busied themselves, then, to prove Harnack wrong, but the proof was not easy. His conclusions were based on long lists of words and sentences taken from various parts of the *Acts* and the Third Gospel, and compared both with one another and with other New Testament writings. The lists were accompanied by copious observations on the grammar. the style, the doctrinal concepts, etc., all of which converged to indicate one sole author for all of the *Acts* and for the Third Gospel. Such arguments, based solely on internal evidence, could be effectively answered only by arguments of the same kind which proved the contrary. It was necessary to show that the language, the style, the concepts, etc., indicated there was more than one author or editor for the text of the two works, and this, evidently, could not be done. At the most, Harnack was answered in general terms, to the effect that the Paul of the Epistles is quite different from the Paul of the *Acts,* and therefore the author of the latter could not have been Paul's companion on his journeys. Special emphasis was placed on the miracles — a real Achilles heel for Harnack where his colleagues of the "lay dogma" were concerned — and it was maintained that whoever narrated such legends could not have been either an eyewitness or a very intelligent person. But Harnack's lists remained intact, and they are still waiting to be answered (§ 98).

134. In the past thirty years several works have been published by independent critics on the sources of Paul's biography. Besides those in which the approach is negative on principle, there are many others which are more cautious and considered. In fact, it may be said that in general the moderates predominate slightly. With regard to the Epistles, almost no one denies the authenticity of *Galatians, Romans, 1* and *2 Corinthians, 1 Thessalonians, Philippians, Philemon.* Several doubt that of *2 Thessalonians, Colossians, Ephesians,* and almost all deny that of the three pastorals (except for a few fragments at the most), and even more, that of the *Epistle to the Hebrews.* As for the *Acts,* we shall briefly mention some of the more representative works.

A work of quite moderate tendency in general is *The Acts of the Apostles*,[15] edited by F. J. Foakes-Jackson and Kirsopp Lake, to which various scholars have contributed. It is a fine arsenal of scientific information, but lacks continuity of judgment, since the various collaborators — about twenty — express their own opinions, often contradicting one another. For example, in Volume II, C. W. Emmet sides with tradition in assigning the *Acts* to Luke, while H. Windisch, who ties in in part with the Tübingen School, assigns them, in the same book, to the period between 80 and 110, and considers them a rewrite of one of Luke's works, which at times contradicts the Pauline Epistles. The two volumes (IV and V) of translation and commentary also keep to the middle of the road and suspend judgment on various questions.

135. One of the chief collaborators in this work, H. J. Cadbury, published a long study on the character of the composition of both writings "Third Gospel — Acts."[16] The two books, he finds, are parts of one work, written by one author. Whether he is unknown or whether he is Luke, as tradition says, has little interest for Cadbury, who assigns very little importance to tradition. But he does think the one author is certainly a person of broad culture — a versatile aristocrat of his times — who followed the rules for historiography of the first century and used sources varying in kind and value, but among them neither the Epistles of Paul nor Flavius Josephus. However, his statements agree in general with the data in the Epistles, just as they have often been confirmed by archaeological findings. The whole writing is to be considered, at least probably, an apologia of Jesus, the Church, and Paul, in historical-expository form, addressed to Theophilus, an important personage who could have exercised great influence on Paul's trial at the end of his first imprisonment in Rome.

E. Mayer's position is practically the same as Harnack's. Like him, he accepts the "lay dogma" and therefore rejects all that is miraculous, but also like Harnack he accepts almost all that tradition tells us about the Epistles and the *Acts*.[17] The latter, he agrees, are the work of Luke, the author of the Third Gospel and Paul's companion in his travels. They have a strictly historical value (except for the miracles, for which Luke merely accepts the popular belief) and their historicity finds astonishing confirmation in the Epistles. The author of the we-sections and the passages in the third person plural is one and the same person,

---

[15] Vol. I, *Prolegomena 1: The Jewish, Gentile and Christian Backgrounds*, London, 1920; Vol. II, *Prolegomena 2: Criticism*, 1922; Vol. III, *The Text of Acts* (critical edition by J. H. Ropes), 1925; Vol. IV, *English Translation and Commentary*, 1933; Vol. V, *Additional Notes*, 1933.

[16] *The Making of Luke — Acts*, London, 1927.

[17] *Ursprung und Anfänge des Christentums*, III, *Die Apostelgeschichte und die Anfänge des Christentums*, Stuttgart, 1923.

and the last nine chapters form a compact and indivisible whole. Paul's sojourn in Ephesus is historical fact, and so is his visit to Athens and the discourse on the Areopagus. At every step the author of the *Acts* shows that he has lived in Paul's milieu and has assimilated his thought. The historical figure of Paul is the one revealed by combining the features portrayed in the Epistles and those in the *Acts*.

136. From this relatively moderate stand, we go to the extreme left, although there are, of course, several intermediate positions between. The extreme left, as we shall see, is represented by A. Loisy, but his influence is also apparent in the works of those less extreme. To the latter belongs M. Goguel[18] who, though he rejects the data of tradition, shrinks from the conclusions of the extremists. The author of the *Acts*, he thinks, is not Luke but someone who reworked Luke's writing, inserting information taken from other sources. It is also probable that this rewriting itself was revamped by a later editor. The sources are not used verbatim but are clothed in the author's own literary style. The *Acts* is connected with the Third Gospel but derives nothing from the Pauline Epistles — which it sometimes contradicts — nor with the writings of Flavius Josephus. On the whole, while it is not a true historical work, the *Acts* contains much sound historical material and, in fact, constitutes one "of the most essential foundations for the history of early Christianity." The date of its composition falls between 80 and 90. A. Omodeo[19] also is a nonextremist but closer to the left and more dependent on Loisy. His writings, however, had no influence, particularly because of his lack of philological background (later he devoted himself to research on the Italian Risorgimento).

137. Loisy became the chief representative of the extreme left wing only gradually, as he abandoned one by one the more conservative positions he had taken. Even after his two commentaries on the *Acts*,[20] the last phases in the development of his thought are marked by publications which refer to the whole New Testament and therefore include the *Acts* and the Pauline Epistles.[21]

The problem Loisy had to resolve was the following. For him Jesus was merely an exalted visionary who was expecting the end of the world within a very short time. Absorbed in this expectation, the visionary preached to the crowds for a few months until he was captured in Jerusalem and put to death.[22] With this premise established, the question immediately arises how this "historical" Jesus, an insignificant Galilean peasant,

---

[18] *Le Livre des Actes,* Paris, 1922.

[19] *Prolegomeni alla storia dell'età apostolica,* Messina, 1921; *Paolo di Tarso, apostolo delle genti, ibid.,* 1922.

[20] *Les Actes des Apôtres,* Paris, 1920; abridged edition, *ibid.,* 1925.

[21] These are: *La naissance du Christianisme,* Paris, 1933; *Remarques sur la littérature épistolaire du Nouveau Testament,* Paris, 1936.

[22] Cf. *The Life of Christ,* pp. 198–212 (§§ 210–221).

ignominiously executed in public about the year 30, should reappear in the Pauline Epistles as the glorious Christ, the Kyrios, the Being above all creation, the Son of God. Since the Epistles begin about A.D. 51, how could this process of limitless sublimation, of deification, which sat the Galilean visionary on the right hand of God, be accomplished in the twenty-year period between 30 and 51? Another basic consideration is the fact that this process took place among the Jews, not among the Greeks or Romans. These pagans deified simple mortals one after the other with no difficulty. A decree of the Roman Senate was all that was necessary to seat on Olympus an emperor who had just died. But among the Jews it would have been the acme of absurdity to equate any human being whatever to the God Yahweh, to God the eternal, invisible, ineffable, whose very name no one was permitted to utter. Moses himself, the great lawgiver of the Hebrews, had never received anything resembling divine honors from them. This, then, was the problem Loisy had to solve.

138. He solved it by assigning to Paul the major responsibility for the divinization of Jesus. In the first place, Paul had not known Jesus personally and so did not have a very vivid impression of his earthly life and human reality. In addition, Paul was Jewish by birth but he had very little of the Jewish spirit. Born and educated in Tarsus, in a Hellenist environment and an atmosphere of religious syncretism, he was familiar with the mystery religions, he had heard of the gods who brought "salvation" and unconsciously his mind had absorbed the vague concept of a redemption, and this idea stayed with him many years, in a kind of state of incubation. When just the right occasion presented itself the idea took on body and life, and Paul identified the principle of salvation and redemption, not with some evanescent Dionysius or twilight Isis, but with this same Jesus of Nazareth, about whom many witnesses had given him testimony. This Jesus, besides being the Messias of the Hebrews, was truly the One who had wrought the redemption and salvation of the whole human race through his passion and death.[23]

---

[23] Loisy set forth these ideas in a study, *La conversion de saint Paul et la naissance du Christianisme*, which appeared in the *Revue d'histoire et littérature religieuses*, 1914, pp. 289–331. Here are a few of his statements: "One cannot conceive without difficulty and many refuse to accept the fact that Paul was converted to the faith of a contemporary Jewish preacher, whom he regarded as the manifestation of a divine being who descended from heaven to save men by being crucified. This would, in fact, have been difficult to imagine if Paul had known Jesus personally, but everything indicates that he had never seen him" (p. 305). — "With respect to Jesus' personality, close as it was to him in time, Paul, therefore, could have had only a vague impression, and we must not be surprised to find this impression almost nothing" (p. 306). — "Paul was not born in Palestine but in Tarsus, where he grew up and probably spent most of the years before his conversion. He was born, then, in a pagan country, in an environment of religious syncretism. On the old national

Now this solution of the problem was very definite and very clear, except that it seemed to be stitched together from sheer affirmations for which there was no proof. Still worse, these statements were flatly contradicted by the sources, since both the *Acts* and the Epistles give us a Paul not only different from but the exact opposite of the Paul depicted in Loisy's solution of the problem. The Paul of the sources was 100 per cent Jewish, a Pharisee, educated in the most orthodox schools of Jerusalem, extremely zealous in the matter of the national traditions and extremely hostile to any compromise with foreign ideologies, the implacable enemy of idolatry in any form. In short, he was a man who would have done anything but build the bridge between the God Yahweh and the gods of the mystery religions, even if the main pillar were to be the Hebrew Messias. How, then, could Paul have been the one to build this bridge?

139. Loisy understood that proofs were necessary. That is, it was necessary either to change the features of the Paul of his solution or those of the Paul of the sources. Loisy chose the second alternative, and set about to sketch the historical portrait of Paul by the usual method of "selection" from the sources. Leaving the Epistles aside for the time being, he began with the *Acts*.

In his two commentaries on the *Acts,* Loisy took up and developed an idea already set forth by Gercke (1894) and more explicitly by E. Norden (*Agnostos Theos*, 1913). According to this theory the *Acts* together with the Third Gospel were originally an authentic writing of

---

religion, related to the ancient religions of Syria and Asia Minor, Hellenist divinities had been grafted and other oriental cults had also been introduced, notably the cult of Mithra, of which Cilicia was one of the principal centers at the beginning of the Roman Empire. What impression these pagan religions made on Paul's mind, he himself never took the time to observe, and he does not tell us anywhere. . . . He must have known their spirit especially, and it must have penetrated his own without his noticing it" (pp. 308–309). — "The mysteries lacked a definite doctrine on the divinity; their myths of salvation lacked a point of contact with history; the moral ideal, toward which they tended more or less to rise, lacked a basis in the very myths which were to uphold it. Now the Christian mystery had everything the pagan mysteries lacked, thanks to Judaism and the Gospel of Jesus" (p. 329). — "Paul did not suspect what an advantage it was for the Christ of the mystery to have behind him Jesus of Nazareth. It is useless to show how wavering and inconsistent is the legend of god-saviours when one wishes to examine it closely. Their earthly work was done in the shadows of the most distant past, we do not know when, and even if we knew when, we do not know how. How much more clearly did the person and work of the Christian Savior emerge! He was born in the time of Augustus; he had preached at Tiberias; he had lived in Palestine; he had been crucified in Jerusalem by order of Pontius Pilate. The Pauline myth of the Redemption appeared as history. . . . Finally, the things one could recount of Jesus, his teaching, his life, his attitude at death, gave him a figure worthy of the role of salvation which had been attributed to him. His morality was pure, and his life had been as noble as his moral teaching. . . . What a contrast between the passion of Attis, even that of Osiris or Dionysius, and the Passion of Christ!" (p. 330.)

Luke. But in the second century an editor transformed the whole work to such a degree that today only fragments of the original remain scattered here and there through the composition of this editor. Luke's writing, composed about the year 80, was worthy of its author, a well-informed historian, and a clear and accurate writer. The individual who revised his work was, so far as the *Acts* was concerned, an "unscrupulous advocate," a "forger," a "falsifier," an "adulterator," "one who invents for the pleasure of inventing," who has "atrociously mutilated, cut, revamped, doctored, interpolated," in a word, who has perpetrated a "perpetual camouflage."[24]

Despite this cataclysm, Loisy felt competent to reconstruct in large measure the general outlines of Luke's work. The prologue, now reduced to a stump, originally gave a summary of the contents, which covered the period from the resurrection of Jesus to the death of Paul and probably to the death of Peter. Then came the narrative proper: first, a summary of the appearances of the risen Christ in Galilee; then the disciples' return to Jerusalem where they begin to preach the Christ; the formation of a group of Greek converts, directed by the seven deacons, and notably by Stephen, who preach the imminent parousia and the abrogation of the Hebrew Law; Stephen is stoned and the Greek Christians driven from Jerusalem while the Jewish Christians remain there undisturbed; the former spread their doctrines in various places and found a community in Antioch to which they admit many pagans; at this time Paul is converted, who is also a Greek and who had not been in Jerusalem at all when Stephen was stoned; the conversion is recounted briefly (in Luke's original writing) as a purely internal and spiritual matter; Paul and Barnabas begin to preach in Syria and Cilicia, and this makes it urgent to solve the matter of the observance of Jewish practices, for the Jewish Christians in Jerusalem are still awaiting the parousia of Christ. The Christians of Jerusalem then begin to accept the more liberal views of the Hellenist Christians. The persecution of Agrippa I breaks out, and in it James and his brother John (the Evangelist) are put to death together. Peter, who has taken refuge in Antioch, engages in the well-known controversy with Paul, who then departs for his travels through Asia Minor, and subsequently Macedonia, Achaea, and Ephesus, without returning again to Jerusalem. He returns after the events in Ephesus and is arrested. Then comes the journey to Rome, followed by the two years in prison and his conviction and death in the years 60–62. Probably the writing went on to describe the persecutions of Nero and the death of Peter.

140. This was the outline of Luke's original work according to Loisy. Everything else we read in the *Acts* today is legendary and tendentious

---

[24] *Actes*, 1920, *passim*.

material introduced by its enterprising rewriter. In this category, for example, are the accounts of the Ascension, Pentecost, Paul's conversion on the road to Damascus, the episode of the centurion Cornelius, the importance of the Twelve under the primacy of Peter in Jerusalem, the voyage of Paul and Barnabas to Cyprus, the episode of Sergius Paulus, of Gallio, and a number of other incidents, and especially all that was miraculous or supernatural. Instead of these falsifications, Luke's writing contained information on the Hellenist Christians, the conversion of Luke himself, the trial and death of James and John, the controversy in Antioch, and many other subjects, including the trial of Paul in Rome. All this information was suppressed by the reviser because of express hostility.

The aim of this reviser, in fact, was to show the imperial authorities in Rome that the Christian religion was the true Judaism, and therefore merited their protection. And another purpose, but one which he felt more deeply, was to magnify the Roman community, exalting Peter at the expense of Paul, and this betrays the fact that the whole revision of Luke's work was accomplished at the express desire of the Roman Church, and the person who falsified the narrative was one of the rulers of that same Church. Once the falsification was accomplished, Luke's original work was taken out of circulation and no trace whatever remained of it.

141. For this radical alteration in the history of early Christianity — which is in reverse precisely the alteration the reviser of Luke's book supposedly accomplished — Loisy marshals conceptual and philological proofs. The conceptual proofs are managed as follows: every time a passage in the *Acts* contradicts the outline of Luke's original work as reconstructed by Loisy, the latter concludes it was the work of the reviser. The philological proofs follow the usual procedure: Whenever there is a construction that is a bit awkward, or an uncommon expression, or mention of an idea already expressed, or the thought is not developed directly, these are considered so many proofs of the intervention of the editor. On the other hand, where the style, syntax, the logical development of the thought all flow smoothly, this shows the shrewd skill of the editor, who was able to disguise his interpolations quite well, although it cannot be doubted that that is what they are.

142. Now, the story reconstructed by Loisy may be justified by his own eschatological theory regarding Jesus' preaching and by his own philosophical premises, but certainly not by the documents. If Luke's original writing disappeared without trace as soon as the revision was published, the inventiveness of a modern scholar is not quite enough to reconstruct it unless he is trying his hand at fiction. As for philological proofs of this type, the impression they make today on scholars familiar with Semitic or Greek-Semitic documents is weaker than ever. If we

applied the same philological methods to texts in a completely different sphere, such as Caesar's *Gallic Wars* or Dante's *Divine Comedy*, we could easily conclude — on the basis of internal evidence alone — that several authors and even more rewriters had operated on them. And if no one dreams of drawing these conclusions it is because of external testimony, not internal criticism. For Loisy the external evidence for the *Acts* had no value. But he forgot that to define the tiniest fragments of eventual sources, the internal evidence of a Greek-Semitic text like the *Acts* is even more untrustworthy than texts like the *Gallic Wars* and the *Divine Comedy*.

This disparagement which Loisy kept piling on his imaginary rewriter — and sometimes on contemporary scholars who disagreed with him[25] — produced on calmer minds the opposite reaction from what he intended, since they clearly revealed the methods he was using to impress the reader.

143. When he finished his critical work on the *Acts*, Loisy was only at the halfway mark since there still remained the Paul of the Epistles, the one so easily called the "Gnostic" Paul, the one who claimed to be the Apostle of the Gentiles through the will and the revelation of Christ, who declared the Hebrew Law abolished, who preached the incarnation of the Son of God, who unveiled the mystery of the Christ, hidden for centuries and but now made manifest in Jesus, in short the one who initiated the transition from early Christianity, which was purely eschatological, to later Christianity, which was already becoming sacramental and ecclesiastical. What an evolution had taken place in these twenty years between the death of Jesus and the first Epistle (§ 137)! But was not this period too short to allow for so profound a change? And could Paul have been the chief author of so great and so sudden a revolution just because, in his youth in Tarsus, he had had some acquaintance with the pagan mysteries and their rites of salvation? And yet, even if the false Paul of the *Acts* were erased from the picture, the Paul of the Epistles remained to testify that the great

---

[25] For example, often (*Actes*, 1920, pp. 42–48), Loisy refers disparagingly to Harnack's works on the *Acts* as an "apologia." On page 45, there is a malicious little treatment of the same works, with reference to their "significance and their role in the general movement of German culture in these last few years" (since Loisy is writing in 1920, he seems to be referring to the Pan-Germanism prevailing before World War I. Perhaps Harnack had done for Pan-Germanism what Loisy's unscrupulous rewriter had done for the Roman Church?) — On page 48 he concludes by saying that "the apologetics of Harnack, though more scholarly and more subtly skillful than that of the editor of the *Acts*, will not seem any less audacious." — Now, if there was one person who should not have used certain inferences, it was Loisy himself. It would have been so easy for Harnack to have replied by asking him if all the fuss and fury he was displaying against his supposed forger of the *Acts*, presumably a high dignitary of the Roman Church, did not derive perhaps from some personal quarrel he had had with that same Church. (Loisy was an unfrocked priest under major excommunication of the Roman Church.)

revolution had really taken place, and in that short time, and with Paul chiefly responsible. On thinking it over calmly, Loisy recognized that to solve the question completely there was nothing for it but to treat the Epistles as he had the *Acts*, otherwise, his demolition of the latter was not only useless but actually disproved by the Epistles if these were left intact. And so he bent himself to the second task.

144. With regard to the Epistles, Loisy shared, up until 1921 and for some years later, the ideas prevailing among the rationalist scholars, namely, that the authentic letters were *Galatians, Romans, 1* and *2 Corinthians,* and even *1* and *2 Thessalonians, Philippians, Colossians,* and *Philemon,* although additions and alterations must have been made in some of these too.[26] These epistles were thought to fall between the years 50 and 61. But the considerations mentioned above forced Loisy to change his mind. If the Epistles belied his theory it was necessary to abandon, not the theory, of course, but the Epistles. Was it necessary, then, to accept the conclusions of Bruno Bauer and the Dutch School, which had declared they were all entirely false (§ 128)? No, not this, because Loisy had used various historical data in the Epistles to prove false the Paul of the *Acts*, so if he rejected them completely he would have to begin his first demonstration all over again. The only thing to do was to employ the usual method of "selection," that is to accept or reject the various passages according to whether or not they fit the theory.

And that is what happened. But we shall not follow Loisy through his new operation, since it is easy to imagine what it was after our experience with his work on the *Acts*. As we have already said,[27] Loisy, following the trail of J. Turmel, took apart, piece by piece, the epistles considered authentic, he extracted the elements which in his opinion attested the historical Paul, and discarded on the heap of falsifications, the elements which portrayed the "gnostic" Paul. Among the latter was

---

[26] "(The question of the authenticity) has been debated so long and in such detail that the discussion may be regarded as boring, and, in any case, as almost closed. . . . There is nothing more personal and less conventional, either in form or content, than the apologetic sections of the Epistles to the Galatians and the Corinthians. . . . In the main, these documents throb with life, and they reflect neither the condition nor the activity of the Christian communities toward the middle of the second century. . . . Even the doubts raised regarding the first epistle to the Thessalonians, the epistles to the Colossians and Philemon, do not seem well founded when one examines these writings with a better sense of reality. . . . This does not mean that the epistles whose substantial authenticity seems indisputable have come down to us without alteration or additions. . . . There seem to be such additions in the first to the Thessalonians, in the first to the Corinthians and in the epistle to the Romans" (A. Loisy, *Les épîtres de saint Paul,* in *Revue d'histoire et de littérature religieuses,* 1921, pp. 76–78).

[27] Cf. *The Life of Christ,* pp. 208–210 (§§ 219–220); pp. 578–579 (§ 548).

also the passage in which Paul attributes to Jesus the institution of the Eucharist, which Loisy doubted to the point of denial.[28]

145. This extreme position elicited anguished protests from scholars who were Loisy's faithful disciples[29] and respectful reservations from his cordial admirers[30] because it seemed the master had lost his sense of proportion. But the disagreement of his disciples made no impression on him. He had, after all, never shown them any particular attention, and he imperturbably pushed ahead on his own road. And here are his last and definite conclusions, presented as "the most important result of (his) criticism" by Loisy himself: "In this manner the gnostic Paul was created, who, especially in the Epistle to the Corinthians, puts forth the thoroughly exaggerated claim that he is, by the special desire and by special revelation of the Christ, the sole apostle of the whole pagan world, the sole depository of a sole revelation, that is to say, the revelation of the mystery, under the different forms and definitions which this mystery affects in the major and the minor Epistles. Conflicting with this fictitious Paul is the fiction of the Twelve and of Peter, the primary source, in fact, the only source it is claimed, of the Christian apostolate, a fiction coupled in Asia with the fiction of the beloved disciple, who also authored a library, the Apocalypse, a Gospel, Epistles. . . . The most important discovery of our criticism may well be the fact of this radical counterfeiting of this historical Paul — the preacher of the primitive eschatological catechesis, broadened slightly, as it had been by the missionaries in Antioch, in order to gain the adherence of the pagans by sparing them the strictures of the legal observances — and of the mystical Paul, with his arrogant pretensions, his constant and tiresome boasting, the coarse insults he hurled against the early disciples, who presumably had Jewish sympathies, a personage impossible to explain in the framework of early history, but explainable if considered to be a person speaking in the name of Christian groups which claimed to be the inheritors of Paul's tradition and who in reality were introducing into it, not the principle of universal salvation through faith in the risen Jesus, a principle admitted without too much difficulty from the beginning, but the mystery of salvation through mystic union with a Savior come from on high and resurrected in glory."[31]

146. And with this conclusion to his criticism of the Epistles, Loisy's task was finished. But in reality he had ended by proving a very differ-

---

[28] Cf. A. Loisy, *Les origines de la Cène eucharistique*, in *Congrès d'histoire du christianisme. Jubilé Alfred Loisy*, Vol. I, Paris, 1928, pp. 77–95.

[29] Cf. E. Bonaiuti, in *Religio*, January, 1936, p. 67.

[30] M. Goguel, *La relation du dernier repas de Jésus dans 1 Cor., 11, et la tradition historique chez l'apôtre Paul*, in *Revue d'histoire et de philosophie religieuses*, 1930, pp. 61–69.

[31] *Les origines du Nouveau Testament*, pp. 331–332.

ent thesis from the one he had set himself to prove. He had proposed to explain how the historical Paul, in the brief span of twenty years, had deified the man Jesus and made him become the Son of God, the Redeemer of mankind (§ 137). Instead he proved — or thought he had proved — that there were two Pauls to deal with. One was the historical Paul, the eschatological preacher of the imminent second coming of Christ, and to this personage could be attributed certain passages in the *Epistle to the Romans* and the one to the *Galatians*. The other was a counterfeit Paul, the mystic or gnostic dreamer, who preached the concept of salvation, wrought by the Redeemer Christ and communicated through the sacraments; and the rest of *Romans* and *Galatians*, along with almost all the other epistles in their entirety, are to be attributed to this fictitious Paul.

But Loisy was unconcerned at this change of thesis. One thesis was as good as another because in the last analysis they were all provisory and peripheral solutions, that is — as he himself said (§ 122) — they were *hypotheses.* The real *thesis,* the enduring central *thesis,* was the elimination of the supernatural Paul through the application of the "lay dogma."

147. We have no intention of raising the alarmed protests of Loisy's followers. On the contrary, we find that his logic was impeccable, that he drew the legitimate and ultimate conclusions from his principles. His followers were illogical when they turned coward and abandoned him to become awkward conservatives. Once entered upon that descent one has no right to stop; he must go to the bottom of it. And at the bottom lies the pure and simple negation: either the complete obliteration of the historical Paul, as Bruno Bauer and some of the Dutch School would have it, or something equivalent, a Paul reduced to shadow, as Loisy had it.

After all, this fate is for Paul morally just. Christ his Master had admonished: "No disciple is greater than the Master." Modern criticism decrees daily a new crucifixion for that Christ, since it denies his historical existence altogether or at the most leaves him scarcely a shadow of it.[32] Paul could not claim better treatment from the same critics than his Master. It is only natural, then, that they decree for Paul a perennial decapitation.

"I die daily," Paul had asserted while he was yet alive (1 Cor. 15:31), and he might repeat the same assertion today in view of the way his moral inheritance is treated in the name of science. During his lifetime, he died every day to fill up in his body "what is lacking of the sufferings of Christ" (Col. 1:24), and this he still continues to do because the passion of Christ endures through the centuries in the Mystical Body of Christ.

---

[32] Cf. *The Life of Christ,* p. 207 (§ 218); p. 211 ff. (§ 221 ff.).

But after this repeated death Paul imitates Christ his Master. He rises again more alive than before, and every mortal blow he receives is for him a gain. He declares it himself unceasingly from his tomb in Rome, on which are sculptured his own words: "For me . . . to die is gain" (Phil. 1:21).

VII

Chronology of Paul's Life

---

148. Chronological Table:

Dates (A.D.)	Events in Paul's Life	Documents	Paul's Writings	Contemporary Events
1–5	Birth of Paul	Acts 7:58; Philemon 9		
13–18 (?)	Beginning of studies in Jerusalem	Acts 22:3; 26:4		Death of Augustus accession of Ti berius, August 19 A.D. 14
36	Stoning of Stephen, Conversion of Paul	Acts 7:58; 9:1–19; 22:4–20; Gal. 1:13–16		Pilate is procurator 26–36; death o Jesus Christ: 30
36–39	Sojourn in Damascus, in Arabia, and again in Damascus	Acts 9:20–22; Gal. 1:17; Acts 9:23–25		Death of Tiberiu accession of Calig ula, March 16, 3
39	First journey to Jerusalem, and fifteen-day sojourn there	Acts 9:26–28; Gal. 1:18–20		
39–43	Sojourn in Tarsus	Acts 9:29–30; Gal. 1:21–24		Death of Caligula accession of Clau dius, January 24, 4
43–44	Sojourn in Antioch	Acts 11:25–26		
44	Famine, and journey (to bring the contributions) to Jerusalem	Acts 11:27–30; 12:25		
45–49 (50)	FIRST MISSIONARY JOURNEY (Cyprus and Asia Minor)	Acts 13–14; 2 Tim. 3:11		
49 (50)	Apostolic Council in Jerusalem	Acts 15:1–35; Gal. 2:1–10		Claudius expels th Jews from Ron (cf. Acts 18:2)
49 (50)	Dispute with Cephas in Antioch	Gal. 2:11 ff.		
(49) 50–(52) 53	SECOND MISSIONARY JOURNEY (Asia Minor, Macedonia, Achaea)	Acts 15:36–18:22 (cf. Gal. 4:13–15		
50 (51)	Philippi	Acts 16:11 ff.		
51	Thessalonica	Acts 17:1 ff.	1 Thessalonians	

Dates (A.D.)	Events in Paul's Life	Documents	Paul's Writings	Contemporary Events
51–53	Corinth	Acts 18:1 ff.	2 Thessalonians	Gallio proconsul in Achaea, 52–53 (51–52)
53–58	THIRD MISSION-ARY JOURNEY	Acts 18:23–21:17		
53	Galatia-Phrygia			
54–57	Ephesus	Acts 19:1 ff.	(54) Galatians (?) (56) 1 Corinthians	Death of Claudius; Nero elected emperor, October 13, 54
57	Departure from Ephesus Sojourn in Macedonia Journey to Illyria (Rom. 15:19)?	Acts 20:1–6	2 Corinthians	
57–58	Corinth (three winter months)	Acts 20:3	Galatians (?) Romans	
58	Journey. Arrest in Jerusalem	Acts 20:3–23:25		
58–60	IMPRISONMENT IN CAESAREA	Acts 24–26		Porcius Festus, procurator, 60–62
60–61	Sea voyage, shipwreck at Malta. Arrival in Rome	Acts 27–28:16		
61–63	FIRST IMPRISON-MENT IN ROME	Acts 28:17–31	Colossians, Ephesians, Philemon, Philippians	
63–64	Journey in Spain			
64–	Sojourn in Italy		Hebrews (?)	Burning of Rome, July, 64
64–66	Journey in the Orient (Ephesus, Crete, etc.) Macedonia, Nicopolis	1 Tim. 1:3; Titus 1:5; 3:12	1 Timothy Titus	
66–67	SECOND IMPRISONMENT IN ROME	2 Tim. 1:15–18; 4:9–21	2 Timothy	Revolt of Judea, 66–70
67	Martyrdom			
				Death of Nero, June 6, 68

149. In the following pages, I shall explain the reasons why I have chosen the dates in the above table. As we shall see, most of them are approximate at best. Others seem to be more probable than the dates assigned for certain of these events by other authors.

Birth of Paul — The year of Paul's birth is not to be found in any documents. It may be deduced indirectly from two incidental references. One is in the Epistle to Philemon, 9, where Paul calls himself "an old man" (πρεσβύτης), which would imply, in the common usage of the term, that he was at least over sixty. Since the letter was written between the years 61–63, this would mean he was born in the early years of the Christian Era, if not before.

The other reference is even more vague. On the occasion of Stephen's stoning, the date of which may be fixed with sufficient certainty in the year 36, Paul is called νεανίας (Acts 7:58), a term the Greeks used to designate both an adolescent not yet twenty or a man nearing forty. Taking the mean between these two and considering the fact that Paul is presented to us immediately afterward as a person with a certain authority in carrying out the persecution of the Christians (Acts 8:3), we may reasonably suppose that he then was between thirty and thirty-five years of age. This again would place his birth in the first years of the Christian Era.

If, then, Jesus was born in the year 748 A.U.C., six years before the Christian Era,[1] Paul was a little younger than he by three to eight years.

150. *Studies in Jerusalem* — From his native city Tarsus, Paul went to study in Jerusalem (Acts 22:3), "from his youth" (ἐκ νεότητος — *ibid.*, 26:4). There is the same uncertainty here as in the preceding date, but we can overcome it in part by referring to the customs of practicing Jews with regard to education. One rule, attributed to Judah the son of Tema, establishes: "At the age of five, reading [of the Bible]; at the age of ten, the Mishna; at the age of 13 [the observance of] the commandments; at the age of 15 the Talmud; at the age of eighteen, marriage, etc." (Mishna, *Aboth*, V, 21). This rule belongs to a time much later than that of Paul's youth, but, assuming that it reflects the customs already prevalent in the first century A.D. we may conclude that Paul went to Jerusalem a little before his fifteenth birthday, or between the years A.D. 13 and 18.

How long his course of studies in Jerusalem lasted, or whether he remained there for some time after his course was completed, it is impossible to determine in any way.

151. *The Stoning of Stephen. The Conversion of Paul* — The first of these events occurs shortly before the second, perhaps a few weeks before (cf. Acts 7:60; 8:1–3; 9:1 ff.). But in what year did they take place?

The positive information we possess is as follows: When Stephen is killed, the new Christian community is already greatly developed both in number (Acts 4:4; 5:14; 6:7) and internal organization (*ibid.*, 4:32; 6:1 ff.), and the faith has spread outside of Jerusalem and Palestine as well (*ibid.*, 8:5 ff.; 9:2). This would lead us to suppose that some time had passed, that is, several years, since the death of Jesus in the year 30.

There is another consideration which helps to determine the number of years. During the trial and death of Stephen there is no interven-

---

[1] Cf. *The Life of Christ,* pp. 155–157 (§§ 173–174).

tion at all on the part of the Roman procurator, who should have appeared at some point since he alone had the right to pronounce or to approve the death sentence.[2] He had had to do this at the trial of Jesus, and his approval should have been necessary for Stephen's sentence of execution since legally it was the same kind of case. And the Roman procurator himself should have been the same, namely, Pontius Pilate, who was in office from the year 26 to 36, and who — as it appears from Jesus' trial — was not at all disposed to renounce this right nor to lend it readily to the service of the Sanhedrists, whom he depised. Instead, in Stephen's case, we find only the Sanhedrin in action with its crowd of satellites, and there is not the slightest reference to the Roman magistrate. Why?

In all probability because Pontius Pilate was no longer in office, having been deposed by his superior, Vitellius, Legate to Syria, and sent to Rome to answer before the emperor the charges brought against him by the Jews.[3] The Sanhedrin, then, had taken advantage of the fact that the procuratorship was empty, or occupied at best by the inexperienced Marcellus (Pilate's successor), and had made a show of authority in the stoning of Stephen. A similar case occurred in the year 62, at the death of the procurator, Porcius Festus, when the Sanhedrin had James the "brother" of Jesus stoned.[4]

If we suppose that the stoning of Stephen took place in these circumstances, that is, in the year 36, then we find that six years had passed since the death of Jesus, allowing sufficient time for the development of the Christian community as mentioned above.

152. *Sojourn in Damascus, in Arabia, and again in Damascus* — This succession of events is arrived at by weaving together the account in the *Acts* and in the *Epistle to the Galatians*. As soon as he was converted, Paul went to Damascus, and having begun immediately to preach faith in Jesus the Christ, he remained there "for some days" (Acts 9:19). This first sojourn in Damascus, which was after all a short one, is not mentioned in *Galatians*, 1:17, which speaks only of his retiring into Arabia and then of his "return" (note the word, which implies a previous sojourn) to Damascus. On the other hand the *Acts* (9:20–25) does not mention Paul's withdrawal into Arabia and treats the two sojourns in Damascus as one.

If his conversion took place in the year 36, then so did his first short stay in Damascus, and immediately afterward the beginning of his withdrawal in Arabia. How long this lasted we do not know, but it was probably no more than a few months (which is perhaps indicated also in the expression "some days" in reference to Paul's general preach-

[2] Cf. *ibid.*, p. 24 (§ 22); p. 54 (§ 59); p. 609 ff. (§ 576 ff.).
[3] Cf. *Storia d'Israele*, II, p. 442 (§ 338).
[4] Cf. *ibid.*, II, p. 466 (§ 415).

ing in Damascus: Acts 9:20), and it was followed by his return to Damascus. It is certain that his withdrawal to Arabia and the second sojourn in Damascus together did not last beyond the third year after his conversion (Gal. 1:18). This would bring us to the year 39.

In this year Paul, to escape an ambush of the Jews, had to flee from Damascus by night with the aid of disciples, who let him down over the walls of the city in a basket. And this was because "the governor under King Aretas was guarding the city" (2 Cor. 11:32; cf. Acts 9:25). This was Aretas IV, King of the Nabateans, on whom Tiberius had in 36 waged a useless war.[5] How does it happen that now in 39, a governor of this same Aretas was lording it so mightily in Roman Damascus that he tried to capture Paul, a Roman citizen, in order to please the Jews? It has been supposed that this "governor" was a representative of Aretas, sent to the suburbs of Damascus to protect the interests of the Nabatean Arabs, who were numerous in the districts around the city. But it is very improbable that the Romans would have tolerated the representative of an enemy king, and such an enterprising one, if they had been the masters of Damascus and its environs. Therefore there is much more likelihood in the other theory that Caligula, who succeeded Tiberius in 37, had ceded Damascus to Aretas, merely to reverse the policies of his predecessor, just as he had done in other instances. For example, in 40 he ceded to Herod Agrippa I the tetrarchate that had belonged to Herod Antipas.[6] This theory is supported also by the fact that while there are Damascus coins with the effigy of Tiberius there are none with that of Caligula (or of his successor, Claudius — § 32). Besides, it dovetails very well with the series of events in Paul's life, for it means he fled the city when it no longer belonged to the Romans but to Aretas. Since Aretas died in the year 40, Paul's flight occurred before that and after Caligula's accession to the throne, which took place in 37. This brings us once more to approximately the year 39, as above.

153. *First Journey to Jerusalem* — This presents no difficulty. According to *Galatians,* 1:18–20, the journey took place "after three years" Paul's conversion and was followed by a two weeks' stay with Peter in Jerusalem. The term "three years" may be a round figure, and we may allow a difference of a month or two either way.

Sojourn in Tarsus — After the two weeks spent in Jerusalem, Paul went to Tarsus in Cilicia by way of Caesarea (Gal. 1:21; Acts 9:30). Tarsus was the center of Paul's activity until Barnabas arrived to take him to Antioch. That was a year before Paul's second journey to Jerusalem, which — as we shall see shortly — took place in 44. Therefore, Paul stayed in Tarsus about four years, from 39–43.

---

[5] Cf. *ibid.,* II, p. 427 (§ 371).
[6] Cf. *ibid.,* p. 450 (§ 395).

Sojourn in Antioch — Paul remained in Antioch "a whole year" (Acts 11:26), that is, until his journey to Jerusalem in 44. The "whole year" was from 43 to 44.

154. *Famine, and Journey* (*to Bring the Contributions*) *to Jerusalem* — When the general famine was prophesied, the Christians of Antioch collected relief for the community of Jerusalem and sent it there by means of Barnabas and Paul (Acts 11:27–30). This is the so-called "journey with contributions." When did it take place?

It should be noted that the famine which occasioned it lasted for several years, was more or less serious in extent, and spread through various regions. It is recorded in Rome at the beginning of the reign of Claudius (Suetonius, *Claudius*, 18; Dion Cassius, IX, 11, 1–3), that is, in 41–42, and there is mention of it again in the eleventh year of Claudius' reign (Tacitus, *Annales*, XII, 43), A.D. 52. Apart from other regions, for Judea we have the testimony of Flavius Josephus (*Antiquities of the Jews*, III, 320; XX, 51, 101) for the period under Tiberius Alexander, who was procurator from 46–48. These years were perhaps the worst for Palestine, but the general famine must have started even earlier, and the above-mentioned journey is to be associated with its first beginnings. It is to be noted also that in the account in the *Acts* (12:1), the journey is associated with the death of Herod Agrippa I, which occurred "at this time," that is, while Paul and Barnabas were still in Jerusalem after bringing the contributions from Antioch (12:25). Agrippa died in the spring of 44.[7] This, then, was the year of the journey.

The journey itself is not mentioned in the *Epistle to the Galatians* (2:1–10), which refers instead to a later one to Jerusalem on the occasion of the Apostolic Council. The reason for the omission is simply that Paul is not narrating in this epistle each single event in his life. He merely wants to show the Galatians that he received his Gospel not from men but from Jesus Christ (1:11–12). Mention of the journey with contributions served no purpose here, since it was an act of Christian brotherhood and not of the apostolic ministry. Besides, when they came to Jerusalem with the contributions, Barnabas and Paul had been directed to the "elders" of the community (Acts 11:30), while there is no mention of their meeting the Apostles. Since Agrippa's persecution was raging at the time, the Apostles were either in prison like Peter, or had probably fled elsewhere as Peter did after his liberation (12:1–17).

Some scholars maintain that the "journey with contributions" is the same one mentioned in *Galatians*, 2:1 ff. But it is sufficient to compare this text with the account in *Acts*, 15:2 ff., to see that the subject of the

---

[7] Cf. *ibid.*, II, p. 454 (§ 399).

two is the same both as to persons, events, and circumstances. This means it is the journey to the Apostolic Council, which was quite a different journey from the journey with contributions. This is, after all, the opinion of ancient authors (Irenaeus, *Adv. haer.*, III, 13, 3: Tertullian, *Adv. Marcion.*, v, 2), and is shared by the majority of modern scholars. The journey with contributions was, therefore, the second we know Paul made to Jerusalem after his conversion. The third was to attend the council.

155. *First Missionary Journey* — On his return from the journey with contributions, Paul stayed in Antioch for a while, but we do not know how long (Acts 13:1–3). Then, with Barnabas and John Mark, he undertook his first missionary journey across Cyprus, Pamphylia, Pisidia, Lycaonia, returning over the same route to Antioch. There he stopped again for "no little time" (Acts 14:27). Then followed the journey to the Apostolic Council, which did not take place before the year 49.

It is not possible to determine the length of the two sojourns in Antioch or of the missionary journey in between. The voyage alone must have taken at least three years, if we remember that they traversed the length of the island of Cyprus (Acts 13:6) and, it would seem, evangelized it with some thoroughness. This must have required several months in Cyprus alone. Taken together, then, the journey and the two sojourns in Antioch occupied the years from 45 to 49 and perhaps to 50.

156. *The Apostolic Council* — Paul himself gives us the date for this Council in the *Epistle to the Galatians*. After narrating his conversion, he says that "after three years" (1:18) he went to Jerusalem, and this was his first trip to the city, as we pointed out above (§ 153). He then continues: "Then after fourteen years I went up again to Jerusalem with Barnabas . . ." ("Ἔπειτα διά δεκατεσσάρων ἐτῶν πάλιν ἀνέβην κτλ.: 2:1). But what marks the beginning of these fourteen years, his conversion or the preceding journey to Jerusalem? If we consider the former, then, since the conversion occurred in 36, the Council took place in 49 (or 50, always, of course, in round figures). If we take the second alternative, seventeen years (3 plus 14) would have had to elapse between the conversion and the Council, and it would be necessary either to set the conversion three years earlier or the Council three years later. Strictly speaking the text itself permits both interpretations. In fact, on the basis of the Greek words, ἔπειτα διά . . . πάλιν, it is somewhat more natural to argue that the fourteen years begin with the previous trip to Jerusalem. On the other hand, the entire context seems to indicate that Paul is thinking of his conversion, the beginning of his "new life," and at the same time of his apostolate, with which he is concerned here. Then the "fourteen years," like the three-year period mentioned earlier, would refer back to his conversion. As we noted above (§ 151), there are several reasons for setting this in the year 36, and which would prevent our setting it earlier. It would be even more difficult to set the Council three years later, according to the data we shall examine in a moment. For all of these reasons we consider that Paul, in his nervous and condensed style, was counting the fourteen years from the time of his conversion. In that case the Council took place in the year 49 (or 50).

Dissension with Peter in Antioch — Everything indicates that this happened shortly after the Apostolic Council. Note that Barnabas also is involved in the incident (Gal. 2:13) and that he shortly afterward left Paul in Antioch (Acts 15:37 ff.).

157. *Second Missionary Journey* — There are two short periods to note between the return of Paul and Barnabas from the Apostolic Council and the beginning of the second missionary journey. One was of "some time" (Acts 15:33), and the other of "some days" (Acts 15:36). Taking them together and allowing for the discussions between Barnabas and Paul and the preparations for the journey (Acts 15:37–39), it may be supposed that a month or two was involved, after which Paul set out again. This must have occurred at the end of 49, or better at the beginning of the year 50.

This second voyage took Paul across Syria and Cilicia into Lycaonia, then to Phrygia and the "Galatian country" (Acts 16:6), and as far as Troas. Sailing to Europe, he stopped in Philippi, Thessalonica, Athens, and Corinth. The journey, which lasted about three years, gives us two important chronological references, both during Paul's stay in Corinth. Upon his arrival in this city, Paul met a Jew by the name of Aquila and his wife Priscilla, "who had recently come from Italy . . . because Claudius had ordered all Jews to leave Rome" (Acts 18:2). We know of this edict of Claudius from Suetonius (*Claudius*, 25),[8] who, however, does not give us the date. Orosius (*Histor.*, VII, 6) assigns the edict to the ninth year of Claudius' reign, which was 49. Since Orosius uses as his authority Flavius Josephus, who does not mention the edict, his date does not seem to have any guarantee. On the other hand, it does dovetail perfectly with the other chronological data we possess. If Aquila left Rome in 49, he could have reached Corinth in 50 or 51 and there have been joined by Paul.

158. The other reference has to do with Paul's meeting with the proconsul, Gallio. During the first eighteen months, and perhaps more, Paul spent in Corinth (Acts 18:11; cf. 7) he was not disturbed by the Jews. If he arrived in Corinth in the first half of 51, this would bring us to the second half of 52. At this time, the Jews rose up against him and accused him before the tribunal of the proconsul, Lucius Junius Gallio, brother of the philosopher Seneca. But Gallio dismissed the charges and left Paul undisturbed. He remained in Corinth for some time (Acts

---

[8] Cf. *Storia d'Israele*, II, p. 223 (§ 196).

18:18). Therefore, the year of Gallio's proconsulship in Corinth must coincide with the time when Paul had already been in the city eighteen months. Happily a famous fragment of inscription found in Delphi and published in 1905[9] helps us determine the time of Gallio's proconsulship. The inscription consists of twelve incomplete lines, and reproduces a letter written by the emperor Claudius to the city of Delphi. By filling in the gaps as far as possible we gather the following data: The letter was written while Gallio was in office, since the sixth line says, "(Ju)nius Gallio my friend and proconsul of Achaea." In addition, it was written after Claudius had been proclaimed emperor for the twenty-sixth time (second line). From other documents we learn that the next imperial proclamation (the twenty-seventh) took place before the first of August in 52. Therefore the twenty-sixth was anterior to that date. We also know that the twenty-fourth such acclamation had occurred not long before the twenty-fourth of January in 52, while we know nothing of the twenty-fifth. Nevertheless, there can be no doubt that the twenty-sixth acclamation took place between January and July of the year 52. Sometime within these few months, therefore, Claudius wrote the letter reproduced in the inscription and at the same time Gallio was proconsul in Achaea. But when did the latter take office? This point is more difficult to establish because the information that has come down to us from the ancient writers is not too certain. In any case, Gallio was unquestionably in office in May of the year 52, and probably had not been in Corinth very long. About this time, Paul was denounced to his tribunal. This seems to be adequately explained by the fact that Gallio was a new magistrate, and in bringing their charges the Jews were trying to put one over on the "new man," even though Paul had been living in Corinth for more than eighteen months.

After the encounter with Gallio, Paul remained in Corinth for some time still (Acts 18:18), and then left for Ephesus. From there, passing through Caesarea-by-the-sea, he went for a brief visit of greeting to Jerusalem (18:22). Finally he went to Antioch, thus ending his second missionary journey. This all took several months. Afterward, having spent "some time" (18:23) in Antioch, Paul departed once more for a third voyage. Chronologically this all fits together perfectly. It must have been spring of the year 53, the good season for traveling.

159. *Third Missionary Journey* — In this third voyage Paul concentrated directly on the "Galatian country" and Phrygia (Acts 18:23) and in these regions he must have spent the rest of the year 53 and part

---

[9] It was published by E. Bourguet, *De rebus Delphicis imperatoriae aetatis capita duo* (Montpelier, 1905). It would seem that Bourguet was unaware of the extraordinary importance of the inscription, but it soon became the object of careful study; cf. A. Deissman, *Paulus*, 2nd edition, Tübingen, 1925, pp. 203–233.

of 54. Then he went to Ephesus, where he remained two years and three months (19:8, 10), and again an unspecified length of time (19:22), or for about three years in all (20:31). Taking this as an approximate figure, we conclude that Paul's sojourn in Ephesus lasted for the rest of 54, through 55 and 56, and a good part of 57.[10]

Departure From Ephesus — This must have occurred about May in 57. There followed a stay of some months in Macedonia, in Philippi. The trip to Illyria (Rom. 15:19) — if Paul went to the interior of this region and did not stop instead at the border — probably took place in this period. Then Paul returned to Macedonia.

From Macedonia he went down to Corinth, where he remained three months, in the winter between 57 and 58.

Journey. Arrest in Jerusalem — From Corinth, Paul traveled by land to Macedonia and there, in Philippi, he celebrated Easter in 58 (Acts 20:3–6). He then went down the western coast of Asia Minor, hurried along by his desire to spend Pentecost in Jerusalem (20:16). After touching at Tyre and Caesarea, he arrived in Jerusalem, where he was imprisoned. This was approximately May in the year 58.

160. *Imprisonment in Caesarea* — Paul was imprisoned under the procurator, Antony Felix, and spent two full years in prison in Caesarea. Then the new procurator Porcius Festus took office (Acts 24:27).

The new magistrate began his term in the year 60, probably late in the summer.[11] Some scholars, comparing a passage in Flavius Josephus (*Antiquities of the Jews,* XX, 182) with one in Tacitus (*Annales,* XIII, 14–15) have assumed that Felix was recalled by Nero in 55, since his brother, Pallas, interceded for him at his trial. Pallas had been very powerful in court but he lost all favor in the year 55. However, this is one of the many instances in which we are not to follow Flavius Josephus. Pallas in fact fell from grace in the first weeks of Nero's reign and before the death of Britannicus (February, 55); and in the three months of Nero's rule there was not time for the supposed events to have taken place (the recall of Felix to Rome, his journey from Palestine, the setting up of the trial, the intercession of Pallas, etc.). There are various reasons, which it is not necessary to discuss here, for taking the year 60 as the beginning of the procuratorship of Porcius Festus, and the majority of scholars do agree on this year.

Sea Voyage, Shipwreck at Malta, Arrival in Rome — These events occupied the period between the autumn of 60 and the spring of 61. In

---

[10] In all probability, Paul's sojourn in Ephesus was not uninterrupted. In the autumn of 56 he had to make a quick trip to Corinth, from where he returned directly to Ephesus. But this question is best treated by itself in the context of other data (§§ 473, 491).

[11] Cf. *Storia d'Israele,* II, pp. 465–466 (§§ 413–414).

addition to the length of time spent sailing and at the secondary stops along the way, the stop at Malta alone lasted three months (Acts 28:11), that is, through the winter.

First Imprisonment in Rome — We have explicit testimony that this lasted a full two years (Acts 28:30), but it may also have lasted a few months longer under another form. These two years take us from the spring of 61 to that of 63. If the period of imprisonment was somewhat longer, it would bring us to about the middle of the same year.

Here our principal guide, the *Acts of the Apostles*, ends. For the later events listed in the table, from the "Voyage to Spain" to the "Martyrdom" we must have recourse to other documents. For the time being let us use the dates as listed above.

VIII

Paul the Writer

---

161. In the twelfth century Christian art began to picture Paul with
a sword, and this became a regular feature of his portrait in later
iconography. Does the sword represent only the martyrdom of the
Apostle? Or, in the mind of the historian, may it not symbolize more
rightly the spiritual weapon he was the first among the disciples of
Christ to use, the weapon of writing? After so many centuries it has lost
none of its temper nor its keenness.

We may note that Christ left no writings. He himself was the living
"word of God . . . and efficient and keener than any two-edged sword"
(Heb. 4:12).

Paul gives us his own evaluation of himself as a writer when he declares that he is "rude in speech, yet . . . not so in knowledge" (2 Cor.
11:6). He does not consider himself an expert and subtle craftsman,
but a man who feels profoundly what he wants to express. The word
(λόγος) is inadequate, but his knowledge (γνῶσις) is full.

162. From Paul's statement we should conclude that he was an eloquent writer. Quintilian, who was the great expert on this subject,
warns us that true eloquence is the fruit, not of literary artifice but of
feeling and strong conviction,[1] and both of these Paul possessed in
abundance. Strictly speaking Quintilian has in mind the author conscious
of his art, who succeeds in clothing his deep feeling in a skillfully prepared form, like the sculptor who pours the molten bronze into the
mold he has laboriously perfected beforehand.

But Paul is not that kind of craftsman. He is not a professional writer.
He is conscious only of the thought he wishes to express. He works
only with his metal, and he pours it into the first mold that happens to
come to hand without bothering to perfect it. This unfinished style is
certainly a defect, but it is at the same time the reason for his greatness,
for it makes him an unconscious artist, a writer who unintentionally
often achieves great literature. That is the judgment on Paul's eloquence
given by Augustine, another expert on the subject: "As we do not affirm

---

[1] *Pectus est quod disertos facit, et vis mentis.*

that the Apostle sought out the precepts of eloquence, so do we not deny that eloquence sought out his wisdom" (*De doctrina christ.*, IV, 7).

The elegant Isocrates, who for ten years assiduously worked over his *Panegyric* and took so long to polish and perfect it that he finally published it when it no longer served any purpose, that is, when the peace he recommended in the oration had already been concluded, this Isocrates is the pure "man of letters" for whom the word is everything, the thought is only the pretext for its use. A short while later Demosthenes reached the highest peak of human eloquence, clothing his flaming emotion in perfect form. Even today, on reading his *De corona* one is awed by his mastery of expression and shaken by the power of his thought. Paul is the exact opposite of Isocrates. He would be glad to dispense with words if he could communicate his thought without them. But since there is no substitute for this opaque and cumbersome material he treats it disdainfully, "for the material is unresponsive" (*Paradiso*, I, 129).

163. This comparison between Paul "rude in speech" and authors like Isocrates and Demosthenes may seem farfetched and inopportune. But we intended it merely as a reference to famous and celebrated standards. The same comparison seems to have been made in the third century by the pagan Cassius Longinus, called because of his learning the "philologist" par excellence, or the "living library." He is supposed to have expressed the following opinion: "Standing therefore at the peak of all eloquence and Greek feeling are Demosthenes, Lysias, Aechines . . . Isocrates, Antiphones: after them Paul of Tarsus, whom I declare also the first example of the assertion which is not exposition."[2] Paul is not to be equated with the preceding Greek orators, but he is worthy to follow them insofar as he represents better than anyone else "non-expository eloquence," that is, the type of eloquence which — as Longinus said elsewhere — is not a demonstration but strikes the imagination and the feeling. This judgment might well have been passed by a pagan philologist, who could not evaluate the argumentative force of Paul's long passages of reasoning, while there is no reference whatever to the Christian content of Paul's writing. A Christian critic would have

---

2 Κορωνὶς δ' ἔστω λόγου παντὸς καὶ φρονήματος ἑλληνικοῦ Δημοσθένης, Λυσίας, Αἰσχίνης, . . . Ἰσοκράτης, Ἀντιφῶν: πρὸς τούτους Παῦλος ὁ Ταρσεύς, ὅντινα καὶ πρῶτον φημὶ προιστάμενον δόγματος ἀναποδείκτου (in J. A. Fabricius, *Bibliotheca greca*, Hamburg, 1711, p. 445; but the list of Greek authors, which is not certain, is according to the reading of Ruhnken). To this passage Fabricius adds the observation: *Postrema de Paulo Apostolo a Christiano homine adiecta sunt.* But this opinion, not supported by any, is unconvincing. On the other hand, J. L. Hug, *Einleitung in die Schriften des N. Test.*, II, 4th edition, Stuttgart and Tübingen, 1847, pp. 285–288, lists good arguments to show that the expressions and thought of the clause in question correspond to others in the authentic writings of Longinus, and that the latter, who was acquainted with Christianity might very well have expressed this opinion. In any case, since there may be some doubt as to its authenticity, we quote it merely as being probable.

certainly been more emphatic in his praise and would not have failed
to mention the Tarsene's religion.

164. When Paul began one of his writings (except perhaps as he
began to grow old) his spirit must have been in a state of feverish agitation, compressed, needled by a thousand ideas all fighting for expression at once. He ponders a while to push these swarming thoughts into
some order, finally chooses one idea, and begins to expound it. But in
the middle of his exposition, a word he has just used evokes another idea
that seems to him indispensable, and leaving the first hanging in mid-
air, he inserts the second. And even in this second concept he is apt to
thrust a short parenthesis to make room for some particular reflection
that has crossed his mind at the moment. Then he closes the parenthesis,
and the insertion, and goes back to finish his original exposition.

But it is never certain that he will finish an explanation he has begun
or bring a sentence to its logical conclusion. When Quintilian's "strong
conviction" becomes violent — as it so often does in Paul — the sentence
may remain unfinished, because as he writes other concepts flash across
his mind and black out the thought he is developing. This is what the
grammarians call "anacoluthon."

At other times — and always because of the pressure of crowding
thoughts — Paul seems intent upon saving time, ink, and paper, and
he sets his ideas down in tight summary fashion which the ancients
perhaps called tachygraphic (and we might call telegraphic). If four
clauses are necessary to the sentence, Paul expresses two and lets the
reader fill in the rest. This is the "ellipsis" of the grammarians.

165. We give only one example of each of these, although Paul's style
abounds in anacolutha, ellipses, and similar stylistic liberties.

An example of a sentence broken up by parentheses within parentheses
may be taken from the very beginning of the Epistle to the Romans
(1:1–7) which starts off as follows: "Paul, the servant of Jesus Christ
. . . set apart for [i.e., to preach] the gospel of God. . . ." At this point the
word "gospel" unfurls before Paul's eyes a marvelous vision, and he
cannot refrain from inserting a commentary: "which he had promised
beforehand through his prophets in the Holy Scriptures, concerning his
Son. . . ." The mention of the Son of God cannot be passed over without
some word of explanation, and this is inserted in a long parenthesis: "(he)
who was born to him according to the flesh of the offspring of David;
who was foreordained Son of God by an act of power in keeping with
the holiness of his spirit, by resurrection from the dead: Jesus Christ
our Lord, through whom we have received grace and apostleship to
bring about obedience to faith among all the nations for his name's
sake; among whom are you also called to be Jesus Christ's — " This
finishes both insertion and parenthesis and Paul now goes back to his
original thought and ties up his sentence: "to all God's beloved who are

in Rome, called to be saints: grace be to you and peace from God our Father and from the Lord Jesus Christ."

166. Or let us take an example of a sentence begun in one way and ended in another. Paul intends to show that the Hebrew Law offers many advantages in comparison with the natural law, and here is his reasoning (Rom. 3:1 ff.): "What advantage then remains to the Jew or what is the use of circumcision? Much in every respect. First indeed because the oracles of God were entrusted to them [the Jews]. For what if some of them have not believed? Will their unbelief make void the fidelity of God? By no means! . . . etc." And his reasoning rushes through a length of compelling argumentation but we wait in vain for the conclusion to his first statement. The adverb "first" ($\pi\rho\hat{\omega}\tau\text{o}\nu$ $\mu\acute{\epsilon}\nu$) leads us to expect that there will be a "secondly" or a "besides" ($\check{\epsilon}\pi\epsilon\iota\tau\alpha$ $\delta\acute{\epsilon}$), but it never comes. Afire with his subject, Paul has forgotten the grammatical sequence and left it unfinished.

The third example will serve to illustrate what we have called his telegraphic style. Paul pictures the Jewish people as an olive tree from which several branches have been broken. On this tree there has been grafted a twig from a wild olive, which, however, has grown and flourished on the old stem. The twig represents the Gentiles, who have been grafted onto the divine revelation already entrusted to the chosen people. There arises the danger that it will grow proud and disdain the broken branches of the tree. But Paul warns against this in a sentence which, if regularly constructed, would read something like this: "Do not boast against the branches, for if you do you are wrong, since you must remember that you do not support the stem, but the stem supports you." Paul, almost as if in a hurry to defend his countrymen, compresses the thought into these few words: "Do not boast against the branches. But if thou dost boast, still it is not thou that supportest the stem, but the stem thee" (Rom. 11:18).

167. These, however, are exceptions and Paul's style is not always so zigzag and breathless. When the little boat of his inspiration is caught by one of the winds that prevail across his skies, he unfurls his sails and, though his sea is always tumultuous, the boat skims it swiftly. The most impetuous of these winds is, in fact, a veritable whirlwind — his love for Christ. In its wake follow two others less lofty but also impetuous, and these are his love for his fellow Jews who reject the Christ and his hostility toward the Judaizing Christians who reject the liberty of the Gospel.

His love for Christ finds genuinely lyric expression, as in the following passage: "Who shall separate us from the love of Christ? Shall tribulation, or distress, or persecution, or hunger, or nakedness, or danger, or the sword? . . . But in all these things we [more than] overcome ($\acute{\upsilon}\pi\epsilon\rho\nu\iota\kappa\hat{\omega}\mu\epsilon\nu$) because of him who has loved us. For I am sure that neither death, nor life, nor angels, nor principalities, nor things present, nor things to come, nor powers, nor height, nor depth, nor any other creature will be able to separate us from the love of God, which is in Christ Jesus our Lord" (Rom. 8:35–39).

Immediately after this we find a passage of moving warmth, inspired by Paul's affection for his countrymen who reject the Christ. It is as if the winds across Paul's sky abruptly take turns blowing him swiftly along his course, and the wind of his joyous love of Christ has yielded place to his sorrowful love for the Jews: "I speak the truth in Christ, I do not lie, my conscience bearing me witness in the Holy Spirit, that I have great sadness and continuous sorrow in my heart. For I could wish to be anathema myself from Christ for the sake of my brethren, who are my kinsmen according to the flesh; who are Israelites, who have the adoption as sons, and the glory and the covenants and the legislation and the worship and the promises; who have the fathers, and from whom is the Christ according to the flesh, who is over all things, God blessed forever, amen. It is not that the word of God has failed. For they are not all Israelites who are sprung from Israel . . ." (Rom. 9:1–6).

168. When he clashes with the Judaizing Christians, Paul flames both with his love of Christ and pity for his countrymen. There is no compromise between the circumcision which has been abolished and the Gospel which has been inaugurated. Let those who favor these compromises come forward and show their letters of credit. Paul will answer: "But wherein any man is bold — I am speaking foolishly — I also am bold. Are they Hebrews? So am I! Are they Israelites? So am I! Are they offspring of Abraham? So am I! Are they ministers of Christ? I — to speak as a fool — am more: in many more labors, in prisons more frequently, in lashes above measure, often exposed to death. From the Jews five times I received forty lashes less one. Thrice I was scourged, once I was stoned, thrice I suffered shipwreck, a night and a day I was adrift on the sea; in journeyings often, in perils from floods, in perils from robbers, in perils from my own nation, in perils from the Gentiles, in perils in the city, in perils in the wilderness, in perils in the sea, in perils from false brethren; in labor and hardships, in many sleepless nights, in hunger and thirst, in fastings often, in cold and nakedness. Besides those outer things, there is my daily pressing anxiety, the care of all the churches! Who is weak, and I am not weak? Who is made to stumble and I am not inflamed? . . ." (2 Cor. 11:21–29). If this is not eloquence, nothing is. It is precisely that type of eloquence which Horace means when he says, "he who profoundly feels his subject will lack neither eloquence, nor clarity of order."[3] Here Paul feels and makes his reader feel with him. This is eloquence.

---

[3] *Cui lecta potenter erit res, nec facundia deserit hunc nec lucidus ordo* (*Ars poetica*, 40–41). We might observe incidentally that this passage was imitated literally

169. But even apart from the heat of controversy, Paul can be eloquent especially when he speaks of the distinguishing mark of the
Christian, which is love. There are many other, though briefer passages
into addition to the famous encomium of charity (§ 486). We shall
refrain from quoting them here, but cite instead two short texts which
illustrate the tenderness of Paul's affection.

Writing to the Galatians, whom he made Christian and who now are
in danger of being alienated from him, he says: "Have I then become
your enemy, because I tell you the truth? . . . my dear children (τεκνία),
with whom I am in labor [of childbirth — ὠδίνω] again until Christ is
formed in you! But I wish I could be with you now and change my
tone . . ." (Gal. 4:16–20). And to the Thessalonians: ". . . while in your
midst we were as children: as if a nurse were cherishing [in her arms —
θάλπῃ] her own children, so we in our love for you would gladly have
imparted to you not only the gospel of God, but also our own souls;
because you had become most dear to us. For you remember, brethren,
our labor and toil. We worked night and day so as not to be a burden
to any of you while we preached to you the gospel of God. You
are witnesses and God also, how holy and just and blameless was
our conduct towards you who have believed; inasmuch as you are
aware of how we entreated and comforted each one of you, acting
towards you as a father towards his children, declaring to you that
you should walk worthily of God, who called you unto his kingdom and
glory. . . . For what is our hope, or joy, or crown of glory, if not you
before our Lord Jesus Christ at his coming? Yes, you are our glory and
joy" (1 Thess. 2:7–12–20).

170. Whenever Paul senses a lessening of or a threat to one of his
great loves, he gives vent to sudden outbursts, which are instructive
from the psychological viewpoint because they reveal the "man" Paul
lingering under the operation of grace. In these instances he does not
always check himself in time, and he tosses in crude expressions which
more effectively express his feeling. Writing to the Philippians (3:7–8)
he says that all he had before esteemed as gain he now counted a loss
(ζημία) for love of Christ. Immediately afterward he repeats the same
word twice: all is loss, he has lost everything in comparison with the
knowledge of Christ. But he is not yet satisfied. The word "loss" is too
colorless, it does not bring out the immense distance between all the
things of the world and Christ. So he uses another, declaring that for
him all these things are dung (σκύβαλα).

Again, Paul is anxious about his beloved Galatians because he per-
ceives the Judaizing Christians are working on them. The latter have

---

by D'Annunzio (*La Nave*, II Episodio) a kind of modern Isocrates, an adorer of the
word, though devoid of sincere emotion.

gone to Galatia to preach that even after the coming of Jesus the Messias, circumcision is necessary. And why not? Circumcision, the distinctive mark of Abraham and of all the Chosen People, can never be abolished. It is a tiny cut, yes, but of measureless consequences; everything depends on it. And here Paul explodes. Not a small cut at all. Those zealots should cut deeper! "Would that those who are unsettling you would mutilate themselves!" (Ὄφελον καὶ ἀποκόψονται κτλ. Gal. 5:12).

171. The years, as always, had their effect on Paul's style too, blunting its edge and muting somewhat its vibrations. His style, which especially reflects the man in Paul, as in every author, shows us in his last Epistles a new phase of his spirit, a more even mood. The old wrestler has become the calm victor. In this state of mind, he finds expressions of almost idyllic serenity: "As for me, I am already being poured out in sacrifice, and the time of my deliverance is at hand. I have fought the good fight, I have finished the course, I have kept the faith. For the rest, there is laid up for me a crown of justice, which the Lord, the just Judge, will give to me in that day; yet not to me only, but also to those who love his coming" (2 Tim. 4:6–8). The metaphors are from the games in the circus which Paul had perhaps seen as a boy in Tarsus. He entered the arena of life in honor of Christ, and he knows that he has given a good account of himself in various contests, including his writing. Now, serenely, he awaits the crown.

* * *

172. There has been a great deal of discussion, perhaps too much, as to whether Paul's writings are letters or epistles.

Deissman, a great student of Greek papyri, took these as his point of reference and found that Paul's writings are similar to the letters of Egyptian peasants or soldiers preserved in these papyri; that is, they were written for a specific occasion and were not intended for the public in general. Above all, they have no literary pretensions. Therefore, he concluded, they are letters and not epistles. The epistle, properly so called, has in fact three characteristics which are the exact opposite of the letters mentioned above; that is, they treat of general rather than specific matters, and usually at great length; they are intended essentially for the public, and above all they do aim to be literary: "The epistle differs from the letter as the historical drama from a passage of history, or a dialogue of Plato from a confidential conversation."[4]

Deissman may be right to a certain extent. But the question was badly stated in postulating a sharp distinction between letters and

---

[4] A. Deissman, *Paulus*, 2nd edition, Tübingen, 1925, p. 7; cf. by the same author, *Licht Vom Osten*, 4th edition, Tübingen, 1923.

epistles, since between the two extremes is a whole scale of mixed forms which reflect the influence of one or the other in varying degree. Many writers, both ancient and modern, have written true letters, addressed to individuals and relating to specific matters, but with a literary purpose in mind as well, sometimes because they foresaw they would be preserved and collected. Therefore, a simple letter may have a literary purpose. On the other hand, a letter may very well treat of general things just as an epistle does. It may be addressed, not to the public in general, but to a group of individuals which is large enough to be almost the equivalent of the "public." And it may be as long as or longer than an epistle. For example, a letter of this type might be sent by an archaeologist to a group of colleagues recounting his examination of certain ruins, in technical style and perhaps with the addition of certain general observations. To which of the two categories would such a writing belong? Common sense would say it belongs to both, that it is an epistle-letter, for it has the private character of a letter and the other features of the epistle. This common sense approach is to be applied to that scale of mixed forms mentioned above, though it does not respect the clear division fixed even by Deissman. Too often the categories established by scholars do not correspond to the realities of everyday life.

173. Paul's letters belong to this intermediate group, and are to be defined singly according to the circumstances of their composition. Fundamentally they are letters, because they have no literary pretensions, they were occasioned by specific circumstances and sent by an individual to a more or less large group of other individuals. But it should be noted that these letters were circulated beyond the group of immediate addressees, and this happened while Paul was still alive and at his express wish.[5] Therefore, in fact if not in name they were "public" writings. Besides dealing with specific circumstances they also contain general philosophico-theological principles and broad historical views, and are sometimes quite long and full. These features bring them more or less close to the form of the epistle. Apart from the letter to the Hebrews, which has all the characteristics of the epistle, the one to the Romans very closely approaches the same type. Other writings have less

---

[5] Paul himself commands that his *Epistle to the Colossians* (4:16) be read to the Laodiceans, and vice versa. His epistles to the Corinthians are addressed to the Church in Corinth, it is true, but also to the faithful "in every place" (1 Cor. 1:2) and to those "that are in the whole of Achaia" (2 Cor. 1:1). He warns the Thessalonians (2 Thess. 2:2) against letters falsely sent them in his name. This may also be interpreted to mean that the senders of the false letters were exploiting a custom that had grown up among the different Christian communities to circulate his epistles from one to the other. This is apart from the question as to whether or not the letter to the Ephesians was actually a "circular" letter addressed to various churches (§ 624 ff.).

of the epistle. The note to Philemon remains a short letter in the strict sense, although it does contain greetings to those who hold meetings in his house (Philemon 2).

174. It is also very true that felicitous discoveries of papyri, preserved

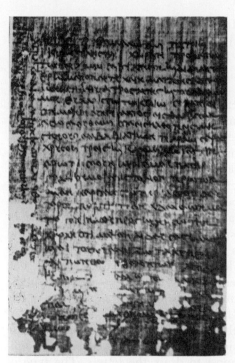

Letter From Apion to Epimachus

by the sands of Egypt, give us new elements for evaluating the literary dress of Paul's letters. These papyri contain numerous strictly personal letters, which provide several points of comparison, in style and vocabulary, with the Pauline writings. There is the same cordial familiarity, the same division into three sections (§ 181). Without going into long descriptions, we may take as an example a little letter of the second century A.D. found among the papyri of Fayyum.[6] In it, Apion, a young Egyptian of the village of Philadelphia, who has enlisted in the imperial Roman navy and is stationed at the naval base of Misenus (Naples), writes to his father Epimachus:

"Apion to [his] lord and father Epimachus many greetings. First of all, I pray that you are well, and that strong in all things, you are happy together with my sister and her daughter and my brother. I give thanks to the lord Serapis[7] for when I was in danger at sea he saved me immediately. When I entered Misenum, I took [as] viaticum[8] from Caesar three *aurei*. And I am getting along well. I beg you, however, my lord father, to write me a short letter, first about your good health, secondly, about that of my brothers, and thirdly that I may kiss your hand for you have brought me up well, and for this reason I hope to make progress soon, the gods willing. Greet for me Capiton and my brothers and Serenilla and my friends.

---

[6] The Greek text is in *Aegyptische Urkunde aus dem Königl. Museen zu Berlin, Griechische Urkunden*, II, 423.

[7] The god Serapis, cf. § 66.

[8] *Viaticum;* in the Greek text βιάτικον. This was for traveling expenses. The "three *aurei*" were a good sum equivalent to 300 sesterces (one *aureus* = 25 *denarii;* 1 *denarius* = 4 sesterces). The value of the *aureus* corresponded roughly to about $5.50; hence Apion got about $16.

I sent you a small picture of myself with Eucthemone. My name is Antonius Maximus.[9] I pray that you are in good health. Centuria Athenonice. Serenus [son] of Agathus-Daemon[10] . . . and Turbo [son] of Gallonius send greetings to you. . . .

[over][11]

"In Philadelphia to Epimachus from his son Apion. Given in the first cohort of the Apameans of J[ulia]n . . . to the *libellarius*[12] by Apion" [who was to give it to Epimachus his father].

*   *   *

175. Here let us anticipate a little and consider some aspects of the physical act of writing in Paul's time.

The letters were usually written on papyrus. Thin vertical strips, about a yard in length and a few inches wide, were cut from the Egyptian papyrus plant. These were joined lengthwise, and then reinforced by another layer of strips placed crosswise. The two layers, compressed together, formed a sheet of "paper." The English word "paper," like the French *papier* and the German *Papier*, derives from the name of the plant that furnished the strips. The sheets varied in thickness and price. One of the better types was the hieratic, which was about ten or twelve inches wide. For ordinary letters, which were usually brief, one sheet was sufficient. For the longer letters, one sheet was glued to the margin of the next until the required space was obtained. This series of sheets was then rolled up and formed a *volumen*.

176. The writing was done with ink and reeds or sharpened goose quills. When the papyrus was of inferior quality, writing became difficult, and the scribe was forced almost to draw the letters. The type of writing varied according to the material used and the skill of the scribe. From the same period we have examples of writing in uncial characters, semiuncial, large cursives both regular and irregular, and also very small cursives. But if one were not a professional scribe, he probably preferred to use the semiuncial characters or at least the large and clear cursives since they were much easier to make and clearer to read, even if they took a longer time to write. We may argue that Paul was among this number from the few lines he added in his own hand at the bottom of the letter to the Galatians (6:11): "See with what large letters I am writing to you (πηλίκοις; ὑμῖν γράμμασιν ἔγραψα) with my own hand!"[13]

---

[9] Apion, the writer, took this new name when he entered military service.

[10] This is a proper name, "Good-Daemon."

[11] The part which follows was written on the outside of the letter (§ 181).

[12] The *libellarius* (Greek, λιβλαρίῳ) was a kind of sergeant in the auxiliary cohorts.

[13] This passage is sometimes cited as a proof of Paul's alleged eye sickness (§ 198). To avoid such fanciful interpretations it is sufficient to consider the passage in context and within the framework of circumstances in which letters were written in ancient times.

↑ Sappho (?) With Stylus and Writing Tablets. Herculaneum, Naples: National Museum (Alinari)

Papyrus — *Panegyric* of →
Isocrates (First Century)

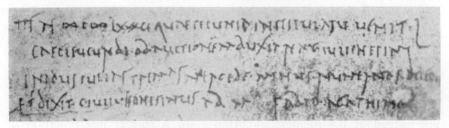

Cursive Writing Found in Pompeii, Dated 10 May, A.D. 54.

He wanted the Galatians to pay close attention to that last passage, which sums up his whole stern letter, and he stopped dictating to the amanuensis at this point and wrote himself, tracing more heavily than usual his own large script, which was perhaps already familiar to his addressees (§§ 180, 511).

If the letter was a short one, it was folded and then sealed with pitch or wax. The name and address was written on the outside, and sometimes also that of the bearer or bearers, or the intermediate stops. If it was a long letter, the *volumen* or roll was enclosed in an envelope (*paenula*), which was then sealed, or else it was wrapped in another sheet of papyrus which was tied with a small cord and then sealed.

177. The physical act of writing letters like those of Paul was a long and heavy labor which we find it hard to imagine today. Apart from the mental effort of crystallizing difficult and subtle concepts and phrasing them adequately, the length of the text alone required several days' writing. But since Paul probably devoted only the hours of the evening or the nighttime to his letters (for he worked by day to earn a living), and since a scribe ordinarily could not work more than two or three hours at a stretch (he wrote crouched on the ground and holding the paper on a tablet in his left hand), we must conclude that ordinarily Paul's epistles were in the writing several weeks.

Recent minute calculations have yielded the following conclusions.[14] If we suppose that Paul, as is very likely, used the hieratic papyrus, he could get about 140 words on each sheet. Various references in ancient authors indicate that it took about one minute to write three syllables and an hour for seventy-two words. Naturally, these figures are approximate, but taking them as the average and as a basis, we find that the earliest epistle, *1 Thessalonians* which has 1472 words, must have taken ten sheets of papyrus and more than twenty hours' writing time. The longest epistle, that to the Romans, which contains 7101 words, required fifty sheets and more than ninety-eight hours' writing time. The shortest, the note to Philemon, with 335 words, required almost three sheets and more than four hours.

178. We repeat that these figures are not to be taken at their strict arithmetical value, but only as an approximate index. Since the writing time was divided into two or three hours at the most per so many working days, the *Epistle to the Romans* must have kept Paul busy for a minimum of thirty-two days (three hours a day for a total of ninety-eight hours) or a maximum of forty-nine days (ninety-eight hours at two hours a day). The same goes proportionately for the other letters.

These calculations may seem merely an exercise in erudition, but they are instead of the greatest importance for a correct interpretation of Paul's letters. The most recent criticism, which has concentrated almost exclusively on an internal analysis of the writings, has taken great care to point out the abrupt transitions from one subject to another, apparent interruptions in the logical development of the thought, regressions and repetitions, sudden changes in style and construction, and similar features. To point out all of these things is quite correct, but it is not equally correct to conclude from them — as is so often done — that they are due to some interpolator, or to the fusion of two different writings, or to other modifications which were not the work of the author. To draw such conclusions is to be historically unrealistic.

179. As we have just seen, work on the *Epistle to the Romans* probably lasted from about thirty-two to forty-nine days. But this is an optimistic figure, since it assumes that during all that time Paul was undisturbed either by his usual illnesses or adversaries, or the ordinary

---

[14] Cf. O. Roller, *Das Formular der Paulinischen Briefe: ein Beitrag zur Lehre vom antiken Briefe,* Stuttgart, 1933.

preoccupations of the ministry, and could therefore devote all those consecutive evenings or nights uninterruptedly to the writing of the letter. But how many unforeseen incidents may have occurred during that period, obliging Paul to suspend his beloved writing for several evenings at a time and thus postpone the completion of the work. Allowing for such interruptions we may well suppose it took two months and even longer to finish this one epistle. It is hardly any wonder, then, to find the features of style mentioned above either in this or in other writings which took so long to finish and which were a first draft, so to speak, composed by a man who did not pay the slightest heed either to style or literary elegance.

180. In ancient times, because of the work involved, people did not ordinarily write their letters themselves but dictated them to slaves who were scribes or amanuenses, generally adding a word of greeting in their own hand at the end. But they might write the entire letter themselves on special occasions or to persons who were very dear. Paul had no slaves, but he often dictated to friends or disciples. They probably lent their services all the more willingly since they knew he spent his days handling the heavy weaver's tools and prickly goats-hair so that by evening his hands were stiff and tired. At the end of the letter, however, he added a greeting in his own familiar script and in some cases he wrote the whole letter himself. The amanuensis for the long letter to the Romans was a certain Tertius (Rom. 16:22). For the *1 Thessalonians,* Sylvanus (Silus) and Timothy may have taken turns, for the former appears later to have been Peter's amanuensis too (1 Pet. 5:12). We have explicit evidence of Paul's signature and personal greetings in *1 Corinthians* (16:21), *Colossians* (4:18), and *2 Thessalonians* (3:17). In the last, Paul warns his readers that this signature is "the mark in every letter" (to distinguish his epistles from false ones circulated under his name). But even where the greeting and signature are not explicitly stated to be Paul's, this is implied. The passage in *Galatians* (6:11 ff.) is equivalent to a signature, since the verb is in the aorist tense (ἔγραψα), which was customarily used in letters in ancient times with reference to the time when the recipient would be reading it, and therefore it was equivalent to our present tense (cf. Philemon 19–21; 1 Pet. 5:12; 1 Jn. 5:13 – Greek text). Many early interpretations considered that Paul had written the entire epistle to the Galatians in his own hand, in the belief that the verb referred to the preceding part of the letter (§ 176). The note to Philemon does seem to have been written entirely by Paul (Philemon 19–21).

181. Paul's epistles followed the customary pattern of the time. The ancients divided their letters into three parts. The first was the "title" or salutation (*praescriptum*), containing the name of the sender and the recipient and accompanied ordinarily by a few words of greeting and praise. For example, Cicero begins a letter to his brother: "Marcus to [his] brother Quintus, greetings"; to his family: "Tullius sends greetings to his Terentia and little Tullia and Cicero."[15] The second part was the body of the letter, varying, of course, in length, and the third part was the conclusion, which was usually very brief and might be omitted altogether. Sometimes it contained the date and place of writing, more often the greetings of the writer or of other persons. For example, the above-mentioned letter of Cicero to his brother ends simply: "The Ides of June, Thessalonica"; that to his family: "Farewell, my beloved ones, farewell. October fifth, Thessalonica." Before his divorce, Cicero is sometimes even more affectionate with his wife: "Farewell, my Terentia; I seem to see you, and so languish in tears. Farewell. November 30."[16] And there are many other similar examples. The address (*inscriptio*), written on the back of the sheet of papyrus after it had been folded and sealed, or on the wrapper (§ 176). is not to be confused with the first part or salutation (*praescriptum*). It served only until the letter was delivered, and if the letter was recopied, this part was omitted, if it had not been already destroyed when the letter was opened. In the case of Apion's letter quoted above (§ 174), the address is preserved, since it was written on the back of the letter itself.

182. This three-part division was also used by the Greeks. The populace abounded in greetings from the writer and others to the recipient and others, as Apion's letter also shows. And the same division was followed in the decree of the Council of the Apostles, drawn up in the form of a letter (§ 359), just as it was faithfully followed by Paul in his Epistles (with the exception of the one to the Hebrews).

In the salutation, for the usual "greetings" (*salutem* — χαίρειν) used also in the decree of the Council, Paul substitutes the words "grace and peace," interwoven at times with observations or wishes. And his conclusions, instead of being confined to the usual "farewell" (*valete*), which the Council also used, are expanded to include other comments and wishes of various kinds, and the list of greetings in his own name and from others is often quite long.

Paul usually devotes the first part of the body of the letter to abstract discussions, on faith, etc., and the second part to concrete matters; but the division is not always clear cut, and he sometimes mingles the two.

* * *

183. And finally, a few observations on the language Paul used. It is the Greek of the *koiné*, the Greek spoken by the great majority of people both of the middle and upper classes as well as the plebeians.

---

[15] *Tullius s(alutem) d(icit) Terentiae et Tulliolae et Ciceroni suis.*

[16] *Vale, mea Terentia; quam ego videre videor: itaque debilitor lacrimis. Vale. Pr. Kal. Dec.*

But Paul's Greek is much closer to that spoken by the educated than by the populace. Although he was Semitic by birth and education, he had learned Greek as a child, and when he grew up he possessed a real familiarity with its syntax and a broad vocabulary. Just as he paid little attention to style, he bothered very little, and for the same reasons, about the purity of the language, and so we do not find in him the studied elegance of the writers of his time who cultivated the Attic Greek, although his occasional quotations from pagan authors (§ 232) show he was not unacquainted with them. Semitisms are to be found in his Epistles, and they are natural in a Semitic author who is treating Hebrew subjects and constantly using the Hebrew Scriptures. The same phenomenon occurs in varying degree in the other New Testament writers. Recently discovered papyri, however, show that some forms, previously considered Semitisms, are not so really, but were commonly used in the Greek of the *koiné*.

184. Paul, however, stamped the imprint of his own personality on the Greek he chose to use. Some words he used with new meanings, or at least new shades of meaning. At times he forms new verbs (especially compounds with the preposition σύν) or new combinations of words to express new ideas, and he presses participles into service when he does not have the word he wants. With these and other expedients he succeeds in building the first arsenal of technical expressions for Christian theology.

From this viewpoint, his merit as well as his audacity is immeasurable. At the end of the same century, John contributed to the same arsenal his majestic term *Logos*, giving it a meaning quite different from the one it had among the Greek philosophers or Alexandrian Jews. And John's audacity, too, was great, especially in view of the significance which he gave that word. In any case, the author of the Fourth Gospel could well cite in his own defense the many audacities of Paul, and the numerous technical terms he had contributed a half century before to the theological arsenal he inaugurated.

185. It was possible to evaluate the consequences of Paul's initiative only some centuries later, when new circumstances required the coining of still other terms. The terrible Aryan controversies which during the whole fourth century buffeted the East and the West, popes and emperors, priests and laymen, raged around a single word, a single term, which was to express with precision a Catholic concept: was the Divine Word ὁμοούσιος, *consubstantial*, with the Father? This word was the "sign of contradiction," around which a whole century battled. The Christological controversies, which came afterward in the fifth century, also had their "sign of contradiction," two words, the concepts of which were debated by the whole world. Was there only one ὑπόστασις, *person*, in Christ or were there two? Was there one φύσις, *nature*, in him or were

there two natures? The precise significance of these words was then
established, and they became technical terms of Christian theology.
And for this reason they too were deposited in the arsenal begun by
Paul.

When, a few centuries earlier, Paul spent the long evenings in his
workshop, leaning perhaps against his loom and worrying his beard
with nervous fingers as he dictated to Tertius, who squatted on the
ground with a writing tablet on his knees and a lantern beside him on
the floor — in those long evenings, Paul founded Christianity's first university of theology.

IX

Paul's Physical Appearance

---

186. Reliable sources tell us nothing certain or specific about Paul's physical appearance. We are faced here with the same lack of data we encountered for the appearance of Christ.[1]

Some passages in his writings have been interpreted to imply certain physical characteristics, but only by reading into them something they really do not say. For example, since Paul was lowered from the walls of Damascus "in a basket through a window" (2 Cor. 11:33), it has been argued that he was small of stature, otherwise he would not have fit in the basket. But the incident itself proves nothing. In the first place, we are not told that our fugitive was completely hidden inside the basket and the lid closed over him. He might have used it merely as a kind of support in his descent over the wall; he might have knelt or crouched in it leaving the greater part of his body exposed. Or it might have been one of those huge baskets (Hebrew: *sal*) mentioned in the *Mishna* (*Shabbath*, XVI, 3), which contained enough small loaves of bread for a hundred meals. This amount of bread was of much greater volume than a man's body.

At times in the past, the etymology of Paul's Latin name, which means "little," "slight," has been used to prove he was of small build. But since we know Paul had both names, Saul and Paul, from childhood (§ 228), their meaning proves nothing. It is as if everyone named Leo, or Rose, or Felicia, must be truly as brave as a lion, or beautiful as a rose, or as happy as happiness. The name *Paul* was a common one in Roman history. The Apostle himself met a Roman proconsul in Cyprus whose name was Sergius Paulus (§ 324).

187. A so-called "proof" has been deduced from the passage in which Paul refers to the remarks of his opponents in Corinth: "For his letters — they say — are weighty and telling, but his bodily appearance is weak and his speech of no account" (2 Cor. 10:10). But the proof is an apparent one only. Here the expression "bodily appearance" does not refer to his stature or other physical characteristics, but to his attitude

---

[1] Cf. *The Life of Christ*, pp. 174–177 (§§ 189–193).

when present in contrast to the tone he assumed in his letters. In other words, Paul's adversaries were accusing him of being harsh and imperious in the letters he wrote from afar, but meek and conciliatory when he was present among them. This is clearly evident from the context (2 Cor. 10:1–2; 11:7; 13:9–10). Speaking of his manner and not of his physical appearance, he says he has made himself small ($\tau\alpha\pi\epsilon\iota\nu\acute{o}s$), i.e., humbled himself, in order to exalt the Corinthians (10:1; 11:7).

The passage in which Paul reminds the Galatians that he evangelized them "on account of a physical infirmity" (Gal. 4:13) refers to an illness from which he was suffering at the time (§ 197) and not to his stature as some have thought.

Little or nothing can be deduced from the episode in Lystra, whose inhabitants believed Barnabas and Paul to be two gods descended among men, and decided Barnabas was Zeus and Paul was Hermes (Acts 14:11–12; § 243). Some have concluded that Barnabas was taken for Zeus because he was older, more solemn in appearance, and more majestic in build, while the Lystrians thought Paul was Hermes, the messenger of Zeus, because he was short and slight. In reality, we know nothing of the age or the appearance of Barnabas, but we are told explicitly that Paul was believed to be Hermes because he was the one who did the talking (*ibid.*, 12) while Barnabas maintained a majestic silence, befitting the father of the gods. The mistaken identification, then, was based not on a physical characteristic but on a characteristic function, so to speak. If the reason had been physical, we should have to conclude that Paul was a charming and handsome young man, for that is the way Hermes is ordinarily portrayed.

Since the authoritative documents say nothing about Paul's appearance, we may glance at the way later generations pictured him in writing and in art.

188. The most ancient description of Paul seems to be that handed down in the legend of St. Thecla (§ 90, note). It was already well known at the end of the second century (cf. Tertullian, *De baptismo*, 17; Jerome, *De viris illustribus*, 7), was circulated in several writings, and according to modern authorities (Harnack, etc.) it must contain a kernel of historical truth. In the

Armenian Drawing of Paul and Thecla
(from *Dict. Arch. Chrét.*)

Acts of Paul (3) which derive from this legend, we find the following description of the Apostle: "[he was] a man of small stature, with a bald head and bow legs, of good carriage ($\epsilon\mathring{v}\epsilon\kappa\tau\iota\nu\acute{o}\nu$). His eyebrows met, and his nose was rather large [and he was] full of grace, for at times he seemed a man and at times he had the face of an angel."[2]

In a writing falsely attributed to John Chrysostom, Paul is called the "mouth of Christ" and the "lyre of the spirit," and is then described as being a man three cubits tall, who "goes beyond the heavens."[3] The "three cubits" of height, a little over four feet, comes as no surprise, since, as we have seen, the same height was assigned to Christ by a Cyriac document of the fourth century and a Byzantine document of the ninth.[4]

189. In the middle of the sixth century, we obtain the following description of the Apostle from John Malalas: "In life Paul was short ($κονδοειδής$), bald, with gray beard and head, a fine nose, light bluish eyes, eyebrows that meet, a fair complexion, of florid aspect, with a thick beard, smiling by nature, wise, gentle, affable, sweet, animated by the Holy Spirit, a wonder-worker."[5]

In the dialogue *Philopatrides*, 12, which has been wrongly attributed to Lucian but was composed instead toward the end of the tenth century, Paul is described as "a Galilean, bald in front ($ἀναφαλαντίας$), with a large nose; traveling through the air, he had penetrated to the third heaven, learning there every beautiful thing. . . ."

At the beginning of the fourteenth century, Nicephorus Callistus says: "Paul was small and slight in bodily size, built as if on a curve and slightly bent, white-skinned, with signs of premature aging, his head without hair, his glance full of grace, his eyebrows arching downward. His nose was handsomely curved and dominated all his face, his beard was thick, rather pointed and grizzled, as was his hair."[6]

If we add up the data in this written tradition, we find substantially the same description as that in the *Acts of Paul*, with the addition, at the most, of some unimportant detail deriving from isolated legends or individual fancy. Paul is stylized as a short, bald man with a thick beard and prominent nose, his eyebrows meeting, his legs somewhat bowed, but on the whole a man of dignified appearance and bearing.

190. When we come to pictorial art, we are on older and somewhat surer ground. Although in the case of Jesus, the fact that he was born, lived, and died in Palestine was a serious obstacle to the production of any contemporary image of him since Jewish orthodoxy absolutely forbade any portrait of living beings for fear of idolatry, the same obstacle

---

[2] L. Vouaux, *Les Actes de Paul et ses lettres apocryphes*, Paris, 1913, pp. 150–152. The same work (pp. 104–112) maintains that the writing originated in Asia between the years 160–170.

[3] In *Principes Apostolorum*, etc., in Migne, *Patr. Gr.*, 59, col. 493.

[4] Cf. *The Life of Christ*, pp. 175–176 (§§ 191–192).

[5] *Chronographia*, X, in Migne, *Patr. Gr.*, 97, col. 389.

[6] *Ecclesiast. Hist.*, II, 37; in Migne, *Patr. Gr.*, 145, col. 853.

did not obtain in Paul's case, for he was a Roman citizen and had lived a long time outside of Palestine.

Theoretically speaking, it is, therefore, possible that some portrait of Paul was made quite early either by an artist who had had the opportunity of observing him or at least on the basis of descriptions furnished by those who had. Eusebius tells us (*Hist. Eccl.*, VII, 18, 4) that he had seen paintings of Peter and Paul, which he attributes to persons of pagan origin who had been helped by them. Whatever judgment is made on the authenticity of the portraits, this information from Eusebius does confirm the abstract possibility mentioned above.

The search for the earliest monuments which may have preserved an authentic iconographic tradition takes us to Italy, and practically speaking to Rome, where Paul lived the last years of his life and where he died, and where, given the abundance of artists, a portrait was an easy matter.

191. But we must begin with an unpleasant setback. A medallion preserved in the Vatican Christian Museum represents Peter and Paul in profile, looking at each other. It was reportedly found by Boldetti in the cemetery of Domitilla, it was studied by G. B. de Rossi, and was considered to belong probably to the second century. In fact, since the cemetery was located on a farm belonging to the Christian Flavii, who were related to the imperial family of the same name, it was supposed that the medallion had belonged to one of the Flavii and had been "wrought either by one who had seen the Apostles,

Medallion of Peter and Paul
Attributed (probably wrongly)
to the Second Century

or at least by some one who knew those who had known them."[7] But this rosy theory it now seems must be abandoned. A recent (and to date unpublished because of the opposition of the above)[8] very careful examination reportedly proves that the medallion is a forgery of the seventeenth century.

192. Hence we must come down to the fourth century for the first

---

[7] O. Marucchi, *Pietro e Paolo a Roma*, 4th edition, ed. by C. Cecchelli, Turin, 1934, p. 152.

[8] To date there has been a report by E. Romagnoli at the fifth meeting of the *Società dei Cultori di Archeologia Cristiana* held in Rome June 14, 1945. The *Osservatore Romano* carried the story on June 17, 1945.

↑ Catacombs of Domitilla, Fourth Century

Catacombs of SS. Peter and Marcel- ➤
linus, Fourth and Fifth Centuries ↓

Frescoes Depicting Paul — Fourth and Fifth Centuries

Icon of Paul — Fourth or Fifth Century (from Cecchelli, *Iconografia*)

Peter and Paul — Stained Glass — Fourth Century (from Cecchelli, *Iconografia*)

Paul — Stained Glass — Fourth Century (from Cecchelli, *Iconografia*)

The Capture of Paul — From the Sarcophagus of Junius Bassus — Fourth Century (from Cecchelli, *Iconografia*)

Peter and Paul — Marble Sketch — Fourth or Fifth Century (from Cecchelli, *Iconografia*)

sure examples, and these are first of all the frescoes in the catacombs. To the first half of the fourth century belongs a fresco in the catacombs of Domitilla,[9] in which Paul appears opposite Peter. The features are indistinct, the hair black but thin on top, the beard pointed in the typical cone shape. The whole face has the form of a pear upside down.

Another portrait in the catacombs of Domitilla belongs to about the year 348.[10] Paul, the only figure extant, is portrayed very much as above. The head is large and out of proportion, the hair black and thin, the beard pointed, and the face has the same pear shape.

The catacombs of SS. Peter and Marcellinus have preserved a large group of frescoes of the fourth-fifth centuries, in which Paul, too, is portrayed.[11] Here the hair is not so thin or so black, the beard is pointed, but the pearlike contour of the face is less marked because of the prominent ears.

In addition to the catacomb frescoes, an icon of the fifth-sixth centuries has special value[12] because while portraying Paul as a man of middle age, it gives us the same general features as the two frescoes in the catacombs of Domitilla: namely, the hair thinning on top but otherwise thick and black like the beard, which is pointed; and conspicuous again is the general pear-shaped contour of the face.

193. Among the mosaics, the most ancient is that in the apse of St. Pudentiana in Rome, which dates back to the end of the fourth century: here the hair is quite thick, even on top, and black; the beard is black and rather rounded. To the second half of the fifth century belongs the portrait in the Catholic baptistery at Ravenna,[13] which gives us a rather square face, only a slight baldness, and a black beard which is rounded instead of pointed.

The stained-glass windows are also very interesting, representing either Paul alone or with Peter.[14] They date back to the fourth century, and show Paul more often bald than not, and with a pointed beard.

194. As for sculpture, the sarcophagus of Junius Bassus of the fourth century merits first place. It is preserved in the Vatican Grottoes. There Paul is pictured perhaps twice: once probably in the center background on one side of Christ (Peter is on the other), and the second time certainly in the lower right in the scene of his capture.[15] The two pictures

---

[9] G. Wilpert, *Le Pitture delle catacombe romane*, Rome, 1903, Plate 154, with details in Plate 179.

[10] *Ibid.*, Plates 181 and 182.

[11] *Ibid.*, Plates 252 and 254.

[12] C. Cecchelli, *Iconografia dei Papi*, I, S. *Pietro*, Rome, 1937, Plate VII, lower right.

[13] C. Ricci, *I mosaici di Ravenna*, Rome, 1932, fasc. II, Plate M.

[14] Cecchelli, *op. cit.*, Plate VI.

[15] G. Wilpert, *I sacrofagi cristiani antichi*, Rome, 1929–1936, Plate XIII; Cecchelli, *op. cit.*, Plate III, lower right, and Plate IX. The figure in the center background according to Wilpert (text, Vol. I, p. 37, n. 4) is not Paul but James the Less.

differ from each other and from the other portrayals mentioned thus far. The figure next to Christ is an idealized Paul, almost youthful, with thick curly hair and a round beard. In the scene of his capture he is bald and is wearing a short beard.

Fragment of Sarcophagus With Figures and Names of Paul and Thecla (Rome: Museo del Campidoglio)

Sarcophagus of Junius Bassus. Christ Between Peter and Paul — Fourth Century (from Cecchelli, *Iconografia*)

Crude but forceful is a marble sketch with the two faces of Peter and Paul, preserved in the museum at Aquileia and dating from the fourth-fifth centuries.[16]

195. A fragment of sarcophagus, earlier than the fourth century, offers a curious little scene of a boat at sea, with a man in the stern guiding the rudder, and another in the prow handling the sail.[17] Near the man at the rudder is cut the name PAULUS. Below and center, sculptured on

---

[16] Cecchelli, *op. cit.*, p. 45.
[17] Wilpert, *Sarcofagi*, Plate X, 3.

the side of the boat, we read Thecla, as if it were the name of the craft.

Figures in ivory begin to appear in the fourth century.[18]

We certainly are not to think that the likeness in these various works of art is a photographic one, or even faithful in detail. The most we can hope for is a certain constancy in the reproduction of a "type," the essential features of which may be very ancient and may reflect Paul's own lineaments, either because they derive from earlier likenesses no longer extant or from descriptions of the Apostle given by persons who had seen him. As a theory this presents no difficulties.[19] In actual fact we find that a common "type" does emerge from the majority of these representations, and more clearly, as is quite natural, from the paintings and stained-glass windows than from the mosaics and sculptures.

It is the "type" we have in the fresco of the catacombs of SS. Peter and Marcellinus, confirmed, as it were, and clarified by the icons: a Paul who is almost bald, with a black pointed beard, a long neck, a rather thin face, which in its general outline suggests an upturned pear.

---

[18] Cecchelli, op. cit., Table XI.

[19] This is substantially the same conclusion as that reached by Wilpert, which he based on the monuments, of which he possesses a masterly knowledge: "In the cases where the princes of the Apostles are individualized, the painters did not consider it necessary to point them out to the spectator by affixing their respective names. . . . We may conclude that the basis for the above-mentioned portrayals of the princes of the Apostles represents, if not an actual portrait, certainly a more or less accurate knowledge of their physical appearance and that this knowledge was very widespread among the Christians of Rome, at least from the end of the third century. On the basis of this theory, for St. Paul there are the data which unanimously indicate as characteristic features, the bald head and long beard" (Wilpert, Pitture, p. 106, text).

X

Paul's Health

196. The question of Paul's physical appearance is associated more closely than is at first apparent, with that of his health.

His life was one long journey from region to region under the stimulus of an idea. He traveled first within Palestine as the persecutor of Christ, and then as his herald throughout almost all the known world, especially from the year 45, when he began his first missionary journey. The twenty years from then until his death can be summed up no better than in his own words (although this passage was written in the year 57): "In many more labors, in prisons more frequently, in lashes above measure, often exposed to death. From the Jews five times I received forty lashes less one. Thrice I was scourged, once I was stoned, thrice I suffered shipwreck, a night and a day I was adrift on the sea; in journeyings often, in perils from floods, in perils from robbers, in perils from my own nation, in perils from the Gentiles, in perils in the city, in perils in the wilderness, in perils in the sea, in perils from false brethren; in labor and hardships, in many sleepless nights, in hunger and thirst, in fastings often, in cold and nakedness. Besides those outer things, there is my daily pressing anxiety, the care of all the churches! Who is weak, and I am not weak? Who is made to stumble and I am not inflamed?" (2 Cor. 11:23–29.)

It is possible to estimate approximately that in his first missionary journey Paul covered over 800 miles, in his second at least 1100, and in his third over 1350, without counting his later voyages. And all of this traveling was usually done on foot, through regions which were in large measure inhospitable and dangerous, with no conveniences or comforts of any kind, eating when and what he could, sleeping when and where he could, working with his hands to earn his keep in the longer intervals between journeys, and carrying in his heart the thousand stinging cares which could not fail to have their effect on his body too. Now, a man who could live that kind of life for long years either had a constitution of steel or a will that could force what it wanted from a weak body.

197. Yet we know that Paul, despite his remarkable stamina, suffered

160

a very serious illness in the year 50, and that from the year 43 he
endured a mysterious infirmity from which he never succeeded in freeing
himself. Both these facts merit a brief examination.

We learn of his serious illness on the occasion of his preaching among
the Galatians. "And you know that on account of a physical infirmity
I preached the gospel to you formerly; and though I was a trial to you
in my flesh, you did not reject or despise me; but you received me as
an angel of God, even as Christ Jesus. . . . For I bear you witness that,
if possible, you would have plucked out your very eyes and given them
to me" (Gal. 4:13–15). From this we conclude that the evangelization
of the Galatians had been fortuitous, in the sense that Paul was taken
ill during one of his journeys and was forced to interrupt his travels,
stopping among the Galatians until he recovered. Seeing a design of
Divine Providence in the circumstance, Paul took advantage of this stay
to evangelize his cordial hosts, both during and after his convalescence.

We are not told what the illness was. It probably did not last long,
but it was certainly quite serious and of a nature to render the sick
man repugnant to those who saw him. We gather this from the fact that
Paul, grateful for what the Galatians did for him at the time, recalls
that they neither rejected nor despised him. This latter verb in Greek
is ἐκπτύω which means literally, "spit out." It was in fact a superstitious
custom when visiting persons with repulsive illnesses to spit in front of
the patient in order to drive out the evil spirit that had lodged within
him.[1] The good Galatians, who must have certainly admired the patience
and serenity with which Paul bore his affliction, did not show any disgust
as usual, nor did they "spit out" in front of him. In fact, in their affection
for him they would have been ready to "pluck out their eyes" if that
would have done him any good.

198. These are the facts we know. From them modern scholars have,
however, drawn quite different conclusions. For some, Paul in Galatia
suffered violent attacks of epilepsy, a disease to which he was supposedly
subject, since the custom of "spitting out" to exorcise the evil spirit
obtained especially when visiting epileptics. Others think that he suffered a violent and disfiguring disease of the eyes, which to them explains
the readiness of the Galatians to pluck out their eyes for him,[2] i.e., to
heal, at least in desire, the stricken member.

---

[1] Here are a few passages which testify to this custom: *Isti qui sputatur morbus
interdum venit* (Plautus, *Captivi*, III, 4 [550]). *Comitialem propter morbum despui
suetum* (Pliny, *Natur. hist.*, X, 33 al. 23). Epilepsy especially was called a "comitialis
morbus," since if an attack occurred during a meeting, the deliberations were
nullified, for it was considered an evil omen. Theophrastus says that a superstitious
man, when he sees a lunatic or an epileptic, is struck with horror and spits in his
[own] bosom" (μαινόμενόν τε ἰδὼν ἢ ἐπίλεπτον, φρίξας εἰς κόλπον πτύσαι) (*Characters*,
XVI, *Superstition*).

[2] The blindness Paul suffered for three days after his conversion (Acts 9:8–9)

But both these deductions go far beyond the premises. Given the custom of "spitting out," it is difficult to see why it was practiced only in front of epileptics and not before persons suffering from, say, small-pox, erysipelas, pneumonia, or any one of a number of diseases accompanied by high fevers and delirium. At the time it was a common belief that all illnesses accompanied by convulsions or seizures of any kind were due to evil spirits, and therefore it would have been possible to apply the prophylactic of "spitting out" to any one of them. The argument for the eye disease based on the Galatians' willingness to give their eyes for Paul is even weaker, since the expression "to pluck out one's eyes" is a figure of speech still prevalent in various modern languages, and means merely a willingness to undergo the greatest sacrifice for another. Some have noted wryly that if one insists upon the literal meaning of this expression, it is necessary to conclude that Paul also had a serious illness of the neck, since he himself says that Prisca and Aquila have "risked their own necks" to save his life (Rom. 16:4). This expression, too, is still a common figure of speech.

All we know, therefore, is that he had a serious illness among the Galatians, but what it was we cannot possibly say. The conjectures about it have been all the more numerous in that it has been associated with the other ailment which Paul himself tells us about.

199. In the year 57, in his letter to the Corinthians, Paul recounted what had happened to him fourteen years earlier, that is, about the year 43: "I know a man in Christ who fourteen years ago — whether in the body I do not know, or out of the body I do not know, God knows — such a one was caught up to the third heaven. And I know such a man — whether in the body or out of the body I do not know, God knows — that he was caught up into paradise and heard secret words that man may not repeat. Of such a man I will boast; but of myself I will glory in nothing save in my infirmities. . . . And lest the greatness of the revelations should puff me up, there was given me a thorn for the flesh (σκόλοψ τῇ σαρκί), a messenger of Satan, to buffet me. Concerning this I thrice besought the Lord that it might leave me. And he has said to me, 'My grace is sufficient for thee, for strength is made perfect in weakness'" (2 Cor. 12:2–9). With regard to the words σκόλοψ τῇ σαρκί we must note that the σκόλοψ is not a single thorn but a mass of thorns, something between a nettle and the skin of the hedgehog. This multiple "thorniness" seems fixed in Paul's "flesh" and gives him no peace. It is caused by Satan; that is, it functions as his minister or messenger (ἄγγελος) but in reality it is permitted by God so that Paul may not become proud. The "thorniness" is fixed in his "flesh," or body, because

---

cannot be adduced to support the theory of this supposed ophthalmia. That was an extraordinary and isolated attack, which was soon over and left no consequences (§ 286).

there its effects are felt immediately, and through them Paul is to learn humility. That is why God, despite Paul's insistent prayers ("three times") does not free him from it but leaves him to be refined in the crucible of pain.

200. Given Paul's own words, we may without hesitation accept the opinion of many of the Fathers, Greek and Latin, who interpreted them to mean a chronic and tormenting ailment.[3] This coincides with the belief prevalent among the Jews that Satan or his ministers were directly responsible for the physical and mental illnesses of the human race, and especially the more serious diseases.[4] But here too we lack the information for a diagnosis of the ailment, since the metaphor σκόλοψ, or "thorniness," is hardly a precise term.

The question then arises whether Paul's illness in Galatia was an attack of this chronic ailment, or whether it was a different sickness altogether. Strictly speaking, neither alternative can be excluded, although it seems much more probable that there are two different ailments involved. The illness in Galatia was marked by some very evident and repugnant manifestation. If this were true of the chronic "thorniness" it is difficult to see how Paul could have led a life of constant journeying going always to different centers where he was entirely unknown and where, therefore, he would run the immediate risk of being "rejected or despised" as an object of disgust. But apart from that, his mention of his chronic illness to the Corinthians has all the appearance of a confidence. He seems to be revealing something they did not know about him, although he had stayed among them more than a year and a half during his first sojourn in their city. The Corinthians, then, did not suspect this chronic ailment, nor had they become aware of it during his prolonged stay with them. It seems reasonable to conclude, therefore, that it was neither evident nor accompanied by any repulsive manifestation as the illness in Galatia had been, and that the two maladies were quite different.

201. Nevertheless modern scholars have multiplied conjectures on the nature of the ailments, especially those who consider both to be one

---

[3] It is true that some of the later Fathers, and many later writers of ascetics supposed that this referred, not to an actual illness, but to temptations to incontinence aroused in Paul by the "angel of Satan." But Paul tells us himself that he was a celibate, living in perfect continence, nor does he suggest in any way that this caused him any particular difficulties (1 Cor. 7:6–9). After all, we may well ask whether these Fathers are attempting to give the true interpretation of Paul's words or whether they are speaking rather as shepherds of souls, moral advisers, and using a free adaptation for their own purposes; this would be all the more true of writers of ascetics.

[4] Jesus, speaking of the woman who had been stooped for eighteen years through arthritis or paralysis, says: "This woman, daughter of Abraham as she is, whom Satan has bound, lo, for eighteen years . . . " (Lk. 13:16). Cf. *The Life of Christ*, pp. 69, 459 (§§ 78, 455).

and the same disease. If we gathered all the diseases suggested by ancient and modern scholars we should have quite a little treatise on pathology. Paul's illness has been diagnosed as urinary stones, toothache, acute and painful deafness, gout (Nicetas), hemorrhoids, a *morbus iliacus* or intestinal disease (Thomas Aquinas), rheumatism (Renan), sciatica (Dächsel), leprosy (Preuschen). Ramsay and several other modern scholars vote for malaria, which Paul contracted, they think, in the swampy and infested regions of Pamphylia. The theory that it was the classic form of epilepsy, suggested by K. L. Ziegler, was warmly championed by M. Krenkel (1890), and many others followed this trail. In support of it, attention was called to the supposedly similar cases of Julius Caesar, Mohammed, Cola di Rienzi, Ferdinand of Spain, Cromwell, Peter the Great, Napoleon, and many artists and writers, who are all supposed to have been epileptic. This was the period in which the theories of C. Lombroso were prevalent concerning the kinship between lunacy (or epilepsy) and genius (including religious genius), theories not at all displeasing to the rationalists who were busy with the history of the origins of Christianity. But others replied that not only were the cases of the above personages clearly incorrect or very doubtful, but even in Paul's case, historically speaking, a castle of gratuitous premises had been mounted, which, medically speaking, was sheer quackery.[5] Many other scholars, while not going so far as epilepsy, opted for the more general field of neuropathology. Among the suggestions in this category, we have an eye disease of nervous origin, hysterical phenomena, neurasthenia, exhausting attacks of nervous origin. Tertullian had thought of headaches with an auricular syndrome,[6] which expressed in modern terms might be a neuropathic ailment.

202. After such a hospital tour, I have no intention of suggesting a hundredth illness as a possibility. The most sensible view would seem to be that held by some scholars that it is useless to keep multiplying conjectures, which are hazardous at best since we do not have sufficient or necessary information. But I should like to call attention to an analogous experience, which does have its importance.

From the passage quoted above (§ 199), it is evident that Paul considers his unknown infirmity to be intimately associated with his rapture to the "third heaven" and paradise. To him it is a medicine given him by God to prevent his growing proud. The remedy, then, must have been administered shortly after the ecstasy, to forestall a temptation to pride that might well have been immediate. This consideration rather quashes the theory of Ramsay and his followers that Paul contracted

[5] The best answer was given by a professor of neurology in Halle, A. Seeligmüller, *War Paulus Epileptiker? Erwägungen eines Nervenarztes*, Leipzig, 1910.

[6] *Anima . . . quae in apostolo colaphis, si forte, cohibebatur per dolorem, ut aiunt, auriculae vel capitis* (*De pudicitia*, XIII, 16).

malaria in Pamphylia during his first journey in 45–48. Even supposing that the Apostle caught malaria in the year 46 (during his long sojourn in Cyprus), that would be at least three years after the ecstasy, which took place in 43. That is too long a time to wait for a spiritual remedy administered against an immediate temptation. It is reasonable to suppose that Paul felt the first "buffets of Satan," the first symptoms of the infirmity, in 43, or at the latest in 44, while he was still living privately in Tarsus or just after he went to Antioch to begin his ministry there.

203. What is involved, then, is a physiological phenomenon which Paul himself — the only competent witness — considers intimately connected with the mystical phenomenon of his ecstasy. The mysterious ailment, therefore, is not to be considered by itself, but within the whole framework of mystical experiences and their physiological consequences. It is unhappily true that the great field of mysticism is one least explored by true science, partly because of old materialistic prejudices. A comparison of similar cases, however, even if it be exterior only, may shed some light on one and the other and illumine certain aspects of the experiences involved.

Among truly mystical souls, we have the most abundant and most authentic data on Teresa of Ávila. Her writings are a model of simplicity, sincerity, and also — insofar as this is possible in mystical experiences — of penetrating clarity. It is precisely these gifts which induce her in the middle of a description of some mystical state, to warn us that she herself does not know how these things take place in her nor what their essence is. We are not concerned here with that essence,[7]

---

[7] We might, however, consider two or three short passages, since they may help us to understand Paul when he says he does not know whether his ecstasy occurred "in the body or out of the body," and that he "heard secret words that man may not repeat."

Says St. Teresa, "The soul, while thus seeking after God, is conscious, with a joy excessive and sweet, that it is, as it were, utterly fainting away in a kind of trance: breathing, and all the bodily strength, fail it, so that it cannot even move the hands without great pain; the eyes close involuntarily, and if they are open, they are as if they see nothing. . . . He who has had experience of this will understand it in some measure, for it cannot be more clearly described, because what then takes place is so obscure. All I am able to say is, that the soul is represented as being close to God; and that there abides a conviction thereof so certain and strong, that it cannot possibly help believing so. All the faculties fail now, and are suspended in such a way that, as I said before, their operations cannot be traced. . . . The will must be fully occupied in loving, but it understands not how it loves; the understanding, if it understands, does not understand how it understands — at least, it can comprehend nothing of that it understands: it does not understand, as it seems to me, because, as I said just now, this cannot be understood. I do not understand it at all myself" (*The Life of St. Teresa of Jesus*, trans. by David Lewis, Newman Book Shop, Westminster, Md., Chap. XVIII, 14, 19, pp. 144, 147).

Elsewhere we find: "This utter transformation of the soul in God continues only for an instant; yet while it continues no faculty of the soul is aware of it, or knows

but it may be helpful to see if there is some experience of the Saint of Ávila that bears an analogy to the mysterious infirmity of Paul.

204. Teresa's autobiography, ended in 1565, tells us that throughout her life she was habitually ill: "I am never, I believe, free from great pain, which is sometimes very acute, especially about the heart."[8] Note that Teresa endures these illnesses in the midst of intense activity, amid constant and exhausting travels, temporal worries, and the most serious spiritual anxieties. All of this is reminiscent of the journeys, worries, and anxieties of Paul (§ 196).

But when and in what circumstances did Teresa's chronic ailments begin? She herself answers this question in her autobiography, shortly after the account of her religious profession (November 3, 1537). Born in 1515, she was not yet twenty-five when she suffered a violent heart ailment accompanied by frequent fainting spells. She was taken from her monastery to undergo treatment, which instead caused her great harm. There followed a severe crisis, in which she lost all consciousness and was believed to be dead. Her grave was dug and the funeral solemnities performed for the repose of her soul.[9] But she survived the crisis, and soon afterwards, ". . . so great was my distress, that our Lord alone knoweth the intolerable sufferings I endured. My tongue was bitten to pieces; there was a choking in my throat because I had taken nothing, and because of my weakness, so that I could not swallow even a drop of water; all my bones seemed to be out of joint, and the disorder of my head was extreme. I was bent together like a coil of ropes — for to this was I brought by the torture of those days — unable to move either arm, or foot, or hand, or head, any more than if I had been dead, unless others moved me; I could move, however, I think, one finger of my right hand. Then, as to touching me, that was impossible, for I was so bruised I could not endure it. They used to move me in a sheet, one holding one end and another the other. . . . I remained in this state, as I have already said, more than eight months; and was paralytic, though getting better, for about three years. I praised God when I began to crawl on my hands and knees."[10]

205. These are the physiological facts. But with a simultaneousness

---

what is passing there. Nor can it be understood while we are living on the earth — at least, God will not have us understand it, because we must be incapable of understanding it. I know it by experience" (*ibid.*, Chap. XX, 24, p. 170).

And again: "When Our Lord brings a soul on to this state, He communicates to it of His greatest secrets by degrees. True revelations — the great gifts and visions — come by ecstasies, all tending to make the soul humble and strong, to make it despise the things of this world, and have a clearer knowledge of the greatness of the reward which our Lord has prepared for those who serve Him" (*ibid.*, Chap. XXI, 15, p. 183).

[8] *Op. cit.*, Chap. VII, 18, p. 49.
[9] For these facts, cf. *ibid.*, Chap. IV, 6 ff., p. 19 ff.; Chap. V, 14 ff., p. 30, etc.
[10] *Ibid.*, Chap. VI, 1–2, pp. 33–34.

no less perfect than it is surprising, Teresa's first mystical experiences take place. In the same pages in which she describes the beginnings of her illness we find interwoven data like the following: ". . . our Lord had already bestowed upon me the gift of tears . . . our Lord began to comfort me so much in this way of prayer, as in His mercy to raise me to the prayer of quiet, and now and then to that of union, though I understood not what either the one or the other was, nor the great esteem I ought to have had of them. I believe it would have been a great blessing to me if I had understood the matter. It is true that the prayer of union lasted but a short time: I know not if it continued for the space of an *Ave Maria;* but the fruits of it remained."[11]

This "prayer of quiet" and "prayer of union" are the mystical states which Teresa later discusses at length, illustrating them with a fineness of penetration that only daily experience could give her. And just as she journeyed through these various mystical states the rest of her life, so also were physical infirmities in varying degree her constant companions, as she herself has told us (§ 204). It would seem the one followed the other as shadows follow the light. They rise together, proceed together, and set together. The fact that they are simultaneous is important. It seems an experience entirely parallel to that of Paul, namely, a mystical experience which has immediate repercussions on physical health.

We cannot pretend to diagnose Teresa's physical sufferings. But two points seem quite certain, namely, that they were the effect and not the cause of the mystical experience, and they were not due to common hysteria notwithstanding certain superficial similarities and their evidently nervous character. We would be disposed to attribute a similar set of ailments to Paul if the documents authorized us to do so. Instead they speak only of the buffets of Satan, permitted by God as a remedy after a mystical experience.

And who is competent to analyze such remedies as these, administered by the heavenly Physician?

---

[11] *Ibid.*, Chap. IV, 8–9, pp. 20–21.

XI

Charisms in Early Christianity

---

206. Let us in imagination look in on a liturgical gathering of a Christian community of Palestine or Syria toward the end of the first century.

It is the day after the Sabbath, which the Christians have already begun to call the Lord's Day in memory of the resurrection of Christ.[1] As the faithful enter the meeting room they greet one another with the kiss of peace and then take places around a table on which is a goblet filled with wine and a tray full of bread that has been broken. First a prayer is recited aloud and passages are read from the holy books. At the end an "elder" pulls the goblet and the tray toward him. All present concentrate their attention on them as they recite aloud in unison: "We thank thee, Our Father, for the holy vine of David thy son, which thou hast revealed to us through Jesus thy Son. To thee be glory for ever and ever!"

After a brief pause, they continue: "We thank thee, Our Father, for the life and the knowledge which thou hast revealed to us through Jesus thy Son. To thee be glory for ever and ever! As this [bread which is] broken was scattered over the mountains and being gathered has become one, so may thy Church be gathered from the ends of the earth into thy kingdom; since thine is the glory and the power through Jesus Christ forever and ever!"[2] The "elder" then recites a prayer, which also includes the words pronounced over the bread and wine by Christ at the Last Supper. When he has finished, those present humbly confess their sins[3] and then each one with greatest reverence eats a morsel of the bread and drinks a sip of wine.

207. After this they recite in unison: "We thank thee, Holy Father, for thy holy name, which thou hast fixed in our hearts, and for the

---

[1] Cf. the *Didachè*, XIV, I. It is known that this writing, which is of the greatest historical importance and was considered inspired by some of the Fathers, originated toward the years A.D. 70–90, or shortly after Paul's death. Its place of origin is Palestine or Syria more probably than Egypt.

[2] *Ibid.*, IX, 1–4. Note that the blessing of the wine precedes that of the bread. The author is probably of Jewish origin and reflects the prescriptions of the *Mishna, Berakoth*, VI, 5; VIII, I, 8.

[3] Cf. *Didachè*, XIV, 1.

Preparation of the Fractio Panis in a Private House
(Reconstruction — "Amici delle Catacombe")

knowledge and the faith and the immortality which thou hast revealed to us through Jesus thy Son. To thee be the glory forever and ever! Thou, Omnipotent Lord, hast created all things for thy name's sake, and thou hast given food and drink . . . and life eternal through thy Son. For all these things we thank thee, for thou art powerful. Thine be the glory forever! Be mindful, O Lord, of thy Church, and deliver her from every evil and perfect her in love of Thee, and gather her, the Sanctified, from the four winds into the kingdom which thou hast prepared for her; for thine is the power and the glory forever and ever! May thy grace come and may this world pass away! Hosanna to the God of David! If any is holy, let him come; if he be not holy, let him repent. Maran-atha! Amen!"[4]

During this time, and especially at the taking of the bread and wine, a new spirit has permeated the gathering. Everyone seems mysteriously transformed and appears to be waiting for some important event, which is, however, usual at their gatherings. A time of recollection and prayer follows, but there is something provisory about it, as if an interruption is momentarily expected.

208. Suddenly one of those present rises to his feet. His face is flushed, his gaze fixed heavenward, and his two arms raised at his sides in the manner of the *orantes*. His body quivers as if pervaded by some inner force. The prayer is interrupted as all fix their eyes on him. After a moment or two he begins to speak impetuously. Each word is spoken with precision and unwavering confidence. The impassioned discourse flows on without the slightest hesitation while the face of the speaker

---

[4] Cf. *ibid.*, X, 2–6.

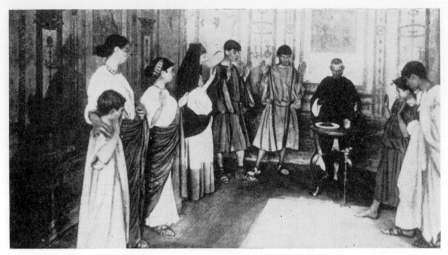

Celebration of the Eucharist in a Private House
(Reconstruction — "Amici delle Catacombe")

registers the various emotions he experiences as he talks. It seems now
to be confidence and again anxiety, sometimes the expression is one of
horror, but more often it is one of jubilation and joy. The listeners do
not understand his words. The language in which they are uttered is
to them a book closed with seven seals. But the general content of the
book they do understand, and they, too, experience the varying emotions of confidence and anxiety, of horror and jubilation and joy as they
are reflected in the speaker's face. A mystical emotion has pervaded the
gathering, and everyone present seems to have caught through the expressive features of the orator a glimpse of a world of ecstatic sublimity,
while his words have kindled mysterious feelings in their hearts.

Then the discourse becomes calmer, slower, and finally ceases altogether. When the speaker has resumed his seat, another rises and he too
assumes an inspired attitude as he speaks. But his words are quite clear,
for he uses the language of the region, and he begins by saying he
will translate the discourse just delivered in an unknown tongue. He
speaks with compelling penetration and calm poise as he recalls, clari-
fies, and confirms the emotions experienced by the gathering during the
preceding discourse. The listeners once again contemplate the same
world of ecstatic sublimity, but it is now clearer and more definite. They
experience the same mysterious emotions as before, but more keenly and
more deeply.

209. And now the second speaker is silent. Everyone is absorbed for
a time in his own thoughts, reflecting on what he has seen and heard,
when suddenly there is a noise at the door. An old man comes in supported by a young woman in mourning. They excuse themselves for

Orante. Catacombs of Domitilla
— Fourth Century

their lateness. The man, who is the young woman's father, is ill and barely able to drag himself along. The woman was widowed a few weeks before, and was delayed at home to care for her small children. They are extremely poor. The two are greeted with affectionate solicitude and sympathetic questions. Finally, one of the faithful exclaims: Brethren, let us pray the Lord that he may deign to deliver his servant from his infirmities! — He then approaches the old man, who is seated limply on a stool, places his hands on the sick man's head, and prays, while all the others join in the prayer. Suddenly, the sick man seems to shudder from head to foot; then he rises strongly and firmly from his seat. His face is alive with health and well-being. He declares he has been cured. And praise and thanksgiving rise to the Lord from all present.

210. The young widow also seems to lose a little of her sadness, but she is not altogether serene. Her face still wears the shadow of past grief and future suffering. Then another one of the faithful approaches her and begins to speak to her quietly. His words are those of a tender brother, of one who shares the same high faith, the same supreme hope, and the same love which the widow feels for the husband she has lost and for her little ones who are alive and unhappy. His words inspire a deep sense of beatitude, such as is felt only by those who have suffered greatly, and so radiant and ineffable is it that it seems both to sweeten the suffering and to gladden the tears. His compassionate words have a compelling effect on the young woman, and the real force of their significance seems to penetrate her innermost being. Soon she is transformed. As her father was healed in body, she is healed in spirit, and she feels ready and able to continue her sorrowful journey in serenity and peace of soul.

We might go on inventing other little scenes and examples, but let us return now to the documents.

✿   ✿   ✿

211. These documents attest that in the first decades the social life of the Church was accompanied by special phenomena, the aim of which

was to strengthen and to develop its life. This is not an isolated or unique fact. It has clear analogies in the physical world. At the beginning of physical life a provident nature ensures the first nutritive elements to sustain it. Plant seeds have a reservoir of food elements to nourish them through the long period of germination in the earth. Newborn infants have a proper nourishment in their mother's milk (cf. 1 Cor. 3:2). Similarly the beginnings of the spiritual life of the Church were accompanied by phenomena such as those described above, which today are known collectively as *charisms*.

Paul, who among all the early Christian writers speaks of them most frequently and at greatest length, calls them *charisms* ($\chi\alpha\rho\acute{\iota}\sigma\mu\alpha\tau\alpha$: Rom. 12:6), "spiritual [gifts]" (1 Cor. 12:1) or simply "spirits" (1 Cor. 14:12, 32). The reason for these synonyms is clear, for the charism is the fruit of *charis* ($\chi\acute{\alpha}\rho\iota\varsigma$), *grace,* and the single source of all the charisms is he who is called the *Spirit* par excellence (1 Cor. 12:4) and is *God* (*ibid.,* 6). Hence these gifts of the Spirit are called "spiritual [gifts]" or "spirits."

212. The purpose of these charisms, still according to Paul, is *usefulness* (*ibid.,* 7), not the usefulness or profit of the individual who possesses and exercises a particular charism but the collective or social usefulness of the whole Church. Paul, in fact, proceeds immediately (*ibid.,* 12 ff.; cf. Rom. 12:4 ff.; Eph. 4:4, 11 ff.) to contemplate the Church as one body, of which the faithful are the members. Each member of the body has its specific function, not for its own exclusive advantage but for the good of the whole organism. Some charisms are intended "as a sign, not to believers but to unbelievers" (1 Cor. 14:22), insofar as the faithful perceive a spiritual inferiority in the unbelievers who lack their particular charisms and therefore derive from that perception the above-mentioned collective usefulness or "profit." Second, the unbelievers may recognize their own inferiority and as a consequence turn to the faith (*ibid.,* 24–25).

213. Paul gives us a list of charisms no less than four or five times, but nowhere does he indicate the list is complete, while sometimes he uses equivalent but different terms for the same charism. Two lists, one with nine and the other with eight terms, appear in the same writing (1 Cor. 12:8–10; 28–30):

Word of Wisdom	Apostles
Word of Knowledge	Prophets
Faith	Teachers
The Grace of Healing	Miracles
The Working of Miracles	Gifts of Healing
Prophecy	Services of Help
The Discerning of Spirits	Power of Administration
Various Kinds of Tongues	Various Tongues
Interpretation of Speeches	

Shortly afterward in the same writing we find another group of terms, which, however, is not intended as a list (1 Cor. 14:25): hymn, instruction, revelation, tongue, interpretation.

The other two lists are as follows: prophecy, ministry, teaching, exhortation, giving, presiding, showing mercy (Rom. 12:6–9); apostles, prophets, evangelists, pastors, teachers (Eph. 4:11).

Let us examine these lists briefly.

214. We attempted to illustrate four of these charisms in the imaginary Christian gathering described above. The first speaker, who immediately after the Eucharist delivered a discourse in an unknown language, possessed the charism of "various tongues," which was also called glossolaly. The second speaker, who translated the discourse into the language of the region, had the charism of the "interpretation of tongues." The believer who placed his hands on the sick man and praying healed him had the gift of healing. The last, whose words consoled the widow, had the gift of showing mercy.

Strangely, the gift of tongues, which seems to us the most interesting and most excites our curiosity, is the least esteemed by Paul, and we shall therefore treat it last. Let us try to determine the character of those which are less obscure.

215. The charism of *apostle* did not denote the twelve collaborators chosen by Jesus, but certain zealous Christians who, disregarding worldly interests and human consideration, dedicated themselves to the diffusion of the Kingdom of God in word and in work, and especially in those localities where it was unknown. The *Didachè* (XI, 3–6) recommends that wherever an apostle appears he is to be "received as the Lord," but he is not to remain in one place more than a day, or at the most two. On leaving he is to receive no money but only the food necessary for his journey.

The *evangelist* was par excellence the bringer of the good tidings or gospel.[5] His duty, it seems, was to strengthen the work of the apostle, consolidating what the latter had begun. Naturally the term *evangelist* here does not denote the author of one of the four Gospels.

Of special importance is the charism of *prophecy*. The prophet's function was similar but not equal to that of the prophet of the Old Testament.[6] His words were for "edification and encouragement, and consolation" (1 Cor. 14:3). He could also reveal the secrets of another's heart (*ibid.*, 25) and predict future events. According to the *Didachè* the prophet "speaks in the Spirit" (XI, 7), he has the right, after the celebration of the Eucharist, to give public thanks to God according to his own inspiration (X, 7) and enjoys various privileges within the

---

[5] Cf. *The Life of Christ*, p. 94 (§ 109); cf. also the passage in Eusebius (*Hist. Eccl.*, III, 37) quoted there which describes the *evangelist*.

[6] Cf. *Storia d'Israele*, I, p. 381 ff. (§ 418 ff.).

communities already established (XIII, 1–6). This is the charism Paul most heartily endorses (1 Cor. 14:1 ff.) because of its direct efficacy in the community. According to the *Didachè* (XIII, 4) some communities lacked a prophet.

216. The three charisms of *teacher* (διδάσκων, διδάσκαλος), the *word of wisdom*, and the *word of knowledge,* must have been basically the same, although differing in certain specific aspects. We do not have any clear notion of them today. Perhaps the *word of wisdom* (λόγος σοφίας) was common to the prophet, while the *word of knowledge* (λόγος γνώσεως) was the property of the teacher. The first appealed for the most part to the emotions, the second to the intelligence and learning. All three must have been intended generally to lead to the knowledge and the love of Christ's teaching through the ministry of the word. The *Didachè* (XV, 2) informs us that the teacher received the same honor as the prophet. Hermas' *Shepherd* makes frequent mention of him also (Mandat., IV, 3, 1; *Similit.,* IX, 15, 4; etc.).

The three charisms of *faith, healing* (ἰάματα), and the *working of miracles* (ἐνεργήματα δυνάμεν) also seem to have something in common since they all had to do with miraculous acts. This gift of *faith* is not the simple acceptance by the intellect of religious truth although it presupposes this. It is rather the absolute certainty that the power of God will intervene miraculously in a specific physical fact to prove its sovereignty. On several occasions Christ himself had praised the effectiveness of such faith if not of this particular charism.[7] While the *grace of healing* was exercised on the human body, that of *miracles* referred to other prodigies not always in the physical field.

217. In the moral field, we find the two charisms listed as *exhortation* (παρακαλῶν) and the *discerning of spirits* (διακρίσεις πνευμάτων). The first seemed to have particular efficacy in complementing the work begun by the prophet (cf. Rom. 12:8 with 1 Cor. 14:3), confirming and corroborating the beginnings of faith. The second must have bestowed special perception in judging, among so many enemies of early Christianity, the mental attitudes of others, the better to guard against the "perils from false brethren" (2 Cor. 11:26). Probably the possessor of this gift was the natural advisor of the head of the community, although the charism itself did not go with those of "administration."

The latter were the four of *pastor, presiding* (προιστάμενος), *ministry* (διακονία), and the *power of administration* (κυβερνήσεις) although the precise nature of each and the differences among them escape us today. In general we may consider that these charisms assisted those charged with directing the community, in temporal matters too, before a regular hierarchy was formed.

218. The two charisms of *giving* (μεταδιδούς) and *services of help*

---

[7] Cf. *The Life of Christ,* pp. 355–358 (§§ 349–351), p. 411 (§ 405).

(ἀντιλήμψεις) served to relieve material distress, while that of *showing mercy* (ἐλεῶν) was concerned with moral misery, although here, too, a precise distinction is not possible. The *giver* distributed what he had and what he could earn to the poor, for the Spirit impelled him to hold as his life's supreme ideal the aphorism of Christ preserved for us by Paul: "It is more blessed to give than to receive" (Acts 20:35). The gift of *services of help* must have been exercised for the benefit of the sick or the needy of various categories, such as prisoners, those persecuted under pagan laws, and similar cases of necessity. As for the gift of *showing mercy*, we know only what the term itself tells us. We attempted to illustrate this with the incident of the widow consoled (§ 210).

In *1 Corinthians*, 14:6, 26, we find mention of the gift of "revelation" (ἀποκάλυψις), which was probably the effect of the charism of prophecy. The same might be said of the *hymn* also mentioned in *1 Corinthians*, 14:26, which refers to extemporaneous compositions of jubilation in poetic form. This perhaps explains the precept in the *Didachè* (X, 7): "To the prophets it is permitted to render thanks as they will," that is, in the form they wish. This took place after the celebration of the Eucharist (§ 207).

219. There remains the charism which today seems the most curious but which in ancient times was the most spectacular. Paul considers it as pretentious as "sounding brass or a tinkling cymbal" (1 Cor. 13:1), if it is not accompanied by inner virtue. This is the gift of *various kinds of tongues*. Paul uses several phrases to refer to it: *tongues, to speak with tongues, to have tongues, to pray in a tongue*. Modern scholars have made for it the technical term *glossolaly*.

We can arrive at only an approximate definition of this charism. It was not, certainly, the gift of making oneself understood at one and the same time by various persons speaking different languages, as a means of facilitating the diffusion of Christ's teaching among foreign peoples. Nor was it — as several modern scholars have supposed — an outpouring of inarticulate and senseless sounds, with some conventional foreign phrase thrown in from time to time, the whole discourse presumably the outbust of someone in a state of psychic exaltation. No, the glossolalist spoke a real language, which was quite articulate and distinct, and with it he expressed specific and ordered concepts; in other words he pronounced a real "discourse" (1 Cor. 14:9, 19), such as a prayer to God, a hymn, a blessing, a thanksgiving (*ibid.*, 14–17). In fact, various compositions "in tongues" could be precisely translated (*ibid.*, 5:27), which would obviously have been impossible in the case of inarticulate sounds with no meaning.[8]

---

[8] The Greek grammarians used the term γλῶσσαι for archaic words either no longer in use or used with particular meanings. Quintilian is referring to these

220. It is also certain that the listener, at least ordinarily, did not understand the glossolalist when he spoke. Paul implies that more than once, as for example when he asks: — If you speak a blessing under the inspiration of your charism, how can the faithful who is uninstructed answer Amen? "For he does not know what thou sayest" (1 Cor. 14:17). He goes further and applies this statement to himself, since he, too, has this gift (*ibid.*, 18, Greek text), and asks: "If I come to you speaking in tongues what shall I profit you?" (*Ibid.*, 6.) He immediately explains why it would profit them nothing. He would be like a flute or a harp producing confused sounds but not a melody, or a trumpet blowing disconnected signals, but not the traditional call to arms. "So likewise you — unless with the tongue you utter intelligible speech — how shall it be known what is said? For you will be speaking to the empty air" (*ibid.*, 9). Listening to the glossolalist, therefore, would be like listening to someone from a foreign country speaking his unknown tongue, in which one might distinguish the various sounds without seizing their meaning. "If, then, I do not know the meaning of the language, I shall be to the one to whom I speak, a foreigner; and he who speaks, a foreigner to me" (*ibid.*, 11). The reason is that "he who speaks in a tongue does not speak to men but to God; for no one understands, though he is speaking mysteries by the Spirit" (*ibid.*, 2).

When he uttered his discourse the glossolalist was in an extraordinary, ecstatic state, and addressed himself to God rather than to his fellow men. Nevertheless the men who heard him, even without understanding him, felt to some degree the spiritual "contagion" of his extraordinary state and shared, by reaction, his mystical exaltation.[9] Paul says that if an unbeliever or an uninstructed person should chance to enter a Christian gathering where many glossolalists were talking at once, he would think he had stumbled into a convention of lunatics (μαίνεσθε: *ibid.*, 23).

221. Paul suggests the psychic state of the glossolalist where he says that when he prays in a tongue his spirit (πνεῦμα) prays but his mind, or understanding (νοῦς) is unfruitful (*ibid.*, 14). This indicates that the glossolalist acted under the impetus of the charism, that is, pervaded by the Spirit, but his understanding remained passive and with-

---

when he says: *Potest (puer) interpretationem linguae secretioris, quae Graeci* γλῶσσαι *vocant, dum aliud agitur, ediscere,* etc. (*Instit. Orat.,* I, 1, 35). Some scholars have therefore considered that the charism of the γλωσσολάλοι consisted of an impetuous rattling off of strings of words like these. The assumption is tendentious and contradicted by what we do know of glossolaly, and first of all by the fact that the discourse of the glossolalist was organic and made sense.

[9] There is a similar phenomenon associated with prophecy in the Old Testament; cf. *Storia d'Israele,* I, p. 384 ff. (§ 421 ff.).

out spiritual fruit, for when the charismatic inspiration ceased, his mind retained no clear or precise knowledge of it. Some general impression did remain, however, and when the phenomenon was over, the glossolalist's mind seemed as it were suffused with a luminous mist that inspired delight, to which Paul refers when he says that "he who speaks in a tongue edifies himself" (1 Cor. 14:4).

But the prayers of the early Christians were primarily community prayers, not individual ones. For this reason Paul wishes the charism to benefit the whole gathering, not just the glossolalist alone, and so he prescribes that the discourse "in a tongue" be followed immediately by an interpretation. Those who had the gift of "interpreting tongues" translated into everyday idiom the words of the glossolalist (1 Cor. 14:5, 27). If there is no interpreter present, Paul commands the glossolalist to keep silent in public, and to "speak to himself and to God" (*ibid.*, 28) for his own personal edification.

222. The light spiritual intoxication which the glossolalist experienced in the exercise of his charism could and did lead to abuses. Sometimes several of them took to speaking at once, and since those present caught some of their exaltation, the gathering — as Paul himself said (§ 220) — seemed quite mad. Or worse still, the room resembled the atrium of one of those pagan temples where fortunetellers and soothsayers delivered the oracles of their deities, gesticulating and raving in the frenzy of their prophetic inspiration and communicating the same excitement to the crowds watching them.

Now, this resemblance, however superficial, was not to be tolerated, for "what harmony is there between Christ and Belial? . . . And what agreement has the temple of God with idols?" (2 Cor. 6:15–16). To prevent these abuses some believed all public exhibitions of glossolaly should be stopped. But Paul, who does not endorse them completely, says rather: "Do not hinder the gift of speaking in tongues" (1 Cor. 14:39). He goes even further, ". . . I should like you all to speak in tongues" (*ibid.*, 5), provided, of course, that order and decorum were properly respected. Paul's criterion may be summed up in the following passage: "When you come together each of you has a hymn, has an instruction, has a revelation, has a tongue, has an interpretation. Let all things be done unto [the] edification [of all]. If anyone speak in a tongue let it be by twos or at most by threes, and let them speak in turn (ἀνὰ μέρος); and let one [only] interpret" (*ibid.*, 26–27).

223. What was the language used by the glossolalists? We do not know; nor do we know whether it was always the same tongue or whether it differed from one occasion to the next. When Paul says, "If I should speak with the tongues of men and of angels . . ." (1 Cor. 13:1), he seems to be referring to a set of human languages and to

another of angelic tongues.[10] The quotation from *Isaias* (28:11 ff.), which Paul cites a little later, refers to a human though barbarous tongue, the Assyrian, which he compares then to the language of the glossolalist (1 Cor. 14:21). From both these instances it might seem legitimate to conclude that the "tongue" may have been at times a human language, although a very rare one or one unknown to the majority, for example the idiom of some still barbarous or far-distant region. In that case, if a native of such a region were present, he would understand the glossolalist even without an interpreter. On the other hand, if at other times the language was some mysterious idiom, known only by virtue of the charism, then we have no basis for any conjecture at all.

224. How long did the charisms last? We have noted that there is greater mention of them in Paul than elsewhere, but he is not the only one to speak of them. Other, and later, Christian writers mention the phenomenon as observable in their own times, and we have already referred to some of their testimonies in this regard.

We find, however, that certain charisms are no longer mentioned after apostolic times, which would indicate that they had died out or were extremely rare. Others appear to be still common enough at the end of the first century and during the second. At the beginning of the third century, there remain only "traces" ($\check{\iota}\chi\nu\eta$), as Origen says (*Contra Cels.*, I, 46; II, 8; etc.; in Migne, *Patr. Gr.*, II, 7, 5, 808, etc.). But in the fourth century the Fathers speak of them as something long past and no longer observable.[11]

At the end of the first century three charisms are clearly attested in the *Didachè*, that of *apostle* (XI, 3, 4, 6), that of *teacher* (XIII, 2; XV, 1–2), and especially that of *prophet* (X, 7; XI, 3, 7–11; XIII, 1, 3–4, 6; XV, 1–2). While we find no definite references in the epistles of Ignatius of Antioch and the letter of Polycarp, there are several references elsewhere to the charisms of *teacher* and *prophet*.[12] Some-

---

[10] According to the rabbinical legends there were seventy human languages, because that was the number of nations in the world (cf. Gen. 10). When the Law of Sinai was delivered, every word that came from the mouth of God divided into seventy languages (Talmud babli, *Shabbath*, 88b), and Moses also set forth the Law in seventy languages (*Genes. Rabba*, XLIX, 2). These seventy languages were taught to the Hebrew Joseph by the angel Gabriel, who knows them all, but the other angels know only Hebrew (*Sotah*, 33a; 36b). Therefore it is necessary to pray in Hebrew if one wishes the angels to carry the prayer to the throne of God.

[11] Not relevant to our subject here are similar phenomena which appeared in heretical Christian movements from ancient Montanism down to the Camisards, Irvingites, Jansenists, and the present-day Pentecostal sects; nor may we consider here the non-Christian religions. For all of these cf. E. Lombard, *De la glossolalie chez les premiers chrétiens et des phénomènes similaires*, Lausanne, 1910; E. Mosiman, *Das Zungereden geschichtlich und psychologisch untersucht*, Tübingen, 1911.

[12] *Epist. of Barnabas*, XVI, 9; Hermas, *Shepherd*, Vision, III, 5, 1; Mandat., XI, 7 ff.; etc.

times there is a vague allusion to the charisms of *discerning spirits,* *healing,* and one or two others. Irenaeus seems to refer to the gift of tongues in this passage: "We hear many brethren in church who have charisms of prophecy, and who speak tongues of every kind through the Spirit" (*Adv. Haer.,* V, 6, 1).

225. That the charisms should decline and gradually die out in less than two centuries was, after all, in the natural course of things. Their very purpose implied their eventual disappearance, as Paul had foreseen. He foretold the day would come when in Christian gatherings, no one would speak in prophecy, nor in tongues, nor with the charism of knowledge (1 Cor. 13:8). All of these things were opportune or necessary while Christianity was a fragile seedling which needed reserve nourishment in order to grow (§ 211). During that period the believers were as children, and "when I was a child, I spoke as a child, I felt as a child, I thought as a child. Now that I have become a man, I have put away the things of a child" (1 Cor. 13:11). During those two centuries Christianity became a robust tree with many strong roots to provide its sustenance. Her followers had become mature men; they had ceased to stammer and spoke a harmonious language.

What was that sustenance and that language? It was what Paul had set at the peak of the pyramid of charisms, as their crown and ultimate goal: charity.

If I possess — he had said — all the charisms, and possess them in high degree, and "do not have charity, it profits me nothing" (1 Cor. 13:1–3). But even when the various charisms will have all disappeared, "charity never fails" (*ibid.,* 8).

Biography

Birth and Early Youth

226. "I am a Jew, and I was born at Tarsus in Cilicia" (Acts 22:3).
Thus does Paul introduce himself to the mob of Jews in Jerusalem
who are rioting against him; and the statement seems to introduce him
as well to the whole world. Although a Jew, then, he was born outside
of Palestine, the holy land of Judaism. He was born among pagans in
the cosmopolitan city of Tarsus (§ 1 ff.), but in one of those ethnic
groups which the Jewish Diaspora had scattered throughout almost all
the world. There he first saw the light between the years 1 and 5 of
the Christian Era, or about the time that Jesus, who may have been
from three to eight years old (§ 149), was an unknown child in Nazareth.

In contradiction to this definite information concerning Paul's birth
in Tarsus (cf. Acts 21:39; 9:11) stands the statement of Jerome, who
says that he was born in the village of "Gischala of Judea," from where
he emigrated to Tarsus with his parents when the village was conquered by the Romans. It should be noted, however, that Jerome gives
us this information twice, the first time diffidently as a "fable,"[1] but
later without reflecting any doubt. The statement, besides being a
direct contradiction of Paul's own words, encounters various geographical and chronological difficulties. Gischala was a large village,
not "of Judea," but of northern Galilee. Flavius Josephus refers to it
frequently since the John who was one of the chief leaders of the
insurrection against the Romans in the years 66–70 came from there.
It was conquered by Titus in the autumn of 67 (*Wars of the Jews,* IV,
84 ff.), that is, when Paul had already died or was nearing death.

It may be, however, that Jerome's statement contains a particle of
truth if it is interpreted to refer to a time before Paul's birth. It is
possible, for example, that his father was taken away as a slave by
the Romans when Quintilius Varus (the one whose death at Teuto-
burg so delighted the Germans) in 4 B.C. devastated a good part of

---

[1] *Talem fabulam accepimus: Aiunt parentes apostoli Pauli de Giscalis regione fuisse
Judaeae: et eos, cum tota provincia romana vastaretur et dispergerentur in orbem
Judaei, in Tarsum urbem Ciliciae fuisse translatos: parentum conditionem adulescentu-
lum Paulum secutum;* thus in the *Comm. in ep. ad Philem.,* 23 (in Migne, *Patr. Lat.,*
26, 617 al. 643), which was written a little before the year 389.

Galilee, although Gischala receives no special mention in this connection (*Wars of the Jews,* II, 66 ff.; *Antiquities of the Jews,* XVII, 286 ff.). It is also possible that Paul's grandfather emigrated from Gischala, not as a slave, but of his own accord and for business reasons, just as many other Jews left Palestine. This might explain how Paul enjoyed Roman citizenship from birth (§ 229).[2]

227. Although outside the land of their ancestors, Paul's family preserved that tenacious attachment to its national and tribal origins, which was always a characteristic of Semitic people.[3] Thus Paul can state specifically that he was "of the race of Israel, of the tribe of Benjamin, a Hebrew of Hebrews" (Phil. 3:5). He was a descendant of the small but warlike tribe of Benjamin which had given the nation its first king, Saul. And Paul's parents, in scrupulous observance of religious precepts, had him circumcised on the eighth day after his birth (*ibid.*) giving him the very name of Saul (Hebrew: *Sha'ul*), which means "Asked [of God]."

If Paul boasts that he is a "Hebrew of Hebrews," after recalling his descendance from Israel and Benjamin, he undoubtedly does so in order to distinguish himself from the "proselytes" of Judaism, and he also wishes to refer to the spirit of strict orthodoxy which reigned in his family and in which he was brought up. Although they lived in a foreign land among idolaters, the flame of national-religious faith never waned, and the members of his household remained "Hebrew of Hebrews" both in feeling and in action. And, to keep that flame alive, the child was in due time sent to study in Jerusalem.

228. Besides the Hebrew name Saul, the child also had a Roman name, Paul. This in no way indicates that his parents had any leanings toward Greco-Roman ways. The use of a double name was most frequent at the time among the Jews both of Palestine and of the Diaspora, and it was especially convenient in dealing with Greco-Romans, who invariably distorted the pronunciation of Semitic names. For this reason foreign names were chosen which had some rough assonance with the Hebrew name. Thus in the period of the Machabees, there had been a High Priest Jesus who had taken the name Jason (Jeshuᵃ: Ἰάσων); and shortly afterward another high priest, Eliaqim, had changed his name to Alcim (Ἐλιακίμ: Ἄλκιμος).[4] Or

---

[2] Photius repeats the information that Paul's family was from Gischala (*Ad Amphiloch.,* 116; in Migne, *Patr. Gr.,* 101, 687), but his source is unknown. He does say, however, that Paul was born in Tarsus; his parents were taken away as slaves during a "Roman war."

[3] Cf. *The Life of Christ,* p. 237 (§ 240).

[4] These two priests favored Hellenism and were therefore opposed to the religious-nationalist movements of the Machabees. Judas Machabeus sent as his ambassadors to Rome two faithful followers, who had Greek, or Hellenized, names, Eupolemus and Jason (1 Mach. 8:17).

the second name might be entirely different, as Alexander Janneus (Jonathan) and Alexander Salome of the Hasmonean dynasty and, in the New Testament, John Mark, the author of the second Gospel, and Jesus Justus (Col. 4:11). The inscriptions in the catacombs testify to this same custom in the earliest Judaism in Rome.[5] The child born in Tarsus was given a second name, a Latin one, which sounded like his Hebrew one: Saul, Paul.

In the documents, the Apostle is called Paul for the first time after his meeting with the proconsul, Sergius Paulus, during his first missionary journey: "But Saul (also called Paul) . . ." (Acts 13:9). This does not mean he took the name as a result of that meeting. It is a subtlety on the part of the author of the *Acts*, who gives the Apostle his Hebrew name while he is working among Hebrews, and at this point begins to use his second name, which is more suitable when he enters the Greco-Roman world. This is the opinion expressed, with perfect historical sense, by Origen[6] and is to be preferred to other early opinions suggested by baseless analogies or arbitrary derivations.

229. No other definite information regarding Paul's family has come down to us, except for the incidental mention (Acts 23:16 ff.) that he had a married sister, whose son was in Jerusalem in the year 58, when he rendered his uncle a genuine service (§ 553). But we do not know this nephew's age, or whether he lived in Jerusalem or merely chanced to be there at the time, or whether he was pursuing his studies as his uncle had done. Nor do we know whether or not his mother was in the city with him.

Paul was a Roman citizen by birth (Acts 22:28); therefore his father must have had Roman citizenship, but how he obtained it we do not know. If it is true that Paul's father or some ancestor emigrated from Gischala to Tarsus (§ 266), one or the other may have become a citizen either by being freed or by paying a price. Paul, who could boast from his youth that he was a "Hebrew of the Hebrews," certainly never imagined how useful it was going to be in later years to be able to state also, "I am a Roman citizen."

Paul was educated in keeping with his family's tradition. He says he was "a Pharisee, the son of Pharisees" (Acts 23:6; cf. Phil. 3:5), and recalls that he had made a name for himself as the zealous guardian of the traditions of his ancestors (Gal. 1:14; cf. Acts 22:3). This indicates that his training was guided by the strict rules governing the

---

[5] According to the count made by J. B. Frey, *Corpus Inscriptionum Judaicarum,* I, Vatican City, 1936, pp. LXVI–LXVIII, more than half the Jews mentioned in the inscriptions in the catacombs of Rome have a Latin name or cognomen, almost two fifths have a Greek name, and only a seventh have a Hebrew or Aramaic name by itself.

[6] *Comment. Epist. ad Rom. Praefatio,* in Migne, *Patr. Gr.,* 14, 837.

observance not only of the written Hebrew law but also the oral rabbinic "tradition" (§ 76). Therefore, at about the age of five, Paul began to learn the letters of the Hebrew alphabet and to spell out his first Hebrew words in the Bible (§ 78). Gradually he was taught the practice of the various legal observances, and therefore — as Jesus, too, was doing in Nazareth at about the same time[7] — he began to recite the basic Hebrew prayer, the Shema', to attend the synagogue on the Sabbath, and to observe the other rabbinical precepts.

230. In addition to this spiritual training he was also taught a manual skill. It was a basic rule that a "man is obliged to teach his son a trade: whoever does not teach his son a trade teaches him to become a thief" (Tosephta, *Qiddushin*, I, 11). For if it could reasonably be expected that an intelligent child like Paul might one day become a learned rabbi, a manual trade not only would not be an obstacle in his future career, but would rather favor and adorn it. The most famous doctors of the Law engaged in some manual trade or craft in addition to their teaching,[8] so that later we find the aphorism: "Rabban Gamaliel[9] son of R. Juda ha-Nasi says: The study of the Law

Ancient Type of Loom Still Used
in Asia Minor

together with a trade is a fine thing, for being busy with both makes one forget sin. All study of the Law not coupled with labor is vain, and an incentive to sin" (*Aboth*, II, 2).

Paul was taught a trade common in the region, that of "tentmaker" (σκηνοποιοί: Acts 18:3). The Cilicians raised large herds of mountain goats that had thick, shaggy coats, from which were woven a stiff, rough cloth. It made an excellent tent for journeys and was used for various similar types of covering. This rough haircloth took its name

---

[7] Cf. *The Life of Christ*, p. 265 (§ 263).

[8] *Ibid.*, p. 149 (§ 167).

[9] This is not Gamaliel, the teacher of Paul, but Gamaliel III, who lived two centuries later. His father, Judah ha-Nasì, is the one who codified the *Mishna* (§ 78).

from the region and was called *cilicium*. Some ancient writers have thought that Paul was instead a tanner, that is, that he prepared the hides for tent coverings.

This trade, learned as a boy, was for him a kind of human citizenship, which, together with his Roman citizenship, helped him throughout his life. Even in the midst of the thousand occupations and preoccupations of the Christian apostolate, he always earned his living with this trade in order not to be a burden to the faithful, and he liked to show his hands calloused from the rough work of the loom, exclaiming ". . . these hands of mine have provided for my needs and those of my companions" (Acts 20:34; cf. 1 Cor. 4:12; 1 Thess. 2:9; 2 Thess. 3:8).

231. From the preceding, it is obviously unnecessary to point out that the exercise of a manual trade in no way implied that Paul's family was in straitened circumstances financially. On the contrary, the fact that he was sent to Jerusalem to study suggests, if not wealth, a certain level of comfort, since his support in so distant a place involved considerable expense, which most of the Jews of the Diaspora, however pious and zealous, could not afford. Though we have no explicit proof, it is quite probable that the income of Paul's family derived from a successful workshop for weaving the haircloth mentioned above, owned and operated by his father.

Paul's first teacher must also have been his father, who in the evening probably taught his small son the first letters of the holy alphabet and told him, as one tells a child, the outstanding events of scriptural history. At the same time, the little fellow attended the elementary school for Jewish children, which was usually[10] next to the synagogue of the district, and to which he would be taken by one of his father's servants, who also acted as a "tutor." When Paul later writes to the Galatians (3:24) that the Hebrew Law has been a tutor in Christ, he was perhaps thinking of that old servant. And when he says to the Corinthians (1 Cor. 4:15) that he is a father to them and not a tutor, he may perhaps be thinking of the profound difference which even as a child he had noticed between the ways of his own father and those of the servant.

232. When he was a little older, Paul could have attended one of the many Greek schools which abounded in Tarsus (§ 4). But we are nowhere told that he did attend them, nor would his father's sentiments permit us to suppose he did. The Pharisees unanimously and universally mistrusted Greek learning. One rabbi decreed energetically: "Cursed is the man who raises swine, and cursed is he who teaches his son Greek knowledge" (*Baba* qamma, 82 b Bar.). Another inquired

---

[10] Cf. *The Life of Christ*, pp. 59–60 (§§ 63–64); p. 318 (§ 314).

if he could study Greek learning, since he had already studied the
entire Hebrew Law, and in reply this verse was quoted him (Josue
1:8): "Let not the book of this law depart from thy mouth: but thou
shalt meditate on it day and night," and the conclusion drawn and
applied to his case was: "Go and seek the hour which is neither day
or night, and devote that hour to the study of Greek culture" (*Mena-
hoth,* 99b). Paul's father, as a strict Pharisee, must have subscribed to
the view of these rabbis, and therefore his son's name never appeared in the roll books of the pagan schools of Tarsus.

Nevertheless many modern scholars suppose that Paul as a boy did
attend these schools. As proof, they cite the fact that he could write
well in Greek, that he quotes the classic authors, and that he is familiar with Greek customs. But this is not proof enough. There were
a great many things an alert and intelligent boy could learn outside
of school, especially in a cosmopolitan and cultured city like
Tarsus. Just as today boys in the Orient speak two or three languages
fluently which they have learned from daily use, so Paul learned Aramaic, which was spoken in his home, and Greek spoken both at home
and in the city. When a person speaks and writes a language from
childhood, he acquires a certain literary skill in it also.

Paul's quotations from the classics are only three, and they amount
to very little. One is a hemistich from his contemporary, Aratus,
Phenomena, 5 (but substantially the same phrase is to be found in the
hymn to Jupiter by Cleanthes, 5) which says: "For we are also his
[Jupiter's] offspring" (Acts 17:28). One is a line from the *Thais* of
Menander: "evil companionships corrupt good morals" (1 Cor. 15:33).
The third derives from the *Oracles* of Epimenides: "Cretans, always
liars, evil beasts, lazy gluttons" (Titus 1:12). Now phrases like these
are not learned quotations, but common sayings of the proverb type,
which could be picked up in everyday conversation. It would not be
necessary to attend a regular boys' school to learn them.

Even less proof is furnished by Paul's allusions to Greek customs,
weapons, games, etc. They may be explained by the interest that
any intelligent boy has in the things going on about him in a large city.

233. On the other hand, Paul displays no thoughtful or trained appreciation of natural or artistic beauty. He travels over land and sea
in every region, certainly encountering many landscapes of great scenic
beauty. He visits Greek cities which are shrines of ancient aestheticism,
where at every step he could have come upon some masterpiece of
world fame. He comes West and enters a world utterly different from
anything he has known before and completely dominated by the concept of *imperium militare.* But he gives no indication of having been
impressed by any of these things, and in his writings there is never the

briefest description — even by way of metaphor — of a mountain view or quiet gulf, of a painting or statue or imposing edifice or army drawn in battle array. And yet, how often the boys his age in the Greek schools must have been assigned written and oral compositions on such topics. If as a man Paul ignores them in his writings, it is natural to suppose this is due, among other reasons, to a lack of formal training in such composition in his childhood. It is only an indication, but it coincides with the other considerations that suggest Paul did not attend pagan schools.

His school, for profane matters, was the everyday life of the city. When he describes in detail the soldier's armor (and this might have been worn by any Roman legionary or by the pretorian guard in his Roman prison), mentioning the belt, cuirass, shoes, shield, helmet, and sword (Eph. 6:14–17; cf. 1 Thess. 5:8), he derives in part from Hebrew models (cf. Isa. 11:5; 59:17; Wisd. 5:18 ff.) and in part from early recollections. As a child Paul may very well have played soldier with his small friends and fashioned paper helmets and wooden swords to make the game more real. When he mentions the athletes competing for the prize in the races in the stadium and the rugged training they undergo (1 Cor. 9:24–27; cf. Phil. 3:14; 2 Tim. 4:7–8), he is again drawing on personal recollections. He could as a boy have witnessed the games in the stadium in Tarsus. Or if his father was strict and refused him permission to go to the stadium, he may have listened eagerly while his playmates described what went on there. When he refers to the "theatron," or "spectacle" (1 Cor. 4:9) unfolding before the world and the angels, this, too, is probably the echo of some boyhood recollection.

234. In one shop or another, perhaps in his own father's weaving shed where he worked, he frequently saw clients come to settle their accounts. When the correct number of coins had been set in a row on the counter, the shop owner thumbed through a sheaf of loose papers, took one out and showed it to the client, and then tore it up in his presence. This was the "chirograph," or note in which the client stated his indebtedness and which was destroyed upon payment of the debt. The custom served Paul later to describe the canceling of a debt immeasurably greater (Col. 2:14).

More than once, as he wandered through the market place, he must have watched a slave being freed. Before the judge stood the owner and the slave, who had managed to scrape together the sum necessary for his ransom. The slave handed the money to the judge, who in turn handed it to the owner. The latter then declared he no longer had any legal right over the slave, and the judge pronounced him a free man. The ceremony of the ransom, or redemption (ἀπολύτρωσις) was accomplished. But Paul's memory of it remains a vivid one and one day it serves as a metaphor to describe a ransom or redemption that was infinitely greater (Rom. 3:24; Col. 1:14; Eph. 1:17).

235. Other early impressions gathered when the whole city of Tarsus was his schoolroom are reflected later. Curiosity must have made the boy Paul, on his way through the streets or the market place, stop now and again to listen while some placid Epicurean philosopher ladled out human happiness to a crowd of listeners, or a solemn-faced Stoic unwound his "diatribe" (§ 54); and his child's mind will have comprehended little or nothing at the time of their excursions into logic. But some vague recollection will have lingered, to come to the surface again when in later years he encounters Epicurean and Stoic philosophers in the agora of Athens and enters into dispute with them (Acts 17:17–18).

Perhaps, too, some night in springtime, he had been awakened suddenly by frenzied cries and deafening noises that came from a building near his house. The next morning he would ask his father what had happened, and the latter, who seemed in a very black mood that day, would answer evasively, perhaps with some muttered curse on those "dogs" of idolaters. But naturally a boy like Paul would not be satisfied. When he went out, he would keep asking this one and that one until some playmate, perhaps the son of a pagan priest, would explain in great secrecy that in that building on the previous night there had taken place the rite of initiation into the "mysteries" of Dionysius (§ 71). The screaming was done by those being initiated, who had eaten the food of the mystery, had been infused with the spirit of the god, and had attained union with the divinity and their own salvation. Mysteries? Union with the divinity? Salvation? What did these things mean? The boy Paul does not understand, but his curiosity is satisfied for the moment and he thinks no more about them. But he does not forget them entirely and as a young man he perhaps studies their exact meaning. Later still, when in his workshop he is dictating letters with his characteristic nervous energy and creating the first theological terms of Christianity (§ 185), he recalls these phrases and definitely refutes their meaning.

236. When Paul was about thirteen years old, it became necessary to make some decision regarding his future. Extremely intelligent and deeply attached to the spiritual heritage of his family, he could profit greatly if his future activity were concentrated on that heritage. The material patrimony of the household was more than sufficient, and in any case Paul could always carry on his father's business. But the moral patrimony was never great enough; it must be constantly increased by whoever felt keenly the honor of being a descendant of Abraham and a son of the Divine Law. If the boy Paul should one day become a Doctor of that Law, one of those impressive "teachers of Israel," to whom the whole nation bowed in reverence, what an honor for the whole family, and what pride for his father! The house could not be so honored by a high priest or a king as by a Doctor of the Law, "because royalty has 30 requisites and the priesthood 24, but the Law is acquired with 48" (*Aboth*, VI, 6). How could an honor so great be achieved? However well disposed, the boy could not attain the 48 requisites in Tarsus, where schools of the Law were lacking. Those most learned in Judaism in his native city could teach him something more, perhaps 10 or at the most 20 of the requisites, but not all 48. Thus after some partial progress, the same question would have to be faced all over again. It was much better to solve the matter from the beginning and start the boy definitely on the road to his goal. In that case, the only answer was Jerusalem.

Paul's father perhaps mulled this over in his mind a long time. Then one evening he called Paul to him and asked him if he would like to go and study in Jerusalem. And the answer was a glad yes.

Shortly afterward Paul left Tarsus for the Holy City. He may have been fourteen years old. It was between the years 13 and 18 of the Christian era (§ 150).

237. In Jerusalem Paul went to the school of Rabbi Gamaliel the Elder (§ 75). The new student's preparation was a good one, in fact excellent. With regard to the written Law — the basis of all learning (§ 78) — Paul must have known the Bible very well, both the original Hebrew text and the Greek version of the Septuagint. In a pious Jewish family, the Bible was the spiritual encyclopedia of the children, practically their one book, and between reading and reciting it they learned whole passages by heart. Paul's training in the oral law or "tradition" (§ 76) was not so advanced. He knew the *halakah* through the pious observances of his family and the *haggadah* from conversations at home and sermons in the synagogue but not much more of either, so that this whole field was still to be covered systematically. But apart from his formal training, the spiritual disposition of the new student was altogether excellent. He had come to Jerusalem as a thirsty deer to the spring, and he desired nothing but to quench this thirst at the pure fountain of the wisdom of Israel, which he was to learn at the feet of his great teacher.

The usual lesson method was to begin with a passage from the Bible. The rabbi read it in the Hebrew text, translated it into Aramaic, and then illustrated it both by recalling the various interpretations of it given by previous rabbis and by comparing it with the *haggadah*. And finally there was student discussion, led by the rabbi and aimed at deducing from the passage the proper precept of the *halakah*. The precept and the "case," or concrete example, were the object of the whole lesson, which was conducted according to the exegetical rules already noted (§ 76 ff.).

For the students, the immediate result of the lessons was increased mastery of the Bible and constant progress in the knowledge of "tradition," whether of the *halakah* or *haggadah*. And Paul, even after his conversion to Christianity, reflected this early formal training.

238. The Bible seems an essential part of all his writings. In the history of Christian literature no other writer derives so much from the Bible as Paul until three centuries later, when we come to Aphraates, the "Persian Sage," who had also received an essentially biblical training. In his letters Paul quotes the Bible directly more than eighty times, and the scriptural allusions and reminiscences are even more numerous. He rarely quotes from the Hebrew text, perhaps two or three times. Ordinarily he quotes the Greek of the Septuagint, which was the version commonly used by the Jews of the Diaspora. At times he seems to be drawing upon another Greek text, which may have been that of Aquila.

Since he knew the Bible substantially by heart, he ordinarily quotes from memory and the differences in wording show he was thinking more of the concept than the exact phrasing. Sometimes the quotation is used to illustrate a point, sometimes it is modified slightly to make its meaning clearer, and sometimes two or more concepts derived from different passages are fused together.[11]

239. From the dialectic viewpoint, Paul's use of the Bible is similar to the way the rabbis used the historical accounts both in the Bible and in the *haggadah* (§ 77, note). In addition to the simple or literal meaning, he sees in certain events narrated in Scripture a much higher and recondite spiritual significance, insofar as the event itself is a prefiguration of another event. Thus Adam is the "type" ($\tau \acute{u} \pi o s$) or figure of the future Christ (Rom. 5:14; cf. 1 Cor. 15:21–22, 45, 49). The institutions and ceremonies of the Old Testament are "a shadow of things to come, but the substance is of Christ," that is, the substance which throws the shadow is the New Testament (Col. 2:17). And again the events which happened to the Hebrews as they cross the Red Sea and the desert are "examples" (1 Cor. 10:6), which happened to them "as a type" (*ibid.*, 11) and are cited with reference to Christ (*ibid.*, 4, 9).

240. At other times Paul uses phrases or expressions from a scriptural text but not with their literal meaning. This type of interpretation was common among preachers in the synagogue, who "adapted" quotations to point a moral or instruction, apart from their strict exegetical meaning. A very clear example of this (Rom. 10:18) is Paul's use of the text of Psalm 19 (*Vulg.* 18:5), without quoting it directly: "Their

---

[11] For this and other information cf. F. Prat, *The Theology of St. Paul*, New York, 1926, I, 411–417.

voice has gone forth into all the earth. . . ." The psalm is referring to the cosmic harmony of the heavens which is poured over the earth, while Paul "adapts" the passage to refer to the Gospel message which is being diffused throughout the human race. Sometimes this device is more complicated and is applied not to simple words or phrases but to events in the Bible, as was the custom in the homiletic Jewish *Midrashim*. To this type belong Paul's allusion to the manna with reference to the collection for alms among the Corinthians (2 Cor. 8:15; cf. Exod. 16:18), and the complicated parallel between Moses, whose face is veiled, and the unbelieving Jews, whose hearts are veiled (2 Cor. 3:7–18; cf. Exod. 34:33–35). The most complicated parallel of all is that between the Justice of the Jewish Law and the Justice of the Christian Faith. The latter is personified and speaks in her own name the biblical maxims which, besides being modified, would seem attributable to the former (Rom. 10:5–9; cf. Deut. 30:11–14). The correct interpretation of these and similar texts in Paul cannot be arrived at unless one keeps in mind each time the particular use he is making of a given biblical quotation, and the fact that this use derives from the formal training he received in Jerusalem.

241. For Paul's indebtedness, apart from the Bible, to Jewish tradition, even for historical events, the case of *2 Timothy*, 3:8, is instructive. Here he mentions Jamnes and Jambres, or Mambres, as the ancient adversaries of Moses, referring undoubtedly to the Egyptian magicians who opposed Moses (Exod. 7:11, 22). But these two names, as Origen noted, do not appear anywhere in the Bible, while they do appear in the Targum (Jonathan on *Exodus*, 1:15, 7:11; *Numbers*, 22:22) and in other Jewish writings. There existed also a special apocryphal writing entitled the "Book (or Penance) of Jamnes and Mambres," which is mentioned not only by Origen, by the so-called *Decree of Gelasius*, and other Christian documents, but seems to have been known to pagan authors also, such as Pliny (*Nat. Hist.*, XXX, 1, 11), Apuleius (*Apolog.*, or *De Magia*, c. 90), and the Neo-Platonist Numenius (in Eusebius, *Praep. evang.*, IX, 8; cf. Origen, *C. Cels.*, IV, 51), who name with Moses either one or both of these adversaries. It is probable that this apocryphal writing dates back before the Christian Era. From these facts, Origen (in Migne, *Patr. Gr.*, 13, 1637) and Ambrosiaster (in Migne, *Patr. Lat.*, 17, 521) concluded that in the above-mentioned passage Paul is quoting the apocryphal writing: but this conclusion is neither necessary nor even very probable. It is much more likely that, like the Targum, he derives here from the great fund of oral tradition of the *haggadah*. This is the conclusion quite rightly arrived at by Theodoret, in the fifth century, who assumed that Paul took the two names from unwritten Jewish teachings (in Migne, *Patr. Gr.*, 82, 847).

242. It was in this kind of intellectual pursuit that Paul spent his time in Jerusalem. How long he remained "at the feet of Gamaliel," if and when he left Jerusalem, where he went from there and what he did next, we do not know. We may perhaps assume that he attended Gamaliel's lessons for three or four years, or until he was about eighteen years old, the usual age for marrying (§ 150), and that he then returned to Tarsus, both to assume his responsibilities in the family business and to begin in the Jewish community there his activity as a Doctor of the Law, fresh from the schools of the Holy City. But this is all conjecture. Even if it corresponds to the fact, however, Paul was absent from Jerusalem more in body than in spirit, and even in Tarsus he must have kept in close contact with the Sanhedrin and the learned Pharisees of the capital, since later on he suddenly reappears on the scene as their authorized representative. This suggests that the elders of Jerusalem had followed from afar the career of this young man, who had been formed and trained among them (Acts 22:3), and just as they had bestowed their approval on him as a student, they now entrusted him with responsibilities and duties.

243. When he came to the capital to begin his studies, Paul had entered upon his puberty, which among Orientals is precocious and impetuous. In Jerusalem he would not have seen the unrestrained license that reveled in Tarsus, but even in the Holy City not everyone was a model of virtuous moderation. If the Sadducees ostentatiously followed many of the customs of their foreign overlords, the Pharisees of daily life (not the ideal Pharisees of the *Mishna*) were too often whitened sepulchers, not to mention the pagans who flocked to the city especially after the Roman administration had set up its headquarters there. How did the young Paul react to the external temptations in his surroundings? As a man he confesses he feels within his body a "law of sin" which is in conflict with the "law of God" and which makes him a prisoner (Rom. 7:21–23). How did he conduct himself in this conflict between the two laws?

It was to be expected that some among the most recent scholars should decide that Paul lived for a time a dissolute life, either in Jerusalem or in the period immediately following his stay there and before his conversion. His remorse for the excesses he had committed, the inefficacy of the Jewish Law to relieve his spirit, his aspirations for a higher life, were all psychological elements which influenced his conversion. And when Paul speaks with such impassioned vividness of human frailty and the conflict between the mind and body of man (Rom. 7:7–25), he is not speaking theoretically or from hearsay, according to these critics, but out of the memory of his former transgressions.

Reasoning like this tempts the malicious suspicion that the biographer may be projecting himself into his subject. We reject the temptation, but the argument does sound like something in a pulp magazine and is clearly refuted by the evidence. In the first place, if we are to consider that the above-mentioned passage reflects Paul's personal experience,[12] then what of the earlier passage in the same writing (*ibid.*, 1:24–32) which is a list of the most infamous vices (§ 46). It is no answer to say that Paul was speaking here of pagans, since what a pagan does a Jew may do also, and before God there is no difference between Greek and Jew (*ibid.*, 2:1–11). Must we conclude then that Paul was altogether a cesspool of vice? Besides, positive testimony gives us a Paul who is anything but dissolute. He himself, telling his story to Agrippa and referring to witnesses, asserts that from his youth in Jerusalem he had lived as a strict Pharisee (Acts 26:4–5). Elsewhere he assures us he has always scrupulously observed the Jewish "traditions," much more so than his contemporaries (Gal. 1:14), and finally he tells us that his former life as a Jew was "blameless" (ἄμεμπτος — Phil. 3:6). Let us believe Paul himself then, leaving the pulp stories to their fate, and conclude that before his conversion Paul lived his Pharisaism entirely and wholeheartedly, carefully observing all the minute precepts of the Law, which he had learned from his teachers and which he considered the framework of his spiritual happiness. And that is why his Pharisaic zeal exploded into furious hatred against nascent Christianity, which was demolishing that framework.

244. When he was eighteen years old Paul might have married (§ 150) and, in fact, was practically under obligation to do so. Celibacy was never regarded with any favor by the Hebrews, and one rabbinic aphorism says that God watches until a man is twenty years old to see whether or not he takes a wife, and if he has not married by that time, then God curses him (*Qiddushin*, 29b). The average Israelite could have as many as four wives and even more, as the Talmud permits, but it seems polygamy was not considered decorous for a Doctor of the Law, and Paul was in this latter category.

In all probability, however, he never married. Clement of Alexandria (*Stromata*, III, 6, in Migne, *Patr. Gr.*, 8, 1157) supposes that Paul was married, deducing this from the passage in his epistle (Phil. 4:3) where he addresses a person called γνήσιε σύζυγε. But who is the person designated by this epithet? The etymological meaning of the word σύζυγος is "one joined," but not necessarily in matrimony. It has also the generic meaning of "colleague" or "comrade." In addition it may also be a proper name, *Syzygus*, as some of the early writers thought.

---

[12] Cf. W. Kümmel, *Römer 7 und die Bekehrung des Paulus* (in *Untersuch. z. N. Test.*, 17), Leipzig, 1929. Cf. also § 518 and note.

Finally the adjective γνήσιε is masculine, and the whole phrase would seem to mean "my loyal comrade" (or "my loyal Syzygus" with a play on the meaning of the name), and therefore not a wife (cf. § 383). In fact, almost all the ancient writers — Tertullian, Jerome, Epiphanius, John Chrysostom, Theodoret, etc. — held that Paul was unmarried.

An even stronger argument is to be found in *1 Corinthians*, 7:8, where he advises his readers to remain unmarried, using his own state as an example. There remains the theoretic possibility that when he wrote this he was a widower, having lost his wife perhaps while still a young man. But historically speaking, this would have to be proved and not merely supposed, especially since it does not accord so well with Paul's exhortation to remain unmarried. If he had been a widower, it would have been easy to answer: Then why did you marry when you were young? — It is, therefore, legitimate to suppose that Paul's great zeal as a Pharisee for the study and observance of the Law led him to renounce marriage, as other rabbis had done, although this was the exception.

245. This period of Paul's life, which for us is completely shrouded in obscurity, goes from the end of his studies in Jerusalem to his re-appearance there at the stoning of Stephen. The end of his schooling may have come in the years between A.D. 16–22 (§ 242), while Stephen's martyrdom, in our view, occurred in the year 36 (§ 151). We must remember, however, that during this time Paul may have gone to Jerusalem on several different occasions, especially in the later years when he had acquired a solid position of authority with the Sanhedrin (§ 242). If we grant this, then the question arises whether or not he ever met Jesus personally.

Chronologically, this was clearly possible. Jesus' public life started at the beginning of the year 28[13] and continued until the Pasch of the year 30. Most of it was spent first in Galilee and then in Judea. Now, during those two and one half years, Paul, on his way down from Tarsus, could have crossed Galilee and visited Judea and Jerusalem. On some such occasion, he might have met Jesus. In fact, however, everything leads to the conclusion that such a meeting never took place, and that Paul never saw Jesus during his lifetime, neither during his public ministry nor at the time of his trial and death. Paul himself never mentions having met Jesus, while if the meeting had taken place he would hardly have neglected to say so, since it would have been to his distinct advantage, especially where those who challenged his apostleship were concerned. If he had taken part in Jesus' trial before the Sanhedrin and his crucifixion — as others have sup-

---

[13] Cf. *The Life of Christ*, p. 157 ff. (§ 175 ff.).

posed[14] — he would not have hidden the fact, just as he did not conceal his part in persecuting "the name of Jesus of Nazareth" (Acts 26:9) and in Stephen's martyrdom (Acts 22:20). On the other hand, Paul states specifically more than once that he has seen the immortal Jesus the Christ after his resurrection (1 Cor. 9:1; 15:8), thus bolstering his claim to be an apostle.

246. Even the passage in *2 Corinthians*, 5:16, does not refer to a meeting with Jesus on earth. The text reads: "So that henceforth we know no one according to the flesh. And even though we have known Christ according to the flesh, yet now we know him so no longer." This last clause, "now we know him so no longer," is enough to exclude the possibility of Paul's having met Jesus. For if we have once met a person we cannot say that we do not know him. Paul's real meaning is clarified by the twice-repeated phrase "know according to the flesh" ($\kappa\alpha\tau\grave{\alpha}$ $\sigma\acute{\alpha}\rho\kappa\alpha$), which shows he is referring to a moral knowledge of a person, namely, the judgment or evaluation one makes of a person. In the past, before accepting Christ's doctrine, Paul had judged him according to human standards ("according to the flesh"), deciding that he could not be the Messias, because he did not have the attributes of the true, triumphant national Messias awaited by the Jewish people, and therefore the Sanhedrin had good cause to condemn him. When, however, Paul discovered in Jesus the Redeemer of the human race who had died for all men (*ibid.*, 15–16), he ceased to judge him "according to the flesh," and judged him instead according to "the love of Christ [which] impels us" (*ibid.*, 14). In conclusion, we may be practically certain that Paul never saw Jesus either before or at the time of his crucifixion.

247. During this, to us, obscure period of Paul's life, the Good Tidings brought by Jesus was also passing through that obscure period of activity that had been foretold in the Gospel parable.

Through the night, the small pinch of leaven the housewife has kneaded into the dough works secretly and steadily, and in the morning she finds her kneading trough full to the brim. In the Jewish populace, Jesus had set a spiritual leaven, hardly visible, hardly noticeable, and then the night had fallen. The elders of Judaism had carefully covered

---

[14] No evidence has been cited in support of this theory because none exists. As for the passage in *Galatians*, 3:1, which some have called a "vivid" description of Jesus crucified and therefore written by an eyewitness, it is sufficient to read it to understand its true meaning. The other arguments brought forward have all been prompted by some theory of criticism: some want to make the Third Gospel derive from Paul alone (excluding the more general apostolic catechesis); others wish to build up the psychological reasons for Paul's conversion (i.e., a reaction to the shattering spectacle of Jesus' crucifixion); and so on, but all these theories are sheer invention.

and sealed the trough, confident that the leaven would disintegrate and
everything remain unchanged. But from the very outset, there was a
ceaseless murmur and a gentle crackling now and then which made
them suspect the leaven was not smothered after all but was busily at
work. Worried at last, they opened the trough to find to their great
indignation that the leaven had pervaded and transformed the mass.
The indignation exploded into persecution. The ferment must be
suppressed.

One of the most indignant and one of the most zealous in persecution
was Paul.

248. In the five or six years between Christ's death and the stoning
of Stephen, the Church had made notable progress. Immediately after
the Ascension the entire Church consisted of some 120 persons gathered
in Jerusalem (Acts 1:15) and perhaps a few hundred scattered elsewhere. Ten days later, at Pentecost, 3000 persons were converted by
Peter's discourse (*ibid.*, 2:41) and their number increased "day by day"
(*ibid.*, 47).

The religious authorities of Jerusalem, and especially the Sadducees,
took action on a first (4:3 ff.) and second (5:17 ff.) occasion, and put
the Apostles in prison. But they went no further, because, among other
reasons, at the meeting of the Sanhedrin Paul's teacher Gamaliel (§ 75)
exhorted them not to go too far, since the movement might be from God
(*ibid.*, 34 ff.). Naturally, the movement kept growing and became especially widespread among the Jews who were not born in Palestine but
in the Diaspora and whose customs and language were Greek even
though for varying reasons they came often to Jerusalem. They were
the Hellenist Jews.

249. Those converted to the Good Tidings lived in common. They
were most faithful to the instructions given them by the Apostles, to
the "breaking of the bread," and to prayer, and they gathered usually
in the part of the Temple called Solomon's Porch (Acts 3:11; 5:12).[15]
They were Jews and they had no intention of repudiating Judaism. They
believed in Jesus and considered themselves Jews who had attained the
goal of Judaism in the Messias Jesus and were expecting their fellow
Jews in time to reach the same goal. But if "of the rest, no one dared
to associate with them" (5:13) in their particular community life, this
in no sense meant a schism, but merely a short period of waiting. They
were the first fruits of the tree and the others would ripen soon.

In the meantime, therefore, the first Christians in Jerusalem continued to frequent the synagogues as usual, many of which had been
built and were maintained by the different communities of Hellenist
Jews who, when they came to Jerusalem from the various cities of the
Diaspora, found their own center in their own synagogue. A rabbinic

---

[15] Cf. *Storia d'Israele*, II, p. 400 (§ 348).

legend, certainly exaggerated, claimed there were 480 synagogues in Jerusalem. Although the figure was not that high, there were undoubtedly very many, and we find separate mention of the synagogue of the "Freedmen" — the Jewish freedmen from Rome — that of the Jews of Cyrene, of Alexandria, of Cilicia, and of the Roman province of Asia (Acts 6:9).[16]

250. The fact that the Christian converts attended the synagogues naturally gave rise to constant public disputes, since the Jews who rejected Jesus as the Messias would demand an explanation from the Hellenist Jews for their acceptance of him, and the latter were more than ready to enter into discussion in the hope of spreading their faith.

In fact, the Hellenist Christians seem to have been the most active and zealous in proselytizing and that is why the hatred of the Jews piled up against them particularly, culminating finally in persecution. And within nascent Christendom itself, they formed not only the far larger and perhaps predominant group, but they were also distinct in language, customs, and other aspects of daily life from the Palestinian Christians. Because at a certain point in their community life with the Palestinian Christians, the widows of the Greeks were neglected, the first seven deacons were appointed, most of whom, if not all, belonged to the Hellenist group. Their duty was the administration of the material effects of the community, but at the same time they were charged with spreading the faith, especially among the Jews of the Diaspora. Among the first deacons was one who had been born a pagan and had then become a Jewish "proselyte," Nicholas of Antioch. There was also Philip the "evangelist," whose charism describes his activity (§ 215) and who had four daughters who were also gifted with charisms (Acts 21:9). And above all there was Stephen who paid for his activity with his life.

251. Meanwhile, through the efforts of the Apostles, who devoted themselves "to the ministry of the word" (Acts 6:4), and the courage of the deacons and other Hellenists in engaging in disputes with their adversaries, "the word of the Lord continued to spread, and the number of the disciples increased rapidly in Jerusalem; a large number also of the priests accepted the faith" (*ibid.*, 7).

This aroused Paul's utter wrath when he came to Jerusalem in the year 36. That members of the sacerdotal class should accept the new faith, Paul could explain easily enough. They were almost all Sadducees, who shamelessly followed pagan ways, and the few who were not Sadducees certainly did not share his Pharisaic views either. In any case, this was no time to hesitate. Sadducees or Pharisees, all must unite against the common enemy that threatened to overrun Jerusalem, Palestine, the Diaspora, and beyond, no one could foresee where. It was enough to watch that Stephen who "was working great signs and won-

---

[16] *Ibid.*, II, p. 215 (§ 191); p. 220 (§ 195).

ders among the people" (Acts 6:8). Could they allow an ignorant faker
to continue such a scandal? He must be confounded and humiliated!
He must be shamed in the presence of the people; it must be made
clear in a public disputation that he was completely ignorant of the
most elementary parts of the Hebrew Law! With Stephen destroyed,
action would then be taken against the others on the authority of the
Sanhedrin, and the matter would be settled once and for all. In all
probability this was more or less the plan of action which Paul supported enthusiastically; or he may even have been its principal author.

252. The public debate with Stephen took place accordingly, and Jews
of the various Hellenist synagogues, including that of Cilicia among
whom Paul counted his best friends, participated in it. The outcome,
however, betrayed their expectations. The discussion, which was both
long and animated, turned on a variety of questions, and many opponents rose to challenge Stephen, but they "were not able to withstand
the wisdom and the Spirit who spoke" (*ibid.,* 10).

This failure led to a more radical measure, which would in fact hasten
the carrying out of the established plan by advancing the intervention
of the Sanhedrin. False witnesses were suborned, who declared they
had heard Stephen speak blasphemous words against Moses and God.
The crowd was aroused, the Elders and Scribes came running, and
they together dragged Stephen off to the Sanhedrin. The desired
"united front" had been achieved. The three groups composing the
Sanhedrin — High Priests, Ancients, and Scribes[17] — set aside for the
moment their conflicting principles, whether Sadducean or Pharisaic,
and acted with one accord. Before judgment was passed, the accused
had been prejudged.

253. The charge brought against Stephen was partly false and partly
true. The false part echoed the charges brought six years before against
Jesus, for Stephen was accused of having spoken irreverently of the
Temple and the Hebrew Law. The true charge was linked with the
new faith, for Stephen had declared that the Messias Jesus would establish a new spiritual order, abolishing the function of the Hebrew Temple
and changing the "traditions" the Pharisees considered fundamental
(*ibid.,* 13–14). Stephen defended himself in a discourse, which is reported with exceptional fullness in the *Acts* (7:2–53), but this account is
evidently a summary nevertheless (§ 112). It is of singular importance
as a historical document, for it gives us some idea of the apologetic
method used by the Hellenist Christians in their controversies with
Judaism.

Stephen goes back beyond Moses to summarize the history of the
Jewish people from the time of Abraham, following the general outline
of the Bible narrative but not without introducing certain elements from

---

[17] Cf. *The Life of Christ,* p. 53 (§ 58).

the *haggadah* (§ 76). This broad historical view serves to point out the economy of salvation ordained by God for the whole human race rather than for Israel alone, and the superiority of the worship given by man to God in sincerity of spirit in contrast with the worship offered him only physically in places consecrated by custom. As the historical exposition proceeds, the discourse charges the Jews with attacking these two cardinal points of the divine economy and of opposing incessantly the work of God for man. And it closes with these harsh words: "Stiff-necked and uncircumcised in heart and ear, you always oppose the Holy Spirit; as your fathers did, so you do also. Which of the prophets have not your fathers persecuted? And they killed those who foretold the coming of the Just One, of whom you have now been the betrayers and murderers, you who receive the Law as an ordinance of angels and did not keep it."

254. This was too much. At the charge that they did not observe the Law, the Scribes and Pharisees of the Sanhedrin lost all the control they had forced themselves to keep until then out of respect for the formalities of the trial. They gesticulated and gnashed their teeth at him threateningly. At this Stephen ceased speaking to his earthly judges. He added only the text of his own sentence given in the presence of his heavenly judge. Raising his eyes to heaven, he stood a moment in contemplation and then exclaimed: "Behold, I see the heavens opened, and the Son of Man standing at the right hand of God" (7:56).

A storm of cries and curses drowned his words. The Sanhedrists "stopped their ears" to hear no more blasphemies and rose to their feet. The younger ones rushed at him to inflict immediately the penalty fixed for his crime. The Sanhedrists were joined by their satellites and the mob, and Stephen was dragged out to his execution.

255. It is almost certain that Paul was present at this scene in the Sanhedrin. He refers to it clearly enough himself when, speaking in general of his persecution of the Christians, he states, "and when they were put to death, I cast my vote against them" (Acts 26:10). The reference to Stephen here seems inescapable, since he was the first and most famous of those put to death. On the other hand, it does not seem legitimate to conclude, from the mention of the vote, that Paul was actually a member of the Sanhedrin and cast a vote against Stephen. To all appearances, no vote was taken, and Stephen's conviction was implicitly decreed in the angry reaction against him. Here the term *vote* seems to be used figuratively, namely, to indicate Paul's part in instigating the conviction, his consent to it, and his co-operation in the execution, just as in another passage he says of Stephen's death ". . . I was standing by and approved it, and took charge of the garments of those who killed him" (Acts 22:20). In addition, we have no other indication that Paul was a member of the Sanhedrin, while his youth sug-

The Trial and Stoning of Stephen (Basilica of S. Lorenzo al Verano)

gests he would still be considered too immature for this supreme council of Judaism.

We have already stated the reasons why we do not think the Roman magistrate had anything to do with Stephen's trial, although he was responsible for the execution of the death sentence pronounced by the Sanhedrin (§ 151). The violent manner in which it was carried out seems to confirm our explanation.

256. Nevertheless, the execution was carried out in strict conformity with the precepts of the Hebrew Law. It was almost as if his executioners were anxious to refute in this way the condemned man's charge that the Scribes and Pharisees of the Sanhedrin did not obey the Law. Now he could see for himself how these illustrious teachers knew how to observe the Law! So the screaming mob dragged Stephen outside the city, as was prescribed by the Law (Lev. 24:14). The Law decreed that blasphemers like Stephen were to be stoned to death by all the people (*ibid.*, 16) and this was the punishment chosen. And finally, the Law required that two or three official witnesses be present at the execution, and these were to throw the first stones (Deut. 17:6–7). This, too, was observed.

For greater freedom, the witnesses took off their cloaks. Paul ran solicitously to take charge of them, for in his zeal he seemed with this gesture "to stone with the hands of all" (Augustine).

The place chosen for the execution was a hollow. The condemned man descended into it and his executioners stood around him. As the first stones of the witnesses struck him, Stephen stood praying: "Lord, Jesus, receive my spirit" (Acts 7:59). But then the shower of missiles hurled by the mob beat him to the ground. "And falling on his knees, he cried out with a loud voice, saying, 'Lord, do not lay this sin against them!' And with these words, he fell asleep" (*ibid.*, 60).

257. The word for "witness" in Greek is "martyr." And so in the Church Stephen became the protomartyr, that is, the first witness of Christ. But what of that other witness, the witness of Jewish Law, who stoned him vicariously through the hands of those he was serving? Is there not some bond between that first witness of the new order and the last witness of the old?

This observation seems quite obvious today after twenty centuries, but on that day the last one to whom it would have occurred was unquestionably Paul himself. He must have felt a warm glow of satisfaction on that day. At last serious action was being taken to ensure respect for the Law and "tradition." Had he spent his entire youth studying the Law and "tradition" merely to be able to decide whether one could eat an egg laid on the Sabbath (§ 88) or read on the Sabbath day by the light of a lamp lit by a pagan (§ 86), and then have to stand by idle while those dirty Christians systematically destroyed the Law? Not at all! They were to continue now as they had begun; they must go on with the plan (§ 251) until all the Christians were destroyed. In the Bible had not *herem* (a "war of extermination") been decreed more than once against the ancient Canaanites?

258. And the plan was in fact carried out. The direct intervention of the Sanhedrin was obtained[18] and a methodical persecution of the new faith began. It was directed almost solely against the Hellenist Christians, for they had been the most zealous in challenging the Jews and also because in Jerusalem they were like unwanted guests, people to be sent back to their place of origin or in any case outside the "Holy City." The Hellenists, in fact, scattered throughout the various districts of Judea, Samaria, and elsewhere. The Apostles, on the other hand, because they were Palestinians, were able to remain in Jerusalem, and were probably undisturbed (Acts 8:1).

But the inflexible Paul was keeping watch. And he shrewdly noted that the victory gained for the time being was only an apparent one,

---

[18] The intervention of the Sanhedrin is clear from *Acts*, 22:5 (Greek text); 26:10 (cf. 9:1–2). This unusual activity on the part of the Sanhedrin may serve to confirm the thesis that the office of Roman procurator was either unfilled or was held by a new and inexperienced magistrate (§ 151).

if it did not actually worsen the situation. Even if the more prominent Hellenist Christians had been scattered, their families and many others less prominent still remained in Jerusalem. In the first place, then, these had to be reduced to helplessness. Then the refugees must be pursued, because, scattering through Palestine and beyond, they could spread everywhere the cursed plague they carried with them. Having analyzed the situation, Paul went immediately into action.

259. He began with Jerusalem. Luke sums up what happened there in these words: "Saul was laying waste the Church (of Jerusalem); entering house after house, and dragging out men and women, he committed them to prison" (Acts 8:3).[19] The verb "laying waste" ($\dot{\epsilon}\lambda\nu\mu\alpha\acute{\iota}\nu\epsilon\tau o$) derives perhaps from Luke's medical vocabulary, for a body suffering a serious illness was a "wasted" body, like a region laid waste or ravaged by the enemy. The fact that the verb is in the middle imperfect tense emphasizes the duration of the devastation, which must have lasted several days and was carried out carefully according to a well-organized plan. Paul and the inquisitors he was directing forced their way into the most suspect houses, preferably those marked as meeting places, and all the Christians surprised in them, both men and women, were taken off to prison. The severity of the persecution is explicitly confirmed by Paul himself when he says: "Beyond all measure I persecuted the Church of God and ravaged it" (Gal. 1:13).

In a few weeks the situation in Jerusalem seemed under control and the persecution was extended to the Diaspora. Paul would give the enemy no truce, and he immediately appealed to the Sanhedrin for authority to take action against the Jewish centers outside of Palestine which gave most cause for suspicion. Theoretically the Sanhedrin's authority extended over all Jews throughout the world.[20] Practically, its effectiveness among the Jews of the Diaspora varied more or less according to circumstances, but it was still considerable in the great foreign cities near Palestine which harbored large Jewish communities. Such, for example, was the city of Damascus, very near Palestine and with a very large Jewish population (§§ 32–33). Since Paul had, besides, many indications that the city was seriously infected with Christianity, he made it the first object of his new measures.

260. It is probable that the Sanhedrin had no particular desire to extend the persecution to Damascus or anywhere else outside of Palestine. The supreme council could still remember the gentle words of Gamaliel, who had warned it to use prudence and tolerance (§ 248). Besides, the cautious Sanhedrists always considered it a risky business to become involved in the affairs of Jews in other regions. But the fiery Paul must have pleaded and exhorted until he succeeded in winning

---

[19] This is the author's translation (Trans.).
[20] Cf. *The Life of Christ,* p. 53 (§ 58).

them to his view. His old teacher, Rabbi Gamaliel, merited every veneration as always, but he must have become a little senile by now, old before his time. How could anyone counsel tolerance toward the viper which all Israel was hatching in its bosom? All the Sanhedrists had to take action, the Sadducees to affirm their authority abroad, the Pharisees to safeguard the Law and the ancestral "tradition." So in the end Paul carried the day and obtained letters addressed to the synagogues of Damascus, authorizing him to do there what he had done in Jerusalem, namely, investigate, make arrests, and bring the prisoners, men and women, back to Jerusalem.

261. The day Paul set out for Damascus, armed with the letters of the Sanhedrin and accompanied by a solid escort of armed men, must have been one of the happiest days of his life up to that moment. His happiness lay not so much in the satisfaction he had in bending the Sanhedrin to his viewpoint, as in his consciousness of the soundnesss of that viewpoint. Now at long last he felt himself a true defender of Israel. The office of the ancient prophets had been transmitted to the Scribes and Doctors, and just as the prophets had taken up the sword to defeat the enemies of Israel, now the Scribes and Doctors must fight against the infamous Christians. Blessed was his father who had sent him to study the Law in Jerusalem, and blessed his own constancy in that study. Now he was reaping the fruit; now he felt ready, like a second David, to fight the battles of Yahweh (1 Kings 18:17; cf. Num. 21:14), like another Jeremias "to root up and to pull down, and to waste and to destroy" all the enemies of Israel (Jer. 1:10).

This was no artificial or superficial excitement. It was rather a profound conviction that he was accomplishing a most noble and holy work. Every Christian out of the way was one obstacle less for the triumph of the Law, which embodied all justice. Certainly many individuals have held convictions of this kind in every religion, but rarely with the unshakable firmness of Paul, in whom — again like the ancient prophet — all was solid as "a pillar of iron, and a wall of brass" (Jer. 1:18).

In this frame of mind, he set out for Damascus.

Paul's Conversion

262. On April 2, 1912, a great ocean liner left England for New York on its maiden voyage. It was a masterpiece of naval engineering, equipped with the latest devices and luxurious fittings, and launched with proud confidence in its ability to surmount any danger of the sea. Even its name proclaimed its boast, the *Titanic*. This, its first voyage, which was to serve as model for a long series of similar trips, was to be one long revel of sumptuous living within and uncontested dominion over the elements without.

And the first part of the journey augured well. But in mid-ocean, the unexpected happened. On a calm bright starlit night, while music and dancing filled its bright salons, the liner smashed full speed ahead into a glistening white mountain of ice that rose suddenly in its course. All the safety precautions were useless. The ship sank rapidly, and of the 2350 persons aboard only half were saved.

The journey of the fiery Pharisee to Damascus morally speaking paralleled the voyage of the *Titanic*. The pilot, Paul, was unshakably sure of himself, the master of his course, who had foreseen every eventuality. Suddenly, across his path, rose a white mountain and he rode headlong into it. Perhaps it was the mountain the prophets had spoken of in other times, when they had foretold:

> "And in the last days the mountain
>   of the house of the Lord
>   shall be prepared on the top of mountains,
>   and it shall be exalted above the hills,
>   and all nations shall flow into it.
> "And many people shall go, and say:
>   'Come and let us go up to the mountain of the Lord,
>   and to the house of the God of Jacob,
>   and he will teach us his ways,
>   and we will walk in his paths:
>   for the law shall come forth from Sion,
>   and the word of the Lord from Jerusalem'"

> (Isa. 2:2–3; cf. Mich. 4:1–2).

On the shore at the foot of the divine mountain lies the wreckage of all the ships that have foundered there through the centuries, whose pilots have then sought refuge on the summit.

263. There were several routes from Jerusalem to Damascus, both main roads and secondary ones. Perhaps Paul took the shortest route along the comfortable Roman road which went first to Sichem, then bearing slightly to the right (without touching the city of Samaria) passed through Beisan-Scythopolis. From there it went up the Jordan valley to Lake Tiberias, where it divided: one branch went east of the lake passing through Hippos and leading straight across the desert to Damascus; the other circled the lake on the west side, touched the cities of Tiberias and Magdala, and crossed the Jordan south of Lake Huleh, from where it went to Damascus. It is likely that Paul followed this second route, although somewhat longer, since it traversed the country of Jesus where he might perhaps gather firsthand information regarding the relatives and friends of his hated enemy. The whole trip was about 180 to 200 miles. A caravan like Paul's, mounted and well organized, could cover it in seven or eight days (allowing for the Sabbath rest). The journey went well, in fact, until the very end, when the unforeseen happened.

264. The great event occurred "about noon," on the open road, when the company was already near Damascus (Acts 9:3; 22:6; 26:13).[1] Probably the city was not only in sight, but so short a distance away that a blinded and weakened man could easily be led the rest of the way without having to be carried (9:8).

As Paul and his escort approached the city, a bright light flashed from heaven and shone about him. Dazzled and bewildered, he fell prostrate to the ground. Then he heard a voice speaking to him in Aramaic, "Saul, Saul, why dost thou persecute me?"

Paul's bewilderment deepened. A swift examination of conscience reassured him somewhat. He was persecuting the Christians, but they were the enemies of the God of Israel and therefore God could not but approve his conduct. He asked anxiously, "Who art thou, Lord?"

And the mysterious voice gave him an answer that was indeed unexpected: "I am Jesus whom thou art persecuting. It is hard for thee to kick against the goad!"[2]

---

[1] The three or four traditions, or better, legends, current today in Damascus regarding the site of Paul's conversion have no foundation in fact. Relatively ancient is the one which sets it at Kaukab on the road to Galilee about three hours' walk from Damascus. But the distance makes us question this. Completely recent and arbitrary is the site commonly pointed out in the suburbs of Damascus near the Eastern Gate; close by, tourists are also shown the window in the city walls through which, later, Paul was let down in a basket. Neither deserves credence.

[2] The phrase "to kick against the goad" — the goad used by peasants to prick the oxen — was a very common one in ancient times. It is found in Pindar (*Pyth.*, 2, 94), Aeschylus (*Agam.*, 1624), Euripides (*Bacch.*, 795), Terence (*Phormio,* 78).

The Valley of Barada Near Damascus

265. As the light had blinded him, this answer now blacked out his mental vision, his judgment of human events. The whole world seemed suddenly to have turned upside down. The Jesus whom he had pushed into the abyss of his hatred, now appeared to him at the summit of all things. He was not only a "lord" but "the Lord" in the highest meaning of the term. Paul could see him standing before him, but above all he could feel his presence in his innermost spirit. His declaration, "I am Jesus," had penetrated Paul's very soul and elicited a spontaneous and irrepressible assent. There stood his archenemy, suddenly revealed in strength and power! And he, Paul, was persecuting him by persecuting his followers. It was a terrible thing to recognize the error he had followed until then, but it was impossible to kick against a goad so strong. The truth was too evident to be denied, and Paul must reverse his whole view of the universe. Lost in utter moral confusion, what was he to do?

The question came spontaneously from his stunned heart, "Lord, what wilt thou have me do?"

The voice answered: "Arise and go into the city, and it will be told thee what thou must do."

266. Meanwhile, Paul's companions were watching in puzzled fright.

There is a similar one in *Ecclesiastes*, 12:11. It is likely that an Aramaic form of the proverb was common in Palestine. As Jesus used popular parables and everyday sayings to teach while on earth, so now Christ glorified uses an everyday proverb. Some have maintained that the form of the proverb derives from Euripides. If this is so, then it is due to the Greek translator, because the phrase was spoken in Aramaic. After all, the proverb, in its Greek form, may well have derived from a poetic source.

At the sudden flash of light, they too had fallen to the ground, and now they were trying to figure out what had happened. They had heard the mysterious voice, but indistinctly and confusedly, and without being able to see who spoke. In the silence that followed they saw Paul rise to his feet, but he stood still where he was, feeling before him with his arms outstretched. And to their astonishment they noticed that though his eyes were wide open he could see nothing. He was blind.

Being practical men, when they realized what had happened, their first reaction was to get away from so dangerous a spot as soon as possible. They could talk it all over later in safety. So they took Paul by the hand and led him, as quickly as they could, into the city.

The shipwreck had been sudden and final. There was nothing left of the past. There was everything to be rebuilt for the future. Paul had to leave the shattered craft at the foot of the mountain and climb to the summit. There, as Moses had before him, he would hear the voice of God.

267. The episode, which marks the death of Paul the Pharisee and the birth of Paul the Apostle, is not given in detail in any of the Epistles. At most, Paul mentions it only incidentally.[3] This is natural. He was not writing for the benefit of twentieth-century scholars but to meet the circumstances that developed in the churches he had founded. The faithful were very well acquainted with this key event in their teacher's life, and he had no time to waste repeating what they already knew so well. On the other hand, the episode is told three times in the *Acts:* the first time (9:3–19) Luke gives it to us as part of the narrative; the second time (22:6–16) he records Paul's discourse to the angry mob in the Temple of Jerusalem, in which he describes his conversion; the third time (26:12–18) it is recounted again in Paul's discourse before the procurator, Porcius Festus, and King Agrippa.

The three accounts are substantially the same, even in the various details, although naturally they are not identical. Luke's account is straight narrative style; Paul's two accounts of his conversion are in oratorical style, and it should be remembered that the first was addressed to a seething crowd, the second to a pagan magistrate and a Jewish king. The difference in audience is sufficient to explain the differences in presentation, slight as they are.

268. Certain discrepancies in content have also been pointed out. One account (9:7) describes Paul's companions as standing ($\epsilon \dot{\iota} \sigma \tau \acute{\eta} \kappa \epsilon \iota \sigma \alpha \nu$) speechless after the apparition, while another (26:14) states that they all fell to the ground. This is hardly worth quibbling over. Paul's companions could have fallen first and then scrambled to their feet, from fright if from nothing else. Besides the Greek verb may also mean to

---

[3] The principal references are 1 Cor. 9:1, 15:8; 2 Cor. 4:6; Gal. 1:13 ff.; Eph. 3:7–8; Phil 3:12.

remain in a given state of mind for some time, which here would indicate they remained in a state of speechlessness for some time.

Again, one narrative (9:7) has it that Paul's companions heard the
mysterious voice (ἀκούοντες τῆς φωνῆς) but saw no one, while another
(22:9) says they saw the light but did not hear the voice (τὴν δὲ φωνὴν
οὐκ ἤκουσαν). But the verb "to hear" in Greek has a double meaning,
the general one "to hear" a sound, and the more specific meaning "to
understand." One may hear someone speak without *understanding* him,
or *hear* someone call without *understanding* whom he is calling. If
we compare the two accounts (especially in the Greek text, with its
disjunctive particles [μὲν . . . δέ] we find that the contrast here is
between the visual and aural perceptions of Paul's companions and
those of Paul himself. The former see the light but no other person,
while Paul sees the light and Jesus who is speaking to him. The former
hear the mysterious voice but do not understand what is being said,
while Paul both hears and understands.[4] The care with which both
accounts record the part played in the episode by Paul's companions
would indicate a desire to present them as partial but disinterested
witnesses of the event itself.

269. Another discrepancy has been pointed out which involves the
events that followed the apparition on the Damascus road. In the third
account (26:16–18) Christ himself, at the end of the vision, announces
to Paul his vocation as Apostle to the Gentiles. In the second (22:14–15)
it is Ananias who tells Paul this when he meets him later in Damascus
(§ 285). It should be noted, however, that Ananias was expressly charged
by Christ to give Paul this message (9:15–16) and therefore his authority
in doing so derives from divine authority. Consequently the third account
skips the intervention of Ananias and attributes the announcement directly to Christ. This more summary presentation was more convenient
on this third occasion, for Paul was speaking to the pagan Porcius Festus
and the Romanized King Agrippa, to whom the name of Ananias would
have meant nothing, while the command of a divine apparition would
have authority even for them. Here, too, Paul's training in the Bible is
apparent, for in the Old Testament the words of a messenger from God
are ordinarily treated as the words of God himself. On the other hand,

---

[4] As proof of this double use of the verb "to hear," it has been pointed out that
in 9:7 it is used with the genitive, to mean the simple perception of sound, while
in 22:9 it is used with the accusative to mean the perception of meaning, i.e., "to
understand." Many scholars have used this argument, stating that in the Greek the
use of one case or the other determines the meaning of the verb, "to hear." But
is this true, actually? Just to cite one example it is enough to notice how these
same two accounts tell of Paul's hearing Jesus call him. In one he "heard a voice
saying to him: 'Saul, Saul, why dost thou persecute me'" (with the accusative, 9:4,
and also in 26:14); and in another Paul himself says, "I heard a voice saying to me,
'Saul, Saul . . .'" (with the genitive, 22:7). And there are other similar examples
in the *Acts*.

in the second account Paul is addressing the Jews clamoring against him in the Temple and so he is more than careful to describe the intervention of Ananias, whom they held in high esteem (22:12), and thereby profit from the testimony of a Jew who was entirely acceptable to his listeners.[5]

In conclusion, these slight variations make the three accounts much more interesting. The *concordia discors* we pointed out in the sources for the life of Christ[6] is to be found here, too, though to a lesser extent, and for the same reasons. The testimonies are drawn from different sources and travel different roads, but all converge toward the same goal. In the documents a *concordia discors* is much more interesting and of greater historical value than a *concordia concors*.

* * *

270. Paul's conversion is, in the history of the origins of Christianity, the most important event after the resurrection of Christ, and its consequences the most decisive. In fact, for those who consider — wrongly — that Paul is the real author of the concepts of Christianity, his acceptance of Jesus marks the beginning of the new religion while Jesus' resurrection is for them simply an article of the new faith.

It is obvious that the rationalists who do not accept the resurrection of Jesus cannot accept Paul's conversion as it is narrated in the sources. But here too they are obliged to find an explanation for the spiritual change in Paul, that is, to replace the narrative of the sources with a "rational" one, as they reconstruct it. There have been several attempts at this. They begin at about the same time as the efforts on the life of Christ[7] and follow the same pattern. They all agree absolutely in excluding any supernatural element, in obedience to the "lay dogma" (§ 120 ff.), and exercise unlimited freedom in rejecting or distorting the documentary evidence and assuming facts clearly excluded by this evidence.

271. The very first efforts[8] in this regard were concerned only with

---

[5] The fact of Paul's vocation communicated to him by Ananias is not to be confused with the confirmation of that vocation which Paul later receives in a vision in the Temple. He speaks of his vision immediately afterward in the same discourse to the rioters (22:17–21), but it is a separate episode.

[6] Cf. *The Life of Christ*, p. 126 ff. (§ 146 ff.).

[7] Cf. *ibid.*, p. 183 ff. (§ 197 ff.).

[8] The earliest of these seems to have had an unexpected result. In the first half of the eighteenth century in England "two scholars at Oxford, to end the travail of their spirits, set for themselves as a direct and careful study for the approaching long summer holiday a twofold task: to demonstrate that the resurrection of Jesus and the conversion of the Apostle were inanities. When they met again both found they had become convinced of the contrary. One of them, Lord Lyttleton, published an elegant study: *Observations on the conversion and Apostleship of Saint Paul* (London, 1747), which was translated and published in French under the more comprehensive title: *La religion chrétienne démontrée par la conversion et l'apostolat de Saint Paul* (Paris, 1754)." Thus A. Vitti in *Biblica*, 1942, p. 379; the source

the external aspects of the event, and tried to explain what had actually happened on the road to Damascus. These were the incredibly ingenuous days when the Heidelberg professor, H. E. G. Paulus, was explaining away the miracles of the Gospel, including Jesus' resurrection, with his naturalistic method.[9] Jesus had never risen from the dead because he had never died. He had merely swooned, and he had gradually revived in the sepulcher, thanks to the period of rest and the pungent odors of the ointments, and had then emerged to all appearances risen from the dead. This explanation seemed to some German scholars of the time a most convenient explanation for Paul's conversion. One fine day, Jesus, who had recovered as outlined here, met his fierce persecutor Paul near Damascus and abruptly challenged him, rebuking him severely. Taken by surprise and frightened by Jesus' harsh reproach, Paul was converted. And that explains everything.

Explanations like these have today something of the flavor of museum pieces, but the method implicit in them is far less archaic than it seems. It was used at least in part for some time afterward although more casually and confidently. Even the latest theories tack on, as an auxiliary argument, some external fact which allegedly influenced Paul's sudden conversion.

272. In any case this awkward use of the naturalistic method seemed too crude to gain much credit. Obviously some other method was necessary. In the first place the texts must be screened as usual and then the inner aspects of Paul's psychological drama examined. The external circumstances became secondary in importance or altogether negligible.

As for the texts, there was little to sift and choose. Many scholars rejected the resurrection of Lazarus with the argument that it was narrated only once, in the Fourth Gospel, while the Synoptics fail to mention it.[10] But there are three accounts of Paul's conversion and all substantially the same. The only thing to do, then, was to cast suspicion on all three, with the assertion that they all derive from the editor of the *Acts,* who invented the entire episode and then was tiresome enough to repeat himself.[11] At the most, there may have occurred on the road to Damascus some sudden manifestation of the inner struggle tormenting Paul, some outburst reflecting his psychological crisis. But the episode certainly did not take place as the three accounts in the *Acts* claim it did.

273. This approach was brought to the fore by C. Holsten, who from 1861 on made the psychological aspects of Paul's conversion the special

---

quoted in the note is W. H. Griffith Thomas, in *International Standard Bible Encyclopedia,* 4 (1915), 2568.

[9] Cf. *The Life of Christ,* p. 184 (§ 198).

[10] Cf. *ibid.,* p. 503 (§ 493).

[11] Thus E. Bonaiuti, *San Paolo,* in *Profili,* n. 77, Rome, 1925, pp. 8–9.

object of his research.[12] He was the disciple of Baur (§ 125) and seemed almost to be taking over his teacher's task, for Bauer himself had become discouraged and decided that no psychological or dialectic analysis could solve the problem of Paul's conversion. Holsten viewed it as an intellectual crisis in a mind already predisposed. Paul was an epileptoid, according to Holsten, extremely sensitive and given to transferring intellectual impressions to visions and ecstasies. After an obscure period of passive acceptance of the Jewish religion, his spirit suddenly awoke, grew prideful, rejected the old concepts, and contemplated an entirely new intellectual vision. This was the liberation of his mind, the first "vision" of Christ, which was followed by a whole series of other hysterical-ecstatic visions. Thus began that "immanent act" of his mind which constituted his conversion.

Holsten was completely convinced of this explanation, and with him A. Hilgenfeld and a few others. Many more, however, disagreed, and notably W. Beyschlag, whose reply was a penetrating one.

274. A psychological explanation was also proposed by O. Pfleiderer in 1890, who, however, stressed the moral aspects and the Christian elements which supposedly influenced the conversion. According to his theory, Paul had been shaken by Stephen's serene tranquillity in death and was tormented by constant remorse. This impelled him to enter into discussions with the Christians whom he persecuted and imprisoned after Stephen's execution, and thus as his remorse increased, his mind received new impulses toward Christianity. At the same time he felt increasingly the inadequacy of the Jewish Law to effect man's liberation, and at a given moment he asked himself if this liberation had not actually been wrought by the Jesus who died on the cross and who so closely resembled the Just, suffering for the good of others, of whom the Hebrew Scriptures spoke (Isa. 53). Contributing indirectly was the fact that Paul was impetuous and inclined to swing from one extreme to the other. Some slight influence was exerted also by external circumstances when, near Damascus, Paul emerged suddenly from the parched roads of the desert to the pleasant gardens surrounding the city. In short, this complex of factors vanquished the persecutor as he was about to begin the persecution and converted him suddenly from enemy to friend. Nevertheless, toward the end of his exposition, Pfleiderer, with unexpected perception, admits that despite all these "proofs" the problem is not completely solved, and so he leaves a margin of possibility for "a religious revelation in the strictest sense of the word."

275. Renan's explanation (*Les Apôtres*, 1869, Chap. X) was charac-

---

[12] The history of these studies and the bibliographical references are to be found, for the earliest period, in E. Moske, *Die Bekehrung des hl. Paulus,* Münster i. W., 1907; for the later period in E. Pfaff, *Die Bekehrung des hl. Paulus in der Exegese des 20. Jahrhunderts,* Rome, 1942.

teristically eclectic-aesthetic. Among the various elements he gathered
here and there, he assigned most importance to external circumstances,
for here the writer-artist in him took wing. When he could describe a
psycho-physical-sentimental drama against an appropriate landscape he
was in his glory and tossed off one marvelous page after another.

In Renan's view, Paul is approaching Damascus to begin the persecution of the Christians "but like all strong souls he was close to loving
what he hated." Having heard of the apparitions of Jesus, he seemed
almost to "see the sweet face of the master" contemplating him "with an
air of pity and tender reproach." At the same time his function as executioner was becoming increasingly odious to him, he was tired from the
journey, his eyes were red and sore, with perhaps the beginning of an
inflammation. And now toward the end of the journey he emerged from
"the sun-scorched plain into the cool shade of the gardens." All this
brought on a kind of attack "in the sickly and deeply shaken frame of
the fanatical traveler. For pernicious fevers, accompanied by reactions
in the brain, are completely sudden in those regions."[13] Probably a storm
broke at the very same moment, for "the slopes of Hermon are the
point where thunder of incomparable violence forms, and the calmest
persons cannot travel unmoved through those terrifying rains of fire."[14]
Now all is clear. In an attack of pernicious fever, Paul mistook a flash of
lightning for an apparition of the "sweet master," a crash of thunder for
his voice, and was thereupon radically changed for the rest of his life
even to the point of martyrdom. But this solution of the problem creates
another with regard to Renan himself. Did he, endowed as he was with
no little intelligence, really believe his own sparkling pages, or was it

---

[13] These "pernicious fevers," with their "reactions on the brain," are dark brush
strokes which Renan adds for greater dramatic effect, but there is no truth in them.
When he tells us in a note that he suffered such an attack at Byblos and was fully
aware — unlike Paul — that he was having hallucinations and not visions, we
can only admire his perspicacity and deplore his bad luck, especially since Byblos
is such a comfortable and pretty place on the seashore. I myself have been much
more fortunate than Renan. I have traveled hundreds of miles in and about Damascus,
in Cilicia, in Galilee and the rest of Palestine, around Antioch and through Syria,
at the peak of summer heat as well as in other seasons, and I have invariably
been immune from "pernicious fevers" and also — so far as I know — from "reactions
on the brain." I never even heard them mentioned. The only case I have ever heard
of is this one of Renan's.

[14] Here again the reader must not be frightened. These descriptions make no
claim to geographical accuracy; they are intended only to be artistic. Hermon is a
very high and majestic mountain, and like all high mountains it causes currents of
air and sudden atmospheric precipitations accompanied by the usual thunder and
lightning. But I have never seen any "terrifying rains of fire" there nor have I ever
heard anyone speak of them. Renan was probably thinking of Dante's rain of fire
in the *Inferno* (XIV), and considering himself here quite rightly an artist rather
than a historian or geographer, he transported the fiery rain to Mt. Hermon. He
had proper permission from Horace: *Pictoribus atque poetis quidlibet audendi semper
fuit aequa potestas.*

enough for him if they were believed by the Voltairean cavaliers and the "precious" ladies of the Paris drawing rooms?

276. The twentieth century has gone more deeply into the psychological explanations of Paul's conversion. Frequently these do not discuss whether the crisis really took place on the road to Damascus or whether the whole scene is to be considered pure fiction. When rare mention is made of the episode, it is usually to extract from it some external circumstance which helped in a secondary way to bring on the crisis itself.

The spiritual factors which prepared the way for the crisis are the same ones adduced before, with, at the most, some difference in explanation or the addition of a new element offered by more recent research. Many scholars hold that Paul had an early predisposition to this crisis because, according to them, he suffered from a sense of deep spiritual discomfort in the Jewish Law. Some believe that this discomfort reached the point, even before his acceptance of Christ, where he was inwardly convinced that the Law could not give man the freedom he was anxiously seeking. Others, however, claim Paul was aware that man, in his state of sin and guilt, could not observe the precepts of the Law, which in itself was good and divine. The only positive proof presented for this inner struggle is the passage in the epistle to the Romans (7:7–25) where he speaks of the conflict in man between the flesh and the Law, and which is supposedly autobiographical (§ 243). As for the efficient cause of this spiritual discomfort, many scholars find it to be the influence of the Hellenist intellectual world in which Paul was born. A certain few consider it the influence exerted on him by Gamaliel's teaching, which was the broad and liberal type like the school of Hillel (§ 75) in contrast to the rest of Pharisaism, which was dour and narrow-minded. And various other causes and reasons are attributed besides.

277. To these rather negative factors must be added the positive influences which attracted the bewildered Paul to the new religion. Only a minority assumes that Paul had met Jesus during his life on earth (§§ 245–246) and had been deeply impressed by him. Many others, however, base their theories on the great attraction they think certain concepts of the oriental religions had for Paul, especially the Persian belief in a "first Man," or the concept of a savior-deity who suffers and dies, as in the mystery religions (§ 281). Concepts like these Paul supposedly transferred to Jesus of Nazareth. Some favor the idea of an apocalyptic Messias such as we find in later Judaism, while others maintain that the Hellenist Christians had a different concept of the Messias Jesus from that of the Jewish Christians of Jerusalem, and that Paul was taken with the Hellenist concept. This presupposes necessarily that he was not in Jerusalem for the stoning of Stephen and the subsequent persecution of the Christians.

These are the principal factors in Paul's presumed psychological conditioning (there are many others omitted here for brevity's sake). Rarely is any one of them advanced by itself. Rather two or more are presented as acting simultaneously in order to make a stronger case. Some explicitly claim Paul was psychopathic. Others add some external, physical factor. And at times, the discussions and theories end unexpectedly with a vague confession of doubt, dictated as it were by scientific prudence, and the admission that the event can never be probed definitively.

278. As an example of an explanation that is at once cautious and eclectic we may quote Loisy (*Actes,* 1920, p. 395 ff.). He is diffident about the very idea of a psychological conditioning; but unable to ignore it, he treats it in a vague and roundabout manner. Paul was no longer sure of the Jewish Law, of its perfection, its moral efficacy, and its power to attract pagans. He was, besides, in "a mental state bordering on the psychotic." Actually, his thoughts were permeated, despite himself, with the Christ he was fighting, and one fine day, in a mental crisis, Paul's own thinking, somehow or other, imposed Christ on his own mind by a hallucination strong enough to disconcert his will and literally subjugate him to the impression of his dream. The external scene artificially assumes a kind of electric atmosphere, which suggests some analogous external phenomenon. As for Paul's companions they must have been a fiction of the narrator, who had to have someone on hand to lead Paul into the city when he was blinded.

And finally, not a few rationalist scholars reject completely all attempts at a psychological explanation and declare that Paul's conversion is and will remain an insoluble problem. Even more numerous are the Protestant scholars who openly consider it the consequence of a supernatural intervention.

279. As the reader will have noticed, all the theories which are preoccupied solely with eliminating any supernatural element delineate for us a Paul entirely different from the Paul of the documents. It is as if, in attempting to explain the conversion of Augustine, various scholars described him as a great general ruined by the envy of his colleagues, who as a consequence gave himself to God; or a great statesman defeated by his political opponents, who then dedicated himself to God; or a lover passionately but vainly devoted to a certain woman, who when rebuffed turned to God instead. No one of these theoretical Augustines would be the Augustine of the *Confessions,* who has told us in that very work how his conversion came about. And anyone who ignores this work and substitutes for it conflicting narratives may describe different types of Augustine, more or less shrewdly or skillfully, but they will all be sheer fiction, while the only historical Augustine will still remain the Augustine of the *Confessions.* The same may be said of Paul. The various Pauls portrayed in the theories mentioned above may all be more or less ingeniously drawn, but they are pure fiction. The historical Paul is the Paul of the documents.

280. Now, it is certainly very easy and very convenient to reject a statement in the documents because it is a little unmanageable, or to invent some necessary detail out of whole cloth even though it is in direct contradiction to the documents. This is the way to write historical romance, perhaps, but not history. And what is worse, this kind of romance is subject to the most humiliating refutation.

Sometimes the refutation is direct and immediate. For example, we have just noted that for Loisy Paul's companions were invented by the narrator. But Loisy dared to assert such an absurdity simply because he was a library scholar who had never attached any importance to archaeology or historical geography and who knew nothing of the customs of the Orient. Therefore he did not know that in the East no voyage of any real length is ever undertaken except in caravans. There was all the more reason to suppose that Paul had a good escort with him, since his journey was to last seven or eight days (§ 263) and he was going to Damascus not on a pleasure trip but to carry out a mission of authority and violence.

Other refutations are less obvious but no less decisive. The theories examined above give us a Paul tormented with remorse, or in great spiritual travail, or deeply influenced by Hellenist thought, etc. But these are sheer assumptions and furthermore are contradicted by all we know of Paul. Tormented by remorse? Rather he must have been jubilant both in his conscience and before God for having gotten rid of Stephen and the other enemies of the Law. Was he not the irreproachable Pharisee, intensely alive with his ideal and wholly dedicated to it? What remorse would a rabid Byzantine iconoclast of the eighth century have felt if he had been responsible for the collapse of a good number of churches on the faithful gathered within them? Making the necessary allowances, Paul on the road to Damascus was relatively in a somewhat similar frame of mind.

281. Was Paul ill at ease in the Law? We have no intention of glossing over his observations on the Law, but let us remember that they were made after the episode on the road to Damascus and not before; they are the result of that event and not its cause. To reverse the picture and assume that Paul would have dared to judge the Law in that fashion before the Damascus episode childishly begs the question. Far from being ill at ease in the Law, Paul was quite happy and comfortable in it like his rabbi colleagues described in the *Mishna*.

Would a rabbi of pure fiber like Paul, educated in the most orthodox schools of Jerusalem, be influenced by Hellenism and the oriental religions? Would his mind have been slowly corrupted by the concepts of the mystery religions or the Persian belief in the Primal Man to the point of breaking under the strain and transferring these concepts to Jesus of Nazareth? The answer is simple. Can we imagine Savonarola hailing with glee the *Carnival Songs* of Lorenzo the Magnificent? Or a Bellarmine delighting in and recommending the writings of Luther? If so, then we may perhaps imagine a rabbi like Paul accepting pagan religious concepts from any and every source. Had he not read a thousand times in the Hebrew Law that idolatry was the supreme crime for an Israelite, and that foreign cults were an adultery which the chosen nation, should it accept them, would commit against her spouse Yahweh? If it had been permitted, he would not have hesitated to repeat against all idolatrous cults the energetic gesture of Phinees, which won so much praise in the Bible (Num. 25:7 ff.; Ps. 106, *Vulg.*, 105:30; 1 Mach. 2:25, 54) and was later referred to by Paul himself (1 Cor. 10:8)? After all, it is enough to read the treatise *Abodah Zarah*, which the *Mishna* devotes to idolatrous worship, to understand historically the utter hostility with which Paul and his colleagues regarded the most tenuous ramifications of idolatry. But when his story is written *a priori* rather than according to the documents, this testimony is easily slighted.[15]

---

[15] The idea that many of the concepts Paul expresses in his epistles derive from the mystery religions seems to be one of those epidemic theories which break out now and then among scholars, and after the contagion has raged awhile it dies down and eventually disappears. The "mystery" epidemic was spread chiefly by R. Reitzenstein, in *Die hellenistischen Mysterienreligionen* 1910 (3rd edition, Leipzig, 1927), which is very rich in scientific information and very poor in logic. Among the many who followed him is A. Loisy, who, as usual, developed someone else's ideas in a series of articles (1911–1914) later gathered into one volume called *Les mystères paiens et le mystère chrétien*, Paris, 1919. Several independent scholars of great reputation remained immune from the infection, however, such as A. Harnack, A. Schweitzer, C. Clemen, Ed. Meyer (and, in part, Fr. Cumont and J. Toutain), and naturally the Catholic critics, whose reaction, however, was out of all proportion to the danger. Today traces of the epidemic remain, but it has lost much of its virulence. Certainly no one denies that Paul had some knowledge of the mystery religions and that some of the terms he uses are to be found in the terminology of these cults (i.e., μυστήριον, ἀποκάλυψις, τέλειος, γνῶσις, ἐμβατεύω, etc.). But the problem is this: in the second place, did Paul take these terms from the mystery religions or from common everyday usage; and in the first place, were the concepts they denoted for Paul the same they denoted in the mystery religions, or were they entirely different? There is nothing more treacherous in religious matters than to conclude that concepts are the same because the same or similar terms are used, or because there is some general analogy between one rite and another (the *Logos* of the Fourth Gospel, and the frequent ablutions in various religions teach us something in this regard). In any case, it is something to be considered in connection with the judgment expressed above but too easily neglected, namely, that Paul had an insuperable aversion, first as a rabbi and then as a Christian, to everything that was associated with the idolatrous practices of the pagans (cf. 2 Cor. 14–16). I do not wish to develop the question here, for it has been abundantly discussed by others. Cf. M.-J. Lagrange, in *Revue Biblique*, 1920, pp. 420–446 (a review of Loisy's *Les mystères*, etc.); J. G. Machen, *The Origin of Paul's Religion*, London, 1921, pp. 211–290; U. Fracassini, *Il misticismo greco e il cristianesimo,*

282. Consequently it has even been claimed that Paul was not such a fiery and zealous Pharisee after all, and to give this assertion some sort of foundation, it was denied that he had ever studied in Jerusalem under Gamaliel. But if it is convenient to deny arbitrarily anything that embarrasses a theory, it is all the more reasonable to refute such denials on the authority of the documents — granted always that the intention is to write history and not fiction, that the Augustine of the *Confessions* is preferred to the warrior, statesman, or lover Augustine.

The other theories that have been proposed are even more fragile, and have found few followers. Paul was not influenced to accept Jesus because he had previously assimilated the concept of the apocalyptic Messias which was widespread in later Judaism. Apart from other considerations, if we compare carefully this concept of the Messias — as set forth in the various apocalyptic writings — and Paul's concept of the Messias Jesus, as reflected in his writings, we find the two are completely different.[16]

Nor is there any more substance to the theory that Paul was psychologically conditioned by the fact that he had absorbed the Hellenist-Christian concept of the Messias Jesus which conflicted with that of the Jewish Christians. First of all, this theory makes the gratuitous assumption that the Rabbi Saul was influenced by the Hellenist Christians, for which there is no evidence, while it quite wrongly rejects his sojourn in Jerusalem before his conversion, for which there is very good evidence. And here again a comparison between Paul's belief and that held by the rest of Christianity refutes the hypothesis, for there is complete agreement between the two.[17]

283. In conclusion, then, why was Paul converted? He tells us himself, with a phrase rich in overtones: "Christ Jesus has laid hold of me" (Phil. 3:12). The Greek verb $\kappa \alpha \tau \epsilon \lambda \acute{\eta} \mu \phi \theta \epsilon \nu$ may also be translated "I was taken by surprise," "I was vanquished," "I was taken as prey," and was used to denote a person or thing unexpectedly overtaken by a given event, i.e., a soldier made prisoner, a prize won in a contest, game taken in the hunt.

He was, in short, suddenly and unexpectedly taken by the Christ Jesus who, with wisdom and patience aforethought, had watched him and trailed him, and had suddenly pounced upon him ($\kappa \alpha \tau \alpha$) and taken possession ($\lambda \alpha \mu \beta \acute{\alpha} \nu \omega$) of him. The invisible Archer had watched and stalked him from early times, for he had chosen him from his mother's womb (Gal. 1:15). On the road to Damascus, as we have seen, he took unerring aim and his arrow pierced the living flesh of the prey,

---

Citta' di Castello, 1922; L. de Grandmaison, *Jesus Christ*, Paris, 1931, II, pp. 510–561; L. Allevi, *Ellenismo e cristianesimo*, Milan, 1934.

[16] Cf. J. G. Machen, *op. cit.*, p. 173 ff.

[17] Cf. *ibid.*, p. 119 ff.

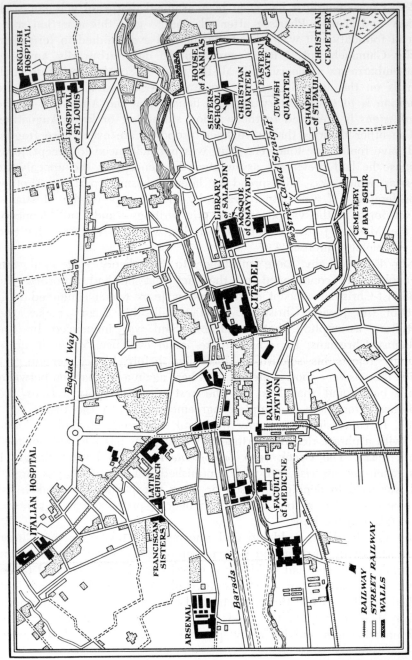

Damascus

but how that inscrutable weapon tamed and dominated and transformed its proud quarry at one blow, we do not know nor shall
we ever know.

These are God's secrets.

*   *   *

284. Led slowly by the hand (§ 266) Paul entered Damascus. Given
his weakened condition, his companions decided what he needed first
was rest, and they brought him to the house of a certain Judas,
probably the best known innkeeper in the local Jewish community.
The house was situated on one of the better streets of the city, called
"Straight" (Acts 9:11), which crossed all of Damascus from East to
West and was lined with a double portico. Considerable ruins of
the latter are still extant, and so is the ancient name of the street
translated into Arabic (*Darb al-mustaqim*), which today is narrower
but follows more or less the same route as in ancient times. In this
comfortable inn, Paul remained "for three days" and "he could not
see, and he neither ate nor drank" (*ibid.*, 9). The physician Luke could
not fail to note the physiological effects of the great encounter.

These effects were, after all, perfectly natural. After what had
happened to him, and with no idea of what the future held for him,
Paul was in a state of utter bewilderment. The darkness in his eyes
seemed also to shroud his spirit. Or rather, there was light in his
spirit, but it was indistinct, like a luminous mist in which he could
not yet discern anything definite.

He had been told that when he entered the city he would be
directed as to what he must do next (§ 265). But by whom? And
how? By a man or an angel? Would there be another vision? Paul
had no idea. And while waiting for the luminous mist to be transformed
to clear perception, as he had been promised, he prayed (*ibid.*, 11).
To whom? Unquestionably to Yawheh, the God of Israel as he had
always done in the past. But now he prayed also to Jesus, whom
he had hated so much in the past but whom he suddenly found to
be his master in the innermost recesses of his soul.

285. There was a disciple of the new religion, named Ananias, who
was highly respected both in Damascus and in Jerusalem as "an observer
of the Law" (Acts 22:12). When and under what circumstances Ananias
had accepted the new faith we do not know. He may have been one
of the Christians who fled Jerusalem to escape persecution (§ 258).
Certainly he knew Paul by reputation as the persecutor of the Christians
in Jerusalem and he also knew of his mission in Damascus (9:13–14).
Perhaps, as a prominent Christian, he would have been one of the
first Paul had to imprison. "The Lord" — Jesus — commanded him in
a vision to go to the way called Straight, to the house of Judas and

Air View of Damascus

visit a man of Tarsus, named Saul, who was at that moment praying
there.[18] When Ananias objected because of what he knew of the man,
the Lord replied: "Go, for this man is a chosen vessel to me [Hebraism
for "chosen instrument"], to carry my name among nations and kings
and the children of Israel. For I will show him how much he must
suffer for my name" (*ibid.*, 15–16).[19] And Ananias obeyed.

---

[18] At this point in the narrative we find the passage: "And he saw a man named
Ananias come in and lay his hands upon him that he might recover his sight"
(9:12). The subject of the verb *saw* is unquestionably Paul, and Ananias' actual
visit is narrated immediately afterward (verse 17). The exegetical explanation is
difficult and further complicated by the textual problem, since the entire passage
is lacking in an important codex. Some critics think it was added later from some
other source (cf. the note to § 119 on the "Western text"). If we keep the passage,
as all the critical editions do, it may be explained either as a bit of information from
the narrator himself (as the Vulgate treats it), or as a statement made to Ananias
by the Lord, who is speaking to him, but both explanations encounter serious
difficulties: they would imply a vision Paul had simultaneously with that of Ananias.
Cf. the comments on the *Acts*. Some scholars, obsessed with the idea of the mystery
religions, find a parallel for this double vision in the initiation rites described by
Apuleius (*Metamorphoses*, XII), who, however, belongs to the latter half of the
second century A.D.

[19] As we have already said (§ 269), in the third account it is not Ananias but
Christ himself who states that Paul is ordained to be the Apostle to the Gentiles:
"For I have appeared to thee for this purpose, to appoint thee to be a minister and
a witness to what thou hast seen, and to the visions thou shalt have of me; delivering
thee from the people and from the nations, to whom I am now sending thee, to open

If we accept the site commonly pointed out today as the place where the house of Ananias stood, in the Christian sector of the city, a little north of the eastern end of the way called Straight, it was a short distance from here to the house where Paul was staying. Having entered in, Ananias, "laying his hands upon him . . . said, 'Brother Saul, the Lord has sent me — Jesus, who appeared to thee on thy journey — that thou mayest recover thy sight and be filled with the Holy Spirit.' And straightway there fell from his eyes something like scales (ὡς λεπίδες), and he recovered his sight, and arose, and was baptized" (*ibid.*, 17–18).

286. This is the skeleton account given us by Luke. But certainly Ananias and Paul had many other things to say to each other even by way of mutual explanation, which have not been recorded for us. Ananias, then, is the bringer of physical and moral light to Paul. He causes him to recover his sight and "be filled with the Holy Spirit."

It is very likely that Ananias possessed the charism of "healing" (§ 216) and used it in Paul's case as he had in others. When he had laid his hands on him, there fell from Paul's blinded eyes "something like scales." Is this phrase to be taken literally or metaphorically? Did some tissuelike substance actually fall from the blinded eyes, or did Paul regain his sight *just as if* something like that had been removed? Several scholars prefer the second or metaphorical interpretation. But the whole structure of the sentence (the "like" directly governing "scales") suggests a literal meaning. It may also be noted that the narrator, the physician Luke, is always careful to observe and note physiological details. There is no foundation, however, to the theory that this is a proof of the ophthalmia, or eye disease Paul is supposed to have had (§ 198, note). Since the cure was miraculous it would have healed such an inflammation anyway, even if there had been one.

287. His body having been restored to light through the cure and his spirit through the infusion of the Holy Spirit, Paul "was baptized." He had undoubtedly heard of baptism as the basic rite for the followers of the Christ Jesus, and Ananias gave him further instructions on its efficacy (cf. Acts 22:16). Hence he received it immediately and was officially incorporated into the society of the Christ Jesus. Perhaps the baptism took place in the comfortable house of Judas, where the ample jars for ablutions stood always filled, for Damascus was well provided with water.

After presenting Paul to us as a new Christian and describing his birth into a new spiritual life, Luke takes a last clinical look at his

---

their eyes that they may turn from darkness to light and from the dominion of Satan to God; that they may receive forgiveness of sins and an inheritance among those sanctified by faith in me" (Acts 26:16–19).

physical life, and observes: "And after taking some food, he regained his strength" (*ibid.*, 19).

After three days spent without eating or drinking this was to be expected, and yet there is a subtle moral undertone to the observation. Paul, in becoming a Christian, did not become a fanatic. In fact, he was further than ever from that state of fakir exaltation which several years later induced forty of his fellow countrymen to swear that they would neither eat nor drink until they had killed him (Acts 23:12, 13). Not Paul. Having become a Christian, he eats and drinks and builds up his strength. With spiritual equilibrium there comes also physical equilibrium.

Paul's First Years as a Christian

288. Great converts to Christ have never lost their individual charac-tertistics, they have merely sublimated them. The psyche of the convert remains essentially the same but it is raised to an immeasurably loftier sphere. Francis of Assisi had been a poet before his conversion and he remained a poet after it. Ignatius of Loyola had been a soldier and he continued to be a soldier, organizing and commanding a troop to which he gave the military name of "company," and writing a manual of tactics and strategy which he called "exercises." Before the time of Francis and Ignatius and innumerable others, Paul, too, followed this rule. The "man" in Saul remained in Paul. The first was the Pharisaic Rabbi, the second was instead the Christian Apostle.

Consequently, from the very beginning his innate impetuosity thrust him immediately into action as a Christian. Could a man of his tem-perament ever have remained idle, especially after an encounter like that on the road to Damascus? In the city Paul openly joined the Chris-tians although he, too, continued to attend the synagogue. There, in one of the explanatory discourses which all present were permitted to give, he began to preach that "Jesus is the Son of God" (Acts 9:20). What Stephen had done only a few weeks before in Jerusalem, Paul was doing now in Damascus, almost as if he had taken up the moral heritage of his victim. What happened next was entirely foreseeable. "And all who heard him were amazed and said, 'Is not this he who used to make havoc in Jerusalem of those who called upon this name, and who has come here for the purpose of taking them in bonds to the chief priests?' " (*Ibid.*, 21.)

But this first endeavor as Apostle was a brief one and lasted only "for some days" (*ibid.*, 20). As we concluded above from the examination of the documents (§ 152), Paul immediately afterward left Damascus and withdrew into Arabia.

WITHDRAWAL TO ARABIA. FLIGHT FROM DAMASCUS

289. We do not know the reasons for this withdrawal into Arabia; we can only guess at them. It is not very likely that Paul left Damascus to escape the threats of the Jews incensed by his sudden conversion.

This had been too recent for him to fear such threats, which, in any case, were probably not yet evident since the Jews would not have been too well informed about the change that had taken place in him. It is possible, however, that Paul had acquaintances in some city or town of Arabia and had special reasons for going there. Or he may have gone to preach his new faith.

Bedouin Nomads in the Syrian Desert

Damascus: The City Wall With Dwelling Atop It

But what region is meant by *Arabia?* The term is a vague one, for at that time it denoted all the broad territory beyond the Jordan, extending northward as far as upper Syria, eastward to the Euphrates, and south to the Red Sea. These regions were, besides, far less deserted than they are today and boasted many prosperous centers. Did Paul go to one of these towns, not too far from Damascus? Perhaps. Then this would explain why the sojourn here is not mentioned separately in the *Acts* but is treated as part of Paul's stay in Damascus. But it may also be that the reference is to some solitary region of the Arabian desert. Some have thought of Mount Sinai (cf. Gal. 4:25). It is certainly possible that Paul, after the complete upheaval that had taken place in his soul, felt the need of solitude for a while, the better to orient himself, to adjust his thoughts and personal relationships in the new spiritual world in which he now found himself. It was not a rare thing for Jews to live alone in the desert for religious reasons. Only fifteen years after Paul's conversion, Flavius Josephus, still an adolescent, lived for three years in the desert with a hermit named Bannus for love of the ascetic life (*Life*, 11–12). Paul may have done the same thing for the reasons mentioned above.

290. This sojourn in Arabia probably lasted only a few months, after which Paul returned to Damascus. There he resumed his polemical preaching: "But Saul grew all the stronger and confounded the Jews who were living in Damascus, proving that this is the Christ" (Acts 9:22). If in the first few days after his conversion, the Jews of Damascus had had some doubts about his new attitude, these were certainly dispelled by now. Perhaps information had come in the meantime from Jerusalem which, together with his recent behavior, showed he had turned traitor completely. The shepherd had become wolf. This discovery led to the same decision Paul had taken or at least approved with regard to Stephen (§ 252). The traitor must be eliminated. Therefore "as time passed on the Jews made a plot to kill him" (*ibid.*, 23). But Paul learned of the conspiracy, probably from some Christian not suspected by the conspirators, and took the necessary precautions.

The Jews had won over to their viewpoint, perhaps with bribes, "the ethnarch of the King Aretas," and guards were set day and night at the city gates to prevent Paul's escape (§ 152). But he remained in hiding, probably in some Christian home within the walls of the city but built against the walls themselves. This custom of building houses on and against the walls existed in ancient times in the Orient (Jos. 2:15), and still persists today, especially in Damascus. One night, according to a fixed plan, Paul tucked himself the best he could into a huge basket, was lowered through a window of the house, and was set down outside the closely guarded walls.

The trick was not unusual. Huge wicker baskets were commonly used to transport loads of small objects (§ 186), as well as to lift or lower heavy loads to or down from the upper stories. Until a few years ago, travelers visiting the fortress monastery of St. Catherine on Mount Sinai were lifted up to it in a basket of this kind. David had fled in similar fashion through a window, as Paul had certainly read more than once in the Bible (1 Kings 19:12). But the ancient example of the heroic king never quite succeeded in erasing from Paul's mind the intense repugnance he felt at having to flee like a thief, and eighteen years later he recalled the episode as a painful humiliation (2 Cor. 11:30–33).

Three years had passed since his conversion. It was the year A.D. 39 (§ 152).

VISIT TO JERUSALEM. SOJOURN IN TARSUS

291. When Paul slipped out of his basket at the foot of the Damascene walls, he quickly and cautiously put as much distance as possible between himself and the city and headed south for Jerusalem. Had he gone north to Tarsus, his homeland, he would have found relatives and friends and with them comfort and security. But the homeland of his spirit was now Jerusalem, not the Jerusalem of the good Gamaliel, and much less that of the Sanhedrin, but the Jerusalem of Peter. In fact, he tells us himself that he went to the Holy City *to explore* (ἱστορῆσαι) Cephas (Gal. 1:18).

"To explore" is a rough and not entirely literal translation, but it seems to me the meaning closest to the idea of the original. The Greek root may in fact be used with reference to a captain who reconnoiters a given area for military reasons,.or figuratively for someone who wishes to become acquainted directly and somewhat thoroughly with some famous person or celebrated object.[1] If Paul went to Jerusalem, then, it was to make the personal acquaintance, and possibly to learn to know very well, the person called Cephas and also Peter. In fact, so anxious was he to know Peter that in the fifteen days he stayed with him he seemed to neglect everything else, for he tells us, "I saw none of the other apostles, except James, the brother of the Lord" (Gal. 1:19). Why was Paul so anxious to establish relations with Peter? For the moment, we may conclude that the visit was connected with the change in him begun with the vision on the Damascus road and grown increasingly deeper in the three years that followed (§ 301).

292. But when he arrived in Jerusalem Paul was met at first with great mistrust. "He tried to join the disciples, and they were all afraid of him, not believing that he was a disciple" (Acts 9:26). The mistrust was indeed well founded. Only three years before, he had laid waste the Christian community in Jerusalem (§ 259). Then there had been rumors, it is true, that he had been converted up there in Damascus, but who could tell how much truth there was in those rumors, especially since communication between Damascus and Jerusalem was not very easy at the time, first because of the war between Herod Antipas and King Aretas[2] and then because of the new regime in Damascus (§ 152). But the mistrust was short-lived, and a Christian of authority, named Joseph and also Barnabas, of the tribe of Levi and a native of Cyprus (Acts 4:36), gave official guarantee for Paul.

"But Barnabas took him and brought him to the apostles, and he told them how on his journey he had seen the Lord, that the Lord had spoken to him, and how in Damascus he had acted boldly in the name of Jesus" (*ibid.*, 9:27).

---

[1] There are several clear examples in Flavius Josephus, a contemporary of Paul. Vespasian went to the Dead Sea "for an exploration" (καθ' ἱστορίαν — *Wars of the Jews*, IV, 477; the same expression used with the same meaning occurs in III, 443). Josephus knew personally a valorous Roman soldier (ἱστόρησα — *ibid.*, VI, 81) and carefully observed the famous statue of salt into which Lot's wife had been converted (same expression, *Antiquities of the Jews*, I, 203).

[2] Cf. *Storia d'Israele*, II, p. 427 (§ 371).

This intervention on the part of Barnabas suggests that he was fully informed of Paul's conversion and subsequent activity and that he had known him for a long time. Since he was a Hellenist Jew from Cyprus, which lies opposite Tarsus, some have thought that he knew Paul from early youth, either in Tarsus or in Jerusalem at the school of Gamaliel. Barnabas' authority was decisive. But the "apostles" to whom he brought Paul could not have been the entire college of the Twelve, nor even the majority, since Paul tells us that on that occasion he had seen only Peter and James the "brother" of the Lord. It was a qualitative majority, however, for Peter was the head of the group and James enjoyed the singular prerogative of being related to Jesus.

Almost as if to confirm this newly won confidence of the Christian community Paul did as he had done in Damascus. During those fifteen days he began to dispute with the Hellenist Jews in the city, assuming once again the heritage of Stephen and in the very places where the martyr had preached. The reaction was exactly the same as that in Damascus. The Jews, indignantly recalling his quite different behavior three years earlier, "sought to kill him. When the brethren came to know this, they took him down to Caesarea and sent him away to Tarsus" (Acts 9:29–30).

293. Paul's sudden departure from Jerusalem probably satisfied the unexpressed desire of the local community. Since the persecution he had directed, the Christian community in Jerusalem had not been disturbed and was now "in peace" (*ibid.*, 31). All of a sudden here was their former persecutor disturbing that peace again, even if this time he came in the role of defender. His intentions may have been the very best, but his fiery polemical methods were not the most opportune, and the new preacher would do better to choose some other place for his efforts. If these worries were not explicitly told Paul, he certainly must have guessed them and fortunately he shared them.

Later, speaking to the angry mob of Jews in the same city, he said that during his sojourn in Jerusalem (certainly this one of the year 39) while he was praying in the Temple, he was caught up in an ecstasy and saw Jesus, who said to him: "Make haste and go quickly out of Jerusalem, for they will not receive thy testimony concerning me." In reply Paul had recalled his persecution of three years before and the execution of Stephen, as if to argue that after what had happened then his testimony today for the faith would be that much more compelling. But Jesus answered: "Go, for to the Gentiles far away I will send thee" (Acts 22:17–21). The wishes of the community and the command of the vision coincided, and so Paul's departure was immediate.

294. The journey from Caesarea, the principal port of Jerusalem, to Tarsus must have been made by sea. If, therefore, Paul says that after Jerusalem he went "into the regions of Syria and Cilicia" (Gal. 1:21), he is not referring to his itinerary at this time but merely indicating in general terms the regions he visited in the following years. His stay in Tarsus was a long one this time, lasting from 39 to 43, and the phrase just quoted implies that during this period he carried on a certain amount of missionary activity both in Tarsus and the surrounding territory (*Cilicia*) and in the country around Antioch (*Syria*). Christian communtiies in Syria and Cilicia are mentioned shortly afterward (Acts 15:23, 41) but we are not told whether they were all founded by Paul. This is especially true for those of Syria, which probably spread out from Antioch. In any case, in these various areas Paul may have strengthened already existing communities or founded new ones, without, however, being completely absorbed by this apostolic activity. For the time being his principal activity was within himself.

Actually, we know very little about the external events from Paul's conversion to the end of his stay in Tarsus, a period which lasted a good seven years (from 36 to about 43). We should like also to be able to describe the whole complex development that was taking place within Paul's spirit at this time and which was certainly much more important than the external events. But unfortunately, this spiritual growth remains jealously hidden, and we can manage only a glimpse or two, which seems almost an intrusion.

295. Luke, speaking of Jesus at about the age of two, says that in Nazareth "the child grew and became strong. He was full of wisdom and the grace of God was upon him" (Lk. 2:40). And again, when Jesus was twelve, he tells us that he "advanced in wisdom and age and grace before God and men" (*ibid.*, 52). What the physician-evangelist recounts of the Child Jesus, the historian must repeat for the Apostle Paul, from both the theological and psychological viewpoints. Jesus' birth as a man took place in Bethlehem, Paul's birth as an apostle, on the road to Damascus, but both events were followed by a period of growth and strengthening, which for Paul was this seven-year period just mentioned. Later, using the phrase of his disciple Luke, he says that all Christians must grow and become strong spiritually until they attain "perfect manhood, to the mature measure of the fullness of Christ" (Eph. 4:13).

In the Damascus vision Paul was invested with the mission of apostle, but the stunned bewilderment with which he received the investiture shows that though he already understood many things relating to it there were many more he did not know. Here, too, we have an eloquent parallel. Mary had received an even higher mission when she was chosen to be the mother of Jesus, and many things hidden from every other human creature she learned on that occasion. Nevertheless Luke — who has told us some of these things — describes the bewildered surprise of Mary and Joseph when they found the Boy Jesus in the Temple, and he tells us that "they did not understand the word that he spoke" in reply to their puzzled questioning.[3] There is no bewilderment unless there is lack of knowledge (*they did not understand*), and such a lack may exist in minds that know a great many things. Like Mary, Paul, in the period immediately following the vision on the Damascus road, was in a state of bewilderment and wonder, of ignorance mixed with knowledge, and from then on he began to "grow and become strong" as an apostle. The bewilderment yielded to wonder, the ignorance dwindled before the growing knowledge.

296. This development took place both by ordinary and extraordinary means, for grace does not do violence to nature but rather depends on its co-operation. They work together, not in fits and starts, but along a smooth and steadily ascending path. To say that Paul's theology derives only from the Damascus vision is a historical and psychological error. The vision came first both in time and in order of importance, but it was followed by various others, to which Paul alludes incidentally and almost reluctantly. Just as in the Damascus vision Paul learned, among other things, of his mission as apostle, so in subsequent visions he learned still other things especially related to that apostolate.

The rationalists are entirely free to consider these revelations purely human phenomena — a subconscious development of various concepts, the fruit of psychic exaltation, or high points in a given spiritual condition, etc. — but then they must prove that these interpretations explain historically the Paul of the documents. It is certain that these revelations constitute the essential features of the apostle, and if these are erased almost the whole figure disappears. Paul himself insists a great deal on the importance of these revelations for his apostolate, and declares specifically that the Gospel he is preaching derives from them: "For I give you to understand, brethren, that the gospel which was preached by me is not of man. For I did not receive it from man, nor was I taught it; but I received it by a revelation of Jesus Christ" (Gal. 1:11–12). This solemn declaration, which is one of the high lights of the *Epistle to the Galatians*, reappears in more or less explicit terms elsewhere (1 Cor. 11:23; 15:1–3; Eph. 3:3), and is supported by historical fact.

297. We have already mentioned two of these particular revelations, which occurred during the period under review, that is, from Paul's conversion to the year 43. One is the vision in the Temple of Jerusalem in the year 39 (§ 293). The other is the vision in which he was caught up to the third heaven and with which is associated his mysterious malady; this occurred about the year 43 (§ 199). The content of this last revelation not only is not given us, but we are told specifically it consisted of "secret words that men may not repeat." It is not to the point, therefore, to try to discuss this field of highest mysticism. On the

---

[3] Cf. *The Life of Christ*, p. 263 (§ 262).

other hand, certain of Paul's teachings during his apostolate he attributes to revelations. His teachings on the Eucharist to the faithful of Corinth he received from Christ: "For I myself have received from the Lord what I also delivered to you" (1 Cor. 11:23; note the emphasis on the pronoun *I* in the Greek text). Speaking of marriage and virginity to the same Corinthians, he gives them various criteria which are not his but the Lord's (7:10), while others are not from the Lord but his own (7:12). In another passage he states explicitly that he has no commandment to give in the name of the Lord and is speaking only as trustworthy counselor (7:25). With regard to the just who are still alive on the day of the parousia, Paul's teaching is "in the word of the Lord" (1 Thess. 4:15), with reference, most probably, to a personal revelation.

298. He is guided by revelations not only in his teaching but in external acts, especially those which are the most decisive for his ministry. He went to the Apostolic Council in Jerusalem, where he submitted for approval the Gospel he had been preaching to the Gentiles, "in consequence of a revelation" (Gal. 2:1–2). When he wanted to evangelize the province of Asia he was stopped "by the Holy Spirit" (Acts 16:6), and immediately afterward "the Spirit of Jesus" kept him from going into Bithynia (16:7). But in compensation another "vision one night" called him to Macedonia (16:9–10), and again in a vision at night the Lord appeared to him in Corinth confirming his ministry in this new territory (18:9–10). He receives other communications from the Holy Spirit during his journey to Jerusalem before his imprisonment (20:22–23; 21:4, 11). And finally, as a prisoner, two nocturnal visions, one in Jerusalem (23:11) and the other on the stormy sea (27:23), assure him he will reach Rome.

In addition to this extraordinary source of personal revelation, we must remember Paul's ordinary source, which was direct dependence on the living Church. From both sources, and not from one only, does the majestic stream of Paul's ministry flow.

299. Dependence on the living Church means, in this case, dependence on the primitive Christian catechesis, which we treated at length elsewhere.[4] We pointed out that from Paul's writings we might glean a short "Life of Jesus" independent of the canonical Gospels, inferior to them in quantity of data but not different in kind of biography.[5] The portrait of Jesus sketched incidentally in Paul's writings is a much smaller one than that in the four Gospels, but the form is the same in both instances. Where, then, did Paul derive the features of this portrait, that is, the elements of the biography and teaching of Jesus? Only from personal revelations? From them yes, but also from the early Christian catechesis.

---

[4] Cf. *ibid.*, pp. 92–98 (§§ 106–113).
[5] Cf. *ibid.*, p. 91 (§ 103).

At the beginning of his Gospel Luke informs us that before starting to write he had followed "up all things carefully from the very first [or, for a long time]" and that in doing so he had followed the example of previous narratives others had undertaken to write "even as they who from the beginning were eyewitnesses and ministers of the word have handed them down to us." Luke thus tells us that he has taken his material from the early catechesis, for the "eyewitnesses" and the "ministers of the word" he mentions were precisely the ministers of this catechesis. If Luke did this, we may well believe that as a faithful disciple of Paul he was in this as well as in other things following his master, who in the period just after his conversion must have had recourse to the common catechesis like all the others newly won to the Good Tidings.

300. But the early catechesis derived from the whole apostolic college, from which alone it received its authority and value. Its various ramifications had not yet appeared at the time of Paul's conversion. What later became the particular catechesis of John was still within the entire patrimony of the apostolic catechesis; much less was it possible to speak of a catechesis peculiar to Paul and addressed especially to the Gentiles. Now this "global" catechesis of the apostolic college could be attributed, practically speaking, to the head and representative of that college, Peter. Peter's catechesis, for which we have clear testimony in the *Acts*,[6] was still the common catechesis of the apostolic college. It was later, with the diffusion of Christianity, that this common fund spread out in parallel ramifications (*Paul, John*) more suited to the new branches sprouting from the main trunk of the Church. In addition, it was still handed on by word of mouth; the first official writing did not appear until shortly afterward in the *Logia* of Matthew, which is our first canonical Gospel.

Was Paul familiar with some writing that dealt with the life and teachings of Jesus? We have no certain data in this regard. These writings, of varying character and origin, were "many" even before the years 62–63, when Luke published his Gospel (Lk. 1:1). If Paul did read any of them, it must have been later, when his missionary journeys were already in full career. In the first years after his conversion he could not have read them for the simple reason that they did not yet exist. The scant decade intervening between the death of Jesus and Paul's visit to Jerusalem to visit Peter (30–39), was too short a time for such writings to have been produced and circulated.

301. From this documentary information, we may draw some conclusions regarding Paul's reason for coming to "explore" Peter. We have already said in general that this was somehow connected with his conversion and consequent spiritual rebirth (§ 291). We may now state

6 Cf. *ibid.*, p. 97 (§ 113).

more specifically that he undoubtedly desired to consult the one who, besides being head of the Apostles, was also the chief source of the common catechesis.

The first rudiments of this catechesis Paul had received from Ananias when he was baptized (§ 287). He must have learned other elements from the faithful of Damascus during his two sojourns in that city, and later his knowledge widened and became surer in his contacts with the Christian communities of Syria (§ 294). But what he learned from these external sources must have been summed up and fused with inner revelations. The information in the catechesis confirmed the visions Paul had during this period, and in turn the visions enabled him to penetrate ever more deeply the inner significance of the catechesis.

Let us take as an example the rite of the Eucharist, which Paul said had been given to him by the Lord (§ 297). This was a historical fact in the life of Jesus for he had instituted the Eucharist "on the night on which he was betrayed," and as such it was certainly included in the instruction on the life of Jesus given the catechumens in preparation for baptism. In addition, it was also a part of the liturgy, for the gatherings of the Christian communities were based essentially on this rite. Did Paul not learn of it, then, when he was prepared for baptism by Ananias? Did he not join in the celebration of the rite when he took part in the gatherings of the faithful in Damascus and Jerusalem, and later in Syria and elsewhere? There would seem to be no doubt that he did. Then how is it true that he received the teaching on the Eucharist "from the Lord"? It is legitimate to assume that he was absorbing this doctrine from within and without at the same time, that is, from personal revelation and from the liturgical catechesis. One source confirmed and clarified the other, and Paul, combining the two, ascribed the whole teaching to its highest source. The mystical doctrine which he sets forth now and then on the Eucharist (1 Cor. 10:16–17) seems to derive from particular revelations rather than from the general catechesis. Similar assumptions may be made with regard to his teachings on matrimony, baptism, etc.

302. Nevertheless, the supernatural enlightenment Paul received was an exceptional source of instruction. Paralleling it in part was the ordinary source, the catechesis. The personal revelations communicated just so much, but certainly not all that Paul would have wished. They had to be supplemented by a careful study of the catechesis. And there was a great deal Paul needed to know as an ex-rabbi, as a Christian, and as an apostle.

As an ex-rabbi he possessed an excellent knowledge of the Bible, but transferred now to Christian doctrine, many things must have suddenly seemed obscure to him at first in the over-all vision of the divine economy for the redemption of man. If the Messias was Jesus of

Nazareth, what was to be the fate of Israel, which had rejected him? What was to become of the Law of Moses after the coming of the Messias? What would be the fate of the pagan peoples who gave no thought at all either to the Law or to the Messias? Then, there were many details to be learned both of the life and the teachings of the Messias Jesus, which had surely been foreshadowed in the Messianic prophecies in Scripture. Did not a deep knowledge of the actions and sayings of Jesus[7] confirm his Messianic dignity in the light of the Bible? Nor was this enough. The Messias Jesus had established certain rites which were to be performed by the faithful, and he had instituted a kind of hierarchy to direct those who believed in him. But what were these rites exactly, how many were there, and what precisely was their spiritual value? How did they fit within the general framework of Jesus' teaching? How was this hierarchy constituted? What relation was there between this hierarchy of the Messianic time and the previous theocratic-national hierarchy of the people of Israel?

These questions and many others undoubtedly came to Paul's mind in the first period of his conversion. Many of them were answered in the personal revelations granted him, and by the early catechesis; and finally he sought the source of this catechesis, and went up to Jerusalem to visit Peter.

303. During the fifteen days spent in "exploring" Peter, a great deal was confirmed and clarified for Paul, and he learned many new things also. It is not difficult to imagine Paul eagerly posing question after question, bringing up one topic after another, and Peter answering him with the serene certainty of the eyewitness and the impassioned sadness of one who loves.

Perhaps on some sunny afternoon they go out of the house together, and when they have gone beyond the northern wall of the city, Peter points to a rocky knoll near the city gate and says simply: "Golgotha." Then slowly and with infinite sadness he perhaps murmurs half to himself, "His mother was there . . . and John . . . I was not!"

Possibly they walk to a tomb of a type common in Palestine, set a short distance away from the mound. And Peter says: "Here is where they brought him as soon as he had died. But after the Sabbath, the women came, and his body was not there. Mary ran to tell me and I rushed here with John. . . . I went in first, there, through that little outer door. His body was not there, but I 'saw the linen cloths lying

---

[7] Paul has preserved one saying (*logion*) of Jesus for us (Acts 20:35): "It is more blessed to give than to receive," which he quoted in a discourse in the year 58 to the elders of Ephesus convened at Miletus. His manner of quoting it suggests that his hearers were familiar with it. Perhaps they had heard it before from Paul himself. Whether Paul learned it from the catechesis, or from Peter, or from some other source we do not know. It occurs nowhere else in the New Testament.

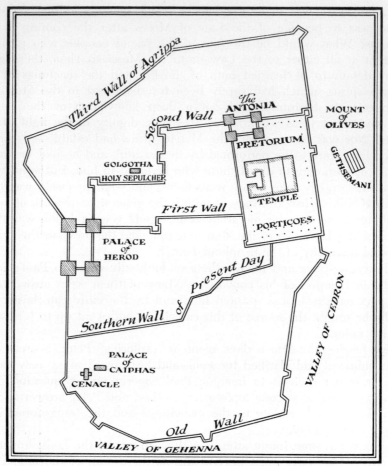

Site of Christ's Passion

there, and the handkerchief which had been about his head, not lying with the linen cloths, but folded in a place by itself' (Jn. 20:6–7). I came away. Mary stayed . . . and a little later she saw him, there near that tree, and she spoke with him . . . and she ran to tell us all, but we . . . did not believe her. . . ." They come back into the city then and traversing the greater part of it go toward the eastern end. As they walk along Peter continues his story: "But on the same day, he appeared to me too. . . ." Perhaps Paul interrupts here to say: "Yes, I know. He was seen by you, and after that by the Twelve. Then he was seen by more than five hundred brethren at one time, many of whom are with us still, but some have fallen asleep. After that he was seen by James, then by all the Apostles. . . ." And Peter in his turn interrupts: "And you saw him too, on the road to Damascus."

"Yes," Paul replies, "as you know 'last of all, as by one born out of due time, he was seen also by me'" (1 Cor. 15:5–8).

304. As they emerge from the city again, they perhaps go down into the Cedron valley and climb up the road beside the Temple to the garden of Gethsemani. Peter continues: "That night, after the Paschal supper, we all came here. It was a place he loved. Most of us went to sleep in that little hut over there near the entrance . . . but he told me and James and John to follow him further into the garden. . . . And when he had come under that olive tree, he 'began to feel dread and to be exceedingly troubled. . . .' And he moved away from us a little, about a stone's throw, and fell to the ground and began to pray: 'Father, if it is possible, let this cup pass away from me. . . .'"

Paul gazes in silence a long time at the spot Peter has pointed out to him, and murmurs perhaps: ". . . in the days of his earthly life, with a loud cry and tears, (he) offered up prayers and supplications to him who was able to save him from death" (Heb. 5:7).

Peter's face is once more veiled with sadness as he adds: "Yes, brother Paul. And while he was praying with a cry and tears, the three of us got lazy and careless and fell asleep. Every time he wakened us, we went back to sleep again. Then Judas came with the soldiers. They seized and bound him, there, between those two olive trees. . . . I attacked one of them and cut off his ear with my sword — but he healed him. Then we all ran away . . . all of us . . . and I with the rest of them. . . ."

305. They leave Gethsemani in silence and walk over the same route taken by the Master on that last night. Finally they reach the south-western quarter of the city and stand in front of the high priest's house. Approaching the door, Peter points inside to the courtyard, saying: "Here — they took him in here to judge him. And they locked him in that cell there at the end of the courtyard. He was in there several hours, and he was mocked and struck and spit upon. I was pacing back and forth between this entrance and the courtyard. Three times — do you understand, brother Paul? — three times I said I did not know him. Then the rooster crowed, just as he had said it would, but I kept on denying him. . . . And it crowed again, as they were taking him back into the cell after they had questioned him. And he looked at me — as only he could. Not a word, not a single word did he say. . . . But I could not bear that look. . . . I was completely undone. Somehow I crept out here and leaned against this corner of the wall, right here, and wept. O how I wept that night, and how I weep every night when I hear the crowing of a cock."

Paul, too, is deeply moved, and perhaps he answers: "My brother, the Lord has forgiven you. But what shall I say of myself? You at least did not persecute him. But I . . . I 'am not worthy to be called an apostle, because I persecuted the Church of God'" (1 Cor. 15:9).

Peter says: "Do not say this, Paul. You had never seen him in the glory of the transfiguration, as I had seen him. You never saw him humble himself to wash your feet as I had seen him do to me. Come, I will show you now where that happened."

306. Peter takes Paul to a humble dwelling not far from the house of the high priest. They mount to the second floor and enter a large room (Mk. 14:15) where Peter explains: "Here we held our last supper. John and I had made the preparations (Lk. 22:8). Jesus' couch was there in the center of the semicircle. I was on one side of him and John on the other.[8] And there, beside John, was Judas. . . . We began to argue who was first among us, and Jesus, as if to answer us, got up and girding up his robe, he began to wash our feet. He began with me. . . . You understand, Paul? He began to wash my feet. . . ."

"And did he wash the feet of Judas?" Paul asks.

"Yes, Judas' too, and then — then he broke the bread in commemoration of himself. All this you know, Paul. . . ."

"Yes, Jesus himself has revealed it to me. On the night in which he was betrayed (he) took bread, and giving thanks broke, and said, 'This is my body which shall be given up for you; do this in remembrance of me.' In like manner also the cup, after he had supped, saying, 'This cup is the new covenant in my blood; do this as often as you drink it, in remembrance of me' (1 Cor. 11:23–25). But tell me, Peter, what did you think when you heard these words?"

"For a moment we were stunned. But then we remembered a discourse Jesus had given us near Capharnaum many months before, when he had told us we must eat his flesh and drink his blood to have life everlasting. Many disciples at that time were scandalized and left Jesus, but we stayed. And when Jesus said to us: 'Don't you want to go too?' I answered, 'Lord, to whom shall we go? Thou hast words of everlasting life, and we have come to believe and to know that thou art the Christ, the Son of God' (Jn. 6:68–69). Bless those words! In this room, that night, the Lord's mysterious discourse at Capharnaum was suddenly very clear."

For a long time, they remain in thoughtful silence in the upper room, and then Peter, pulling himself away from his memories says: "My brother, it is already late. Let us go home. And obeying the words of the Lord, we shall break bread together with our brethren this evening in memory of him."

307. Though Paul's growth in strength and wisdom as an apostle is based on these two elements we have been discussing, namely, the revelations made to him directly and the apostolic catechesis, we must not exclude his own personal contribution. For in his mind he meditated and worked over and molded these two elements, adapting them to the

---

[8] Cf. *The Life of Christ,* p. 570 (§ 542).

field of action to which he had been called. At the time of his conversion, Ananias had told him in the name of Christ that he was to be the Apostle to the Gentiles (§ 285), and this had been confirmed for him in the vision in the Temple (§ 293). Now the God of the Jews and of the Gentiles was one God, and their redeemer Christ was one and the same, and therefore the teaching to be given one and the other must be one and the same; only the method of presentation might differ. Paul, ordained for the Gentiles, prepared a special method for presenting Christ's teachings to them. To this end, some of the elements he wished to emphasize may have been given him in relevations, while others derived from his study of the basic catechesis. He himself added his own conclusions, associations, and reflections, for his mind was filled from his youth with meditation on Scripture. From this long labor emerged what Paul calls firmly "my Gospel."[9]

308. Paul's case is not unique. Fifty years later the Apostle John finished "his Gospel" after a long labor much like Paul's. John's particular catechesis also derives from the basic apostolic teaching, but the elements he selected were quite different from those chosen by the three preceding synoptic evangelists. John worked over his material for more than half a century, bringing out concepts not particularly stressed before and using completely new terms, just as Paul had done. The preparation of the new type of catechesis, or the "new" Gospel of John, had the practical aim of defending Christ's doctrine against its new Gnostic enemies, just as Paul's aim was its diffusion among the Gentiles. John's Gospel takes a different road from that of the Synoptics, but it arrives at the same goal. Paul's catechesis beats a path different from Peter's, but both come to the same place in the end.[10]

309. This identity of goal was openly recognized by both Paul and the other Apostles and agreed upon, as it were, on one solemn occasion. At the end of his first missionary journey, when Paul went to the Apostolic Council in Jerusalem (§ 355), he did so in order to receive official approval of "his gospel" from the elders of the first Christian community: "And I conferred with them on the gospel which I preach among the Gentiles, but separately with the men of authority; lest perhaps I should be running, or had run, in vain" (Gal. 2:2). The result was all that Paul could have wished or expected:

". . . the men of authority laid no further burden [i.e., correction] on me. On the contrary, when they saw that to me was committed the

---

[9] The expression appears in Rom. 2:16, 16:25; 2 Tim. 2:8; and as "our gospel" — an editorial plural — in 2 Cor. 4:3; 1 Thess. 1:5; 2 Thess. 2:14; and in equivalent expressions in 1 Cor. 15:1; Gal. 1:11, 2:2. As for the ancient opinion given by Jerome, that the phrase "my gospel" refers to Luke, cf. *The Life of Christ*, p. 114 ff. (§ 135).

[10] For the relation between John's "new" Gospel and the Synoptics, cf. *The Life of Christ*, p. 145 ff. (§ 164 ff.).

gospel for the uncircumcised, as to Peter that for the circumcised (for he who worked in Peter for the apostleship of the circumcised worked also in me among the Gentiles) — and when they recognized the grace that was given to me, James and Cephas and John, who were considered the pillars, gave to me and to Barnabas the right hand of fellowship, that we should go to the Gentiles, and they to the circumcised" (*ibid.*, 6–9).[11]

From this episode, which Paul recounts to the Galatians he has evangelized, he draws a clear conclusion (*ibid.*, 7–9). If anyone should come to the Galatians to preach another gospel different from that of Paul, let him be accursed, even if he were an angel come down from heaven. And the reason is that there "is not another gospel" (*ibid.*, 7). In short, what Paul calls "my gospel" was substantially the same as that of Peter and the elders of the Church of Jerusalem[12] and had their full approval.

310. To sum up, then, this is more or less the way we may reconstruct the period from Paul's conversion to the end of his sojourn in Tarsus (A.D. 36–43). His active apostolate during this time was probably quite limited. The work of preparation and formation for his future apostolate, however, which we have just attempted to examine, must have been very intense. If his stay in Arabia was spent in some desert place and lasted some time, it was well suited to favor this inner formation. But even during his sojourns in Damascus and Tarsus, he progressed and attained increasingly "perfect manhood, to the mature measure of the fullness of Christ" (§ 295).

And now he was ready. To begin, he awaits only some divine bidding, like the soldier who has oiled and readied his weapons and waits only the nod of his commander to plunge into battle. As for the world, what did it matter to him any longer? The greatest rewards the world could offer were for him as σκύβαλα (§ 170), in comparison with love for Christ. "With Christ I am nailed to the cross. It is now no longer I that live, but Christ lives in me" (Gal. 2:19–20). But there is yet much to do. What is lacking of the sufferings of Christ must be filled up (Col. 1:34), completed by sufferings with him and for him in the propagation of his Gospel. His greatest desire would be "to depart and to be with Christ, a lot by far the better" (Phil. 1:23). But he must be patient and suffer and labor for Christ himself, that is, for his faithful (*ibid.*, 24). And so he is "hard pressed from both sides" — and caught between

---

[11] The elders added to this division of labor a practical recommendation that Paul as he worked among the Gentiles send some material assistance to the poor of the community of Jerusalem: "provided only that we should be mindful of the poor, the very thing I was eager to do" (Gal. 2:10). The community in Jerusalem was in fact in very straitened circumstances (§ 317). Paul had already brought them the collection from Antioch (§ 154), but their circumstances remained difficult for many years, and Paul never forgot to collect help from the Gentile communities for the poor of the mother church.

[12] A similar thought is implicit in 1 Cor. 15:11.

his desire to be united with Christ in the world beyond and to work for him here on earth. Yet he is serene. Whatever happens, "Christ will be glorified in my body, whether through life or through death. For to me to live is Christ and to die is gain" (*ibid.*, 20–21).

Who was more worthy to grasp in his hand dominion over the world, a man of Paul's spirit or the emperor on the Palatine, with his thirty-odd legions scattered throughout the known world? If the world is ruled by thought, the answer is Paul; if it is ruled by force, then Caesar wins.

History has chosen between the two.

ANTIOCH

311. While Paul was preparing himself in Tarsus, Christ was preparing the field of his apostolate.

In persecuting the Church in Jerusalem, Paul had feared, with complete justification, an increasing diffusion of the new religion. The Christians who fled Jerusalem to escape Paul's persecution scattered not only through Palestine, but traveled "all the way to Phoenicia and Cyprus and Antioch, speaking the [Gospel] word to none except to Jews only" (Acts 11:19). The refugees, then, did spread the faith, but only among the *Jews*, which is the term Luke uses for the followers of the Jewish religion in general, whether they are Hellenists of the Diaspora or Palestinians. Apparently these missionary refugees thought the rule Christ had followed in his earthly life, who had been sent "to the lost sheep of the house of Israel" (Mt. 15:24) and not, directly, to the pagans, applied also to them. In the meantime, however, the new religion had penetrated Samaria, a region which had become heretical in ancient times and pagan in recent times. In addition, Peter himself, in Caesarea, had given Baptism to the centurion Cornelius, who, though a "proselyte" of Judaism, was a pagan by birth, as were his relatives and friends (Acts 10:24, 48). Unquestionably the horizon of Christian teaching was widening even in Palestine. But the most decisive growth, which was to mark the beginning of the world-wide avalanche, occurred outside the holy land of Israel.

312. Among our refugee missionaries, there were some who were "Cyprians and Cyreneans, who on reaching Antioch began to speak to the Greeks[13] also, preaching the Lord Jesus" (11:20). These hardy souls who addressed themselves to the pagan Greeks were Hellenist Jews, natives of Cyprus or Cyrene. We do not know them by name, but it is very possible that some of them are named shortly afterward, when the prominent members of the Christian community of Antioch are

---

[13] The reading "Greeks" ("Ελληνας) alternates in the codices with "Hellenists" ('Ελληνιστάς); almost all the critical editions prefer the former, and rightly so because in the context the contrast is between the *Greeks* (pagans) and the *Jews*, not the Hellenists and Palestinian Jews.

listed: "Simon, called Niger, and Lucius of Cyrene, and Manahen, the foster-brother of Herod the tetrarch" (13:1). We have no other information concerning them, but we may suppose, for reasons which are neither certain nor negligible, that the Simon called Niger is the same Simon who a few years before had helped Jesus to carry his cross.[14] On the other hand, there is no basis for the theory some have advanced that Lucius the Cyrene is Luke the author of the *Acts*. In the first place, the name is not the same — Lucius is not the equivalent of Luke — and neither is the country of origin, for the early testimonies invariably give Antioch as Luke's native city but never Cyrene. If Luke was not among the Cyprians and Cyreneans who first had the courage to preach Christ to the "Greeks" of Antioch, however, he was certainly one of the most precious and eager conquests of the new religion and he was both a Greek and an Antiochene (cf. § 317, note).

313. This zeal immediately bore abundant fruit. "And the hand of

---

[14] The reasons are substantially these. We noted (cf. *The Life of Christ*, p. 112, § 133; p. 632, § 604) that Paul in his *Epistle to the Romans* sends especially affectionate greetings to a certain Rufus and his mother and that these two persons were respectively the son and wife of Simon of Cyrene. Listed just before a Lucius who is from Cyrene we find this *Simeon* (equivalent to Simon) described with the epithet *Niger* or dark (of face). The suspicion arises that he is from Cyrene too, like Lucius, and that the epithet indicates he was from North Africa. But, we repeat, this is only conjecture.

Antioch of Syria — A Panorama

the Lord was with them, and a great number believed and turned to the Lord" (11:21). The news of this spiritual flowering reached Jerusalem and the authorities there sent Barnabas to Antioch. We know that Barnabas came originally from Cyprus (§ 292), like some of those preaching in Antioch, and undoubtedly he shared their opinion about the necessity of evangelizing the pagans. What he saw when he reached Antioch filled him with joy, "and he exhorted them all to continue in the Lord with steadfast heart; for he was a good man and full of the Holy Spirit and of faith" (11:23–24). But besides this, the good Barnabas was a practical man, and he immediately saw that hard work was necessary if a flowering so full of promise was to be followed by a rich harvest. The first need was for laborers for the harvest, as Jesus had mentioned (Mt. 9:37–38). But where to find them, well prepared and suited to this work, that is, free from the nationalistic prejudices against the pagans common among the Jewish Christians?

One such laborer Barnabas did know, and he was most suitable from every viewpoint. But for some years now he had been living apart and in a distant place, and who could tell whether he would be willing to move to Antioch? Barnabas decided to try him anyway, and the better to succeed he sent neither letters nor messengers but went himself to invite the future evangelizer in person. And here are the few brief words with which this great event is described for us: "And he went forth to Tarsus to look for Saul, and on finding him he brought him to Antioch" (Acts 11:25–26).

314. If Barnabas chose Paul on that occasion, it must have been because he knew that at his conversion Ananias had foretold his apostolate among the Gentiles (§ 285). The harvest in Antioch seemed custom-made for one who was to evangelize the pagans. Whatever the future field of Paul's activity was to be, Antioch was the entrance gate. After this first encounter, Paul, "filled with the Holy Spirit and with faith," would be ready to go where he would. Paul's visitor probably used some such argument as this when he had found him in Tarsus. For his part, Paul, who was awaiting some divine bidding, recognized it in the invitation of his old friend. In fact, it seemed as though the one who had introduced him to the Apostles in Jerusalem (§ 292) was now introducing him to the pagan world for which he knew he was ordained. And so Paul went with Barnabas to Antioch. It was the year 43.

315. What happened after Paul's arrival in Antioch is also told us with an economy of words out of all proportion to the information they contain: "And for a whole year they took part in the meetings of the church and taught a great multitude. And it was in Antioch that the disciples were first called 'Christians'" (*ibid.*, 26). In the "great multitude" mentioned here there must have been not only pagans of the lower classes but also those of some social standing — as, for example,

Luke – and perhaps a few wealthy aristocrats. The event was of such extent and renown, that it gave rise to the name "Christian."

The epithet was undoubtedly coined by the pagans, not as a religious denomination but merely as an everyday description and not without a suspicion of good-natured mockery. The Antiochenes, seeing the "great multitude" gathering to follow the "Christos," considered them almost his "party" and called its members *Christianoì*, an epithet similar to "Caesareans," "Pompeians," given to the followers of Caesar's or Pompey's party, etc. Some scholars have thought the epithet was fashioned by the Roman magistrates of Antioch, because the suffix – *ianoì* – is of Latin origin, while the Greek suffix would have given us a word like *Chrìstioi* or *Christikoì*. But the conclusion is not a necessary one, for there are other examples of mixed Greek and Latin epithets, which reflect the influence of the language of the governors on the language of the region.[15] It was, then, a popular name without any religious connotation, but it gives us a glimpse of the extent of the event which inspired it.

316. This was also the first permanent result of Paul's apostolic activity. That "whole year" in which he and Barnabas worked intensely among the pagans of Antioch produced something which already bears Paul's imprint, namely, its everlastingness. It is moving to note that while the Christian community of Antioch disappeared through the centuries, absorbed in the whirlpool of human events, its name "in the world endureth still and shall endure" (*Inferno,* II, 60–61). This symbolic everlastingness appears as soon as Paul appears, almost as if it were his seal. As long as there is in the world a disciple of the Messias Jesus, he will be called by the name given the "great multitude" conquered by Paul in Antioch. The *nomen* (name) is an omen.

In Palestine, the Jews still called the disciples of Christ "Nazoreans," and the epithet given them in Antioch seemed to foretell the new roads the new faith was to travel. The motive center of Christianity in the world now became Antioch, the spiritual arsenal set up as an advance post in the heart of paganism. Jerusalem remained the mother church, both of the Nazoreans and the *Christianoì*, the general headquarters of the Good Tidings, but in practice the weapons to conquer the world for the Gospel were to come from the field staff rather than headquarters, from Hellenist Antioch rather than Jewish Jerusalem. When Christian liturgy in the seventh century instituted in Gaul a commemoration

---

[15] A summary of the question is to be found in A. Ferrua's *Christianus sum,* in *Civiltà Cattolica,* 1933, II, pp. 552–556; III, pp. 13–26. Naturally, some have denied the Antiochene origin of the epithet "Christian," maintaining instead that it was of later origin. Half a century ago, the Protestant Blass replied: *Vanissima ipsaque specie argumenti destituta sunt quae contra fidem huius testimonii Lucani e quibusdam prolata sunt.* There is not much point in arguing with those who make negation a fetish. It gives them an importance they do not deserve.

of the Antiochene chair of Peter, in addition to the older feast of the Roman chair, it rightly fixed the itinerary of Christianity's general staff, which in its gradual transfer from Jerusalem to Rome deposited its spiritual ammunition for a time in the arsenal of Antioch.

JOURNEY OF THE COLLECTION. PREPARATIONS IN ANTIOCH

317. The relations between the new church in Antioch and the mother church remained very cordial. In fact the good news Barnabas sent to Jerusalem prompted the departure for Antioch of some members of the community who were distinguished for the charism of prophet, for it was within the very function of those so gifted to spend themselves for the good of others (§ 215). And they came, not only to strengthen the new community spiritually but to seek material help for the Christians of Jerusalem. In the Holy City the faithful were living in great poverty. This was caused in part perhaps by their holding their property in common (§ 249 ff.), which after some time must have caused serious inconveniences. But an even greater factor was the first signs of the famine already raging in various regions of the Roman Empire (§ 154).

The famine was foretold by Agabus, one of the "prophets" who had come from Jerusalem. He spoke, no doubt, in virtue of his charism at one of the liturgical gatherings of the Antiochene Christians. It is probable according to some of the documents[16] that our narrator Luke was also present at this gathering. The announcement was made on such authority and the fact was so compelling that there was no discussion. It was decided to send help to the mother church, almost in recompense for the spiritual help received from her. All of the disciples gave according to their means and the sum was sent to Jerusalem with Barnabas and Paul.

This is the journey of the collection and it took place in 44 (§ 154).

318. Their stay in Jerusalem was not very long, both because their mission was merely to consign and distribute the help sent from Antioch and in particular because the community in Jerusalem was now being harassed by the persecution of Herod Agrippa. James the Elder, the brother of John the Evangelist, had been killed.[17] Peter had been imprisoned and miraculously freed, and to escape further arrest he had

---

[16] At this point in the narrative in the *Acts* (11:27–28) four or five codices and versions insert this passage: "There was much joy [at the arrival of the charismatics of Jerusalem]. When we had all gathered together, one of them named Agabus spoke, saying . . . " Several critics consider this passage authentic; if it is, it must be added to the we-sections (§ 92), and it would be the first of them. Also, it would indicate that Luke was already a Christian at this time, i.e., in the year 44.

[17] John the Evangelist was also killed at this time according to a few more imaginative critics who have their own reasons for getting rid of him in a hurry (cf. *The Life of Christ*, p. 136, § 156).

gone "to another place" (Acts 12:17). The only Apostle left in the city
was James the Less, "the brother of the Lord," protected by the great
veneration the people had for him. The ordinary faithful had either
fled or were living more or less in hiding. The death of Agrippa, shortly
after Peter's flight, probably occurred while Barnabas and Paul were
still in Jerusalem (§ 154).

In these circumstances fraught with danger, Paul had no opportunity
to "explore" Peter again or any of the other Apostles. Yet he must have
gained something in knowledge of the historical catechesis during this
new visit to the holy places. When he and Barnabas set out again for
Antioch they were no longer alone, for they were "taking with them
John, who was surnamed Mark" (ibid., 25). He is the future author of
the Second Gospel. We know that he was the cousin of Barnabas, and
that the home of his mother, Mary, in Jerusalem was a meeting place
for Christians. In fact, Peter took refuge there right after his miraculous
escape from prison.[18] We also know that Mark was probably the youth
who fled naked when Jesus was arrested in Gethsemani[19] and that both
the house in which the Last Supper was held and Gethsemani itself
may have been the property of his family.[20] May we not speculate a
little on the information Paul received from an eyewitness like Mark?
He must have gathered a number of significant details in Mary's house,
which he undoubtedly visited several times if, in fact, he did not lodge
there with Barnabas who was related to the family. The very fact that
Mark decided to follow them to Antioch might well have been the consequence of the zeal-filled conversations held in that house, where
everything reminded one of Jesus. It is likely, then, that this visit to
Jerusalem was of some use to Paul as a new "exploration," not of Peter
but of other authoritative witnesses.

319. Mark followed Barnabas and Paul to Antioch, as Paul had followed Barnabas (§ 314), to be a laborer in the spiritual vineyard. But
in the meantime, the horizons had grown wider and the projects more
numerous. The community in Antioch was seething with life, an expansion beyond its limits was vaguely foreseeable, and new workers
therefore were most opportune. The conversations in Mary's house in
Jerusalem had won Mark to these new prospects, but did he possess
the long and special preparation that Paul had when he was called from
Tarsus by Barnabas?

At first all went well. Back in Antioch the three resumed their zealous
activity and this continued for an indefinite time. One day, however,
the divine bidding for which they had been dimly and somewhat fear-
fully waiting became clearly evident. During a liturgical gathering, at

---

18 Cf. *The Life of Christ*, p. 107 (§ 127).
19 *Ibid.*, pp. 113–114 (§ 134); pp. 593–594 (§ 561).
20 *Ibid.*, p. 560 (§ 535); p. 586 (§ 554).

Antioch: View From Mt. Silpius

which Barnabas, Simeon Niger, Lucius the Cyrenean, Manahen (§ 312), Paul, and others gifted with charisms were present, "the Holy Spirit said, 'Set apart for me Saul and Barnabas unto the work to which I have called them'" (Acts 13:2). The Spirit must have spoken through one of the charismatics present, and the authenticity of the message was recognized by the other "prophets and teachers" gathered with them (*ibid.*, 1). In all probability it was not unexpected but corresponded to some prayer of the community or to some private revelation previously received by Barnabas and Paul. The ardor of spiritual conquest had been kindling the community for some time and they had been making plans and praying to God to know his will. He revealed it as we have seen.

320. After this illumination from on high, various days must have been spent making and discussing plans and preparing the means and methods for a successful missionary enterprise. To what pagan region should they go? To Cyprus, to southern or central Asia Minor, to Ionia, to Macedonia or Achaia? All of these regions must have been thoughtfully considered, the advantages and disadvantages they offered carefully weighed; what Jewish communities were there to which the missionaries might go before addressing themselves to the pagans; what acquaintances they had in those communities to whom letters of recommendation might be addressed. All the various angles were considered, for if those fervent Christians were endowed with charisms, they were also endowed with great practical good sense, and while they contemplated the reign of Christ in heaven, they squarely faced the realities on earth. But none of this preparation is narrated for us. We are told only of the election of Paul and Barnabas, and that "having fasted and prayed and laid their hands upon them, they let them go" (*ibid.*, 3).

The discussion did not produce a plan complete in every detail. The more distant and difficult regions like Macedonia and Achaia had undoubtedly been rejected, and it was agreed that for a first attempt it might be wise to begin with an easier territory and then proceed further if all went well at the beginning. If they began with the more modest course, the Holy Spirit would direct the missionaries to other areas. The first stopping place was to be Cyprus for obvious reasons. Barnabas was from Cyprus, and there were "Cyprians" among those who had first preached to the "Greeks" of Antioch (§ 312). Paul himself, if he had not on occasion actually visited the island, which lay just opposite Tarsus, might easily have had acquaintances there. Their contacts were ready made, then, in Cyprus and this was a great advantage. After Cyprus, the missionaries could decide where to go next.

Thus began Paul's first missionary journey. It was the year 45 (§ 155).

The First Missionary Journey

321. There is a subtle suggestion in Luke's narrative that only two of the three who set out were missionaries. "So they [i.e., Paul and Barnabas] sent forth by the Holy Spirit, went to Seleucia and from there sailed to Cyprus. On their arrival at Salamis they began to preach the word of God in the synagogues of the Jews; and they had also John as assistant" (ὑπηρέτην — Acts 13:4–5). So it was only Barnabas and Paul who were "sent forth by the Holy Spirit," and under his guidance began their activity in Salamis. But John, or Mark, did not enjoy this prerogative; he was simply the "assistant" to the two true missionaries. This serves to prepare the reader for Mark's future defection.

The route taken by the three travelers was the usual one. From Antioch they went to its harbor Seleucia (§ 31) and sailed from there to Salamis on the island of Cyprus (§ 35). There their missionary activity began.

CYPRUS

322. The first evangelists, and Paul in particular, always went first to the Jews to preach the Messias Jesus, and if they rejected the message, then turned to the pagans. The nation which had been the chosen one of God had a right to this priority even though the Messias Jesus had extended its privileges to all nations. Once this right had been duly respected, no other privilege was reserved for the Jews, who were now made equal with all the other nations. The best way to reach the Jews was to attend the synagogue and take advantage of the custom which permitted anyone present to address the gathering.[1] The procedure is described by Luke in his account of Paul's discourse in the synagogue of Antioch of Pisidia (§ 331).

Paul invariably followed this custom. In his discourses in the synagogues he always tried to convince the Jews on the basis of Holy Scripture that the Messias they foretold was Jesus of Nazareth, for he fulfilled in himself all that the Scriptures had attributed to him. It was, therefore, a systematic, historical-biblical exposition, set forth in the usual method of rabbinical exegesis (§ 77 ff.). Sometimes

---

[1] Cf. *The Life of Christ*, p. 62 (§ 67).

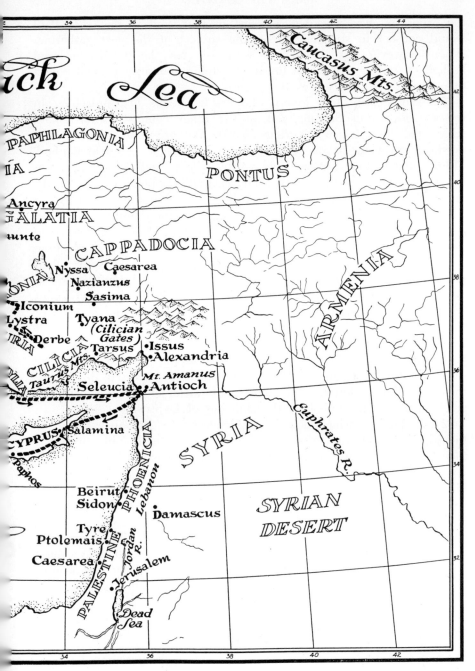

Paul's First Missionary Journey

the exposition was accepted, at least in part, and in that case Paul would consent to speak again on the subject at the next gathering. When, however, his conclusions were rejected, he openly declared he had no further obligation toward his fellow countrymen and would therefore address himself to the pagans.

323. We are not told exactly the result of this first preaching in the synagogues of Salamis, nor in the other centers on the island where the Jews were numerous (§ 35). We are told only that the missionaries "went, passing through the whole island as far as Paphos" (13:6); that is, they traversed almost the whole length of Cyprus from the eastern to the western coast. The account is obviously a summary one and must refer to several months' work. The distance between Salamis and Paphos is about 100 miles, and there must have been several villages and towns along the route with almost always some community, however small, of Jews. Even if they stopped only long enough in each one to sow the spiritual seed and make sure it had taken root, the weeks and months must have passed swiftly.

We may assume indirectly that the result of all these weeks of activity was not slight. We are given no details about the reaction of the evangelized Jews as in other instances. On the other hand, if Barnabas later returned to Cyprus with Mark (Acts 15:39), he must have done so not only for personal reasons, but also to see to the results of this first mission. As the missionaries traversed the island, they undoubtedly left behind them small nuclei of Jewish Christians, among whom there rose later the churches of Cyprus.

324. In Paphos, which was the residence of the Roman governor of the island (§ 35), the missionaries were unexpectedly able to widen their field of activity. They first addressed themselves to the Jewish community, it seems, and their discourses in the synagogue were highly successful, so much so that throughout the city the newcomers were the main topic of conversation. Even the governor heard of them, probably as learned philosophers come to Paphos on private business. The governor at that time was Sergius Paulus, whom Luke correctly calls the *proconsul* (ἀνθύπατος) because Cyprus was at that time a senatorial province and governed not by a propraetor but by a proconsul of praetorian rank.[2] Luke also introduces Sergius Paulus as a "man of

---

[2] Luke was accused in the past of being in error when he called Sergius Paulus *proconsul* instead of *propraetor*. The governors of Cyprus had been propraetors when it was an imperial province but in 22 B.C. it had become a senatorial province and its governors were proconsuls (cf. the passages in Strabo and Dion Cassius referred to in § 34). A Greek inscription found in Soli, a city on the western coast of the island, has the phrase ΕΠΙ ΠΑΥΛΟΥ (ΑΝΘ)ΥΠΑΤΟΥ "under Paul the proconsul," which almost certainly refers to this Sergius Paulus. The inscription was found and published by the American consul on Cyprus, L. Palma di Cesnola, *Cyprus, Its Ancient Cities, Tombs and Temples,* London, 1877, p. 425.

discernment" (σύνετος), and this seems to be confirmed by Pliny the Elder's mention of a Sergius Paulus as the source of his information, probably on Cyprus,[3] who may well be the same person. In any case, the administrative affairs of the island, which was a quiet place and off the beaten track, did not keep the proconsul too busy; and being a cultured man with an inquiring turn of mind he filled his leisure hours with congenial friendships and conversations with learned men, for whom his house stood always open. From all of them he hoped to learn new things, even from the magicians, astrologers, and similar devotees of the occult sciences, who enjoyed so much prestige at that time as various Roman authors attest.

325. Now, among the friends of the proconsul, a Jew named Bar-Jesus ("son of Jesus") had particular authority. Luke calls him a "magician" and "false prophet." But it should be remembered that the term *magus* almost always denoted a person of some learning and sometimes of good moral standing also.[4] From the context here we may suppose that Bar-Jesus was not a coarse or ignorant man but one well versed in the learning of his time, including the occult sciences. Luke calls him also a "false prophet," which suggests that among the sciences he cultivated the art of divination, on the basis of which he probably paraded himself as a messenger of God and spoke in God's name.

---

[3] *Nat. hist.*, Books II and XVIII, in the summaries at the beginning of the work, in the respective lists *ex auctoribus*. The passages which mention Cyprus are II, 90, 97, 112 (al. 88, 96, 108); XVIII, 12, 57 (al. 7, 25).

[4] Cf. *The Life of Christ*, p. 249 (§ 252).

Ancient Paphos — Ruins of the Temple of Aphrodite

Actually, for a Jew in those times, the temptation to claim to be God's messenger was particularly strong, and a few years later the false prophets were mushrooming all over Palestine.[5]

It was this quality of "prophet" that caused the conflict between Bar-Jesus and the missionaries. Perhaps he had heard them speak in the synagogue and immediately understood that their ideas and his were poles apart. When the proconsul became interested in the new arrivals, Bar-Jesus probably tried to prejudice him against them, but without success. Sergius Paulus sent for the interesting strangers to hear their views. It was said in the city that they spoke of a certain Jesus who, having died a few years ago and risen again, brought new life to all mankind without distinction as to race. Well, let them set forth all their teaching; he was quite ready to accept what was good in it. This candid and independent attitude was not too rare among honest minds in those days of widespread skepticism, and Luke describes it by saying that the proconsul "sought to hear the word of God." He was, then, a well-balanced individual who preferred to hear and judge for himself, rather than be influenced by the opinions of others, even learned persons like Bar-Jesus. He probably spoke with the missionaries more than once, and from the beginning seemed susceptible to their arguments, especially those of Paul, who was probably the principal speaker.

326. Bar-Jesus was present, and his attitude is described by Luke as follows: "But Elymas, the sorcerer (for so his name is translated),[6] opposed them, trying to turn away the proconsul from the faith" (Acts 13:8). Paul's argument probably followed the general outline he chose for pagans. He began with the natural knowledge of the one God, then spoke of the God revealed first to the Hebrews through the patriarchs and Moses and then to the whole human race through the Messias Jesus, and, finally, he set forth Jesus' teachings and the facts of his life. Bar-Jesus probably did not oppose this argumentation very strongly at first while Paul was speaking of the natural knowledge of God, but when he came to Hebrew history and especially to the teachings of the Messias Jesus, the Jewish sorcerer and the Christian ex-rabbi must have clashed violently, while the argument raged

---

[5] Cf. *Storia d'Israele*, II, p. 465 (§ 412).

[6] This parenthesis is difficult. It cannot refer to the name *Bar-Jesus*, which has quite a different meaning (as above), but is to be understood to mean "Elymas, the magician, for thus (*magus*) is his name (Elymas) interpreted." But what is the meaning and derivation of *Elymas?* Many think it comes from the Arabic *'alim*, "learned," and if one is "learned" in the occult sciences he is also a *magus*, or magician; but this does not solve certain morphological and conceptual difficulties. It might possibly derive from the semitic root 'LM to "bind," with reference to the magician's powers over the occult.

through quotations from Holy Scripture and interpretations of various kinds. But at a certain point, "Saul (also called Paul)[7] filled with the Holy Spirit, gazed at him and said, 'O full of all guile and of all deceit, son of the devil,[8] enemy of all justice, wilt thou not cease to make crooked the straight ways of the Lord? And now, behold, the hand of the Lord is upon thee, and thou shalt be blind, not seeing the sun for a time.' And instantly there fell upon him a mist of darkness, and he groped about for someone to lead him by the hand" (Acts 13:9–11).

327. Paul, too, had found himself in a similar condition on the road to Damascus, blind and needing someone to lead him by the hand (§ 266). But he had already yielded to his opponent, while here the consent of the man struck blind was lacking. Naturalist explanations have been advanced for this incident also. The sorcerer was of a neuropathic constitution, so that, shocked by Paul's words and practically hypnotized by his look, he suffered a temporary clouding of his vision. This merely proves that these critics rather tiresomely resort to the same methods over and over again.

We are not told the subsequent fate of Bar-Jesus. Of Sergius Paulus we are told: "Then the proconsul, seeing what had happened, believed and was astonished (ἐκπλησσόμενος) at the Lord's teaching" (ibid., 12). If he "believed" he acknowledged at least intellectually the truth of Christianity, but did he also acknowledge it officially by receiving baptism? We do not know, although we may consider it implicit in the verb "believed." His position as a high official of the Roman Empire was not a serious obstacle to his baptism, for at this time (A.D. 45) Rome did not yet have anything against Christianity, and it was immaterial whether a magistrate in the provinces became Christian, was initiated in the mysteries of Isis, or gave his name to some Pythagorean sect.

ANTIOCH OF PISIDIA

328. The episode of Sergius Paulus concludes the missionaries' sojourn in Cyprus. It had been on the whole a fruitful one, and the conversion of the proconsul especially had opened their hearts to brighter hope. With no definite itinerary established (§ 320) the missionaries left the island for the mainland to the north. But as soon as they had arrived, an unhappy incident occurred in the little company, which was,

---

[7] This is the first time the Apostle is called Paul in the Acts; cf. § 228.

[8] Since his name was Bar-Jesus, i.e., "son of Jesus," there is the temptation to think that the epithet "son of the devil" is intentionally opposed to this name, with reference to Jesus of Nazareth. Since the magician did not have the reverence for Jesus' name which Paul had, the contrast so clear to us would have been lost on him.

Perge — Theater and Nymphaion

perhaps, not altogether unforeseen. "Putting to sea from Paphos, Paul and his companions came to Perge in Pamphylia; but John left them and returned to Jerusalem" (*ibid.*, 13).

The crossing from Cyprus to Pamphylia was not a long one. They landed in Adalia, and shortly afterward reached Perge, about nine or ten miles from the sea (§ 10). But even this short trek showed that Pamphylia was quite different from Cyprus. If there in Perge at the foot of the Taurus Mountains, the countryside was wild and desolate, what might they not expect once they entered that mountain territory, on impossible roads, with no conveniences whatever and at the complete mercy of highwaymen? John, or Mark, may have had some such thoughts at Perge, but probably other considerations had already been disturbing him for some time.

329. Note that here the little caravan of travelers is referred to with a new expression "those with Paul" (οἱ περὶ Παῦλον). Up to this time the head of the company had been Barnabas. Now it is Paul, and the others are "those with" him. This new phrase undoubtedly reflects a new situation. At their departure from Antioch and during the first part of their stay in Cyprus Barnabas was the leader, but as their missionary activity was intensified, Paul took the leadership as the natural consequence of that very activity. He was the initiator and the leader, and the others, inevitably, became "those with Paul." As long as they remained in Cyprus Barnabas had the advantage of being in his own country, and therefore was particularly useful because of his acquaintances there. But even this advantage had considerably diminished toward the end as they entered the pagan milieu of the proconsul, and had ceased altogether when they left the island. John Mark must have noticed this *diminutio capitis* of his cousin Barnabas, and young as he was, he did not like it very much. Now here was this new adventure, when they must throw themselves into the ravines and swamps of Pamphylia, an adventure which was, as usual, Paul's idea, and which the good Barnabas did not have the firmness to oppose. But was this wise or prudent?

Mark was quite ready to admire Paul's indomitable energy, but he could not see why they all had to think as he did or follow him wherever he took it into his head to go. A novice at traveling and away from his country for the first time, he was probably homesick, and the thought of his mother's house grew more and more compelling every day. He contrasted his gentle mother Mary, the solicitous hostess of Peter escaped from prison, with this volcanic Paul who never seemed to need any sleep or food; his comfortable and pious Jerusalem with this savage Pamphylia, the lair of devils and robbers. So as they were about to leave Perge for the interior, Mark decided to go home and took the sea route for Jerusalem.

Paul felt Mark's defection deeply and remembered it for a long time (§ 370). Barnabas did not dare follow his cousin and remained with Paul. After all, they probably excused the young man's departure since he had had no specific preparation for the present task (§ 319), and was really not of the number who had been "sent forth by the Holy Spirit" (§ 321).

330. With Mark gone, Paul and Barnabas resumed their journey from Perge, heading due north toward the center of Asia Minor. Following the river Caister, they took the road that led first to Adada and then to Antioch of Pisidia, and thus came immediately to the Pamphylian range of the Taurus mountains.

A Roman Traveler Settling Accounts With an Innkeeper (Louvre — Paris)

The distance from Perge to Antioch was about 130 miles but the route was so difficult and dangerous that the journey took at least six or seven days. The road was barely a mule path, which first plunged into the ravines cut by the river Caister, and then climbed up toward the tableland of Pisidia to about 3000 feet above sea level, where it meandered among the snowy peaks, across lonely heaths, and through thick forests. There were mountain streams to ford, or a new path to find where a landslide had blocked the old one, or thick wild vegetation to be chopped away. Everywhere lurked the threat of the old bands of highway robbers, constantly increased by runaway slaves, who made a good living on the merchants traveling back and forth. Nowhere could the traveler hope to find, at the end of an exhausting day, any better shelter than some tumbled-down caravansary where he could expect to eat only what he had brought with him, sleep on the ground in the chill mountain air, and be awakened by the howling of the hungry wolves prowling around the neighborhood. Only beyond the Taurus, along the more traveled road of the plain, could one find one of those wretched little inns, pictured sometimes in archaeological documents, where one might spend a reluctant night, and leave early the next morning after paying an exorbitant price to the ill-famed innkeeper.

But Paul and Barnabas took these hardships in stride, sustained by the thought that if this difficult route could be traveled by merchants in pursuit of gain, by Roman legionaries for military training, and by imperial functionaries in the fulfillment of the duties of their office, so much the more could it be traveled by the Apostles of the Messias Jesus for his glory. Between the fourth and fifth day, the journey became easier. The road led along the coast of Lake Egherdir (§ 27) through an Alpine landscape, and after another night or two spent along the way, they arrived in Antioch.

331. As usual, Paul and Barnabas went first to the Jewish community. It was probably quite large since the city had a thriving trade in hides, and the travelers undoubtedly had letters of introduction to someone there. They lost no time in beginning their mission and went to the synagogue on their first Sabbath there. The synagogue was attended not only by those who were Jewish by race, but also by the non-Jews who were attracted to the religion of Israel and who were divided into two classes, a lower one of the devout or "God-fearing," and a higher one of "proselytes."[9] Paul is to meet pagans affiliated with Judaism almost everywhere throughout his travels.[10] Perhaps the word had spread that there were two strangers

---

[9] Cf. *Storia d'Israele*, II, p. 245 (§ 213).
[10] *Ibid.*, II, p. 243 (§ 211).

Antioch of Pisidia

with new ideas in town, and the meeting may have been more crowded than usual with non-Jews.

The procedure was the usual one, and Luke describes it thus: "And entering the synagogue on the Sabbath, they sat down. After the reading of the Law and the Prophets, the rulers of the synagogue sent to them saying, 'Brethren, if you have any word of exhortation for the people, speak.' Then Paul arose, and motioning with his hand for silence, said, 'Israelites and you who fear God, hearken . . .'" (Acts 13:14–16). It is almost the same scene as that of Jesus' last discourse in the synagogue of Nazareth before being driven from his village (Lk. 4:16–30), except that the author gives us only the beginning of Jesus' discourse[11] but quite a long summary of Paul's.

332. Again the exposition follows Paul's usual outline (§ 326). But this time, since he is speaking to people who already believe in the one God, he omits the observations on the natural knowledge of God and begins with the revelation of God to the Hebrews. He goes on then to the revelation through Jesus, strengthening his exposition with allusions to the Messianic passages in Holy Scripture. Of particular importance is his conclusion: "Be it known therefore to you, brethren, that through him forgiveness of sins is proclaimed to you, and in him everyone who believes is acquitted of all the things of which you could not be acquitted by the Law of Moses" (Acts 13:17–41).

The novelty of the argument and the specific facts presented with regard to Jesus must have made an impression. But the high point in the discourse was the comparison between the inadequacy of the

[11] Cf. *The Life of Christ*, pp. 366–368 (§ 358).

Law of Moses for justification and the actual justification wrought
by faith in Jesus. The Jews with Pharisaic leanings sniffed a little
heresy in these words, a whiff of rebellion that boded no good. On
the other hand the non-Jews, the affiliated "fearing God" and the
"proselytes," saw in them the dawn of a day made radiant by the
sun of spiritual freedom. In any case, the subject was too intricate
to be exhausted in one gathering. So at the end of this day's meeting
the rulers of the synagogue and others asked the two missionaries to
come back on the next Sabbath to speak of these things again. There
were other more enthusiastic listeners who could not wait a whole week
and asked them right away to explain what they had said. For Paul
and Barnabas, this lively interest was the effect of the "grace of God,"
and this guided their reply. "Many of the Jews and the worshipping
converts went away with Paul and Barnabas, and they talked with
them and urged them to hold fast to the grace of God" (*ibid.*, 43).

333. During that week, the news spread through the entire city.
Not only the Jews but the pagans, both Greek and Oriental, both the
learned and the tradesmen, came to know that on the next Sabbath
there would be a discourse in the synagogue by a certain Jew from
Tarsus, who was a Roman citizen and had once persecuted a certain
Jesus of Nazareth, but then had joined his party, after seeing him
alive one day near Damascus and becoming convinced that he was
a kind of semigod, or that personage the Jews called the Messias. It
was said that the orator, educated in Tarsus, was a skillful and
vigorous speaker, and it would certainly be interesting to hear him
develop this theory of independence from the Jewish Law and of
spiritual freedom with which he had terminated his previous talk.
For this modest little city the event was an extraordinary interruption
in its monotonous life of trade and commerce, and so it happened
that "the next Sabbath almost the whole city gathered to hear the
word of the Lord" (*ibid.*, 44). The phrase, "the word of the Lord,"
is precise from the narrator's viewpoint, but psychologically more
accurate is the expression in Codex D ("Western text": 119, note),
which says that the city came to hear "Paul." What had captured
their interest was the speaker, with these new ideas, whereas the
crowd knew little or nothing yet about the "word of God."

Now the size of Paul's audience considerably irritated the elders:
"On seeing the crowds, the Jews were filled with jealousy" (*ibid.*, 45).
What were all those pagans doing there? Had they come to con-
taminate the synagogue with their unclean presence? Or did they
hope to hear in the synagogue, no less, that the Law of Moses was
inadequate? Or that before God a Greek or a Barbarian or a Scythian
was as good as a Jew? Let this Paul of Tarsus try to defend such
nonsense and everyone would see the welcome that awaited him.

334. Paul's second discourse here is not recorded for us. Only the above-mentioned Codex says vaguely that "he gave a long discourse on the Lord," Jesus. But we may deduce the substance of it from analogy. The concepts on justification set forth in the previous talk are typical Pauline ideas which appear also in the epistles to the Romans and the Galatians. In speaking especially of Jesus this time, he must have declared that he was the Messias predicted by Scripture, that he had died and had risen from the dead, that his death had brought redemption to all men without distinction, thus abolishing the Law of Moses and the other privileges of the Jews, and other similar concepts as set forth in his epistles. This assumption is strengthened by the reception the Jews gave the discourse, for they "contradicted what was said by Paul, and blasphemed" (*ibid.*, 45). To whom were these "blasphemies" or insults addressed? To the heretic, Paul, undoubtedly, but by implication to Jesus also, the subject of the heresy, whom Paul later called the "stumbling block for the Jews" (1 Cor. 1:23).

It is easy to reconstruct the scene. As Paul proceeded with his argument, the Jews tried to demolish its dialectic structure (very much as the radical critics today attempt to do with his letters and the narrative of the *Acts*). They rejected his testimony, distorted the meaning of the biblical quotations, and had recourse to insult especially, showering their scorn on Jesus, his life and teaching, and everything concerned with him. Then when Paul declared that, in the kingdom of the Messias Jesus, the Jew is on a par with those of any other race, that the Gospel has taken the place of the Law of Moses, while the non-Jewish listeners must have applauded noisily, the Jews lost all control. A tempest of insults broke over Paul's head, violent threats were hurled at the renegade, the traitor, and he could no longer make himself heard above the din.

335. But Paul had foreseen this turbulent epilogue and was prepared for it. He remained standing on the platform from which he was speaking, paying no attention to the cries and threats flung at him. He exchanged a few words with Barnabas who was standing near the dais, and they both continued to wait. As soon as the hubbub had subsided enough for him to be heard, they both spoke out with serene assurance: "It was necessary that the word of God should be spoken to you first, but since you reject it and judge yourselves unworthy of eternal life, behold, we now turn to the Gentiles" (Acts 13:46).

The schism had come. Paul and Barnabas did not set foot in the synagogue again, but this did not mean they were idle. Their final declaration, that they abandoned the Jews to preach to the Gentiles, had delighted the latter, who immediately and gladly accepted their instructions. The gatherings were held now, not in the synagogue, but

Iconium: Caravansary of the Seljuk Period

in some shop or private home or garden, as chance permitted. But they were no less fruitful because of this. These pagans in search of the light flocked to the meetings, so that gradually "the word of the Lord spread throughout the whole country" (*ibid.*, 49). The news spread easily. Those who had attended one of the meetings and found consolation in what they had heard there spoke of it to relatives living in the same house, to the merchant from a distant village in town on business, to the soldier who had come down from the mountain garrison to get his orders at headquarters. Many of them became interested, attended the gatherings, and also found consolation there, and in their turn spread the news among their acquaintances and friends. The two missionaries must have spent themselves going from one place to another, inside and outside the city, perhaps enlisting the help later of some neophyte endowed with the necessary charisms (§ 211 ff.). Every once in a while, when the brief period of instruction was finished, groups were taken to the bank of some stream and baptized.

336. The work here must have lasted several months, perhaps more than a year, since the movement could not "spread throughout the whole country" of Antioch in a few weeks. The Jews did not observe these results of Paul's preaching without some anxiety. At first they thought they had ended the nonsense when they expelled the two missionaries from the synagogue. Now they discovered that they possessed a spiritual authority of their own, which in no way derived from the synagogue, and which had, in fact, become more active and effective after their expulsion. Yet they could not tolerate a rival altar of this kind, which had so much in common with Judaism. How to suppress it? To reopen the discussions was not very opportune since Paul was not one to be easily confounded. There was nothing left but to have recourse to the authorities, just as the Jews had done in Damascus where Paul was obliged to escape in a basket (§ 290).

"But the Jews incited the worshipping women of rank and the chief men of the city, and stirred up a persecution against Paul and Barnabas and drove them from their district" (*ibid.*, 50). This time, it was not money which counted so much, as it had in Damascus, but social position. The pagan women affiliated with the Judaism of the Diaspora were always numerous, not only among the "worshipping" and "God-fearing" but also among the "proselytes," because they were not faced with the serious inconvenience of circumcision, which almost always kept the men from this higher grade. In Damascus all the non-Jewish women, except for a few, were affiliated with Judaism (§ 33). In Antioch of Pisidia, the social influence of the more prominent of these women was used, through their husbands and relatives who had offices or position in the city, to put an end to the scandal. It was easy to find the legal pretexts for a desired end, given the privileged position the Jews enjoyed in the Empire.

The "persecution," which is barely mentioned, might have carried with it some of the trials Paul recalls having endured (2 Cor. 11:23–25). He may have been dragged to the synagogue to receive the regulation thirty-nine strokes of the lash,[12] which he tells us he suffered at least five times in his life. Or he may have been flogged by the civil magistrates, which happened on three occasions. Perhaps he was sentenced for several days to prison, which from then on comes to be his lodging more and more frequently. We know nothing definite about this, however. In the end, a "popular" uprising, carefully prepared by the instigators concerned, drove the two missionaries from the city.

337. And this time, too, they were well prepared for what happened. When, beaten and bruised, they were driven from the city, they "shook off the dust of their feet in protest against them" as Jesus had taught them to do (Mt. 10:14), "and went to Iconium." Far from being discouraged when one field of activity was shut to them, they immediately found another elsewhere. And the new Christians they left behind them in Antioch shared their sentiments, for "the disciples continued to be filled with joy and with the Holy Spirit" (Acts 13:52). Perhaps these disciples had heard from Paul and Barnabas that when the Apostles had been scourged by the Sanhedrin in Jerusalem, "they departed from the presence of the Sanhedrin, rejoicing that they had been counted worthy to suffer disgrace for the name of Jesus" (Acts 5:41). The con-

---

[12] Cf. *ibid.*, p. 57 (§ 61); pp. 59–60 (§ 64).

viction had grown among the neophytes that the kingdom of the Messias Jesus could not be spread without trials and sufferings, and they rejoiced when they could contribute their own sufferings to its diffusion.

These paradoxical sentiments were not peculiar to the neophytes of Antioch and Pisidia, but were characteristic of Paul himself, who dared to boast: "Wherefore I am satisfied, for Christ's sake, with infirmities, with insults, with hardships, with persecutions, with distresses. For when I am weak, then I am strong" (2 Cor. 12:10). But neither had Paul invented this reversal of ordinary human reactions. He had learned it from the supreme paradox, the Sermon on the Mount.[13]

ICONIUM

338. The trip from Antioch of Pisidia to Iconium, which occurred perhaps at the beginning of the year 47, was a little over a hundred miles. Accompanied perhaps by a few zealous neophytes from Antioch, the two missionaries crossed the parched and desolate tablelands which stretched between the two cities and were the classic type of Asiatic steppe. In the less marshy areas, and those less covered with saline incrustations, wandered large flocks of sheep and goats, which furnished the material for the many weaving shops of Iconium. There probably were numerous Jews in the city (§ 25), attracted by its trade. As soon as he arrived, Paul easily found means to exercise his own trade in one of the weaver's shops run by a fellow Jew, thus earning his living with his own hands, as was his custom (§ 230).

339. But at the same time he began his spiritual labors, addressing himself first to the Jews again: "Now it came to pass at Iconium that they went in the same way into the synagogue of the Jews and so spoke that a great multitude of Jews and of Greeks believed" (Acts 14:1). It is clear that this, too, is a highly condensed report, since the conversion of a "great multitude" must have been the result of a relatively long period of activity. The subsequent events, which resemble the occurrences in Pisidian Antioch, are also extremely condensed. The Jews who rejected the teaching of the missionaries "stirred up and poisoned (ἐκάκωσαν) the minds of the Gentiles against the brethren" (ibid., 2). We may easily recognize among these Gentiles, not only people of the humbler social classes, but the rich industrialists and those with most influence in civic affairs.

Nevertheless, the persecuted Apostles did not yield, but "stayed a long time, therefore, acting fearlessly in the Lord, who gave testimony to the word of his grace by permitting signs and wonders to be done by their hands" (ibid., 3). We find in full play, then, the charisms with which the missionaries were endowed and whose direct purpose was the diffusion or the strengthening of the faith (§ 211). The Jews had

---

[13] Cf. ibid., p. 322 (§ 318).

nothing to set against this unfurling of spiritual forces except material force. And they used it.

"But the people of the city were divided, some siding with the Jews and some with the apostles. But when there was a movement on the part of the Gentiles and of the Jews with their rulers to insult and stone them, hearing of it, they escaped to the Lycaonian cities Lystra and Derbe and the whole country round about, and there they went on preaching the gospel" (*ibid.*, 4–7).

340. The final scene was substantially the same as that in Antioch of Pisidia. Given Paul's paradoxical criteria, he must have been "satisfied" with this persecution too (§ 337), concluding that the work done in Iconium had been blessed by God since it had ended in what seemed from the human viewpoint complete failure. And the Iconian neophytes, like those of Antioch, no doubt "continued to be filled with joy and the Holy Spirit." Paul's success as a missionary lies in this topsy-turvy reversal of human standards. Man fails always. But God always triumphs. It is the secret of the Sermon on the Mount, which too often has not been understood by critics and philosophers.[14]

LYSTRA

341. The two missionaries fled from Iconium probably in the first months of the year 48, and took refuge in Lycaonia, in the little city of Lystra (§ 28), which lay about thirty miles to the south. The surrounding country was a desolate steppe, infested besides by highwaymen, with whom a century earlier Cicero had had a great deal to do at the time of his proconsulship in Cilicia. There was little or no industry in

---

[14] Christian legend inserts the episode of Thecla in this sojourn at Iconium. A summary follows: As Paul and Barnabas leave Antioch of Pisidia, a certain Onesiphorus (cf. 2 Tim. 1:16) comes to meet them. Paul's appearance (cf. § 188) had been described to him in a dream so that he would be able to recognize him. At Iconium Paul preaches in the home of Onesiphorus. Thecla, a rich and learned young lady, who lives in a nearby house, listens to Paul's preaching without seeing him. Deeply impressed by his discourse on virginity, she refuses to marry Thamyris, her betrothed, and she persists in her refusal despite his pleadings and those of her mother. They appeal to the local court, and Paul is imprisoned as a magician. Thecla succeeds in going to visit Paul secretly in prison, but is surprised there by her mother and Thamyris. Paul and Thecla are reported to the judge. He is scourged and expelled from the city. She is condemned to be burned for her obstinacy. The burning pyre, however, is extinguished by a sudden downpour, and Thecla flees to join Paul. She follows him to Antioch where she refuses to marry Alexander the Syrian. Again brought before the judge she is condemned to the wild beasts, but they do not touch her, and she is then thrown into a pit full of snakes, which show her the same deference. She is then set free and returns to Iconium, from where she goes to Seleucia in Isauria. Here she converts a great number to Christ and dies at an advanced age. As we noted before (§ 99, note; § 188), the legend may contain a kernel of historical truth, especially in the first episode relating to Iconium, but it is difficult today to extract that kernel from the rest. The legend was widespread in the Greek Church and was known also to the Latin Fathers (Ambrose, Augustine).

Fourth- or Fifth-Century Ivory — Paul and Thecla in Iconium. Stoning of Paul at Lystra. London: British Museum. Ivory of the Fourth or Fifth Century (from Dalton, *Catalogue of Early Christian Antiquities in the British Museum*)

the city itself, and not many Jews had come there. We do not know whether or not there was a synagogue, although there always was one in the Jewish communities of the Diaspora no matter how small.[15] But there were Jewish families in Lystra (cf. Acts 16:3), with one of which the refugees lodged, probably that of Timothy, who is to figure prominently in Paul's next journey (§ 372).

In these circumstances, the missionaries were obliged to direct their activity almost exclusively to the natives of the place, the Lycaonians, simple and unlettered polytheists, who, though they understood more or less the international language, Greek, usually spoke Lycaonian, some fragmentary inscriptions in which are still extant. The Hellenism which had penetrated as far as Lystra had, as usual, transformed the local divinities, probably nature gods (§ 59), fusing them with the Greek deities and had given them Greek names. And so the Lycaonians of Lystra worshiped Zeus and Hermes. They had a temple to Zeus situated — it would seem — near the gate of the city (Acts 14:13). They also knew the legend, of Phrygian origin but well known in the Greco-Roman world, of the aged couple, Philemon and Baucis, who had received Zeus and Hermes disguised as mortals in their humble cottage, and were rewarded by having their wishes granted (Ovid, *Metamorph.*, VIII, 620 ff.).

342. One day, near the temple of Zeus, Paul was talking to a group who had gathered there, either for some feast in the temple or for the market held at the city gate. Barnabas stood near him silently. As always in such crowds, there were beggars poking around asking alms. In fact, one of them, lame from birth, had laboriously pushed his way through

---

[15] Cf. *The Life of Christ*, p. 58 (§ 62).

the group listening to Paul, and he stood listening too with great attention. The orator was speaking of a certain Jesus, who was the Son of
God but who had become man and had lived among men in order to
save them. And this unhappy beggar had immediately applied this to
himself. If this Jesus was saving people, who had more need of being
saved than he himself, who had borne misfortune since his birth? The
keen hope kindled in him was clearly reflected in his face. Paul, experienced speaker that he was, followed the effect of his words in his
listeners' faces, and he noticed the emotion of the cripple. "Gazing at
him and seeing that he had faith to be cured, [he] said with a loud
voice, 'Stand upright on thy feet.' And he sprang up and began to walk"
(Acts 14:9–10).

In several of the miracles wrought by Jesus, the essential prerequisite
had been faith.[16] Here Paul, using the same criterion, noticed that the
lame man "had faith to be cured." To be sure, the salvation brought by
Jesus and preached by Paul was a spiritual one, not a physical cure.
But the first did not exclude the second; in fact, it might even require
it if it could profit the spiritual salvation of the person cured or others.
The lame man was certainly thinking of his own cure. Paul, by virtue
of his charisms, saw that the cure could benefit the bystanders too and
so he worked the miracle.

343. In reality, the good effects came only later, while the first reaction was awkward and embarrassing. "Then the crowds seeing what
Paul had done, lifted up their voice saying in the Lycaonian language,
'The gods have come down to us in the likeness of men.' And they
called Barnabas Zeus, and Paul Hermes, because he was the chief
speaker" (ὁ ἡγούμενος τοῦ λόγου). The identification with the two gods was
probably prompted by the episode of Philemon and Baucis, and the
Lycaonians thought they were seeing a repetition of it. Astonished at
the cure and surprised by the perfect resemblance, they began to

---

[16] Cf. *ibid.*, p. 335 ff. (§ 349 ff.); p. 411 (§ 405).

Lystra (from Ramsay, *The Cities of St. Paul*)

shout in Lycaonian, since that was their everyday language. But it was
unknown to Paul and Barnabas, and at first they did not understand
that they had been mistaken for two gods. If Paul was identified with
Hermes, this had nothing to do with his physical appearance, as we
have already pointed out (§ 187) but was due to the fact that he was
the "chief speaker" of the two.

Up to this point, all went smoothly enough, and the Lycaonians assumed
that the two supposed gods were glad to have been recognized and so
enthusiastically acclaimed. But the scene changed when the acclaim was
followed by action, which could be understood without any knowledge
of Lycaonian. "And the priest of Zeus that stood at the entrance to the
city[17] brought oxen and garlands to the gateways, and with the people
would have offered sacrifice." All was now clear to the missionaries.
The people were about to perform an act of idolatry in their honor
no less!

"But on hearing of this, the apostles Barnabas and Paul rushed into
the crowd, tearing their clothes, and shouting 'Men, why are you doing
this? We also are mortals, human beings like you, bringing to you the
good news that you should turn from these vain things to the living
God who made heaven and earth and the sea and all things that are
in them. In the generations that are past he let all the nations follow
their own ways; and yet he did not leave himself without testimony,
bestowing blessings, giving rains from heaven and fruitful seasons, filling your hearts with food and gladness'" (Acts 14:14–17). The two
Apostles tore the hems from their tunics to show their indignation at
this impromptu deification, for — as we know[18] — this was a Jewish custom at times of great distress or grief. The little discourse is adapted to
the Lycaonian mentality, used to a nature form of worship (§ 59) and
recalls them to the principle of the true God, the author of nature, not
without concepts and phrases from the Hebrew Bible. Their reaction
to the ceremony begun in good faith may seem a little excessive to us
today, but we must remember that they were Jews with a deep and
traditional horror of anything bordering on idolatry. And this serves
to confim further the absolute conflict between Paul's thought and any
possible idolatrous source (§ 281).

344. The immediate result of Paul's little speech was to stop the sacrifice, but its later consequence was to provoke a too radical change in
the opinion the untutored Lycaonians had formed of the two of them.
The missionaries had confessed that they were men like the rest. There-

---

[17] The expression is not clear (τοῦ Διὸς τοῦ ὄντος πρὸ τῆς πόλεως). It may have a
locative meaning: "of Zeus (whose temple) is in front of the city"; or a figurative
meaning: "of Zeus who protects the city." I prefer the locative meaning. Also "the
gates" seem to me to be the gates of the temple rather than of the city.
[18] Cf. *The Life of Christ*, p. 600 (§ 568).

fore, concluded the disillusioned deifiers, they worked miracles through magic like so many other preachers wandering around at the time. They must be let alone but at the same time it would not do to trust them blindly. They must be watched because they might some day use their mysterious powers to harm or trick the people, as many of these other preachers did.

An indefinite period of time followed while Paul and Barnabas continued their preaching without being disturbed and won a number of disciples (*ibid.*, 20). But Jews from Antioch and Iconium changed the Lycaonian neutrality to open hostility. They had not forgotten the moral defeats they had suffered and they had heard that the two missionaries were in Lystra continuing to spread their propaganda with great success. A "punitive expedition" was soon organized and, with the probable help of Jews in Lystra, led to definite action, which is again condensed for us in this summary fashion: "But some Jews arrived from Antioch and Iconium; and after winning over the crowds, they stoned Paul and dragged him outside the city, thinking that he was dead. But the disciples gathered round him and he got up and re-entered the city. The next day he set out with Barnabas for Derbe" (*ibid.*, 19–20).

345. Again, it is not hard to reconstruct what happened. The Jews from abroad probably work secretly for a few days, buying persons of influence and persuading the crowd that the two Apostles are common tricksters and dangerous sorcerers. Then Paul is challenged to a public debate, for which the audience is hand-picked and well coached. During the discussion, they begin to cry out against this man who blasphemes against Moses and disturbs the peace of the city. The regular punishment of stoning is decided upon, as it was for Stephen (§ 256), and immediately executed. Paul faints under the blows and is thought to be dead. The executioners hurry to drag him outside the city, both because that is required by Jewish law and because their conscience is not quite comfortable so far as the civil magistrates are concerned. Outside the city, dogs and vultures will ensure the disappearance of the body during the night. At nightfall, in order not to be seen, the disciples go out to care for his body, and instead save Paul. But he does not wish to expose the Christians of Lystra to further persecution, and the next day he leaves the city secretly, perhaps on muleback because of his wounds, and goes to Derbe.

If Paul lodged in Lystra at the home of Timothy (§ 341), his wounds were dressed that night by Lois and Eunice, the grandmother and mother of Timothy respectively, whom Paul later recalled with affection (2 Tim. 1:5), just as he also reminded Timothy of the persecution he endured not only in Antioch and Iconium but also in Lystra (3:11). The persecution in Lystra, at least physically, had been much more serious than the previous ones. The stoning Paul received then is mentioned specifically in the long list of his tribulations (2 Cor. 11:25), and he may be referring to the scars left by that stoning when he says he bears "the marks of the Lord Jesus" in his body (Gal. 6:17). Just as the fugitive slaves were branded with the mark of their owners (§ 613) so Paul is branded as a slave of Christ by the scars he received for his glory.

Gudelissin — the Site of Derbe (from Ramsay, *The Church in the Roman Empire*)

DERBE

346. Derbe (§ 26) was situated about forty miles southeast of Lystra. The activity of the two missionaries in this little village is summarized even more briefly than usual. We are told only that "after preaching the gospel to that city and teaching many, they returned . . ." (Acts 14:21). But even from these brief words we may gather that the stay in Derbe was not a short one, for it would have taken at least a few months to "teach many disciples." If we add to these the months spent in Lystra, we come to the latter part of the year 49 (§ 155). Among the disciples converted at this time, we recognize the Gaius of Derbe who later accompanied Paul (20:4). Perhaps the missionaries had stayed at his house.

When, toward the end of their stay in Derbe, Paul and Barnabas began to plan the return journey, they had a convenient itinerary to take them back to their starting point. They could continue eastward through Isauria, and crossing the Taurus Mountains at the Cilician Gates (§ 7), reach Tarsus after a journey of some two hundred miles. From Tarsus it was easy to get to Antioch of Syria, from where they had started. But this route was rejected, for the special reason that the two missionaries were anxious to see once more the communities they had founded during the past four or five years and to strengthen them in the faith. It was decided therefore to retrace their steps, stopping briefly in the same cities as before. In the meantime, Paul and Barnabas had undoubtedly received news from time to time from the new communities, and were convinced their visits now would be timely. On the other hand, to reappear in the places from which they had been invariably forced to flee, no longer presented the same dangers since time had passed and most of the local magistrates had changed. After all, if they were prudent and did not appear at public gatherings no one would pay any attention to them. The return journey is described to us thus: "They returned to Lystra, Iconium, and Antioch, reassuring the disciples and exhorting them to continue in the faith, and reminding them that through many tribulations we must enter the kingdom of God." Then after Paul and Barnabas had imposed hands on the elders presented to them (χειροτονήσαντες δὲ αὐτοῖς) "in each church with prayer and fasting, they commended them to the Lord in whom they had believed" (Acts 14:21–23).

347. This, then, had been the real purpose for revisiting the new communities, to provide a stable organization for them. After the departure of their founders, the new Christian communities had been isolated, except for intermittent letters they may have received from Paul and Barnabas. Separated now from the local synagogues, the neophytes gathered to pray in private homes, finding solace in the charisms with which they were generously endowed (§ 211 ff.). But such a state of things could be temporary at best. During this second visit, the two founders establish a true organization. They ordain the elders they have chosen in each community after listening to the opinion of the brethren. Placing their hands upon them they make them the ordinary directors of the respective communities and give them authority to preside over the gatherings and to conduct the services of worship. Thus organized, the various communities became so many cells, each living its own life but all bound together within the Mystical Body of Christ, of which they formed a part.

At the end of their tour of the different communities, the two missionaries arrived once again in Pamphylia, and we are told simply that this time they also evangelized Perge (§ 328). From there they went down to the port of Adalia where they set sail for Syria and finally returned to Antioch (*ibid.*, 25–26).

The Council of Jerusalem:
Dissension at Antioch

348. The child developing in its mother's womb already has a life of its own distinct from that of its mother, even though it is as yet incomplete and dependent on the mother's life. But during this period of formation it is being prepared gradually for its own independent life by a provident nature. And even when the child has been born, there is still a slender cord binding him to his mother. Only when this has been cut does the new life become completely independent.

It is historically accurate to say that the Christian Church — in its externals — was conceived and formed in the womb of the Jewish Synagogue, and that for a certain length of time its life was united with that of the latter, although it was distinct from it and clearly directed toward complete independence. The last tie binding it to the Synagogue was the observance of the rites prescribed by the Law of Moses. Once this was severed, the Church acquired an autonomous life, entirely independent of the Synagogue.

349. The one who dared to cut this bond, with incalculable consequences for the history of mankind, was Paul. In this sense he may be said to have "delivered" the Church.

Five centuries earlier Socrates had claimed to be the midwife of the spirit, saying that for the minds of his followers he continued the profession of his mother Phenaretes, who had been a midwife. The figure was quite appropriate. But Socrates cut nothing, declared nothing abolished, and, except for the intemperances of the Sophists, rejected nothing. His function was not bold. It was limited to helping the minds of his disciples to give spiritual birth.

On the other hand, Paul's boldness, evaluated historically, is enormous. He cut a religious tradition that had lasted thousands of years. He declared abolished a code which was the sole foundation of the life of an entire nation, and, besides that, he declared it abolished in the name of the same divine authority which had promulgated it. He rejected as valueless now the letter of that code which was the boast, the pride, the prerogative, the nobility of a whole nation, and for which thousands of martyrs had given testimony.

Nor did he act lightly, with only a dim perception of the consequences of his boldness. On the contrary he foresaw them very clearly, and his heart wept at the thought of them: "For I could wish to be anathema myself from Christ for the sake of my brethren, who are my kinsmen according to the flesh; who are Israelites, who have the adoption as sons, and the glory and the covenants and the legislation and the worship and the promises; who have the fathers, and from whom is the Christ according to the flesh . . . etc." (Rom. 9:3–6 – § 167). These words are enough to reveal Paul's full awareness of the gesture he was making. And yet he cut this last tie with unwavering resolution, though his hand trembled with emotion. What were his reasons for this? They are to be found in our narrative.

350. On their arrival in Antioch from Asia Minor Paul and Barnabas "called the church together and reported all that God had done with them, and how he had opened to the Gentiles a door of faith" (Acts 14:27). The "door of faith" opened to the Gentiles was a typical expression aptly describing the deep impression the recital of Paul and Barnabas made on the Christians of Antioch. It was the whole pagan world being opened to the Gospel, the numberless multitudes and boundless regions which tomorrow would enter the Kingdom of the Messias Jesus. Before this radiant vision, how small and narrow seemed little Palestine and the strip of Syria where the Good Tidings had been heralded until then. How thin and scattered seemed the groups of Christians organized up to that time. The gathering must have thanked heaven with deep emotion for the assistance rendered the missionaries in the past, and grandiose plans for the future began to take shape that this vision of the pagan world conquered for Christ would come true as soon as possible. Paul and Barnabas remained in this enthusiastic environment "no little time" (*ibid.*, 28), for the rest of the year 49 and perhaps the beginning of 50 (§ 155).

It is not hard to explain this enthusiasm among the Antiochene Christians, some of whom had been converted from Hellenistic Judaism, more liberal in its views than that of Palestine, but the majority from paganism (§ 312 ff.). Neither one nor the other thought it necessary to impose special conditions on the pagans desiring to enter the Church, except faith in Christ and baptism. If some of the Hellenist Jews wanted to continue the observance of certain Jewish ritual precepts after their conversion they were perfectly free to do so, according to their own consciences, but without imposing these same precepts as obligations on others. There was no obligation whatever. The converted

pagans had never observed the Jewish precepts, and therefore they had
no reason whatever to observe them now. And for that matter neither
did the Hellenist Jews since their acceptance of Christ had replaced and
sublimated their dependence on the Law of Moses, freeing them from
that temporary Law. These attitudes explain the enthusiasm which filled
the Christians of Antioch when they heard that God "had opened to
the Gentiles a door of faith."

351. But the Palestinian Jews did not see things exactly the same way.
They too opened the door to the Gentiles, but only halfway, admitting
only those who accepted the Jewish rites. Their arguments were based,
they thought, on Jesus' teachings. Jesus had declared he had come not
to abrogate the Jewish Law but to complete it (Mt. 5:17). Had he not
faithfully observed this Law himself? Had he not directed his preaching
to the Jews alone, specifically excluding the non-Jews (§ 311)? In any
case, it was quite clear that the covenant God had made with Abraham
could not be abolished, just as it was evident God's promises could not
fail to be fulfilled. If circumcision and the other Jewish rites required in
that covenant were abolished, then God's promises were denied. Heaven
forbid! The nation of Abraham was to have been the elect of God for all
eternity, distinguished precisely by the rite of circumcision. On this
there could be no doubt. The difference now was that since the Messias
had come, the Gentiles too could be accepted as followers of the Christ,
provided they were incorporated into the chosen nation of God by
accepting circumcision. Therefore the "door of faith" was opened to all,
yes, but with a small vestibule in front of it, represented by the Jewish
Law. Anyone who did not come through the vestibule could not reach
the door.

Against this line of reasoning stood the case of the centurion, Cornelius, who, although he was an uncircumcised pagan, had been received
into the Church by Peter (§ 311). But his case was the exception and not
the general rule, for Peter himself had had to justify his action before
the general meeting, appealing to the explicit command he had received
from God to act in that manner (Acts 11:1–18).

352. The majority of Palestinian Christians held these views. But their
most typical and zealous exponents are easily recognizable in the priests
of Jerusalem who had been received into the faith (6:7) and the
converted Pharisees who later openly requested the observance of the
Jewish Law (15:5).

Was this a question of religion or of race? It was both, for in the
history of Israel, religion and race had been fused. The Israelites adored
the true God, Yahweh, because they were the descendants of Abraham.
Now that the Messias had come, this fact still retained all its ancient
value. But now those who did not have in their veins the blood of
Abraham could compensate for this with a substitute. They could accept

circumcision and the rest of the Law, and only on this condition could they be disciples of the Messias Jesus.

Whether or not this was a purely racial issue is not relevant to the present discussion. What is pertinent is the fact that Paul opposed this thesis with all his strength — this same Paul who has been called a fanatical Jew in our day by certain abysmally ignorant rulers.

353. The first conflict between the two currents of thought occurred in Antioch. Some time after the return of Paul and Barnabas, there arrived in that zeal-filled community certain Jewish Christians from Palestine, who categorically told their fellow Christians, converted from paganism: "Unless you be circumcised after the manner of Moses you cannot be saved" (Acts 15:1). While this statement intimated that essentially they were not Christians at all, it also closed the "door of faith" which they had jubilantly contemplated as open to the Gentiles. Who would dare now to speak of the Messias Jesus to the pagans, if circumcision and other Jewish rites were an essential prerequisite for becoming Christian? Circumcision had already been a serious obstacle to the diffusion of the Jewish religion, and very few men had entered the group of "proselytes" precisely because it was required of them (§§ 331, 336). And to this must be added the precepts regarding the Sabbath rest, the purity of foods, contact with pagans, and that whole interminable set of rules which accompanied the pious Jew in every act of his daily life (§ 80 ff.). To demand all that of a pagan was to shut the "door of faith" in his face. It meant two things, that the Christians of Antioch were not true Christians, and that they were not qualified to invite other pagans to become Christians. It nullified what had been done in the past. It precluded anything for the future.

354. But naturally, there was no passive acceptance of this statement. The information we have indicates that the reaction was immediate and energetic, and its principal leaders were Paul and Barnabas: "And when no little objection was made against them by Paul and Barnabas, they decided that Paul and Barnabas and certain others of them should go up to the apostles and presbyters at Jerusalem about this question" (15:2). The procedure was a normal one. Since neither side would yield, it was decided to refer the matter to the mother church for a decision. The question was such as to involve a general principle and could compromise the future propagation of the Church. Hence it was necessary to appeal to the highest authorities of the Church for a norm that would be valid for always. The highest authorities of the whole Church were the "apostles and presbyters" of Jerusalem, whose powers were recognized by the community in Antioch.

The faithful gathered in meeting chose Paul as a delegate but this corresponded to a revelation he himself had had in this regard (§ 298). He took with him a young pagan convert of Antioch who was all zeal and action. His name was Titus (Gal. 2:1), and he was destined to become one of Paul's most trusted collaborators.

355. Their journey took place toward the end of the year 49, or more probably the beginning of 50 (§ 156), and was made by land. They went down through Phoenicia and Samaria, stopping in the Christian communities along the way and "relating the conversion of the Gentiles and they caused great rejoicing among all the brethren" (Acts 15:3). In Jerusalem they were received by a general meeting of the faithful there, composed of three distinct groups (*ibid.*, 4). The highest of these was that of the Apostles, and in the city at that time were James the "brother" of the Lord, Cephas (Peter), and John, the future evangelist. These were considered the "pillars" (Gal. 2:9). Next in authority were the presbyters, who advised and worked with the first. And finally, there was the congregation of the faithful. To this assembly the delegates reported both on their work and on the question which they had been sent to discuss. But in addition Paul spoke of the problem privately with the elders of the community, and also about "his Gospel" (§ 307), and they probably had more than one conversation on these matters.

The result, as we know (§ 309), was full approval for Paul's Gospel and a division of the areas to be evangelized. Thus the dissension in Antioch with regard to the observance of Jewish rites was also resolved by implication. Paul's particular Gospel did not impose these rites; in fact, it excluded them. Therefore, if "his Gospel" was approved, the rites were excluded at least for converts from paganism, to whom Paul addressed his teaching. Having obtained this approval from the elders, namely, the Apostles, Paul had already won his battle.

356. But the partisans of the Jewish observances were far from giving up the fight. As we might expect, they were Pharisees (Acts 15:5), but Paul, their former colleague, calls them "false brethren" who had infiltrated the community to destroy the spiritual liberty brought by Christ and return it to the slavery of the Law (Gal. 2:4). They must have worked quietly at first, since there was little to hope for from the elders, and then forced the issue openly on a particular case. Crying scandal, they denounced Titus, Paul's young companion, because he had not been circumcised and declared that he therefore could not participate in the Christian assemblies with the scrupulous observers of the Jewish precepts. Let him be circumcised and his status thus regularized. But the question concerned the general principle far more than an individual case. So far as an individual case was concerned Paul might have given in since for him the rite no longer had any validity, and later, for practical reasons, he permitted the circumcision of Timothy (§ 373). But since Titus' case had been presented to attack the basic principle, Paul did not yield and Titus was not circumcised.[1]

---

[1] Paul tells us explicitly that Titus was not circumcised (Gal. 2:3). Some modern

Even after this defeat, the Judaizing Christians did not admit they were beaten, but continued to busy themselves in secret. In reply, Paul continued to defend his thesis, certain of the explicit or implicit support of the Apostles. At another meeting attended by the Apostles and presbyters (Acts 15:6), the faithful of Jerusalem and the delegates from Antioch (*ibid.*, 12), there was a long debate during which each side naturally refused to budge from its position. The decision was reached only when the highest authorities rose to speak.

357. The first of these was Peter. His discourse, preserved for us in outline summary, might be called a document *ante tempus* of the papal curia in Rome, well balanced, penetrating, and above all realistic. The question had to be solved not on the basis of personal judgments but of reality. Peter demonstrated this reality on three points: first, he recalled that the evangelization of the Gentiles had already begun some time ago, referring in particular to the conversion of the centurion Cornelius, which he himself had had to justify (§ 351). Then he pointed out that those earlier pagans who had been converted had received the charisms of the Holy Spirit just as well as the converted Jews even though they did not observe the Law of Moses. And finally, he defined this Law as an intolerable yoke which no Jew had actually borne in its entirety, and against it he set the Grace of the Messias Jesus, which alone could bring salvation to both pagans and Jews (*ibid.*, 7–11).

When Peter finished, "the whole meeting quieted down." The protests and personal observations which had prolonged the discussion fell silent. There were no further objections. Peter had spoken. But the delegates from Antioch were not silent. They had new material to add to Peter's argument. "Then the whole meeting quieted down and listened while Barnabas and Paul told of the great signs and wonders that God had done among the Gentiles through them" (*ibid.*, 12). These facts, gathered in the experience of the first missionary journey just ended, confirmed Peter's thesis. If God had worked those wonders among the uncircumcised Christians, it was a good sign that he was pleased with them even though they were uncircumcised.

358. Nevertheless, one point remained to be clarified: what did James the "brother" of the Lord think of all this? He enjoyed great authority among the Christians because of his relationship to Jesus and his position as Apostle, and he was also held in great esteem by the pious Jews because of the consummate austerity of his life.[2] His general prestige

---

scholars have nevertheless taken it upon themselves to circumcise him, claiming that the next sentence in the epistle is grammatically awkward and obscure. They reason, therefore, that Paul was still smarting at the memory of his defeat and was attempting to conceal Titus' circumcision. The argument is a curious one since it attaches no importance to Paul's clear statement of fact and claims to find in an obscure sentence something it does not say at all.

[2] Cf. *Storia d'Israele*, II, pp. 466–467 (§ 415).

had made him a point of contact between the Jews and Christians of
Jerusalem. A phrase of Paul (Gal. 2:12) has led to the inference that
a group of Judaizing Christians centered about him particularly and
perhaps used his name in order to gain acceptance of their own ideas.
On this particular occasion the one dim hope of the Judaizing partisans
was James. If he spoke he would perhaps save something of their position, which had just been demolished by Peter. And James did speak,
but while his discourse confirmed the general opinion held of him as
a man deeply attached to Judaism, it disappointed the secret hopes of
the Judaizers.

He immediately took his stand with Peter. The converts from paganism
were not to be disturbed with Jewish precepts. On the other hand, they
were to show a certain regard for the converts from Judaism by abstaining from certain practices to which the pagans attached no importance. He listed four prohibitions which we shall examine presently
(Acts 15:13–21).

359. The discourses of Peter and James formed the basis for an official
document, namely, the "decree" emanating from the council to solve
the question proposed by the delegates from Antioch. Here is the text
in its "Eastern" form: "The brethren who are apostles and presbyters
send greeting to the brethren of Gentile origin in Antioch and Syria
and Cilicia.

"As we have heard that some of our number have disturbed you with
their teaching, unsettling your minds, persons to whom we had given
no instruction, we have decided, being assembled together, to select
representatives and send them to you with our beloved Barnabas and
Paul: men who have pledged their lives for the name of Our Lord
Jesus Christ. We have therefore sent Judas and Silas, who themselves
also by word of mouth will give you the same message. For the Holy
Spirit and we have decided to lay no further burden upon you but this
indispensable one, that you abstain from things sacrificed to idols and
from blood and from what is strangled and from immorality; keep yourselves from these things, and you will get on well. Farewell" (Acts
15:23–29).

The "Western" version (§ 119, note) differs slightly from this "Eastern"
text in that the "Western" codices enumerate only three prohibitions
(omitting the "things strangled") and add instead the precept of charity
not to do unto others what one does not wish for himself. It is practically certain that the original text is that of the "Eastern" version, while
the "Western" is a modification made in the second or third centuries
in order to have it serve as a little moral code, almost a catechism, for
Christians converted from paganism. The modification has no relation
to the historical circumstances which elicited the decree, while by adding

the precept of charity it inserts another subject which had never been questioned at all.[3]

360. The first part of the decree, then, declares that pagan converts have no obligation to submit to circumcision or other precepts of the Jewish Law ("no further burden, but, etc."), thereby rejecting the claims of the Jewish Christians who came to Antioch to enforce the rite of circumcision. But the pagan converts are not the only Christians of the Diaspora. Their colleagues are converts from Judaism. Therefore, the ex-pagans are to abstain from certain practices which, though indifferent in themselves, are by ancient tradition abominable to the ex-Jewish brethren, and thus pay them the deference of Christian charity. At the end, for good measure, they are reminded to abstain from other practices which are illicit in themselves and extremely common among pagans.

The first three prohibitions concern practices abominable to the Jews, namely, eating the meat of animals sacrificed to idols, "blood," and the meat of animals butchered without having been previously bled (that is, "strangled"). The fourth prohibition is directed against fornication, which is illicit *per se*.

The first three were included substantially in the seven precepts of the sons of Noah ("Noachic precepts"), which, according to rabbinic legislation, had to be observed by non-Israelites living in Israeli territory (*Sanhedrin*, 56 b). The meat of sacrificial animals was abominable because it was believed that in eating it one participated as it were in the idolatrous sacrifice in which it had been offered. Blood or the meat of animals not previously bled was abominated because of the very ancient belief among Semitic people — accepted by the Mosaic Law (cf. Gen. 9:3–4; Lev. 17:10–14) — that the blood was the seat of the soul, and by eating it, therefore, one absorbed the soul of the animal with all its brutish qualities.

361. In practice, however, it was not an easy thing in those days to abstain from such meats if one lived in a pagan community, for they were sold in the markets along with other meats since the pagan buyers attached no importance to their source. But at least in the meals taken together, the *agapes*, in a Christian community, the ex-pagans were to abstain from these foods out of respect for the ex-Jews. The precept was in essence a precept of charity, to be observed out of deference to those whom Paul later called "weak" (Rom. 14:1 ff.; cf. 1 Cor. 10:23 ff.) and who would have been scandalized to see their Christian colleagues eating abominated food. When the occasion of scandal ceased to exist so did the precept, since there was no longer any need for the particular form of fraternal charity on which it was based.

---

[3] These four prohibitions, without the precept of charity, appear elsewhere in the "Eastern" text (Acts 15:20; 21:25), and in the "Western" with the same variations.

Nevertheless, these prohibitions were respected for a very long time in the Church and even after the danger of scandal had disappeared. Not only in the year 177 did the martyrs of Lyons declare that as Christians they could not eat blood (in Eusebius, *Hist. Eccl.*, V, I, 26), but even in succeeding centuries down to the Middle Ages we encounter unexpected echoes of this early "abomination" due unquestionably to the great authority of the apostolic decree as well as to sporadic inveterate customs difficult to eradicate.

362. The fourth and last prohibition concerns fornication. According to some scholars this term (πορνεία) refers only to marriage contracted within certain degrees of kinship forbidden by Jewish Law. But this is hard to prove, while the word itself usually meant, especially among pagans, sexual intercourse between unmarried men and women. If special mention is made of fornication, even though it is forbidden by the natural law, this was due to the fact that it was so widespread among pagans as to have acquired an apparent legitimacy from common consent.

Cicero undertook to defend it explicitly, on the grounds that it was the common practice: ". . . When has this not been done? When has it been reproved? When has it not been permitted? In short, when has it happened that a thing which is licit is not licit?" (*Pro M. Coelio,* 20.) Many other pagan writers of about the same time jest about it or in other ways attest its prevalence.[4] So widespread was it and so deeply rooted that much later, after four centuries of Christianity, it could exert the influence on a young catechumen, son of a fervent Christian, which is documented in the first books of the *Confessions of St. Augustine.* Besides, fornication had penetrated many pagan cults as an ordinary adjunct, and had thus received an almost religious legitimacy (cf. 15, 31, 35, 41, 71, 72, etc.). Given this pagan mentality, it was opportune to recall to ex-pagan Christians, at least at the end of the decree and *ad abundantiam,* that it was intrinsically unlawful.

363. As the text itself tells us, the decree was sent to Antioch with Judas and Silas, representing the community of Jerusalem and accompanied by Barnabas and Paul, who thus returned to their headquarters. Of Judas we know only that he was called Barsabbas (Acts 15:22), "son of Sabbas" ("of the Old One"). This same patronymic was attributed also to the Joseph nominated with Matthias to take the place of Judas Iscariot in the college of Apostles (Acts 1:23). If the two were brothers — as it would seem from the patronymic — this Judas must have been an early Christian, perhaps a disciple of Jesus, and consequently would have had great authority in the community of Jerusalem. The other messenger, Silas, appears later as Paul's companion, and is cer-

---

[4] Horace, *Satires,* I, 2, 31; Terence, *Adelphi,* 101; Seneca, *Controv.,* 2, 4 (12), 10; Quintilian, *Instit. orat.,* 8, 3, 48; besides the entire *Satyricon* of Petronius Arbiter.

tainly the same person as Sylvanus mentioned in his epistles. Like Paul, he too was a Roman citizen (16:37) and was probably a Hellenist Jew. Both of them, Judas and Silas, were distinguished by the charism of prophet (§ 215).

The messengers and the decree, read in public, were greeted with great joy by the community in Antioch while the two "prophets" with their charismatic discourses kindled even further the zeal and ardor of the Christians there. Then Judas returned to Jerusalem while Silas remained in the community, whose missionary zeal appealed directly to his own spirit.

The grave problem had in substance been solved with a victory for Paul, since the council's decision had sanctioned his fundamental principle of the separation of the Church from the Synagogue. Yet in his letters Paul never alluded to the decree, even when he is treating the same subjects it contemplates and even though it was the document of his victory. Was this humility or does it imply disagreement with the first three prohibitions? We do not know. But it is certain that if there was any disagreement it concerned only those aspects of transitory value which today have disappeared altogether. On the fundamental question, of perennial validity, there was full agreement, and this was achieved by virtue of the principles defended by Paul.

❊   ❊   ❊

364. Nevertheless an explicit dissension did occur shortly afterward between the two principal artificers of that decree and it related precisely to applying the above-mentioned prohibitions. It is the famous dissension at Antioch, the only data concerning which is to be found in Paul's epistle to the Galatians (2:11 ff.).

We may conclude that this took place immediately after the council of Jerusalem, both from the sequence of events as set forth in the epistle and from the fact that Paul and Barnabas were still together in Antioch, which sets the time a little before Paul's second missionary journey (§ 370). Peter went from Jerusalem to Antioch during this time, perhaps for reasons related to the evangelization of the Gentiles, for although the center of this activity was Antioch it was of decided interest to the head of the mother church in Jerusalem. Since he was staying for some time among the Christians of Antioch, the majority of whom were converted pagans, he freely adapted himself to their customs. Hence he entered their houses, ate with them, took part at the *agapes* at which no one worried whether or not the meat served was that of sacrificial animals, or unbled, or unclean according to the Jewish Law. These things Peter did freely and broad-mindedly, although he was applying to himself, a Jew, what the letter of the decree accorded the converted pagans. But Peter legitimately went beyond the letter to the spirit of the decree, and this granted him, a convert from Judaism, the same liberty accorded those converted from paganism. Besides, charity was safeguarded, for no one was scandalized by his association with the ex-pagans.

365. In the midst of this idyl, however, along came some Judaizing Christians from Jerusalem again. They were "certain persons" who had come "from James" ($\tau\iota\nu\grave{a}s$ $\grave{a}\pi\grave{o}$ $^{\prime}I\alpha\kappa\acute{\omega}\beta\sigma\upsilon$), that is, they belonged to the group centering around the highly authoritative "brother of the Lord." These had perhaps been sent by James, for whatever reason, but they easily used his name to give prestige to their own tenets (§ 358). On seeing Peter's conduct among the ex-pagans, they again cried scandal, thus inaugurating the long line of Capitoline geese who have always pretended to save the Rock of the Church in much better fashion than its strategic defender. The alarmed clatter of the geese impressed Peter, who, in the charitable hope of restoring peace and quiet "began to withdraw and to separate himself" from the ex-pagans, "fearing the circumcised" (Gal. 2:12). But the example of the head of the Apostles could not fail to have its influence on the others. "And the rest of the Jews dissembled along with him ($\sigma\upsilon\nu\upsilon\pi\acute{\epsilon}\kappa\rho\acute{\iota}\theta\eta\sigma\alpha\nu$), so that Barnabas also was led away by them into that dissimulation" (*ibid.*, 13).

The Judaizing Christians from Jerusalem could not ask for more. They had been defeated in the doctrinal field by the decree of the council, but they were now vindicated in actual practice. The example of an Apostle like Peter, avoiding contacts with the ex-pagans, proved that the Jewish precepts were still completely in force despite the decree of the council. If Peter had spoken in the council in favor of abolishing that Law and approved the decree, he had done it under pressure from that troublemaker Paul — the geese cackled — but the real Peter was once more in evidence here, avoiding the ex-pagans of Antioch. Things must be as they were before, then; the ex-pagans on one side and the ex-Jews on the other. Both were part of the Church of the Messias Jesus, yes, but in two completely separate compartments. A descendant of Abraham was too noble a soul to be in the same compartment with a Greek or a Roman, and the circumcised were far too holy to mingle with those who did not have this distinction!

366. These arguments, from practice to principle, Paul clearly divined; and he forestalled the danger by removing their foundation. "But when Cephas came to Antioch, I withstood him to his face, because he was deserving of blame ($\kappa\alpha\tau\epsilon\gamma\nu\omega\sigma\mu\acute{\epsilon}\nu\sigma s$ $\mathring{\eta}\nu$)." These words show that Paul openly and frankly opposed Peter "to his face" and not behind his back as the Judaizers are wont to do. But they in no way imply a violent or arrogant attitude on his part. To disarm the Judaizers, Paul appealed to Peter, speaking with the zeal which was his special gift but also with the charity which was the prerogative of all early Christians.

367. And yet this episode, so human and so Christian in its essence, has been interpreted in the most varied ways. It is unnecessary to say that the early Lutherans took great delight in it, visualizing a violent scene insulting Peter (a little reminiscent of the insults Luther was hurling uninterruptedly against the pope of Rome). These do not merit any reply. In early times, Clement of Alexandria supposed that the Cephas named here was not the Apostle Peter but one of the seventy-two disciples of Jesus (in Eusebius, *Hist. Eccl.*, I, 12, 2). This opinion, although it was espoused by later scholars and even by some in our own time, has no proofs in its favor and many indications against it. Various ancient writers, and Jerome especially, supposed that the dissension in Antioch was a little scene fixed up in advance by Peter and Paul in order to foil more effectively the intrigues of the Judaizers. But the observations offered by Augustine (epp., 40, 75, 82, in Migne, *Patr. Lat.*, 33) demolished once and for all this theory. What is certain is that Paul was convinced Peter's conduct was mistaken and harmful, and it is equally certain that he remonstrated with him vigorously.

"But when I saw that they [Peter and his imitators] were not walking uprightly according to the truth of the gospel, I said to Cephas before them all: 'If thou, though a Jew, livest like the Gentiles, and not like the Jews, how is it that thou dost compel the Gentiles to live like the Jews?'" (Gal. 2:14.) The admonition was perhaps given in a general meeting of the community, to remedy the unfortunate impression created among the ex-pagans at being abandoned by Barnabas, so recently their zealous teacher. The reasons Paul adduced were the key points of his doctrine. A Jew converted to Christ knows he is not justified by the works of the Jewish law but by his faith in Christ. If then, though justified by his faith in Christ, he claims he still needs the works of the Law, he shows he is still a sinner and thereby declares that faith in Christ is not sufficient. To abandon the Law for the faith is not a sin. It means abandoning what has been abolished for what has been inaugurated, to exchange a former death for a new life, otherwise Christ has died in vain (*ibid.*, 15–21).

368. The error which caused Paul to remonstrate with Peter was one of conduct, not of doctrine, as Tertullian noted, in his usual curt style: *Conversationis fuit vitium, non praedicationis* (*De praescr.*, 23). Peter had not denied any of the doctrinal principles established by the council of Jerusalem. But in practice he did not conform to them on this occasion, thinking in good faith that he would thus avoid conflict and trouble. The early Protestants who cited the episode in Antioch as proof of the fallibility of the pope of Rome fell into an obvious historical mistake. In addition they confused the infallibility of the teacher with the peccability of the Christian in action, not knowing, perhaps, that the pope of Rome confesses his sins and mistakes like any other ordinary Catholic Christian.

Paul does not tell us the result of the episode, but there is no reason to doubt that Peter accepted his protest affectionately and modified his behavior accordingly. The Apostles lived only for the propagation of the Good Tidings, and whatever was useful to this end was for them always welcome, especially if it came from a zealous evangelizer like Paul. Hypersensitivity and petty personal pride had no place among them, endowed as they were with charisms and completely dedicated to Christ.[5]

369. If the episode in Antioch was essentially an act of charity — *libera in Paulo ad arguendum, humilis in Petro ad obediendum* (Augustine) — there is also charity in Luke's silence on the subject. An Antiochene himself, he undoubtedly knew of the incident, while Paul had probably spoken of it incidentally more than once. Yet he does not mention it at all. Why?

If we consider the circumstances well, it seems inevitable to conclude that this silence on the part of the informed but prudent Luke was prompted both by his veneration for the head of the Apostles and his devotion to the discipline of the Church, and probably also by an explicit recommendation of Paul.

Luke wrote the *Acts* about fifteen years after the episode had taken place, when the situation had completely changed and the Judaizing Christians were no longer a serious danger in the Church but were either diminishing in number or withdrawing from it altogether. In such circumstances was it opportune to keep talking about a human weakness committed with every good intention by the head of the Church? Would retelling it now not offer ammunition to the new enemies of the Church and its hierarchical constitution?

An objective historian is not obliged to give all the facts in his possession if these do not fall within the general framework of his story. The framework of the *Acts* is the general fact of the diffusion of the Church in the world (§ 91) and not the detailed chronicle of its diffusion, much less the criteria which governed it. Thus the episode in Antioch was irrelevant to his theme, and Luke could omit it without prejudice to his objectivity and truth as a historian.

The Hebrew Scriptures offer a far more striking example of such

---

[5] It might be well to note here the observations on this incident of Francis de Sales, who was a keen psychologist, with an excellent knowledge of the New Testament, and above all a great saint. He notes the "humility and gentleness with which St. Peter received the correction which St. Paul made to him notwithstanding that he was his Superior. We do not know which is the greater, the courage of St. Paul in reproving St. Peter, or the humility with which St. Peter accepted the correction for something he thought it wise to do and in which he had every good intention" (*Les Oeuvres de S. Francois de Sales, Entretien,* XVI, tom. VI, Paris, 1685, p. 286).

omission. The books of the *Chronicles* (*Paralipomena*) omitted from the story of King David the adultery and subsequent murder he committed, although both these crimes had already been narrated in the books of *Kings*. As the author of the *Chronicles* passed over these two unsavory deeds out of respect for the great King of Israel, so Luke quietly omitted the weakness of Peter, out of "respect for the high keys" (*Inferno,* 19, 101).

The Second Missionary Journey

370. The exultation of the Antiochene community over the spiritual freedom sanctioned by the apostolic decree was immediately reflected in missionary zeal. Paul suggested to Barnabas that they return to visit the Christian centers they had established on their previous journey. Barnabas was quite ready for such a trip but he wanted to take with him again his cousin, John Mark, who had left them at Perge to return to Jerusalem (§ 329). This suggests that Mark had meanwhile come to Antioch, perhaps in Peter's company, attracted by the fervid activity of that community. But Paul would have none of Mark; in his opinion he could not be counted on after his previous defection.

The discussion between the two was a lively one. The physician Luke says there was a "paroxysm" ($\pi\alpha\rho o\xi\nu\sigma\mu\acute{o}s$) between them, that is, a state of exasperation (Acts 15:39). And for all their argument they could come to no agreement. Beneath Paul's charisms there lingered the "man" with all his rough tenacity (§ 288), which became even more inflexible when a cause he considered just was involved. For his part, Barnabas, who had been so accommodating on the previous journey, yielding to Paul the direction of the mission (§ 329), refused this time to give in and be separated from his young cousin. This is what appears on the surface. If there were other hidden and perhaps loftier motives under these appearances, we do not know.[1] In the end they separated "from each other, and Barnabas took Mark and sailed for Cyprus" (*ibid.*, 39).

---

[1] We may turn again to St. Frances de Sales for a few reflections on this episode: "It is a remarkable thing that the Lord has permitted that many things, truly worthy of being written down, which the Apostles had done, are buried in deep silence, while this imperfection which the great St. Paul and St. Barnabas committed together has been recorded: it is undoubtedly a special Providence of the Lord, who has thus wished it for our particular instruction. They were both going to preach the Holy Gospel, and they were taking with them a young man named John Mark, who was a kinsman of St. Barnabas; and these two great Apostles fell into a dispute, whether they should take him with them or whether they should leave him behind, and finding that they held opposite views on this matter and could come to no agreement, they separated one from the other. Now tell me, must we be troubled when we see some fault in ourselves, when the Apostles also committed them?" (In *Oeuvres, op. cit., Entretien*, XIV, v. VI, p. 244.)

The separation, however, did not ruin their friendship. Later Paul speaks of Barnabas with deference (Gal. 2:9; 1 Cor. 9:6) and his lack of confidence in Mark eventually disappeared. He later accepted him among his companions and depended on him a great deal (Col. 4:10; Philemon 24; 2 Tim. 4:11). Barnabas, whose return to Cyprus was certainly prompted by missionary motives (§ 322), disappears at this point from the story of early Christianity, and we hear no more about him except in later legends.

Silas, who had all the qualities of a good missionary (§ 363), now became Paul's companion and they departed immediately from Antioch to begin the second missionary journey. It was the end of the year 49, or more probably the beginning of 50 (§ 157).

371. Paul was heading for new fields of endeavor but he did not forget the old. He decided to visit first the communities he had established in Asia Minor, from where he would proceed as the Spirit prompted him. He therefore took the direct route they had rejected on their return from the previous journey, namely, the road which connected Derbe, across the Taurus range, with Tarsus and Antioch (§ 346).

From Antioch, Paul and Silas crossed Mt. Amanus at the "Syrian Gates" (§ 7), entering Cilicia from Syria. Along the way they stopped in the various communities founded in these two regions, where Paul was already known (§ 294), and "strengthened the churches" (Acts 14:41). Leaving Cilicia, undoubtedly from Tarsus, they braved the crossing of the Taurus Mountains at the "Cilician Gates" (§ 7). If the ascent of the Taurus in Pamphylia five years before had been difficult (§ 330) this was considerably more arduous and dangerous. On the second day's journey the road, which could hardly have been worse, plunged into narrow mountain passes, from which only a sliver of sky was visible above. Our two travelers had to wade mountain streams and clamber over rocks where landslides barred their path. They could hear the rumble of distant landslides and the cries of wild beasts from their mountain lairs among the crags. They were quite likely to meet bands of robbers, for these fastnesses had been inhabited by thieves for centuries, or come upon the decaying bodies of animals or men abandoned along the way. But never once would they encounter a village or a house or a shelter for the night. At the early setting of the sun, they had to stop beneath the shelter of a tree or some overhanging rock, eat the little they had brought with them, roll themselves in their cloaks and sleep on the ground, after making the sign of the cross to protect themselves from the dangers they were risking for the glory of Christ. There was nothing else to do. The "Cilician Gates" were, and still are, a deep narrow fissure in the mountain rock. On either side of the path, the cliffs rise for several hundred feet and are so close together that one might cross from one to the other on an ordinary piece of board. At the narrowest point the Romans had set a gate and stationed a small body of guards. The gate served as an excellent post for military and police surveillance.

372. Having crossed the Taurus, the two travelers could contemplate the endless plain of Lycaonia stretching beneath them. This had to be

The Cilician Gates (from Schweinitz, *In Kleinasien*)

crossed too and it presented different though no lesser difficulties. In springtime, when the journey probably took place, the plain was green with vegetation but swampy, and travelers unfamiliar with the paths risked sinking into the soft marsh mud. In Paul's time there was a great deal of pasturing on the plain and the many flocks offered some means of obtaining food, just as the shepherds' huts offered some shelter.

After about ten days of travel, the two missionaries arrived in Derbe (§ 346), but we are told nothing about this first stopover. From here they went on to Lystra, where they perhaps lodged in Timothy's house as before (§ 341). It is certain that at this time Timothy was attracted within Paul's orbit never to leave it again. The young man's father was probably dead. He was an affectionate, delicate, almost timid, and very devout youth (2 Tim. 1:4 ff.), reflecting perhaps the pious and feminine upbringing given him by his mother, Eunice, and his grandmother, Lois, both fervent Jewesses. He was not circumcised because his father, perhaps a Greek or Roman employee, had been a pagan. The youth had become a Christian with his mother and grandmother during Paul's previous sojourn among them. During the Apostle's absence, Timothy had been active in keeping alive the flame of the new faith not only in Lystra but also in the environs, so that "he was highly thought of by the brethren in Lystra and Iconium" (Acts 16:2).

This kind of novitiate was a good sign in Paul's view. He had noticed Timothy especially and he suggested that he become his co-worker. The invitation probably appealed not only to the inclinations but to some secret hope of the young man, and he accepted without hesitation. And so the number of three missionaries, desired by Barnabas, was now rounded out.

373. But there was still some difficulty with regard to the new recruit. The fact that Timothy was not circumcised, although he was the son of a Jewess, might elicit the usual recriminations from the Jews the missionaries encountered along the way. There were so many difficulties to be expected from the Jews that it seemed sensible to avoid this one at least. The rite, according to Paul, had been abolished and was useless. But it was admissible to observe it still for reasons of charity and the keeping of the peace. For these practical reasons, Paul circumcised Timothy.

This was in no sense a repudiation of the thesis he had defended at the Apostolic Council (§ 356). The latter dealt with the matter as an obligation, while Paul's action here involved only its permissibility. In Jerusalem the Council had discussed whether the rite was necessary for salvation in Christ, but no one had declared it an illicit act for anyone desiring to undergo it for the traditional reasons. The rite in this instance was determined by practical considerations, which in no way implied that it was obligatory. This seems quite evident. Nevertheless some scholars have rejected this particular information in the *Acts* with the argument that Paul, having refused to circumcise Titus, could not now circumcise Timothy. These scholars, who compose history in conflict with the documents, should note that Paul later practices other Jewish rites (§§ 448, 540), and he does so according to his usual principle, "I have become to the Jews a Jew that I might gain the Jews" (1 Cor. 9:20). It is the same principle he follows in Timothy's case and is based on practical charity, not doctrinal necessity.

374. Timothy, who was about twenty years old (cf. 1 Tim. 4:12), had known the Hebrew Scriptures from childhood (2 Tim. 3:15). After he joined Paul, he received the "laying on of the hands" both from him (2 Tim. 1:6) and from the council of elders (1 Tim. 4:14). He became Paul's secretary and accompanied him almost everywhere, including Rome and Jerusalem, represented him on various occasions, was associated with him in a number of epistles, and received two from him after he had left him.

Leaving Lystra, the three missionaries visited other Christian communities established during the previous journey, communicating to them the decisions reached in the decree of the Apostolic Council. "So the churches grew stronger and stronger in the faith and increased in numbers daily" (Acts 16:5).

Having finished visiting the fields of his former activity, Paul now turned to new pastures. What region to choose among all those still hidden from the Good Tidings? Paul's thought turned to the province of Asia (§ 12 ff.), which had a dense population and a number of

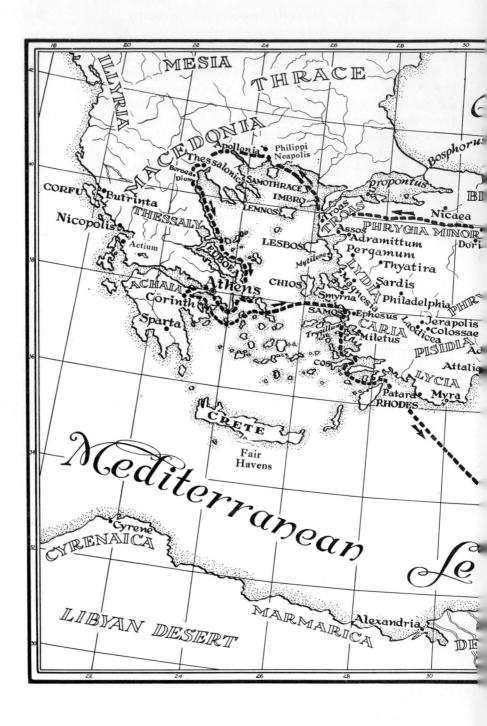

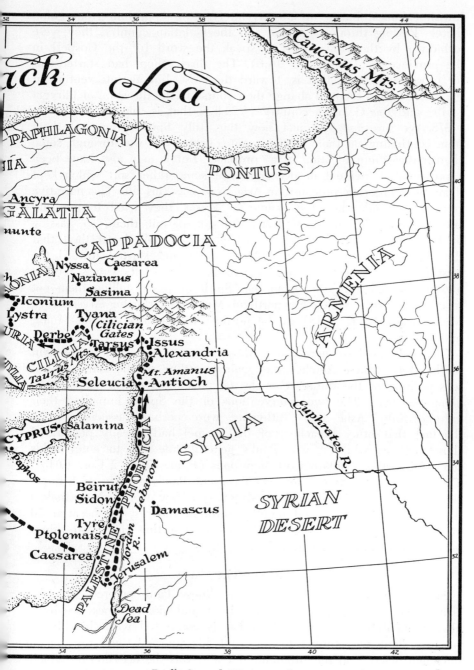

Paul's Second Missionary Journey

Jewish colonies, but a mysterious intervention kept him from going there: "Passing through Phrygia and the Galatian country, they were forbidden by the Holy Spirit to speak the word [of the Gospel] in the province of Asia" (Acts 16:6). The three, then, had started out for proconsular Asia, that is, toward the west, but an intervention of the Spirit caused them to change their course in the direction of Phrygia (§ 19) and the Galatian country (§ 23 ff.), that is, toward the north.

375. We are not told just how the Holy Spirit prevented them from continuing on their original route. Perhaps it was through some charismatic communication of a "prophet," but it may also have been a providential incident or occurrence of some other sort which kept them from entering proconsular Asia. Nor was this all. The narrative continues: "And when they came to Mysia, they tried to get into Bithynia, but the Spirit of Jesus did not permit them; so passing by Mysia, they went down to Troas" (ibid., 7–8). We learn, then, that the three missionaries left northern Galatia and started toward the west again, but when they approached Mysia (§ 17) there was another mysterious communication from the "Spirit of Jesus" telling them not to enter Bithynia, which lay north of Mysia. So, skirting Mysia, they went toward Troas (§ 18) in the northwestern corner of Asia Minor, by the sea.

Obviously we have here one of those summary accounts so frequent in the Acts, which sketches the general outline of the itinerary but tells nothing of the duration or the circumstances of the stops made along the way. The two interventions of the Spirit, impeding their entrance into "Asia" and "Bithynia," were perhaps associated with the fact that other preachers of the Gospel had already penetrated those regions, while it was Paul's general rule not to enter fields plowed by others, but to work new ones (Rom. 15:20; 2 Cor. 10:15). The author of the Acts, anxious to present Paul's activity in Europe, skims over this sojourn in Asia Minor in a few words. Nevertheless it must have lasted several months, through the rest of the year 50 and perhaps the beginning of 51, and during that time two things of particular importance occurred.

GALATIA

376. One important event was the illness Paul suffered, not the "sting of the flesh" (§ 199), but the brief and violent illness we have already mentioned (§ 197). The other is connected with this illness, because Paul was forced to interrupt his journey and stop in an unknown place. And this unintentional stop was the occasion on which he evangelized the Galatians the first time (Gal. 4:13–15). From this we must conclude that the unknown place was in the "Galatian region," which Luke tells us Paul had traversed. Besides, those evangel-

ized by Paul "formerly" were real "Galatians," as he calls them in his epistle; that is, they inhabited the northern part of the Roman province of Galatia, where the Galatian tribes had settled, together with the central zone as far as Ancyra, at the time of their invasion (§§ 23-24).

Two Views of Ancyra in Galatia

This information solves the question of the recipients of the letter Paul addressed to the "Galatians." All the early interpretations, down to the late nineteenth century, held the opinion that Paul was addressing himself to the real "Galatians," that is, the inhabitants of the northern part of the province of the same name. But for almost a century now many scholars have preferred the inhabitants of the southern section of the province, and according to this view, the epistle was addressed to the Christians of Antioch of Pisidia, Iconium, Lystra, and Derbe, whom Paul had evangelized during his first journey.

On the contrary, the fact is that these latter people could never have been called "Galatians" for the simple reason that they were, and were called, Pisidians or Lycaonians, just as they spoke a language called Lycaonian (§ 343). Nor did their administrative incorporation into the province of Galatia in any way cancel out their separate names, as the inscriptions prove (§ 24). Besides, if Luke here says that the three missionaries crossed the "Galatian region," he undoubtedly means the territory of the Galatian tribes in the northern part of the province and not the province in general, because the missionaries were coming from Pisidia and Lycaonia, which were part of the Roman province of Galatia, and so they were already within the province. Therefore, having been "forbidden by the Holy Spirit" to evangelize proconsular Asia, they passed through Phrygia and the "Galatian region" properly so called, while remaining within the boundaries of the province.

Other subtle reasons advanced in support of the theory of southern Galatia are learned quibbles and do not weaken these clear and solid reasons on which the old interpretation is based.

377. The condensed narrative of the *Acts* must be supplemented by the information in the epistle to the Galatians. We then learn that the three missionaries, because of Paul's illness, stopped in some undetermined place in the Galatian region. Their arrival was a highly important event for the inhabitants for, in addition to their many admirable qualities, they had the defect of an insatiable curiosity. Julius Caesar, who was personally acquainted with their ancestors in Gaul, often speaks of their curiosity together with a certain levity and impulsiveness of character. According to the Roman author, the Gauls had the habit of stopping a traveler or peddler, crowding around him to hear what he knew or had heard along the way, and on the basis of this gossip immediately making important decisions.[2] As for the Galatians themselves, the orator, Themistius, in the fourth century A.D., sketches them with the same colors, for he says they were intelligent and docile, but when the cloak of a philosopher appeared in their midst, they clung to it like iron to a magnet.[3]

We may well imagine, then, that the three missionaries immediately became the chief topic of conversation throughout the countryside. Paul, though his illness was repugnant, was given affectionate care by these cordial peasants, and he himself tells us that they were ready to pluck out their eyes for him (§ 197 ff.). At the same time, they were curious to know who the three unknown travelers were, where they were going, and how they happened to be there, what news they brought from the countries they had been traveling through, and what their political and religious ideas were. Naturally their curiosity was put to good use by Silas and Timothy first, while Paul was ill, and then by Paul himself during and after his convalescence. So these simple peasants were evangelized, and though their conversion had been incidental so far as Paul's program was concerned, it was no less effective than others he had planned and prepared for.

378. The missionaries' success was spectacular. Paul was received as "an angel of God, even as Christ Jesus" (Gal. 4:14). It seems certain that there were Jews in the Galatian region, but they must have been few in number and not acrimonious, for Paul's first preaching here

---

[2] *De bello gallico*, II, 1; III, 10; IV, 5.
[3] *Orat.*, XXIII, p. 229.

went off smoothly and quietly without the usual opposition from the Jewish camp, as though he were speaking only to well-disposed pagans. But it was not long before Judaizing Christians, from outside the region, came poking in among them, and the second time Paul visits his beloved Galatians (§ 450 ff.) he finds the sowers of discord already busy. The Galatians, as if to evidence their light and volatile nature, were not entirely insensible to the flattery of the troublemakers, and Paul admonished them with heartfelt exhortations during his second sojourn among them (Gal. 1:9; 4:16; 5:3). Notwithstanding this the danger grew, and when Paul heard of it he wrote his wavering flock the epistle which quivers with indignation and affection (§ 504 ff.).

When Paul had fully recovered his health and his profitable stay among the Galatians was over, he and his companions resumed their journey to Troas (§ 18) and thus drew near Europe. There, not far from the Troy of Homer, Paul waited. Two mysterious communications had kept him from the province of Asia and Bithynia; the guidance had been negative. But he perhaps foresaw some positive message which would direct him to a new field of labor.

379. The wait was not a long one, and it was brightened by the joy of meeting a beloved friend, who became another companion for the journey. This was Luke. Since the *Acts* (16:10 ff.) uses the first person plural (§ 92) to narrate the departure from Troas, we conclude that the narrator joined the group in this city or shortly beforehand.

How did Luke happen to be in these parts? He may have had personal matters to attend to in Philippi in Macedonia, where he left Paul (16:40) and later joined him again (20:6), and the most convenient harbor from which to sail to Macedonia from northwestern Asia Minor was Troas. We may suppose that in all likelihood he made periodic visits both to Philippi and Troas in the exercise of his profession as a physician, for in those times the more well-known disciples of Aesculapius traveled a great deal. We might permit ourselves a further conjecture and suppose that Luke had learned of Paul's recent illness and with all solicitude set out to look for him to help him, catching up with him in the country around Troas. Whatever the truth of the matter, Luke found Paul in good health and asked about his future plans. Upon learning that he had no fixed goal at the moment but was waiting for God to guide him, Luke probably did not fail to draw his attention to Macedonia.

380. Perhaps one day while they were both walking along the harbor of Troas, Luke pointed in the direction of Macedonia. It was the country just beyond Tenedos, the island sacred to Apollo lying opposite the port. It took just a few hours' sailing to get there, and it was a country of great hopes. Luke, who knew it well, was sure of this, and he would be most happy to ask his numerous acquaintances there to help the missionaries. In fact, did Paul see those men there in the harbor with full cloaks and broad-brimmed hats? They were Macedonian merchants. And Luke, who had a long familiarity with their character, was sure that many of them could be easily won to the Good Tidings.

Paul's heart must have beat a little faster at all this, like a merchant's when he sees the opportunity for an unusual profit. But he waited for some divine bidding. He could not decide by himself. Before lying down on his straw mat to sleep that night he must have prayed the Lord of all souls for a long time to illumine his mind with regard to the proposal made him by his good friend the physician.

Then Paul fell asleep and his prayer was answered. Luke tells us that "Paul had a vision one night; a Macedonian was standing, appealing to him and saying, 'Come over into Macedonia and help us'" (Acts 16:9). The man in the vision perhaps appeared clad in a full cloak and broad-brimmed hat like those worn by the Macedonian merchants Paul had seen that day in the harbor. His urgent invitation to come to Macedonia removed every doubt as to the meaning of the vision. The next morning Paul told his vision to the other three and found them in full agreement. Luke, including himself in the narrative for the first time, continues: "As soon as he had the vision, straightway we made efforts to set out for Macedonia, being sure that God had called us to preach the gospel to them" (*ibid.*, 10). They departed immediately afterward.

PHILIPPI

381. The four men who sailed that day from Troas represent a historical fact of incomparable importance, the irruption of Christianity in Europe. They were not truly the first Christians to touch European soil, for by this time (A.D. 51) the Gospel had undoubtedly reached Rome and other centers. But we know nothing of other evangelizers and their work may be represented symbolically by the four missionaries setting out from Troas.

A century earlier Julius Caesar had thought of making Troas the center of the Roman Empire (§ 18) instead of Rome. Paul, who had been looking to Rome, has a similar but reverse plan, for he leaves Troas with the intention of making Rome the cen-

Kavalla (from Monmarché et Tillion, *Les pays d'Europe*)

Philippi — General View of Forum

ter of the kingdom of Christ. Caesar's plan was not too grandiose for the means at his disposal, but it failed. Paul's plan was palpably a paradox, and yet it triumphed. This is characteristic of Christianity's diffusion, to triumph in the most contrary circumstances.

The sailing was without incident. The 175 miles between Troas and Neapolis (Kavalla) were covered in two days, including a short stop on the island of Samothrace at about the halfway mark. The missionaries disembarked at Neapolis (§ 37) and reached Philippi (§ 37), the most important city in the district,[4] on foot in two or three hours.

382. At Philippi there were so few Jews they did not have a building for a synagogue. On the Sabbath they gathered in an "oratory" (*proseuchè*) in the open air near a stream of water not far from the city,[5] the water being necessary for the ablutions prescribed by the Mosaic Law. Some have thought the stream was the Gangites (§ 37), which flows less than two miles west of the city, but it may have been one of the many springs which had given the city its ancient name, *Krenides* ("Fountains").

---

[4] The phrase in apposition to Philippi is very obscure: "which is the first city in the district of Macedonia, a colony" (Acts 16:12). The passage varies in the codices; nor is it clear whether the adjective "first" refers to the importance of the city or to the fact that it was the first of a series Paul visited on his journey. Both interpretations, as well as others that have been suggested, offer certain difficulties. Or was the adjective a kind of honorary epithet, meaning "outstanding" or "noteworthy"?

[5] Cf. *Storia d'Israele*, II, p. 227 (§ 199).

Faithful as always to his custom of preaching first to the Jews, Paul and his companions attended the gathering in this "oratory" on their first Sabbath in the city. It did not seem very promising. There were only women present, some of whom were pagans by birth and affiliated to Judaism in the class of the "devout." But Paul was not discouraged. "And a certain woman named Lydia, a seller of purple from the city of Thyatira, who worshipped God, was listening: and the Lord touched her heart to give heed to what was being said by Paul" (Acts 16:14).

"Lydia" (i.e., "the woman from Lydia") was more of a surname than a real name, because Thyatira — as we have seen (§ 17) — was often assigned to the region of Lydia instead of to Mysia. It was a colony of Macedonians and a great market center for purple, which accounts both for the woman's presence in Macedonia and for her occupation. This was probably a lucrative one and assured her a certain degree of financial comfort, as we may judge from her subsequent actions.

When she had been sufficiently instructed, she was baptized with her whole family. She may have been a widow, but in any case she had good sense and energy enough to head both her family and her business. When her whole household had become Christian, she approached the missionaries and said: "'If you have judged me to be a believer in the Lord, come into my house and stay there.' And she insisted upon our coming" (*ibid.*, 15).

383. If the woman "insisted" it is clear that at first they declined her invitation. As usual, Paul was unwilling to be a burden to anyone, and they preferred to stay in the humble merchant's inn, where they were lodging, than in her well-appointed home. But the woman made almost a moral issue of it. They had judged her worthy to enter the spiritual house of the Lord; did they not judge her worthy to receive them in her home? They had to accept, even though the relative luxury of their new quarters might be embarrassing to their missionary spirit. Later, writing to the Christians of this city, Paul recalls that in all Macedonia he had consented to receive help in money only from them (Phil. 4:10–20), and it is not difficult to recognize as the principal contributor the wealthy "seller of purple."

Paul's meeting with Lydia was too tempting for Renan to let pass without weaving around it a little idyl to his own romantic taste. Paul, he decided, married Lydia. The basis for his view is the expression "my loyal comrade" which may also be translated "loyal Syzygus" (Phil. 4:3) and which we have already indicated refers to a man and not a woman (§ 244).

384. We have no other information about Paul's sojourn in Philippi between this incident and the episode which closed it. But we may be sure that it lasted several months and was both active and fruitful. Paul's method was the same as that in his first missionary journey. From acquaintances made among the Jews, other contacts were gradually developed; here in Philippi these were almost all with pagans. From house to house, from quarter to quarter, then to the suburbs of the city and finally to towns at a little distance, the missionaries made their way, until finally there was a sizable nucleus of disciples of the Good Tidings. We have no hint of opposition from the Jews in the beginning, and this is not surprising since they were so few in number. The establishment of this first church in Europe was accomplished easily enough, and the thought of it remained always for Paul a source of pride and consolation. Twelve years later, addressing himself to these his first sons, he speaks with special affection: "For God is my witness how I long for you all in the heart of Christ Jesus" (Phil. 1:8). — "So, then, my brethren, beloved and longed for, my joy and my crown . . ." (4:1).

Paul soon found zealous co-workers among the first neophytes, and especially among the women. Mentioned among them are Evodia and Syntyche "who have toiled in the gospel" with Paul (4:2–3). Among the men, in addition to the problematical Syzygus (§ 244) we find a certain Clement (4:3) — whom some early writers identify with Clement of Rome, probably wrongly — and especially Epaphroditus. The latter, whom Paul praises generally and calls "my brother and fellow-worker and fellow-soldier" (2:25–30; 4:18), went from Philippi to Rome while Paul was in prison, to bring him help from the community. In Rome Epaphroditus fell seriously ill, but afterward returned to Philippi bearing with him the epistle of the prisoner (§ 629 ff.).

385. In conclusion, the establishment and organizing of the new community had gone well enough for Paul to be completely satisfied. But was it possible anywhere to form a group of disciples of the Messias who had died on the cross without their having to bear a cross in some fashion themselves? How did it happen that at Philippi they did not encounter anything like the underhanded intrigue of Pisidian Antioch (§ 336), or the popular uprising of Iconium (§ 339), or the stoning in Lystra (§ 345), which had given a characteristic Christian flavor to the first missionary journey? Paul must have found his work in Philippi somewhat savorless on this account, and he was worried. Perhaps he prayed God to season his labors a little with the paradox of the Sermon on the Mount (§ 337), otherwise he would not be too sure that he had toiled for Christ and with Christ. The assurance came at the end of his sojourn in Philippi, almost as a seal and guarantee. There was a persecution.

386. The episode is described so well in Luke's restrained account, that it would be foolish to paraphrase it: "Now it came to pass as we were going to the place of prayer that a girl met us who possessed a divining spirit and brought her masters much profit by soothsaying. She followed Paul and ourselves and kept crying out saying, 'These men are servants of the most high God and they proclaim to you a way of salvation.' This she did for many days; until Paul, being very much grieved, turned and said to the spirit, 'I order thee in the name of Jesus Christ to go out of her.' And it went out that very moment" (Acts 16:16–18).

The girl, or slave, was one of the many women fortunetellers common in pagan religions, who were perhaps possessed. This one in particular possessed a "spirit Python" ($\pi\nu\epsilon\hat{v}\mu\alpha$ $\pi\acute{v}\theta\omega\nu\alpha$) who was believed to be the special spirit of soothsaying and divination.

According to mythology (Ovid, *Metamorphoses*, I, 443 ff.), Python was the serpent who in ancient times pronounced the oracles at Delphi, but Apollo killed him and gave the oracles in his stead. This is the origin of the epithet Pythian applied to the god and the name Pythia given the priestess of Apollo at Delphi. But the Greek writers also called a ventriloquist "python," and the little slave girl in question may have been one, as Augustine thought (*De civit. Dei*, II, 23). Whatever the case may be, the girl pronounced oracles, divined the future, and performed the other extraordinary and spectacular acts which the pagans expected from those who possessed the mysterious power of Pythian Apollo. Paul naturally·did not believe in Apollo and considered instead that the girl was possessed by a devil, like the many others who had been freed by Christ, as he himself had recounted so many times to his catechumens. It is true that this "spirit Python" seemed benign and not malicious, for he declared that the missionaries were "the servants of the most high God" and were proclaiming "a way of salvation." But Paul, far from placing any faith in these protestations, considered them rather a stratagem of the devil. He remembered in fact that "the unclean spirits" had been very obsequious before Jesus and proclaimed: "Thou art the Son of God" (Mk. 3:11), but he had driven them out nevertheless. Paul, who is careful to imitate Christ (1 Cor. 11:1), does just that on this occasion and uses his charismatic power to drive out the "spirit Python."

387. But then came the consequences. The girl had "masters," perhaps a group of pagan priests who shrewdly exploited her and gained "much profit" thereby. But once she had been exorcised, this source of profit suddenly dried up and their business was ruined. And this led to trouble, as Luke also tells us: "But on seeing that their hope of profit was gone, her masters seized Paul and Silas and dragged them into the market place to the rulers; and bringing them to the magistrates, they said, 'These men are making a great disturbance in our city; they are Jews and are advocating practices which it is

Philippi — Northern Side of the Forum (from Collart, *Philippes*)

against the law for us to adopt or observe, since we are Romans' "
(Acts 16:19–21). In the market place or forum stood the tribunal,
presided over by the "archons" or "strategoi" (§ 37), who were actually
duumvirs of the Roman colony. The accusation was made before these
magistrates. The real reason — the loss of a good business — was not
mentioned at all, while the accusers skillfully wove together concern
for the public order ("they are making a disturbance"), anti-Semitism
("they are Jews"), and fidelity to Roman customs. There was more
than enough here to impress the judges.

388. In fact, during the public discussion the crowd grew furious
against the accused, and the archons, influenced by the excitement of the
mob, took summary action. The defendants were two foreign vagrants
after all. What point was there in wasting time with questions,
witnesses, pleas, and similar formalities? Two good-for-nothing troublemakers, who came disturbing a tranquil Roman colony, are to be put
in their place with a few swift measures.

In the first place, before the session is over, the rod. The traditional
command to the lictors rang out: *Submovete* — push back the crowd.
Despoliate — strip the condemned. *Verberate* — strike them with the
rods taken from the fasces.

The crowd shouts its satisfaction. The accused try to make themselves heard above the shrieks of the mob but no one pays any
attention to them, convinced they are uttering the usual pleas and
lamentations of those condemned to the rod. The scourging is

administered with great severity, but that is not enough. To be on the safe side, they must be imprisoned and guarded with special care. The jailer, careful to carry out the full order, shuts the two bruised and bleeding prisoners in an inner cell and locks their feet in the stocks.

389. Finally Paul could be satisfied! That night, as he stretched his wounded body on the damp hard ground, he had the certainty that the community in Philippi was blessed by Christ and that here too he had labored for Christ. The persecution proved it! "I am filled with comfort, I overflow with joy in all our troubles" (2 Cor. 7:4).

Paul tells this to Silas, lying near him, and hears without surprise that his companion feels the same way. Theirs was "a perfect joy." The faithful were gathered at that hour, perhaps in Lydia's house, to pray for them and to celebrate the supper of the Lord, and their one regret was that they could not be with them, instead of here in prison where they could hear only the hoarse voices of the other prisoners cursing and swearing in the darkness. To be with them in spirit at least, they began to recite the prayers and sing the hymns commonly sung at the Christian gatherings. Perhaps in some sweet oriental chant they sang the paradoxical teachings of the Sermon on the Mount, "blessed are they that mourn . . ."; "blessed are they that suffer persecution . . ." (§ 337). Luke tells us in fact that "at midnight Paul and Silas were praying, singing the praises of God, and the prisoners were listening to them" (Acts 16:25).

For the thieves and murderers shut up in there, the thing was incomprehensible. Pray, when cursing was more to the point? Sing hymns, when it would be better to smash the stocks and break down the doors? Or did these two strange characters have some mysterious relationship with a powerful spirit, whom they were invoking now to come and free them?

390. In fact, that is just the way it seemed not long afterward. Here, too, Luke's account cannot be matched: "And suddenly there was such a great earthquake that the foundations of the prison were shaken. And at once all the doors flew open, and everyone's chains were unfastened. And the jailer, roused out of sleep and seeing that the doors of the prison were open drew his sword and was about to kill himself, thinking that the prisoners had escaped. But Paul cried with a loud voice, saying, 'Do thyself no harm, for we are all here.' Then calling for a light, he ran in and trembling for fear fell down before Paul and Silas; and bringing them out, he said, 'Sirs, what must I do to be saved?' And they said, 'Believe in the Lord Jesus, and thou shalt be saved, and thy household.' And they spoke the word of the Lord to him and to all who were in his household. And he took them at that very hour of the night and washed their wounds; and he and all his family were baptized immediately. And taking them into his house, he set food before them, and rejoiced with all his household over his faith in God" (Acts 16:26–34).

It is clear that Luke's intention is to recount not only an earthquake, but a miracle. And as usual the rationalists accept the earthquake but reject the miracle. Earthquakes are not infrequent on the Balkan peninsula, and one more or less makes no difference.

But an earthquake which opens barred prison doors and, above all, unfastens prisoners' feet from the stocks has never occurred and cannot occur naturally. It requires an exception to physical laws, and that is a miracle. But not for the rationalists. For them it is better to call it a legend added to the story later.

But the narrator Luke is practically an eyewitness and an impartial one. That makes no difference! In this and similar cases, we must deny Luke is speaking, or at least that he is an impartial eyewitness. That, in essence, is the reasoning of the defenders of reason.

391. Paul and Silas had in part foreseen the miracle — or something equivalent. Perhaps it was not too much of a surprise for the other prisoners who had reflected on their praying and singing.

But the jailer was in a quite different state of mind. Awakened by the earthquake, he was frightened first of all because of his own responsibility, which was serious if the prisoners had escaped. When Paul reassured him on this score, he recovered himself and realized that something mysterious was involved in what had happened. Probably he knew that Paul and Silas were preaching a new religion. Then both their conduct in prison and the effects of the earthquake led him to conclude that their religion was the true one. Perhaps he had more than once heard the slave girl announce that they were proclaiming a way of "salvation." Remembering this, he asked them what he must do to be "saved." His simplicity and fervor were sufficient guarantee for Paul, who after a brief instruction baptized him and his whole family. The Holy Spirit would do the rest afterward.

The welcome little supper, which baptizer and baptized took together, brought the whole affair to an affectionate and appropriate close.

392. But there were others in the city who were not quite at ease, and these were the *strategoi* of the day before. Their procedure in judging the two strangers had been altogether too hasty and might lead to very unpleasant consequences. Perhaps, when the judgment was over, they had received information about the accused from someone who knew them and was not carried away by the fury of the mob. Lydia may have sent such a person or accompanied him herself to the judges, for she had both the means and the motive to make the magistrates listen to her. In the end, they must have been convinced that the two they had condemned were neither guilty nor vagrants but enjoyed instead a certain undefined authority. Thus they could appeal to the Roman authorities of the province, showing that they had been condemned contrary to all Roman law. The Western version (§ 119, note) adds as another reason that the magistrates had been frightened by the earthquake. This is quite likely. If they had learned that the two prisoners were preaching a new religion, it would be natural for their pagan minds to link the earthquake with the unjust condemnation.

The result was that "when day came, the magistrates sent the lictors with the instructions, 'let these men go.' And the jailer reported these words to Paul: 'The magistrates have sent word that you are to be released; now therefore come forth and go in peace.' But Paul said to them, 'They have beaten us publicly and without trial, although we are Romans, and have cast us into prison; and now are they going to put us out secretly? By no means, but let them come themselves and take us out.' The lictors reported these words to the magistrates, and on hearing that they were Romans they were alarmed and came and appealed to them; and taking them out, besought them to leave the city. And leaving the prison they went to Lydia's house, and after seeing the brethren and encouraging them, they departed" (Acts 16:35–40).

393. The magistrates' fright at hearing that Paul and Silas were Roman citizens was fully justified. We have a precise judgment from Cicero in this regard: "If a Roman citizen is bound, it is a misdeed, if he is struck it is a crime, and if he is killed it is almost parricide,"[6] and this statement was based on explicit legislation. The *lex Valeria* of 509 B.C. had prohibited the striking of a Roman citizen without a previous and explicit popular decision. The *lex Porcia* of 248 had prohibited scourging a Roman citizen for any reason whatever. The magistrates had directly violated both these laws and had besides condemned two Roman citizens without a regular trial and without listening to their defense, which procedure was emphatically forbidden in Roman law. Hence their fright.

The consequences could have been very serious and extended to the whole local Roman "colony" as had happened in similar instances. Nor would the excuse that Paul and Silas were Jews by birth have done them any good. Race did not count in the case of those with Roman citizenship, and a few years later Flavius Josephus lays special blame on Gessius Florus, the last Roman procurator of Judea, for having violated this law with respect to the Jews: "What no one [had dared] before, Florus then dared, causing to be scourged and nailed to the cross men of equestrian rank, whose race was Jewish but whose dignity was Roman" (*Wars of the Jews*, II, 308).

---

[6] Cf. *The Life of Christ,* p. 626 (§ 597).

394. How did it happen the two accused did not declare their Roman citizenship before the tribunal? Probably because what took place there was more of a riot than a trial, and between the shouts of the crowd and the excitement of the magistrates, they could not make themselves heard. But when they saw that the magistrates, still unaware of their Roman citizenship, wanted to set them free only to cancel out the irregularity of their procedure, then they made known that citizenship, which was the most serious element in the case. The effect was immediate. The magistrates yielded completely, and came in person to beg pardon and appeal to them. But still terrified at what they had done, they insisted that the matter be kept quiet and begged the two offended Romans to leave the city.

Paul saw no difficulty in this, for if they remained against the wishes of the magistrates, they would have found themselves in constant friction with them. So shortly afterward, he and Silas departed, after having exhorted and bade farewell to the community of faithful in the home of Lydia. From the fact that the narrative at this point is again told in the third person plural, we deduce that Luke remained in Philippi. This was probably due to the desire to leave with the new community a kind of vicar, who, besides being filled with fervor, was also well acquainted with the city (§ 379). As for the third missionary, Timothy, we are not told explicitly that he left with Paul for Thessalonica and then Beroea, but we do find him with Paul later in Beroea (Acts 17:14; § 406) and the salutations in the epistles to the Thessalonians indicate he was well known to them. He must have made their acquaintance, therefore, together with Paul and Silas.

THESSALONICA

395. Leaving Philippi, the missionaries crossed Amphipolis (§ 37) and Apollonia and arrived in Thessalonica (§ 38) after a journey of about 120 miles. The Jews in Salonika today represent about one half the population, and in the (Thes)Salonica of Paul's time they must have been very numerous also. This was probably the reason why it was the first stop after Philippi.

Upon his arrival, Paul immediately began his double activity, that of earning his living and of winning souls. He lodged with a certain Jason, probably a Jew originally named Jesus (§ 228), and found the opportunity to exercise his trade (§ 230) either with him or elsewhere, so that later he reminded the Thessalonians he had "worked night and day so as not to be a burden to any of you" (1 Thess. 2:9; cf. 2 Thess. 3:8). He took up again, then, his weaving of tent cloth, right after having made a journey of 120 miles on foot and before the wounds he received at Philippi were completely healed. But his work yielded little, and in time the missionaries must have been in rather difficult financial circumstances. We surmise this from the fact that Paul twice consented to take help from Philippi (Phil. 4:16; § 383).

396. His spiritual labors began as usual among the Jews in the synagogue. There "for three Sabbaths, he reasoned with them from Scripture; explaining and showing that the Christ had to suffer and rise from the dead, and that this is the Christ, even Jesus, whom I preach to you" (Acts 17:2–3). The passages referred to were the Messianic texts from Scripture, particularly those which foretold the

Thessalonica — The Harbor

sufferings of the future Messias. And this was precisely the greatest obstacle to overcome. For the Jews looked forward to the Messias as the supreme national hero, who would march triumphantly from victory to victory, whereas Paul described him as a poor, humble artisan who had died on the cross.

Only "some" of the Jews believed (*ibid.*, 4) as the result of the discussions in the synagogue, but Luke, summing up the Apostle's missionary activity here, adds that a large number of God-fearers [and] the Greeks, and not a few women of rank[7] were also converted. The "God-fearers" or "worshipers" were those affiliated with Judaism and for the most part were won over in the synagogue. But through

---

[7] The conjunction *and* after *God-fearers* occurs in only a few codices, but it is the most authoritative reading conceptually. The God-fearers — or worshipers — were those affiliated with Judaism, while the *Greeks* in Luke's narrative are usually the pagans; the "large number" came from both these groups. The epistles to the Thessalonians indicate the majority of converts in that community were ex-pagans.

them, and thanks to intense activity outside the synagogue as well, the many Greeks who were still pagan were also won. It is noteworthy too that there were a number of women of rank who accepted the new faith. While the image of the Messias, suffering and dying on the cross for the salvation of all humanity, was rejected by the majority of Jews, it was accepted by many pagans. The former were offended by this humiliation of the Messias and the idea of equality between Jews and pagans in the kingdom of salvation, but the latter saw in the humiliation the price of salvation and in that equality the glorification of human dignity.

397. The careful assistance given the neophytes was an exhausting labor for the missionaries, and especially for Paul. After having spent the greater part of the day at his loom, and despite the weariness of his hands and limbs, he would perhaps go to instruct a group of catechumens gathered to wait for him in some shop. Later he might stop in a house where a whole family desired to be instructed for baptism. On his way home, he might visit some woman of rank anxious to question him about certain points in his teaching, and perhaps as he left her home, he was stopped by a group of slaves in the courtyard eager to know if there was "salvation" for them too. When he reached home late in the evening, perhaps a Jewish elder was waiting for him to discuss certain passages in Scripture, and they would converse for long hours by the light of a lamp as Jesus had done with Nicodemus. Finally, before stretching out on his straw mat to sleep, he probably asked Silas and Timothy about their day's work — had they visited the sick man who had asked for them; had they reconciled the two catechumens who were quarreling; had they explained clearly to the group of slaves preparing for baptism that fornication and deceit are never permissible, and that on becoming

Thessalonica — Suburbs of the City

Christian they must abandon these old habits and no longer behave like the "Gentiles who do not know God" (1 Thess. 4:4–5).

When he thought back over that whole exhausting activity, he seemed to have been a busy nursemaid for a distracting crowd of small children, and that is how he describes himself later with mingled humor and emotion in the passage already quoted (§ 169). But in Thessalonica, as elsewhere, the missionaries were well assisted by neophytes endowed with charisms, who later carried on their work (cf. 1 Thess. 5:12). It is certain that charisms must have abounded in the community, even to miracles, and this was the principal reason for its rapid and stable development (1:5).

398. The missionaries' success was indeed great. There was no lack of trouble, but it was mingled with joy. The Thessalonians received "the word in great tribulation, with joy of the Holy Spirit" (1:6). With this formation the neophytes soon became an example and an inspiration for communities both far and near. Almost a year later, Paul could say, "so that you became a pattern to all the believers in Macedonia and Achaia. For from you the word of the Lord has been spread abroad, not only in Macedonia and Achaia, but in every place your faith in God has gone forth, so that we need say nothing further" (1:7–8).

Paul's praise of these neophytes gives us a glimpse of one of the chief spiritual impulses which led to their conversion: "You turned to God from idols, to serve the living and true God, and to await from Heaven Jesus, his Son, whom he raised from the dead, who has delivered us from the wrath to come" (1:9–10). They were attracted to Christianity, then, not only by the concept of the Messias Jesus, who had died and risen from the dead, as Paul had recounted in the synagogue, but also by the expectation that this Messias would return from heaven and save his disciples from the wrath to come. Paul had undoubtedly spoken of Christ's second coming to other communities he founded, but we have no indication that this element of his teaching made elsewhere the same impression it did in Thessalonica.

399. As we know,[8] there had been more or less widespread among the Jewish people, since the first century B.C., an expectation of some grandiose event which would change the course of human things. The "present world," compounded of injustice and grief, would be replaced by the "world to come," of justice and happiness. But there were differing opinions as to how this was to take place. Some, more feverish in their expectation but less numerous, foresaw a sudden cataclysm, a cosmic conflagration which would destroy the "present world," while immediately afterward the Messias, descending from the

---

[8] Cf. *The Life of Christ*, p. 197 ff. (§ 209 ff.); p. 544 ff. (§ 523 ff.).

heavens, would inaugurate the "world to come," the eschatological kingdom of God. On the day of the "wrath to come," at the universal judgment, the faithful Israelites would be gathered into the kingdom of God — alive, or resurrected if they had died before — while the reprobate pagans would be overwhelmed by divine wrath.

Other Jews, however, and these were the majority, envisaged a gradual change. First the Messias would come and establish the kingdom of God, not an eschatological but an earthly kingdom, and thus the "present world" would begin to be destroyed, for the Messianic kingdom would mark the triumph of Israel over the pagan nations. It would last for an indefinite period of time, and only at the end of this period would the "present world" be replaced by the eschatological "world to come."

400. In addition, at this period of Paul's life (A.D. 51), vague aspirations for a general rebirth or renewal were also pervading the pagan world. The great, burdensome mass of the Roman Empire grew increasingly heavier, while its ancient splendor grew dimmer and dimmer in the palace of the Caesars. The lunacies of Caligula had been followed by the turpitude of Messalina. When she was murdered in 48, Agrippina dominated the scene with her intrigues; three years later she was finally to rid herself of the weakling Claudius by poisoning him. Many wondered where all these things would end. What was to become of the Empire, governed by a female tyrant and a weakling, when the Parthians rose in the east and the Barbarians in the north? At the same time many "prodigies" kept occurring one after the other: earthquakes, comets, rains of fire, monstrous offspring born to both humans and animals, a flock of vultures nesting on the Capitoline, a bolt of lightning which struck the monument of Drusus, the father of Claudius, while the doors of the temple of Jupiter opened by themselves.[9] What did all these "prodigies" mean? Evidently the gods — so thought the learned and the populace alike — were warning against some imminent event. Some tremendous happening was about to take place, and the course of human events would be utterly changed.

Even before Paul's coming, the Thessalonians must have been familiar with both these expectations, that of Israel through the many Jews living among them, and that of the pagans through the general relationship between their city and the center of the Empire. And the parallel between the two expectations could not have failed to impress even the most skeptical. Then Paul had come, and in his instructions he had reported to them in detail the eschatological dis-

---

[9] Tacitus, *Annales,* XII, 43, 64; Suetonius, *Claudius,* 46; Dion Cassius, LX, 35. Note, however, that these prodigies are assigned in general to the last years of Claudius' reign, that is, to before the year 54.

Thessalonica — Arch of Galerius

course of Jesus to his disciples the Tuesday before he died. From Paul the Thessalonians learned that Jesus too had foretold something similar to what both Jews and pagans were awaiting.

401. In the first place, the most holy building in the whole world, the Hebrew Temple of Jerusalem would be destroyed, and not a stone of it would be left standing upon a stone. Then the great "tribulation" would burst over them, accompanied by the "beginning of sorrows"[10] — wars, earthquakes, and famines in various places. Then, "after that tribulation," the sun and the moon would be darkened, the stars would fall from heaven, and immediately afterward there would be the "parousia" of the Son of Man. Jesus would descend on the clouds from heaven, in power and glory, and would gather his elect to him from the four corners of the world.

All this Jesus had foretold quite specifically. But he had not been specific with regard to the time when all these things were to take place. Or better, he had been precise enough about the time of the great tribulation. He had used the comparison of the fig tree. When its branches begin to swell and the tiny leaves to bud, it is a sign that summer is near, and he had concluded by saying that all would come to pass within the present generation, that is, within about forty years. But with respect to the time of the parousia, he had stated briefly that only the heavenly Father knew the day and the hour but no one else, not even the angels in heaven nor the Son.

---

[10] For all these terms in the eschatological discourse of Jesus and for their interpretation, cf. *The Life of Christ*, pp. 544–555 (§§ 523–531).

402. As they reflected on these statements of Jesus and compared them with the Jewish and the pagan expectations, the Thessalonians became gradually convinced of the imminence not only of the great tribulation but also of the parousia of the glorious Christ descending from heaven. Since Jesus had neither affirmed nor denied the imminence

Environs of Thessalonica

of the parousia, the neophytes of Thessalonica — as other communities of Christians elsewhere, for that matter — assigned it to the same time as the great tribulation and believed it would happen within their own generation. Within about forty years, therefore, the glorious Christ descending from heaven would replace the "present world" of iniquity and sin with the "world to come" of justice and glory, and there he would gather his elect from the four corners of the world.

Had Paul taught them the parousia was imminent? We shall discuss this later (§ 430 ff.). In any case, what he said to praise them was true, that they had been converted "to serve the living and true God, and to await from heaven Jesus, his Son, whom he raised from the dead, who has delivered us from the wrath to come" (§ 398).

403. In Thessalonica, then, as in Philippi all went well — so well, that Paul must have begun to worry again at the lack of trials and difficulties, for without them he did not seem to be working for Christ. But Christ soon set his mind at rest with a genuine tribulation, whose source was as usual the Jews. The imperturbable Luke recounts it in a few words: "But the Jews, moved with jealousy, took certain base loafers and forming a mob, set the city in an uproar. They attacked Jason's house and sought to bring them out to the people; but not finding them, they dragged Jason and certain brethren before the magistrates of the city, shouting, 'These men who are setting the world in an uproar have come here too, and Jason has taken them in; and they are all acting contrary to the decrees of Caesar, saying that there is another king, Jesus'" (Acts 17:5–7).

Loafers in ancient times were never lacking in the forums and market places. Cicero gave them the picturesque epithet *subrostrani*, for they invariably gathered about the rostrum where an orator was speaking, and they applauded or heckled according to who had paid them. In Thessalonica they had been paid by the Jews and so they espoused their cause.

Screaming patriotism and loyalty to Caesar, these "representatives of the popular mind" marched through the city and gathered in front of Jason's house, where Paul was lodging. But their quarry, Paul and Silas, was not there. They had probably been warned in the meantime and departed hastily. For want of a better victim then, they took Jason and dragged him before the magistrates who presided over the "[assembly of the] people" (§ 38). The most that poor Jason could be accused of was sheltering Paul. But the demonstrators, the better to impress the magistrates, implicated him in the far more serious charge of favoring those who violated Caesar's edicts and set against Caesar another "king, Jesus." This was high treason, a *crimen maiestatis*.

404. It is quite likely that Paul, speaking to the Christians of the kingdom of God, had given Jesus the title of "king," but in the same sense in which Jesus himself had told Pilate he had a kingdom (Jn. 18:36), or with the eschatological meaning of Paul's own statement that "our citizenship ($\pi o\lambda i\tau\epsilon\upsilon\mu a$) is in heaven, from which also we eagerly await a Savior, our Lord Jesus Christ" (Phil. 3:20). The zealous informers had heard of this title given Jesus and had tacked their treacherous accusation to it.

The magistrates of Thessalonica were not so impulsive or precipitous as those of Philippi (§ 388). They imitated rather the attitude of Pontius Pilate before the same charge against Jesus. They must have recognized, from long familiarity, the *subrostrani* who were clamoring about something every day in front of their tribunal, and they had a fairly good estimate of the sincerity of this zeal they now displayed for Caesar. On the other hand, the magistrates could not answer merely: "Get away, you paid fakers! How many drachmas a head did you get from the Jews to put on this show?" Certain things cannot be said in public. The magistrates were afraid of consequences, and so they divided the evil in two, a little as Pontius Pilate had done. Luke tells us they were "stirred" by the stand taken by the rioters, and they "accepted bail ($i\kappa a\nu\acute{o}\nu$) from Jason and the rest and then let them go" (Acts 17:9). Just

what the "bail" was we do not know. It may have been a sum of money
or a pledge for the future. For the magistrates it was a loophole through
which they could escape the present embarrassment without too much
violence to their conscience. And Jason and the other Christians went
home to their own houses.

405. Even after this, however, the people did not calm down. To
avoid further trouble, "the brethren straightway sent Paul and Silas
away by night to Beroea" (*ibid.*, 10). Paul was by now quite accustomed to these sudden departures from the communities he founded.
It was a sign for him that all was going well, according to the paradoxical
principles of the Sermon on the Mount (§§ 337, 385).

After a journey of about three days, toward the southwest, Paul and
Silas arrived in Beroea (§ 38). It must have been after the beginning
of the year 51. Their stay there was not a long one, neither was it
stormy. This remote little city was for Paul a place of calm and quiet
if not of rest. As usual, he went first to the synagogue, where he was
well received, for these Jews — Luke says — "were of nobler character
than those of Thessalonica" (*ibid.*, 11). Paul's preaching interested them
so much that they began to study Scripture eagerly to see if it confirmed what Paul said. "Many of them became believers, and so did
no small number of prominent Gentiles, women and men" (*ibid.*, 12).
These Gentiles, for the most part, must have been affiliated with Judaism.
Among them was Sopater, the son of Pyrrhus, who later joined Paul
(20:4).

This fruitful activity and tranquil sojourn was interrupted by the usual
jealousy of the Jews. When it was learned in Thessalonica where Paul
was staying and what he was doing there, the customary expedition was
organized to go and stir up trouble in Beroea. To prevent unhappy consequences, the neophytes sent Paul to the coast, probably to the port
of Dium which was about forty miles from Beroea. Perhaps Paul himself had expressed the desire to leave Macedonia altogether to get away
from his implacable persecutors.

406. Silas remained in Beroea, and with him Timothy, who here reappears in the narrative (§ 394). From Dium or some harbor nearby,
it was possible to reach Athens in three or four days of sailing, rounding
Cape Sunium to the south, and this seems to be the route taken by Paul
instead of the overland route which led down across Thessaly and took
about twelve days. The Western version, however, supposes that Paul
traversed Thessaly. It is also a curious fact that Paul's traveling companions stayed with him as far as Athens and then returned home. This
has led to the conjecture that Paul at the time was suffering a severe
attack of his illness (§ 199 ff.) and could not be left alone; but it is
merely a conjecture.

When Paul bade his escort farewell in Athens he charged them to tell

Cape Sunium — the Southern Tip of Attica, South of Athens

Silas and Timothy to come to him as soon as possible. They did in fact join him later, not in Athens but in Corinth (Acts 18:5). To this period belongs the journey of Timothy, whom Paul sent to visit the communities of Thessalonica, and during that time Paul remained "at Athens alone" (1 Thess. 3:1–2), that is, without Silas either. Among the various explanations offered to reconcile these data, the most natural seems to be that Timothy and Silas joined Paul immediately in Athens. Then Timothy was sent to Thessalonica and Silas somewhere else (perhaps to Philippi), and when their missions were completed they both joined Paul again in Corinth.

ATHENS

407. To think of Paul in a state of aesthetic excitement the first time he walked through the enchanting city of Athens would be a serious historical error. The "man" in him was a combination of the leveled ruins of a former rabbi and the superstructure of the Christian Apostle. His spiritual life was completely and utterly concentrated on religion. Nothing else elicited a response in his spirit, any more than the racing form might interest a student of philology, immersed in his codices and papyri. In fact, the comparison is a weak one. The philologist might be disinterested in horse racing but not hostile to it. Paul, both as an ex-rabbi and a Christian Apostle, was directly hostile to everything he saw along the streets of Athens, to all that went to give it its special character. His state of mind is described with psychological accuracy by Luke when he says: "Now while Paul was waiting for them [Silas and Timothy] at Athens, he was exasperated ($\pi\alpha\rho\omega\xi\acute{v}\nu\epsilon\tau o$) to see how the city was wholly given to idolatry" (Acts 17:16).[11]

408. The visitor in Athens today cannot help a feeling of excitement,

---

[11] The streets were literally filled with statues as well as temples, as we learn from various ancient authors (i.e., Livy, XLV, 27). Some have cited in this regard the passage of Petronius Arbiter (*Satyricon*, 17): "Our country is so full of divinities that in it you may more easily find a god than a man." But it is not clear that temples or statues are meant here by "divinities," nor that the country is Athens.

even if he is a fervent Christian and although he knows the objects he is admiring are but a small relic of the splendid beauty that adorned the city in Paul's time (§ 40). But there have been twenty centuries of Christianity, and idolatry as such has disappeared. The objects admired no longer have any religious significance but remain merely the legitimate creations of art. To Paul, however, they were something

General View of Ancient Athens

quite different. In the first place, the statues and paintings were illicit artistic creations for an ex-rabbi since the Hebrew law forbade the portrayal of any human being. Besides, they attested and favored the impiety of idolatrous worship for they were filled with religious meaning which was quite legitimate in the minds of those who adored them, but which for Paul was blasphemy against the true God.

Here, too, Renan could not resist a purple passage. Trembling before the statues of Athens, he exhorts them to tremble too because an iconoclast has arrived in the city, that little unpleasant Jew Paul, who has decreed their destruction and has raised the hammer against them. This theatrical apostrophe might in Renan's day have squeezed a dutiful tear or two from his sentimental audience, fluttering after culture, but it leaves the historian cold. The fact is that whatever remains of those works of art was saved in great measure by the Christianity preached by Paul, while the barbarian nations which rejected Christianity threw most of them into the fire to make plaster of them. Paul was concerned with religion and not aesthetics, there is no doubt of that. But once religious principles were safe, he could also exhort: "For the rest, brethren, whatever things are true, whatever honorable, whatever just, whatever holy, whatever lovable, whatever of good repute, if there be any virtue, if anything worthy of praise, think upon these things" (Phil. 4:8). Among "these things" there might well be the fine arts, provided of course there was nothing in them harmful to religion.

The statues of Athens, however, were a direct denial of Paul's religious principles, for they were idols in everyday use. And this accounts for Paul's exasperation when he saw them.

409. The Jewish colony in Athens was not very large but it did have a synagogue. Paul attended it to explain his teaching to the Jews and the "devout," but it would seem he made very little impression on them. He then tried casting his net in other waters and, addressing himself to the pagans, "he had discussions . . . in the market-place every day with those who were there" (Acts 17:17).

Athens: Theater of Dionysius

Most of Athenian life was carried on in the public places, and the heart of that life was the market place. The Athenians did everything there: they bought and sold and traded; they discussed politics; and they besought their gods. In one corner a rhetorician harangued the crowds, while in another a strolling player parodied the mannerisms of celebrated personages. On one side of the portico enclosing the agora the Stoics had installed themselves to study the doctrines of Zeno. Opposite them the disciples of Epicurus were elaborating the philosophy of their master. Strangers from far-off regions, dressed in the garb of pilgrims, arrived every now and then and described the powers of some unknown oriental god, the efficacy of an unknown rite, or the magic virtues of mysterious stones or plants.

The Athenians crowded the agora every day and spent much more time there than in their own homes. Idle, talkative, mocking, greedy for news, they were busy trying to see and hear everything that was going on, one moment watching a juggler in open-mouthed delight, and the next minute listening to a Platonic philosopher discuss the eternal ideas; now storming with questions a merchant just arrived from India, and now carefully noting the responses of an Egyptian soothsayer predicting the fate of the Empire or explaining a set of love philters. Luke briefly describes the crowd in the market place when he says, "Now all the Athenians and the visitors there from abroad used to spend all their leisure telling or listening to something new" (*ibid.*, 21). Various pagan writers concur in this description, beginning with Demosthenes and Thucydides, who mention particularly the levity, loquacity, and curiosity of the Athenians.

410. Mingling with this crowd, Paul did not feel lost but painfully "alone" (1 Thess. 3:1). He looked upon all these seekers after novelty with the eye of the assiduous student of the Bible. Like the vision in Ezechiel (34:5 ff.), they seemed to him a flock of sheep with no shepherd, "scattered upon the face of the earth." Paul was ready to tell them about their lawful shepherd, the Messias Jesus. But how would they receive his message? In any case, he must try to reach them; and try he did.

The first with whom he established contact must have been those with whom "he had discussions . . . in the market-place every day." They perhaps did not pay too much attention to him, more interested in the news brought by the Indian merchant or the responses of the Egyptian fortuneteller than in his teachings about Jesus. But Paul did not lose courage, and kept searching for someone who would become interested enough at least to enter

The Agora of Athens

Athens: The Portico of Eumenes. At the Right, the
Slopes of the Acropolis (Alinari)

into discussion with him. His persistence was observed and some
philosophers became curious about what he was saying. "And then
even[12] some of the Epicurean and Stoic philosophers debated with
him; and some said, 'What is this babbler[13] trying to say?' But
others, 'He seems to be a herald of strange gods,' because he proclaimed to them Jesus and the resurrection. And they took him and
brought him to the Areopagus, saying, 'May we know just what this
new doctrine taught by thee is? For thou bringest some strange things to
our ears; we wish therefore to know what these things mean'" (Acts
17:18–20).

411. Since Paul "proclaimed Jesus and the resurrection," these philosophers concluded that he was "a herald of strange gods," and their
conclusion was not mistaken. Their coupling of "Jesus and the resurrection" in that fashion was most probably due — as John Chrysostom
pointed out[14] — to the fact that they understood the word "resurrection"
to be the name of a goddess. There were in Athens shrines to Compassion, Modesty, Victory, and even to Insult and Impudence. A foreign

---

[12] Note this *even* ($\kappa\alpha\iota$), which seems to indicate previous unfruitful attempts.

[13] For "babbler," the Greek has $\sigma\pi\epsilon\rho\mu o\lambda\acute{o}\gamma os$, the etymology of which is "gatherer
of seeds." It was originally an epithet of the crow and the magpie, and later of
beggars, who gathered up the kernels of grain spilled in the market place. It then
came to be used figuratively to mean "a gatherer of words," a talkative person, a
demagogue, and the like. In the present text it seems to imply that Paul, at no
particular loss for words, had no philosophical concepts.

[14] *In Acta Apost. Homil.*, 38, 18.

preacher might well be talking to them about a goddess named Resurrection. Jesus and Resurrection seemed to them a perfectly normal pair of gods, male and female, similar to many other divine couples that inhabited their Pantheon. Mohammed fell into a similar misunderstanding when he heard Christian teachers preach the Divine Trinity of the Father, Son, and Holy Spirit. In Arab the word "spirit" (*ruḥ*) is feminine, and Mohammed thought it designated a woman, the wife of the Father and mother of the Son, whom he then identified with the Virgin Mary.[15]

412. And so Paul went to the Areopagus. Originally this name indicated a hill east of the Acropolis, which was reached from the market place by a steep stairway carved in the rock. On the top of this hill, in the open air, the ancient Athenian tribunal had met, whose special function was to pass judgment on murderers. Legend interpreted the name to mean "hill of Ares," the god of murder and of war, equivalent to the Roman Mars, and it meant practically "hill of murder." Legend also said that on that hill Ares had been judged for a murder by the other gods. In reality, the name had originally meant "hill of the *Arai*," the Eumenides or Furies, for on its slope there was a temple dedicated to them where those acquitted by the tribunal offered sacrifice (Pausanias, I, 28, 6). Later, the name Areopagus clung to the tribunal itself, even when it no longer met on the hill but in the market place in the Royal Portico (*Stoa basileios*). In Roman times, the authority of the tribunal had in a sense increased, for it had become a kind of senate to safeguard the ancient traditions of the city, with authority to pass judgment on religious, moral, and cultural questions. We know from Plutarch (*Cicero*, 24) that Cicero tried to have the Areopagus express a desire and request that the philosopher Chratippus remain in Athens to teach the youth.

413. The question arises, therefore, whether Paul appeared on the hill or whether he was taken before the tribunal meeting in the market place. There are reasons which are not negligible in favor of his appearance before the tribunal, but all things considered it is more likely that he was taken up on the hill. The text itself, in its most obvious meaning, prompts this interpretation, for it says they took him "on" the Areopagus (ἐπὶ τὸν Ἄρειον πάγον). Besides, there is no hint in the entire episode that Paul was officially questioned by a tribunal and much less that he was the object of a specific "writ of impiety" as Socrates had been 450 years before. There is no accusation, no cross-examination, no discussion, and no sentence. Nor did Paul speak as a defendant before a panel of judges, but as any private citizen to other individuals who

---

[15] *Koran*, Surah 5, 116; cf. 5, 77 and 4, 169: for these passages cf. the Arab commentators on the *Koran*.

wanted to hear what he had to say, and at a certain point dismissed him because they were bored and disappointed. If the little group of philosophers — for they could not have been many — took Paul "on" the Areopagus, it was probably because they wanted a quieter place for discussion than the crowded and noisy agora. On the top of the hill there were steps cut in a semicircle in the rock, where the judges used to sit. The speakers, the defendant and the plaintiff, used to take their places on two stones opposite them. And we may imagine the scene this time was much the same. The philosophers sat on the steps. Paul spoke to them standing "up in the midst of the Areopagus" (Acts 17:22). And here is what he said, according to Luke's summary.

414. "Men of Athens, I see that in every respect you are extremely religious. For as I was going about and observing objects of your worship, I found an altar with this inscription: 'To the Unknown God.' What

Areopagus of Athens (Alinari)

therefore you worship in ignorance, that I proclaim to you. God, who made the world and all that is in it, since he is Lord of heaven and earth, does not dwell in temples built by hands; neither is he served by human hands, as though he were in need of anything, since it is he who gives to all men life and breath and all things. And from one man he has created the whole human race and made them live all over the face of the earth, determining their appointed times and the boundaries of their lands; that they should seek God, and perhaps grope after him and find him, though he is not far from any one of us. For in him we live and move and have our being, as indeed some of your own poets have said, 'For we are also his offspring.'

"If therefore we are the offspring of God, we ought not to imagine that the Divinity is like to gold or silver or stone, to an image graven by human art and thought. The times of this ignorance God has it is true overlooked, but now he calls upon all men everywhere to repent; inasmuch as he has fixed a day on which he will judge the world with justice by a Man whom he has appointed, and whom he has guaranteed to all by raising him from the dead" (Acts 17:22–31).

The little group on the Areopagus listened more or less attentively up to this point. But when they heard him speak of resurrection from the dead they decided they were wasting time. Some of them, probably the Epicureans, began to laugh and sneer. The others, perhaps the Stoics, said a little more politely — well, well, "we shall hear thee again upon this matter" (ibid., 32). And the meeting came to an end.

415. Paul, who became Greek to the Greeks and a Jew with the Jews to win all men to Christ (1 Cor. 9:20–23) had approached the mentality of the Greeks as much as possible in order to persuade them to accept his teaching. His discourse, in fact, has a different tone entirely from his talks to the Jews — that in the synagogue of Pisidia (§ 332) for example. Here he makes no reference to the Bible but quotes instead a pagan poet, Aratus (§ 232). He does not allude to the revelation of the Old Testament but speaks instead of the knowledge of God attained by human reason, as various Greek philosophers had done and as — in almost the same place — Socrates had testified with his death. In addition, at the very beginning of his discourse, we may note the *captatio benevolentiae*, common to ancient orators, when Paul says he had noticed that the Athenians were very religious (ὡς δεισιδαιμονεστέρους), a statement found not only in various Greek writers (Sophocles, Isocrates, etc.) but also in the Jew Flavius Josephus (*C. Apion.*, II, 130). Also in accordance with the oratorical customs of the time is the argument from a present fact, in the mention of the altar he has seen in an Athenian street, bearing the inscription "To the Unknown God."

416. Pausanias attests (I, 1, 4) that along the streets from the harbor of Phalerus to Athens, there were various altars dedicated to unknown gods, and other ancient authors also record the existence of similar altars in other places, but the inscriptions are in the plural. Jerome states definitely — on what basis we do not know — that the inscription Paul had seen was not in the singular but the plural, but that he quoted it in the singular for the sake of his argument (*in Titum*, I, 12). There were dedicatory inscriptions to one god, however, who for some reason or other had not been identified. One of these is mentioned by Diogenes Laertius (*Epimen.*, I, 10), and such an altar is still extant on the Palatine hill in Rome. The text of the inscription on this altar is as follows: *Sei Deo Sei Deivae Sacr(um) — C. Sextius C(aii) F(ilius) Calvinus Pr(aetor) — De Senati* [sic] *Sententia — Restituit*. The present altar, then, is a restoration or substitution for the previous altar made by order of the Senate. The C. Sextius Calvinus who was charged with the restoration was probably the son of the Calvinus who was consul in the year 124 B.C. In fact, the letters of the inscription indicate it belongs to about the year 100 B.C. We have here, then, a single deity, to whom in Rome in Republican times an altar was dedicated, for reasons we do not know, nor do we know whether it was a god or goddess.

417. Paul's argument aimed to prove that God, the creator of all things and all men, can and must be known by all men, and this by virtue of what men understand with their reason when they observe his works. For God is not far away but near all men, and they live immersed in him almost as fish in the sea. They may seek him like persons blindfolded groping ($\psi\eta\lambda\alpha\phi\dot\eta\sigma\epsilon\iota\alpha\nu$) for someone in their midst, until they "find" him, catching hold of him and recognizing him. But historically men have not found God. They have erred and mistaken for the true God statues of gold, silver, and stone, and so the human race has passed through long periods "of this ignorance."

At this point Paul leaves the field of natural reason and enters that of supernatural revelation, declaring that God has recently called upon men to repent, that is, to change their manner of thinking ($\mu\epsilon\tau\alpha\nu\circ\epsilon\hat\iota\nu$).[16] The reason for this is that God "will

Altar on the Palatine to the Unknown God
(Palatine Administration Photo)

judge the world with justice" through a Man destined for that office. And in order that the authority of this Man may be evident and well known, God has given him the necessary credentials by raising him from the dead. Here Paul intended to go on and name this unknown Man, the Messias Jesus. But his listeners had had enough.

418. It is not surprising that various modern scholars will have none of the discourse on the Areopagus either. Some of them, like U. Wilamowitz and E. Norden, were outstanding classical philologists but

---

[16] Cf. *The Life of Christ,* p. 268 (§ 266).

not so expert in their knowledge of Jewish religious thought. Others belong to the ranks of those New Testament critics for whom the progress of science is essentially the rejection of the documents. It is unnecessary to note that among the latter we find Loisy (§ 139 ff.). In their opinion the discourse was invented at the beginning of the second century and its author was inspired by a piece of information in Philostratus' life of Appollonius of Tyana (VI, 3), to which he added certain historical concepts. On the other hand, many other well-known scholars and rationalists, and Harnack[17] to begin with, have favored the authenticity of the discourse, demonstrating how fragile are the reasons alleged to the contrary and how acrobatic are the conclusions deduced from them. In actual fact, the authenticity of the discourse is finding increasing acceptance.

419. The discourse on the Areopagus was a failure. Contributing to this perhaps was some difficulty with the choice of language, or a somewhat stiff or awkward manner of presentation, which would not have predisposed Paul's meticulous auditors in his favor. But the real reason was the supernatural element, which disconcerted his listeners the moment it was mentioned. They had hoped to hear arguments filled with wisdom, and instead they were being told a foolish old wives' tale about the resurrection of the dead. This was neither serious nor dignified, nor did it merit any discussion.

After nineteen centuries things seem to be very much the same. Apart from this particular discourse, the rationalist critics accept almost all the statements in the *Acts* and Pauline epistles, provided no supernatural element is involved. But as soon as there is the slightest hint of the supernatural they imitate Paul's audience on the Areopagus. There is, however, this difference, that Paul was forced by circumstances to interrupt his discourse, while today, after nineteen centuries, he still has not interrupted the broader discourse addressed to the whole world. He himself had clearly foreseen this partial failure of his preaching on earth: "For the Jews ask for signs, and the Greeks look for 'wisdom'; but we, for our part, preach a crucified Christ — to the Jews indeed a stumbling-block and to the Gentiles foolishness. . . . For the foolishness of God is wiser than men, and the weakness of God is stronger than men" (1 Cor. 1:22–25). It may be that Paul was thinking here of the result of his discourse on the Areopagus. Certain it is that he did not consider it a failure, but listed it among his "victories" after the stoning at Lystra (§ 345), the scourging at Philippi (§ 388), and the various times he had been forced to flee during his previous missions. These were the paradoxical victories of the Sermon on the Mount (§§ 337, 385, 405). His words still preach today and will continue to preach the

---

[17] *Ist die Rede des Paulus in Athen ein ursprünglicher Bestandteil der Apostelgeschichte?* in *Texte u. Untersuch.*, 39, 1, Leipzig, 1913.

"foolishness" of "Jesus crucified," instead of the "wisdom" which men expect. This "wisdom" will continue to reject the "foolishness" and proclaim its failure. But Paul will continue to mark these apparent failures in the list of his victories, proving by facts that his "foolishness" does not fail and never surrenders. It is the fundamental law of the history of Christianity.

420. But the sojourn in Athens did bear some little fruit: "Certain persons however joined him, and became believers; among them were Dionysius the Areopagite and a woman named Damaris, and others with them" (Acts 17:34). Just a few isolated persons, then. Among them the most prominent was Dionysius, whose epithet "Areopagite" indicates that he must have been a member of the tribunal (§ 412), but we know nothing else about him. In the second century, Dionysius of Corinth states that his namesake the Areopagite was the first bishop of Athens (in Eusebius, *Hist. Eccl.*, III, 4, 10; IV, 23, 3). Toward the end of the fifth century an unknown but sharp-witted author published several writings under the name of the Areopagite, and quite skillfully sustained the fiction.

This tiny group of converts was a handful of seed for the future Church in Athens, but the seed sprouted slowly and with difficulty. Paul afterward seems to have taken no further interest in Athens. In later centuries we have scant and obscure information on the progress made there by Christianity, while it is certain that in the fourth century Athens was still for the most part pagan. The reason lies in the character of the city itself, which had become an academy filled with ancient glories but empty of any worthy heirs to those glories. Her citizens chattered about Socrates but without imitating his life, much less his death. They spun sophistries on Plato and Aristotle, but without penetrating the content of their thought. They were arrogantly indifferent to everything else, confident in the sense of their own superiority, and they filled their idle lives with the practice of hedonistic principles.

Paul never found again an obstacle greater than this indifferentism. In the jealousies of the Jews there was some satisfaction; in the violence of the pagans, he rejoiced; but the inert indifference of the Athenians enervated him. He was like an expert navigator who indomitably weathers any storm, but who is defeated by an exhausting calm.

Shortly afterward, therefore, he left Athens for Corinth. It was between the spring and summer of the year 51.

CORINTH

421. If during the short trip between Athens and Corinth, Paul took stock of his situation, he must have been reminded of the biblical episode of David, an unarmed youth with nothing but a shepherd's sling and a few stones, on his way to attack Goliath, a giant more than twice his size and completely armed.

However optimistically his experience in Athens might be interpreted on the basis of the Sermon on the Mount (§ 419), it was still humanly speaking a failure. Besides this, he knew Corinth by reputation and he had no illusions about what to expect there. He was going as the herald of the Messias Jesus to a city which was enthusiastically practicing its own religion, oriented about two well-defined deities, the god Money and the goddess Lust. The god Money was adored in the shops and other buildings crowding Corinth's two harbors (§§ 41–42), with their busy and all-absorbing traffic in every kind of merchandise going to and coming from all parts of the world. His companion was the goddess Lust, who was adored more or less everywhere throughout the city. The temple of Aphrodite on the summit of the Acrocorinth was served by more than a thousand prostitutes (§ 41), who lodged in charming houses surrounding the temple, but in practice the whole city was a

Corinth: Ruins of the Theater (from *Enciclopedia Italiana*)

branch of the shrine. The epithet of the goddess of the temple had a very exact meaning. She was called Aphrodite *Pandemos*, that is, "of all the people." Not only the rich merchants of the harbor and other citizens of the city, but also foreigners from distant lands, attracted by its reputation for refined delights, streamed to the temple and its dependencies and poured into it enormous wealth. Lust and license prevailed everywhere, not only unbridled but ostentatious. It had its influence on the language, too, for the Greeks had coined the verb "to corinthize" and the epithet "Corinthian girl" to denote the kind of life lived there and its devotee. There was also the phrase "Corinthian sickness" to indicate the physiological consequences of that life. But this last expression inspired no fear in the worshipers of the goddess any more than the monument in the cemetery erected to a famous temple prostitute, Lais, who was portrayed as a lioness tearing and devouring her prey (Pausanias, II, 2). Neither health nor money was spared in the service of the goddess, for the reason so frankly stated by the Roman who had carved on his tomb: *Balnea vina venus corrumpunt corpora nostra, sed vitam faciunt balnea vina venus.*[18]

422. To a city like this Paul dared to go and preach "Blessed are the poor . . . ! Blessed are the clean of heart . . . !" What could this small and helpless David expect to achieve against the armor-clad Goliath? At the most, another failure, like that in Athens! Notwithstanding all this Paul was determined to try. He knew he would find corruption in Corinth but not the arrogance and pride of Athens, and he feared pride of the intellect much more than pride of the flesh. Against pride of the flesh he had the medicine of the charisms, but against pride of the intellect, the charisms were far less effective, because their epitome was charity (§ 225), which intellectual pride repudiates.

423. As he entered Corinth, this presumptive conqueror of the city was in quite wretched circumstances. He had no material means, for his loom-calloused hands had been idle a long time due to constant traveling and perhaps also to attacks of his mysterious illness. He was in extreme need to the point of suffering hunger (1 Cor. 4:11) until help came from the community of Macedonia, which he accepted because he was forced to by circumstances (2 Cor. 11:8–9), while he maintained

The Corinthian Canal

his independence by not accepting anything from anyone in this new field of labor. Morally he was suffering because, among other reasons, he had no news of the communities of Macedonia. Anxious over the fate of his beloved neophytes exposed now to many trials, he had sent Timothy and Silas there from Athens, while he remained alone (§ 406), but they had not yet returned nor sent any news.

His accounts then were on the debit side, both physically and spiritually. Only Christ was left to him, and trusting in him alone he entered Corinth. Later, when he recalled his arrival in the city, he reminded the

---

[18] Cf. *The Life of Christ*, p. 124 (§ 144).

dust from his feet and here he shook his garments, but the moral significance of the gestures is the same.

426. Free now of his obligation to the Jews, Paul found headquarters close by. Titus Justus, a pagan affiliated with Judaism and probably a member of the local Roman colony, offered him his house which adjoined the synagogue. Paul accepted the offer and from then on held his meetings there. These were attended by some Jews but in much greater number by pagans, and soon yielded fruit. Crispus, who was the ruler or president of the synagogue,[20] was converted with all his household and so were many pagans. Paul incidentally mentions various names among these first neophytes: a certain Stephanas and his household were the "first-fruits of Achaia," and were baptized by Paul himself, although he usually did not baptize (1 Cor. 1:16–17; 16:15); he also baptized the afore-mentioned Crispus and the Gaius who was later his host (Rom. 16:23). Also mentioned are a certain Fortunatus and an Achaicus (1 Cor. 16:17), and among the first converts we may consider Erastus, the city treasurer (Rom. 16:23), and Tertius, who was Paul's amanuensis when he dictated the epistle to the Romans (§§ 180, 185). Many women were also converted, and among them we have the names of Chloe, who seems to have been the head of a wealthy family (1 Cor. 1:11), and Phoebe. The latter was the deaconess of the community founded in the Corinthian port of Cenchrae (§ 41) and materially assisted many of the brethren including Paul himself. In all probability it was she who brought from Corinth the epistle to the Romans (cf. Rom. 16:1–2). There are references indicating that several of these neophytes soon began to work with Paul both in his ministry and in the various tasks of organization.

427. The great majority of converts, however, were from the lower classes or were slaves, who were very numerous in Corinth (1 Cor. 1:26; 7:21; 12:13). Raised amid the social dregs of a thoroughly corrupt city, it was natural that even after their conversion they should reflect the mentality and customs in which they had been formed. Paul reminds them of this later, in frank terms that are not surprising in view of Corinth's degeneracy (§ 421): "Do not err; neither fornicators, nor idolators, nor adulterers, nor the effeminate, nor sodomites, nor thieves, nor the covetous, nor drunkards, nor the evil-tongued, nor the greedy will possess the kingdom of God. And such were some of you, but you have been washed, you have been sanctified, you have been justified in the name of our Lord Jesus Christ, and in the spirit of our God" (1 Cor. 6:9–11). To set such a flock on the straight path Paul had to work intensely and for a long time. And so deeply rooted were the old habits that some years later he had to admonish them again in a letter to correct moral

---

[20] Cf. *The Life of Christ,* p. 59 (§ 64).

abuses which were extremely serious but seemed nonetheless natural and legitimate to these people in whom vice was inveterate (§§ 474, 479, 481 ff.).

428. But all this work of purification could not fail to arouse hatred and persecution. Today it was a girl taken from her lover, tomorrow a husband brought back to his wife, or a youth extricated from the vicious life of his family. The malcontents must have been quite numerous and, touched to the quick, they did not stop with protests but went on to actual persecution. Here they found natural allies in the Jews of the adjoining synagogue. These were on the one hand deeply irritated by the conversion of the ruler of the synagogue, Crispus, and, on the other, they hardly looked with favor on all the goings on in the house of Titus Justus since that heretic Paul had installed himself there. On the outside, persecutions from pagans and Jews alike; on the inside, wave after wave of mud and filth, of the most humiliating and shameful kind. These were the circumstances in which Paul found himself after a few months' labor in Corinth.

His anguish, which must have been immeasurable, is barely hinted at in one of his epistles (1 Thess. 3:7) while there is no mention of it at all in the *Acts,* which does recount instead his liberation. It is as if Luke omitted the malady in order to record the cure, and since this was nothing less than a vision, we may understand how deeply discouraged and bewildered Paul must have been: "And one night the Lord said to Paul in a vision, 'Do not fear, but speak and do not keep silence; because I am with thee, and no one shall attack thee or injure thee, for I have many people in this city'" (Acts 18:9–10).

Humanly speaking, it was difficult to see these "many people" in Corinth. Very visible indeed were the innumerable "panderers, barrators, and similar filth," to use Dante's phrase (*Inf.,* XI, 60), but was it these people who were destined to become disciples of Christ? Like his ancestor Abraham, Paul, "hoping against hope believed, so that he became the father of many nations" (Rom. 4:18). Trusting in the vision, he was confident he would become the spiritual father of the "many people," and he continued his efforts with renewed vigor, remaining in Corinth another eighteen months (§ 158).

429. Since Corinth was a great trading center, the Good Tidings radiated from the city to the surrounding districts. We have specific information of a community in Cenchrae, which, of Corinth's two harbors, was the farther from the city (§ 41). Less specific but more significant is the statement that there were Christians in "the whole of Achaia" (2 Cor. 1:1), but we do not know how many there were nor where.

The gradual liberation of the first catechumens of Corinth from their moral degradation, and their progressive acquisition of Christian spirituality were powerfully aided by charisms, which appeared in extraordinary abundance and strength in this community. We have already discussed the charisms (§ 211 ff.). Here we need only recall that Paul is the ancient author who deals with them at greatest length, and he does so in the first epistle to the Corinthians, written a few years after the foundation of the Christian community there. This sheds some light on the spiritual life of the community in Corinth and by analogy on the others also.

THE TWO EPISTLES TO THE THESSALONIANS

430. But while Paul remained in Corinth, his thoughts were often elsewhere. Recounting for the Corinthians the long list of his tribulations (§ 168), he reminds them that in addition to his external trials, "there is my daily pressing anxiety, the care of all the churches! Who is weak, and I am not weak? Who is made to stumble and I am not inflamed?" So while he was pursuing the work of evangelizing Corinth with energy and ardor, he was worrying about the communities founded in Pisidia, Lycaonia, Galatia, and Macedonia, and anxiously awaiting news of them. From his beloved Thessalonica, Timothy brought welcome news upon his long-awaited arrival in Corinth (§ 425), and this is substantially what he reported.

Things on the whole were going quite well there. The neophytes remained steadfast in the faith despite their various trials and tribulations. They preserved a great affection for Paul and desired constantly to see him again, although there were some among them who called him an ambitious flatterer and shrewd opportunist. But there were several shadows across this bright background. Here and there, old pagan customs were lifting ugly heads, especially fraud and fornication. More serious still was their expectation of the parousia (§ 402). The Thessalonians had become generally convinced that the advent of Christ in his glory was to take place within a very short time and they were acting accordingly. Some abandoned themselves to complete inertia, indifferent to all the occupations of daily life. Others were deeply grieved because members of their families had died meanwhile and they thought these dear departed would somehow be relegated to an inferior place on the day of the great parousia since they would not participate with them, who were alive, in the great triumph of the glorious Christ.

431. When Paul heard these things, he found some consolation in the thought of the constancy and fidelity of the neophytes, but he was all the more disturbed by their ideas of the parousia. He would gladly have set out to explain in person to his beloved converts how matters really stood. But how could he leave Corinth now, how interrupt the labor that promised so well here, too? He could go to Thessalonica only in spirit, by writing a letter containing the admonishments required by the circumstances. And that was what Paul did. The first epistle to the Thessalonians is in itself the oldest writing in the New Testament. It was composed between the end of the year 50 and the beginning of 52.

When the various labors of the day were over, probably late in the evening, Paul began to prepare the material for his letter. We have already noted that the first epistle to the Thessalonians required ten sheets of papyrus and more than twenty hours of writing (§ 177). This means that if Paul worked at it two hours a night, he must have spent about a dozen evenings in some corner of his weaver's shop, meditating on the proper words and phrases and dictating them slowly to his amanuensis. The latter, seated on the ground, with the writing tablet on his knees, patiently traced the letters and syllables on the papyrus as Paul dictated. Peering into the dim lamplight, we seem to recognize in the amanuensis one of Paul's companions, Timothy or Silas (Sylvanus), both of whom are named in the beginning of the letter. It is likely that they took turns, alternating by the hour or the evening (§ 180). A summary of the letter follows.

432. After the customary greetings (§ 181), Paul expresses his affectionate regard for the recipients of the letter and his joy at their exemplary conduct. He then recalls the beginning of his ministry among them, praises their constancy in their trials, and tells them he is desolate that he is unable to visit them although he ardently desires to do so. He reminds them that he sent Timothy to them from Athens because of his great anxiety for them, and expresses his sense of consolation at the good news which Timothy has brought from them. He then exhorts them to live holy lives, to flee fornication, fraud, and sloth.

As for those who have died, the Thessalonians are not to grieve, for as Jesus died and rose again, so will the faithful who had died in him follow him: "For this we say to you in the word of the Lord, that we who live, who survive until the coming of the Lord, shall not precede those who have fallen asleep. For the Lord himself with cry of command, with voice of archangel, and with trumpet of God will descend from heaven; and the dead in Christ will rise up first. Then we who live, who survive, shall be caught up together with them in clouds to meet the Lord in the air, and so we shall ever be with the Lord. Wherefore, comfort one another with these words" (1 Thess. 4:15–17).

433. Up to this point Paul has sketched a general view of the parousia using traditional terms from the Old Testament, which are to be found also in the eschatological discourse of Jesus.[21] And he has included

---

[21] Cf. *The Life of Christ*, pp. 549–550 (§ 527). For the relationship between the epistles to the Thessalonians and the early Christian catechesis, cf. J. B. Orchard, *Thessalonians and the Synoptic Gospels*, in *Biblica*, 1938, pp. 19–42.

himself among those "surviving" at the time of the parousia for the obvious reason that he is still alive. He thus tried to calm the anxiety of the Thessalonians, assuring them that when the parousia occurs, the dead and the living will share equally in the glory. Then he discusses the time of the parousia. The transition is also reminiscent of the eschatological discourse, in which Jesus dealt first with the signs that are to precede the "great tribulation" and the parousia and then with the time when the latter will take place.

Of this Paul says, "But of the times and seasons, brethren, you have no need that we write to you, for you yourselves know well that the day of the Lord is to come as a thief in the night. For when they shall say, 'Peace and security,' even then sudden destruction will come upon them, as birth pangs upon her who is with child, and they will not escape" (5:1-3). He concludes with various recommendations, among them that the letter be read to all the brethren. The final words, "The grace of our Lord Jesus Christ be with you," were probably added in Paul's own hand.

434. At the first opportunity, the epistle was sent to Thessalonica, but it did not accomplish the purpose for which it was written. After all, the letter said nothing that its recipients did not already know. That the day of the parousia was not known, that it would come suddenly, were things the Thessalonians had heard from Paul himself when he was instructing them. But that did not exclude the possibility that it might happen tomorrow, just the same, or within a month or a year, nor did the letter itself exclude these possibilities. Their conviction, therefore, remained unchanged.

Shortly afterward, someone coming from Macedonia to Corinth told Paul that the Thessalonians remained fervent and zealous Christians, but they were still eagerly awaiting the imminent parousia, for reasons we shall presently examine. Therefore, the number of those living in complete idleness had greatly increased, many of whom were not even bothering to procure food for themselves. Since in a few days, or at most a few weeks, the "present world" was to yield to the "world to come" (§§ 399, 402), what need was there to work in order to have food? They might as well stop working for these few weeks or even days, since before very long they would all be seated at the sumptuous messianic banquet (Lk. 12:37). At this piece of information, Paul, no less indignant at their idleness than at their perfervid expectation of the parousia, wrote the second epistle to the Thessalonians, shorter but more peremptory than the first, and sent, perhaps, two months later.

435. After the usual felicitations and exhortations, the letter takes up the matter of the parousia and this time Paul says: "We beseech you, brethren, by the coming of our Lord Jesus Christ and our being gathered together unto him not to be hastily shaken from your right mind, nor terrified, whether by spirit, or by utterance, or by letter attributed to us (ὡς δι' ἡμῶν) as though (ὡς ὅτι) the day of the Lord were near at hand" (2 Thess. 2:1–2).

The allusions here . . . "spirit" . . . "utterance" . . . "letter" . . . indicate the elements which prompted the attitude of the Thessalonians. In the meetings of the community, there were faithful who were — or thought they were — endowed with charisms, and speaking either in tongues or in prophecy (§ 215), they would declare in the name of the Spirit that the solemn event was imminent. Some one of them had gone further and had written a letter in Paul's name stating that the event was about to take place.[22] Such was the hysteria of these neophytes that they did not shrink from these tricks in order to persuade the others of their own belief.

436. Paul, however, rejects it and immediately gives his reasons: "Let no one deceive you in any way for [the day of the Lord will not come][23] unless the apostasy comes first, and the man of sin is revealed, the son of perdition, who opposes and is exalted above all that is called God, or that is worshipped, so that he sits in the temple of God and gives himself out as if he were God. Do you remember that when I was still with you, I used to tell you these things? And now you know what restrains him, that he may be revealed in his proper time. For the mystery of iniquity is already at work; provided only that he who is at present restraining it, does still restrain, until he is gotten out of the way.

"And then the wicked one will be revealed, whom the Lord Jesus will slay with the breath of his mouth and will destroy with the brightness of his coming.

"And his coming is according to the working of Satan with all power and signs and lying wonders, and with all wicked deception to those who are perishing" (2 Thess. 2:3–10). After these admonitions, Paul exhorts the Thessalonians to avoid those who preach idleness because the parousia is imminent and who eat though they do not work. Let them rather imitate him, Paul himself, who has always worked to earn his bread and "if any man will not work, neither let him eat" (3:6–12).

At the end, Paul added in his own writing, "I Paul, greet you with my own hand. This is the mark of every letter. Thus I write" (3:17). It was customary in ancient times for the sender of a letter to add some word of greeting at the end in his own hand (§ 180). Here Paul adds a brief greeting in his own handwriting ("Thus I write") which will

---

[22] The allusion to the "letter" seems to indicate a forgery; others prefer to consider, as Thomas Aquinas did, that it refers to the preceding, authentic letter which was erroneously interpreted. There are arguments for this second view also although it does not seem so well founded as the other (cf. 2 Thess. 3:17).

[23] This bracket is lacking in the text. It is one of the instances where Paul, absorbed in his thought, leaves the sentence grammatically incomplete (§ 164 ff.).

distinguish his letters for the Thessalonians from other forged letters that may come their way.

437. It may be that now for the Thessalonians Paul's thought on the parousia was clear, both with regard to the time of its occurrence and the signs which were to precede it. In addition to the two epistles, which we share with them, they had received Paul's own oral instructions, to which he himself referred them and which formed a kind of advance commentary on the letters. We possess the letters but not the commentary, and so for us Paul's thought is clear enough with regard to the time of the parousia, but quite obscure so far as the signs are concerned.

For Paul, the time of the parousia is absolutely unknown, as Jesus himself had taught in the eschatological discourse. Besides, as he writes, there is no indication whatever that the great day is near. This is undoubtedly the lesson of the second letter. The question then arises how to reconcile this teaching with the statement in the first letter that "we who live, who survive until the coming of the Lord," shall not be more favored than those who have died but "shall be caught up together with them in clouds to meet the Lord in the air." Does this first person plural, "we," mean Paul was convinced he would be alive at the time of the parousia?

438. If we confine ourselves to the literal meaning, it seems impossible to find any agreement not only between the two letters, but between the first and second parts of the first letter in itself. If Paul was sure he was going to be alive at the parousia, he could not insist that its time was absolutely unknown and that it would come "as a thief in the night," as he says in the first epistle. In that case, the Thessalonians were much sharper than he, and their state of "alert" could teach him how to prepare for a thief.

Are we to consider, then, that in the interval between the first and second letter Paul changed his mind, that he first believed in the imminence of the parousia and then became disillusioned because of the delay? The interval between the two letters was very short, two or three months perhaps (§ 43), and there is nothing to indicate that in so short a time Paul's thinking had undergone so radical a change on the subject. In fact, we have direct proof that he had not changed his thinking at all since, when he later wrote his first epistle to the Corinthians (15:51–52), he set forth the same ideas as those in *1 Thessalonians* (§ 488, last note).

439. Another suggested solution is to consider *2 Thessalonians* apocryphal either in whole or in part. It then presumably is not Paul's letter but the work of a forger, at least in the passage in which he contradicts the first letter on the subject of the parousia. Thus the alleged conflict between the epistles is definitely eliminated. But the same result could be obtained by declaring the first letter apocryphal and the second authentic. Why reject the second, then? The reason is clear. The exponents of this theory are followers of the eschatological school — although not all of them — according to which Paul was expecting the end of the world at any moment (§ 137) just as the Thessalonians were. Thus they reject the second letter because this clearly denies that Paul had any such expectation. There are no other reasons for rejecting it.

It is the same method as that used by the Tübingen school. To sift the documents, the disciples of Tübingen used their own particular touchstone, the conflict between the Jewish Christians and the Hellenist Christians (§ 125). The touchstone of the eschatologists, on the other hand, is the imminence of the parousia, but they use it the same way and declare false all documents which do not stick to the magnet. Those who find this method "historical" are welcome to it. Those who consider it *a priori* reasoning, which seeks to prove *idem per idem*, will relegate eschatologism to the same limbo as the Tübingen school.

440. Why, then, did Paul in his first letter speak of "we who live, who survive until the coming of the Lord"? For the reason that he is eminently the Apostle of the Mystical Body of Christ, namely, the Church (§§ 621, 622, 634), and therefore he is referring to this permanent society rather than to individuals. He views the entire Mystical Body rather than its separate members. He speaks of the parousia from the viewpoint of the permanency of the Church, and the maxim he gives is to be true so long as the Church endures. When the parousia will take place he does not know, for it may happen within a brief time or "in the ages to come" (Eph. 2:7). But whenever it happens, there will be the faithful who are dead and the faithful who are still alive, and both will share equally in the glory.

Paul is contemplating these two perennial categories of the Church, although he is speaking from the viewpoint of the living, since he is still alive himself. But the principle will remain true, whether stated now by Paul or by some believer "in the ages to come." Individuals are transitory, while the structure of the Church is perennial. This means that the principle stated by Paul will be reiterated "in the ages to come" with the same truth as it was uttered the first time. The "we" in Paul's statement expresses the sense of Christian collectivity which he feels to a supreme degree. If the parousia comes when he has died, his "we" will still be valid, for the future brethren will represent him in that perennial category.

It may be objected that it is not natural to express third person concepts in the first person. But it should be noted that while Paul does not exclude the possibility that the parousia will come during his lifetime, he does not exclude the other alternative either. He affirms nothing regarding the time and therefore speaks from the viewpoint of his present state, which is among the living. The rest becomes clear within the framework of Christian collectivity and the concepts he expresses elsewhere. Certainly a modern writer might have expressed himself differently, with clear distinctions, distinct hypotheses, and a list of premises. But Paul is neither a modern writer nor does he ever abandon the condensed and elliptical style which is characteristic of him (§ 164 ff.).

441. As for the signs which are to precede the parousia, what Paul says to the Thessalonians, after prudent reflection and by way of completing his previous oral instructions to them, may be summed up as follows. Before the advent of the glorious Christ, there will be an "apostasy." On that occasion the "man of sin" will be revealed, who will attempt to take the place of God. But for the present, this cannot happen because of him "who is . . . restraining him," although the "mystery of iniquity" is already at work. But "the Lord Jesus will slay [him] with the breath of his mouth" (a messianic phrase deriving from *Isaias*, 11:4), so that the parousia of Jesus in glory is to be set against the parousia of the "wicked one." The latter, as the emissary of Satan, will act "with all power and signs and lying wonders," but he will be overcome by the parousia of the glorious Jesus.

How are these various points to be interpreted? The "apostasy" which will inaugurate the great conflict refers certainly to a defection, but to what kind of defection and on whose authority? And who is "the man of sin, the son of perdition, who opposes and is exalted above all that is called God, or that is worshipped, so that he sits in the temple of God and gives himself out as if he were God"? Caligula in fact had tried to sit in the Temple of Jerusalem, commanding that a statue in his honor be erected therein, and this had made an enormous impression on the Jews. This had happened about a dozen years before, in the year 40,[24] but when Paul is writing to the Thessalonians no such danger is evident. And to what does the expression "what restrains him" (τὸ κατέχον) refer, balanced a little further on by the expression "he who is at present restraining it" (ὁ κατέχων)? Is it an actual personage, or a symbolic personification? And what of the other allusions obscure to us?

442. To us today this great drama is a closed book, sealed with seven seals. And that is the way it seemed to the various interpreters of ancient times, including Augustine who says frankly: "I confess I absolutely do not know what he meant"[25] Nevertheless, modern scholars, as is natural and right, have attempted to break one or another of the seals in the hope of being able to read a few lines of the book.

---

[24] Cf. *Storia d'Israele*, I, 447 (§ 393).
[25] *De civitate Dei*, XX, 19, 2.

What we can state with certainty is that similar concepts had already appeared in the Old Testament (Dan. 7:8 ff.; 11:36 ff.). In early Christianity there was the current belief that in opposition to Christ there would rise an archadversary, who was given the name of Antichrist. The idea of the antichrist was undoubtedly included within the ordinary catechesis, for the recipients of the first epistle of John read: "You have heard that Antichrist is coming" (that is, "will come") (1 Jn. 2:18; cf. 4:3). Besides, this real and great antichrist already has precursors, as it were, who have begun his work and prepared his coming, and who are therefore so many antichrists (1 Jn. 2:18; 2 Jn. 7).

443. It is natural then to compare this antichrist of the apostolic catechesis with the "man of sin" of Paul, to whom is attributed the "mystery of iniquity" which, though hidden, "is already at work" (ἐνεργεῖται) in antithesis to Christ. And to confirm this, note that the antithesis between Christ and the antichrist is resolved in the antithesis between the "mystery of Christ" and the "mystery of iniquity." Paul speaks of the former several times (Eph. 1:9; 3:3, 4, 9, Greek text; Col. 1:27; 2:2; 4:3, Greek text), for just as the "mystery of iniquity" is already in action, so the "mystery of Christ" is developing progressively. This mystery is so broad that it extends not only over all mankind without distinction as to race (Eph. 3:5–9; Col. 1:26–29), but to all creation, for its purpose is "to re-establish (ἀνακεφαλαιώσασθαι) all things in Christ, both those in the heavens and those on earth" (Eph. 1:10). Therefore, as a result of this fundamental antithesis between them, the mystery of the antichrist will have the same broadness of scope in the contrary sense; that is, its purpose will be to turn away from Christ and to re-establish in the antichrist all things in heaven and on earth.

In reality, on the basis of this data, the ancient exegetes in general identified the "man of sin" with the antichrist, considering the latter to be an actual person and not the personification of an idea. But except on this one point there was great divergence of opinion. This is especially true of the phrases "what restrains him" and "he who is restraining him," with regard to which we may note the opinion of certain early writers (Irenaeus, Jerome), accepted by many modern scholars, that the expression refers to the Roman Empire, which, being stably governed by a wise legislation, was considered a guarantee of order and peace.

444. It would be perhaps impossible and certainly valueless to enumerate the various persons or things identified through the centuries with the various signs listed in Paul's epistle. They are usually mere flights of fancy, which was free to wander through a field so suited to its exercise, and often carry with them tendentious insinuations.

One such theory, which found great credence among various

Protestant sects not only at the beginning of the Reformation but also in quite recent times, is that the antichrist is the Pope of Rome. Naturally "what restrains" this antichrist is Protestant teaching. There is no doubt that if religious questions had the influence over the masses they once had, the antichrist would be identified with Hitler or Stalin, Churchill or Mussolini, Roosevelt or the Mikado, depending on the viewpoint. And he "who is restraining" would be in each case the one in each pair not chosen as the antichrist. The principle is the same as that in the old Protestant exegesis.

In the Middle Ages, many identified the antichrist with Mohammed. Several modern scholars, basing their views on the historical circumstances of Paul's time, interpret the antichrist as Simon Magus or the legendary Nero-come-to-life-again (Tacitus, *Hist.*, II, 8–9). For others, the apostasy is a political revolt against the Roman emperor in general, who is considered the antichrist, while "what restrains him" is the various governors of the Roman provinces, who, knowing the needs and desires of the people, restrain the emperor's aspirations to self-deification.

445. The theories which identify the phrases with facts and personages of Paul's time are in all likelihood mistaken.

In the first place, it nowhere appears that Paul attributed any particular importance to the political events and circumstances of his day. Writing to his neophytes, he warns them that "our citizenship (πολίτευμα) is in heaven" (Phil. 3:20), implying that political affairs in general barely touched the sole of his sandals.

In addition, as we have just noted, heaven is involved in the conflict between the "mystery of iniquity" and the "mystery of Christ" for dominion over all things in the heavens and on earth. The struggle between these two mysteries transcends the political and terrestrial; it is altogether cosmic. Paul states that he wishes "to enlighten all men as to what is the dispensation of the mystery [of Christ] which has been hidden from eternity in God, who created all things; in order that through the Church there be made known to the Principalities and the Powers in the heavens . . ." (Eph. 3:9–10). Thus, in his concept, the victorious affirmations of the Church on earth are gloriously echoed in the heavens among the Principalities and Powers and other angelic hierarchies. The angels, then, participate in the conflict between the "mystery of Christ" and the "mystery of iniquity," on the side, of course, of the former. Now the concept of a cosmic struggle with repercussions on the earth is not peculiar to Paul. It is to be found in both the Christian *Apocalypse* (12:7 ff.) and in the abundant apocalyptic literature of the Jews.[26] This shows once again that Paul's thought derives both from the common apostolic catechesis and from certain concepts of contemporary Judaism.

---

[26] Cf. *The Life of Christ*, pp. 75–77 (§§ 84–86).

It is our opinion that the signs Paul describes to the Thessalonians as forerunners of the parousia are directly related to this cosmic struggle, and it is in this — and not in contemporary political realities — that we must seek the meaning of the various allusions, and especially the phrase, "he who is restraining." In any case, even here, any interpretation would be mere theory, more or less plausible, and nothing more. The seven seals which clasp the mysterious book could be broken with accuracy and certainty only by Paul himself or by some one of the Thessalonians who heard his oral teaching on the subject.

❈   ❈   ❈

446. Paul's successful apostolate in Corinth after he left the local synagogue must naturally have displeased the Jews not a little. After tolerating him for eighteen months (§ 428) they tried to get rid of him by appealing to the proconsul, Gallio (§ 158). He had probably been in office only a few months, and the Jews, who had been busy gathering information about him, had good hope that he might favor them. One day, they "made a concerted attack upon Paul and took him before the tribunal, saying, 'This fellow is persuading men to worship God contrary to the Law'" (Acts 18:12–13). Which "Law" was this, the Jewish or the Roman? The accusers did not specify, perhaps on purpose, the better to impress the proconsul, but they surely meant the Jewish Law. The Roman law might be considered to be implicitly involved since the Jewish religion was recognized and protected by Roman legislation.

But Gallio did not swallow the bait. When he realized what was going on, he interrupted Paul, who had begun to speak in his own defense, and said to the accusers drily: "If there were some question of misdemeanor or serious crime, O Jews, I should with reason bear with you. But if these are questions of word and of names and of your Law, look to it yourselves; I have no wish to decide such matters.' And he drove them from the tribunal" (*ibid.*, 14–16). The Jews had sadly miscalculated. They had hoped to find the proconsul a solicitous patron, and instead they found him not only the blood brother of Seneca, but the spiritual brother of the philosopher enemy of the Jews.[27]

447. When the crowd, which perhaps did not have much liking for the Jews either, saw the proconsul order his lictors to clear the space in front of the tribunal so quickly, it took advantage of the scene to stage a demonstration. "Then they all seized Sosthenes, the president of the synagogue, and beat him in front of the tribunal; but Gallio paid no attention to it" (*ibid.*, 17). The hapless Sosthenes must have been either the successor or the colleague of the ruler of the synagogue,

---

[27] Cf. the quotation from Seneca in Augustine's *De civitate Dei*, VI, 10.

Corinth — Street to the Lecheum and Stairway of the Agora

Crispus, who had become a Christian (§ 426). The poor man, who may have instigated the Jewish action against Paul, paid in his person the anti-Jewish prejudices of the mob. Unwittingly he had the honor of taking Paul's place in the flogging which usually concluded the trials instituted against the Apostle. If this Sosthenes is the same person whom Paul, in his letter to the Corinthians (1 Cor. 1:1), calls "Sosthenes our brother," we may conclude that his misfortune had brought him to Christianity, perhaps because of the interest Paul took in him after the beating. But the identity is not certain, since there is no evidence except the same name.

We have no information about further relations between Paul and Gallio. They must both have been victims of Nero and perhaps in the same year. Gallio, who became involved in the conspiracy of Piso, was forced to kill himself shortly after the suicide of his brother Seneca (Tacitus, Annal., XV, 73; XVI, 17).

After the encounter with Gallio, Paul remained in Corinth "some time longer" (Acts 18:18; § 158), perhaps a month or two. Then, with Aquila and Priscilla, "he sailed for Syria," leaving Corinth through its eastern harbor, Cenchrae. Nevertheless it was not a direct voyage, for from Cenchrae he went to Ephesus, in Asia Minor. Probably there was no boat sailing directly to Seleucia, the port of Syria.

448. Immediately following is the curious information that the three of them, Paul, Priscilla, and Aquila, departed "having shorn his head in Cenchrae. For he had a vow." Who had made the vow, Paul or Aquila? Grammatically, the phrase may apply to Aquila, who is the

last named in the text. But from the context it would seem to refer to Paul, who is the subject of the narrative. The vow he was under was associated with the ancient Hebrew rite of the "Nazarite" (Num. 6:2–21), but it had perhaps been mitigated in substance and duration. A few years later, Queen Bernice, whom Paul met (§ 571), took this same vow and on that occasion Flavius Josephus furnished the following explanation: "There is the custom that those suffering from some illness or other trial take a vow, thirty days before the day on which they are to offer sacrifices, to abstain from wine and to shave their hair."[28] We do not know Paul's reason for taking the vow. But it is significant that he who asserted the Christian's independence from the Jewish Law should still practice certain of its observances. This confirms what was said above. Paul considered the Jewish rites still permissible but no longer obligatory (§ 373).

The stop at Ephesus was a brief one to service the ship, but since it included a Sabbath he took advantage of the fact to go to the synagogue and set forth his teaching. He must have aroused considerable interest, because the Jews begged him to remain longer. He did not consent although he did promise to return later.

449. He set sail again, disembarking this time in Caesarea of Palestine. From here "he went up to pay his respects to the church and then went down to Antioch" (Acts 18:22). Jerusalem is not named, but the verb "to go up" was the usual one to indicate a journey to Jerusalem, and the word "church" with no qualifying epithet indicates the mother church of that city.

The stop in Jerusalem was a very short one too, just long enough for a greeting. Paul may have been in a hurry to reach Antioch, but it is also possible he did not linger because of the Judaizing movement which prevailed there. These Judaizing Christians had not subsided after Paul's victory at the Apostolic Council in 49, nor did they view with much pleasure the hordes of pagans he admitted into the Church without requiring that they be circumcised. Their welcome to the returned missionary, therefore, may have been a chilly one. Paul, for his part, could sense that these set and narrow Judaizers did not have much in common with him and, in order not to arouse the old arguments, he hurried off to Antioch, the fervid missionary center where he was more at ease.

His arrival in Antioch brought to a close his second missionary journey. He had left the city around the end of 49 and the beginning of 50. He returned at the beginning of the year 53.

---

[28] *Wars of the Jews*, II, 313. The School of Shammai also prescribed the thirty-day period for those entering Palestine from abroad (*Mishna, Nagir*, III, 6).

The Third Missionary Journey

450. Luke's account of the third missionary journey begins in the most laconic fashion. It seems the author's tendency to skim over events which occur in regions he has already mentioned and hurry on to new fields. In the present instance he says only that Paul, on his return to Antioch, "after spending some time there . . . departed, and traveled through the Galatian country and Phrygia in turn, strengthening all the disciples" (Acts 18:23). As we have already noted (§ 159), this summary statement refers to a quite long period of time. Paul must have left Antioch in the spring of 53 and spent the rest of the year and part of 54 in the Galatian region and Phrygia, reaching Ephesus in the same year. Luke dwells at some length upon his sojourn in Ephesus, for this is new territory, but he skips the Galatian region and Phrygia, which have been discussed before. It is our present task to try to fill in both parts of Luke's outline as far as possible.

If Paul went directly from Antioch to the Galatian country, he again followed the route of his second journey, that is, through the "Cilician Gates" (§ 371). But when he had crossed the Taurus, instead of proceeding east in the direction of Derbe, Lystra, and Iconium, he headed north, across Tyana, Sasima, and Caesarea of Cappadocia, and entered the Galatian country from the east. This time, then, he skipped the communities of Lycaonia and Pisidia, founded during his first journey, and hurried on to his beloved Galatians.

451. This second sojourn among the Galatians is deduced from his epistle (Gal. 4:13), where, recalling his first stay among them — on the occasion of his illness — he says that he evangelized them "the first time" (τὸ πρότερον: § 116, note). When he was writing the letter (§ 505), therefore, he had evangelized them a second time and this was on the occasion of this third missionary journey. His going to the communities of Galatia, rather than those of Lycaonia and Pisidia, was probably determined by information he received which had caused him some concern. Worried that the purity of their faith may have been undermined by ill-intentioned persons from without, he hastened to these well-loved converts, "strengthening" them — as Luke tells us —

in their inexperience. Subsequent events showed that Paul's suspicions were well founded (§ 504).

452. An unerring spiritual strategist, Paul had for a long time been aware of the important position of proconsular Asia. The following among its innumerable gulfs were important for their commerce: Pergamum (§ 17) at the mouth of the Caicus; Smyrna at the mouth of the Hermus (§ 13); and to the south, Ephesus at the mouth of the Cayster. Below the promontory of Mycale, where the Great Meander flowed into the sea, lay Miletus.

In addition to these principal cities, there were many others of great

Ephesus — Ruins of the Stadium

importance in the province. In the discourse Flavius Josephus attributes to King Agrippa II, in which he attempted to dissuade the Jews of Jerusalem from war against Rome, the number of cities in the province of Asia is given as 500, and this is probably drawn from official documents.[1] The province was undoubtedly one of the most thickly populated in the whole Empire. The port of Ephesus was in direct communication by sea both with Rome and all the West and with Egypt and Palestine in the south, while numerous land routes linked it with the regions of the East as far as Persia and India. It was not without reason that the Romans, who were also expert strategists, had stationed the headquarters of the proconsul in Ephesus (§ 21).

453. On his arrival in the city this time Paul found material assistance awaiting him. Aquila and Priscilla were still there (§ 448) and no doubt Paul lodged with them. He also began to work again in their

---

[1] *Wars of the Jews*, II, 366; the same figure occurs in Philostratus, *Lives of the Sophists*, II, 1, 4. The number varies in other documents.

shop, and in addition he unexpectedly found a small group of semi-Christians.

Since Paul's first visit, a "certain Jew named Apollos, a native of Alexandria, came to Ephesus. He was an eloquent man, and mighty in the Scriptures" (Acts 18:24). The Hellenist name *Apollos* was the abbreviation of Apollonius or Apollodorus. The fact that he came from Alexandria, the great Jewish center of Egypt,[2] indicates in general what his intellectual information had been. If he was not actually a pupil of Philo, he must have followed the exegetical school of Scripture of which Philo was the most prominent exponent. The latter, using an allegorical method, tried to reconcile Moses with Plato. It is in this sense that we must understand the phrase "mighty in the Scriptures."

But we have more important information concerning Apollos' spiritual formation: "He had been instructed in the Way of the Lord, and being fervent in spirit, used to speak and teach carefully whatever had to do with Jesus, though he knew of John's baptism only" (*ibid.*, 25). This baptism is the rite of John the Baptist,[3] which had great success in Palestine, spreading from there throughout the Diaspora. Apollos is a case in point, but there is even greater evidence in the Fourth Gospel, the first chapters of which underline more than once the full accord between John the Baptist and Jesus, showing the former's frank and open submission to Christ (cf. 1:15 ff.; 3:23 ff.). This indicates that at the end of the first century when this Gospel was written, its author was still concerned with disciples of John the Baptist who were dissenting from the Messias Jesus or at least unaware of him. Apollos' knowledge of him was not complete. He taught "carefully ($\dot{\alpha}\kappa\rho\iota\beta\tilde{\omega}\varsigma$) whatever had to do with Jesus," but that does not mean he taught all that was known of him. What he taught was exact, but he did not have the whole, and perhaps not even the main part, of Christian teaching.

454. Nevertheless his zeal impelled him to speak of Jesus in the synagogue of Ephesus, just as Paul did elsewhere in his travels. Here Aquila and Priscilla heard his discourses and immediately noted the accuracy of what he said and his lack of full knowledge. So they "took him home and expounded the Way of God to him more precisely [that is, with greater fullness]" (Acts 18:26).

Apollos accepted what they told him with no difficulty. Undoubtedly they also told him of their recent stay in Corinth with Paul and the flourishing Christian community founded there. This, perhaps, prompted him to go to Corinth, both to perfect his own knowledge of the catechesis and to become acquainted at firsthand with a Christian

---

[2] Cf. *Storia d'Israele*, II, p. 211 ff. (§ 190 ff.).

[3] Cf. *The Life of Christ*, p. 270 ff. (§ 268 ff.); p. 293 (§ 291).

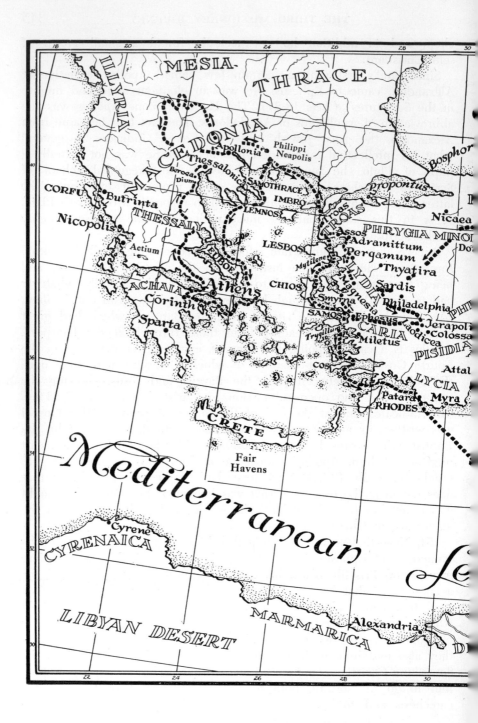

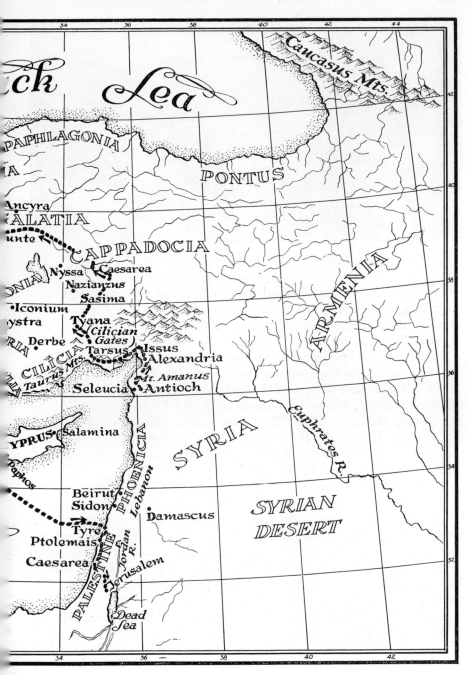

Paul's Third Missionary Journey

Ephesus — Street and Library of Celsus

community. The disciples he had won in Ephesus, who were in reality only half Christian, wrote recommending him to the Christians of Corinth, with whom they corresponded perhaps through Aquila and Priscilla. "On his arrival there he was of great service to those who had believed, for he vigorously refuted the Jews in public and showed from the Scriptures that Jesus is the Christ" (*ibid.*, 28).

455. All this had happened before Paul reached Ephesus during his third journey. When he arrived he found about twelve disciples of Apollos. He asked them, "Did you receive the Holy Spirit when you became believers?" They were a little perplexed at the question and answered, "We have not even heard that there is a Holy Spirit."

"How then were you baptized?" Paul persisted.

"With John's baptism," they answered.

This brief dialogue, while it gives us a glimpse into the formation of these semi-Christians, also indicates the signs by which the first true Christians recognized the baptism of Jesus. These signs were the manifestations of the Holy Spirit, who was received in Baptism. Finally Paul explained to them, "John baptized the people with a baptism of repentance, telling them to believe in him who was to come after him, that is, in Jesus."

Paul's explanation is in perfect agreement with the first chapters of the Fourth Gospel as mentioned above. These converts, who had come only halfway, accepted the explanation and "were baptized in the name of the Lord Jesus; and when Paul laid his hand on them, the Holy Spirit came upon them, and they began to speak in tongues and to prophesy" (19:2–6).

The most obvious and natural interpretation of these words is that

there were two distinct rites here, the baptism and the laying on of
the hands. Paul performed the latter, but we are not told he had
also baptized them. Considering that his usual rule was not to confer
baptism himself, we may conjecture that it was given by Aquila or
one of Paul's companions. Whatever the case may be, at the second
rite, the laying on of the hands, the newly baptized received the Holy
Spirit, who manifested himself through the charisms already discussed
(§ 211 ff.). The neophytes now bore the evident marks of their faith.
The two rites, though separate, were performed one after the other,
so that as soon as an individual became a Christian, he was immediately
able to manifest himself as such. In fact, the two rites — baptism and
confirmation — were coupled for many centuries in the Church, since
they were almost always administered to mature persons converted
to Christianity. But gradually, as it became the general rule to baptize
infants, the two rites were no longer administered at the same time,
for the infant needed to be made a Christian, but he could not of
himself manifest that quality.

Ephesus — Ruins of the Gymnasium

456. At the same time, Paul, again according to his custom, was
attempting to evangelize the Jews. For three months he went to
the synagogue to preach the Messias Jesus and it does not seem that
at first he encountered any particular difficulty. But in time the same
old hostilities began to sprout and grow, and so, just as in Corinth,
Paul left the synagogue and established a center for his activity elsewhere. In Ephesus this was "in the school of one Tyrannus" (*ibid.*, 9).

The *scholé* of the Greeks (Latin, *schola*) was, strictly speaking, a
place for carrying on intellectual pursuits or for imparting or receiving
regular instruction. Rooms for these purposes were to be found in all

the "gymnasia," among the other rooms used as libraries, for exercising, baths, etc. In one, you might listen to a rhetorician declaiming or commenting on a Greek lyric poet; in another a group of philosophers would be discussing Stoicism or Epicureanism; in yet another a teacher might be conducting a course of lessons in eloquence. In the intervals, or when the lesson or discussion became boring, one could go out into the courtyard to stretch his legs or chat in the sunshine. This Tyrannus, whose school was host to Paul, may have been a Greek rhetorician (as his name implies, though we know nothing else about him), who gave lessons in such a room rented for the purpose. When the lessons were ended, the room remained empty and he sublet it to Paul for the hours when he was not using it, thereby adding to his earnings at the same time.

457. The "Western text" (§ 119, note) gives us the hours in which Paul occupied the room, that is, "from the fifth to the tenth hour" of sunlight,[4] or from about eleven in the morning until four in the afternoon our time. The ancients, in fact, were very early risers.[5] The day's business (*negotia*) began at dawn and continued until near noon. The afternoons were reserved for leisure (*otia*), that is, physical exercises, pastimes, amusements, etc. Tyrannus probably finished his lessons around eleven and then left the room to Paul.

Paul had been working at his loom since the first light of dawn. While his hands set the warp and woof of his goat-hair canvasses, his mind set the pattern of the discourse he was to give in the school of Tyrannus. For him there were no hours of *negotia* and *otia*. There was the one and only business to which his entire activity was dedicated, the message of the Christ. He perhaps ate something on his way from the shop to the "school," and there he was, ready to speak of Christ until sunset.

458. The dispassionate Luke, who gives only part of the story and lets us glimpse the rest for ourselves, adds laconically, "Now this went on for two years" (*ibid.*, 10). That Paul had great physical resistance despite his mysterious malady is quite evident from his journeys (§ 196). But it is even more evident in the life he led here, which would have tired any strong man in a few months. We must remember that for Paul there was never — in late evening, at night, or in some rare scrap of time otherwise unoccupied — a moment of calm or rest. In addition to his "anxiety for all the churches" (2 Cor. 11:28) he had founded and with which he maintained close contact, he had to spend himself a thousand ways for all those who came to hear him and were preparing to become Christian, continuing, in other words, on

---

[4] For the ancient method of telling time cf. *The Life of Christ*, p. 635 (§ 607).
[5] This custom is evident also in Jesus' trial before Pilate; *ibid.*, p. 609 (§ 576).

a much larger scale, the incessant and detailed activity in which he had spent himself in Thessalonica (§ 397).

And all this in the midst of the unremitting hostility of the Jews, who could not forgive this schismatic for the success of his independent activity.

Not long afterward Paul reminded the presbyters of Ephesus: "You know in what manner I have lived with you all the time since the first day that I came into the province of Asia, serving the Lord with all humility and with tears and in trials that befell me because of the plots of the Jews; how I have kept back nothing that was for your good, but have declared it to you and taught you in public and from house to house. . . . Watch, therefore, and remember that for three years night and day I did not cease with tears to admonish every one of you" (Acts 20:18-20, 31). And from Ephesus itself he wrote to the Corinthians: "To this very hour we hunger and thirst, and we are naked and buffeted, and have no fixed abode. And we toil, working with our own hands. We are reviled and we bless, we are persecuted and we bear with it, we are maligned and we entreat, we have become as the refuse of this world, the offscouring of all, even until now!" (1 Cor. 4:11-13.) This, in substance, was the kind of life Paul led for three years (§ 159) in Ephesus.

Ephesus — The Ancient Aqueducts

459. Undoubtedly there was something extraordinary in him which upheld him in the midst of the storm. Luke helps us understand this when he tells us the extraordinary results of this intense activity: ". . . All who lived in the province of Asia, both Jews and Gentiles, heard the word of the Lord. And God worked more than the usual miracles by the hand of Paul; so that even handkerchiefs and aprons were carried from his body to the sick, and the diseases left them and the evil spirits went out" (Acts 19:10–12). These "handkerchiefs" were large ones used in the Orient for wiping the forehead, and the "aprons" were those used by workmen and so by Paul too at the loom. The fact that these objects were sought by the Ephesians anticipates in a certain sense the cult of relics which developed later in the Church.

The rationalists find the mention of these "miracles" distasteful and in obedience to their "lay dogma" explain them away as legend. They do not realize that the careful Luke is giving us also a psychological reason for Paul's enormous success, whereby the Good Tidings spread from Ephesus more or less throughout the whole province of Asia. Having rejected Luke's reason, they have to find another which will explain this success historically. And when they have found it, those who do not accept the "lay dogma" will invoke for their part the antidote of good sense. The fact remains that Paul, after a few months of that activity and working of miracles, had become famous throughout Ephesus, as is evident from the episodes which Luke narrates immediately afterward. But first let us consider a moment the summary information that the Gospel was spread throughout the province of Asia.

460. Paul's position as evangelizer in Ephesus is precisely summed up in the words he himself writes from Ephesus to the Corinthians: "For a door has been opened to me, great and effective" ($\dot{\epsilon}\nu\epsilon\rho\gamma\acute{\eta}s$ — 1 Cor. 16:9). It was the door which opened directly on the populous and cosmopolitan hinterland of the city (§ 452). The irradiation of the Good Tidings from Ephesus to the 500 cities of the province came about gradually through the innumerable contacts and relations of the various persons always coming and going in the capital; many of them heard Paul, mostly by chance. Naturally, he must have fostered these contacts, tenuous at first, then gradually stronger and more extensive. It was the same method he had used before in Antioch of Pisidia (§ 335) and more or less elsewhere. Luke tells us nothing of all this activity, which must have been singularly extensive. He gives us only the results, and this we can check in part against the information in other sources.

About forty years later the book of the *Apocalypse* was written, which is addressed "to the seven churches that are in Asia" (Apoc. 1:4), and these were the churches of Ephesus, Smyrna, Pergamum, Thyatira, Sardis, Philadelphia, and Laodicea (1:11; 2–3). Now as early as the end of the first century, these communities are not only well organized but appear to be afflicted with trials of various sorts, and some seem even to have entered on a period of decline. This leads to the conclusion that their foundation had not been recent but went back at least a few decades. This would bring us, if not to the time of Paul's sojourn in Ephesus, to the period immediately following it.

Laodicea — Ruins of the Stadium

Other information is to be found in Paul's own epistles. While he was a prisoner in Rome, a scant ten years after his stay in Ephesus, he writes to his neophytes in Asia Minor, and from these letters we gather the information which follows.

461. Along the river Lycus, Christian communities had arisen in the cities of Laodicea, Colossae, and Hierapolis (§ 20), the first two a short distance apart on the left bank of the river to the south, the third on the right bank to the north. Paul was well acquainted with these communities and solicitously followed their progress, but he had not founded them nor had he ever visited them (Col. 2:1; cf. 1:4, 9; 4:13 ff.) although he wrote the Colossian community the epistle which has come down to us.

The principal herald of the Good Tidings in those regions was Epaphras, a wealthy Greek of Colossae. This is certain so far as his own city is concerned (Col. 1:7–8), and is very probable in the case of Laodicea and Hierapolis (4:13). Since there was busy traffic between Colossae and Ephesus, we may conclude that Epaphras met Paul on some trip to the latter city, listened to his preaching in the school of Tyrannus, and was converted to Christianity so whole-heartedly that he immediately became its missionary when he returned to his own country.

He soon had helpers, but we do not know whether he converted them there or whether they were converted by Paul in Ephesus.

Probably the Philemon to whom Paul addressed the epistle extant today (Philemon 19) was converted by Paul. The community gathered in his house in Colossae, and with his wife Appia he had greatly contributed to the spread of the Gospel (*ibid.*, 1–2). In Laodicea, on the other hand, the community met in the home of a certain Nymphas (Col. 4:15). The name must have been an abbreviation of Nymphodorus and does not designate a woman.

462. Of these three churches, only that of Laodicea is mentioned in the list in the *Apocalypse*, but that does not mean the other two declined rapidly after the death of Paul.

With respect to Hieropolis (or Jerapolis), the information extant from ancient times gives rise to ambiguities because of the changes which have occurred in place names and the fact that many towns had the same name. There were many cities named Hierapolis in the Roman Empire, and there were two in Phrygia, one in Phrygia *Prima* or *Pacatania* (§ 19) in the valley of the Lycus, and the other to the northeast in Phrygia *Secunda* or *Salutaris,* not far from Synnada. The latter was more frequently called Hieropolis and was assigned from the fourth century on to Phrygia Minor, a designation for what in ancient times was northern Phrygia. It is quite probable, however, that from early times there was contact between the two cities of this name in Phrygia. It seems likely that the Hierapolis in the Lycus valley was the native city of Papias, who flourished around the year 120 and to whom we are indebted for the few ancient external data regarding the information in the Canonical Gospels.[6] There was also a bishop of Hieropolis toward the end of the second century, the Abercius who in his famous epitaph tells us he has visited both the community in Rome and those of Mesopotamia, with Paul (1.12 — that is, his writings) as a traveling companion. The Hieropolis of Abercius is not the one in the valley of Lycus, however, but the one near Synnada.[7] Abercius' special reference to Paul leads us to infer nevertheless that he is associating his own city with the one of the same name in the writings of the Apostle, since the latter city is also called Hieropolis in some of the ancient documents.

463. These are the certain data which have come down to us regarding the group of churches along the river Lycus, and they permit us to add a little to the summary information in Luke regarding the evangelization of the Roman province of Asia. For the rest, there is only conjecture.

Might not other converts of Paul in Ephesus, for instance, have

---

[6] Cf. *ibid.*, p. 93 (§ 107); p. 98 (§ 114); p. 108 (§ 128), etc.

[7] Cf. A. Ferrua, *Della patria e del nome di S. Abercio,* in *La Civiltà Cattolica,* 1943, IV, pp. 39–45.

Epitaph of Abercius. Second and Third Centuries. Rome: Christian Museum of the Lateran

imitated the zealous activity of Epaphras and carried the Christian message in other directions? Did no one go to Thyratira, the city of the good Lydia, the mistress of the purple dye sheds in Philippi (§ 382)? May not some one of Paul's disciples have founded the church in Miletus, where Paul later called a meeting of the presbyters of Ephesus (Acts 20:17) and where later still he left the sick Trophimus (2 Tim. 4:20)? In Smyrna, in the first decade of the second century, we find the bishop Polycarp, who in his letter to the Philippians (3:2) specifically recalls Paul's "letters"[8] to them and appears to be very well acquainted with the Apostle's writings. Is it not possible that the first to preach in the city of Smyrna, so well represented in post-apostolic Christianity, was someone of Paul's disciples sent there from Ephesus? Such conjectures might be continued at length, but they would serve no practical purpose.

Certainly true, then, is Luke's general statement that "all who lived in the province of Asia . . . heard the word of the Lord," for the seed of the Gospel was sown throughout the whole populous area, and it immediately took root and sprouted beneath the brilliant sun of Paul. Later, when this sun had set another rose to shine upon this Gospel harvest. Toward the end of the first century, John the Apostle settled in Ephesus, and from there Christianity received the last of its Gospels, the "spiritual" Gospel.[9]

464. Meanwhile, Paul's fame as a wonder-worker in Ephesus was too great to escape imitation. There were Jewish exorcists in the city who, out of hostility to Paul, tried to obtain the same results with the same methods. They thought the "magic formula" Paul used to free the possessed automatically produced its good results of itself,

---

[8] Polycarp uses the plural although there is only one epistle from Paul to the Philippians extant today. Polycarp may have been familiar with more than one, or his term may include the letters to the neighboring Thessalonians. Probably, however, it is a *plurale generis.*

[9] Cf. *The Life of Christ,* p. 136 ff. (§ 156).

Ruins of Hierapolis in the Lycus Valley

and they tried using it too. Among them were the seven sons of a
certain Sceva, of a family of Jewish high priests. Two of them tried
to exorcise a demoniac in the name of the Jesus preached by Paul,
"but the evil spirit answered and said to them, 'Jesus I acknowledge,
and Paul I know, but who are you?' And the man in whom the evil
spirit was sprang at them and overpowered them both with such
violence that they fled from that house tattered and bruised"
(Acts 19:15-16).

465. This humiliating encounter became known through all Ephesus
and resulted only in increased prestige for Paul. Another consequence
was that "many of those who believed kept coming, and openly
confessed their practices. And many who had practised magical arts
collected their books and burnt them publicly; and they reckoned
up the prices of them, and found the sum to be fifty thousand
pieces of silver" (*ibid.*, 19). These "books" are the *Ephesia grammata*
discussed in § 16.

The wide circulation of these magic scrolls is also evidenced by
the fact that several of the neophytes had used them before their
conversion and still kept them in their houses. The failure of the
Jewish exorcists opened their eyes on this score, high-lighting the
impotence of magic and the power of Paul. The great public bonfire
of magic writings was almost a reparation for the past and a public
manifestation of their new belief. Nor is it necessary to wait for
Savonarola's time to find examples of bonfires of impious or obscene
writings, for they also occurred in the pagan world (Livy, XL, 29).
The cost of the material burned was impressive. both because of the

quantity of writings thrown on the pyre and the high price at which they sold. The "fifty thousand pieces [drachmas] of silver" was equivalent to about 9200 gold dollars, an enormous sum for those times.

466. It was late in the third year of his sojourn in Ephesus when Paul began to think of leaving. The new community was now solidly established and it had fervent leaders. The Holy Spirit would take care of the rest. Ephesus was not the whole world, and Paul felt he was called elsewhere. He planned therefore to go toward Jerusalem, passing through Macedonia and Achaia, saying to himself, "After I have been there, I must also see Rome" (Acts 19:21; cf. Rom. 15:23).

But before setting out, Paul prepared the communities he intended to visit. "So he sent two of his assistants, Timothy and Erastus, to Macedonia, while he himself stayed on for a while in the province of Asia (Acts 19:22). This Erastus must be a different person from the Erastus who was the city treasurer in Corinth (§ 426). As for Timothy, this mission in Macedonia with Erastus was not the same as that in Corinth mentioned in *1 Corinthians* (4:17; 16:10) which had a different purpose and must have occurred before this. But we shall discuss this presently for, because of the complications which had arisen in the community of Corinth (§ 473 ff.), this last period of Paul's stay in Ephesus involved various difficult questions, some of which are merely hinted at. Let us consider first Paul's departure from Ephesus, which did not come about as he had planned, but as a result of an unexpected incident, a riot of the silversmiths in the city.

467. The narrative of this episode is historically one of the most vivid and colorful in the *Acts,* and so I shall quote it directly.

"For a silversmith named Demetrius, by making silver shrines of Diana, brought no small gain to the craftsmen; and these he got

Smyrna

together, along with workmen of like occupation, and said, 'Men, you know that our wealth comes from this trade; and you see and hear that not only at Ephesus but almost over the whole province of Asia, this man Paul has persuaded and turned away numbers of people, saying, "Gods made by human hands are not gods at all." And there is danger, not only that this business of ours will be discredited, but also that the temple of the great Diana will be regarded as nothing, and even the magnificence of her whom all Asia and the world worship will be on the decline.' On hearing this they were filled with wrath and cried out, saying 'Great is Diana of the Ephesians.'

"And the city was filled with confusion, and they rushed by a common impulse into the theatre, dragging along the Macedonians Gaius and Aristarchus, Paul's fellow-travelers. But when Paul wanted to go before the people, the disciples would not let him; and some of the Asiarchs who were friends of his sent to him and begged him not to venture into the theatre. Meanwhile, some were shouting one thing and some another; for the assembly was in confusion, and most of them did not know why they had gathered together. Then some of the crowd called upon Alexander, as the Jews were pushing him forward; and Alexander, motioning with his hand for silence, wanted to give an explanation to the people. But as soon as they saw that he was a Jew, they all with one voice for about two hours shouted, 'Great is Diana of the Ephesians.'

"But when the town clerk had quieted the crowd, he said, 'Men of Ephesus, what man indeed is there who does not know that the city of the Ephesians is a worshipper of the great Diana and of Jupiter's offspring? Since therefore this is undeniable, you ought to be calm and do nothing rash. For you have brought these men here who are neither guilty of sacrilege nor blasphemers of your goddess. Therefore, if Demetrius and the craftsmen with him have a complaint against anyone, court days are kept and there are proconsuls; let them take action against one another. And if you require anything further, it shall be settled in the lawful assembly. For we are even in danger of being accused of riot over today's uproar, since there is no culprit whom we can hold liable for this disorderly gathering. And with these words he dismissed the assembly" (Acts 19:24–40).

468. The psychological accuracy of this description is striking. The majority of that noisy crowd ran to the theater only because of certain vague rumors, and they stayed there for hours shouting their acclaim for the goddess Diana without knowing exactly why. It is a typical impulsive and irrational mob.

The only ones who do know what the tumult is about are Demetrius, the silversmith, and to a lesser degree the craftsmen he has been haranguing. They had some interest in the rioting since they formed the guild, as it were, of silversmiths. Such guilds (συνεργασίαι) are mentioned in several inscriptions and they were powerful influences in the economic and social life of the Greek cities. Our Demetrius,[10] if not

the head of the guild of Ephesian silversmiths, was certainly one of its most influential members, a kind of large-scale contractor who furnished work to the craftsmen and more humble artisans. His workshops daily produced hundreds of the little shrines (ναίσκοι, aediculae), which were reproductions of the great temple of Diana and enclosed a small statue of the goddess. The large ones could be set up outdoors, while the smaller ones served as offerings in the temple or were used for private devotions at home. These objects were very popular with pilgrims, and they were made also in cheap materials like stone and terra cotta,

Coin of Valentinian I With the Image of the Shrine of Diana of Ephesus

but those of Demetrius were of precious metals and therefore yielded a rich profit. But one gloomy day, this shrewd contractor noticed that his

[10] An English scholar, Hicks, identified him with a Demetrius who is named in an inscription from Ephesus, but this seems mistaken. Cf. W. M. Ramsay, *The Church in the Roman Empire before A.D. 170*, 9th edition, London, 1907, the seventh chapter of which deals with Paul's sojourn in Ephesus. For the social aspects of life in Ephesus, cf. V. Chapot, *La province romaine proconsulaire d'Asie*, Paris, 1904.

Ephesus — Theater

industry was seriously threatened by the new religion Paul was preaching, and he plunged in to save the situation, arousing his workers as quoted above. Thus he indirectly gives us some measure of the success Paul had achieved "not only at Ephesus, but almost over the whole province of Asia."

469. After their master's harangue, Demetrius' craftsmen started off for the theater shouting all the way. The theater was the usual place for meetings, and as they proceeded they were joined by numerous idlers and curious passers-by until the crowd was swelled out of all proportion. Some of Demetrius' dependents who were better informed went to find Paul at home, but when they failed, they dragged out "Gaius and Aristarchus, Paul's fellow-travelers."[11] When Paul heard what was happening he wanted to go to the theater immediately, anxious to free his companions, but his disciples would not let him expose himself to the danger involved. It is significant that the same advice was given him by "some of the Asiarchs who were friends of his." This shows that he was well liked by the magistrates (§ 22), although they were in all probability not Christian.

Meanwhile, the tumult in the theater was increasing, and adding to the general commotion was the fact that the new arrivals did not even know why they had come. At a certain point the Jew Alexander[12] appeared on the scene, but this part of the episode remains obscure. Perhaps he was pushed forward by the Jews who felt that they, too, were threatened since they did not worship Diana either, and he was "to give an explanation" for his coreligionists disclaiming any responsibility for Paul. But the crowd would not let him speak because he was a Jew. And so the confusion and the uncertainty increased, and the only thing the mob could find to do was to shout "Great is Diana of the Ephesians" for a couple of hours.

470. Finally "the Scribe (γραμματεύς) of the people" intervened. He was a kind of town clerk; his office was a very important one in Ephesus and is mentioned in the inscriptions. He was evidently a calm and practical man, and he turned the mob to a sensible realization of what was happening. With shrewd skill he first dissipated their apprehensions regarding the temple of Diana, which no one had profaned in any way. As for the rest, if Demetrius and his workmen had any grounds for complaint, they could take proper legal steps and not resort to mob

---

[11] This *Gaius* is a Macedonian and not to be identified with Gaius of Derbe (§ 346) or Gaius of Corinth (§ 426). *Aristarchus* was a Thessalonian (Acts 20:4) and was later Paul's companion on the journey to Rome (27:2) and in prison there (Col. 4:10). It is quite probable that these two witnesses were the ones who gave Luke an account of the episode.

[12] We know nothing of him. Some thought he was "Alexander, the coppersmith," mentioned by Paul as an opponent in 2 *Timothy* 4:14 (cf. 1 Tim. 1:20), but there exists no positive proof for this. Alexander was a very common name.

Ephesus — Entrance to the Theater

action. The Roman authorities were not to be fooled with; they might easily suspect some sort of political and seditious skullduggery in a disorderly gathering like that, for which no one could give a good reason.

The authority of the speaker and above all the good sense of his observations calmed the mob, which, now that it had finally discovered what the hubbub was about, went quietly home, their throats somewhat the worse for wear.

The danger to Paul, notwithstanding the happy outcome of the affair, had been a serious one, certainly more serious than appears from our reading of the episode today. When Paul a few months later in his epistle to the Romans (16:3–4) speaks of "Prisca and Aquila, my helpers in Christ Jesus, who for my life have risked their own necks," he is probably referring to what they did to save him at the time of the riot of silversmiths. Paul was lodging with them (§ 453) and the rioters must have gone to their house looking for him, and not finding him dragged out Gaius and Aristarchus instead. But just how the couple risked their lives to save Paul we are not told.

471. An even more obscure reference is in 1 *Corinthians,* 15:32, where Paul says: "If [speaking] as men do, I fought with beasts at Ephesus . . ."

Some ancient writers, deriving from the apocryphal *Acts of Paul* (§ 90, note), interpreted these words literally to mean that the Apostle had been exposed to wild beasts in the stadium at Ephesus. Undoubtedly, however, Paul is here using a metaphor for some serious trial he endured at the hands of men as implacable as beasts. The same metaphor and the same verb (θηριομαχέω) were used a few decades later by Ignatius of Antioch, who wrote to the Romans (5:1) that he was fighting with beasts, with ten leopards to be precise, who were the ten soldiers escorting him to Rome. Paul could not have been exposed to actual beasts, protected as he was by his Roman citizenship (§ 39). What metaphorical beasts does he mean then?

Since these words were written in the first months of the year 56, they cannot refer to the riot of the silversmiths, which took place in 57. They refer, therefore, to some serious plot against him, perhaps on the part of the Ephesian Jews, about which we have no information. There is a clear allusion to the silversmith episode, however, as well as to other trials suffered toward the end of his sojourn in Ephesus, in the emphatic little passage written in the autumn of 57 from Macedonia: "For we would not, brethren, have you ignorant of the affliction which came upon us in Asia. We were crushed beyond measure — beyond our strength, so that we were weary even of life. Yes, we have been carrying within our very selves, our death sentence . . ." (2 Cor. 1:8–9). In any case, it is very probable that these various tribulations were somehow associated with one another and that the riot of the silversmiths was one outburst in a more or less habitual state of affairs, although it is the only one we know about.

472. Was Paul imprisoned in Ephesus? Theoretically this is possible,

Ephesus — Street From the Theater to the Gymnasium

but in actual fact there is no evidence that he was. A short time later, writing to the Romans (16:7), he sends his greetings to Adronicus and Junias, his "fellow-prisoners" (συναιχμαλώτους) but we do not know whether this refers to an imprisonment in Ephesus or elsewhere. If in Ephesus, it must have been a very short one like that in Philippi (§ 388 ff.). It is not likely that Luke would have omitted the mention of a prolonged stay in prison during a period of such intense activity. This argument is all the more valid as answer to those who assume — as some moderns have done (§ 566) — that it was in Ephesus Paul wrote the so-called captivity epistles. These epistles were written when Luke was with the prisoner (Col. 4:14; Philemon 24), and so it is even more unlikely that he would have omitted mention of a long imprisonment in Ephesus. This theory, like so many of recent date, is not well founded.

The riot of the silversmiths was the final act in the series of Paul's tribulations and determined his departure from Ephesus. Among other considerations was his desire not to expose the new community to greater persecution. Therefore, "when the tumult had ceased, Paul sent for the disciples and encouraged them; then he took leave of them and started for Macedonia" (Acts 20:1), that is, he set out on the journey he had already planned (§ 466).

But before leaving Ephesus with Paul, let us examine for a moment the questions mentioned above (§ 466), which connote another broad field of trials and difficulties for Paul. These are the trials which he called "his daily pressing anxiety, the care of all the churches" (§ 430). These worries and anxieties, which in Corinth led him to write twice to the Thessalonians, were caused here by certain happenings in the community in Corinth, which were indeed stormy ones.

THE TWO EPISTLES TO THE CORINTHIANS

473. Let us take as our guide here a chronological outline. Paul's sojourn in Ephesus, we noted, includes part of the year 54, the whole of 55 and 56, and a part of 57, since he left the city in about May of the latter year (§ 159).

The Year 55 — Toward the end of this year Paul wrote an epistle to the Corinthians (1 Cor. 5:9) which is no longer extant and which preceded by some months the *First Epistle to the Corinthians* we now possess. Later he received disquieting news about the Corinthian community, brought to him in Ephesus by "those of the house of Chloe" (1 Cor. 1:11), and he sent Timothy to Corinth (4:17; 16:10).

The Year 56 — Some months before Pentecost Paul, anxious over Timothy's mission, began another letter, which is the extant *First Epistle to the Corinthians* (16:8). While he was writing it, or shortly before he had begun, there arrived from Corinth a delegation composed of

Stephanas, Achaicus, and Fortunatus (16:15–17), who did not have encouraging news either (5:1; 11:18) and who probably had brought with them a letter from the community asking Paul for certain directives (7:1 ff.).

The Year 56: Summer-Autumn — Timothy returned from Corinth to Ephesus, bringing disconcerting information about his mission and the effect of *1 Corinthians.* Paul therefore decided to go personally to Corinth. This visit, which is not mentioned in the *Acts* at all perhaps because it was so short, was his second and is implicitly attested in his own words (2 Cor. 12:14; 13:1–2, Greek text). In addition to being so brief, it was made "in sorrow" (2:1) because of the condition in which he had found the community. Seeing that the evil could not be cured in so short a time, and unable to remain away from Ephesus for long, he returned to the latter city immediately, intending to do his best for the deteriorating community from a distance.

The Year 56 — Toward the end of the year Paul postponed, through pity, an immediate return to Corinth to punish the culprits (2 Cor. 1:15, 16, 17, 23; 2:1; 13:2). Meanwhile he sent Timothy to Macedonia to prepare the communities there for his arrival (Acts 19:22; § 466) and sent a very severe letter to Corinth. This is the letter written "with many tears" (2 Cor. 2:4; 7:8), which is not extant and which would be chronologically the third of the epistles to the Corinthians.

The Year 57 — Toward the beginning of the year Paul, still greatly worried over conditions in Corinth, sent Titus there to see what effect the letter written "with many tears" (2 Cor. 7:5–7; 12:18) had had, telling him to return by land and wait for him in Troas (2:12–13).

The Year 57 — In about May of this year the silversmith riot forced Paul to leave Ephesus suddenly. When he reached Troas, Titus had not yet arrived. His anxiety for Corinth impelled him to go on to Macedonia in the hope of meeting Titus sooner (2 Cor. 2:12–13; Acts 20:1). He did finally meet him there and found that he brought rather good news (2 Cor. 7:5–7).

The Year 57: Summer-Autumn — From Macedonia Paul wrote the *2 Corinthians,* which has come down to us and which was actually the fourth letter sent the community. He probably traveled at this time as far as Illyria.

The Year 57–58: Winter — Paul went to Corinth for the third time and stayed there three months (Acts 20:2–3). There he wrote the epistle to the Romans (Rom. 16:1; cf. 16:23 with 1 Cor. 1:14), which follows by some months the letter to the Galatians (§ 505).

474. Let us now examine the facts as arranged in this outline.

Of the letter, now lost, written to the Corinthians toward the end of the year 55, we know no more than Paul's reference to it later (1 Cor. 5:9), when he mentions he had told them not to associate with the immoral. Though it is no more than an isolated mention, it is significant because it indicates that not a little of their former moral taint still clung to the neophytes of Corinth. Besides, this admonition had been wrongly interpreted. Some persons, perhaps with the tendentious purpose of discrediting Paul, had interpreted it to mean that Paul commanded the Christians of Corinth to break off all relationships with immoral persons of any class or group. Was this possible in a city like Corinth, which was one whole brothel (§ 421)? Paul patiently explained he did not mean this, "otherwise you would have to leave the world" (1 Cor. 5:10). He had told them only to avoid those neophytes who were not yet completely free of their old habits. From the year 55, then, Paul was seriously worried over moral conditions in Corinth.

475. Shortly afterward, worries of another kind were added. Members of the household of a certain Chloe, a Corinthian lady who was in frequent contact — perhaps for business reasons — with Ephesus, had arrived in the city and reported to Paul that dissensions and conflicting factions had sprouted in the community on the isthmus. Some boasted they were Paul's disciples, others that they were followers of Apollos, still others opted for Cephas, while some declared simply that they were followers of Christ. They would not have been the caviling Greeks of the decadence, these Corinthians, if they had not split into so many separate parties, each with its own standard and prompt to condemn opposing factions. It was not a matter of genuine scission. These were rather diverse currents which gloried in a famous name, just as later in the universities students rallied about the name of one famous professor or other, though all belonged to the same university. This rivalry had been stimulated either unwittingly or purposely by preachers who had come to Corinth after Paul's departure and had had their influence on the proverbially volatile Corinthians.

One of these had been Apollos. His flowery eloquence and winged allegories (§ 453) had conquered quite a number, who perhaps compared his style with the stiff unliterary Greek of Paul's discourses. Other preachers had followed Apollos. From Jerusalem came a number of Judaizing Christians armed with letters of recommendation from the great Apostles of the Holy City, and a particular group had clustered about them. Since they referred constantly to Cephas, contrasting him perhaps with Paul, this group considered themselves as the special disciples of Cephas. Others, ignoring human names, formed the group "of the Christ." These may have been persons who, confident in their charismatic gifts, felt they were illumined directly by Christ without any human intermediaries, or they may have been Palestinian immigrants who had known Christ personally during his mortal life and therefore considered their status one of special privilege. And finally, one group, irritated by all these novelties, declared themselves the adherents of him who had first spoken of the Christ in Corinth, and this was "the group of Paul."

476. One of the first to become concerned over this crumbling of Christian unity was Apollos, who had been a partial and involuntary cause. Toward the end of 55 he had left Corinth and returned to Ephesus, where he told Paul what was happening, and this confirmed the news brought by Chloe's people. The very fact that he left the scene of his unsought triumphs shows his displeasure that his name had become a sign of discord. Paul, however, had complete confidence in Apollos and generously recognized the contribution he had made to the solid organization of the Corinthian community (1 Cor. 3:6). He tried to persuade him to return to Corinth to reconcile all the little factions, but Apollos was unwilling to go (16:12).

Despite these facts, some modern critics have considered Apollos the archadversary of Paul in Corinth, a tricky and tenacious opponent from whom Paul had to defend himself with tact and almost in fear. This is another example of fictionalized "criticism" which ignores or distorts explicit historical evidence. Paul was hardly the man to be afraid of Apollos if the latter had been his enemy. He had quite boldly taken issue with Peter in Antioch (§ 364 ff.), and he was altogether capable of taking issue with Apollos even more openly and directly without having recourse to childish tricks and subterfuges.[13] Much less would he have begged the wolf to return to the fold by insisting he go back to Corinth. On the other hand, a few years later, Paul shows special respect for Apollos (Titus 3:13), which indicates his esteem for him was unchanged.

Naturally, Apollos had had as little to do with the group which took his name as Christ and Cephas and Paul had had with the others. The real culprits were the troublemakers who used the names for their own partisan purposes. And the community threatened to disintegrate.

477. When Apollos refused to return to Corinth, Paul sent Timothy, hoping that he would manage to resolve the many difficulties, including the matter of the factions. In addition, he sent a letter to Corinth to help Timothy's mission. This is the *First Epistle to the Corinthians* as we possess it, and these are the circumstances of its writing. Paul was about

---

[13] An example of one of these, adduced as a very convincing proof, is that when Paul said that "the doctrine of the cross is foolishness to those who perish (ἀπολλυμένοις), but to those who are saved, that is, to us, it is the power of God" (1 Cor. 1:18), he is supposedly alluding to Apollos. The Greek participle *apolly-mènois* contains the reference, no less! No one, however, has suggested what other Greek verb Paul should have used here and in parallel passages as the antithesis of "saved," nor is there any explanation of how the Corinthians managed to catch the reference immediately although no one else has thought of it through the centuries until our own day. Much negative criticism today is based on reasoning of this kind, presented with the utmost seriousness.

to begin dictating the letter, which would have taken several weeks to finish (§ 177 ff.), when Stephanas, Achaicus, and Fortunatus arrived from Corinth. It is even more probable, however, that he had already begun the letter and that the first four chapters were written when the delegation arrived with its unwelcome news and the letter sent by the Corinthians. The fifth chapter, in fact, seems to leap to its subject like a horse under a sudden crack of the whip. The entire epistle treats both the earlier and more recent matters brought to Paul's attention and also replies to the questions set forth in the letter just arrived from Corinth. A summary follows.

478. After the customary courtesies, the epistle takes up the matter of the separate factions, which had been reported to Paul some time before.

There must be no divisions and dissensions in a Christian community, yet in Corinth some say they are of Paul, others of Apollos, others of Cephas, and still others of Christ. What does this mean? "Has Christ been divided up? Was Paul crucified for you? Or were you baptized in the name of Paul?" (1 Cor. 1:13.) Paul is very glad that he personally baptized very few in Corinth, so that his name cannot serve as a pretext for another sect. He has evangelized them only, speaking not with the wisdom of words but with the word of the cross which is the salvation of the elect. God has rejected human wisdom and has made the foolishness of Christian teaching triumph. For the Jews are looking for miracles and the Greeks for wisdom, whereas Christ crucified is a scandal to the Jews and sheer folly to the pagans; but to those who are called he is salvation, whether they be Jews or Greeks. Did the Corinthians themselves not lack perhaps those things the world considered great gifts? Yet through them, God has put the world to shame. From the beginning Paul spoke to them not with human wisdom, but preaching Jesus crucified, and he did this that their faith might be founded on the power of God. In reality, he possesses a wisdom unknown to the world and revealed to him by the Spirit of God which searches all things. Paul does not speak of this to sensual men, but to the spiritual. The Corinthians are still sensual, like "little ones in Christ" (3:1), and cannot take the solid food of grown men, as their behavior demonstrates.

Who is this Paul and this Apollos, in whose names they are divided? They are both ministers of God, each in his fashion. "I have planted, Apollos has watered, but God has given the growth" (3:6). Paul was the engineer who laid the foundation and others have come to build upon it. But the foundation is and always will be Jesus Christ, and whatever is built on it, whether it be of precious material or of wood or straw, will be tried in fire on the day of the Lord. The Corinthians are not to be led astray by names, in which they think they may take pride. "Therefore let no one take pride in men. For all things are yours,

whether Paul, or Apollos, or Cephas; or the world, or life or death; or
things present, or things to come — all are yours, and you are Christ's,
and Christ is God's" (3:21–23). Paul and the other Apostles are the
ministers of Christ and the stewards of the mysteries of God. Their
conduct is to be judged not by men but by the Lord when he comes.
And yet, behold. The Corinthians are filled, they are rich, they are
powerful, while Paul and the other Apostles have become a spectacle
to the world, both to angels and men, appearing as fools, weaklings,
without honor, suffering hunger, thirst, nakedness, and every privation.
But Paul reminds the Corinthians of these things with affectionate irony,
for he desires to admonish them as a father. Among the many tutors
they may have, he is their real father in Christ. And finally he tells them
he has sent Timothy to them (§ 477) until he can come himself (Chaps.
1–4).

480.

479. Paul then abruptly takes up the question of morals.[14] He has
learned of the serious things that have happened among the faithful of
Corinth, so serious, in fact, that like immorality is not found even among
the pagans. A Christian has dared to marry his own widowed step-
mother, and the brethren have boasted of it instead of driving the
incestuous man from their midst. But Paul, spiritually present among
them, delivers the body of the culprit to Satan that his soul may be
saved on the day of the Lord. The Corinthians should be prudent. Let
them cast from their midst all leaven of malice, and let them be as
unleavened bread for their Pasch, which is Christ. In his previous letter
Paul has urged them not to associate with the immoral (§ 474) but he
was not referring to pagans; he meant the neophytes who had not yet
freed themselves from their old habits. The faithful are not even to take
food with brethren of such evil conduct (Chap. 5).

480. Then comes the matter of the pagan courts, or tribunals.[15] If a
Christian has a complaint against a brother, does he dare appeal to a
pagan court for justice and ignore the justice of his brethren? Do not
the Corinthians know that the Christians one day will judge the world
and the angels? The most humble of the faithful are competent to judge

---

[14] The abruptness of this transition is evident. Given Paul's taut and nervous style
and the length of time required to dictate the letters, it might perhaps be explained
by the fact that he here began to concentrate on a different subject. It seems more
likely, however, that it was occasioned by the news brought him from Corinth
(§ 477): "It is actually reported that there is immorality among you, and such
immorality as is not found even among the Gentiles . . . " (5:1).

[15] The question of the pagan courts also seems related to information just brought
from Corinth: a Christian had brought a fellow Christian before the civil court,
composed of pagans. To evaluate Paul's reply properly, apart from the spiritual
element, it should be noted that the Jews had their own courts, recognized by the
Roman authorities both in the Diaspora and in Palestine especially (cf. *Storia
d'Israele*, II, p. 224, § 197; p. 433, § 376).

worldly matters. It is already an evil thing when questions of this kind arise among the faithful, for it would be better to suffer the wrong in patience. In any case, they are not to go before pagan judges. And above all, they must not permit such lawsuits to arise among them by committing fraud and injustice. These old habits of the Corinthians were abolished too when they became Christian (6:1–11).

481. The question of immorality is treated again. Some neophytes think that having acquired liberty in Christ they can go on committing fornication, which, after all is a natural thing, like the digestion of food: "Food for the belly, and the belly for food" (6:13). Not at all. "The body is not for immorality, but for the Lord." Besides, in baptism the Christian becomes a member of Christ. "Shall I then take the members of Christ and make them members of a harlot?" The temple of the Holy Spirit must not be profaned: "Do you not know that your members are the temple of the Holy Spirit, who is in you, whom you have from God, and that you are not your own?" (6:12–20.)[16]

482. Then follow the answers to the various questions in the letter sent Paul by the Corinthians. — To abstain from the use of marriage is a good thing, but for the avoidance of fornication it is better to use it. The husband has a duty in this regard toward his wife, and she toward him. Each has authority over the body of the other. To abstain from intercourse is licit, provided it be by common consent, for spiritual reasons and for a short time. Paul would wish all to be as he[17] but let those marry who cannot imitate him. To the married, the Lord, not Paul, commands "that a wife is not to depart from her husband, and if she departs, that she is to remain unmarried or be reconciled to her husband. And let not a husband put away his wife" (7:10–11).[18] If only one spouse become Christian, the marriage remains. But if the nonbeliever leaves the other, the Christian spouse is free.[19] In general, everyone remains as he was before his conversion, circumcised or uncircumcised, slave or free; all are equal before Christ (7:1–24).

483. Virginity and Widowhood — With regard to virginity, Paul does not have a precept of the Lord to give the Corinthians. He can only advise them according to his own experience. "I think, then, that this is good on account of the present distress (διὰ τὴν ἐνεστῶσαν ἀνάγκην) — that it is good for a man to remain as he is" (7:26), namely, without a

---

[16] Note that Paul condemns fornication solely for Christian religious reasons, with no reference to philosophical, social, or hygienic arguments against it. While he certainly must have been aware of these, he considered them of slight efficacy in comparison with the sublimity of the Christian reasons. Mystical incorporation in Christ is the great foundation of Paul's moral teaching.

[17] That is, free from matrimonial ties. Cf. § 244.

[18] For this passage and its relation to early Christian catechesis, cf. *The Life of Christ*, p. 487 (§ 480).

[19] This is the "Pauline Privilege."

wife, as Paul is.[20] But if a man has a wife he must not seek to be freed. If he is unmarried he is advised not to take a wife. Those who marry do nothing wrong, but they "will have tribulation of the flesh." The reason for this advice is explained immediately afterward. "But this I say, brethren, the time is short; it remains that those who have wives be as if they had none; and those who weep, as though not weeping; and those who rejoice, as though not rejoicing; and those who buy, as though not possessing; and those who use this world, as though not using it, for this world as we see it is passing away. I would have you free from care. He who is unmarried is concerned about the things of the Lord, how he may please God. Whereas he who is married is concerned about the things of the world, how he may please his wife; and he is divided" (7:29–33).[21] The same is true of women. A father may well give his daughter a husband before her youth is gone, but he would do better

---

[20] The eschatologists translate the phrase "present distress" as "imminent (or urgent) fate," and consider it a reference to the parousia, the imminence of which makes marriage impracticable. But it should be noted that almost the same phrase occurs again shortly afterwards, ἀνάγκη . . . ἐπίκειται (1 Cor. 9:16), where Paul speaks of the necessity he is under to preach the Gospel. Philologically the parallel is striking: ἐνεστῶσαν = "instant"; ἐπίκειται = "is incumbent."

Its application to matrimony is in the following verse: "Yet such will have tribulation of the flesh," that is, the complex of cares and responsibilities involved in marrying and having children, which in Paul's view are an obstacle to a higher Christian life. The expression in itself in no way refers to the parousia, while from the context it is evident it refers to married life and the anxieties it entails.

[21] This passage is the war horse of the eschatologists. As they interpret it, if "the time is short," this means that the parousia is imminent. "This world as we see it is passing away" means that the world is about to come to an end at the parousia. The parousia, they claim, is the "great idea" of the entire conceptual content of Paul's writings. — Paul's thought must be judged within the whole framework of his writings and activity. Is he speaking here, as many have assumed, of the death of the individual, for whom at that time the world passes away? This in our view is making Paul say what he did not want to say. He is speaking of an "end," which is not far off, but he does not say that this may be only the death of the individual. We must not forget that the time of the parousia is for him absolutely unknown (§ 437 ff.); it may happen in a short time or in "the ages to come" (§ 440). His teaching on this subject scrupulously follows the eschatological discourse of Jesus. This "end" will occur with the parousia, certainly, if this should take place in a short time; if it does not, then the "end" will come for each individual with his death. But in either case, "the time is short" (συνεσταλμένος — "abbreviated") since much time has passed already and the "end" will not be long in coming in one way or another: "therefore, while we have time, let us do good . . . " (Gal. 6:10), and those who wish to may renounce matrimony for this purpose. The eschatologist interpretation of this passage is one-sided; Paul wrote and worked without stating or denying anything with regard to the time of the parousia. If the certain imminence of the parousia was his "great idea," it should be reflected in every page he wrote; but we find no reference to it in certain basic writings (Galatians, Ephesians, etc.) and only a limited number of incidental mentions (Romans, § 522, note; Philippians, § 633, note) and one fuller treatment (Thessalonians, § 431 ff.). In his daily conduct Paul acted as though the parousia were anything but imminent. He foretold that before the parousia "the full number of the Gentiles" and all of Israel would be

Frescoes Around the Entrance to a Cubicle.
Catacombs of SS. Peter and Marcellinus
—Third Century (Pontifical Institute of
Christian Archeology)

not to have her marry. The widow, too, may remarry, but she would do better to remain a widow "in my judgment. . . . And I think that I also have the spirit of God" (7:25–40).

484. Things Sacrificed to Idols[22] — The Corinthians are to be guided by knowledge but also by charity. To eat meats sacrificed to idols is not illicit in itself, since the idol is nothing and only the one true God exists. Nevertheless some whose knowledge is not perfect think these meats are not licit, and in charity one must abstain from eating them in order not to give scandal to the weak. By way of analogy Paul cites his own example as Apostle. The Corinthians undoubtedly recognize him as an Apostle; would he not therefore have a right to the community's support, and also to take with him a Christian woman as housekeeper "as do the other apostles, and the brethren of the Lord, and Cephas? Or is it only Barnabas and I who have not the right to do this?" (9:5–6.) This right is evidenced also by examples from the Old Testament. Yet he does not avail himself of it in order not to place any obstacles in the way of the acceptance of Christ's Gospel, and he wishes to preach free, making himself all things to all people in order to win them to Christ. As athletes in the stadium observe strict abstinences in order to receive the prize, so he chastises his body, accepting every sacrifice in order to obtain the incorruptible crown. Many facts in the Old Testament, foreshadowing the New, warn that concupiscence and idolatry are to be avoided and God's help is to be sought in times of

---

converted (Rom. 11:25–26), but how could all this come about within the space of a few months or even years? In his later pastoral letters, he gave directions for organizing the various communities on a stable and lasting basis; if the world were going to end the next day, practically, this was useless; it would have been much more sensible to proclaim a general sit-down strike as the Thessalonians had done (§434). — (It is true that for this very reason the pastoral letters have been rejected as apocryphal, but this is a *petitio principii* which does not merit discussion.) — Cf. also § 489, note.

[22] For sacrificial meats, cf. § 360 ff.

Eucharistic Banquet (Second Century) Catacombs of Priscilla
(Pontifical Institute of Christian Archeology)

temptation. Nor is it permissible to attend idolatrous banquets: "The cup of blessing that we bless, is it not the sharing of the blood of Christ? And the bread that we break, is it not the partaking of the body of the Lord?" But in contrast those who partake of idolatrous banquets become associates of devils. "You cannot drink the cup of the Lord and the cup of devils; you cannot be partakers of the table of the Lord and of the table of devils" (10:21). In practice, they must be careful not to scandalize others. Let them eat freely the meat sold in the market without asking whether it comes from sacrificial animals or not, and let them accept invitations to dine in the homes of pagans. But if it is explicitly said that the food has been sacrificed to idols, one should not eat it, in order not to disturb the consciences of others.[23] All is to be done for the glory of God and for love of neighbor. They are to imitate Paul in this as he imitates Christ (8–11:1).

485. Christian Gatherings. The Agape and the Eucharist — In religious gatherings women are to veil their heads, both to show submission to man and their respect for the angels (11:10).[24]

---

[23] Since the number of sacrificial victims at times was in the hundreds or thousands, the public markets were not uncommonly stocked with such meats.

[24] In pagan Tarsus women were usually well veiled when they went out (§ 5), but in Corinth this custom was not observed. Paul asks that women veil their heads at least in religious gatherings for symbolic reasons: in the Orient, to go with uncovered head signified authority and dominion, while a covering over the head indicated submission and respect. In the Christian hierarchy, man is the head of woman, Christ the head of man, and God the head of Christ (11:3; cf. Eph. 5:23). The reference to the angels is not clear; it seems to take for granted that they are invisibly present at liturgical gatherings.

As for the meal taken in common, or the *agape*,[25] it is not to be held in so many separate groups, while some come who are hungry and others who are drunk. Let them eat their suppers at home; the *agape* is to be held with fitting decorum, in equality and charity, and for the purpose of celebrating the "Lord's Supper" (11:20). With regard to this "Supper," or the Eucharist, Paul states: "For I myself have received from the Lord (what I also delivered to you), that the Lord Jesus, on the night in which he was betrayed, took bread, and giving thanks broke, and said, 'This is my body which shall be given up for you; do this in remembrance of me.' In like manner also the cup, after he had supped, saying, 'This cup is the new covenant in my blood; do this as often as you drink it, in remembrance of me. For as often as you shall eat this bread and drink the cup, you proclaim the death of the Lord until he comes.' Therefore whoever eats this bread or drinks the cup of the Lord unworthily, will be guilty of the body and blood of the Lord" (11:23–27). One must examine himself well, therefore, before

---

[25] We do not have much information on the origins and nature of the *agape*. It was undoubtedly a meal taken in common, both as an expression of brotherly love and as a form of assistance to the poor. It was different from the "Lord's Supper," at which the Eucharistic rite was celebrated, although in early times the one generally preceded or followed the other on the same occasion. Since the abuses mentioned here by Paul persisted, the *agape* was completely dissociated from the "Lord's Supper," and after that it gradually disappeared from use. — For Paul's comments on the Eucharist and the relationship of his teaching to the rest of the early catechesis, cf. *The Life of Christ*, pp. 573–579 (§§ 544–548).

Celebration of the Eucharist in the Catacombs of Rome
(Reconstruction — "Amici delle Catacombe")

partaking of the Lord's Supper, for if he partakes of it unworthily he eats and drinks his own judgment (11:28–34).

486. Charisms: Charity[26] — The charisms all come from the Holy Spirit and they are all for the common good. They are different as the members of the body are different, but each contributes to the general well-being of the organism. Let the Corinthians aspire to have the nobler charisms, those which contribute to the edification of the community. But there is one thing which is more excellent than all the charisms, and that is charity. Paul writes here his winged "encomium," which has something of the cadence of a hymn.

"If I should speak with the tongues of men and of angels,
  but do not have charity,
  I have become as sounding brass or a tinkling cymbal.
And if I have prophecy
  and know all mysteries and all knowledge,
And if I have all faith so as to remove mountains,
  yet do not have charity,
  I am nothing.
And if I distribute all my goods to feed the poor,
  and if I deliver my body to be burned,
  yet do not have charity,
  it profits me nothing.
Charity is patient,
  is kind; charity does not envy,
[Charity] is not self-seeking,
  is not provoked,
  thinks no evil,
Does not rejoice over wickedness,
  but rejoices with the truth;
[Charity] bears with all things,
  believes all things,
  hopes all things,
  endures all things.
Charity never fails,
  whereas prophecies will disappear,
  and tongues will cease,
  and knowledge will be destroyed.
For we know in part and we prophesy in part;
  but when that which is perfect has come
  that which is imperfect will be done away with.
When I was a child, I spoke as a child,
  I felt as a child, I thought as a child.

---

[26] For this whole subject, cf. §§ 206–225 above.

Now that I have become a man, I have put away
   the things of a child.
We see now through a mirror in an obscure manner,
   but then face to face.
Now I know in part,
   but then I shall know even as I have been known.
So there abide faith, hope and charity, these three,
   but the greatest of these is charity" (13:1–13).

Among the charisms, prophecy is to be preferred to the gift of tongues. The latter edifies the individual, but the former the whole community. In their gatherings, let two or three speak in turn, and let them be followed by an interpreter. Two or three prophets may speak, but women are not to speak in the gatherings (Chaps. 12–14).

487. The Resurrection of the Dead — Paul has already instructed the Corinthians that Christ died for our sins, was buried, and rose again. The resurrected Christ appeared to Cephas, then to the Twelve, and then to more than 500 of the brethren together, some of whom are still alive, then to James and to all the Apostles. Finally he appeared also to Paul, as to one born out of due time, since he is the least of the Apostles and unworthy to be called an Apostle because he has persecuted the Church of God.[27] If, then, Christ is risen, how can some of the Corinthians say that the dead shall not rise again?[28] The lot of Christ is the lot of his followers. If there is no resurrection for the dead, neither is Christ risen. And if Christ is not risen, Paul's preaching is vain, and the faith of the Christians is vain. And if the Christians place their hope in Christ for this life only, they are the most unhappy among men. But Christ is certainly risen: "For since by a man came death, by a man also comes resurrection of the dead. For as in Adam all die, so in Christ all will be made to live" (15:21–22). The first fruits of this resurrection is Christ; the harvest — those who have believed in him — will come at the parousia. He will triumph over all his enemies, the last of which is death. Then he will give his Kingdom to his Father. That they did believe in the resurrection was attested by the custom in Corinth of being baptized for their dead.[29] It is also attested by the life of constant abnegation led by Paul for the faith.

---

[27] Cf. also *The Life of Christ*, p. 653 (§ 626).

[28] The fact that even among the Christians of Corinth there were some who denied the resurrection of the dead gives us an indication of the environment in which early Christianity was working there. It also helps us to understand further the laughter with which Paul's discourse on the Areopagus was received (§ 414).

[29] This is the only mention we have of this curious custom, and it tells us very little: if a catechumen died before being baptized, it was the custom in Corinth for a relative to be baptized for (ὑπέρ) him. It was not a true proxy but some form of prayer for the deceased; how it was understood by the "stand-in" himself we do not know. Paul refers to the custom without giving any judgment on it. He merely argues from it that it is an implicit admission of the resurrection of the dead. Later

488. But some will ask how the dead will rise and what sort of bodies they will have then. This is nonsense. It is as the seed which does not sprout until it has first died in the earth. Thus the human body is sowed in the corruption of death and rises in incorruption. ". . . what is sown a natural body rises a spiritual body. If there is a natural body, there is also a spiritual body. So also it is written, 'The first man, Adam, became a living soul' [Gen. 2:7]; the last Adam became a life-giving spirit. But it is not the spiritual that comes first, but the physical, and then the spiritual. The first man was of the earth, earthy; the second man from heaven . . ." (15:44–47).[30] The Christians, who bear the likeness of the earthy man, will also bear the likeness of the heavenly. There follows a solemn announcement: "Behold, I tell you a mystery: we shall not all sleep [die], but we shall all be changed — in a moment, in the twinkling of an eye, at the last trumpet.[31] For the trumpet shall sound,

---

the custom was taken over by certain heretical sects, and it became an actual substitution rather than a proxy.

[30] The terms used in this passage were common in the Greek world and derived from Platonic philosophy, which considered man to be composed of three elements: the body, the *psyche,* and the *pneuma.* The *psyche,* or "soul," was common to both man and the unreasoning animals. Man was different from the latter by virtue of the *pneuma,* or "spirit." All three terms occur in *1 Thessalonians,* 5:23. However, the terms *psyche* and *pneuma* were sometimes used in a sense different from their original meaning, and this happens in Paul's writings on occasion also, especially when he is using the adjectives derived from these terms, as in the present passage. He sometimes uses the term *pneuma* to mean the Holy Spirit, and the adjective to mean something in relation to the Holy Spirit. The expressions in this passage have been interpreted in a special lexicon as follows: σῶμα ψυχικόν, translated here as "natural body," "is the body subject in this life to the psyche or vegetative soul, made servant to procreation and nutrition (as against the σῶμα πνευματικόν, or 'spiritual body,' subject only to the spirit, the glorified and rational mind)"; the "spiritual body" is the "body informed by the *pneuma,* completely subject to and tempered by the spirit and made to serve it in the noblest activities of the glorified mind (cf. the body of man in ecstasy)" — Fr. Zorell, *Novi Testamenti lexicon graecum,* pp. 635 and 469. Commentaries usually discuss these matters at some length.

[31] The reading, "we shall not all fall asleep but we shall all be changed . . . " is attested by the great majority of Greek codices and ancient quotations, and is in complete harmony with the rest of the passage. The Vulgate reading, "we shall all indeed rise, but we shall not all be changed," has in its favor almost no Greek testimony. There is very little in favor of still a third reading, "we shall indeed fall asleep, but we shall not all be changed." The last two readings are unquestionably due to alterations on the original text (the first reading), on the assumption that Paul is speaking here of the different fate of the just and the sinners at the last judgment. Instead, Paul is speaking of the parousia, at the occurrence of which there will be some Christians still alive ("we shall not all sleep") and others who have already died; both will undergo a change. Since he is still alive he cannot but include himself in the category of the living, that is clear. But the pronoun "all" indicates one might well pass from the category of the living to that of the dead before that time, and this applied to Paul as well as to anyone else. This is the same mode of expression discussed in connection with the epistles to the Thessalonians; that is, Paul is speaking of the two perennial categories of the Church, and he

and the dead shall rise incorruptible and we shall be changed. For this corruptible body must put on incorruption, and this mortal body must put on immortality. But when this mortal body puts on immortality, then shall come to pass the word that is written, 'Death is swallowed up in victory. O death, where is thy victory? O death, where is thy sting?'

"Now the sting of death is sin, and the power of sin is the Law. But thanks be to God who has given us the victory through our Lord Jesus Christ" (Chap. 15).

489. Conclusion — Let the Corinthians also take up a collection for the brethren, as Paul has requested the churches of Galatia to do. Let each one put aside what he can on the first day of each week, and when Paul arrives he will send the whole sum to Jerusalem. He will come after he has passed through Macedonia, and will perhaps spend the winter in Corinth. But he is going to stay in Ephesus until Pentecost. He urges them to receive Timothy well and to send him back, for he is waiting for him. Apollos, although Paul earnestly besought him to go back to Corinth, is unwilling to do so. Greetings and salutations follow. And then: "I Paul greet you, with my own hand. If any man does not love the Lord Jesus Christ, let him be anathema! Maranatha!" (Chap. 16.)[32]

490. The letter was dispatched to Corinth at the first opportunity and probably reached its destination around Easter of the year 56. The effect Paul hoped it would have was to be fostered and strengthened by Timothy, who was in Corinth for that purpose. But the desired effect was wholly lacking. A few months later, in the summer, Timothy returned to Ephesus and reported that neither he nor Paul's letter had made very much impression. The petty little cliques persisted as before, the various abuses still continued more or less, and Paul's admonitions from afar did not carry enough authority to be heeded. In Corinth the troublemakers who had insinuated themselves into the community were subverting it and causing its disintegration, and if the situation was not remedied as soon as possible, it would all collapse. But what was the remedy?

Perhaps Timothy himself suggested that Paul visit Corinth, even if

---

naturally places himself in the one to which he belongs as he writes (§ 440). Again there is no preoccupation here with the time of the parousia; whenever it occurs, it will overtake both categories. The instruction given the Corinthians agrees with that given the Thessalonians, and there is no indication that Paul's thinking on the subject has changed.

[32] The expression *Maràn athà* (Μαρὰν ἀθà) is Aramaic and means "Our Lord comes," that is, has arrived. It was probably an exclamation of joy used as a greeting or salutation among the early Christians, as a kind of reminder of the coming of the Saviour and his presence in the Church (somewhat similar to the greeting used in the Russian Orthodox Church at Easter: "Christ is risen!"). The *Didachè* also gives this exclamation (§ 207). Others interpret it, less accurately I think, as an optative: "May our Lord come!" (cf. Apoc. 22:20.) The eschatologists find another argument for their theory in this expression; but again they are arguing *a priori*.

only briefly. His presence was much more authoritative than a letter, and his authority in Corinth was still so great that he could achieve a great deal by going there in person. In Ephesus, it is true, there was a multitude of things to do, but he could permit himself an absence of a few weeks. He could sail on the first ship leaving for Greece. The trip would take two or three days; he could stay in Corinth a few weeks and come right back to Ephesus with the satisfaction of having saved the Corinthian community.

491. Paul yielded to this reasoning and made his "second" trip to Corinth for which we have indirect evidence in his own words.[33] But this journey was also a great disappointment. Timothy had not accurately measured the state of affairs in Corinth, and had judged them to be far less dismal than they really were.

We are not told very clearly what happened on Paul's arrival. We might almost assume he is purposely veiling the episode in prudent reserve, so disgusting and painful was it for him. He alludes in general to one who has grieved not Paul so much as the whole community (2 Cor. 2:5). And again he refers to one who did a wrong and another who was wronged, and though both are unnamed we may suppose from the context that the one who suffered the wrong was Paul himself (7:12). Therefore, when Paul appeared in Corinth not only must he have encountered the resistance of those stubbornly attached to their various factions, but he was also publicly and seriously insulted by a Christian. This may have been a man of evil habits who had been rebuked by Paul.

Though Paul realized how serious matters were, he was not able to stay very long, and soon left Corinth again for Ephesus. He promised, however, that he would soon return to mete out the deserved punishment (1:23). Instead, when he thought it over, he delayed his return through pity, hoping to regain the souls of the Corinthians. He sent Timothy to Macedonia and dispatched to Corinth a letter written "with many tears."[34] The subsequent events are set forth in the chronological table above (§ 473).

---

[33] "Behold, this is the third time that I am ready to come to you" (2 Cor. 12:14). — "Behold, this is the third time that I am coming to you. . . . I have already warned, when present [the second time], and now in my absence I warn again those who sinned before, and all the rest, that, if I come again, I will not spare" (13:1–2). This was written before Paul's sojourn in Corinth in the winter of 57–58, which is the "third time" mentioned here, The *Acts* give us only one previous sojourn, that in which Paul evangelized Corinth. There must have been another, however, which is that here indicated in "the second time."

[34] Ancient interpretations and some modern ones consider that the letter written "with many tears" is *1 Corinthians*. However, it is enough to review the content of this epistle to note that it does not conform in any way to such a title. The incestuous man rebuked in Chapter 5 cannot be identified with the one who publicly insulted Paul; *1 Corinthians*, which is associated with Timothy's mission to Corinth, cannot be at the same time the next letter, which prompted Paul to

492. The months which followed the letter "of many tears" were for Paul most difficult ones. To the mortal trials he was suffering in Ephesus (§§ 471–472), there was added now this thorny woe of Corinth. How would the letter "of many tears" be received? Would it rouse his poor sons from their drunkenness and rekindle their old affection for him, or would it irremediably cut every bond between them?

Unable to repress his anxiety, Paul sent Titus to Corinth for news. He then left Ephesus himself as a result of the riot of the silversmiths, and to his great disappointment did not find Titus in Troas, where they had planned to meet. Troas presented a fine fertile field for evangelization, but the absence of Titus — and of news from Corinth — gave him no peace, and he went on through Macedonia in order to meet his messenger more quickly (2 Cor. 2:12–13). We may imagine the storm seething all that time in the mind of a man like Paul! It was almost as if his life depended on the arrival of Titus. "For indeed when we came to Macedonia, our flesh had no rest; we had troubles on every side, conflicts without and anxieties within" (7:5).

493. Finally Titus appeared, as comforting as a rainbow across the storm clouds. He did not bring a complete calm, but he did bring news that the worst part of the storm was over. The sun was really breaking through. It is in these circumstances that Paul wrote his *Second Epistle to the Corinthians.* A summary follows.

After the initial greetings, Paul thanks God that he has consoled him throughout his severe trials, and he hopes that the Corinthians will share in the consolation, for they have occasioned it. With the intent of paving the way for his arrival in Corinth, Paul justifies his own conduct after the painful incidents he has been through, disclaiming the charges his adversaries had hurled against him (1:1–12).

494. Apologetic Section — He is not a fickle man who easily changes his plans. He had decided to come to Corinth, to go from there to Macedonia and then return to Corinth, and he desired to carry out this plan because he is not one to waver between yes and no. With Paul it is always a "yes" like the perennial "yes" of Jesus Christ before God. Nevertheless he gave up the plan, not from fickleness, but to spare himself and the Corinthians the sorrow of the punishments they deserved. He had sent instead the letter of "many tears" (2:4). The community has punished the one who grieved not Paul so much as all of its members. Now let this punishment be sufficient, and let them show mercy to the guilty one so that he will not be overwhelmed by too much sorrow. Paul has forgiven him also for love of the Corinthians. So great

---

send Titus there. *1 Corinthians,* which is the second epistle to this community chronologically (§ 473), is quite different from the letter of "many tears," which was chronologically the third. For a discussion of whether part of the letter of "many tears" is included in *2 Corinthians,* cf. § 499, note.

is his anxiety for them that he did not want to stay in Troas, where there was great opportunity for evangelization, but set out for Macedonia in order to meet Titus more quickly and have news of them. This news was good news, and so he is more confident now that he is spreading everywhere the fragrance of Christ, for he is not in truth "as many others, adulterating the word of God" (2:17), but with full sincerity he preaches it as it comes from God in Christ.

495. Here, perhaps in response to some inner thought of his own, Paul abruptly asks: "Are we beginning again to commend ourselves? Or do we need, as some do, letters of commendation to you or from you? You are our letter, written on our hearts, which is known and read by all men" (3:1–2).[35] Paul's confidence is not in himself but in God, who has chosen him as a minister of the New Testament, founded not on the letter but the spirit. The Old Testament, although founded on the letter, had the glorious ministry of Moses. Therefore, so much more glorious will be the ministry of the New Testament, founded in the spirit. But in the Old Testament, Moses spoke to the Hebrews covering his face with a veil, and today a similar veil covers their hearts at the reading of the books of Moses. The ministers of the New Testament, however, speak unveiled, for "where the Spirit of the Lord is, there is freedom" (*ibid.*, 17). Conscious of their mission, the Apostles flee all pretense and trickery, but openly and truthfully preach the word of God appealing to the consciences of men before God. And if their Gospel is veiled, it is veiled only for those who are perishing, blinded as they are by the god of this world.

496. What sustains the Apostles in this office is the power of God — always persecuted but never defeated; always bearing in their bodies the sufferings of Jesus that the life of Jesus may be made manifest in them, since he who raised Jesus from the dead will raise them also. Even though the outer man is decaying day by day, the inner man in them is continually renewed, for they look not at the transitory and visible things but the eternal things which are not seen. When their earthly house shall be destroyed like a tent, they will be gathered into an imperishable dwelling in heaven. Meanwhile, "we who are in this

---

[35] The reference in "letters of commendation" includes some, only, of Paul's adversaries in Corinth; others might well have appeared there without such letters. The former were probably Judaizing Christians come from Jerusalem, as noted above (§ 475). Their opposition to Paul, in any case, was personal rather than doctrinal; answering them indirectly, Paul does not enter into the discussion of principles as in his letter to the Galatians, but he does take up the attacks on his person, authority, and conduct. While these adversaries try to discredit Paul, it is certain that they themselves are "adulterating (καπηλεύοντες) the word of God." The Greek word means not only an adulteration such as a dishonest merchant may make in his wares, but also an illegal or fraudulent profit. They were, therefore, also greedy and venal. Paul answers them with his own disinterestedness and aversion to any economic gain.

tent sigh under our burden, because we do not wish to be unclothed, but rather clothed over, that what is mortal may be swallowed up by life" (5:2–4).[36] Since while we are in the body we wander as exiles from the Lord, let us prefer to be exiles from the body and to be at home with the Lord. And whatever our end, let us be pleasing to the Lord, for we must all appear before the tribunal of Christ to receive from him the reward or punishment for our deeds.

497. Paul hopes that the Corinthians will judge him to be sincere. Not that he wishes to commend himself to them again, but he does want to warn them against the presumptuous who are slandering him. In all he does he is impelled by the love of Christ who has died that all may have life in him. Nor does he any longer know anyone according to the flesh, not even Christ.[37] He knows only the new creature risen from the universal reconciliation in Christ. With respect to this reconciliation, "on behalf of Christ, therefore, we are acting as ambassadors, God, as it were, appealing through us" (5:20). Let the Corinthians, then, accept his exhortation and his ministry, which is that of an Apostle always suffering tribulations, defamed and beaten, yet always patient, truthful, and powerful. "We are frank with you, O Corinthians; our heart is wide open to you. In us there is no lack of room for you, but in your heart there is no room for us. Now as having a recompense in like kind — I speak as to my children — be you also open wide to us" (6:11–13). Let the Corinthians not make common lot with unbelievers. What has light in common with darkness, or Christ with Beliar? Let them trust in him. "We have wronged no one, we have corrupted no one, we have taken advantage of no one" (7:2). The Corinthians are Paul's glory, and amid his innumerable trials, he is filled with joy because of them. In Macedonia when he was oppressed by unspeakable anxieties, he was consoled by the arrival of Titus who brought him their affectionate greetings and the message of their regret for the painful episodes that had occurred. He did cause them sorrow with his severe letter (the one of the "many tears"), but he is glad now because in making them sorry he led them to repentance: "For behold this very fact that you were made sorry according to God, what earnestness it has wrought

---

[36] The "tent," or earthly dwelling, is the body. When this has died, the Christian will be gathered into an imperishable dwelling in heaven. First must come, however, the difficult passage of death. Therefore, the Christians sigh and wish they might be "clothed over" (ἐπενδύσασθαι) with the heavenly dwelling without being first divested of the earthly. This can happen only if they are still alive at the time of the parousia; "if indeed (εἴ γε καὶ) we shall be found clothed, and not naked," that is, without our mortal bodies. Here again, Paul indicates as before (§§ 440, 488) that some will be still alive at the time of the parousia, though he does not know when it will take place.

[37] For the discussion of this passage, see § 246.

in you, nay, what explanations, what indignation, what fear, what yearning, what zeal, what readiness to avenge! In everything you have showed
yourselves to be innocent in the matter.[38]

"If then I did write to you, it was not for the sake of him who did
the wrong, nor for the sake of him who suffered the wrong; but to make
clear the zeal we have for you, before God" (*ibid.*, 11–12). Titus personally was consoled, too, by the attitude of the Corinthians (1:13, 7:16).

498. Exhortation for the Collection — The brethren of Macedonia,
though very poor, have collected a great deal for the poor (of Jerusalem). The Corinthians, who began to take up this collection the year
before (8:10; 9:2)[39] should compete with the Macedonian Christians
in generosity. This is not a command but an exhortation. Think of Jesus
Christ, who being rich became poor that all men might be enriched by
his poverty. Titus and two other brethren sent by Paul are charged to
collect their offerings. They are most worthy persons, and Paul is on
his guard "lest anyone should slander us in the matter of our administration[40] of this generous amount. For we take forethought for what is
honorable, not only before God, but also in the sight of men" (8:20–21).
Paul exhorts them again to be generous and to accept his messengers,
reminding them of the divine reward for their charity (Chaps. 8–9).

499. Polemical Section — Abruptly, and with no reference to what has
preceded, Paul enters upon a strictly polemical passage which continues
to the end of the epistle.[41] They say that he is timid when he is among

---

[38] These words show that the letter of "many tears" and the coming of Titus
had made a deep impression. The Corinthians had energetically tried to make amends
for what had happened and to dissociate their responsibility from that of the one
"who did the wrong," that they might once more enter into Paul's good graces.

[39] This is an important chronological indication, which, taken with 1 *Corinthians*,
16:1, shows that quite a bit of time had elapsed between the writing of 1 *Corinthians* and 2 *Corinthians*, in which the facts noted above could have taken place,
i.e., Paul's second trip to Corinth, the writing of the letter of "many tears," etc.

[40] This statement is made as a precaution against the calumnies of his venal
adversaries.

[41] The transition is as abrupt here as at the beginning of Chapter 5 of 1 *Corinthians* (§ 479), and this passage returns to a subject already treated in the first
seven chapters of the letter. A number of theories may be advanced to explain this.
Perhaps at this point the slow task of writing the letter was interrupted for a time
by some external event (Paul's journey to Illyria?), and when it was resumed, Paul
had received more detailed information about his cunning adversaries in Corinth.
Hence he treats with greater emphasis and precision the subject taken up in the first
seven chapters. Or perhaps Paul, satisfied with the good news which Titus had
brought him, first answered his adversaries in general terms, with the deliberate
intention of demolishing them systematically in the last part of the letter. Greek
orators on occasion used this device, and it would have been natural for one of
Paul's character to use it intuitively. Whatever the degree of likelihood in these
various theories, they at least do not conflict with the evidence of the codices,
all of which transmit this passage as the last part of 2 *Corinthians*. This is not
true of the other theories which assume that it is a fragment of another letter,
tacked on here later but written either before or after 2 *Corinthians*. These have no

them but fearless when he is absent. Now he trusts that he will not have to show his boldness among them when he next comes to them. He does not act according to the flesh, and he has at his disposal divine weapons which can overcome all arrogance that lifts itself against God. If his adversaries say they are of Christ, he too is Christ's and he can make his authority prevail. It is not true, as some say, that his letters are weighty and telling, while he is weak in appearance and his speech of no account. He can be in his presence just as he is in his letters. Some consider themselves of great importance, measuring themselves by their own standards, but wrongly. Paul measures himself according to the measure Christ has given him, that is, by what he has done for the Gospel among the Corinthians without invading the commission of others.

500. The Corinthians must bear with him if he speaks foolishly! But he is jealous of them, as of a pure virgin whom he has espoused to Christ, and he fears that their faith will be seduced as Eve was seduced by the serpent. If in fact someone should preach to them another Jesus, not preached by Paul, or another Spirit or another gospel, they might well bear with him! "For I regard myself as nowise inferior to the great apostles.[42] Even though I be rude in speech, yet I am not so in knowledge; but in every way we have made ourselves clear to you. Or did I do wrong when I humbled myself that you might be exalted, preaching to you the gospel of God free of charge?" (11:5-7.)

When he was in need in Corinth, Paul did accept help from the brethren in Macedonia but not from the Corinthians. " Why so? Because I do not love you? God knows I do. But what I do I will go on doing, that I may deprive them of the occasion who are seeking an occasion to boast that they are doing the same as we do.[43] For they are false

---

proofs in their favor, especially since the abrupt transition and repetition can be explained in other ways, including those mentioned. The same may be said of the theory that this is a fragment of the letter of "many tears." To bear such an epithet, this letter, however severe it was, must have expressed predominantly Paul's affection for the Corinthians. The passage under discussion here is composed of anger and indignation, without the slightest trace of a teardrop; and Paul might be said to have written it rather with a rod in hand (cf. 1 Cor. 4:21).

[42] These "great Apostles," as the ancient exegetes realized, are not Paul's adversaries, but the true Apostles in Jerusalem, the "pillars" of the Church — Peter, James, John . . . (cf. Gal. 2:9); but Paul's opponents did use their names to discredit him. In doing this, they hoped to remove the chief obstacle to their own profit. That is why Paul insists, in the following passages, on the fact that his evangelizing has never been a financial burden to anyone, and he calls these adversaries "false apostles, deceitful workers. . . ."

[43] This sentence is not clear, but it seems to mean this: Paul will continue to evangelize with no profit to himself, so that his adversaries will not be able to imitate him. They boast of their apostolate and discredit that of Paul, but their own avarice will prevent them from imitating the disinterestedness of Paul's apostolate.

apostles, deceitful workers, disguising themselves as Apostles of Christ. And no wonder, for Satan himself disguises himself as an angel of light. It is no great thing, then, if his ministers disguise themselves as ministers of justice. But their end will be according to their works" (*ibid.*, 11–15). He seems to be speaking thoughtlessly, he knows. But since the Corinthians tolerate so many who boast of themselves, they may let him boast a little too. "But wherein any man is bold — I am speaking foolishly — I also am bold. Are they Hebrews? So am I! Are they Israelites? So am I! . . ." (for the whole passage see § 168). But in reality Paul is not boasting except of his infirmities. There are, besides, the supernatural events: "I know a man in Christ who fourteen years ago . . ." (cf. the entire passage in § 199).

501. Paul has spoken like this to defend his apostolate, since in nothing is he inferior to the "great Apostles" although in himself he is nothing. His apostolate among the Corinthians has been confirmed by every kind of supernatural occurrence, and their community is in no sense inferior to any of the others except that it has been evangelized free. Let them pardon him this wrong! "Behold this is the third time that I am ready to come to you. And I will not be a burden to you; for I do not seek yours, but you. For the children should not save up for the parents, but the parents for the children" (12:14). He will spend himself for them, as Titus has done. But he fears that on his arrival he will find them still divided into factions with the consequent jealousies, contentions, and evil gossiping, and that he will have to weep over the impurities, fornication, and licentiousness of the impenitent sinners. He warns them, as he did the second time, that he will not be indulgent. Therefore let them examine themselves carefully. He writes in this vein so that he will not have to be severe with them when he comes. The epistle ends with the brief conventional greetings (Chaps. 10–14).

502. This letter, which arrived in Corinth at the beginning of autumn 57, must have had the desired effect. The reconciliation between father and son was a warm one, and Paul soon afterward went down from Macedonia to Corinth and spent three months of the winter there between the years 57 and 58. We have no indication of later dissensions with this community. In fact, the epistle to the Romans, written from Corinth during these three months, reflects a tranquillity of spirit which must certainly reflect the recent reconciliation and the peace of the community. The entire episode, which had led through anxious doubts and painful experiences to victory, also had its influence on Paul's spirit, undoubtedly giving rise to many new ideas and revealing ever wider horizons for action.

503. Paul's excursion into Illyria must have taken place during his sojourn in Macedonia. In the letter to the Romans (15:19) he describes the area of the apostolate he has covered thus far as being "from Jerusalem round about as far as Illyricum"; that is, Jerusalem is the south-eastern limit and Illyria the northwestern. Illyria, or Illyricum, corresponds more or less to modern Dalmatia, stretching just north of Epirus and north-northwest of Macedonia. Does Paul mean to include Illyricum or not? Has he evangelized this area as far as the border of Illyria, or did he enter the region to preach the Gospel there too? We do not know. The *Acts* tell us nothing in this regard, but this might be another of the frequent omissions of this book. The narrative does, however, leave a period of time (Acts 20:2) sufficient for a rapid journey into Illyria, where, if conditions were favorable, Paul might have founded some Christian communities like those of adjacent Macedonia. From Illyria, he would then have passed through Macedonia again to go down to Corinth.

THE EPISTLE TO THE GALATIANS

504. The cares and anxieties which have been needling Paul during the last months of his stay in Ephesus are not yet over. If Ephesus was rocking as if from earthquake and Corinth swaying like a tower threatening to collapse, the news which reached him from older communities was not too good either, especially from the Galatians. Paul had visited the Galatians a second time in 54 at the beginning of this third missionary journey (§ 451). He had chosen to go to them rather than to the communities of Pisidia and Lycaonia because of the disquieting news he had heard of the Judaizing Christians who had penetrated among them and were threatening to corrupt the faith of these ingenuous mountain folk. But the visit of their beloved spiritual father had conjured away the danger only for a time, and he left them with the resolve to watch over them in the future even if from a distance.

And he had good reason. The proverbial fickleness of the Galatians soon rose above their sincere affection for Paul, and one sad day the news came to him that the Judaizers were causing spiritual destruction while his beloved neophytes were being won *en masse* by their blandishments. What to do? Circumstances made it impossible for Paul to go to Galatia again now; the same circumstances probably kept him from sending one of his faithful co-workers. Or he may have considered it useless to do this since it would have taken Paul himself to make an impression on the Galatians at this stage. The only recourse was to send them an epistle. This is the extant *Epistle to the Galatians*.

505. But when and where was the letter written? At the beginning of Paul's sojourn in Ephesus between 54 and 55, or while he was in Macedonia or Corinth, between the end of 57 and the beginning of 58? Either is probable. An argument for the former thesis is Paul's exclamation to the recipients of the letter: "I marvel that you are so quickly deserting him who called you to the grace of Christ, changing to another

Gospel" (Gal. 1:6). Our first impression on reading these words is that the spiritual defection of the Galatians was recent and had occurred shortly after Paul had left Galatia. In favor of the second assumption, that the epistle was written later, we have the resemblance in thought between the epistle to the Galatians and that to the Romans, which is so evident that the latter epistle seems an amplification of the ideas in the former, an amplification from the doctrinal viewpoint alone with none of the various preoccupations in the former. This suggests that in the period elapsed during Paul's sojourns in Macedonia and Corinth, he was elaborating in particular the concepts common to both epistles, and that he set them forth differently because of the different purposes of the letters.

This second supposition, though not certain, is the more probable. As for the speed with which the Galatians apparently fell away from Paul's teaching, this might be interpreted to mean a sudden yielding to the repeated blandishments of the Judaizers. Or it may even mean that Paul had had reassuring news, oral or written, about their constancy and faithfulness, which was suddenly belied almost immediately afterward. In conclusion, the letter to the Galatians was written either at the end of 54, or more probably at the end of 57 shortly before the *Epistle to the Romans*. A summary follows.

506. Paul sends his greetings as "an Apostle, sent not from men nor by man, but by Jesus Christ and God the Father who raised him from the dead" (1:1). We do not find here any praise of those to whom the letter is addressed or the usual courtesies. There is a rebuke in their stead. How does it happen that the Galatians, in so short a time, have changed heart and turned to another gospel, which is preached by those who desire only to disturb them and pervert the true Gospel of Christ? "But even if we or an angel from heaven should preach a gospel to you other than that which we have preached to you, let him be anathema!" (*Ibid.*, 8.) Paul means this so intensely that he repeats it. Is he working for men or for God? If he were seeking to please men he would not be the servant of Christ! "For I give you to understand, brethren, that the gospel which was preached by me is not of man. For I did not receive it from man, nor was I taught it; but I received it by a revelation of Jesus Christ" (*ibid.*, 11–12).[44] The Galatians know that he, as a Jew, bitterly persecuted the Church. But when it pleased God, who called him by his Grace, to reveal to him his Son that he might preach him to the Gentiles, he did not take counsel with flesh and blood nor did he go up to Jerusalem to those who were Apostles before him, but he went to Arabia and then returned to Damascus. After three years he did go up to Jerusalem to meet Peter, and remained with him for fifteen days,

---

[44] For the origin and character of "Paul's Gospel," cf. the discussion in § 307; for what follows about Paul's life, cf. also § 152 ff.

but he did not see any of the other Apostles except James. After that, he went into Syria and Cilicia, and the churches of Judea did not know him although they rejoiced at his conversion. After fourteen years, he again went to Jerusalem, with Barnabas and Titus this time, because of a revelation, and he there set forth the Gospel he was preaching to the Gentiles. On that occasion, Titus was not circumcised, although some of the false brethren who had intruded themselves among the faithful demanded his circumcision, attempting to abolish the freedom brought by Christ. But Paul did not yield and defended the truth of the Gospel.

507. In addition, the elders in Jerusalem neither corrected nor amended Paul's Gospel as he set it forth, and all agreed on the respective fields of evangelization they would cover (cf. this passage quoted in § 309). Later, Paul openly rebuked Cephas in Antioch for his conduct, which seemed to conform to the views of the Judaizers (§ 364 ff.), and he said to him: If you who are a Jew live as a Gentile, how can you oblige the Gentiles to live as Jews? We who are Jews by birth, knowing that man is justified not by the works of the Law but by the faith of Jesus Christ, believed in him in order to be justified by his faith and not by the works of the Law. But if, seeking justification in Christ, we also are accounted sinners would Christ be the minister of sin? By no means. On the contrary, if I reconstruct what I have destroyed, I am a transgressor. Instead, I have died to the Law in order to live to God. With Christ I have been crucified, and what lives in me is no longer I, but Christ. I live in the flesh, yes, but I live in the faith of the Son of God, who has loved me and gave himself for me. I do not reject the grace of God. For if justice is acquired by the Law, then Christ died without reason (Chaps. 1–2).

508. The Jewish Law and the Christian Faith — "O foolish Galatians! who has bewitched you, before whose eyes Jesus Christ has been depicted crucified? This only I would learn from you: Did you receive the Spirit in virtue of the works of the Law, or in virtue of hearing and believing? Are you so foolish that after beginning in the Spirit, you now make a finish in the flesh? Have you suffered so much in vain? if indeed it be in vain. He therefore who gives the Spirit to you, and works miracles among you, does he do it by the works of the Law, or by the message of faith?" (3:1–5.) Abraham too believed and it was credited to him as justice (cf. Gen. 15:6). Thus those who have faith are blessed with the faithful Abraham, but those who rely on the works of the Law are under a curse, for it is written: "Cursed is everyone who does not hold to all things that are written in the book of the Law, to perform them" (Deut. 27:26). Christ, on the other hand, who with his death on the cross took upon himself the curse of the Law, has freed us from it, transmitting to us the blessing of Abraham through faith.

A human contract that has been ratified cannot be annulled or altered.

Now God made his promises to Abraham and to his offspring, who is Christ. The Law, therefore, which was made 430 years later than Abraham cannot annul those promises which were made him freely by God. The Law was added because of transgressions; it is a bilateral contract which required the intervention of a mediator, nor is it capable of conferring justice. It functioned as a tutor leading us to Christ, in order that we might be justified by faith. But now that we have Christ through faith and baptism, the tutor is no longer of any use, for all of us, without distinction of race or class, have put on Christ.

509. The heir, as a child, is like a child slave, although he is the master of all, and he is under a guardian until he comes of age: "So we too, when we were children were enslaved under the elements of the world.[45] But when the fullness of time came, God sent his Son, born of a woman, born under the Law, that he might redeem those who were under the Law, that we might receive the adoption of sons. And because you are sons, God has sent the Spirit of his Son into our hearts, crying, 'Abba, Father.' So that he is no longer a slave, but a son; and if a son, an heir also through God" (4:3–7). Once the Galatians were slaves to false gods. But now that they have known the true God, how can they turn again to the "weak and beggarly elements" to become again their slaves? "You are observing days and months and seasons and years.[46] I fear for you, lest perhaps I have labored among you in vain" (*ibid.*, 9–11). Let the Galatians be for Paul what he is for them.

510. They remember that because of an illness, he evangelized them the first time. And they received him then with every affection, as if he had been an angel or Jesus Christ himself (§ 378). Where is that affection now? Then they would have plucked out their eyes for him, and has he now become their enemy because he tells them the truth? Let

---

[45] The phrase "the elements of the world" (τὰ στοιχεῖα τοῦ κόσμου) recurs elsewhere (Col. 2:8, 20; and in part in 2 Pet. 3:10, 12). Among the Greeks, *stoicheia* meant elements in general, either of writing (the alaphabet), or of a given branch of learning (the rudiments; cf. Hebr. 5:12), of a material object (the components), and in later times of the heavens particularly (the planets in Alexandrian astrology). This last meaning developed gradually, penetrated medieval rabbinic thought and led to the concept of angels who guide the planets and of influences exercised by the latter on the destinies of men. The more romantic critics have fallen upon these concepts and, pushing their origins back several centuries, have ascribed them to Paul. It is probable that Paul is using the term with two of its original meanings; that is, he is referring to the first period (the rudiments) of the knowledge of God through which the whole world has passed, the pagans as well as the Hebrews. But this first rudimentary period was also the reign of matter, for both pagans and Hebrews were "enslaved under the elements [components] of the world" — the pagans because, although they knew God by their reason, they ended by adoring material idols (Rom. 1:20 ff.); the Hebrews because they were restricted to the material observances of the Law, which governed them as a tutor governs the heir while he is still a child.

[46] The detailed prescriptions of the Jewish religious calendar, and perhaps, also of the pagan calendars.

them guard against seducers, who are trying to estrange them from him; he is always as an affectionate mother, who suffers again the pains of labor for them (§ 169).

The Law itself directs them to Christ. Abraham, indeed, had a son Ishmael, born of the slave girl, Agar, according to the flesh, and a son Isaac, born of the free woman, Sara, according to promise. This is an allegory of the two Testaments. Agar symbolizes the Old Testament, which brings forth children into bondage, and Sara the New which brings them forth into freedom. And just as Ishmael persecuted Isaac, so now the Synagogue persecutes the Church but it will be driven out as Agar was. We are sons not of the slave woman but of the free. Therefore, let the Galatians preserve the freedom brought them by Christ. If they accept circumcision, Christ will be of no advantage to them. He who is circumcised is obliged to observe the whole Law and falls away from the grace of Christ, for whom only faith which works through charity is valid. Let them take care lest they be corrupted. A little leaven ferments all the dough. He, Paul, has never preached circumcision, because then the stumbling block of the cross would serve no purpose! Let these zealots who preach thus mutilate themselves (§ 170 – 3–5:12).

511. Consequences of the Preceding Question. Various Admonitions — The freedom of the Christians, however, is not license; it is placed at the service of charity. The whole Law is summed up in the precept: Thou shalt love thy neighbor as thyself. This very liberty demands that they conquer the desires of the flesh, for its desires lust against the spirit, and the spirit has desires that conflict with those of the flesh. The works of the flesh are immorality, idolatry, dissensions, party strife, carousings, etc. And those who commit these things will not inherit the kingdom of God. The fruits of the spirit are love, joy, peace, patience, etc. The followers of the Messias Jesus have crucified the flesh and its passions and they act according to the spirit. The Galatians must be patient and mild with one another. They must avoid vainglory and sow in the spirit in order to reap life everlasting (5:13–6:10).

The end of the letter is in Paul's own handwriting. "See with what large letters I am writing to you with my own hand!" (§ 176.) Taking the quill in hand, Paul proceeds to summarize almost the whole letter for these dear big children of his in Galatia. They must not permit themselves to be circumcised. Those who urge them to do so are afraid of being persecuted for the cross of Christ and their aims are worldly. Paul glories in nothing save the cross of Christ, through whom the world is crucified to him and he to the world. For neither circumcision nor uncircumcision is of any account, but a new creature. Let no one give him further trouble now, for he bears in his body the marks of the Lord Jesus (§ 345). A greeting closes this part added in his own hand (6:11–18).

THE EPISTLE TO THE ROMANS

512. We left Paul in Corinth where he spent the three winter months of the year 57–58 in relative calm (§ 502). But the rare intervals of tranquillity in Paul's life were not only brief but far from inactive. It is perhaps not coincidence that Paul's longest writing, which contains the most majestic elaboration of his thought, belongs to this period, for which we have no information on external events. This is the *Epistle to the Romans*.

The calculations noted in the Introduction suggest that the dictation and writing of this letter kept Paul busy for about 100 hours, or anywhere from 32 to 59 days (§§ 177–178). Therefore a half, or a little less than half, of his sojourn in Corinth was devoted to meditating and working out his ideas during the day, so that in the evening he might dictate them to Tertius, his amanuensis for this letter (§ 180).

With it Paul wished to establish direct contact with the Christian community of Rome and prepare his arrival there. He had been thinking a long time of going to Rome and had planned to do so during the third year of his stay in Ephesus (§ 466). Now, having traveled through almost all the Orient, he fixed his sights on the West, which meant Rome first of all and then eventually Spain. It was as if on the threshold of old age, he was unwilling to leave the world before his name was known in every one of its regions, or, to put it more accurately, he could not bear to think that there was a single region in the whole world where the name of Jesus Christ did not resound in blessing. But at that time, the nub of the whole world was Rome; all roads led there. And Paul too aimed his next journey there.

513. Actually Christianity had filtered into Rome several years before (§§ 381, 601). Its precise beginnings there escape us, but there is no doubt that the first evangelizers of the city of the Caesars were not disciples of Paul. Everything points rather to the assumption that they came from among Peter's followers in Jerusalem. When, in Antioch, the various missionary zones had been divided among the Apostles (§§ 309, 355), Peter had been assigned the apostolate among the Jews and Paul among the Gentiles. At first Rome must have fallen within the province of Peter, for the first Christian preaching there was addressed especially to the Jews, who were both numerous and powerful in the city.[47] Very soon, however, ex-pagans began to predominate instead of ex-Jews, so that from the viewpoint of numerical proportion and general character the community began to resemble increasingly the various communities Paul had founded in Asia Minor, Macedonia, and Greece. It was Paul's rule not to enter fields sowed by others, as he himself reminds the Romans (Rom. 15:20; cf. 2 Cor. 10:13), and therefore, strictly speaking,

---

[47] Cf. *Storia d'Israele*, II, p. 220 ff. (§ 195 ff.).

he should not have concerned himself with the Roman community. But the ethnic-Christian character recently assumed by that community might well have been a valid reason for his being concerned with it at least occasionally. After all, the fraternal relationship among the various communities and the evangelizers of different zones might well have been maintained for their mutual edification and to strengthen their common faith (cf. Rom. 1:11–12), and such relations were all the more natural with an eminently cosmopolitan city like the capital of the world Empire.

Add, too, that Paul had learned that the usual troublemakers and sowers of discord were also trying to lead astray the Christians of Rome (16:17–20), and he may have wanted to help confirm them in the true faith even though they were not directly his spiritual children. Even with these reasons, however, Paul intended to respect the province of others, for he planned to visit the community in Rome not as he had visited his own communities in Asia Minor, Macedonia, and Greece, but on his way to Spain (15:24). Things turned out differently later, but at this time, this was his plan with respect to Rome.

As a result, the epistle turned out to be an almost impersonal exposition of doctrine, with scarcely any data about the author and with no direct polemical intent. But since it deals with matters which are at the very roots of Christian belief, it was destined to remain, after the Gospels, the most ample and solemn document of early Christianity. The summary follows.

514. The salutation, which is particularly solemn, is also particularly broken in structure (cf. § 165). Paul thanks God for the faith of the Romans, which is now famous in all the world, and he assures them that he remembers them always, praying that the occasion may come when he may visit them. He has wanted for a long time to see them that he might impart to them some spiritual gift and that he might be comforted with them by their common faith. He is not ashamed of the Gospel, "for it is the power of God unto salvation to everyone who believes, to Jew first and then to Greek. For in it the justice of God is revealed, from faith unto faith, as it is written, 'He who is just lives by faith' [Habacuc 2:4]" (1:1–17).

515. Justification by Faith in the Gospel — Having set forth his thesis in the introduction, Paul then goes on to prove it. The pagans are not justified, for although they may know God by deducing his existence and his attributes from created things, they have not rendered him the homage which is his due and they have fallen away into idolatry. In punishment, God has abandoned them to ignominious passions (cf. the blunt enumeration in § 46 — 1:18–32).

But the man [Jew] who judges his brother judges himself, because he too is guilty before God of the works he has condemned in his pagan brother. The good will be rewarded and the evil punished, first in the Jew and then in the Greek, for God is no respecter of persons. Those who sinned without the Law will perish without it. For it is not those who hear the Law who are just in the sight of God but those who keep it. The pagans, who do not have the Law, have nevertheless its injunctions written in their hearts, and they hear its voice in their own consciences. And all this will appear on the day when God will judge the secrets of men according to the Gospel. But you, who call yourself a Jew, and who boast of your privileges, you who are instructed by the Law and instruct others, why do you not instruct yourself? You who teach others not to steal and not to commit adultery, why do you commit these sins? While you glory in the Law, you dishonor God by transgressing it, and because of your guile the name of God is blasphemed among the pagans! Circumcision is a good thing, yes, provided the Law is observed also. But if the Law is transgressed, circumcision becomes uncircumcision. And the uncircumcised who observes the precepts of the Law will be considered circumcised and will judge the circumcised who does not observe them. The true Jew is not he who appears to be so outwardly, nor is true circumcision that of the flesh. The true Jew is so in spirit and true circumcision is in the heart. Yet the position of the Jews is one of privilege. For even if some of them have not believed, this does not annul the fidelity of God. Jews and Greeks have all sinned, they are all under sin, and no one can boast before God (2–3:20).

516. All, however, both Jews and Greeks, are justified by faith in Jesus Christ, who by his blood became the sacrifice of expiation. Is God only of the Jews? Is he not God also of the Gentiles? He will justify the circumcised by faith and the uncircumcised through the faith. The Law is not abolished but confirmed. Abraham, too, was justified not by his works, for in that case he would have had reason to glory in himself before God, but by faith, for it is written that he believed in God and this was credited to him as justice (Gen. 15:6). And this was done while he was still uncircumcised. Circumcision came later as the seal of the justice of faith, so that he became the father of all the uncircumcised who believe and of all the circumcised who follow in the steps of his faith. And the promises made Abraham were given not through the Law but through the justice of faith. The Law, which was later than the promises, cannot be their prerequisite, for the Law occasioned the transgression of itself, which would be an obstacle to their fulfillment. The promises, on the contrary, will continue to be passed on to the spiritual descendants of Abraham through the faith (3:21–4:25).

517. Faith carries with it the hope of the glory of the sons of God through the merits of Christ. And in its turn, hope is strengthened by

tribulations and "does not disappoint, because the charity of God is poured forth in our hearts by the Holy Spirit who has been given to us" (5:5). If Christ died for us when we were wicked, so much the more should we hope in salvation now that we are justified by his blood. "Therefore as through one man sin entered into the world and through sin death, and thus death has passed into all men because (ἐφ' ᾧ) all have sinned" (5:12).[48] Death is not the punishment for present sins, for it has reigned from Adam until the Law was given through Moses, and it reigned also over those who had not sinned after the likeness of the transgression of Adam, who is a "type" (§ 239) of the future Adam, Christ. But the new Adam has superabundantly restored what was taken from the old. As the offense of the old Adam brought condemnation on all men, so the justice wrought by the new Adam extends to all men for their justification. The practical consequence of the Law was to prevent the transgression from abounding. But where sin has abounded, grace has abounded even more that the reign of sin in death might be replaced by the reign in justice for eternal life through Jesus Christ (Chap. 5).

518. The consequence of all this is that the Christian must sin no more. Those who have been baptized in Jesus Christ have been baptized in his death. Buried with him in his death, the Christian then rose to a new life.[49] United to Christ, as the shoot grafted on the vine, the neophyte, who has participated in his death, will also be at the resurrection. Therefore, Christians must consider themselves dead to sin and alive in Jesus Christ. Sin must not reign in their mortal bodies and they must preserve their members as weapons of justice for God. Before being baptized, they were slaves of sin, but what did that bring them? Death. Now, ransomed from sin, they have become slaves to God, and the fruit of this is sanctification and its end is life everlasting (Chap. 6).

The Romans, expert in law, know that the Law binds a man only so long as he is alive. For example, a married woman is bound to her husband while he is alive, but if he dies she is free to marry again. Now, the Christian is dead to the Law through his incorporation in Christ, that he may belong to him risen from the dead. Not that the Law is sin, but it makes us know sin. I would not have known lust unless the law said: Do not lust. But sin, having found an occasion in this command-

---

[48] The last sentence in the Vulgate is *in quo omnes peccaverunt,* the *in quo* referring to Adam (since *in quo* could hardly be used in place of *eo quod*). This was the common interpretation in the West until the time of Cajetan. The Greek text leaves no doubt that it must be translated as "because," which is the accepted interpretation today.

[49] A reference to the symbolic significance of baptism, administered by immersion, which was the meaning of the Greek verb. The one receiving the sacrament entered the water; his being covered with it was a symbol of burial and his emergence a symbol of the resurrection. The spiritual effects, Paul is saying, parallel the symbol.

ment, inspired in me all manner of desires, "for without
the Law sin is dead" (7:8).
Once I was living without
Law.[50] But when the commandment came, sin revived
and I died, and the commandment that was intended for
life led me to death. The
Jewish Law is good in itself,
but sin uses it as an occasion
to bring death. The Law is
spiritual, but I am carnal, and
sold into the power of sin. I
do not understand what I do,

The Fall of Adam and Eve (Catacombs
of SS. Peter and Marcellinus — Fourth
Century)

for I do not do what I wish but what I detest.[51] If, then, I hate what I
do, I admit that the Law is good. "Now therefore it is no longer I who
do it, but the sin that dwells in me. For I know that in me, that is, in
my flesh, no good dwells, because to wish is within my power, but not
to do good" (*ibid.*, 17–18). I am glad of the law of God according to
the inner man; "but I see another law in my members, warring against
the law of my mind and making me prisoner to the law of sin that is
in my members. Unhappy man that I am! Who will deliver me from the
body of this death? The grace of God through Jesus Christ our Lord!"
(*Ibid.*, 23–25.)[52]

519. The Messias Jesus, through the spirit of life in him, has freed
the Christian from the law of sin and death. What the Law could not
do, God has done, who, sending his Son "in the likeness of the sinful
flesh as a sin-offering, condemned sin in the flesh" (8:3). Therefore
Christians must walk not according to the flesh but the spirit, for the
flesh is inclined to death but the spirit to life and peace. Christians are
not of the flesh but of the spirit, since the Spirit of God dwells in them.
If anyone does not have the Spirit of Christ, then he does not belong

---

[50] We have already pointed out that these passages are not autobiographical
(§ 243), although Paul may be speaking from the experience of his own conscience.
They are rather autobiographical of the whole human race, not of Paul the individual.
The "I" is an editorial first person, and represents the Jew, undermined by sin,
torn by concupiscence, left to his own resources, and therefore not equal to bearing
the burden of the Jewish Law.

[51] Maxims of this kind were very common among the pagans. There is the famous
one of Ovid: *Video meliora proboque, Deteriora sequor* (*Metamor.*, VII, 19–20),
and the other of Epictetus, which says that the sinner "does not do what he wishes,
and what he does not wish to do he does" (*Dissert.*, II, 26, 4).

[52] This is the answer in the Latin of the Vulgate. Very few Greek codices have
this reading. The critical Greek reading is "Thanks be to God," in which the answer
is implied.

Miracle of the Spring, Symbolizing Baptism. Rome: Catacombs of SS. Peter and Marcellinus — Fourth Century (Pontifical Institute of Christian Archeology)

Baptismal Scene. Catacombs of St. Callixtus — Second Century (Pontifical Institute of Christian Archeology)

to Christ. But if the Spirit of him who raised Jesus from the dead dwells within the Christians, then he who raised Jesus from the dead will also bring to life their mortal bodies, by virtue of the Spirit dwelling within them. Those who are led by the Spirit of God are the sons of God. The Christians did not receive a spirit of bondage in order to fear again, but a spirit of adoption as of sons, so that they cry: Abba! Father! Being sons of God, we Christians are also his heirs, co-heirs with Christ, suffering with him that we may be glorified with him. The sufferings of the present time are as nothing compared to the future glory which will be revealed in us.

Creation itself is in eager expectation, longing for the revelation of the sons of God.[53] "For we know that all creation groans and travails in pain until now. And not only it, but we ourselves also who have the first-fruits of the spirit — we ourselves groan within ourselves, waiting for the adoption as sons, the redemption of our body" (*ibid.*, 22–23). But our liberation is in hope, and consequently in waiting for what we yet do not see. Therefore the Spirit comes to the aid of our weakness. "For we do not know what we should pray for as we ought, but the Spirit himself pleads for us ($ὑπερεντυγχάνει$) with unutterable groanings. And he who searches the hearts knows what the Spirit desires, that he

---

[53] Nature itself was disturbed as a consequence of the primordial fall of man; and it too is anxiously awaiting the manifestation of the sons of God, since then it will be reintegrated into its original order and, ransomed from the effects of sin, will also participate in the glory.

pleads for the saints according to God" (*ibid.*, 26–27). For those who love God, all things work together for good, since he has foreordained their vocation to the faith and to glory. God favoring us then, who will be against us? If God has given us his own Son, why will he not give us all other things? Who will separate us from the love of Christ? No one. Nothing — not tribulation, nor distress, nor persecution . . . (cf. § 167 — Chaps. 7–8).

520. The Unbelief of the Jews[54] — Paul is grieved because his countrymen, the Jews, do not believe in the Messias Jesus (cf. the passage quoted in § 167). God's promises have not failed, however, because of this defection. His promises were not given to all the blood descendants of Abraham without distinction. They were addressed only to Isaac, and of the sons of Isaac, only to Jacob and not to Esau. God is not unjust. He freely distributes his favors, not because of man's efforts but of his own mercy. You will say then: Why does God rebuke man? Who can resist God? No, say rather, how do you, a man, dare to ask an accounting of God? Does the clay ask an accounting of the potter? To show his wrath and his power, God endured with patience those who had predisposed themselves to damnation, and he did it also to show forth the richness of his glory upon those who won his mercy. And we are these, called by him not only from among the Jews but also from among the Gentiles. This calling of the Gentiles, to take the place, in part, of obstinate Israel, was foretold by the prophets of the Old Testament. Thus, the Gentiles came to Justice by way of the faith, but Israel, though having a Law of justice, did not attain it because her people did not seek it from faith but from works.

In sorrow over the obstinacy of the Jews, Paul bears witness that they have zeal for God but not according to an exact knowledge (ἐπίγνωσιν), for they wish, as it were, to substitute their own justice for that of God. For the goal of the Law is Christ, unto justice for everyone who believes. The justice of the Law consists in performing its works, but the justice of faith — without bidding us to ascend into heaven or descend into the abyss to seek Christ — teaches us to believe in our Lord Jesus and to profess him openly.

"For there is no distinction between Jew and Greek, for there is the same Lord of all, rich towards all who call upon him" (10:12). But how will the Jews believe in the Christ Jesus if they have not heard

---

[54] Paul faces this question not only because of his own feelings in the matter but rather as a theological question. The obstinacy of the Jews, which was becoming increasingly clearer, in refusing to recognize the Messias Jesus was a serious argument against the theory of universal redemption wrought by Jesus Christ, which Paul has been expounding up to this point. Why was the very nation, once chosen especially by God, now blocking the plans of divine redemption? Why against this luminous horizon did that one dark spot persist, just where one might have least expected it?

him preached? No, this word was preached to the ends of the earth, but they did not accept it, as the prophets of the Old Testament had foretold (Chaps. 9–10).

521. Must we say then that God has rejected his people? "By no means! For I also am an Israelite of the posterity of Abraham, of the tribe of Benjamin" (11:1). In the general defection of the Jews a remnant remained faithful as in the days of Elias. They are those chosen by grace, who saw what the others, being blinded, did not see. But if the blinded have fallen, their fall is not without fruit nor will it last forever. In the first place, "by their offense salvation has come to the Gentiles, that they may be jealous of them" (*ibid.*, 11). Besides, when they shall rise again, the world will derive a good far greater than the harm it received from their fall. For this reason, though he is the Apostle of the Gentiles, Paul does all that he can to save as many Israelites as possible. There follows the comparison of the olive tree, some of whose branches have been broken off and on whose trunk wild olive branches have been grafted (cf. § 166). The branches of the grafted tree – the Gentiles – not only are not to boast against the original tree, which is Israel, but are to remember that one day the broken branches will also be regrafted upon it. "For I would not, brethren, have you ignorant of this mystery, lest you should be wise in your own conceits,[55] that a partial blindness only has befallen Israel, until the full number of the Gentiles should enter, and thus all Israel should be saved," according to the prophecy (*ibid.*, 25–26). For the Israelites are always most dear to God because of their ancestors. And just as the Gentiles were once rebels against God and have now obtained mercy, so the Israelites are rebellious now, but one day they will obtain mercy. balancing the mercy shown the Gentiles. "Oh, the depth of the riches of the wisdom and of the knowledge of God! How incomprehensible are his judgments and how unsearchable his ways! . . . For from him and through him and unto him are all things. To him be the glory forever, Amen" (Chap. 11).

522. Various Moral Admonitions – The Christians of Rome are exhorted to offer their bodies as living, holy sacrifices, pleasing to God. This is the true worship required of them. They are so many members of a mystical body, and therefore let each perform his own proper function for the whole body. The same is to be said of the different charisms they possess (§ 211 ff.). But all of these various duties are summed up in the precept of charity, which makes one forget himself and serve others and forgive all things (Chap. 12).

In their relations with the civil magistrates "let everyone be subject

---

[55] The admonition was a timely one for the Christians of Rome; when Paul was writing these words, the community was composed for the most part of ex-pagans (§ 513), and therefore they might easily be tempted to despise the Jews and consider them shut out from the mercy of God.

to the higher authorities, for there exists no authority except from God, and those who exist have been appointed by God. Therefore he who resists the authority resists the ordinance of God; and they that resist bring on themselves condemnation. For rulers are a terror not to the good work but to the evil" (13:1–3). Christians must be subject to the authorities, not only for fear of punishment, but for conscience' sake. For the same reason, they must pay the tribute. "Render to all men whatever is their due; tribute to whom tribute is due; taxes to whom taxes are due; fear to whom fear is due; honor to whom honor is due" (*ibid.,* 7). Every duty is to be resolved in charity, which is the fullness of the Law. "And this do [the more so because of your] understanding the time [in which you live] for it is now the hour for us to rise from sleep, because now our salvation is nearer than when we came to believe. The night is far advanced; the day is at hand. Let us therefore lay aside the works of darkness, and put on the armor of light."[56] Abandoning all vice and immorality, "put on the Lord Jesus Christ, and as for the flesh, take no thought for its lusts" (Chap. 13).

Those who are "weak in faith" are to be treated with forbearance by those who are strong. If the weak abstain from certain foods and perform special observances on certain days, they are not to be despised by the strong. Vice versa, the strong, who do not observe these abstinences and practices, are not to be judged unfavorably by the weak. Both have the intention of serving the Lord, and this intention is to be respected. In itself, no food is unclean, but do not give scandal to one of the brethren by eating something which to him is abhorrent. Rather give it up for love of peace and for charity. As Christ did, try to please others more than yourself, and let all receive one another as Christ received all, both Jews and pagans (Chaps. 12–15:13).

523. Conclusion. Explanations and Greetings — Paul knows very well that the Christians of Rome are well endowed with knowledge and are able to admonish one another. Nevertheless he has written to give them some few reminders in his capacity as Apostle of the Gentiles, to whom he devotes all his activity. He has preached the Gospel "from Jerusalem round about as far as Illyricum" (§ 503) where the name of Christ had not been heard, for he has not wished to build on the foundations laid by others. Many times he has been prevented from coming to visit them, although he has desired to do so for many years. Now, having no further work in the country where he is, he is setting out for Spain, and on the way he hopes to stop among them before finishing his journey. But for the moment he must go to Jerusalem, to bring the contributions

---

[56] The urgency here bears no inference with regard to the parousia, as the eschatologists would have it, but is to be taken with reference to any "end," before the coming of which one must do good. Cf. § 483, note, for a discussion of *1 Corinthians,* 7:29–33; cf. also § 489, note; § 633, note.

collected for the poor of that community in Macedonia and Achaia. He asks them to pray for him, that he may escape from the intrigues of the Palestinian Jews and that his mission will be acceptable to the faithful in the Holy City (15:14–33).

He commends to them Phoebe, the deaconess of the community of Cenchrae (§ 426), and asks them to receive her and assist her affectionately. There follows a long list of greetings, first to Prisca (Priscilla) and Aquila.[57] Then come a few brief warnings to be on guard against troublemakers (§ 513), greetings from Paul's companions, and a doxology (Chap. 16).

524. Toward the beginning of March in 58, Paul left Corinth. He had decided to go by sea, embarking at Cenchrae and sailing directly for Syria. But at the last minute he was told — most probably by a Christian anxious for the master's safety — that the Jews had made a plot against him (Acts 20:3).

It is not likely that the purpose of the plot was to rob Paul of the considerable sum he was taking to Jerusalem. The Jews of the Diaspora were not pirates, and a money prize that had to be obtained with violence and the murder of a fellow countryman would not have inspired them to such a plot. It was prompted rather by moral reasons, and Paul himself had had a vague presentiment of something of this when, in his letter to the Romans, he asked them to pray that he might escape the unbelievers of Judea (Rom. 15:31). The underlying motive was hatred for the renegade Jew who had become the Apostle of the Messias Jesus.

Acts of violence, even against an individual, were quite frequent at the time among the Zealots who were *Sicarii*.[58] They were motivated, however, not by love of gain but by religious-nationalist fanaticism. Paul must have been marked as a victim by some Zealot leader in Judea, who charged his emissaries abroad to carry out the attack. The occasion was most convenient. The Pasch was approaching and the ships sailing for Syria from the various Mediterranean ports were loaded with Jewish pilgrims on their way to Jerusalem. A well-directed blow at night in some dark corner of the ship, with the aid of accomplices, would get rid of the renegade forever. His body could be easily disposed of in the sea, and he would hardly be missed from among the crowded passengers.

---

[57] This is an exceptionally long list of some twenty-five names. Some scholars maintain that it derives from some other epistle — perhaps that to the Ephesians — since Paul, who had never been in Rome, could not possibly know that many people there. This ignores the testimony of the codices, all of which carry the list as part of this particular epistle. Against the thesis stands the fact that Paul might well have met these persons in the course of his travels, and he sends greetings to as many as he can to show the Romans he is not unknown among them. It has also been correctly pointed out that several names in the list (Junias, Ampliatus, Urbanus . . .) are clearly of Roman origin, and are attested by Roman inscriptions.

[58] Cf. *Storia d'Israele*, II, p. 437 ff. (§ 381 ff.); p. 463 ff. (§ 411 ff.).

The "Meteors" of Thessaly

525. The report of the solicitous Christian saved Paul, however. He gave up his plan to go by sea and chose the overland route, although it was much longer, for it obliged him to go through Macedonia again. It was impossible now to be in Jerusalem for the Pasch. His companions on the journey were representatives of various communities he had founded: Sopater of Beroea; Aristarchus and Secundus of Thessalonica; Gaius of Derbe, Timothy; Tychicus and Trophimus of the province of Asia (Acts 20:4). But at a certain point in the journey — impossible to determine for lack of necessary data in the narrative — the group divided, and one part hurried on ahead to await the others in Troas. Paul crossed Thessaly and went to Philippi, where he met again his beloved Luke. And at this point the narrative returns to the first person plural (§§ 92, 379).

526. Paul spent the Pasch at Philippi. When the eight days of the feast were over, accompanied by Luke and perhaps a few others, he embarked at the port of Neapolis (§ 381) for Troas. This time the crossing must have been rough for it took five days. In Troas they rejoined the rest of the party which had preceded them, and remained there seven days.

Their last day in Troas happened to be the Hebrew "first day after the Sabbath," or our Sunday. It was, therefore, the day the early Christians dedicated to a liturgical gathering of special importance (cf. 1 Cor. 16:2). This one must have been particularly moving because Paul was bidding farewell to the community. As Luke tells it, "And on the first day of the week, when he had met for the breaking of the bread, Paul addressed them, as he was to leave the next morning, and he prolonged his address until midnight. Now there were many lamps in the upper room where we had assembled. And a young man named Eutychus, who was sitting at the window, was overcome with drowsiness and, as Paul addressed them at great length, he went fast asleep and fell down from the third story to the ground and was picked up dead. Paul went down to him and laid himself upon him, and embracing him, said, 'Do not be alarmed, life is still in him.' Then he went up and broke bread and ate, and having spoken to them a good while, even till daybreak, he departed. And they took away the boy alive and were not a little comforted" (Acts 20:7–12).

527. We note that the gathering was held in an "upper room" ($\dot{v}\pi\epsilon\rho\dot{\omega}\omega$). We do not know whether this was the general rule among the early Christians, but we do know that Christ had instituted the Eucharist at the Last Supper in a room above the ground ($\dot{a}\nu\dot{a}\gamma\alpha\iota\omega\nu$). The "breaking of the bread" could only be the Eucharistic rite for which Paul elsewhere uses the same expression (1 Cor. 10:16). The sequence of events is quite clear. On Sunday, the community gathers to celebrate the Eucharist late in the evening, that is, at the hour at which Jesus had instituted it. Paul joins them, for he is leaving the next day and he takes advantage of the occasion to bid farewell to the brethren and give them some last exhortation. Before the celebration of the Eucharist, he addresses them at some length. The young Eutychus falls asleep, tumbles from the window, and dies. Paul goes down, embraces him, and assures the gathering that he is not dead. Returning immediately to the upper room, he partakes of the Eucharist with the brethren, converses with them until dawn, and leaves. The youth had probably been laid on a bed in another room, and we are told only that having escaped death he filled all with consolation.

It is to be noted that the narrative attaches little importance to the episode of the young man, which to us seems the most important. The chief importance, on the other hand, is attributed to the Eucharistic rite, while Eutychus' accident is treated merely as an interruption, and a very slight one. As soon as Paul has embraced the dead youth and reassured the others, the rite is resumed as if nothing had happened, and the meeting continues until dawn. The physician Luke says briefly that the young man was "dead" and then "alive," without giving us any details. When Paul laid himself on the dead youth and embraced him tightly ($\sigma\nu\mu\pi\epsilon\rho\iota\lambda\alpha\beta\dot{\omega}\nu$) we may conclude that, with his deep knowledge of the Bible, he was thinking of Elias and Eliseus, who had performed those symbolic gestures, customary in Hebrew prophetism, over the two dead persons they revived (1 [3] Kings 17:21–23; 2 [4] Kings 4:34–36).

Mytilene (Lesbos) (from Monmarché, *Les pays d'Asie*)

Some rationalists have interpreted Paul's phrase, "life is still in him," to mean that the youth was not yet dead. But that is not what it means. The whole context indicates that in the narrator's mind, the phrase denotes that the youth was alive again after being dead; that is, life was in him because it had been returned to him. The biblical account attributes similar statements to Elias when he raised the child from the dead.

528. The voyage from Troas toward the south was in reality a cargo run. The first stop was at Assos, which lay just behind the promontory south of Troas. It could be reached either by sailing around the promontory, or overland across the base of the promontory in about six hours of travel on foot. We do not know why Paul chose to go by land; he had sent his companions away shortly beforehand by boat, engaging to meet them in Assos.

At Assos, Paul went on board and they sailed for Mytilene, on the eastern shore of Lesbos. It was the most important city on the island.

The next day they sailed between Chios, about level with Smyrna, and the mainland, and the day after that, past Ephesus, entering the straits between the island of Samos and the promontory of Mycale. According to one reading they docked at Trogyllium (Santa Maria). The following day they reached Miletus.

529. Today the traveler who follows Paul's route, along the Ionian coasts of Asia Minor from Troy down to Rhodes, is delighted with the scenery and caught in the fascination of the three thousand years of history which haunt it. In Paul's time those regions were less populated with historic ghosts, but much richer in natural beauty and certainly more flourishing. In all probability, however, he was characteristically unmoved (§ 233) by what he saw about him, for the true world in which he lived he carried within him. This world at the moment was anything but tranquil and serene. Everywhere on his spiritual horizon ominous clouds were gathering.

He decided not to go to Ephesus in order to save time, because he wanted to be in Jerusalem for Pentecost (Acts 20:16). He was going to the Holy City not only to bring the contributions that had been collecting for so long a time and in so many places, but also because he was impelled there by some irresistible urging of his spirit (*ibid.*, 22). He foresaw serious trials awaiting him, however. In the first place, how would the brethren in Jerusalem receive the contributions and their bringer? The end of the epistle to the Romans (15:30–31), which asks for prayers that the offerings may be well received by those brethren, shows that he had some misgivings on this point. It might be that the rigorist current, which was quite strong in Jerusalem, would still be hostile to him and even to the help he was bringing, and would do all in their power to have both rejected. Did the gifts not come, after all, from the uncircumcised? Had they not been gathered by him who wished to abolish the Law? The more intransigent might want to tell such a benefactor what Peter had told Simon Magus: "Thy money go to destruction with thee" (Acts 8:20). It would be a very serious matter if that happened, and Paul suffered the torment of uncertainty.

530. And this was not all. There were external dangers as well. The ending of the same epistle alludes to the unbelievers of Judea, the Zealot-*Sicarii,* who had already concocted one plot against Paul. He must have known quite a bit about the intrigues of these fanatics, for he mentions them again in his discourse at Miletus (Acts 20:19). One plot had failed, but what were these implacable enemies not capable of doing to him when he appeared in Jerusalem? For him to die would be nothing but gain (Phil. 1:21). But what of the communities which he had founded and watched over for so many anxious years, day by day? And his plan to evangelize the West as far as Spain, and his visit to Rome, were these all to vanish at the dagger thrust of an unknown Zealot?

Well, the Lord must provide. Certain it is Paul felt a mysterious warning whispering within him constantly: "I am going to Jerusalem, compelled by the Spirit, not knowing what will happen to me there; except that in every city the Holy Spirit warns me, saying that imprisonment and persecution are awaiting me" (Acts 20:22–23). With these things on his mind, it is clear Paul was not in much of a mood to enjoy the panorama unfolding around the ship; withdrawn within himself, he was reflecting on his immediate future.

531. This state of mind is apparent in the discourse of Miletus (§ 12). From here he sent for the presbyters of Ephesus. While he did not wish to stop in the city itself, in order to save time, neither did he wish to leave the region without greeting and exhorting the representatives of this beloved community. The discourse to the presbyters is reported by Luke. It closely resembles Paul's epistles in language and sums up the

teaching he had given them in Ephesus. It clearly mirrors the Apostle's frame of mind, moved by memories, disturbed by dark forebodings, sustained by hope, and comforted by the testimony of his conscience.

Those he has called together, Paul says, know how he has lived from the first day he entered the province of Asia, serving the Lord with all humility amid many trials and the plottings of the Jews. He has neglected nothing that was for their good, teaching in public and from house to house, and urging both Jews and Greeks to repentance in God (cf. § 417) and faith in Jesus. Now he is compelled spiritually to go to Jerusalem. He does not know what will happen there, but the Holy Spirit in every city has forewarned him that prison and persecution await him. He, however, is not attached to life. What concerns him is the fulfillment of the office assigned him by the Lord Jesus, to give testimony of the Gospel of God's grace. He knows that they, whom he has evangelized himself, will not see him again.[59] While he has no regrets in their regard, he exhorts them to care for themselves and the

---

[59] This is what Paul thought at the time, but he did return to Ephesus again, after his first imprisonment in Rome (§ 635). This suggests that Luke wrote the summary of the discourse and the *Acts*, before the pastoral letters were written, which tell us that Paul did return to Ephesus. If Luke had been familiar with these letters, he might have omitted Paul's prediction.

Miletus — Theater

Rhodes — The City

"flock in which the Holy Spirit has placed you as bishops (ἐπισκόπους),[60] to rule the Church of God" (20:28). He knows that after his departure fierce wolves will creep into the fold, and even among them now listening to him, some will arise and speak perverse things to draw the disciples away. They must be vigilant, therefore, remembering that for three years he has not ceased night and day to exhort each one of them. And now he commends them to the grace of God, who will help them. He has sought nothing from their material possessions, and they know that he has provided for his own needs and those of his companions with the toil of his own hands. He wanted in that way to show them that they were to succor the needy with their toil, and recalled to them the words of the Lord who said, "It is more blessed to give than to receive" (§ 302, note).

532. At the end of the discourse, Paul knelt and prayed with them all. Then they all embraced and kissed him weeping, grieving because he had said they would not see him again. And they escorted him to his ship.

After a stop of perhaps two days, Paul left Miletus and continued his journey with a smaller group of companions. The subsequent narrative implies that Trophimus and Aristarchus were still with him and Luke, but the others were not mentioned again. It is probable that they left Paul in Miletus. On the first day the ship headed for the island of Cos, on the next it reached Rhodes, and the day after that they debarked at Patara in Lycia (§ 11), due east from Rhodes. At Patara, they "found

---

[60] Since the discourse is addressed to the "elders" (πρεσβύτεροι), it is clear that the two terms "bishops" ("overseers") and "elders" here mean the same thing.

a ship crossing over to Phoenicia, and we went on board and set sail. After sighting Cyprus and leaving it to the left, we sailed for Syria and landed at Tyre, for there the ship was to unload her cargo" (Acts 21:2–3).

533. Notwithstanding Paul's hurry, the stop in Tyre was a long one, lasting seven days, probably because the ship was being serviced. But he took advantage of the delay to visit the local community, the origins of which must have gone back to the time of the persecution of the Christians he himself had instigated (cf. Acts 11:19). Some of them, warned "through the Spirit," begged Paul not to go to Jerusalem — to avoid the trials awaiting him there — but they did not succeed in detaining him. When the seven days were up, "we left there and went on, and all of them with their wives and children escorted us till we were out of the city; and we knelt down on the shore and prayed. And having said farewell to one another, we went on board the ship and they returned home" (21:5–6). From Tyre the ship went to Ptolemais, and there, it would seem, the sea voyage ended.

534. Paul stayed with the Christian community in Ptolemais a day, and then, with his companions, set out by land for Caesarea, "where we went to the house of Philip the evangelist, who was one of the seven [deacons], and stayed with him. He had four daughters, virgins, who had the gift of prophecy" (*ibid.*, 8–9). A certain Agabus, who also had the charism of prophet, arrived in Caesarea from Judea at this point. He must have come from Jerusalem and seems to be the same Agabus the "prophet" whom we met in Antioch (§ 317). He performed before Paul one of those symbolic acts used so much by the ancient Hebrew prophets, especially Ezekiel. He took Paul's girdle, and having bound his own hands and feet with it, he proclaimed: "The man whose girdle this is the Jews will bind like this at Jerusalem, and they will deliver him into the hands of the Gentiles!" (*Ibid.*, 11.) On hearing this, from one with the authority of the prophetic gift, all those present, including the narrator Luke, begged Paul not to go to Jerusalem. But he replied: "What do you mean by weeping and breaking my heart? For I am ready not only to be bound but even to die at Jerusalem for the name of the Lord Jesus!" When they saw they could in no way dissuade him, they acquiesced and said, "The Lord's will be done" (*ibid.*, 13–14). Against these warnings, though they came to him indirectly from communications of the Spirit, Paul set his own inner revelations, which gave him an unshakable certainty as to the course he was to pursue. The road for him was the road to Jerusalem, even if it led to prison or the executioner's block. This was the "will of the Lord," and that was enough.

The last lap of the journey from Caesarea to Jerusalem was made, probably with a stop along the way, in the company of some of the Christians from Caesarea who joined the caravan, perhaps to offer their protection en route. In Jerusalem, they secured lodgings for Paul at the home of Mnason, a Cypriot, who had been a Christian for a long time. Since he was of Greek origin, his house was the most convenient for a group of Christians among whom there certainly were some who were uncircumcised. They would not have been readily received in the homes of the Judaizing Christians, and, if they had been, occasions for dissension would have arisen too easily.

This was the fifth visit known to us which Paul made to Jerusalem since his conversion.

Imprisonment in Jerusalem
Imprisonment in Caesarea

---

535. Paul's reception in Jerusalem may be described as "diplomatic" in the familiar sense of the term. But it would certainly have been something less than that — as he himself had feared (§ 529) — had a higher authority not intervened to change the situation, if not in substance at least in appearance. Similar instances are not unknown in every field of diplomacy.

It should be remembered that the community in Jerusalem, comprised both Hellenist Christians and Jewish Christians, with their differing tendencies (§ 350 ff.). The latter were certainly the more numerous and powerful, but over them both stood the highest Christian authorities, the "great Apostles," revered by both groups even though each tried to draw them to its own side. The skillful prudence of these authorities must have been most evident in their ability to keep both groups within the fold with the fewest possible conflicts, persuading now one side and now the other to renounce some preference or prejudice. There was, indeed, a common denominator which could absorb their differences, and this was reciprocal charity, which, according to John's catechesis was the distinguishing precept Jesus had given his disciples, on the eve of his death (Jn. 13:34–35; 15:12), and which Paul's catechesis set at the apex of all the charisms (§ 225). But if that was utterly clear in theory, in actual practice the vagaries of human nature prevented now one group and now the other from rising to such lofty heights. Then the "great Apostles" would suggest some middle course which the two groups could accept to their mutual satisfaction. That was the best the diplomacy of charity could accomplish, to reconcile the distinctive precept of charity with the sluggishness of human nature.

536. Paul's first meeting with the Christians of Jerusalem was a cordial one. "On our arrival at Jerusalem the brethren gave us a hearty welcome" (Acts 21:17). It is easy to recognize in these brethren the Hellenist Christians, who, as soon as they heard of the arrival of the missionaries to the Gentiles, went to greet them and rejoice with them over the good news which they brought. But this is a private meeting, among the faithful of the same group, who can speak freely heart to heart, who have no administrative responsibilities and so do not have to worry about keeping a quiet balance between two opposing factions. Meanwhile, that very evening the news of this important visit spread throughout the community and reached, of course, the ears of its greater and lesser authorities. Since the new arrivals had expressed the desire to be received officially and consign the sums of money they had brought, the presbyters fixed the next day for the meeting and meanwhile discussed how the missionaries should be received.

Undoubtedly there were different views, and some among the minor leaders probably proposed that the offerings collected among the uncircumcised be rejected outright and that Paul's criteria in evangelizing the pagans be openly repudiated (§ 529). Other "elders" perhaps were less radical in their approach and suggested that the offerings be accepted but at the same time that Paul be required to impose on his pagan converts at least the fundamental points of the Jewish Law. Others were content with something less, and, concerned only with their own countrymen, suggested Paul be required to command his Jewish converts to observe the Law even after they were baptized. Such were probably the principal views expressed by the presbyters, almost all of whom were Jewish Christians.

But the meeting was attended also by the only one of the "great Apostles" then present in Jerusalem, James, the "brother" of the Lord. As he listened to these various proposals he must have thought of the stand he had taken on the occasion of the Apostolic Council (§ 358) and how little his attitude was now being imitated. At the end, it is likely that he again expressed his former views on the subject and disappointed once more the elders' hopes. Since, however, the responsibility of the moment rested entirely on his shoulders, he considered it opportune to sweeten the bitter pill of disappointment with a little concession of a practical nature. The result must have been a kind of "agenda" which determined the attitude to be maintained at the next day's meeting, an attitude of charitable compromise and alert prudence.

537. "On the next day Paul went with us to James, and all the presbyters came in. After greeting them, he related in detail what God had done among the Gentiles through his ministry. They praised God when they heard it. . . ." Up to this point, everything is quite clear and natural. The elders listen to this happy report on the diffusion of the Good Tidings and they praise God for it. But they have something to reply right afterward, and the veiled and courteous manner in which they say it does not at all conceal their inner thoughts. We do not know who spoke in reply, but it was probably James himself, in the name of the elders and in accordance with what had been agreed the night before.

Whoever it was, Paul heard himself being told: "Thou seest, brother, how many thousands of believers there are among the Jews, all of them zealous upholders of the Law." This fact is handed to Paul almost as a counterpoise to his tidings of the numerous pagans he has converted. And it was a fact that could not be ignored, since both ex-Jews and ex-pagans acknowledged Jesus as their Messias. The fact was all the more tangible at that particular time in Jerusalem, where innumerable Jews had gathered from the Diaspora to celebrate Pentecost, a good number of whom had accepted the Christian faith although they continued to make pilgrimages as prescribed by Jewish Law. But this fact is followed by another piece of information which, not without prudent artifice, is attributed to these same Jews. "Now they have heard about thee that thou dost teach the Jews who live among the Gentiles to depart from Moses, telling them they should not circumcise their children nor observe the [Jewish] customs."

538. In actual fact, this was not exactly Paul's teaching. He maintained that the pagans who became Christians were not to be concerned with Jewish observances, but, with wise understanding, he was less categorical in the case of Jewish converts. He left it to the individual conscience whether or not to continue the observances of the Law, although he did declare that the Law did not bring salvation and that it had been abolished with the coming of the Messias Jesus. It is true that the ultimate consequence of these principles was "apostasy" from Moses, but Paul had merely set the principles before the disciples of Moses and left their consciences free to choose or not the practical consequences. He understood human nature too well not to treat his countrymen as human beings rather than machines, knowing full well what it cost a man to give up ancient and revered traditions. He himself, after all, had made and kept the vow in Cenchrae (§ 448) from personal piety, and for charity's sake he had circumcised Timothy (§ 373). But the meeting of the elders passed over these subtle distinctions and human considerations, and while attributing the opinion to others, bore down on the question of "apostasy" from Moses.

This was immediately followed by a suggested remedy, offered as affectionate advice. "What then? The multitude is sure to assemble, for they will hear that thou hast come. So do what we tell thee. We have four men who are under a vow; take them and sanctify thyself along with them, and pay for them that they may shave their heads; and all will know that what they have heard of thee is false, but that thou thyself also observest the Law. But as for the Gentile believers, we ourselves have written our decision that they abstain from idol offerings and from blood and from what is strangled and from immorality" (*ibid.*, 18–25).

539. In substance, the remedy was to perform publicly an act which complied with a particular precept of the Jewish Law, that is, the vow of the "Nazarite" (§ 448). Paul was not asked to make any doctrinal statements regarding the validity and efficacy of that Law. He could keep his own views on that matter, but he was to offer a concrete example to dissipate the dangerous rumors circulating in his regard.

What he was being asked to do was not really of great importance. In fact, it is probable that the elders chose that very act instead of another because they had incidentally learned of the same vow made by Paul in Cenchrae five years earlier. Then he had taken the vow from personal devotion. Now let him join the four Christians who had made it and help them fulfill it. It often happened, in fact, that poor people who had taken the vow of the "Nazarite" could not meet the considerable expense involved in performing the sacrifices when the time of the vow was over. In such cases, wealthy persons gained merit by offering them the means of paying for the sacrifices, after which they could shave their heads and be freed from the vow (cf. Flavius Josephus, *Antiquities of the Jews*, XIX, 294).

To indicate that the proposal, moderate enough in itself, was also a just one, the elders alluded at the end of the discourse to the decree of the Apostolic Council, which listed for the converted Gentiles four specific prohibitions (§ 360 ff.). This reference, which may have been also a kind of *do ut des*, reminded Paul that as far as the pagans he had converted were concerned, he was perfectly free since they had no other obligations except those four mentioned. This is explicitly stated in the "Western" version (§ 119, note), which reads: "But as for the Gentile believers, they have nothing to say against thee, for we ourselves have written . . . etc."

540. But despite all this sugar-coating the pill was still bitter enough for Paul, who had to swallow it. The tactful Luke makes no mention of any hesitancy on Paul's part but proceeds immediately to recount how he followed the advice. Nevertheless Paul must have had his moments of hesitation and inner rebellion, or he would not have been the man he was. For the past twenty years, however, the Apostle of Christ had imposed himself on the man Paul. In that decisive moment, he remembered he had written a few months earlier to the Corinthians that he became a Jew with the Jews in order to win them (1 Cor. 9:20). He recalled, too, that in the same letter (13:2) he had said he would be as nothing, even though he could move mountains, if he had not charity. So when put to the test, the Apostle in him restrained the man and obliged him to become once more a Jew, and, in all things, he permitted charity to triumph.

Having accepted the suggestion, Paul the next day went with the four Jewish Christians who had taken the vow, and after performing the prescribed ceremonies of purification, he entered the Temple of

Jerusalem to make the necessary declaration as to when the vow would end and to establish with the priests the day when the required sacrifices were to be offered. For the next seven days, while waiting for the end of the vow, he continued to frequent the Temple with the four Nazarites.[1] The seven days were almost over when the event occurred which changed the whole course of Paul's life.

541. During the Pentecost, the Temple of Jerusalem was crowded with pilgrims from all parts of the Diaspora; and, as we have seen,[2] the Temple was not only the one place of worship and sacrifice for Judaism throughout the world, but also the great meeting place for the inhabitants and visitors in the city. Its "Court of the Gentiles," which pagans also were permitted to enter, was for Jerusalem what the agora, or market place, was for any Greek city. Almost anyone could be found there and practically all business could be transacted there. In this period particularly, when the movement of the Zealot-*Sicarii* was growing by leaps and bounds from month to month, the Temple and the "Court of the Gentiles" was a kind of international listening post and moral fortress, as it later became the actual fortress of the insurgents in the war of 70. Here some passionate nationalist, afire with messianic political visions, harangued the crowd, and there another buttonholed a potential recruit for the cause. There open attacks were ordered on distant rioting villages, while in another corner plans were made to dispatch from this life with a mysterious dagger thrust the government official or eminent Jew who opposed their ideas. All the various threads of the world Diaspora were tied together in the Temple. And therefore to watch over and rule the Temple was to watch over and rule all of Judaism.

The Romans were well aware that this was the nerve center of Palestine and the whole Jewish world, and they kept a permanent cohort of soldiers in the Fortress Antonia, situated north of the Temple and connected with it by an inner passage. The garrison, especially on the occasion of the great feast days, was more or less constantly alerted,

---

[1] This period of "the seven days" is mentioned with the definite article in *Acts*, 21:27, but we have no other information concerning it. As noted above (§ 448), the shortest duration of the Nazarite vow was thirty days (cf. *Mishna, Nazir*, I, 3), during which time one was to abstain from all fermented beverages and not cut his hair. At the end of thirty days, one was released from the vow by sacrificing three sheep and offering oblations in the Temple, and by shaving his head and burning a lock of his hair on the altar with the sacrifice. We have no evidence that shorter periods were also admissible for the vow, such as, for example, seven days. In any case, it is not certain that Paul took the vow himself this time. He was associated with the four Nazarites as a patron, paying the costs of the sacrifices, and perhaps performing with them some secondary rite from personal devotion.

[2] Cf. *Storia d'Israele*, II, p. 399 ff. (§ 348 ff.); p. 464 ff. (§ 411 ff.); *The Life of Christ*, p. 46 ff. (§ 48 ff.).

because the enormous influx of pilgrims filled with nationalist hopes and enthusiasms offered plenty of occasion for rioting, which often grew very serious.

542. Many of these riots are recorded by Flavius Josephus, but it is irrelevant to our purpose to list them here. We may quote, however, his account of one of them: "The false Egyptian prophet drew an even greater misfortune down upon the Jews. He was a charlatan come into the country; and having acquired the reputation of prophet, he gathered about 30,000 of those who were led astray by him. Having led them round and round from the desert to the mountain called 'of Olives,' from there he would have been able to invade Jerusalem with force and, overcoming the Roman garrison, he would have set himself up as ruler of the people, supported by the armed mob which entered with him. But his attempt was prevented by [the Roman procurator] Felix, who went to meet him with heavy Roman infantry, while the entire populace engaged in his defense. But when the conflict began, the Egyptian took flight with a certain few of his followers, while the greater number were killed or captured, and the rest of the crowd scattered to their homes. These having been disposed of, the infection, as in a sick body, appeared again in another place. For charlatans and brigands, gathering together, incited many to revolt and were exhorting them to freedom threatening death to those who subjected themselves to the authority of the Romans. . . ."[3]

To be exact, this episode did not take place within the Temple but in the immediate vicinity, for the Mount of Olives where the Egyptian was encamped was directly opposite the Temple, which was undoubtedly the first objective. In any case, the episode is instructive, both for what it reveals of the general background of the period we are discussing and because the procurator Felix and the false Egyptian prophet are associated with Paul.

543. Of Paul, let Luke tell the story: "But when the seven days were almost over, the Jews from the province of Asia, seeing him in the temple, stirred up all the people and seized him shouting, 'Men of Israel, help. This is the man who teaches all men everywhere against the people and the Law and this place, and moreover he has brought Gentiles also into the temple and has desecrated this holy place.' For they had seen Trophimus the Ephesian in the city with him and they supposed that Paul had taken him into the temple. And the whole city

---

[3] *Wars of the Jews*, II, 261–264; the same episode is retold in *Antiquities of the Jews*, XX, 169–172, where it is stated that 400 of the Egyptian's followers were killed and 200 captured, but the total number is not given. The figure 30,000 here is certainly exaggerated. In *Acts*, 21:38, it is 4000. This type of historical accuracy makes it hard to explain the preference some critics display for Flavius Josephus over Luke — not to mention the many instances in which the former contradicts himself.

was thrown into confusion, and the people ran together, and seizing Paul, they proceeded to drag him out of the temple; whereupon the doors were immediately shut" (Acts 21:27–30).

Paul was being watched, then. The Jewish pilgrims from the province of Asia, and particularly from Ephesus, had seen Paul in the streets of the city with Trophimus of Ephesus (§§ 525, 643) and trailed him from then on in the hope of catching him in the Temple, where they could throw their weight about. The accusation they screamed at the top of their lungs, that Paul had brought Trophimus into the Temple, was not true. But since they had seen Paul there, they easily assumed that Trophimus was there too. In any case, the Christian Trophimus, an ex-pagan and therefore uncircumcised, could very well enter the "Court of the Gentiles." He could not go beyond it into the inner court, however, for the Greek and Latin inscriptions on the wall which separated the two courts forbade pagans entrance to the inner one under penalty of death.[4]

544. The hue and cry raised by Paul's enemies excited the crowd gathered in the Temple, and the tumult quickly spread outside. Other Jews of the city came running, and Paul was dragged from the inner court of the Temple that they might punish him as he deserved. It looked very much like a riot that would end in bloodshed. Therefore the Levites on duty, accustomed by now to these violent demonstrations, hurried to close the gates of the Temple so it would not be desecrated by blood.

But in addition to the Levites, others intervened who were far less acceptable to the rioters and these were the Roman soldiers. They not only were garrisoned in the adjacent Fortress Antonia, but according to Flavius Josephus (*Wars of the Jews*, V, 244), during festival days when disorders could be so easily sparked, they were also stationed, fully armed, here and there along the porticoes. The soldiers on guard, then, sent a messenger posthaste to the Fortress Antonia to report to the tribune in command that the mob was working up to one of the usual riots. The tribune, whose name was Claudius Lysias, immediately called out soldiers and centurions and marched on the scene, where he found a huge crowd trying to beat Paul to death.

But let us turn to Luke again: "And when they saw the tribune and the soldiers, they stopped beating Paul. Then the tribune came up and ordered him to be bound with two chains, and inquired who he was and what he had been doing. Some in the crowd shouted one thing, some another, and as he could not learn anything certain on account of the tumult, he ordered him to be taken into the barracks. And when

---

[4] Cf. *Storia d'Israele*, II, p. 400 (§ 348), for a photograph of these inscriptions, which were discovered in 1871.

he came to the steps [which led from the Temple court up to the Fortress Antonia⁵] he was actually being carried by the soldiers owing to the violence of the crowd; for the mass of the people followed, shouting, 'Away with him!'

"And as Paul was about to be taken into the barracks, he said to the tribune, 'May I say something to thee?' He said, 'Dost thou know Greek? Art thou not the Egyptian who recently stirred up to sedition and led out into the desert the four thousand assassins?' But Paul said to him, 'I am a Jew from Tarsus in Cilicia, a citizen of no insignificant city. But I beg thee, give me leave to speak to the people.'

"He gave him leave, and Paul, standing on the steps motioned with his hand to the people, and when they had become quiet, he addressed them in Hebrew . . ." (Acts 21:32–40).

545. What an extraordinary man this Paul was, but always equal to himself! Here he is half dead from the beating, from which he was rescued by the unexpected intervention of the Roman soldiers. Bruised and bleeding, he is carried bodily to a safe place outside the Temple of his God, which has become so unsafe for him. And instead of drawing breath and binding his wounds, he is concerned not so much over the material Temple from which he has just been dragged as for his countrymen whom he is leaving within, almost as if he were leaving behind him his own soul! What has he to say to these kinsmen who are shouting for his blood?

The tribune Lysias has mistaken him for the rebel Egyptian (§ 542). Paul for the moment tells him only that he is a Jew of Tarsus, without giving him what is for him much more important information (§ 547). Having obtained the permission, he speaks "in Hebrew," that is, in Aramaic. This was the everyday language in Palestine, and naturally as soon as the crowd heard the first words it fell silent, recognizing that Paul was of their race.

546. Paul's discourse to his would-be assassins was substantially an apologetical autobiography.

He tells them he is a Jew, born in Tarsus, educated in Jerusalem at the feet of Gamaliel, according to the strict acceptance of the Law of the fathers, and zealous for God just as they are. He has in the past persecuted the Christian faith, imprisoning its adherents, and the high priest and elders can bear witness to this. When he was sent by them to Damascus to extend the persecution there, he was converted (cf. § 267 ff.). Later, while he was praying in the Temple of Jerusalem, Jesus appeared to him in a vision, commanding him to go out of the city because his preaching would not be accepted there; and he told him he was sending him to distant peoples (§ 293; 22:1–21).

---

⁵ This flight of steps is mentioned by Flavius Josephus in his description of the Fortress Antonia (*Wars of the Jews*, V, 243).

At the statement that Jesus had sent him to the pagans, the multitude, which had been listening quietly, exploded once again. Whether they considered Jesus' apparition to Paul true or false, they could not admit that pagan peoples be judged worthy substitutes for the holy race of Israel, and their protest was expressed with the usual oriental histrionics. The mob shouted, waved their cloaks, and threw dust in the air. At this ugly turn of events, the tribune Lysias ordered the soldiers to take Paul into the barracks. Lysias had understood nothing of the discourse in Aramaic nor the shouting, and puzzled by this new outburst of violence, he thought it best to investigate. Paul had said he was not the Egyptian. Was he then some other revolutionary or troublemaker? Obviously; but what could he have done? And why were the Jews so furious with him? It was best to question the accused and get a confession from him. But to avoid wasting time with the evasions and lies usual with this type of prisoner, Lysias decided to get right on with the scourging. Cross-examinations to the tune of the whip went more quickly and were much more productive.

547. The soldiers carried out the tribune's orders under the supervision of a centurion, and began to prepare the accused for the scourging. But as they proceeded to strip him and bind him over a low pillar, "Paul said to the centurion who was standing by, 'Is it legal for you to scourge a Roman without a trial?'" The episode recalls the incident in Philippi (§ 393). The centurion was quick to realize the seriousness of the situation and suspended the proceedings. Hurrying to the tribune, he said, "What art thou about to do? This man is a Roman citizen!" He hastened to Paul himself and as if to make sure that what he had heard was correct, he asked him: "'Tell me, art thou a Roman?' And he said, 'Yes.' And the tribune answered, 'I obtained this citizenship at a great price.' And Paul said, 'But I am a citizen by birth.' At once therefore those who had been going to torture him left him; and the tribune himself was alarmed to find that Paul was a Roman citizen, and that he had bound him" (22:25–29).

It never entered the tribune's head that Paul might not be telling the truth. It would have been inconceivably reckless to claim Roman citizenship if he did not have it, and in the rare instances when the claim had been fraudulently made, the offenders had been punished by death (Suetonius, *Claud.*, 25). Rather, with a tinge of sadness perhaps, he thinks of the heavy sum he has paid for that precious citizenship. In fact, a short time before, in the reign of Claudius, there had been quite a bit of traffic in this matter and the price of citizenship had fluctuated like that of any commodity (Dion Cassius, LX, 17). Apparently Lysias has secured it when the price was very high, that is, when it first began to be sold, and he had paid dearly for it.[6] Certain that Paul enjoyed the

---

[6] His name indicates that the tribune Lysias was of Greek descent; he probably

rights of citizenship, the tribune was frightened even that he had ordered him bound.[7] In fact his whole conduct of the affair would have been another violation of Roman law if his orders had been carried out completely, since he had ordered the scourging at the beginning of the cross-examination, while the Emperor Augustus had decreed that a trial could not begin with torture (*Digest*, XLVIII, 18, 1).

548. With this worrisome fear knocking on his mind, poor Lysias did not sleep very well in the Fortress Antonia that night. He perhaps spent most of the time trying to puzzle a way out of the whole dangerous business. The fruit of his nocturnal pondering was the decision to implicate as many people as possible and leave the final outcome to others.

"The next day, as he wished to find out the real reason why he was accused by the Jews, he loosed him and ordered the priests and all the Sanhedrin to assemble; and taking Paul forth, he placed him in front of them" (Acts 22:30). And so the Sanhedrin is back on the scene just as it was in the trial of Jesus thirty years before,[8] and it is not impossible that at this time some of those present at Jesus' trial were still alive. If the tribune brought Paul before the supreme tribunal of the Jewish nation, it was not certainly to hand him over into their power. His primary purpose was to find out the exact nature of the charges the Jews were bringing against their countryman, who was a Roman citizen. Second, he wished to show some deference to the Sanhedrin. The charges could only be of a religious nature, and as such had no interest for the tribune however deeply they might interest the Sanhedrin. The Sanhedrin would appreciate this appeal to its prestige, and would be sure to protect the tribune if he had to give an account to his superiors for the irregularity of his conduct against a Roman citizen. In any event, the Sanhedrin would not have the last word in Paul's case, and even though he was referred to the supreme Jewish assembly, Paul was still covered by Roman authority and therefore was under the protection of the tribune.

549. When Paul stood up before the Sanhedrin — according to Luke's account (23:1) — he looked long and steadily at its members. Perhaps he recognized some and was looking for others with whom he had had contact twenty-two years before when the same body had given him the letters authorizing him to persecute the Christians of Damascus

---

added the Roman name Claudius because he had obtained his citizenship under this emperor.

[7] Bound, that is, for the scourging. Paul appears in chains several times afterward (i.e., Acts 26:29), but that was because he was under *custodia militaris*, that is, the custody in which an accused not yet judged was kept (§ 561), and this involved the wearing of chains.

[8] For a description of the Sanhedrin, its functions and relations with the Roman authorities, cf. *The Life of Christ*, p. 53 ff. (§ 57 ff.).

(§ 260). Then he began to speak, declaring first of all that his conscience was clear before God.

At this appeal to an invisible judge, when the defendant was supposed to justify himself before his visible judges, the high priest presiding over the session lost his temper and ordered those standing near the prisoner to strike Paul on the mouth. The high priest then in office was Ananias,[9] whom Paul could not know because he had been elected in the year 47. Or perhaps Paul heard the command but could not determine who had given it. As it echoed through the room, however, there occurred a little scene of great psychological significance.

"Then Paul said to him: 'God will strike thee, thou whitewashed wall. Dost thou sit there to try me by the Law, and in violation of the Law order me to be struck?' But the bystanders said, 'Dost thou insult God's high priest?' And Paul said, 'I did not know, brethren, that he was the high priest; for it is written, 'Thou shalt not speak evil of a ruler of thy people' [Exod. 22:28]" (Acts 23:3–5). The epithet "whitewashed wall" echoes the metaphor used by Ezechiel (13:10 ff.) with reference to the spiritual guides of the Jewish people. In alluding to this biblical passage Paul is speaking as a Jew to Jews and right afterward he purposely quotes another, but the expression "whitened sepulchres" as used by Jesus would have struck no note of recognition in that audience.

550. A comparison of this episode with the trial of Jesus[10] is inevitable. Then the high priest, Annas, grew angry and a zealous servant obligingly struck Jesus for him, while the Lord, with divine serenity, asked him to show how he had offended him. Here the high priest Ananias also loses his temper and orders Paul to be struck. In all probability the order was not carried out, yet Paul's reaction was not exactly a gentle one.

Some have said Paul's reaction was justified, both because the act was illegal and because he had to defend his dignity as a Roman citizen before the tribune, as well as for other reasons. Others have seen in his reply the prediction of the death of Ananias who was later assassinated by his own countrymen. These are all valid observations and deserve to be noted, but in the last analysis, the best comment seems that of Jerome: "Where is that patience of the Savior, who, led as a lamb to the slaughter, did not open his lips; rather he replied with all sweetness to the one who had struck him? We do not belittle the Apostle, no, but we point out the glory of the Lord, who, while suffering in the flesh,

---

[9] For this Ananias, cf. *Storia d'Israele*, pp. 462, 467, 473 (§§ 408, 409, 416, 422). Flavius Josephus (*Antiquities of the Jews*, XX, 205 ff.) describes him as an avaricious and violent man. He was deposed in 59 and was assassinated by the Zealot-*Sicarii* in 66 (*Wars of the Jews*, II, 429, 441).

[10] Cf. *The Life of Christ*, p. 595 ff. (§ 563).

overcomes all insult and frailty of the flesh" (*C. Pelagianos*, III, 4; in Migne, *Patr. Lat.*, 23, 600).

551. Paul's "humanity" is quite evident immediately afterward. The answer he had given the high priest had exasperated the entire assembly. To break that compact hatred he had to break the spiritual unity of his auditors, setting one side against the other. And Paul shrewdly slit the seam that bound the two factions together.

We know that the seventy-one members of the Sanhedrin might be either Sadducees or Pharisees[11] and that the two groups were in complete disagreement.[12] When he began to speak again, therefore, he declared that he was a Pharisee, the son of Pharisees, and that he had been persecuted because of his hope in the Messias and in the resurrection of the dead. These were two of the doctrinal questions on which the factions disagreed. In that explosive gathering, Paul's words touched off the fuse. There immediately arose one of the usual interminable disputes between Sadducees and Pharisees, and the original purpose of the meeting was forgotten.

Was Paul's statement true? In reality, even as a Christian, he continues to call himself a Pharisee (Phil. 3:5) when he refers to his past, and it is perhaps with this same autobiographical intent that he makes the statement now. Had he really been arrested because of his views on these two points of doctrine? From his viewpoint, yes. He was being persecuted as the Apostle of the Gospel, that is, as one who had placed his hope in the Messias Jesus and believed in the resurrection of the dead. If the non-Christian Pharisees were awaiting another future Messias, that was their affair. There was some element of common doctrine between Paul and the Pharisees. And Paul's shrewd perception shows that those who have truly been caught up to the third heaven as he had been still retain a very acute vision of the realities of this world.

552. The dispute Paul had provoked became quite violent. Some of the Pharisaic scribes were shouting that there was nothing blameworthy in Paul, while their adversaries shouted the contrary just as loudly and threatened to attack the defendant. The tribune, who was watching the brawl and was responsible for the safety of his Roman citizen, "fearing lest Paul should be torn to pieces by them, ordered the soldiers to come down and take him by force from among them and bring him into the barracks" (Acts 23:10).

This humiliating human scene was followed immediately by another of divine consolation. "But the following night the Lord stood by him and said, 'Be steadfast, for just as thou hast borne witness to me in Jerusalem, thou must bear witness in Rome also'" (*ibid.*, 11). It was a divine confirmation of his old plan to go to Rome (§ 512).

---

[11] Cf. *ibid.*, p. 53 (§ 58).
[12] *Ibid.*, p. 29 ff. (§ 28 ff.).

553. And so the Jews who had been stalking Paul lost their quarry. But it would not have been the time of the Zealot-*Sicarii* if his persecutors had given up their game so easily. To realize the incredible obstinacy of those people, it is enough to recall what they did a few years later in the war against the Romans. Learning that their previous plan had failed, they made another the next day which had all the aspects of a regular conspiracy, though of a religious nature. More than forty of them gathered together and swore under pain of a curse invoked on themselves not to eat or drink until they had killed Paul. Then they went to the high priest and the elders — that is, the members of the Sanhedrin who were not Pharisees and so were hostile to Paul — and begged them to ask the tribune to bring Paul before the assembly again as if they wished to question him further. The conspirators would see to it that he was killed on the way. But they were too excited to maintain the necessary secrecy. One of them talked too much and news of the plot finally reached a nephew of Paul who was in Jerusalem (§ 229).

The young man rushed to the Antonia to warn his uncle, who was given courteous treatment by the tribune and so could receive his young relative and speak freely with him. When he heard what was brewing, "Paul called one of the centurions to him and said, 'Take this young man to the tribune, for he has something to report to him.' So he took him and brought him to the tribune and said, 'The prisoner Paul called me and asked me to bring this young man to thee, for he has something to say to thee.' So the tribune took him by the hand, and going aside with him asked him, 'What is it that thou hast to tell me?' " (*Ibid.*, 17–19.)

554. When the tribune heard what Paul's nephew had to say, he sent him off, charging him not to tell anyone. He now understood the situation more clearly and decided it was time for the second step in his plan, namely, to pass the responsibility of the final decision on to someone else (§ 548).

An experienced soldier, used to the "imperium," he called two centurions and issued orders: "Get ready . . . two hundred soldiers to go as far as Caesarea. . . ." But perhaps two hundred would not be enough against the aroused Zealot-*Sicarii* prowling about the countryside. The soldiers would be on foot. They would need reinforcements that could move more swiftly. And so he added: ". . . and seventy cavalry and two hundred spearmen." At what hour should they leave? "The third hour of the night," or about nine in the evening. If the secret were kept and they left at night there would be less chance of disturbances. And finally, a thought for the prisoner: "and provide beasts to mount Paul and take him in safety to Felix the governor" (*ibid.*, 23–24).

These orders seemed to take care of everything, and Lysias felt a little easier. The escort of 470 men as far as Caesarea might seem a bit excessive, but at the time it was better to be overprepared. The important thing was for Paul to arrive safely in Caesarea. After that, the procurator could take care of the matter. Lysias had had enough trouble in this whole thorny business. It was also to be hoped that the consideration he had shown Paul, in providing horses for him and his guard, would persuade that Roman citizen not to complain to the procurator that he had been chained and almost scourged at the very beginning of his questioning (§ 547).

555. All that was needed now was the letter or *elogium* Roman law required a magistrate to send to a higher authority when he referred a prisoner to him. The letter contained a description of the case and usually the magistrate's personal opinion. The tribune's *elogium* on Paul to Felix was as follows:

"Claudius Lysias to His Excellency Felix the governor, greeting. Whereas this man had been seized by the Jews and was on the point of being killed by them, I came on them with the troops and rescued him, having learnt that he was a Roman. And wishing to know what charge they had preferred against him, I took him down into their Sanhedrin. I found him accused about questions of their Law, but not of any crime deserving of death or imprisonment. And when I was told of an ambush which they had prepared for him, I sent him to thee, directing his accusers also to state the case before thee. Farewell" (*ibid.*, 25–30).

This document, which has all the marks of authenticity, slants the facts a bit in Lysias' favor. He did not come to Paul's rescue having

Antipatris (Ras-el-Ain): Arab Castle on the Little Mound Which Covers the Roman Ruins

learned that he was a Roman citizen. He learned that later when he had already saved him. Nor does he make any mention of binding Paul or ordering him scourged, but the reasons are obvious. The slight distortion of truth is to make a good impression on his superior; the two omissions are to avoid making a very bad one.

556. The journey was accomplished without incident. The first part was made by a forced march mostly at night, and the first stop was at Antipatris, the modern Ras-el-Ain, about forty miles from Jerusalem, where there was practically no reason to fear attacks from the conspirators.[13] Here, however, the foot soldiers left the escort and only the

cavalry continued with Paul the next day. When they arrived in Caesarea, both the prisoner and *elogium* were consigned to the procurator Felix. The latter asked Paul what province he was from and, upon being told Cilicia, he stated he would hear him when his accusers had arrived. Meanwhile, he ordered him to be guarded in "Herod's palace" (*ibid.*, 35).

557. This "palace" was the royal one Herod the Great had erected when he completely rebuilt the city of Caesarea, a project which took some twelve years. It was now called a "praetorium" because

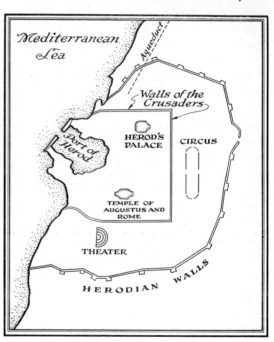

Map of the Ruins of Caesarea of Palestine

the highest Roman magistrate of Judea resided there, it being the custom of Roman officials to take up their headquarters in the royal palaces in the regions subjugated (cf. Cicero, *In Verrem*, IV, 5, 30). The building was quite sumptuous, of Hellenist and utterly pagan inspiration. King Herod Agrippa I had even adorned its rooms with statues of his own daughters, thereby violating a well-known Hebrew prohibition. But when he died in 44 (Acts 12:18–23), the populace invaded the palace, knocked down the statues and dragged them to a brothel, defiling them

---

[13] It was also at Antipatris that the Jews in revolt stopped pursuing the Roman army of Cestius Gallus, which they had routed at Beth-horon (*Wars of the Jews*, II, 554) at the beginning of the war in 66.

obscenely (Flavius Josephus, *Antiquities of the Jews,* XIX, 343–359). The palace had prison cells and rooms for more or less rigorous detention, as befitted the dwelling of an oriental ruler. In one of these rooms, Paul awaited the outcome of this adventure, never imagining certainly that his wait would be so prolonged.

We have nothing to add to what we have already said about Antonius Felix.[14] We might recall, however, Tacitus' statement that he "exercised his royal power with the spirit of a slave, having recourse to every cruelty and lust" (*Hist.,* V, 9).

558. Five days later the plaintiffs arrived from Jerusalem, the high priest Ananias, several elders of the Sanhedrin, and a certain Tertullus, a lawyer who was to plead the charges against Paul. Felix received them, called the accused before him, and opened the discussion of the case.

Tertullus began his harangue with the usual *captatio benevolentiae* addressed to the procurator. Thanks to his foresight and his excellent administration, the Jewish nation lived in great peace. But now, this pest of a man Paul had come to disturb that peace, "a promoter of seditions among all the Jews throughout the world, and a ringleader (πρωτοστάτην) of . . . the Nazarene sect." He had even tried to desecrate the Temple but he had been caught by the Jews. It was enough to question the accused himself; his answers could not help but confirm the charges (Acts 24:2–8). Naturally the claque the high priest had brought with him vigorously seconded the attorney's accusations.

559. The prisoner was then allowed to speak. Paul defended himself with a simple appeal to the very evident facts, not without a reference to the doctrinal matter he had brought up before Lysias and the Sanhedrin.

---

[14] Cf. *Storia d'Israele,* II, p. 463 ff. (§ 410 ff.).

Caesarea of Palestine — the Northern End of the Harbor

He spoke confidently, knowing that Felix had been ruling the nation for many years and was familiar with similar questions. Not more than twelve days before, Paul said, he had gone up to Jerusalem to worship in the Temple, but no one had found him disputing there nor gathering crowds about him in the synagogues or through the city. His adversaries could not prove his words untrue. He admitted that "according to the Way, which they call a sect," he adored the God of his fathers, believing all that was written in the Law and the prophets and sharing the same hope which they affirmed, namely, that there will be the resurrection of the dead, both the just and the unjust. And for this reason he was careful to keep his conscience blameless before God and man. After many years of absence he had returned to Jerusalem to bring material help to his countrymen and make his offerings in the Temple. On that occasion, some Jews of the province of Asia found him in the Temple, purified, and with no crowd about him or disturbance of any kind. They were the ones who should have come to prove their charges, but they were not present. Well, let those who did come state what guilt they found in him when he was brought before the Sanhedrin, unless it be guilt to declare aloud, as he had done, that he was being judged because of his belief in the resurrection of the dead (*ibid.*, 10–21).

560. Felix attached the same importance to Paul's words as he did to Tertullus'. He knew very well that Tertullus' little speech about the deep peace Judea enjoyed under his rule could be taken seriously only as fine irony. But in the procurator's mind the servility of Tertullus and Paul's fancies on the resurrection of the dead were in the same category. Since, however, there seemed to be people who spoke like the attorney and had illusions like the Apostle, it was up to him to see how shrewdly he could exploit the situation to his own advantage. Evidently these particular Jews were baneful charlatans and Paul a deluded fanatic. But he must avoid antagonizing the Jewish bigwigs by acquitting Paul immediately, and at the same time he must make sure whether or not the prisoner had a large crowd of admirers or disciples ready to support his cause. For all his strangeness, Paul was something of an interesting fellow, and conversing with him would help to while away the boredom of the idle hours in Caesarea. So he postponed judgment.

The excuse for the postponement was, of course, bureaucratic. When the discussion was over, the procurator arose and, shrugging his shoulders regretfully, he said, "When Lysias the tribune, comes down, I will decide your case" (*ibid.*, 22). Then he ordered the centurion to keep Paul under guard but to allow him some liberty and not prevent any of his friends from rendering him assistance.

561. This type of custody was called *custodia militaris,* or "military custody." It was much more lenient than the *custodia publica,* or "public custody," which meant confinement in the common prison, such as Paul

had undergone in Philippi (§ 389). Under *custodia militaris*, the prisoner usually resided in a fortress or other guarded place, which was, however, quite comfortable. A chain was fastened to his wrist and to that of the soldier guarding him. "The same chain joins the prisoner and the soldier," says Seneca (*Epist.*, 5, 7). This *custodia militaris* might eventually be relaxed in many ways. For example, the prisoner might be allowed to rent a house or other living quarters, go about visiting his friends, or even remove the chain while indoors. In such cases, the

custodia militaris resembled the *custodia libera,* or "free custody," which was the most lenient, permitting the prisoner to live in the home of some person of authority who, by making a formal pledge or posting bail, guaranteed the prisoner's presence.

Paul, after years of strenuous activity and discomfort in foreign lands, was now forced to almost comfortable inactivity in Israel itself, and this was to last two whole years. What of his trip to Rome? On this score Paul had no doubt. His journey to Rome had been confirmed by his recent vision of Jesus (§ 552), and he was serenely unworried. Cer-

Barbarian Chained to the Wrist of a Roman Soldier: Arch of Septimius Severus — Rome

tainly from a purely human viewpoint the journey seemed now more unlikely and improbable than ever, but from this very human improbability he drew his sense of confidence and certainty, for he recognized in it the paradox of the Sermon on the Mount (§ 405).

562. A few days later Felix summoned Paul to a private and unofficial conversation. This time the procurator's wife Drusilla was with him. Felix had the mania of most plebeians who attain power for marrying into the noblest families. During his lifetime he was "the husband of three queens," as Suetonius calls him.[15] Drusilla, of the family of the Herods, a daughter of Agrippa I, was his third wife, while Felix was

[15] *Ibid.,* II, p. 463 (§ 410).

her second husband. Her first had been Azizus, King of Emesa, who had become a Jew to marry her. But after two years of marriage (in the year 54) his little fifteen-year-old bride left him for Felix, a pagan in religion and a freedman by birth. This laxity of conduct, characteristic of the Herodian family, did not prevent Drusilla from considering herself Jewish, however. At that time, in fact, it was a kind of fad with noble Jewish ladies to interest themselves in the historical and philosophical aspects of religion, as an intellectual exercise and not as an occasion for changing their spiritual loyalties. It is quite possible, therefore, that Drusilla herself had asked to meet Paul, being curious to know this "rebel" against her religion about whom she had heard so much.

We are not given the details of the conversation, but it was obviously a long one and to a certain degree effective. According to Luke, Felix heard what Paul "had to say about the faith in Christ Jesus. But as he talked of justice and chastity and the judgment to come, Felix became alarmed and answered, 'For the present go thy way; but when I get an opportunity I will send for thee'" (Acts 24:25).

Here was Paul speaking of chastity (ἐγκρατείας) to these two who hardly knew the word. It is true Paul followed his discussion of justice and chastity with the judgment to come as a sanction on those who had not practiced these virtues. But it was this very idea of a judgment, perhaps a new concept for his two listeners, which disturbed their guilty consciences and irritated them. If Felix did as Paul preached, he would have to give up the plunder of his subjects and his possession of another man's wife; on this there could be no discussion. And he preferred the plunder and the wife to Paul's teachings: "For the present go thy way. . . ."

563. In fact, this odd preacher might provide a tidy profit for Felix. He might be of a wealthy family, or quite rich from the offerings and donations of his disciples. Had he not just brought large sums of money to Jerusalem to help his coreligionists? And among his innumerable disciples in various regions, there were bound to be many wealthy followers ready to open their purses for him now that he was in prison, and even perhaps to offer considerable sums to purchase his freedom. This was an excellent prospect for Felix and infinitely more attractive than the justice and continence and future judgment preached by his prisoner. This was the game to play, but shrewdly, without showing his hand, and concealing the true reason for this interest in philosophical-religious discussions. This is what Luke tells us: "At the same time he was hoping that money would be given him by Paul, and for this reason he would send for him often and talk with him" (*ibid.*, 26).

It did not take Paul long to understand this little game, but though he probably had no money and certainly had no intention of buying the

Caesarea of Palestine — Medieval Walls of the Harbor
(Built With Ancient Columns)

governor in any case, neither could he refuse to waste his time in conversation with him. But what a humiliation this must have been for one of Paul's proud and fiery temperament. Instead of instructing honest slaves who hungered and thirsted after justice, he was forced to fence with this togaed scoundrel whose hunger was for gold and whose thirst was for pleasure. The persecutions he had endured in Asia Minor, Macedonia, and Greece had been physically much more difficult, yet they had not carried with them the subtle torment of this humiliation. Yet Christ asked this trial of his Apostle, too, as a prerequisite for his going to Rome. Paul understood and endured it for long months.

564. "But after two years Felix was succeeded by Porcius Festus; and as he wanted to ingratiate himself with the Jews, Felix left Paul in prison" (*ibid.*, 27). The procurator was changed toward the middle of the year 60 (§ 160). His decision to leave Paul in prison must have been due either to the fact that he had not obtained the money he had hoped from Paul, or to a desire to lessen somewhat the resentment of his subjects, which might find expression in a package of accusations sent to Rome just as he returned to the capital to give an account of his governorship.

A few codices add a third reason, namely, "because of Drusilla." The phrase parallels that in *Mark* (6:17) "because of Herodias," in the account of the death of John the Baptist. It suggests that Drusilla, irritated by Paul's discourses on continence and the future judgment, took her revenge by demanding — not the death of her censor as Herodias had done — but at least his continued imprisonment. This is quite possible, although the evidence for it is not sufficient.

Caesarea of Palestine — Ruins of Ancient Columns in the Harbor

565. Paul's two years in Caesarea, however, were not wholly inactive. He was allowed to receive visitors when he chose, and this permitted both his disciples to help him and Paul himself to maintain contact with Judea and the communities he had founded in the Mediterranean basin. Besides being the residence of the governor, Caesarea was practically the only harbor in Judea, and from it one could correspond with every point along the Mediterranean. This was most convenient for Paul.

The news of his imprisonment must have soon reached Corinth, Macedonia, Ephesus; and from Ephesus it probably spread to the interior of Asia Minor. It seems logical to suppose that from one or another of these various communities, disciples set out to visit their beloved Master and even to bring him financial aid. The good Lydia, for instance, the owner of the dyeing sheds in Philippi, who had already helped Paul financially (§ 383), might conceivably have sent a comfortable little sum with her greetings to cheer the prisoner. We may imagine Paul's joy when one of these visitors arrived, or how he anxiously asked one from Galatia if those big children there had finally given up the idea that they had to be circumcised (§ 504 ff.), and a visitor from Corinth if the community there had forgotten its mania for factions (§ 475). This is all pure conjecture, of course, but it seems legitimate.

566. It also seems legitimate to make similar conjectures about his writings. It would have been quite natural for Paul to give visitors from far-off communities a letter for the faithful or a note for some one individual. But we have no positive information on this score, since the extant epistles written in prison were composed in Rome (§ 613 ff.), not here or in Ephesus (§ 472).

We do not know whether the faithful Luke took up residence in Caesarea to be with the prisoner, but it would seem more likely that he made frequent visits there instead. It is certain, however, that as soon as the prisoner's departure from Caesarea was decided upon, Luke was with him and ready to accompany him on the voyage, the narrative of which is again in the first person plural (27:1 ff.), indicating the author was an eyewitness. It is also very probable that in these frequent trips to Caesarea and its surroundings Luke made the most of every opportunity to gather from the various persons and places he visited in Judea the material for his great historical work, which constitutes the Third Gospel and the *Acts* (§ 95 ff.) and to which he gave final form later in Rome.

This historical summary might even have been undertaken at the suggestion of Paul, who perhaps saw the value of such a work as he sat in solitary meditation in the praetorium of Caesarea. If Paul did prompt it, then he undoubtedly advised the author and made many suggestions to render the writing adequate and worthy. It is not surprising that a work born under such patronage should bear a certain imprint of the patron (§ 100). Of the New Testament authors, Luke is certainly the one closest to Paul in letter and in concept, as we have already pointed out,[16] so much so that Tertullian declared: "They are accustomed to ascribe to Paul the digest of Luke" (*Adv. Marcion.,* IV, 5).

567. Porcius Festus, who succeeded Felix as procurator, was a good magistrate but did not accomplish all he could have because he was overtaken by an untimely death while still in office.[17] Three days after his arrival in Caesarea, he went up to Jerusalem, the most difficult city in his entire jurisdiction. The Jewish elders immediately appeared before him to present their compliments and also their most urgent requests. First among these was the question of Paul.

That unsavory character had been in Caesarea for two years awaiting sentence, and this must inevitably be a conviction. Would the procurator please be kind enough to delay no longer the penalty which he so richly deserved and which all the Jews had been so anxiously awaiting? Would he have the accused come to Jerusalem? The Sanhedrin would be convoked immediately and would settle this interminable and disgraceful affair in one session. In that way the new governor would inaugurate his term of office with a measure utterly pleasing to the people and he would win the gratitude of the whole nation.

This, substantially, must have been the elders' approach to Festus. In reality, they had gone much further among themselves, having re-

---

[16] Cf. *The Life of Christ,* p. 118 (§ 138).
[17] Cf. *Storia d'Israele,* II, p. 466 (§ 414).

vived their two-year-old plan to ambush Paul and kill him on the way from Caesarea to Jerusalem.

568. Festus' reply was a pure and simple appeal to the law. Paul was in Caesarea, where he himself was returning shortly. The case had been referred to the tribunal in Caesarea and therefore there was no need to transfer the prisoner back to Jerusalem. If the elders had charges to make, they could come as plaintiffs to the court in Caesarea. That was all. But he was making no concessions contrary to the law merely to ingratiate the populace.

After about ten days, Festus returned to Caesarea and the day afterward he held court to judge Paul's case. The Jews, who had come from Jerusalem, immediately deposed a number of serious charges, which they could not prove. From Paul's reply, that he had committed no crime "neither against the law of the Jews nor against the temple nor against Caesar" (25:8), we gather that the accusations fell under these three headings. Only the last, touching Caesar, was within the direct competence of the procurator. The other two came under the jurisdiction of the religious-judicial authorities of the nation, which even under Roman administration continued to function freely, although under the supervision of the latter.

It was, therefore, a case of mixed jurisdiction, which had to be handled with prudence, possibly by arriving at some mutual agreement. Festus, as a man of the law and a prudent governor, tried to find a middle course which would respect both the rights of his tribunal and the prisoner and the sensitivities of the Jews. He turned to Paul and said: "Art thou willing to go up to Jerusalem and be tried there before me on these charges?

"But Paul said, 'I am standing at the tribunal of Caesar; there I ought to be tried. To Jews I have done no wrong, as thou thyself very well knowest. For if I have done any wrong or committed a crime deserving of death, I do not refuse to die. But if there is no ground to their charges against me, no one can give me up to them; I appeal to Caesar.' "

569. The solemn formula had been pronounced: *Caesarem appello.* When a Roman citizen, in whatever region or before whatever court of the empire, uttered this formula, all the jurisdictions depending on the imperial court were automatically annulled for him. The Roman citizen had invoked the supreme jurisdiction of the emperor, his natural chief and governor, and consequently the other governors appointed by the emperor had to withdraw before that appeal and send the prisoner to Rome (except in very special and very rare cases). Even if the trial was about to be finished, as soon as the appeal was made everything stopped and the accused was transferred to Rome. He could neither be convicted nor acquitted by a lower court.

In Paul's case also the formula produced the magic effect: "Then

Festus, after conferring with the council, answered, 'Thou hast appealed to Caesar; to Caesar thou shalt go'" (*ibid.*, 9–12). The brief conference with the councilors, who assisted at the trial and were usually young men starting their careers in the administration, was a simple formality. After Paul's appeal, Festus could do nothing but send him to Rome. As procurator he had no further jurisdiction over him.

570. If in Jesus' trial Pontius Pilate had wrongly washed his hands, Porcius Festus could rub his happily for having extricated himself from the affair without wronging anyone. Those who bit their hands, at least metaphorically, were the plaintiffs, who thus saw their prey escape them. They could, it is true, follow the accused to the court of the emperor, but Rome was not Caesarea and besides it was much farther away. To strike at Paul, was it really worth the trouble to undertake such a long voyage at such tremendous expense and to disturb the powerful but costly protectors the Jews had on the Palatine? It was hardly possible to become involved to that extent. When Paul's trial was begun in Rome, it is probable that none of his accusers from Judea were present (§ 603).

Paul was now sure of going to Rome. When he had thought of this journey in the past, he had hardly imagined he would make it in these circumstances. But on thinking it over, everything could be explained by the phrase he himself had written to the Romans three years before: "Now we know that for those who love God all things work together unto good" (Rom. 8:28). All had been prearranged by God, for the good of him who loved God.

571. Before the journey began, there occurred by chance a little incident to distract the waiting time. There came to Caesarea to greet the new procurator, "King Agrippa and Bernice" (Acts 25:13), with whom we are already well acquainted.[18] Both were children of Agrippa I (§§ 557, 562), and the incestuous relationship between them was the subject of scornful gossip even in Rome. The brother, Agrippa II, was a cultured man, who took an interest in Jewish religious questions. The rabbinical writings record several cases of the Law which he proposed. But his was a purely intellectual learning, and it had no influence whatever on his life. He himself was a skeptic and yielded supinely to the wicked domination of his sister. Bernice had had a couple of legal husbands, perhaps three, to which she added not only her incestuous liaison with her brother, but a more notorious affair with Titus, begun during the Jewish wars in 69 and continued later in Rome. She was, then, a worthy sister of Drusilla, the wife of Antonius Felix (§ 562), and surpassed her in dissoluteness.

Paul's presentation to these two personages came about quite naturally. They stayed in Caesarea several days, in the course of which

---

18 Cf. *ibid.*, p. 455 ff. (§ 400 ff.).

Festus spoke to them of Paul's case. He had inherited a prisoner from Felix and he had been unable to make up his mind about him. The elders of Jerusalem asked for his conviction, but he had told them Roman law did not permit a conviction without a regular trial. When this began, in Caesarea, the plaintiffs had neither charged nor proved that the prisoner had committed a real crime. All they had against him were "certain questions about their own religion [literally 'superstition': δεισιδαιμονίας] and about a certain Jesus, who had died, but who Paul affirmed was alive." He had asked him if he wished to go to Jerusalem but the prisoner appealed to Caesar, to whom, therefore, he had to send him (25:14–21). A case like this naturally interested Agrippa, who had probably heard of Paul, as he undoubtedly had heard of Jesus and of early Christianity (cf. 26:26). And so he said to Festus: "I myself also could have wished to hear the man."

"Tomorrow," said Festus, "thou shalt hear him" (*ibid.*, 22).

572. Particular solemnity was given the occasion next day, which was, more than anything else, a kind of entertainment for the illustrious guests, a diversion from the monotonous life of the province. With great pomp, Agrippa and Bernice entered the audience hall, which was filled with tribunes and prominent persons of the city. And then Paul was brought in, still chained.

The procurator considered it appropriate to speak a few words of introduction. This was the man whose death the Jews had several times demanded, but Festus found he had committed no deed deserving the death penalty. But the accused had appealed to the emperor and so he was being sent to Rome. Festus, however, was wondering what to put in the *elogium* (§ 555) which was to present the prisoner's case to the emperor. Perhaps his guests could suggest what he should write (*ibid.*, 24–27). Immediately afterward Agrippa, to whom the procurator had given the honor of presiding, asked Paul to speak.

This discourse, the last of the great discourses in the *Acts*, closely resembles Paul's discourse to the Jews rioting in the Temple (§ 546); that is, it is substantially an apologia of his life, adapted somewhat here to his different audience. The latter is represented primarily by Agrippa, who also was a Jew, while Festus and the other pagans are in the second row, so to speak.

573. Paul says he considers himself fortunate to be able to speak before King Agrippa, because he knows he is well versed in Jewish customs and controversies. The events of Paul's life are known to all the Jews. He has lived as a Pharisee, and he is now brought to trial because of his hope in the promises made by God to their ancestors, the fulfillment of which is awaited by all the twelve tribes. And is it incredible, perhaps, that God should raise the dead? At first he had thought it his duty to take action against the name of Jesus of Nazareth. Consequently he had imprisoned many in Jerusalem and had cast his vote for many others to be killed (§ 255), and he had extended the persecution even beyond the city. On his way to Damascus, he had been converted (cf. § 267 ff.). After that he had obeyed the divine injunctions received at his conversion, and he had preached in Damascus, Jerusalem, Judea, and to the Gentiles, exhorting them to repent and be converted to God. For this reason the Jews captured him in the Temple and wished to kill him. But he, with the grace of God, will continue to testify to both high and low, teaching nothing that had not been foretold by Moses and the prophets, who had affirmed that the Messias was to suffer and, as the first to rise from the dead, was to proclaim the light to the people of Israel and to the Gentiles (26:2–23).

574. When he heard Paul mention the resurrection, the amiable Festus, who had listened up to this point without too much interest, unconsciously imitated the Areopagites (§ 414). He interrupted the speaker, saying with a loud voice: "Paul, thou art mad; thy great learning is driving thee to madness."

"I am not mad, excellent Festus," said Paul, "but I speak words of sober truth. For the king knows about these things and to him also I speak without hesitation. For I am sure that none of these things escaped him; for none of them happened in a corner.[19] Dost thou believe the prophets, King Agrippa? I know that thou dost."

And Agrippa said to Paul: "In a short while (ἐν ὀλίγῳ) thou wouldst persuade me to become a Christian!" (Acts 26:24–28.)

As Festus' exclamation was one of good-natured teasing, Agrippa's reply is that of an elegant and courteous skeptic. He does not seem to mean that he was deeply impressed, so that "in a short while" or with a little more effort, he could be converted. His remark seems rather intended to disabuse Paul of the idea that he could convert him. Today he might have exclaimed: "Look out, or next you will be converting me."

575. Paul patiently returns the phrase: "I would to God that, whether it be long or short, not only thou but also all who hear me today might become such as I am, except for these chains" (*ibid.*, 29). And his chain jingles as he lifts his hands in a final gesture.

Agrippa, Festus, and the others rise and gradually leave the room, exchanging their impressions: this Paul is a dreamer; he is in the clouds, all right, but he has done nothing that deserves imprisonment or death. Agrippa, the guest of honor, expresses his thought in a few words, for the procurator had shortly before attributed a great deal of importance to his opinion: "This man might have been set at liberty, if he had not appealed to Caesar" (*ibid.*, 32).

---

[19] An allusion to Jesus and the rise of early Christianity, which were notorious throughout Palestine.

He might have been set at liberty from the legal viewpoint, but not from the viewpoint of providence. If Paul had been released, any incident, followed by others one after the other, could have kept him in the East for an indefinite period and he might never have reached Rome. Providence, however, had decreed that he go to Rome and that he go there precisely because he was a Roman citizen.

The Voyage to Rome
Shipwreck at Malta

576. "When it was decided, then, that we should sail for Italy, they consigned Paul with some other prisoners to the care of a centurion named Julius, of the Augustan regiment" (Acts 27:1). With these words, Luke begins his long account of Paul's journey and arrival in Rome, which takes us to the end of the book (§ 115 ff.). The description of the sea voyage is very detailed and reveals not only Luke, the eyewitness, but also Luke, the man of culture and attentive observer. Rich in nautical terms, this description was judged by Mommsen and other eminent historians as one of the most important documents on Greco-Roman navigation, and modern nautical experts who have carefully examined both its historical and technical aspects judge it an excellent piece of work.[1] It is said that Nelson reread this passage from the *Acts* on the morning of Trafalgar.

In 64, four years after Paul's voyage, Flavius Josephus made a similar journey and he, too, was shipwrecked. Of the 600 passengers on board, he was among the eighty who were saved. His account of it, however, takes only a few lines (*Life,* 14–16).

577. The centurion Julius, to whose custody Paul was assigned, proved during the voyage to be a man of fine sentiments and he showed Paul special courtesy. We do not know which cohort is meant by the "Augustan cohort" or "cohort Sebastena," to which we are told he belonged. It may have been one of the five cohorts then permanently garrisoned in Judea, but it is also possible that it was a cohort of the praetorian guard in Rome and that Julius was sent with a detachment as an escort of honor for Porcius Festus when he came to the province. In that case, since the detachment had to return to Rome, Festus might have taken this occasion to entrust Paul and the other prisoners to the centurion.

---

[1] Cf., among others, J. Smith, *The Voyage and Shipwreck of St. Paul,* London, 1886; A. Breusing, *Die Nautik der Alten,* Bremen, 1886, pp. 142–205; W. Stammler, *Apostelgeschichte 27 in Nautischer Beleuchtung u. die ostdeutsche Bibelübers. des Mittelalters,* Berlin, 1931; U. and A. Cesarano, *Verso Roma con l'Apostolo delle genti,* Verona, 1932.

The latter may have been common criminals, destined for the wild beasts in the circuses of Rome.

It was late summer in the year 60, and it was necessary to make haste. Sailing in the Mediterranean was considered dangerous as early as the middle of September. After the first ten days of November navigation normally ceased altogether until the first of March, when, with the beginning of spring, the "Favonian" or westerly winds began to blow. However, there were some exceptions in this period of the "closed sea," as the ancients called it. The first to defy the wintry season had been the pirates, according to Pliny (*Nat. hist.*, II, 47), who observes that in his day the avaricious followed their example. Herod the Great, anxious to save his throne, had also embarked at Alexandria for Rome in the middle of winter in 40 B.C. and had run into serious danger off Pamphylia, though he arrived safely

The Centurion M. Favonius Facile of the XX Legion: Tomb — First Century

at his journey's end (Flavius Josephus, *Wars of the Jews*, I, 279–281).

For want of something better, Julius took a ship at Adramyttium, a Mysian harbor just below Troas (§ 17),[2] which sailed from Caesarea for its home port along the coast of Asia Minor. When the prisoners embarked Luke and Aristarchus of Thessalonica went with Paul (§ 469). These two boarded the ship either as private passengers — since it was a commercial vessel — or more probably they were admitted aboard through the kindness of the centurion, who pretended they were Paul's slaves, for the law permitted that a prisoner who was a Roman citizen might be attended by a pair of slaves.

578. The day after their departure, they docked at Sidon, and here Julius permitted Paul to go on land and visit the brethren of the local community. From Sidon the ship sailed in a northerly direction and, because of the wind from the west, passed under the lee of Cyprus, thereby

---

[2] The Vulgate mistakenly has *navem Adrumetinam,* which means a ship from Adrumetum, a harbor in the province of Africa, just below Carthage.

staying partially within the shelter of the island. When they reached Myra, a harbor of Lycia (§ 11),[3] the centurion transferred his prisoners to a ship from Alexandria which was bound for Italy and they set sail once more.

The new boat was a *navis oneraria* used to transport wheat from Egypt to Rome. It was broad and squat, like all ships of that type, with a tall mast in the center of the hull and a smaller one toward the prow. It could stow about 300 tons or perhaps a little more. Since it was carrying a full cargo and extra passengers, it made very very slow progress against a contrary wind. Hence it took "many days" to arrive off Cnidus, which lay on the southwestern point of Asia Minor opposite Rhodes, although the journey from Myra normally took one day. To find an easier course, the pilot came left toward the south, intending to skirt the southern lee shore of Crete. Having rounded Salmone, the eastern promontory of Crete, which is also mentioned by Strabo (II, 4, 3), they advanced along the southern coast of the island and managed, not without difficulty, to enter a bay called Fair Havens near the town of Lasaea (Thalassa).

Roman Ship. Rome: Museo Torlonia
(Alinari)

579. At Fair Havens they were safe since it was a small oval-shaped bay well sheltered from the sea, but it was not a very suitable place for a long stay. An observation of Luke helps us to evaluate their situation. He says, "much time had been spent and navigation was now unsafe, for the Fast was already over" (27:9). This Fast was Yom Kippur, or the Day of Atonement, on which the Jews were obliged to fast. Since this holy day fell on the tenth day of the month Tishri, it was now about the end of September and the beginning of October, the time when navigation practically ceased and after which it was a serious risk to put out to sea.

The ship's navigators knew this very well but they had a plan which did not seem too hazardous to them. A little farther west on the same southern shore of Crete, there was another harbor called Phoenix, which was much more comfortable and more suitable for wintering than Fair

---

[3] We do not know why the Vulgate reads *Lystra* here instead of *Myra*. We know of no harbor of that name in the region.

Havens. The distance between the two ports was 40 nautical miles and could be covered in a little over a day with any kind of favorable wind. To make this run, which was not reckless, would permit them to unload and store the cargo for the winter, while this was too difficult in Fair Havens. Besides the ship would be better sheltered in Phoenix and the passengers more comfortable through the winter.

The Bay at Fair Havens

580. A little conference was held among the responsible officers. These were first of all the centurion, for since the ship belonged to the imperial merchant fleet he had the highest military rank aboard. Then came the captain (ναύκλ^γρος) and the pilot (κυβερνήτης); and finally Paul too was invited, probably by the centurion who respected him highly.

The centurion seems to have taken a neutral position at first, while the captain and the pilot argued for the short run from Fair Havens to Phoenix. Paul opposed it saying, "Men, I see that this voyage is threatening to bring disaster and heavy loss, not only to the cargo and the ship, but to our lives also" (27:10). But Paul's opinion made no impression. The centurion, who was responsible for the decision, probably considered that his prisoner, however worthy as a person, was not so experienced in these matters as the others, and he might even be a little afraid of the sea. So, as Luke tells us, "the centurion gave more heed to the pilot and the captain than to what Paul had to say" (*ibid.*, 11), and their course was decided upon.

Shortly afterward a light south wind sprang up, which was just what was needed. If they hurried they would reach Phoenix in a few hours and everything would be saved. They weighed anchor and coasted the island. Having rounded Cape Matala, west of Fair Havens, they made good a northwesterly course, keeping close to shore and heading toward Phoenix.[4]

581. But without warning the scene changed, in the sudden and radical manner of meteorological changes in that part of the Mediterranean at that season. A violent wind called Euroaquilo burst down from the mountains of the island against the ship, blowing, that is, from northeast to southwest.

The consequences were immediate: "And when the ship was caught in it and could not face the wind, we gave way and were driven along" (*ibid.*, 15). In a short time they were off Cauda (today Gaudos), a small island southwest of Fair Havens. Since the ship was now running a little in the lee, it was possible to complete one important maneuver. The ship had sailed from Fair Havens towing the small boat used for landing and unloading, and this was now a great danger since the high waves kept tossing it against the hull, causing considerable damage. In this brief interval and with great difficulty the boat was hoisted aboard.

Having furled the sails, they proceeded to "bind" the hull, reinforcing it on the outside with hawsers wound around it and on the inside with shoring. The sailors feared the ship would be driven by the storm into the great Libyan Syrtis, the broad sandy bight between Tripolitania and Cyrenaica, which offered no approach. This would mean the loss of the ship, the cargo, everything. To prevent or at least to delay this disaster, they lowered from the stern the so-called "instrument" ($\sigma\kappa\epsilon\tilde{v}os$). This seems to have been a mass of cordage or a beam held perpendicularly, which functioned as a sea anchor, slowing the speed of the ship as it was dragged along.

582. Now completely out of control, the ship was at the mercy of the raging elements for fourteen consecutive days. It is not hard to imagine the sufferings of those aboard during those two weeks. The small 300 ton ship was tossed on the sea like a nutshell, pitching and rolling and groaning under the merciless pounding of the mountainous waves. Now it perched for a moment in the deep foam of an enormous wave and the next it plunged between two black walls of water. Since there was no inner propulsion, the ship was all the more helpless against the beating of the sea.

During the first night the storm must have worsened and the next day it was thought necessary to lighten the ship. So the deck cargo was thrown overboard; and on the third day, the gear which was not strictly necessary was also thrown over.

Then a period of terror-filled monotony enveloped the crew and the passengers, with no relief or variation as day followed day. Each might

---

[4] Their nearness to shore is expressed in the Greek with the word ἆσσον, which the Vulgate understood as a proper name, *Assos*, the city mentioned in *Acts*, 20:13 (§ 528), near Troas.

be their last. Inside the ship they lay exhausted and moaning in the darkness of the hold amid the reek of vomit and filth. Outside there was no interruption in the mad pounding of the waves; nothing was to be seen but the water washing over them. They had completely lost all bearings. There was nothing they could do. How long would the hull be able to stand the beating of the sea? "As neither sun or stars were visible for many days and no small storm was raging, all hope of our being saved was in consequence given up" (27:20).

583. Disasters of this kind undoubtedly shake an ordinary man and disorient him at least for a time from the moral world in which he usually lives. Did these intermi-

Mosaic — Roman Ship in Port — Third Century Mosaic (Alinari)

nable days affect Paul too? Did they shake him at least partially out of the spiritual world of that Christ in whom he lived? Not at all. On the contrary, from what Luke adds immediately, it would seem Paul set this extraordinary event also within the broad vision of his spiritual world. Besides — suprising as it is — he was not at all unaware of physical realities and was concerned for the lowly requirements of living which the other passengers forgot. Like the later Christian mystics, he showed that while his head might be in the third heaven his feet were firmly planted on the ground.

"Then, when they had eaten nothing for a long time, Paul got up in the midst of them and said, 'Men, you should indeed have listened to me and not have sailed from Crete, thus sparing yourselves this disaster and loss. And now I beg you to be of good cheer, for there will be no loss of life among you, but only of the ship. For last night an angel of the God I belong to and serve, stood by me, saying "Do not be afraid, Paul; thou must stand before Caesar; and behold, God has granted thee all who are sailing with thee." So, men, be of good cheer; for I have faith in God that it will be as it has been told me.' " Then Paul indicated they were to be cast ashore on a certain island (*ibid.*, 21–26).

584. It is quite probable that few listened to this exhortation and that fewer still responded to it. When one has been caught for days in an infernal storm and has had the last drop of life drained out of him by seasickness, nothing makes any impression except relief from the

NAVICVI KARTHAC DISVa

Mosaic: Banner of Carthaginian Sailors (Ancient Ostia)

torment. And here was that strange prisoner standing up and preaching about an island! What island? Where? How could he know about any island nearby when they had been lost for so many days and the sailors themselves, with all their experience, had no idea of their bearings? An angel of his God had appeared to him? Well, that must have been a trick of the imagination, brought on by the cramps in his stomach and nervous reaction. A few may have thought he was speaking with some authority, and among them the good Julius, who had already sensed something extraordinary in Paul.

It is also likely that Paul said these things on the thirteenth day after their departure from Fair Havens. It is certain that on the fourteenth night, as they were being driven to and fro in the Adrian Sea, the crew about midnight began to suspect that some land "was approaching" (*ibid.*, 27). This phrase of the Greek text is vividly expressive of the sailor's viewpoint, since the land seemed to be approaching as the vessel was driven toward it, and it was all the more suitable in those circumstances when for fourteen days they had been at the mercy of the sea hoping for land of some kind to come to meet them. The sea called "Adria" in those days was not only the Adriatic, but also the lower stretch of sea between Sicily on the one hand and Greece and Crete on the other.[5] But Luke learned the name of the sea only later, when

---

[5] Flavius Josephus also calls the sea in which he was shipwrecked the *Adria*, although he was picked up by a Cyrenean ship and landed at Pozzuoli (*Life*, 15–16).

he learned the name of the island on which they landed. On that night itself, he could not have told whether the sea was the "Adria" or the great Syrtis.

585. Feverish with hope, the sailors lowered the lead line, and discovered that the water was only 20 fathoms deep. Since the fathom (ὀργυιά) measured about 6 feet, the depth of the water was only about 120 feet. They took soundings again and got a reading of 15 fathoms. There was no doubt. The land was approaching rapidly even though they could not see it through the darkness of the night and the storm.

Then, for fear the ship would be driven on the rocks, the sailors checked its course by dropping four anchors from the stern, hoping for daylight to reveal the land they were longing to reach. But since they were so close, their danger had in a sense increased and the sailors knew it. Now that it had slowed almost to a stop, would the ship be able to stand the beating of the waves until morning? And if it began to give way, as was very probable, how could they manage to save the passengers, who would undoubtedly crowd the small boat in a panic. It was better, the sailors thought, to look out for themselves first and get to land. Later, if it was possible, they would come back for the passengers.

So they began to lower the boat (§ 581) into the sea, pretending that they were going to cast anchor lines from the bow as well. But Paul, who perhaps had overheard them making their plans, "said to the centurion and the soldiers, 'Unless these men remain in the ship, you cannot be saved.'" This time Paul's warning had an immediate effect. Since their own lives were involved, they drew their swords and cut the lines, letting the boat fall into the water.

586. Daybreak was near and it was easy to foresee a difficult and toilsome day ahead, attempting to save the ship or at least the passengers. But no one remembered that they were physically unprepared for these efforts, since after fourteen sleepless nights and days, in which terror alternated with seasickness and nervous excitement, they could barely stand on their feet. But Paul did think of it, being a mystic and a realist at the same time. It is also possible that Luke, the physician, called the circumstances to his attention. Turning to the people anxiously waiting to leave the ship, Paul said: "This is the fourteenth day that you have been constantly on the watch and fasting, without taking anything to eat. So I beg you to take some food for your safety; for not a hair from the head of any one of you shall perish.' With these words he took bread and gave thanks to God before all and broke it and began to eat. Then all became more cheerful and took food themselves. Now, we were in all two hundred and seventy-six souls on board" (*ibid.*, 33–37).

Some exegetes have interpreted Paul's act here as the celebration of the Eucharistic rite, performed for himself and his Christian companions.

This theory, which is also upheld by some Protestant and rationalist scholars, is by no means to be dismissed as absurd. It is quite possible that the early Christians performed the rite for comfort and consolation under stress, restricting it to the essential acts only. However, it seems more likely that Paul's act of thanks before the breaking of the bread was not the formula for the Eucharist but the usual Jewish prayer before meals, which Jesus had also said at the multiplication of the loaves and at Emmaus.[6]

587. Since in addition to the dead cargo the ship carried only 276 persons, it must have been much smaller than the one on which Flavius Josephus was wrecked, which carried 600 (§ 576). As for the cargo, Luke tells us that as soon as they had finished eating, they threw the grain overboard to lighten the ship.

This grain was the cargo destined for Rome. Some scholars have supposed that this sudden and only mention of "grain" ($\sigma\hat{\iota}\tau o\nu$) was due to an ancient error on the part of some copyist, for by transposing one letter we could read "mast" ($\iota\sigma\tau\acute{o}\nu$) instead. This would be the main-mast, supposedly cut down and thrown into the sea. From the paleo-graphical viewpoint the thesis is attractive, but there is nothing to support it in the context.

588. Luke then describes in detail the next maneuver the sailors attempted. "When it was day, however, they did not recognize the land; but they observed a bay with a sandy shore, upon which they resolved

---

[6] Cf. *The Life of Christ*, p. 383 ff. (§ 373); p. 657 ff. (§ 630).

Malta — A Cove in the Bay of St. Paul

to beach the vessel, if they could. So casting off the anchors they left them to the sea, loosening at the same time the lashings of the rudders; and hoisting the foresail to the wind, they made for the beach" (*ibid.*, 39–40). On seeing a wide bay, then, the sailors decided to head for it even though they suspected the presence of shoals barring the entrance. Once inside the inlet, it would be easy to drive the ship on the beach and ground it.

So they stripped the ship of all anchors and began to use the rudders again. On ancient ships there were two rudders the shape of large oars, one on either side of the hull. Finally they raised the foresail, which was enough to carry the ship with moderate force into the inlet.

589. At first the maneuver seemed to be succeeding, but at the entrance to the bay they ran aground on the shoals. "But we struck a place open to two seas, and they ran the ship aground. The prow stuck fast and remained immovable, but the stern began to break under the violence of the sea" (*ibid.*, 41).

This "place open to two seas" (τόπον διθάλασσον) must have been one of those sand bars not uncommon at the entrance to bays and inlets. They are formed where two opposing currents, the tides of the outer sea and those of the inner meet, and because of the constant force of the waves there, they are always most dangerous to anyone stranded on them. The sailors, who had not noticed the sand bar, struck it head on and the prow drove into it. The results were immediate; while the prow stuck in the sand, the stern was smashed by the waves.

The danger was immediately sensed by all on board, who were naturally seized with panic, and each one rushed to save himself. The soldiers remembered their own responsibilities and the serious penalties they would pay if any of the prisoners escaped. To avoid this difficulty, they decided to kill their charges, but the centurion, who wished to save Paul, forbade the slaughter. He gave orders that those who could swim should make for the shore while the others were to be brought in on planks or other wreckage from the foundering ship. "And so it came to pass that all got safely to land. After our escape we learned that the island was called Malta (*Melita*)" (27:44–28:1).

590. The ancient name of the island, *Melita*, was of Punic origin, that is Semitic. The two islands, Gozo and Malta, were called *Gaudo-Melita*.

A few amateur scholars have maintained that the shipwreck island was not Malta but the island of Melada (Greek: Μελίτη; Latin, *Melite*; Croatian, *Mljet*) which lay off the coast of Dalmatia a little above Ragusa and opposite the Abruzzi on the Italian shore. Since this theory is prompted largely by local pride and has no serious evidence to substantiate it, it is enough to have mentioned it.

On Malta, the place indicated as the site of the shipwreck has great

Malta — General View of the Bay of St. Paul

probability in its favor and is bolstered by very old tradition. On the
northern coast of the island, there is a bay facing east (the direction
from which the ship was coming), called the Bay of St. Paul. Naturally,
its general configuration may have changed somewhat through the centuries, but it has remained more or less a wedge-shaped mirror of water
pushing into the land, and it is surrounded for the most part by friable
rocks. At the foot of the rocks there is some sandy beach all around the
bay, but in all likelihood the sailors headed for the northern shore of
the bay, where the islet of Salmonetta (Selmunett) is separated from
the mainland by a channel. There, where the currents from the sea met
those of the bay and the channel, it was very possible for sand banks
to form, and on one of them the ship was stranded. Today the statue
of St. Paul erected near the channel of Salmonetta, and in addition a
fountain of St. Paul and a chapel in his honor on the southern shore
of the bay, recall the dramatic landing of *San Bulos*, the patron of the
Maltese.

591. When they finally reached land, drenched and exhausted, the
survivors were surrounded by the inhabitants of the island. Luke calls
them "barbarians," according to the Greco-Roman custom of calling anyone barbarian who did not speak a language familiar to the Hellenist
world. But what he says next redounds entirely to their honor: "And the
natives showed us no little kindness, for they kindled a fire and refreshed
us all because of the rain that had set in and the cold" (28:2).

Today, the Maltese speak a mixed Italian-Semitic dialect. The Semitic
elements derive from the ancient Punic language of the island and the
later Arabic influences, which were considerable. In Paul's time, the
islanders must have spoken what was substantially a Punic dialect,

namely, the language of the Carthaginians, which in its turn was a Phoenician dialect. Now the Phoenicians, whose country was just north of and contiguous with Palestine, spoke a language closely related to the Hebrew. Therefore the difference between Punic and Hebrew was, at the most, no greater than that between modern French and Italian, which are both neo-Latin just as Punic and Hebrew both belonged to the northwestern Semitic group. When Paul exchanged the first few words with the helpful islanders that gathered around them, he found they were less "barbarian" than it seemed to Luke, for with the help of a little Hebrew and Aramaic, he succeeded in making himself understood and in understanding them. Others probably came running also who could speak Greek or Latin, and the conversation undoubtedly became general and animated.

592. Since it was about the first of November (§ 579), the fire was a real boon to the shipwrecked company on the shore. After the storm and the cold rain, it was what they needed most. Paul, unable to keep still while others were working, was helping to feed the fire. "Now Paul gathered a bundle of sticks and laid them on the fire, when a viper came out because of the heat and fastened on his hand. When the natives saw the creature hanging from his hand, they said to one another, 'Surely this man is a murderer, for though he has escaped the sea, Justice does not let him live.' But he shook off the creature into the fire and suffered no harm. Now they were expecting that he would swell up and suddenly fall down and die; but after waiting a long time and seeing no harm come to him, they changed their minds and said that he was a god" (28:3–6).

The first reaction of the islanders was entirely natural. The prisoner has barely been saved from the sea, and now as soon as he reaches land he is bitten by a poisonous snake. He must indeed be an incredible murderer, on whom *Dikē* — Justice personified — is determined to inflict due punishment. She has permitted him to escape drowning only to make him suffer a more torturing death. But when this imagined decree of Justice is not fulfilled, the islanders go to the other extreme. He is no ordinary man, for he can neither be drowned nor poisoned. He must be a god. The Lycaonians of Lystra had come to a similar conclusion (§ 343).

593. In the Greek text, Luke uses several medical terms, which it is not necessary to dwell on here. We have his vivid and lively description as an eyewitness, who also is frightened at the sight of the viper dangling from Paul's hand and who watches wide-eyed as he calmly shakes it off into the fire.

The rationalists, of course, do not accept the incident since it is miraculous. They reject it without even discussing it. A few have objected that Malta today has no poisonous snakes. The truth is that Malta has very little fauna at all today and what there is has not been exhaustively studied. Some also maintain that there were poisonous snakes on the island until a century ago. But whatever the case today, it is not inevitable that it was the same twenty centuries ago. How many animals, especially small ones, have ceased to exist over a much shorter period of time?[7] The islanders, who recognized the viper, expected to see Paul swell up and die from the poison, and their experience with such cases is more valid than today's tendentious theories.

Malta — Environs of the Old City

594. When they had been somewhat warmed and dried, the 276 survivors were sheltered — as Luke tells us — in the various homes of the good islanders. But the episode of the viper had its effect, for Paul, with Luke and Aristarchus, and perhaps the centurion Julius with a few others of some standing, were received into the home of Publius, who held large estates in the region and was the "head man" of the island (28:7).

This title of "primus" — or head man — is to be found in various Maltese inscriptions[8] and denoted the "principal" representative of Roman authority in residence, since the island was under the jurisdiction of the praetor of Sicily. It is likely that Publius' house was near the Città Vecchia, or "Old City." This ancient capital of the island is about five or six miles from the bay, and, in the neighborhood, several of these inscriptions which mention the "primus" of the island have been found.

---

[7] The Maltese give St. Paul credit for the absence of poisonous snakes on the island. With all due respect to the piety of this idea, this absence is probably due to the density of population and the scarcity of fauna. The island is one of the most thickly populated in the Mediterranean; there are only three kinds of snakes on it, and it is natural that the poisonous species should have been killed off first.

[8] *Corpus Inscrip. Gr.*, III, 5754; *Corpus Inscrip. Lat.*, X, 7495.

For three days, the guests found cordial hospitality in that comfortable house. Paul unexpectedly repaid this in circumstances which could not fail to be noted in the narrative of the physician Luke. "And it happened that the father of Publius was laid up with fever(s) and dysentery; but Paul went in, and after praying and laying his hands on him, he healed him. After this all the sick on the island came and were cured" (28:8-9). The word "fevers" in the plural indicates recurrent attacks and suggests the so-called "Maltese fever." But we do not have enough information to try a diagnosis. Luke notes the fever and Paul, using the charism of "healing" (§ 216), cures it. Immediately he is obliged to use the charism for many other sick persons on the island, who, as soon as they hear of the first cure, come hurrying to this man who did not die of the snake bite and who has such power for himself and others.

Naturally, such a benefactor is treated with every courtesy and deference. "And they honored us with many marks of honor, and when we sailed, they provided us with such things as we needed" (*ibid.*, 10). This means they were provided with everything, since they had lost everything in the shipwreck.

595. These are the external facts. But what was their spiritual aspect? Did not Paul, who needed only a few days in a place to start preaching the Christ Jesus, preach here on Malta too during the three months he remained there? The *Acts* tell us nothing of this, nor is there any information from other ancient sources. However, Luke's silence is not necessarily a negative one, and it is not only possible but also probable that by the end of Paul's sojourn there was a small Christian community on the island which had sheltered him.

Roman Ship in Full Sail. Beyrouth: Museum (Alinari)

When the stormiest part of the winter was over, they departed once more, that is, in about February of the year 61. "We set sail after three months in an Alexandrian ship with the Twins on her figurehead, which had wintered at the island." The "Twins" were the twin gods, Castor and Pollux, who were the patrons of sailors. Actually, navigation usually was not resumed until a little later, toward the beginning of March. But since the run between Malta and the southern shores of Italy was such a short one, the Alexandrian ship decided to try it in order to save time.

There were no surprises this time. Luke's story becomes almost an

Syracuse — The Greek Theater

outline, like several passages in the *Anabasis* of Xenophon or the *Wars of the Jews* of Flavius Josephus.[9] "We put in at Syracuse, and stayed there three days. Then, following the coast, we reached Rhegium; and one day later a south wind sprang up, and on the second day we arrived at Puteoli, where we found brethren and were entreated to stay with them seven days" (28:12–14). At Puteoli — modern Pozzuoli — they left the ship, and the rest of the journey to Rome was made by land.[10]

596. It is significant that Paul found Christians in Puteoli, and their presence may be explained as usual by the presence of a Jewish community there. According to Flavius Josephus (*Wars of the Jews*, 11, 104) there must have been many wealthy Jews in Dicearchia (Pozzuoli), from which we conclude that before Paul's arrival some of them had been converted to Christianity. They remained in Puteoli seven days, perhaps among other reasons because of some formality involving Julius and the soldiers, and the Christians there hastened to inform the brethren of Rome that Paul had arrived and was about to come to them. Some of the Romans set out immediately to meet the traveler on the road, which could have been none other than the Appian Way.

The representatives of the Roman community went as far as the *Three Taverns,* a stopover for travelers mentioned also by Cicero (*ad Attic.,* I, 13, 1; II, 10; II, 12) and situated about thirty-three miles from Rome, where another road branches from the Appian Way in the direction of Anzio. Others went on as far as the *Forum of Appius,* a few

---

[9] Cf. G. Ricciotti, *Flavio Giuseppe tradotto e commentato,* Vol. I, Introduction, pp. 69–71.

[10] Flavius Josephus also landed at Puteoli after his shipwreck (§ 584, note).

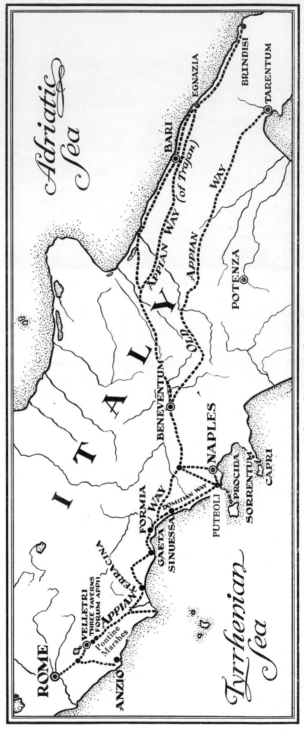

Italy and the Roads to Rome

Panorama From Cape Miseno: Pozzuoli in the Background

miles farther south, which had been founded by Appius Claudius and had become the great gathering place of "sailors, tavern-keepers and thieves" as Horace described it after having stopped there (*Sat.*, I, 5, 2–4). The *Forum of Appius* was on the edge of the Pontine Marshes. There began the *decemnovium*, that is, a straight stretch of road nineteen miles long, beside which ran a canal that went as far as Terracina (Anxur). One could travel by boat on the canal instead of on the road, and it is likely that Paul did travel on a canalboat from Terracina to the *Forum of Appius*. There, and again at the Three Taverns, he met the Christians who had come from Rome, and "when Paul saw them, he gave thanks to God and took courage" (Acts 28:15).

After the stopover at the Three Taverns, the company began the ascent over the Alban Hills, which led past Velletri. The last stop, of the six or seven required for the trip from Puteoli to Rome, probably occurred at Ariccia (Horace, *ibid.*), about sixteen miles from the city. From the top of the Alban Hills Paul looked on Rome for the first time.

597. The Rome of the year 61 was destined to disappear almost completely in the great fire of Nero three years later. It was a jumbled irregular city which had grown through the centuries, district by district, one crowded against the other. Except for the imperial Palatine and the white marble of the Forum at its foot, there was little that could be distinguished from a distance. But surrounding it was a thick network of lines converging on the city from all directions as if in a hurry to reach it. They were the aqueducts and roads over which water, and peoples from every region, came to the mistress of the world.

Perhaps Paul, stopping for a moment to view the panorama spread before him and meditate on that network of roads and aqueducts, thought of the living water of which Jesus had spoken to the Samaritan woman[11] and of those peoples on their way to the house of the God

The Appian Way at Terracina (Anxur)

of Israel, spoken of by the ancient prophets (§ 262), a water and a people which up to that time had reached Rome in too small a measure. He had longed so much to come to Rome precisely in order to circle the fated city with another spiritual network. The water of the Samaritan woman was to have its perennial source in Rome, and from there it would be carried to the most distant regions of the earth. The peoples of the world would travel no more to the hill of Sion, but to the city whose seven hills recalled the seven lights of the golden candelabrum in the Temple of Jerusalem. Such thoughts on the part of a prisoner in chains were foolishness and he knew it; but because they were foolish he had an unshakable faith in them (§ 419). Another recollection helped to sustain that faith. Just as Paul now stood contemplating Rome from the Alban Hills, Jesus thirty years before had contemplated Jerusalem from the Mount of Olives a few days before his death.[12] Jesus had wept then, and his tears now justified the Apostle's hopes.

598. Paul entered the city through the *Porta Capena,* corresponding more or less to what is today the Porta di San Sebastiano. Upon their arrival Julius gave Paul and the other prisoners over to the custody of the officer charged to receive them.

---

[11] *The Life of Christ,* pp. 296–298 (§ 294).
[12] *Ibid.,* pp. 523–524 (§ 507).

According to a few manuscripts this officer was a "camp commander" (στρατοπεδάρχῃ), a title corresponding to that of *praefectus castrorum*, or "camp prefect," among the Romans. But what is the camp, or *castra*, referred to here? Some have thought it meant the barracks of the *milites peregrini* or *castra peregrinorum* between the Coelian and Palatine hills, used to billet transient soldiers and as headquarters for certain police services. This is not impossible, although the certain data we possess on these *castra peregrinorum* are no earlier than the third century. Even if Paul was taken to these barracks, however, where perhaps Julius and his soldiers were billeted, he was transferred immediately afterward to the headquarters of the praetorian guards, namely, the *Castra Praetoria* (its site near the Via Nomentana is still called Castro Pretorio). There he was handed over to the *praefectus castrorum*, who was the officer in charge of the barracks as deputy of the praetorian prefect.

At the time the prefect was Afranius Burrus, a friend of Seneca and like him a Stoic philosopher and former tutor of the young Nero. Burrus, or one of his deputies, must have received Paul from Julius together with the official information regarding his trial. But since the *elogium* written by Porcius Festus (§ 572) had almost certainly been washed into the sea during the shipwreck, there was nothing to do but accept the verbal presentation of the prisoner made by the centurion. This was undoubtedly couched in highly favorable terms, judging from the sen-

Ancient Network of Roads and Aqueducts Between Rome and the Alban Hills

timents the good Julius had displayed toward Paul more than once during the journey, and the result of the presentation was excellent too.

599. "On our arrival at Rome, Paul was given permission to live by himself with a soldier to guard him" (28:16). This meant that instead of remaining a prisoner in the Castra Praetoria, Paul was placed under a very mild form of *custodia militaris* (§ 561). He could stay in any house he chose, but when he went out he must be accompanied by a soldier, to whom he was bound by a chain. In fact, Paul rented a house, one undoubtedly picked out for him by the Christians of Rome, and there he freely received all who came to see him, preaching the Gospel and speaking of the Christ Jesus "with all freedom and unhindered" (28:31).

We have no way of determining where this house was. The tradition which places it at Santa Maria in Via Lata near the modern Corso Umberto, or the other which sets it at San Paolo della Regola

The Consular Way in the Alban Hills

near the modern synagogue or elsewhere are very late and without foundation.[13] We may rather suppose in a general way that it was some house near the Castra Praetoria.

600. As soon as he was settled, Paul began his activity. First of all he wished to clarify his position vis-à-vis the Jews of Rome, who were numerous and powerful and had some protectors in the Imperial Court.[14] Therefore, three days later, he sent word to the leaders of the Jewish community that he would gladly receive them, since he had just arrived from Judea and wished to present himself to them. Without doubt some of these Jewish leaders had heard Paul spoken of as a crazy innovator, but had not been able to form any clear judgment of him.

---

[13] Cf. O. Marucchi, *Pietro e Paolo a Roma*, 4th edition, pp. 148–150; C. Cecchelli, *Gli Apostoli a Roma*, Rome, 1938, pp. 21–22.

[14] *Storia d'Israele*, II, p. 220 ff. (§ 195 ff.).

They accepted the invitation, therefore, in order to make up their minds about him.

When they were assembled, Paul appeared before them chained to his guard. He began by telling them he had nothing against their common nation nor had he come to present charges against it. He had been imprisoned without cause in Jerusalem and had been handed over to the Romans, who wanted to release him since they had found him innocent. But since the Jews there protested, he had been forced to appeal to Caesar, and therefore he had been sent to Rome: "This then is why I asked to see you and speak with you. For it is because of the hope of Israel that I am wearing this chain" (28:20).

601. Paul introduced himself in general terms purposely. This first meeting was not an opportune time to enter into a doctrinal discussion. Equally vague and carefully worded was the reply of the Jews, which was not without a certain tact. They said that up to that time they had received no letters concerning Paul from Judea, and neither had anyone come to speak against him. It would therefore be helpful if he would set a day and explain his thought, since it was well known that the "sect" (αἱρέσεως) to which he belonged encountered strong opposition everywhere (*ibid.*, 21–22).

We gather from this that there was steady correspondence between the Jewish authorities in Jerusalem and the community in Rome (and, indeed, the other communities throughout the Diaspora), since the leaders assembled here were a little surprised, so to speak, that they had received no information about Paul from the Sanhedrin. It is also clear that the Jews of Rome were acquainted with Christianity and with the fact that it encountered opposition generally throughout the Diaspora. But with great tact, they avoid any reference to Christianity in Rome, although the expulsion of the Jews from Rome, ordered ten years before by the Emperor Claudius (§ 157) and occasioned by the riots that had taken place over "Crestus," had been due almost certainly to riots instigated by the Jews against the "Crestiani" or Christians.[15]

602. So they fixed a day and the Jews came in even greater number to take part in the discussion with Paul. "And to them he explained the matter, bearing witness to the kingdom of God and trying from morning till evening to convince them concerning Jesus from the Law of Moses and from the Prophets. And some believed what was said; and some disbelieved; and as they could not agree among themselves, they began to depart, when Paul added this one word, 'Well did the Holy Spirit speak through Isaias the prophet to our fathers, saying . . .'" There follows the passage of *Isaias*, 6:9–10, quoted from the Septuagint, in which the prophet, in God's name, rebukes Israel for her obstinacy. We have

---

[15] Cf. *The Life of Christ*, p. 83 (§ 92).

already discussed elsewhere the meaning of this quotation, cited also by Jesus.[16] To the prophet's words Paul added a final sentence which also had the ring of prophecy: "Be it known to you therefore that this salvation of God has been sent to the Gentiles, and they will listen to it" (28:23–28).

The destiny of Rome had been unwittingly at stake during that discussion. The Jews refused to become citizens of "that Rome where Christ is Roman" (*Purgatorio*, 32, 102), and as a consequence the same citizenship was offered to the pagans, who hastened to accept it. The Jews of Rome refused to accept the invitation to transfer from Mount Sion to the Capitoline, and the Capitoline was occupied by the pagans, who destroyed the Temple of Jupiter which rose there to set up a cross in its place. On Mount Sion the one temple of the God Yahweh was destroyed forever and over the ruins rose the crescent of Islam.

---

[16] *Ibid.*, pp. 373–376 (§§ 363–364).

First Imprisonment in Rome

603. At the end of his journey through purgatory, when he reached the earthly paradise, Dante tells us he turned to ask Virgil a question as usual and to his dismay found that his faithful guide and teacher had disappeared. Fortunately Beatrice was descending at that moment from heaven to take Virgil's place and lead the poet through Paradise, so in the end Dante's loss was his gain.

We are far less fortunate. At this point in our narrative, our faithful guide, Luke, disappears no less abruptly than Virgil, but no Beatrice appears to take his place. We are left alone, not in an earthly paradise, but on an almost deserted heath, and our only guides from now on are doctrinal writings which contain little or no historical data.

We have already noted that Luke, after using twenty-one verses to recount the first days of Paul's sojourn in Rome, sums up the next two years in about twenty words, making no reference to the trial before the emperor's tribunal, although this was the natural conclusion to the last chapters of the book. We also ventured to explain this strange and unexpected close to the narrative (§§ 118–119). It is our belief that the trial ended at the beginning of the year 63 and that Paul was acquitted and released.

A number of factors may have occasioned the long delay before this sentence was pronounced. One may have been the desire to give the accusers of Judea time enough to come to Rome and present their charges. Another likely reason may have been the decision to await the arrival of another written report on Paul from the procurator of Judea, since the *elogium* consigned to Julius had been lost in the shipwreck off Malta (§ 598). The acquittal also must have been determined by various considerations, first, by the prisoner's actual innocence before Roman law, which as yet was not hostile to Christianity; and, second, by the reports of the Roman authorities on the accused, both the oral one given by the centurion Julius and the copy of the written one sent from Judea; and finally, by the very fact that the plaintiffs did not come to Rome from Judea (§§ 116, 570), and therefore the trial lacked its principal motivation, since all the other elements in it favored the prisoner. In view of all these circumstances, an acquittal was inevitable.

And so in the first months of the year 63, Paul regained his complete freedom after five years spent under *custodia militaris*. And he began to think again of his old plans to evangelize the West. During these two years in Rome, however, he had been far from inactive, and it is now our task to inquire into that activity as far as we are able, both with respect to Rome and to places far from Rome.

604. However mild its form, the *custodia militaris* kept Paul from doing two main things, among many others less important, namely, working with his hands and engaging in public discussion in the synagogues and elsewhere. We have noted more than once how important Paul considered his economic independence and his earning his own living. Yet he was not a slave exactly to this rule, and if Providence disposed otherwise, he would accept the humiliation of receiving help and support from others. This was what happened in Rome.

In that vast human beehive, composed of two million persons of every race and circumstance, scarcely a third lived on their own means. The great majority possessed nothing and lived by depending in one way or another on those who did. On the one hand were the ancient patricians and the newly rich, on the other the great crowd of "clients," proletarians, and slaves. Paul became then a "client" of Christian charity. At first his rent and his food were provided by the Christians of Rome who had admired and loved him ever since they had received the epistle he had sent them. Later, the brethren of the communities he had founded in the Orient came to his assistance. As soon as they heard of the prolonged detention in Rome of their beloved teacher, they hastened to send him help. First among them were the Philippians (Phil. 2:25; 4:14 ff.), and among these, certainly, the good Lydia as usual (§§ 382–383).

605. His material needs thus provided for, Paul threw himself more than ever into his spiritual activity. His first efforts in Rome as elsewhere were made among the Jews and, as elsewhere, the discussion in Paul's lodging yielded less than mediocre results (§ 602). But he could not now attend the synagogues in Trastevere and other sections of the city, dragging after him the praetorian guard to whom he was chained. He probably made other efforts to reach his countrymen in gatherings held in his house, but as he repeatedly met with solid resistance, he gradually turned his attention from them to the pagans.

This deepened the split which had already become evident in Rome between Judaism and Christianity; and this in turn inevitably provoked the envy of the Jews against the Christians, who were growing in number and influence. On the first opportunity, the envy found vent in specific charges. Thirty years later, Clement of Rome (1 Cor. 5:2–5) attributes the death of Peter and Paul to "zeal and envy," and, more specifically, the martyrdom of Peter to "wicked zeal" and that of Paul to "zeal and contention." He does not name the source of that zeal, envy, and contention but since he immediately afterward describes the persecution of Nero which followed the great fire of 64 (§ 118), the most natural source historically is Roman Judaism, and this deduction corresponds in every way to the circumstances of the time. This rivalry was the final consequence of the refusal on the part of local Judaism to accept citizenship in "that Rome, where Christ is Roman" (§ 602).

606. After the unbelieving Jews, Paul had to concern himself with the Jews who did believe. At the time of his imprisonment, the community in Rome certainly numbered more ex-pagans than ex-Jews (§ 513). On the other hand, we have no indication whatever, not even in the *Epistle to the Romans*, that the Judaizing Christians of Rome presented any real danger from the doctrinal viewpoint or that Paul had to engage in controversy with them. But there is one curious development. Paul's ceaseless activity quickly turns his house into the center, as it were, of Roman Christianity, and by a kind of wholesome contagion, prompts many others to imitate him in thus spreading the Good Tidings. Among these new preachers, there were some who — as Paul says — "preach Christ even out of envy and contentiousness" (Phil. 1:15). In other words, their aim is not so much to spread the Good Tidings as to spite Paul by setting up a kind of rival altar: "Some proclaim Christ . . . out of contentiousness, not sincerely, thinking to stir up affliction for me in my chains" (*ibid.*, 17). Who were these ill-intentioned preachers?

We note that Paul's expressions — "envy" . . . "contentiousness" — are those used by Clement in describing the Roman milieu, not that both

Praetorian Soldiers — Antonine Column
in Rome

refer to the same persons, but they may well be referring to the same spiritual attitude characteristic of a certain group of persons. And this group is Roman Judaism. Clement is referring to the unbelieving Jews, Paul to some among the Jews who have believed. Although Christian, they resented the rapidly increasing pre-eminence Paul was acquiring in the community and they could not tolerate it. They could not accept that this rebel nomad, after facing Peter down in Antioch and after causing all kinds of trouble for James the "brother" of the Lord and the mother community in Jerusalem, should come to Rome and start lording it over the whole community there. They proposed to show him, therefore, that there could be preachers of the Gospel independent of him. Would faith in Christ die, perhaps, if there were no Paul?

607. These human jealousies, partly nationalistic and in any case petty, had no effect on Paul. They resulted, as a matter of fact, in a wider diffusion of the Good Tidings. And this, quite apart from the intentions which prompted them, was enough for the prisoner of Christ. And so he replied in all simplicity: "But what of it? Provided only that in every way, whether in pretense or in truth, Christ is being proclaimed; in this I rejoice, yes and I shall rejoice [in the future]" (*ibid.*, 15). And he took all the more comfort from the fact that in addition to these who preached from vindictiveness, there were others who were inspired by his good example, who preached "out of good will" (*ibid.*, 15), who acted "out of love since they know I am appointed for the defense of the gospel" (*ibid.*, 16).

Paul himself preached to all who came within the radius of his activity, and first of all, therefore, to the praetorians assigned to guard him. Were not these guards' souls redeemed by Christ, and were they not as great in the eyes of Christ as the emperor of Rome or the high priest of Jerusalem? Every few days a new guard arrived from the Castra Praetoria to relieve the soldier on duty, and fastening Paul's chain to his wrist prepared to spend some time at his side. One may have been an Italian from Cisalpine Gaul, and the next a native of Pannonia, or Norca, or Macedonia, or Galatia, according to the tour of duty. In this constant changing of the guards, Paul had a splendid opportunity to affirm the "catholicity" of the Christian message, and he sought to draw this forced companion of his to Christ. He tried by word and example, undoubtedly, both consciously and unconsciously, sometimes succeeding and sometimes failing. The praetorian guard was inevitably present during the conversations Paul held with his many visitors, and could listen, if he chose, to the long discussions on the Law and Grace, on Moses and Christ. While one guard fell asleep in sheer boredom, the next might become interested and curious.

608. In the intervals between one visit and another Paul must have asked his companion about himself, his country, through which the Apostle perhaps had traveled, about his family and his religion. Then the man would emerge through the soldier's rough exterior, as he melted a little in reminiscence and relived some part of his boyhood for this unknown prisoner, who showed him so much understanding and kindness. However given to vice and brutality the guard might be, he could admire his prisoner's fearlessness, his way of life, so pure that hardly a twelve-year-old girl in Rome could be found to match it, his solicitude for others, his forgetfulness of self, his disdain for money.

What kind of a man was he, anyway? Certainly quite different from those who ruled Rome and the world from the Castra Praetoria and the Palatine. And why did he lead such a peculiar life — no detail of which escaped the guard day or night? Perhaps the guard's curiosity was aroused and he began to ask questions. And the prisoner would reply speaking to him of a certain Christ, who had been poor as the praetorian in his own house, and yet more powerful than the prefect of the Praetorian Guards and the emperor on the Palatine. Often the dialogue remained no more than an exchange of words, again it captured a soul — such are the mysteries of the grace of Christ.

609. But the effects of this prisoner-guard relationship over the months were surprising. The souls captured — human souls hidden beneath the trappings of corrupt and brutalized soldiers — were far more numerous than those who remained indifferent. Writing to the Philippians, Paul could give them this encouraging news: "Now I wish you to know, brethren, that my experiences have turned out rather for the advancement of the gospel, so that the chains I bear for the sake of Christ have become manifest as such throughout the praetorium and in all other places. And the greater number of the brethren in the Lord, gaining courage from my chains, have dared to speak the word of God more freely and without fear" (Phil. 1:12–14).

The Praetorium Paul refers to here is not the barracks of the Castra

Gathering of Christians in a Patrician House in Rome for the Celebration of the Liturgy (Reconstruction — "Amici delle Catacombe")

Praetoria (§ 598) so much as the 12,000 soldiers billeted there, so many of whom succeeded each other as his guard. After a few months, almost the whole camp knew more or less who Paul was and that he was in chains because of Christ. He certainly did not mean to claim that all the praetorians were already Christian or ready to be converted. He states only that he himself and his case were well known among the soldiers, and this was not a disadvantage but rather "an advancement" of the Gospel. Therefore, beside the many who remained hostile or indifferent, there must have been many of good will and others already won. In addition to this moral penetration of the Praetorium, Paul tells us his example has produced the epidemic of preachers noted above, prompting many of the brethren to imitate him with good will, while others did so through envy (§ 606).

610. Another precious reference, but not a very clear one, is to be found in these words of Paul to the Philippians: "All the saints [the Christians of Rome] greet you, especially those of Caesar's household" (Phil. 4:22). There is no doubt that "Caesar's household" is the imperial palace on the Palatine, and that there were Christians there when Paul wrote these words, that is, between 62 and 63. But who and how many there were we cannot say. Nor must we assume that all of these were Paul's converts. In fact, the long list of greetings with which the letter to the Romans ends (§ 523) would suggest that some of the Christians named there were associated with Caesar's household before Paul's arrival in Rome. This does not exclude the possibility, however, that more were converted by Paul.

According to Clement of Alexandria,[1] several of "Caesars' equestrians" invited Mark to write down Peter's catechesis, which they had heard; Mark accepted the suggestion and wrote the Second Gospel at about this time. It is very likely that the Christians of "Caesar's household" mentioned by Paul were freedmen or slaves, for it was in the lower classes of society that Christianity made its first conquests in Rome as elsewhere. The first clearly attested Christians of high social rank in Rome come only later, under the Flavian emperors. For the time of Nero there is the strong supposition that Pomponia Graecina was a Christian, an outstanding woman and wife of the consul Plautius, who according to Tacitus (Annal., XIII, 32) was suspected of a "foreign superstition." She was brought before the tribunal of the family and was declared innocent. All this happened in 58, however, and before Paul's arrival in Rome.

611. Other Roman patricians have been thought Christian (some figure with Paul in the famous novel Quo Vadis?) but more on the basis of a general possibility than of certain historical evidence. We have al-

---

[1] Hypotyp. ad I Petri, 5, 14; cf. The Life of Christ, p. 160 (§ 130).

ready mentioned the alleged correspondence between Seneca and Paul (§ 53), which is unquestionably a later forgery, prompted both by the superficial resemblances between Stoicism and Christianity and by the fact that the philosopher and the Apostle were in Rome at the same time. It is, of course, possible that the two met and talked with each other. (Paul had known Seneca's brother Gallio, who was also in Rome at that time, § 446 ff.), but there is no evidence Paul actually influenced Seneca. Nevertheless, that Paul's activity extended to some of the patricians is both possible and probable. He could leave his lodgings and make visits in private homes, accompanied by his guard, and therefore he could attend the gatherings of the faithful held, especially when Christianity first came to Rome, in the patrician houses opened to them for that purpose by owners who were zealous neophytes.

Paul's helpers during this imprisonment are his former collaborators, some of whom had come purposely to Rome from distant regions. Besides Luke and Aristarchus, his companions during the voyage and shipwreck (§ 577), we are agreeably surprised to find among them Mark, the cousin of Barnabas (Col. 4:10; Philemon 24), which shows their old estrangement (§ 370) had entirely disappeared. This is the sojourn in Rome when Mark wrote his Gospel (§ 610). In this little group of affectionate disciples we find the faithful Timothy (Phil. 1:1; Col. 1:1) and the Tychicus (Eph. 6:21; Col. 4:7) who had accompanied Paul on part of this third missionary journey (§ 525). Also named are a certain "Jesus who is called Justus," of whom we know only that he was Jewish (Col. 4:11), and a Demas who seems not to have been a Jew (Col. 4:14; Philemon 24). The latter left Paul later and went to Thessalonica "loving this world" (2 Tim. 4:10); he was probably an apostate.

Epaphroditus of Philippi (§ 384) and Epaphras of Colossae (§ 461) came to Rome purposely to visit the prisoner, but we shall speak of these later.

612. We find these names mentioned incidentally, but undoubtedly there were others in the group helping Paul. In addition to rendering him material assistance they must also be considered his co-workers in the apostolate, for Paul was certainly not the man to beg pity or commiseration. His zeal had need of helpers to reach those in Rome whom his chains kept him from seeking out himself, just as the visitors who came to him with messages of affectionate devotion from far-off communities were invariably charged with messages and missions on the return journey, all related to the apostolate. For him, to live was Christ (Phil. 1:21), and whoever came near him was drawn within that life. Those who had some other goal for themselves eventually deserted him as Demas did.

His constant vision of Christ did not distract him from the practical aspects of everyday life, but directed and inspired him in its lowliest and humblest happenings. We may take as an example of this the episode suggested in the letter to Philemon.

613. *The Epistle to Philemon.* Paul had been a prisoner in Rome several months, when one day an odd-looking man came to see him. He was poorly dressed, and he looked like one of the slaves who came in such large numbers to hear the Apostle. He spoke Greek badly, with a Phrygian accent, and his manner was cautious and suspicious, as if he were afraid of everyone he met. On being admitted he was visibly startled when he saw the praetorian guard in the same room. Since he was in his own lodgings Paul was unchained at the moment, and, having understood immediately his visitor's embarrassment, he took him into another room so that he might be encouraged to speak freely. What they said to each other we are not told, but it is not hard to reconstruct the scene on the basis of the results of that conversation.[2]

— Who are you? What is your name? (Paul began.)

— I am called Onesimus.

— You are a slave, then (Paul answered with a kind smile). "Onesimus," in Greek, means "useful."[3]

— Yes I am a slave, and my master is one you know, Philemon, of Colossae in Phrygia, whom you converted to your religion (§ 461).

— Indeed I know him, and I am very fond of him. Do you have a letter from him? Did he send you to me?

— No, that is not the case at all. I have run away, because . . . I have stolen. It was a crazy thing to do, I know . . . he treated me so well. But now what am I to do? After stealing and running away, if I am caught you know very well what will happen to me. They'll brand a big *F* on my forehead with a red-hot iron to show everyone I am a Fugitive (§ 345), and then it will be the *ergastulum* or the quarries for me to work like a beast until I die.[4] . . . Philemon must have reported me and the search is on. That is why I have come to Rome, where all the runaways come. But now I see the danger is even more terrible here. The other day I saw the 400 slaves of Pedanius Secundus, the prefect of the city, being marched through the streets to be executed because one of them had killed their master.[5] . . . From then on I have been

---

[2] Since there is so much fictionalized criticism which conflicts with the documentary evidence, we may perhaps be permitted this little reconstruction, which is based on an authentic document.

[3] Slaves were frequently given descriptive names of this kind, just as a horse today may be named Lightning.

[4] The *ergastulum* was a house of correction for slaves. There are various references to these customs in the classical authors; cf., for example, Valerius Maximus, VI, 8, 7; Cicero, *De officiis*, II, 7; Martial, VIII, 75, 9, etc.

[5] This massacre, carried out at the express wish of the majority of the Senate and of Nero, was opposed by the populace but in vain. It happened in the year 62 (Tacitus, *Annales,* XIV, 42–45).

terrified they would catch me any moment. I cannot take any more.
I am worn out. For months I have been running and hiding, and hiding
and running, like a wild animal — unable to rest, nothing but scraps to
eat — no one to talk to . . . ever. I can stand no more. That is why I have
come to you.

— I am glad you did. How did you know I was in Rome?

— A few days ago I met a friend of my master's and yours, Epaphras
of Colossae who follows your religion, too (§ 461). He was always very
good to me before I ran away. I told him everything, and he said to
come to you; he said he would speak to you about me. . . .

— Good. . . . Epaphras has been in Rome several weeks, and he has
brought me much news of our brethren in Colossae. . . . Well, come
now, cheer up. Don't be discouraged. We shall find a way to remedy
the wrong you've done and save you somehow. Your master is a very
good man, and he is a Christian. You, my poor Onesimus, do not know
what this means, to be a Christian!

614. That was all for that day. Paul gave Onesimus some supper, and
that night the slave slept on a mat spread in a corner of Paul's room.
The next morning he felt greatly refreshed and was much less afraid
of the praetorian guard. A little later Epaphras appeared, and he and
Paul talked alone for a long time. Then they called in Onesimus and
told him their plan.

Onesimus was to remain in Paul's house and perform some little
service for him, as if he were his slave. Paul would write to Philemon
and ask him to deed him Onesimus. Given his affection for Paul he was
sure to comply. Then Epaphras, who was the friend of both, could
eventually testify to the transfer before the authorities. Onesimus could
relax now; he had nothing to fear from any search. But he was to remember that the three of them, Paul, Philemon, and Epaphras, were
doing this for him for love of Christ.

Onesimus thought for a moment he was dreaming. Then he looked
about him, and asked, haltingly, where he might meet this Christ, the
head of their religion, to speak with him and thank him. Paul answered
smilingly that one day he would see Christ right there, in his house.

At the end of a few weeks, Onesimus had become a Christian. Night
and day he listened while Paul spoke of Christ to his numerous visitors.
And as he saw how Paul lived entirely forgetful of self, completely absorbed in his Christ, he, too, saw Christ with the eyes of his soul if not
his body, and he decided to become his disciple. And so master and
slave became equals in Christ.

615. There was still Philemon, however, to whom Paul had not yet
had the opportunity to send a letter. Epaphras had come to Rome for
the purpose of working with Paul and he was not yet ready to leave.
Tychicus (§ 611) was about to depart to attend to various matters in

the province of Asia and to carry a letter to the community of Colossae. He could take the letter to Philemon, then. At this point Paul thought the whole matter over. Their first plan had been right while Onesimus was outside the spiritual Christian family and subject only to human laws, but it was no longer just now that he had become their brother in Christ and dependent on the divine law of charity. He talked this over again with Epaphras and decided to send Onesimus back with Tychicus; Philemon would treat him now as Paul had done.

To this effect, Paul wrote his little note to Philemon, which is universally considered a literary gem. For all its brevity, it contains the principles for the solution of serious social questions in the light of Christian morality, and first among these the question of slavery, the difficult problem which paganism waited for Christianity to solve (§ 50). The note was undoubtedly written in Paul's own hand, and it probably took him a little over four hours to pen it (§§ 177, 180).

616. "Paul, a prisoner of Christ Jesus, and our brother Timothy, to Philemon, our beloved and fellow-worker, and to Appia, the sister, and to Archippus, our fellow-soldier, and to the church that is in thy house: grace be to you and peace from God our Father and from the Lord Jesus Christ.

"I give thanks to my God, always making remembrance of thee in my prayers, as I hear of thy charity and of the faith that thou hast in our Lord Jesus and towards all the saints [i.e., the Christians]. May the sharing of thy faith be made evident in full knowledge (ἐπιγνώσει) of all the good that is in you, in Christ Jesus. For I had great joy and consolation in thy charity, because through thee, brother, the hearts of the saints have found rest.

"For this reason, though I am very confident that I might charge thee in Christ Jesus to do what is fitting, yet for the sake of charity I prefer to plead, since thou art such as thou art; as Paul, an old man — and now also as a prisoner of Jesus Christ — I plead with thee for my own son, whom I have begotten in prison, for Onesimus. He once was useless to thee, but now is useful both to me and to thee. I am sending him back to thee, and do thou welcome him as though he were my very heart. I had wanted to keep him here with me that in thy stead he might wait on me in my imprisonment for the gospel; but I did not want to do anything without thy counsel, in order that thy kindness might not be as it were of necessity, but voluntary.

"Perhaps, indeed, he departed from thee for a short while so that thou mightest receive him forever, no longer as a slave, but instead of a slave as a brother most dear, especially to me, and how much more to thee, both in the flesh and in the Lord! If, therefore, thou dost count me as a partner, welcome him as thou wouldst me. And if he did thee any injury or owes thee anything, charge it to me. I, Paul, write it with my own hand: I will repay it — not to say to thee that thou owest me thy very self. Yes, indeed, brother! May I, too, make use of thee in the Lord! Console my heart in the Lord!

"Trusting in thy compliance I am writing to thee, knowing that thou wilt do even beyond what I say. At the same time make ready a lodging for me too, for I hope that through your prayers I shall be restored to you. Epaphras, my fellow-prisoner in Christ Jesus, Mark, Aristarchus, Demas and Luke, my fellow-workers, send thee greetings. The grace of the Lord Jesus Christ be with your spirit. Amen."

617. The humorous tone of this little note of Christian intimacy is quite evident, in contrast to the solemn epistle to the Romans and the heated polemics of *2 Corinthians*. With a pun on the name *Onesimus*, Paul says the slave was *useless* to his old master but he is now *useful* to both the old and the new. Still with a play on the Greek root of *Onesimus*, he hopes to make use (ὀναίμην) of "Useful's" former master. The slave has run away, it is true, but this has proved a good, for now he returns as a brother in Christ. He has stolen and must make restitution? Fine: Paul himself will take care of the matter. There is his signature at the end of the letter for guarantee. With a light change of tone, almost as if he clapped Philemon on the shoulder, Paul reminds him that he owes himself to the Apostle, who has made him a Christian. He then tactfully weaves in a veiled suggestion, hoping that Philemon, who understands the language of charity, will read between the lines. He will undoubtedly "do even beyond" what Paul says. What can this mean if not giving official freedom to the slave who has become his brother?

And finally, Paul tells Philemon to prepare for his arrival. This suggests that the note was written when his trial was almost over and Paul could foresee his acquittal and a subsequent journey to Colossae.

618. Antiquity has preserved for us a few examples of letters in which pagans (Pliny the Younger to Sabinianus) or Christians (papyri) intercede on behalf of runaway slaves or others in similar difficulties, but none of these has the moral significance and delicacy of this little note to Philemon. The fact that it immediately encountered particular veneration is evidenced by the fact that it has been preserved. While many other letters Paul wrote have been lost— i.e., those to the Corinthians (§§ 474, 491), that to the Laodiceans (Col. 4:16), and perhaps one to the Philippians (Phil. 3:1; cf. § 463, note) — although they certainly dealt with matters of doctrine and discipline, this familiar note to Philemon has defied the centuries and is still with us. This indicates that it was passed from hand to hand at first and then widely copied, for everyone found in it not only Paul's usual cordiality but a certain light-hearted freshness which is not apparent in his other writings.

619. *The Epistles to the Colossians and to the Ephesians.* When

Tychicus left Rome shortly afterward accompanied by Onesimus, he carried in addition to the note for Philemon at least two other letters, one addressed to the Colossians (Col. 4:7) and another to the Ephesians (Eph. 6:21). Only a short time elapsed between one and the other, the letter to the Colossians and the note to Philemon preceding the other by only a short interval. Paul had never been to Colossae (§ 461). His letter is based on the information Epaphras had brought him with regard to both the Christian community there and the one in Laodicea, the two being associated for various reasons. The converts in those regions were zealous in faith and charity, but for some time now they had revealed a disturbing tendency to theosophical speculations, which if carried further would eventually turn them from the Christian faith. It is not possible, from Paul's admonitions to them on this score, to deduce the system of doctrine which inspired the speculations, if indeed it was a well-defined and complete system. It seems certain that the prevalence of this tendency among the Colossians reflected a double circumstance: in the first place, the Phrygians had always had a conspicuous proclivity for illuministic theories of a syncretist character; in the second, this was nourished by the activity of certain doctors who, being Jewish, carried particular weight and authority among these neophytes. It is certain that the majority of Phrygian Christians were converts from paganism and not Judaism, but the Jews were numerous in those districts, for more than two centuries earlier 2000 Jewish families had been transferred to Lydia and Phrygia and had multiplied abundantly (Flavius Josephus, *Antiquities of the Jews*, XII, 147–153). As Christian communities sprouted up beside them, the doctors of the Law in these Jewish centers penetrated them bringing with them ideas peculiar to Judaism. Theirs was not the strict, closed Judaism of the Pharisaic schools of Jerusalem, however, but a more liberal form permeated with philosophical and theosophical concepts, and especially rich in those speculations on angelic beings which abound in the writings of later Judaism.

620. We may say in general that these Phrygian Christians took delight in scrutinizing the relations between God and the world, between spirit and matter, and saw scattered throughout the universe crowds of angelic mediators, differing in nature and power, who served as a kind of ladder of communication between the visible and the invisible, the human and the divine. It is likely that the Colossians had given this whole angelic world its technical name, "Fullness," *Plèroma* ($\pi\lambda\acute{\eta}\rho\omega\mu a$). We note in fact that Paul uses the term without explanation, although elsewhere he uses it in other context with its commonly accepted meaning. But while he takes the term from his neophytes Paul corrects its use, especially in its application to Christology.

The neophytes of Colossae were not content to speculate on this angelic world in itself, but mindful that they were Christians, they examined its relationship with the Messias Jesus in whom they believed. They perhaps were personally inclined to consider the Messias Jesus superior to this whole angelic Fullness, but here we may glimpse the influence of the Jewish doctors, who must have raised doubts in their minds on this score. The Messias Jesus might be superior to the less noble and lofty angelic choirs, but not to all, and much less to those most noble hierarchies of the Thrones, Dominations, Principalities, and Powers. He was anterior to all visible creatures, but not to all creatures without distinction including the invisible beings, for in that case he would be an image of Yahweh, the invisible God.

We have no more precise data on the ideas or doubts of the Colossians, but the afore-mentioned elements suggest certain features of the broad systems of Gnosis which developed in the second and third centuries. It would be quite mistaken, however, to attribute to the Christians of Phrygia the specific concepts of later Gnostic thought, and especially to give certain of the terms used by them or Paul the special meanings they acquired later in the subtle development of these Gnostic systems. In addition to the matter of speculation, there was also the question of practical rules with regard to ascetic practices and Jewish legal precepts.

621. A summary of the epistle to the Colossians follows.

The salutation mentions Timothy as well as Paul. The introduction contains a long "encomium" of the Colossians and refers to Epaphras (1:1–8).

Paul prays always for the Colossians, that they may be filled with a perfect knowledge of the will of God, "in all spiritual wisdom and understanding," and that they may conduct themselves accordingly, giving thanks to the Father who has rescued them from the power of darkness and transferred them into the kingdom of his son. "He is the image of the invisible God, the firstborn of every creature.[6] For in him were created all things in the heavens and on the earth, things visible and invisible, whether Thrones, or Dominations, or Principalities, or Powers. All things have been created through and unto him, and he is before all creatures, and in him all things hold together. Again, he is the head of his body, the Church; he, who is the beginning, the firstborn from the dead, that in all things he may have the first place. For it has pleased God the Father that in him all his fullness ($\pi\lambda\eta\rho\omega\mu\alpha$)[7] should dwell, and that through him he should reconcile to himself all

---

[6] Rather, "firstborn of all creation," i.e., born *before* any creature ($\pi\rho\omega\tau\delta\tauo\kappaos$ $\pi\acute{\alpha}\sigma\eta s$ $\kappa\tau\acute{\iota}\sigma\epsilon\omega s$).

[7] Shortly afterward Paul says that in Christ "dwells all the fullness of the Godhead bodily"; here, however, he must be referring to the fullness of "grace and truth" (cf. Jn. 1:14, 16) which is a consequence of the "Fullness of the Godhead."

things, whether on the earth or in the heavens, making peace through the blood of his cross" (1:15–20).

Thus the Colossians, once alienated through their evil deeds, are now reconciled through the death of the divine Son, provided that they persevere in the faith in the Gospel of which Paul is the minister.

Paul rejoices in the sufferings he endures for their sake, for in that way he fills up what is lacking of the sufferings of Christ for his body, which is the Church. He is indeed the minister of "the mystery which has been hidden for ages and generations, but now is clearly shown to his saints" (1:26). To spread the knowledge of this mystery among the Gentiles Paul labors with all the energy which Christ gives him. May the Colossians and Laodiceans, who do not know Paul personally, be increasingly comforted in their hearts by reason of his labors, and may they enter into a full knowledge of the mystery of God, of Christ (1:9–2:3).

622. Let them not be seduced by persuasive arguments ($\pi\iota\theta\alpha\nu\text{o}\lambda\text{o}\gamma\acute{\iota}\alpha$), but let them remain steadfast to the doctrine of Jesus Christ in which they have been instructed. "See to it that no one deceives you by philosophy and vain deceit, according to human traditions, according to the elements of the world [cf. § 509, first note] and not according to Christ. For in him dwells all the fullness of the Godhead bodily, and in him who is the head of every Principality and Power you have received of that fullness" (2:8–10). In Christ they have been circumcised spiritually, and having been buried with him in baptism they have risen with him. God canceled the decree (§ 234) of our condemnation, nailing it to the cross, and he defeated the spiritual forces against us. Let no one, therefore, bother the Colossians with rules and regulations about food and drink, or the observance of feasts, the new moon, or the Sabbath. These old institutions were a shadow of the things to come, but the substance was Christ. They are not to be deceived by those who affect humility and worship of the angels, trusting in their own imaginations but not connected with Christ, who is the head of the whole mystical body. If the Colossians "have died with Christ to the elements of the world," why must they pay any attention — as if still living in the world — to the prohibitions or precepts of human superstition. Those who advocate these observances, with a show of wisdom and asceticism, seek the gratification of the flesh (2:4–23).

623. The Colossians, risen with Christ, are to seek the things that are above, where Christ is seated at the right hand of God, not the things of the earth. They have died and their life is hidden with Christ in God, and when Christ shall appear they too will appear in glory. Let them kill all vice in their bodies, stripping off the old man and putting on the new, which is according to the image of him who created them: "Here there is not 'Gentile and Jew,' 'circumcised and uncircumcised,' 'Barbarian and Scythian,' 'slave and freeman'; but Christ is all things and in all" (3:11).

Let them clothe themselves in all virtues and especially charity. And they will have peace and joy and intimacy with God. Let wives be subject to their husbands, and husbands affectionate and kind to their wives. Let children obey their parents, and let parents not provoke their children. Slaves are to obey their masters with sincerity and simplicity, seeking to honor the Lord, and the Lord will repay them. Masters are to be just and fair with their slaves, mindful that they have a master in heaven. A few brief recommendations follow: to persevere in prayer, praying also for Paul that God may assist him "to announce the mystery of Christ (for which also I am in chains)"; to be prudent in their speech with outsiders (3:1–4, 6).

Other information and advice will be given them by Tychicus, whom Paul is sending to them for this purpose with Onesimus, "our most dear and faithful brother, who is one of you" (§ 615 ff.). He sends them the greetings of Aristarchus, of Mark the cousin of Barnabas, of Jesus called Justus, who are his only fellow workers who are Jews. Epaphras, too, sends greetings, who is praying always and working for the communities of Colossae, Laodicea, and Hierapolis. Greetings, too, from Luke, "our most dear physician," and Demas. "Greetings to the brethren who are at Laodicea and to Nymphas and the church that is in his house. And when this letter has been read among you, see that it be read in the church of the Laodiceans also, and that you yourselves read the letter from Laodicea."

The epistle closes with an autograph: "I, Paul, greet you by my own hand. Remember my chains. Grace be with you. Amen" (4:7–18).

624. As we have already noted, Tychicus took with him from Rome, in addition to the letter for the Colossians, another known today as the *Epistle to the Ephesians* (§ 619). Normally, he would have debarked in Ephesus and therefore visited that community before going to Colossae. But an examination of this epistle poses the question: To whom was it actually addressed?

It is evident at first reading that in form and content this epistle closely resembles that to the Colossians, and this resemblance is even greater than that between the epistles to the Romans and Galatians (§ 505) respectively. The division of content in *Colossians* and *Ephesians* is the same and so are the subjects treated, although in the latter they are dealt with a little more fully. In addition the letter to the Ephesians is completely general and impersonal in character, with no element to indicate it was intended particularly for readers of that city rather than any other. On the basis of any information we have today it might have been read equally well by the Christians of Laodicea, Hierapolis, Miletus, or other communities in the province of Asia (§ 12 ff.). Although Paul had lived for some time in Ephesus and was very well known to the non-Christians and Christians both (§ 469), it contains no personal greetings, in contrast to the epistle to the Romans with its long list of greetings (§ 523) although Paul at that time had never been in Rome.

The only testimony in favor of Ephesus is in the salutation of the letter, but it is far from being certain. In the ordinary editions, it is true, the letter begins: "Paul, an Apostle of Jesus Christ by the will of God to all the saints who are at Ephesus . . ." but the phrase *at Ephesus* is questioned by the critical editions and is rejected altogether by several scholars of every denomination. The reason for this, in addition to the impersonal character of the letter, is the fact that this phrase is lacking in the oldest uncial codices, the Vatican and the Sinaitic (fourth century), and in some minuscule codices, and that it was not known to ancient writers like Origen, Basilius, and perhaps others; furthermore, according to Tertullian (*Adv. Marcion.*, V, 11, 17), Marcion included this letter in his canon as an epistle addressed to the Laodiceans and not to the Ephesians.

625. There have been various attempts to explain these facts.

Some have considered that it was a form letter addressed to several communities, and that several copies were made, therefore, leaving a blank in the salutation for the insertion of the place, i.e., "to the saints who are *at Ephesus* . . ." as in the present instance, or *at Hierapolis* or *at Laodicea*, and so on.

Others have decided that this was the letter to the Laodiceans which Paul mentions at the end of his epistle to the Colossians (§ 623). The substitution of *at Ephesus* for *at Laodicea* was supposedly a *damnatio memoriae* as a consequence of the severe rebuke the church of Laodicea later earned in the *Apocalypse* (3:14–19) because of its decadence; that is, the ill-famed name of Laodicea was replaced by that of the metropolitan church of the region, namely, Ephesus.

Different explanations have found no followers.

On the other hand, not only does the phrase *at Ephesus* occur in the great majority of codices, but ecclesiastical tradition from the beginning of the second century (cf. Ignatius, *Ephesians*, 12, 2) considered that the epistle was addressed to the Ephesians, and this was true also of writers (Origen, Tertullian, Basil, etc.) who did not read the phrase *at Ephesus* in the salutation.

The observations to the contrary certainly have their weight. The question is whether they are more valid than the tradition and whether the conclusions drawn from them are legitimate.

626. It is certain that the form or circular letter with a blank space for the appropriate addressee was unknown in pagan antiquity. This theory, then, ingeniously attributes to Paul's times a modern custom.

The assumption that the letter was addressed to the Laodiceans is a specious one. This theory does not explain what authority might have ordered the *damnatio memoriae* and succeeded in having it carried out so promptly and thoroughly that only Marcion's testimony escaped, especially since in the second century the church of Laodicea had risen from its decadence and could well insist upon its right to have its name restored to the codices. In addition, Paul personally did not know the community of Colossae any more than that of Laodicea (§ 461), yet there are those personal touches and greetings in the epistle to the Colossians which are lacking in that to the Ephesians (if this had been addressed originally to the Laodiceans). In addition, Paul asks the Colossians to exchange epistles with the Laodiceans (§ 623). If the present hypothesis were true there would be no reason for exchanging them since both letters are so much alike (§ 624) that having read one is substantially equivalent to having read the other.

627. The unquestionably impersonal character of the letter may be explained, perhaps, by the fact that Paul intended it not only for the community in Ephesus but for all the communities of the province of Asia for which Ephesus was the head, but this does not mean it was a form letter in the strict sense of the word.

It may be that Paul decided to take advantage of Tychicus' impending journey to send all those communities the same admonitions he had just written out for the Colossians. He developed somewhat further the same concepts (cf. the epistle to the Romans as compared with that to the Galatians: § 505), but he omitted all personal notes or greetings. Tychicus was expressly charged to communicate any information about Paul himself (Eph. 6:21–22), and perhaps also to convey the Apostle's special greetings to specific persons. The oral additions and communications of Tychicus would thus render the letter more appropriate to each community. The epistle, however, was addressed to that in Ephesus, which was the Christian center for all of proconsular Asia. It is true that in the letter to the Colossians Tychicus is also charged with giving additional information (Col. 4:7–9), but in this instance there was also the matter of Onesimus, who is expressly mentioned.

It is possible that when Paul wrote the letter to the Colossians he had not yet thought of writing the other. As the time of Tychicus' departure drew near, he decided it would be opportune to send an epistle to all the communities in the province of Asia, and so he dictated the letter to the Ephesians along the very same lines as the former. The disappearance of the phrase *at Ephesus* may be explained by the fact that in copying the letter some communities omitted it as being no longer necessary or indicated, while other communities copied it as it was. The majority of the codices derived from the latter.

628. A very brief summary of the *Epistle to the Ephesians* follows (cf. that to the Colossians, § 621 ff.).

First Part. — Praise to God the Father who has chosen us, before the foundation of the world, to be adopted as his sons through the grace of Christ, in whom all things on earth and in heaven are re-established (ἀνακεφαλαιώσασθαι). For the faith, the Christians have received the Holy Spirit. Therefore, may they understand the mystery of the salvation wrought in them by Christ who sits at the right hand of God the Father in heaven "above every Principality and Power and Virtue and Domination — in short, above every name that is named, not only in this world, but also in that which is to come" (1:21). Christ is the head of the Church, which is his body. In the Church, Gentiles and Jews are made one, united by the grace of Christ. The wall of separation between the two, that is, the Hebrew Law, has been made void by the redemptive death of Christ, and all now are part of the spiritual edifice whose foundation is the Apostles and prophets, and whose cornerstone is Christ himself. Paul, now a prisoner, preaches this mystery. He has a deeper knowledge of it by virtue of special revelation (3:2 ff.). Therefore he prays God to strengthen the inner man in all the faithful (Chaps. 1–3).

Second Part. — The faithful are exhorted to "preserve the unity of the Spirit in the bond of peace: one body and one Spirit . . . one hope . . . one Lord, one faith, one Baptism; one God and Father of all . . ." (4:3–6). There follow certain rules with regard to the charisms (cf. § 211 ff.); admonitions not to imitate the customs of the pagans, to divest themselves of the old man in order to put on the new; a list of vices to avoid and virtues to practice; the duties of wives and husbands, of children, parents, slaves, and masters (4:6–6:9).

The Christian is a spiritual soldier who fights, not against flesh and blood, but "against the Principalities and the Powers, against the world-rulers of this darkness, against the spiritual forces of wickedness on high" (6:12; cf. 2:2). Therefore he must put on a complete armor, girding himself with truth and having a breastplate of justice, his feet shod with readiness, his shield of faith, his helmet of salvation, and his sword of the Spirit (§ 233).

Tychicus will give them news of Paul himself. The letter closes with general greetings (6:10–24).

629. *The Epistle to the Philippians.* When Tychicus departed with these letters there still remained with Paul another visitor who had come from afar to assist him and instead needed assistance himself. This was Epaphroditus who had brought the prisoner of Christ the financial assistance sent him by his beloved sons in Philippi (§ 604). But during his stay in Rome, Epaphroditus contracted a serious illness, about which we are given no details. (Some scholars have immediately diagnosed this as malaria. Romans find this not only arbitrary but highly unlikely.) For a long time he was in danger of dying, and his convalescence was a long one, long enough, in fact, for the news of his illness to reach Philippi and the communication to come back to Rome that all his brethren there were seriously disturbed at his condition, which saddened him greatly. But by the will of God, the illness was cured, his strength regained, and he was able to undertake the return journey. Much time had passed by now; the second year of Paul's imprisonment was almost over and he could foresee the end of his trial before long.

Naturally so dear a visitor could not depart without a letter from Paul. The news Epaphroditus had brought about the community of Philippi had been good news, and the help had been most opportune. Paul must write them these things and at the same time satisfy his own heart, which was particularly attached to these Christians, his "firstborn" in Europe. It was in these circumstances that Paul dictated the *Epistle to the Philippians,* which is more affectionate, serene, and restful than any of his other writings, and in addition contains some of the peaks of Paul's religious thought. It seems a conversation among friends, gathered about the hearth, but it is a Christian hearth and above it hangs a crucifix. A summary follows.

630. In the salutation, Paul, with Timothy, sends wishes for grace and peace "to all the saints in Christ Jesus that are at Philippi, with the bishops [cf. § 531, note] and deacons."

He thinks of them always and prays for them because of their affectionate association with him from the first day until now, confident that God who has begun a good work in them will bring it to perfection. Paul feels this same affection for them, for they share in his chains and in the defense of the Gospel. God is his witness that he longs for them all in the Heart of Christ Jesus, and prays that their charity may ever abound increasingly in full knowledge and discernment, so that they may be pure and without reproach unto the day of Christ. He tells them that his experiences in Rome have resulted in good for the Gospel. The whole Praetorium speaks of him, and many brethren, with good will or from envy, have begun to preach the Christ (cf. §§ 606–609 for the discussion of these passages). In this the prayers of the Philippians will help him, for he desires nothing but to glorify Christ with his life and with his death. For him Christ is life and death is gain. If he lives, it is to work for the glory of Christ; but if he dies, he will be freed and united with him. This would be much better for Paul, but for the Philippians it is better that he remain, and thus, with this conviction, he stays on. Let their behavior be worthy of the Gospel, so that whether he revisits them or remains absent from them, he may know they are steadfast in one spirit, striving together for the faith of the Gospel and suffering for Christ (Chap. 1).

631. They must have charity and a sense of solidarity and a spirit of self-denial toward one another, each one regarding the others as his superiors and looking out not for his own interests but for those of others. This is the example given us by the Christ Jesus, "who being in the form of God, thought it not robbery[8] to be equal with God: but emptied (ἐκένωσεν) himself, taking the form of a servant [slave], being made in the likeness of men, and in habit [aspect] found as a man. He humbled himself [even more] becoming obedient unto death, even to the death of the cross. For which cause God also hath exalted him, and hath given him a name which is above all names; that in the name of Jesus every knee should bow, of those that are in heaven, on earth, and under the earth: and that every tongue should confess that the Lord Jesus Christ is in the glory of God the Father" (2:6–11). The Philippians, then, are also to be obedient, co-operating for their salvation with what God works in them. Let them be blameless and guileless in the midst of a perverse generation, fulfilling the boast Paul makes of them, to their mutual rejoicing.

He hopes soon to send to them Timothy, his beloved co-worker, who also loves them. He hopes to come to them himself. But meanwhile, he is sending Epaphroditus, who has been gravely ill. He was grieved to learn that they had been anxious because of him. They are to welcome him then with all joy and gratitude for what he has done for them (Chap. 2).

632. They are to beware of the dogs, of the evil companions, of the mutilated.[9] We are the truly circumcised who serve God in spirit and have no confidence in the flesh. Paul, too, might have confidence in the flesh and boast that he was circumcised on the eighth day, that he is of the race of Israel, of the tribe of Benjamin, a Hebrew of Hebrews, as regards the Law a Pharisee, and as for zeal a persecutor of the Church — blameless, therefore, according to the justice of the Law! But these things now, as compared with Christ, he counts no longer a gain but a loss. In fact, he counts everything as loss for him in comparison with the excelling knowledge of Jesus Christ, for whom he has lost all things and now counts them as dung (σκύβαλα, § 170). He esteems only that justice which comes from faith in Christ and the imitation of Christ, whereby one grows like him. May he lay hold of

---

[8] Robbery, ἁρπαγμόν, in the sense of an object snatched and forcibly retained, that is, avidly possessed and jealously guarded, which one never consents to give up. This metaphor is used in describing the attitude of Jesus who was not jealously attached to his equality with God "but rather emptied himself. . . ." It is clear that Christ did not "empty himself" of his equality in divine nature but the external manifestation of the prerogatives of this equality. In so doing, he took "the form of a slave" (in antithesis to "the form of God") and "humbled himself."

[9] A reference to the Judaizing Christians who had penetrated the Philippian community; "mutilated" is here used as a term of disparagement for the circumcised; cf. what follows immediately and cf. also § 170 at the end.

Christ as Christ has laid hold of him! (§ 283.) He has not yet attained this goal but he presses toward it like those who run races in the stadium. He exhorts the Philippians to imitate him, but to beware of the enemies of the cross of Christ, whose god is their belly and who think only of earthly things. But our citizenship is in heaven, from which we await Jesus Christ as Saviour, who will refashion our lowly bodies and render them like his own glorious body (Chap. 3).

633. He exhorts the Philippians, his beloved and dearly longed for brethren, his joy and his crown, to stand fast in the Lord. Those two good women, Evodia and Syntyche, are to forget their old disagreement and be of one mind in the Lord (§ 384). His "loyal comrade" (*syzygus*, §§ 244, 383) is to help them. Let them always rejoice: the Lord is near.[10] Let them pray, that they may enjoy the peace of the Lord and love all that is noble, just, and pure (4:1–9).

The solicitude the Philippians have shown in the past for Paul's needs has now had another occasion to express itself. He, indeed, knows how to live both in privation and in abundance. But he is pleased by the help they have sent him; in so doing they have shared in his affliction. They know that since leaving Macedonia he has accepted help only from them, once or twice, while he was in Thessalonica. What he has received now from Epaphroditus is more than sufficient. It was truly a holy offering, well pleasing to God, and God will reward them.

He sends greetings to all in Christ Jesus. "All the saints greet you, especially those of Caesar's household [§ 610]. The grace of our Lord Jesus Christ be with your spirit. Amen" (4:10–23).

*   *   *

634. As was to be expected, the authenticity of the four letters written in prison, especially *Colossians* and *Ephesians*, has been challenged by a number of radical critics. They lightheartedly reject the testimony of the earliest tradition, which is unanimous in assigning these four writings to Paul (while in rare instances, where the traditional data seems to favor their ideas, they make a great show of it). Their arguments consist mainly of strictly personal judgments on the concepts set forth in the rejected letters and secondarily on philological considerations.

For example, since the Christological teaching and the doctrine of the mystical body of Christ are much more fully developed in *Colossians* and especially in *Ephesians* than in Paul's previous letters, this gives rise to the suspicion that they are not his work — as if Paul had to write down everything he had in his head the first time he penned an epistle, or as if his thought could not undergo a progressive development. The

---

[10] "The Lord is near" — this is another basis of argument for the eschatologists. What was said with reference to the epistles to the Corinthians (§ 483, note) and the Romans (§ 522, note) is valid here too; cf. also § 489, note.

fact that *Ephesians* is a faithful elaboration of *Colossians* proves that it is the work of a forger, who has embroidered the preceding writing, which was perhaps authentic — as if an author could not himself, in special circumstances, elaborate and develop one of his own writings while preserving its general outlines. Finally these letters, and *Ephesians* especially, contain words Paul does not use elsewhere. This is true, but it is also true that they contain other words he has used elsewhere, while the new terms employed are fully justified by the fact that he is treating new subject matter (just as Luke abounds in new words when he describes the voyage and shipwreck, § 99).

But it is useless to persist in replies to such objections, for the true reasons underlying the latter are much deeper than the historical-conceptual or philological arguments adduced for them (§ 120 ff.).

Last Years.
Second Roman Imprisonment. Death

---

635. When the sun sets behind a chain of mountains, darkness does not fall suddenly but is preceded by a period of half-light which outlines a few peaks against the dimming sky. When the shadows close about the peaks, we know the sun has gone although we cannot see the precise point of its setting. And this is somewhat our circumstance with regard to Paul. His first Roman imprisonment ended, and with it the data in the letters he wrote at that time, we enter a period of half-light, in which we may glimpse some certain items of information, but they are extremely few and the connection between them is not clear. They are the few peaks still outlined with light above the sea of obscurity that has fallen over all the rest.

The certain data we possess after Paul was freed from the *custodia militaris* is as follows:

At a given time Paul was in Ephesus with Timothy. From there he departed for Macedonia, leaving Timothy in Ephesus (1 Tim. 1:3).

At another time he was on the island of Crete with Titus, and departed while Titus remained behind (Tit. 1:5).

After his departure from Crete, we find him in Nicopolis, certainly the city of this name in Epirus (§ 43). Before his arrival there he had written to Titus, in Crete, to meet him in Nicopolis (3:12).

At another time when Titus was no longer in Crete but in Dalmatia, Paul, again a prisoner in Rome, wrote to Timothy begging him to come as soon as possible. Before that he had been in Troas and had passed through Corinth and Miletus (2 Tim. 1:17; 4:9–21).

In addition to these facts, we must keep in mind two plans Paul had made in the past which he might have been able to carry out in this period. One was his old project to visit Spain (§§ 513, 523) and the other was his more recent plan to visit Philemon in Colossae, whom he had asked to prepare a lodging for him (§ 617).

But what was the sequence of these certain and probable events?

636. Some have supposed that as soon as Paul was freed he went to Colossae, since this was his most recent plan and he had announced his coming to Philemon. That it was his latest idea may be true, but it is also true that Paul, who was full of plans, still had in mind his older and more cherished hope to go to Spain. Which did he decide to do first, since one journey would take him to the East and the other to the Far West? We do not know, but in all likelihood he went to Spain first, both for the reason mentioned above, and in view of the fact that Spain was for him a new field of endeavor and therefore more attractive. And finally it was much easier to get to Spain from Rome than from elsewhere.

It is almost certain that Paul actually did make this journey to Spain. At the end of the first century, Clement of Rome (*Corinth.*, 5, 7) stated that Paul, "after having taught justice to the entire world and having come to the ends of the West, gave testimony. . . ." The expression the "ends of the West," for someone writing in Rome, could not have any meaning except with reference to Spain. The Muratorian Fragment, about the year 180,[1] speaks precisely of a journey made to Spain by Paul, and in agreement with this we have the apocryphal *Acts of Peter*, the *Acts of Paul*, and the subsequent testimony of many of the Fathers (Athanasius, Epiphanius, Chrysostom, Jerome . . .). Some maintain that these testimonies are based solely on Paul's expressed intention to go to Spain (Rom. 15:24, 28). But this would have to be proved and not merely affirmed, while the earliest testimonies, being of Roman origin, suggest rather that they derive from other local documents.

We have no details concerning this voyage or its results. Paul probably went by sea, but the entire journey could not have lasted very long. After a few months he must have been back in Rome, since it would have been difficult for him to embark directly for Greece and the Orient from Spain.

As for the facts listed above of which we are sure, we can only guess at their probable sequence. One possible reconstruction of these events follows.

637. Paul left for Spain shortly after his acquittal in the year 63, and returned to Rome during the first half of 64. There he found Luke who was finishing his writing of the *Acts* (§ 118). In July of 64 the great fire of Rome broke out, which was followed by the persecution of the Christians. The *Acts* was brought to an abrupt close (cf. § 118), and immediately afterward Paul left Rome, stopping in some unknown town in Italy, from which he sent the epistle to the Hebrews (§ 650 ff.).

This was probably a harbor town where there was a Christian community, like Puteoli (§ 596) or even Ostia or Porto, where inscriptions attest the presence of Jews from early times. Paul took refuge there both to escape the imperial police, which was particularly interested in his capture, and to await a convenient opportunity to sail for the East.

---

[1] Cf. *The Life of Christ*, p. 116 (§ 136).

He succeeded on both counts, and at the beginning of the year 65 he was in Ephesus with Timothy. Here we have certain information as to the facts but not the sequence of time.

After a sojourn of undetermined length, Paul left Timothy in Ephesus and departed for Macedonia, where he wrote the *First Epistle to Timothy*. From Macedonia, stopping perhaps in Corinth on his way, he went to a new zone of activity, going with Titus to evangelize the island of Crete. He perhaps had had this in mind since he had touched there during his voyage to Rome (§ 578). When the work here was well on its way, he left Titus on Crete and went to another place, though we do not know where. Having decided to spend the winter in Nicopolis (§ 635), probably in the year 65–66, he wrote to Titus to join him in that city.

Nicopolis: Ruins of the Theater

The winter in Nicopolis must have been spent in intense activity, preaching the Gospel in the surrounding country, especially to the north, for later Paul sent Titus to Dalmatia (2 Tim. 4:10).

638. Suddenly we find Paul again a prisoner in Rome, from where he dispatches his last writing, the *Second Epistle to Timothy* (1:17). The circumstances of this new arrest are most obscure. It almost certainly did not occur in Rome but in some distant place, where the imperial police, who had been looking for him since his departure from Rome, finally caught up with him.

One or two things in his last letter may shed some tiny bit of light on this event. He says that he left his cloak, his books, and his parchments in Troas (§ 526 ff.) at the home of a certain Carpus (2 Tim.

4:13), and he asks Timothy to bring these things with him when he comes to Rome. This departure from Troas, so sudden that he had not time to take his cloak or the precious writings he had always with him, suggests the circumstances of an arrest here. From Troas he would have been taken to the capital of the province, which was Ephesus (§§ 18, 21), and there his trial would be begun before the tribunal of the proconsul. But the popularity Paul once enjoyed even among the pagans of that city (469) had died away. This time his defenders were few, among them Timothy (1:4), Onesiphorus, Aquila, and Priscilla (1:16–18; 4:19). Many turned coward, however, and abandoned him, and among these were some, like Phigelus and Hermogenes, who least of all should have behaved thus (1:15). His most bitter enemy was Alexander the coppersmith (§ 469, note) who did him "much harm" (4:14–15). From Ephesus, the prisoner, with the usual *elogium* (§ 572), must have been sent to Rome by sea, and he was accompanied by a small group of disciples. But this dwindled along the way, for Trophimus (§ 543) fell ill and stopped at Miletus, Erastus (§ 426, cf. § 466) remained behind in Corinth (4:20), others left through cowardice or from obedience after their arrival in Rome, until one day only the faithful Luke (4:11) was left with the prisoner.

This picture of Paul, in chains again and attended by Luke, is the

Deceased in the Attitude of an Orante. Rome: Catacombs of Domitilla —
Third Century (Pontifical Institute of Christian Archeology)

last we have of him in his writings. It was probably the end of the year
66 or the beginning of 67.

I repeat, however, that this sequence from the year 63 to 67 is pure
conjecture. Too much information is lacking both as to the events themselves and the chronology to permit anything else.

639. *The Pastoral Letters.* The three writings from which we glean
the few pieces of information discussed here are known today as the
Pastoral Letters, since they deal in general with the administration or
government of the churches both with respect to internal organization
and various external dangers. A summary follows.

The First Epistle to Timothy — After the salutation and greeting, Paul
reminds Timothy that he left him in Ephesus that he might oppose those
who teach "fables and endless genealogies" (1:4), which are both useless
and harmful. Some claim to be Doctors of the Law but they are charlatans, who do not know that the Law is good provided it is rightly
used, and that it exists not for the just but for various types of sinners.
This is the doctrine of the Gospel of which Paul is minister, having been
so chosen through the mercy of God although he had been formerly a
persecutor. He commits the same charge to Timothy that he may exercise it differently from the others who "have made shipwreck of the
faith, among whom are Hymeneus and Alexander, whom I have delivered up to Satan that they may learn not to blaspheme" (Chap. 1).

Prayers are to be offered for all men, including kings and all those
in high authority, since God desires all to be saved. There is one God,
and there is one mediator Jesus Christ who gave himself to ransom all
men. Men are to pray lifting up their hands, and women in decent and
unostentatious dress. Women are to listen and not teach (in the Christian gatherings), for they are subordinate to men, and their duty is
childbearing. The bishop (§ 531, second note) must be blameless, married only once, possessed of many virtues, and exemplary in the manage-
ment of his own family. The deacons must be endowed with similar
qualities (2–3:13).

640. Paul hopes to rejoin Timothy soon, but in case of delay, he is
to conduct himself always in conformity with the norm that the house
of God is "the Church of the living God, the pillar and mainstay of
the truth." There follows a brief passage on the "mystery of godliness,"
which is lyric in tone and is taken perhaps from some early Christian
canticle. This mystery is centered in Jesus Christ who was

> Manifested in the flesh,
> Justified in the spirit,
> Revealed to angels,
> Preached to Gentiles,
> Believed in the world,
> Taken up in glory (3:16).

But the Spirit says that in aftertimes there will be many deceits and
hypocrisies. Impostors will appear preaching that marriage is forbidden
and certain foods prohibited. Timothy must fight such doctrines. He
must avoid old wives' tales and train himself in godliness. Notwithstanding his youth, let him be an example to all; he must not neglect
the charism that is in him, granted to him through prophecy with the
laying on of the hands of the presbyterate (3:14–4:16).

Timothy is to treat all the faithful in a manner suitable for their state.
Let him see that widows lead an exemplary life. Those helped by the
community must be sixty years of age, and of respectable and worthy
conduct. Young widows are to remarry. If a Christian has a relative who
is a widow, he is to provide for her so that the community may be able
to provide for the others. The "elders" are to command special respect,
especially those who preach and teach, and accusations against them
are not to be lightly believed. Timothy is not to impose hands except
on those in whom he has complete confidence. Paul tells him to stop
drinking only water and to take a little wine also because of his frequent
infirmities (Chap. 5).

There follow various admonitions regarding slaves and masters, the
preachers of novel doctrine, and avarice. Timothy is exhorted to lead a
blameless life, to admonish the rich, and to protect the deposit of faith
against the lying disciples of false knowledge.

641. *The Epistle to Titus* — There is a solemn salutation in which
Paul draws attention to his prerogatives as a preacher of the Gospel
(this was opportune for a community but recently established — 1:1–4).

Paul has left Titus in Crete that he might appoint "elders" in every
city. (Later they are also called "overseers" or "bishops" — cf. § 531,
note 60.) Those he chooses must be blameless, married but once, and
their children must be believing and of exemplary conduct. They must
not be proud or given to anger but must have the virtues which are
the antithesis of these things. These gifts are necessary that they may
combat the many impostors, most of whom are Jews, and they are especially opportune among the Cretans, one of whose "prophets" has said:
"Cretans, always liars, evil beasts, lazy gluttons" (§ 232). Titus is to
rebuke them sharply, that they may remain sound in the faith and "may
not listen to Jewish fables and the commandments of men who turn
away from the truth" (1:14). These give lip service to God but their
actions deny him (Chap. 1).

There are particular obligations for each station in life: old men,
elderly women, younger women, youths, slaves. All must live justly and
piously in this world, "awaiting the blessed hope and manifestation of
the glory of our great God and Savior, Jesus Christ" (Chap. 2).

Christians are to obey the magistrates and be moderate and mild with
all men; they must divest themselves of their old faults. The goodness

and kindness of God our Saviour has appeared, who through his mercy saved us with the bath of regeneration and renewal of the Holy Spirit poured forth upon us. Titus is to insist upon this doctrine and avoid "foolish controversies and genealogies and quarrels and disputes about the Law." The heretic is to be admonished a first and second time, and then he is to be avoided as self-condemned (3:1-11).

When Paul sends Artemas or Tychicus, then Titus is to join the Apostle in Nicopolis where he intends to spend the winter. He is to help Zenas the lawyer and Apollos on their way. The letter closes with general greetings (3:12-15).

642. *The Second Epistle to Timothy* — After the salutation, Paul thanks God and states that he remembers Timothy constantly in his prayers, longing to see him again. Paul recalls his tears and his guileless faith, which dwelt first in his grandmother Lois and his mother Eunice (§ 372). Let him rekindle the charism of God which is in him, and which he received through the laying on of Paul's hands. Let him not be ashamed to give testimony for our Lord and his prisoner Paul, and let him share the hardships suffered for the Gospel. Let him trust in the power of God who has called us in virtue of the grace bestowed on us in Christ Jesus eternal ages ago and made manifest now through the appearing of the Saviour Christ Jesus. For him Paul suffers these things, but he is certain that Christ guards the deposit entrusted by him to Paul "against that day." Timothy too is to guard the good trust of the teaching he has received from Paul (1:1-14).

Timothy knows that all in the province of Asia have turned away from Paul, including Phigelus and Hermogenes. But Onesiphorus has remained faithful and has not been ashamed of Paul's chains. In fact, he has come to Rome and sought him out diligently until he found him. May God reward him! Timothy also knows very well how much Onesiphorus has already done for Paul in Ephesus (1:15-18).

Timothy is to give the teachings he has received from Paul to trustworthy men. He must fight like a good soldier of Christ Jesus. The soldier does not entangle himself in worldly affairs, so that he may be pleasing to him who has enrolled him in the army. The athlete in the stadium and the farmer in his fields are also of single purpose. Let Timothy remember that Jesus Christ rose from the dead according to Paul's Gospel, for which he suffers chains like a criminal although the word of God is not bound by chains. If we die with Christ we shall live with him, and if we remain faithful to him we shall reign with him (2:1-13).

Timothy is not to dispute with words, but he is to give good example as the upright dispenser of truth. Hymeneus and Philetus have wandered from the truth, saying that the resurrection has taken place already, and they are destroying the faith of some. But Timothy is not to be surprised at the presence of these evil ones because the Church is like a great house, in which there are vessels not only of gold and silver, but also of wood and earthenware. Timothy is to be a gentle teacher, avoiding foolish discussions (2:14–26).

643. In the last days, difficult times will come. Men will be filled with vice although making a semblance of piety. Of this number are those who insinuate themselves into houses and captivate silly women whose heads are full of errors and who are led astray by various desires. Just as Jamnes and Mambres rose against Moses (§ 241) so do these rise against the truth. But they will be confounded. Timothy is well acquainted from experience with Paul's conduct and the sufferings in (Pisidian) Antioch, Iconium, and Lystra, from which the Lord rescued him. All those who desire to live piously in Christ Jesus are persecuted; therefore Timothy must be constant and faithful to the teachings he has received and the examples he has seen. From his childhood he has known Sacred Scripture, which can instruct him to salvation through faith in Christ Jesus: "All Scripture is inspired by God and useful for teaching, for reproving, for correcting, for instructing in justice . . ." (Chap. 3).

Paul charges Timothy to be zealous in spreading and defending the sound doctrine. A time will come when men will not endure the truth but will secure teachers who will please their ears, but he must remain faithful to his office, fulfilling his ministry. "I am already being poured out as a libation, and the time of my departure is impending . . ." (cf. this entire passage in § 171).

The Apostle asks Timothy to hurry and come to him, for Demas has left him (§ 611), Crescens is in Galatia (or Gaul?), Titus in Dalmatia, and only Luke is with him. He is to bring Mark with him for he will be of great help to Paul. He has sent Tychicus to Ephesus. When Timothy comes, he is to bring the cloak, books, and parchments which Paul left in Troas at the house of Carpus. Alexander the coppersmith has done him a great deal of harm. Timothy is to beware of him. "At my first defense no one came to my support, but all forsook me; may it not be laid to their charge. But the Lord stood by me and strengthened me, that through me the preaching of the gospel might be completed, and that all the Gentiles might hear; and I was delivered from the lion's mouth" (4:16–17). At the end, Paul sends his greetings to Priscilla and Aquila and to the household of Onesiphorus. He tells Timothy that Erastus stayed in Corinth, and that Trophimus was left in Miletus because he fell ill. He bids Timothy to hurry and come before the winter. And he closes with greetings from Eubulus, Pudens, Linus, and Claudia.

✱   ✱   ✱

644. A unanimous tradition, attested from the first half of the second century, attributes the three pastoral epistles to Paul. The only dissenter, even among the heretics, was Marcion (the case of Tatian is doubtful), who in his usual fashion rejected the three writings, not on the basis of historical evidence which conflicted with the tradition but because the concepts they contained did not conform to his own ideas. It was not until the nineteenth century that Marcion's judgment and also his method found honor, with this difference that the fixed canons of various schools were substituted for his theological concepts.

The postulates underlying these canons are as follows: the ecclesiastical organization and hierarchy reflected in the pastoral epistles are too highly developed for Paul's time and must belong to the late second century; the heretics indicated in these epistles are actually the followers of the great gnostic currents of the second century, especially that of Marcion, and therefore the epistles are later than these systems. These postulates are buttressed with still other arguments: these letters differ in language and style from those which we are certain Paul wrote; the doctrine of a united and organized Church cannot be Paul's teaching, since he contemplated only the free message of faith in Christ (and, the eschatologists add, the imminent parousia); finally, there is no period in all Paul's life to which these three epistles may be assigned.

645. But as usual the first confident flush of negation was followed by a period of hesitant reflection. The ancient testimonies for the authenticity of the letters could not be accepted, but the *tabula rasa* decreed by the modern critics was perhaps a little excessive. And so the road of compromise was chosen. Many scholars assumed that the three epistles — and especially *Titus* and *2 Timothy* — incorporated several little authentic "notes" written by Paul but rewritten and retouched by later hands. Thus it was possible to introduce the usual method of "selection" to sift the authentic from the false.

Several fragments were thus selected, but naturally they varied from one scholar to the next, and a passage accepted as unquestionably authentic by one critic was rejected as unquestionably spurious by another. Thus there is quite a bit of variation in the "reconstructions." In view of our previous discussion (§ 120 ff.), it is unnecessary to dwell on the lack of basic critical objectivity in these methods. It is only natural, however, to ask how these patient astrologers of scriptural criticism can expect their gratuitous conclusions to be accepted when they themselves do not accept the authoritative testimony of antiquity. One affirmation of the second century in the Muratorian Fragment (and a number of other documents in the present instance) is worth much more than a hundred negations decreed by the disciples of modern theories which are destined to wither in a few decades.

646. The supporting arguments listed above are quite specious.

Is there no period in Paul's life to which these letters can be attributed? There is, if we do not end his life with the *Acts* (§ 116 ff.). If, as various sources indicate, Paul lived for several years after his release from his first Roman imprisonment, we have a period more than sufficient for these three epistles, which in themselves require such a period. Paul had foreseen that his first imprisonment would end not in conviction but his release, and he had expressly stated this in the letters written during this imprisonment.

Paul could not have taught the doctrine of an organized Church? It may be that this does not conform to the doctrine of Paul as envisaged by the Tübingen School or the eschatologists, but it does not follow that these two schools have painted a truer picture of Paul than that in the documents. If we put together the elements of Paul's teaching on the Church which are scattered through his previous letters and the *Acts*, we find that there is agreement between them and what he says — more fully and emphatically — in the pastoral epistles.

The language and style of the pastorals is different from the other epistles? Yes and no. Here, too, the words and phrases have been carefully listed and counted. Of 897 words, 133 are not found in Paul's other writings (excluding the *Epistle to the Hebrews*) and another 171 are not found in Paul's other writings or in the rest of the New Testament — a total, therefore, of 304 words which form the special lexical patrimony of the pastorals as compared with the other epistles. There is also a conspicuous number of special phrases and *hapax legomena*.

647. These indications are true (although more recent calculations differ somewhat and tend to diminish the lexical differences between the two groups of writings) but the conclusion drawn from them is not true, namely, that the author was different.

In the first place, there still remain the majority of the words, almost two thirds of the total, which are found in both sets of writings. And what of the influence on language and style exercised in every age and on every writer by the subject matter he is treating and the circumstances in which he writes? There are abundant examples of this it is unnecessary to cite. Must we demand that in his old age Paul should write exactly as he did in the full flowering of his young energy? And now that he provides with great solicitude for the internal life of the communities, must he use the same choice of words and figures as when he was engaging in polemics with the Judaizers of Galatia? Does not this new subject matter require new terms or a new use of old terms?

It has in fact been noted that the pastorals differ in choice of language from the epistles written during his first imprisonment in far less degree than they differ from the earlier epistles. And this is easily explainable. Paul, during his first imprisonment, is already an older man and is dealing with subjects much closer to the content of the pastorals than that of his earlier epistles. Also to be noted is the lack of any structural outline in the pastorals, which seem to jump from one topic to the next. This, however, is due both to their character and the circumstances in which they were written. Paul is giving practical rules for various occasions or conditions as they come to mind, sometimes interrupting himself or repeating something he has already said. It should also be remembered that 2 *Timothy*, written during his last, harsh imprisonment, must have been composed amid many physical difficulties.

648. There remain the basic postulates for rejecting the authenticity of the pastorals.

It is not at all true that the ecclesiastical organization and hierachy reflected in these letters are too precocious and must be assigned to the late second century. The very contrary is true, namely, that in the first decade of the second century we find this development much more advanced than that reflected in the pastorals. In the letters of Ignatius of Antioch, written between 107 and 108, we find described in detail the hierarchy of an authoritative, established, and resident episcopate.[2] At the peak of this hierarchy is the "overseer" (*episcopus*, bishop), who is the vicar of God and Jesus Christ; subordinate to him are the "elders" or presbyters, who represent the college of the Apostles; and below them are the deacons, who are the dispensers of the mysteries of Christ. "Without these [three groups] it cannot be called a church" (*Trallian.*, 3, 1). This situation is not true of the pastorals, in which the terms "elder" and "overseer" or "bishop" are used interchangeably (Tit. 1:5, 7; cf. also *Acts* and § 531, note), and in which Titus and Timothy are only the vicars of Paul and represent his authority but are not assigned to an established see or permanent residence. This indicates a period of incomplete organization, and therefore anterior to the organization reflected in Ignatius' letters.

This organization was developing and spreading more or less rapidly according to the different regions, but it cannot be maintained historically that at the time of the pastoral letters (A.D. 64–67) the work is already completed as we have it described by Ignatius fifty years later. Clement of Rome, writing to the Corinthians between the years 96–98, speaks of the grade of deacons as separate from that of the "overseers" or bishops (*Corint.*, 42, 4–5) but elsewhere he also calls the latter "elders" or presbyters. To sum up then, the pastorals reflect an ecclesiastical organization which is less developed and complete than that in existence during the first decade of the second century, and therefore they belong to an earlier period; this confirms what tradition tells us with regard to the date of their composition.

---

[2] Texts and references in A. Casamassa, *I Padri Apostolici*, Rome, 1938, pp. 150–153.

649. The other argument against their authenticity is even less founded. The pastorals do not argue against the great gnostic systems of the second century, whether that of Marcion, Valentine, or others, but they do combat certain doctrinal elements anterior to these systems. The antecedents of the Gnosis of the second century are not at all clear, but they certainly go back farther than the great systems designed in that century. We indicated some traces of such elements in the epistles written in prison (§ 619 ff.). In their turn the pastorals indicate that the exponents of these ideas come from Judaism (Tit. 1:10), that they are doctors of the Law (1 Tim. 1:7), that they engender disputes about the Law (Tit. 3:9), impose the precepts of men (1:14), and recount Jewish fables and endless genealogies (1 Tim. 1:4; Tit. 1:14; 3:9). The Jewish coloring is conspicuous in all of these, but it is utterly lacking in the long genealogies of eons and other angelic beings constructed by the great gnostic systems. The Jewish genealogies referred to in the pastorals are those which relate rather to the patriarchs of the Hebrew nation, constructed by the *haggadah* (§ 76 ff.) and preserved in various Jewish *midrashim*, especially in the apocryphal *Book of Jubilees* composed in Palestine in the second century B.C. Naturally these Jewish elements may have been mixed with others of different origin and blended by individual speculations, to which the pastorals do allude but in too vague a manner for us to understand them today. In any case, they are a far cry from the detailed gnostic systems that developed in the next century.

650. *The Epistle to the Hebrews* — A singular writing which the majority of testimonies attribute to Paul and which is known as the *Epistle to the Hebrews* can be assigned to no other time in Paul's life than this twilight period we are discussing.

Often a huge mass of rock stands alone in a stretch of plain encircled by some vast mountain range. No connection between it and the mountains which surround it in the distance is at all evident. It is one of the "erratic masses" detached from the parent range in prehistoric times and carried down into the valley by some geological phenomenon. An analysis of its rock, however, proves it to be of the same composition as that of the encircling mountains. We may not know how or when it became detached but we can be certain of its origin.

This comparison suggests itself spontaneously when we attempt to summarize what tradition and analysis tell us of the relationship between the *Epistle to the Hebrews* and the other writings of Paul.

A reading of the epistle suggests still another comparison. *Genesis* tells us that Jacob covered his hands with goatskin to deceive his blind father Isaac into thinking he was his brother Esau in order that he might steal for himself the paternal blessing due the first-born. Surprised by Jacob's voice, Isaac asked to touch him to make sure of his identity and even then he remained doubtful, exclaiming: "The voice indeed is the voice of Jacob, but the hands are the hands of Esau" (Gen. 27:22). We have a similar reaction on reading *Hebrews*. An analysis says it is Paul but the voice is not the voice of Paul.

651. This was noted as early as the second century. and tradition remained hesitant with regard to this letter for several centuries thereafter. In contrast to its confident assertions with respect to Paul's other writings, it often did not recognize him as author and sometimes denied its authenticity altogether. We must distinguish here, however, between the Western and the Eastern Church, for these two great sectors of Christianity took completely opposite views not only with regard to *Hebrews* but also to the *Apocalypse*. While not a few Greeks denied that John the Apostle was the author of the *Apocalypse* and excluded it from the canon, the Latins unanimously accepted it as the work of John and a canonical writing. On the other hand, while many Latins either did not know the letter to the Hebrews at all or else attributed it to authors other than Paul, or explicitly excluded it from the canon, the Greeks unanimously accepted it as canonical and assigned it to Paul, although some of them supposed that he was not responsible for its literary form.

It would take too long to list the names of the Greeks who do accept the epistle as canonical and Paul's, to whom might be added a few Syrians of the fourth century, and equally long to list the Latin authors previous to the fifth century who hold the opposite view. We shall consider, therefore, merely a few of the most representative testimonies.

652. The highly authoritative Muratorian Fragment does not mention the epistle and neither does Cyprian of Carthage. Tertullian cites it but attributes it to Barnabas and probably does not consider it a canonical writing (*De pudic.*, 20). Gregorius of Elvira[3] also attributes it to Barnabas. In 392 Jerome stated that the letter "among the Romans has not up to the present time been considered [the work] of the Apostle Paul" (*De viris illust.*, 59). But it is evident from the testimony of others and from what he himself says elsewhere that this statement is a little too summary: "It must be said that this letter, which bears the title 'To the Hebrews' is accepted not only by the churches of the Orient but also by all the past ecclesiastical authors of the Greek language as [a writing] of the apostle Paul, although many believe it to be of Barnabas or Clement. Nor does it matter whose it is since it is by a Churchman and is commemorated in the everyday reading in the churches. For if the custom of the Latins is not to accept it among the canonical Scriptures, the churches of the Greeks with equal freedom do not accept the Apocalypse of John; nevertheless we accept both, thus following not the custom of the present time but the authority of the ancient authors" (*Ad Dardan.*, epist. 129, 3; in Migne, *Patr. Lat.*, 22, 1103).

---

[3] Or whoever else was the author of the *Tractatus Origenis de libris SS. Scripturarum*. Cf. the edition of P. Batiffol, Paris, 1900, p. 108.

At the beginning of the fifth century, Augustine was still doubtful of the authorship of the epistle though not of its canonicity. Up until about the year 407 he had listed it among the fourteen epistles of Paul, but from 409 on he avoids citing it as Paul's work and expressly records his doubts as to its author. To evaluate his position correctly, however, it should be remembered that he attended as a priest the Council of Hippo in 393, and as a bishop the Council of Carthage in 397, at which the thirteen epistles of Paul the Apostle "and one of the same [Paul] to the Hebrews" were declared canonical. After Augustine's time it becomes increasingly common among the Latin authors to consider the epistle to the Hebrews the work of Paul, and the previous hesitancies gradually disappear. Thus from the fifth century on the Western and the Eastern churches are in agreement on this matter.

653. The chief reason for the uncertainties is expressed, in the third century, not by a Latin but by the Greek Origen, who states: "The style of the letter entitled 'to the Hebrews' has not that characteristic inexpertness of language of the Apostle, who confessed that he was unskilled in words, that is, in eloquence. On the contrary, the letter is of perfect Greek style and composition. Those who know how to judge differences of expression can attest to this. On the other hand, that the concepts in the letter are admirable and in no way inferior to those in the unquestioned apostolic writings, will be adjudged equally true by those accustomed to reading the apostolic texts. . . . I, for my part, would say that the concepts are those of the Apostle, but the structure and style are of someone recalling the apostolic concepts by way of reducing to writing the sayings of the master. If, then, some churches consider this letter to be one of Paul, they are to be praised for this, for it is not without reason that the ancients have handed it down as Paul's epistle. But only God knows with certainty who did write the letter. Information has come down to us from some according to whom Clement, who was bishop of the Romans, wrote the letter, and from others according to whom Luke, the author of the Gospel and the Acts wrote it" (in Eusebius, *Hist. Eccl.*, VI, 25, 11–14). The observations of the competent Origen, offered also by other ancient authors, still retain their validity today.

654. The style and language of this letter differ greatly from the rest of Paul's epistles. It abounds in *hapax legomena* and contains also many literary Greek expressions which do not occur in the other Pauline writings. The sentence structure is fluid, smooth, rhythmic, and almost entirely free of the abrupt transitions and outbursts which are characteristic of the other epistles. It does reflect the polished eloquence of the Greeks — in contrast to the rough and natural forcefulness of Paul — and from its opening lines rises to a majesty of expression not found elsewhere in the New Testament.

There are no Hebraisms. The manner of quoting the Bible is different from Paul's usual manner with respect to the formula used to introduce the quotations, faithfulness to the exact wording of the text, and the exclusive use of the Septuagint. In conclusion, Origen is quite right when he describes this letter as "completely Greek" ('Ελληνικωτέρα) since this quality is not equaled even by Luke, who is the most Greek of the New Testament authors. If we go from the *Corinthians* or *Galatians* to *Hebrews* we seem to be going from a popular text preserved in the papyri — like the letter of Apion to Epimachus (§ 174) — to a discourse by some classical Greek orator.

Should we suppose that Paul before writing *Hebrews* took a number of lessons from some Alexandrian rhetorician to recast his style completely?

And finally, there is the impersonal character of the letter, which lacks the exordium, with its mention of the recipients, and the good wishes which were habitual with Paul; also lacking are the greetings at the end from or to various individuals. There is simply the statement that "the brethren from Italy send greetings" (Heb. 13:24). Also toward the end, the letter says that Timothy has been set free (undoubtedly from some form of imprisonment) whom, if he comes soon, the writer hopes to see together with the recipients of the letter (13:23). But we know nothing at all about this imprisonment of Timothy and so the reference throws no light on the circumstances in which the letter was written.

655. But an examination of the content of this epistle yields quite different results. Here we find the basic concepts of the Pauline epistles. The doctrines they set forth, as occasion required, with respect to justification, the Law, the redemptive mediation of Christ, his person, are all to be found again in *Hebrews*. Some — like the priestly office of Christ — are more fully developed here, but this is evidently due to the specific aim of this epistle. In any case, these concepts are those already set forth more briefly in the other epistles. Commentators have arranged lists of parallel passages (which space does not permit us to quote) that show clearly that almost all the doctrinal concepts in *Hebrews* are somehow expressed in the other epistles.

This resemblance in content is so great that it not rarely influences the style itself, which, beneath its polish, is reminiscent of the phrases in the other Pauline letters. This is true of the solemn prologue which calls the Son the "brightness of [the] glory and the image (χαρακτήρ) of [the] substance" of God (1:3), just as in the epistles he had been called "the image of God," or "the image of the invisible God" (2 Cor. 4:4; Col. 1:15). Again, the Son has been made "so much superior to the angels as he has inherited a more excellent name than they" (Heb. 1:4), just as other epistles state that he is above every kind of angel and every name (Eph. 1:21), and that he has received a name above every name (Phil. 2:9). Similar parallels may be found throughout.

Adding up the external testimonies and the negative and positive elements of the internal evidence, we come back once more to Isaac's conclusion: "The voice indeed is the voice of Jacob, but the hands are the hands of Esau." The voice is that of someone we do not know speaking in Paul's name, but what he says comes from Paul's mind. This is also the conclusion of antiquity, expressed by Origen and others, namely, that the concepts of the letter are Paul's, but they were set in writing by someone else.

656. Who is this "someone else"? The early writers offered various names, such as Barnabas, Luke, Clement of Rome. Some thought that Paul wrote the letter in Aramaic, the language of the Hebrews to whom he addressed it, and that one of the above-mentioned co-workers then translated it into its present polished Greek form. This theory has been quite rightly abandoned today, since there are so many philological reasons for considering it an original and not a translation.

In recent times, many other names have been proposed: Apollos, Silas, the deacon Philip, Aristion. . . . Chivalry also nominated a woman, Priscilla, on the basis that there is something "feminine" about the letter. But Harnack, who proposed this theory, was perhaps not thinking of Paul's rule that women were not to teach in Christian gatherings (1 Cor. 14:33–34; 1 Tim. 2:12). But these are all conjectures; any one of them is more or less likely theoretically, but none of them is actually demonstrable. For example, Apollos, the polished Alexandrian with his gift for allegory, whom Paul mentions with solicitude in his later years (Tit. 3:13), might well have been the writer of the letter, but who can prove that he was? It is, therefore, more reasonable to repeat with Origen: "Only God knows with certainty who did write the letter."

657. It was undoubtedly addressed to Hebrews, as its title states, although this belongs to the second century. But to what Hebrews and in what country? They are converts from Hebraism and not ex-pagans; this is clear from the whole tone of the letter and the nature of its reasoning, accompanied throughout by quotations from the Old Testament. This is a slight hint as to the particular group of Jewish Christians to whom it was addressed; that is, they must comprise a Christian community whose members were exclusively, or almost exclusively, Jewish converts. Such a community could arise only in Jerusalem or Alexandria, the two most populous and powerful centers of Judaism at that time.[4] But we have no indication that Paul was ever in direct contact with Alexandria, and we possess only the vaguest and barest information on

---

[4] For the importance of Alexandria, cf. *Storia d'Israele*, II, pp. 211–219 (§§ 190–194).

the origins of Christianity in that city. This leaves Jerusalem, to whose Christian community the letter was addressed.

Here, too, are those who argue for various other places, such as Rome, Antioch, Ephesus, Corinth, Thessalonica, Cyprus, Galatia, Lycaonia, Spain, and even other regions. Again we are in the field of pure conjecture, and it is useless to discuss all these suggestions. Only the theory for Rome is not an arbitrary one, although, in the light of documentary evidence, it does not seem probable. We have already noted that when Paul wrote his letter to the Romans, the Roman community was composed predominantly of ex-pagans (§ 513), not ex-Jews. Nor does the worship in the Temple of Jerusalem, which the writer vividly describes as still flourishing, seem a very opportune argument for readers most of whom had not attended it. In addition, the writer sends the greetings of "the brethren from Italy" (13:24). Strictly speaking these could be persons of Italian origin now living elsewhere, who here send greetings to the Romans. But it seems more natural to consider them Jews who send greetings to their fellow countrymen in Jerusalem.

658. The vague designation, "from Italy," may also contain some slight clue. Why did not the writer name the city from which he is writing, or the specific places from which the brethren send greetings? "Italy" says too much and too little, for in Italy were the Jews of Rome as well as the Jews of Puteoli and numerous other Jewish settlements on the peninsula, but obviously not all of these were sending collective greetings. What reason was there for not mentioning any definite place? We have elsewhere noted (§ 637) a possible inconvenience in this, namely, the danger that the letter might fall into the hands of the imperial police, who were looking for Paul, while he remained in hiding, waiting for the opportunity to sail for the East. So vague a term as "Italy" would not have given the police any help, even if the letter were intercepted. If this theory is valid, the letter must have been written between the years 63 and 65.

659. The general conditions in Jerusalem and Palestine coincide with this date. Things were going from bad to worse there, and the country was on the threshold of the war which broke out in 66 and ended in 70 with the destruction of Jerusalem and the Jewish state. Everywhere there was an atmosphere of gathering storm, and the Christians of the local community clearly foresaw that they would be the first exposed to the fury of the hurricane. There had already been a persecution in 62, in which James the "brother" of the Lord had been killed.[5] That same year, the good Porcius Festus had been succeeded as procurator by the rogue Albinus (62–64), of whom Flavius Josephus says "there was no kind of evil which he neglected." Albinus was followed by Gessius

---

[5] For the facts which follow, cf. *ibid.*, II, p. 466 ff. (§ 415 ff.).

Florus, who, also according to Josephus, excelled Albinus in wickedness, and had come to Judea with the attitude of "an executioner sent to execute the condemned." Meanwhile, since the year 62, Jesus the son of Ananus, had been wandering through the streets, crying out incessantly: "A Voice from the East! A Voice from the West! A Voice from the four winds! A Voice over Jerusalem and over the Temple! A Voice over brides and grooms! A Voice over all the people!" And he repeated his gloomy prediction "by day and by night, through all the alleys . . . and on the festival days he cried out more than ever, and though repeating this for seven years and five months, his voice never grew weaker nor did he become weary" (Flavius Josephus), notwithstanding the bloody penalties to which he was subjected. At the same time the Zealot-*Sicarii* were growing more and more aggressive, indulging in slaughter and rapine, while anarchy spread throughout Jerusalem and the whole region.

As a consequence, in the year 66, "many illustrious Jews, as if plunging into the sea from a foundering ship, abandoned the city" (*Wars of the Jews,* II, 556). At about the same time the Jewish Christians of Jerusalem, warned through a charismatic intimation received by one of their leaders, moved to Pella, a city of Perea, "and thus the royal metropolis of the Jews and the whole region of Judea were abandoned by holy men (i.e., Christians)" — Eusebius, *Hist. Eccl.,* III, 5, 3.

660. This epistle was addressed to the Christians before their emigration to Pella, but when circumstances in Jerusalem had already rendered life there most difficult for them. On the other hand, though they had become Christian, they still felt the blood of Abraham in their veins and they had by no means forgotten that they belonged to the chosen nation of God, which could boast — as Paul himself said — that it had received "the adoption as sons, and the glory and the covenants and the legislation and the worship and the promises . . ." (Rom. 9:4–5). Had these solemn prerogatives vanished to nothing? On every side, it is true, there were warnings of impending catastrophe. But the Temple still stood to testify with its majestic rites to the everlasting fidelity with which God maintained his promises. Certainly the Messias who was foretold had come and they believed in him, Jesus. But his coming could not have abolished the ancient institutions of Hebraism but would rather have confirmed and corroborated them, since with him there came also the fullness of time and the kingdom of God on earth. Therefore, these Jewish Christians did not lose hope in the midst of dire predictions and harsh sufferings, but expected to see before long the beginning of an era in which the Messias Jesus would make the Hebrew religion, somewhat Christianized, triumph throughout all the world.

These were, in the view of the present writer, the physical and spiritual circumstances of the recipients of the epistle to the Hebrews, which was written to meet their difficulties and to bring them a word of consolation. A brief summary follows.

661. None of the codices carry for this letter the salutation and introduction in which Paul usually presented himself as the Apostle of Christ Jesus, etc. It is not impossible that it was lost, but it is more probable that it never existed. Some early writers explained this by assuming that Paul, the special Apostle to the Gentiles, purposely omitted any reference to this quality since he was writing here to the Jews. This explanation does seem justifiable, especially if we remember the old differences between the community of Jerusalem and Paul with respect to his apostolate to which, in times so difficult, it was hardly opportune to allude even indirectly. The letter, in fact, calls Jesus "the apostle . . . of our confession" (3:1).

662. *Comparison Between Christ and the Angels* — God, having spoken in various ways to the Hebrew patriarchs, has spoken last of all through his Son. The Old Law was promulgated through the angels, but the divine Son is superior to them, as many passages in Scripture prove. If, then, to transgress the Old Law was a serious omission, how much more serious will be our transgressions against the word of Christ. The divine Son, to whom all things were made subject, was temporarily humiliated in his Passion and death that he might bring about the salvation of men, his brothers; but immediately afterward he became the high priest before God to obtain propitiation for the sins of the people (Chaps. 1–2).

663. *Comparison Between Christ and Moses* — Both were faithful to their office, but Christ is superior to Moses because in the house of God Christ is the Son and the Lord, while Moses was a servant. If those who in ancient times in the desert hardened their hearts against the word of Moses were kept from entering the promised land, with far greater reason those who do not listen to the voice of Christ will be kept from entering into his rest (3–4:13).

664. *Comparison Between the Priesthood of Christ and the Hebrew Priesthood* — Jesus, the Son of God, is the supreme high priest, who passed into the heavens to implore mercy for men, for whose weaknesses he has great compassion. He was called to this office by God just as Aaron was, and he was chosen a priest forever according to the order of Melchisedech. It will be hard for the recipients of the letter to understand this point, because they are not capable of taking so lofty a doctrine and are in danger of regressing and returning to their former ideas. But let them remember that repentance is not granted to those who consciously reject the faith they have once received, for "they crucify again for themselves the Son of God and make him a mockery" (6:6). Nevertheless the writer is confident that they will rise to better things, mindful of the promises made by God to Abraham. The priesthood of Melchisedech was a figure of the priesthood of Christ; just as Scripture tells us that Melchisedech is superior to Abraham and Levi, so the priesthood of Christ is superior to the Levitical priesthood, and he is a priest forever (4:14–7:28).

665. *Comparison Between the Sacrifice of the New Testament and That of the Old* — The high priest Christ, in the heavens on the right hand of God, offers sacrifice in the true tabernacle, built by God and not by man. The tabernacle of the Mosaic Law had two parts, the first of which many priests entered to perform the ordinary rites, but the second only the high priest once a year, to offer the blood of sacrifice in expiation. This was a foreshadowing of the future time, for Christ, by virtue of his own blood, entered truly into the tabernacle not made by hands, working the redemption and establishing the New Testament.[6] Thus while the Old Testament was ratified by the blood of the sacrificial animals, the New was ratified by the blood of the testator and high priest. The sacrifice of expiation was repeated every year in the Old Testament, but, in the New, Christ offered himself once and for all, because in the former the sacrifice had a limited efficacy, but in the latter its virtue is infinite, and perfects forever (8–10:8).

666. *Exhortation to Persevere* — Those receiving this letter are to remain faithful to the justice wrought by Christ, mindful of the punishment threatened to apostates. Let them recall the early fervor with which they endured great trials, and let them rekindle it now that the end is near. Let them keep in mind the admirable example of faith given by Abel, Henoch, Noe, Abraham, Sara, Isaac, Jacob, Joseph, Moses, Josue, the Judges, and the other heroes of the Old Testament. Let them remember above all the example given them by "the author and perfecter of the faith, Jesus, who for the joy set before him, endured the cross, despising shame, and sits at the right hand of the throne of God" (12:2). Let them endure, therefore, until the trial of blood, which will purify them and increase their justice. Let them not imitate the stupidity of Esau, nor those ancient Hebrews who were terrified at the voice of God from Sinai. They are in the city of the living God, which is holier than Sinai (10:19–12:29).

Various Recommendations — Recommended to them are the virtues of charity, hospitality, chastity, generosity, obedience to their superiors. They are not to be led away by "various and strange doctrines," and are to be concerned with grace and not with the useless precepts regarding food. Let them follow the example of Jesus, who was killed outside the gate of the city, let them go out to him, bearing his reproach; for they have on earth no permanent city, but await the city that is to come.

The writer exhorts them to pray for him that he may be restored

---

[6] *Testament* here has the double meaning of *covenant* and *will*.

to them the sooner. He tells them that Timothy has been set free, with whom, if he comes soon, he will visit them. "The brethren from Italy" send greetings (Chap. 13).

* * *

667. Paul's second Roman imprisonment must have lasted several months, between the years 66 and 67. The first and principal wave of the Neronian persecution occurred immediately after the burning of Rome, but it did not end in that year. It had established, at least implicitly, a legal precedent, that "it was not lawful to be Christian" (*non licet esse christianos* — Tertullian, *Apolog.*, IV, 3), and this precedent could always be applied by the civil authorities when political or police reasons required it. The name Christian had become incriminated, and it implicitly carried with it "the punishments connected with the name" (*flagitia cohaerentia nomini* — Pliny the Younger, *ad Trajanum*, 2).

We have practically no information here to guide us, but we may suppose that Paul, sought by the imperial police from the beginning of the persecution and captured in 66, was subjected in Rome to a very detailed trial, both because he was an outstanding representative of the persecuted religion and a Roman citizen and because the period of summary executions was now over and the authorities were using more careful methods.

668. There seems to be an allusion to these methods, together with the length of the trial, in the words of Paul to Timothy: "At my first defense no one came to my support. . . . But the Lord stood by me and strengthened me . . . and I was delivered from the lion's mouth" (§ 643). Some of the early writers, following Eusebius (*Hist. Eccl.*, II, 22, 2–4) interpreted this "first defense" to mean his first Roman imprisonment, and the "lion" as a metaphor for Nero, who was then reigning. But it is certain instead that the phrase, "the lion's mouth," is a quotation from Psalm 22 (Vulg. 21):22, and is intended as a general reference to very serious danger. It does not seem that the "first defense" can refer to the first Roman imprisonment, because after his release Paul had been with Timothy for a long time (§ 635) and would certainly have told him all about that imprisonment and his acquittal. There would be no need, therefore, to give him any information about it here. The phrase "first defense" must allude rather to a preliminary hearing before this second trial, in which Paul succeeded in averting an immediate conviction through a complex of circumstances which today escape us. But he had no illusions. He understood quite well that the conviction had merely been postponed, and with a change of circumstances he would be summoned to another hearing: "I am already being poured out as a libation, and the time of my departure is impending" (2 Tim. 4:6; § 643).

The "lion" could not mean Nero himself, for from the end of the year

66 until the beginning of 68 he was not in Rome, having gone to Greece to give that nation the notorious spectacle of his colossal buffooneries. In this connection, we might note that some have seen a reference to Nero's absence from Rome in the passage in Clement of Rome (*Corint.*, 5, 7) which says that Paul, after having taught the entire world and traveled to the confines of the West (§ 636), "gave testimony under the governors" (μαρτυρήσας ἐπὶ τῶν ἡγουμένων). These "governors" would supposedly be the deputies Nero had left behind to govern Rome, namely, the freedman Aelius and the prefect of the Praetorium, Sabinus, since the other praetorian prefect, Tigellinus, had accompanied the emperor to Greece. If it was Clement's intention to allude here to these two governors, we should have a precious chronological reference, because no one was better informed than he; he was writing on the spot only thirty years after the events had occurred. But this is far from being certain. It is possible, and perhaps more probable, that this is merely an allusion to the well-known passage in the Gospels in which Jesus warns his Apostles that they will be dragged before governors (ἡγεμόνας) and kings for his sake to bear "witness" (Mt. 10:18; cf. Mk. 13:9, Lk. 21:12, and also 1 Pet. 2:14). In that case, Clement would be indicating that Paul had followed Jesus' command, but his phrase would not be a specific reference to the two governors of Rome during Nero's absence.

669. After the "first defense," Paul's imprisonment continued in extremely difficult circumstances, while the foreseeable outcome grew increasingly hopeless. This was not the mitigated form of *custodia militaris* of his first imprisonment, but the *custodia publica* in the common prison together with ordinary criminals (§ 661), where visits of relatives and friends were allowed only with difficulty. A tradition says this was the Tullian prison called in the Middle Ages the Mamertine prison, but there is no evidence for this before the fifth century and therefore it has little authority. Theoretically it is not impossible.[7]

The harsher treatment Paul suffered this time seems to be indirectly suggested here and there in *2 Timothy*: Onesiphorus, who came to Rome to help him, found him only with difficulty after a long search (1:17); in the cold, damp, subterranean prison he would have good use for the cloak he had left in Troas, and he asked that it be brought him with his books and parchments (4:13); he wanted Mark with him, who knew Rome well, so that he could help him carry on his ministry from prison, since the good Onesiphorus had probably departed again and "only Luke" could not accomplish by himself the many duties entrusted to him by the prisoner (4:11); for the same reason he wanted Timothy

---

[7] Cf. O. Marucchi, *Pietro e Paolo a Roma*, 4th ed., *cit.*, pp. 142–144. In the year 71, Simon Bar-Ghiora, principal leader of the Jewish insurrection against Rome, was killed in the Tullian prison: cf. *Storia d'Israele*, II, p. 517 (§ 470) and photograph.

with him, too, and he urged him to come before the winter because of his dark forebodings (4:21). Nevertheless, the money strategically distributed among the soldiers on guard by Luke and some of the brethren ensured occasional visits from other disciples. Among them we have the names of Eubulus, Pudens, Linus, and Claudia, who sent their greetings to Timothy (4:21) and who must have been prominent members of the scattered and decimated Roman community.

Whether or not Timothy arrived in time to give his beloved master his worn cloak and precious parchments, we do not know.

✻   ✻   ✻

670. A few months after this last letter was written, Paul's worst forebodings — or better, his highest hopes — came true. A second hearing was held, and this time the sentence was death.

Within the next day or so Paul, according to Roman custom, was taken outside the city for the public execution of the sentence.[8] A centurion, a maniple of praetorian guards — and in their midst the aging prisoner in chains. Perhaps a group of not unhappy Jews from Trastevere marched along beside the Praetorians, and a little farther behind, a small and silent group of Christians.

Beheading was the only form of capital punishment permissible in the case of Roman citizens, but this must have been preceded by the scourging. When they arrived, therefore, at the place of execution, the prisoner was first stripped and then bound to a block. His thin and weary body then received the last of the many floggings he had endured throughout his life, but this was the most ruthless of all, since he was now an *ex-lex*, a man rejected forever by the law and all humanity.

His bleeding body was bent forward to expose his neck to the headman. There was a curt command from the centurion, the flash of a sword, a thud. The head rolled a little distance, the body collapsed in a pool of blood.

Thus died Paul of Tarsus, a Jew by birth, a Roman citizen by law, once a teacher of the Mosaic Law by free choice, now an apostle of the Christian Gospel by supernatural vocation. Each of these four prerogatives was reflected in his death.

671. The ancient testimonies either are vague or fail to agree with regard to the year of Paul's death.

From Eusebius (*Chronicon*, 1. II, *Olympiad.*, 22, in Migne, *Patr. Gr.*, 19, 544) we might conclude that Paul died in the fourteenth year of

---

[8] Tacitus' description of the execution of a Roman citizen might well be applied to Paul: *Custodia militari cinctus, ne in ipsa urbe conspectior mors foret, ad quadragesimum ab urbe lapidem, via Appia, fuso per venas sanguine, extinguitur* (*Hist.*, IV, 11).

Nero's reign, that is, between July of 67 and June of 68. The fourteenth year of Nero is given by Jerome (*De viris illustr.*, 5), who confirms this indirectly by saying that Seneca had died two years before Paul (*ibid.*, 12). Since Seneca died in April, 65, this brings us again to the year 67. Other isolated documents give instead the year 66 or 68.

Several modern scholars prefer 64, but for the most part they are the same critics who deny the authenticity of the pastoral letters and Paul's last journeys indicated therein and do not need to allow for a period of time to which these journeys may be assigned. They assume, therefore, that Paul fell victim to the persecution which broke out immediately after the burning of Rome. In our opinion, however, the pastorals are authentic, and the sequence of the last journeys as listed above coincides without any particular difficulty with the date of death fixed in 67. This is, after all, the date for which there is the best evidence in the differing ancient testimonies, and is also preferred by many modern scholars.

We know nothing about the day of Paul's death. June 29, which is celebrated in the liturgy of the Western Church, is a conventional date and derives from other facts we shall note presently.

672. A constant tradition attested from the second century sets the place of the Apostle's martyrdom *ad Aquas Salvias*, a site a little over three miles from Rome on the road to Ardea, which lies a little to the left of and not far from the road to Ostia. This uniform tradition, founded on numerous testimonies of ancient writers and visitors to Rome, is in harmony with the data on the end of Paul's life and the Roman customs of the time, and therefore is not open to question.[9]

Immediately after the execution, the body was taken to a place nearer Rome, a little over a mile from the city on the Ostian Way, and was buried in an open cemetery, which has recently been rediscovered. The excavations have turned up several well-preserved burial vaults. Paul's tomb — like Peter's — quickly became a center of special veneration for Roman and foreign Christians.

Until the fourth century no special structure was built over either tomb, but the Christians marked them in some other way, which we do not know. Whatever mark was set on them it must have been clearly visible and of a certain solemnity. We gather this from the statement of the presbyter Gaius, at the beginning of the third century, to Proclus, the Montanist heretic: "I can show you the trophies of the apostles. If, in fact, you will go to the Vatican Hill or to the Ostian Way, you will find the trophies of those who founded this [Roman] church" (in Eusebius, *Hist. Eccl.*, II, 25, 7). The term "trophies" (τρόπαια), repeated twice,

---

[9] For the various texts on this subject, cf. O. Marucchi, *Pietro e Paolo a Roma*, 4th ed., *cit.*, Chaps. III–V and Appendix I.

Graffiti of the Second Half of the Third Century With Invocations to Peter and Paul. Basilica of St. Sebastian — Rome (from A. Fliche and V. Martin, *Storia della Chiesa*, It. tr.)

could mean both the victory over an enemy and the spoils taken from the vanquished and hung on poles, as a sign of triumph, according to the custom of the Roman legionaries. It is clear, in this instance, that if Gaius is sending his opponent to the Vatican Hill and the Ostian Way, he is sure he will find visible signs of some kind which recall the two victors and their respective victories. The *trophies* were undoubtedly the unknown symbols or other marks the Christians had set over the two venerated tombs.

673. In the second half of the third century, we find that in a place called *ad Catacumbas,* in the third mile of the Appian Way and about one mile from the cemetery of Callixtus, there rose a center for the veneration of Peter and Paul together. The explanation which is common today but not unquestioned supposes that in the year 258 both bodies were transferred to this place for reasons we do not know, and were kept there for a short time, after which they were returned to their original tombs. This place was later called *Triclia apostolorum,* and over it was erected, in the reign of Constantine, the *Basilica apostolorum* (today San Sebastiano). There an inscription (*latomia*), dictated by Pope Damasus, said:

Hic habitasse prius sanctos cognoscere debes
Nomina quisque Petri pariter Paulique requiris....[10]

Numerous graffiti executed there by ancient pilgrims contain invocations to Peter and Paul. The graffiti, which are on the *Triclia* and antedate the basilica of Constantine, prove the antiquity of the veneration for that *Memoria apostolorum*.

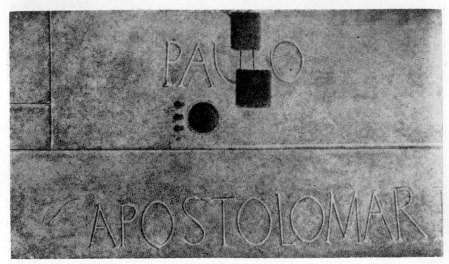

Inscription on Paul's Tomb — Fourth Century

A feast day *ad Catacumbas* on June 29 is documented in the fourth century in the *Depositio martyrum* and later in the *Martyrologium Hieronymianum*. If we compare the readings in the various codices, we may suppose the original text was somewhat as follows: *III Kal. Jul. Romae natale sanctorum apostolorum Petri in via Aurelia in Vaticano, Pauli vero in via Ostiensi, utrumque ad Catacumbas, Tusco et Basso consulibus.* This consulship was in 258, the year in which it is supposed the bodies were transferred. The date *III Kal. Jul.*, or June 29, was taken as the anniversary of the martyrdom of both Apostles in the Western liturgy, while in the oriental liturgies it varies according to place from December 27 or 28 to June 29, as in the West. It is likely

---

[10] Other copies of the inscription have *Hic habitare* . . . (instead of *habitasse*) which would indicate that when Pope Damasus dictated the inscription the two bodies were still *ad Catacumbas*. Recently the whole question of the date of the transferral of the bodies and the length of time they remained there has been reopened; but we cannot go into it here. We confine ourselves to accepting the opinion which, as noted above, is the commonly accepted one but is not certain. For the recent discussion cf. G. Belvederi, *La tomba di S. Pietro e i recenti lavori nelle grotte vaticane*, in the *Bollettino degli amici delle catacombe*, 1943, pp. 29–64; *idem, Le Cripte di Lucina* in *Rivista di archeologia cristiana*, 1944, pp. 3–46.

that in 258 in Rome there was held for the first time a commemoration of both Apostles together *ad Catacumbas,* independent of the veneration offered them at their respective tombs on the Vatican Hill and the Ostian Way.

674. After his victory, Constantine had a basilica built over Paul's original tomb on the Ostian Road. But it was quite small, and fit within the space between the apse and the papal altar of the modern basilica. It faced in the opposite direction also, for its entrance was on the ancient pavement of the Ostian Way, where the apse of the basilica now stands.

In 386 the emperor Valentinian II demolished Constantine's basilica and built another much larger and facing in the same direction as the present one. The construction was continued by Theodosius and others until the time of Gallia Placidia, as numerous inscriptions on the triumphal arch testify. After various restorations through the centuries the Valentinian basilica was destroyed in the great fire of 1823. The few sections left standing were incorporated in the subsequent reconstruction, which gave rise to the basilica we have today.

In the center, around Paul's tomb are sculptured his own words, which so admirably sum up his life: "For me to live is Christ and to die is gain" (Phil. 1:21).

*   *   *

The visitor, sight-seeing in the silent basilica today, admires the shining marble pavement, the smooth columns, the graceful sweep of the arches, the gold ceiling, the soft beauty of the old mosaics, which survived the fire. But in the eyes of his soul there is only one vision — the figure of Paul rising above his tomb, the conqueror of time and space, "Though he is dead, he yet speaks" (Heb. 11:4).

Just before reaching the basilica, the visitor will have noticed a steel tower, which night and day casts its intangible messages into the ether. It was a symbol and a "type." Within the basilica is the millennial tower stronger than steel, the dead still living, who casts without ceasing his message of the spirit to the entire world.

A Summary Glance

What remains today of Paul's work?

In the material sense there is practically nothing left. The numerous and fervent Christian communities he founded in Asia Minor and Macedonia, where Christianity had, as it were, its second cradle, have today all disappeared. The Gospel of Paul was driven from them by the Koran of Mohammed, just as in its turn the Koran is today being driven out by atheistic secularism. The few communities Paul founded elsewhere have wasted to mere shadows. Only the Roman community remains the spinal column of Christianity, but it was not founded by Paul, who always considered it built on foundations laid by others.

In the spiritual sense the precise contrary is true. Paul's work not only persists today in its entirety, but it has grown and spread more than a thousandfold. When we compare it with what it was at the time of Paul's death we cannot help but think of the Gospel parable of the mustard seed. Today Christianity, in large measure, means Paul, just as human civilization in our era signifies in large measure Christianity. The truly civilized man, consciously or unconsciously, is today to some extent a disciple of Paul.

This historical law, whereby an apparent failure is followed by a real triumph, has always guided the destiny of Christianity, and before Paul, it was established, as it were, by Christ himself.

The conversion of the Jews, to which the mission of Jesus was directly addressed, did not take place. The mission failed: in the land of the Jews not only did the doctrine of Jesus not take root, but forty years later the very nation of the Jews was uprooted and cast out. The failure, therefore, seemed complete. But this had been foreseen: "Amen, amen, I say to you, unless the grain of wheat fall into the ground and die, it remains alone" (Jn. 12:24). Thus it is a failure from which is derived the triumph, a death from which life is born. The seed dies to release the fertile plant. Mortal men, in their smallness, fix their eyes on the immediate and temporary victory; God contemplates the eternal future triumph.

Thus it was with Jesus, and thus it was with his great disciple Paul. During his lifetime the Apostle filled the known world with his activity.

"Though He Is Dead, He Yet Speaks"

ideal is Christ, and to this he now devotes, with ardor even more intense, every action of his life. For him, now, to live is Christ (Phil. 1:21) and all else is without value or significance. Who can set up barriers to this ideal? Even in chains, he exclaims confidently: "But the word of God is not bound" (2 Tim. 2:9).

Paul's confidence in himself and his mission carries him always to the front line. Just as he refuses to depend on others for his support and works with his own hands to earn his bread, so he refuses to build on the foundations of others, unwilling to appear vested with others' merits. He sets out on his first missionary journey as the co-worker of Barnabas. But they have gone no farther than Cyprus, still at the beginning of their voyage, when their relationship is reversed and Barnabas is the co-worker of Paul, who has, for practical purposes, assumed the leadership. They prepare to make the next journey together, but before their departure they separate because Paul finds Barnabas' suggestion unwise and refuses to yield in the slightest to the other's view. He resists the authority of Barnabas just as a little before this he had publicly stood up to the authority of Peter, having in view not the latter's office as head of the Apostles, among whom he acknowledges himself the "least" (1 Cor. 15:9), but only the idea with which he was absorbed.

Only those disciples remain with him a long time who are docile and filled with devotion, and who are inspired not so much by their own ideas as by the great idea which Paul has been able to transfuse in them. Apollos, an original thinker, is not with him long, and neither is the experienced Barnabas. But often with him and bound to him throughout their lives, we find the youth Timothy, the neophyte Titus, the adaptable ex-pagan Luke, who become so many extensions of Paul's personality.

And yet this man, born to command and impose his personality on others is above all a man of love. He needs to love others and to feel himself loved, otherwise life has no meaning for him. His eulogy of charity (1 Cor. 13) is inspired, it is true, by his Christian view of the universe, but it also reflects his own temperament. This lyric hymn contemplates men as brothers in God but there is also the feeling that they are comrades in exile on the earth. For Paul's love for men is not a thing of sweet sentimentality or empty attitudinizing, but of sacrifice, devotion, and renunciation. His love represents not only his own natural inclinations but a charity that is willed.

The basic canons of this charity, Paul says, are these: "In humility let each one regard the others as his superiors each one looking not to his own interests but to those of others" (Phil. 2:4); "rejoice with those who rejoice; weep with those who weep" (Rom. 12:15). "Now we, the strong, ought to bear the infirmities of the weak, and not to please ourselves. Let every one of you please his neighbor by doing good, for his edification" (Rom. 15:1–2).

Everywhere Paul encounters sympathy and love, not only as an apostle but also as a man. In Ephesus, some of the Asiarchs, though pagan, are his friends and they take pains to save him from the rioting silversmiths. The neophytes of every community are devoted to him with their whole souls, from those in Galatia who are ready "to pluck out their eyes" for him to those of Corinth who weep and are distressed because they have aroused his angry disdain. To sadden a community to tears it is sufficient to say he would never see them again, as happened in Miletus, and to gladden the faithful in his absence it is enough to announce he will visit them soon, as in the case of the Philippians.

If a man is loved it is a sign that he knows how to win love, for this is the law of "love, which to no loved one permits excuse from loving" (*Inf.*, V, 103). Therefore the sympathy Paul encounters everywhere is a consequence of the warmhearted affection he has for others. Unpolished writer though he is, he finds expressions of shining tenderness for his distant neophytes. He says he has been in pains as of childbirth for them, that he has fondled them as a nurse fondles her own children (Gal. 4:19; 1 Thess. 2:7), that he has them in his heart and longs for them all in the heart of Christ Jesus (Phil. 1:7–8).

He feels everything that happens to them; when one of them is weak, he is weak, when another undergoes some deep spiritual crisis he is aflame (2 Cor. 11:29). These are not mere words. When there is a crisis in the Corinthian community, which threatens to leave him, he is truly inflamed and suffers through several anxious months at the beginning of the year 57. In the absence of news, he first dispatches messages and messengers, and then, unable to contain himself any longer, he hastens to meet the awaited messenger to shorten the intolerable suspense.

The various feelings of so ardent and sensitive a nature are reflected in his impetuous writings. He passes abruptly from anxious agitation to confident serenity, from threats and scorn to understanding affection, from scathing irony to sorrowful exhortation. At one moment he seems defeated and cast down; immediately afterward he rises the conqueror of everyone and everything. He writes with "many tears" and is not ashamed to confess it, but he does not hide the fact that he has a rod within reach (1 Cor. 4:21).

And these stormy transitions occurred in a soul by no means unused to self-discipline and the control of his emotions. Ever since he had been born to Christ, a "new man" had risen and grown great within him; but the "old man" was still there, and between the two there was a truceless conflict destined to last until the last day of his life. There were inner struggles, of the senses and the spirit (Rom. 7:14 ff.); the tactician who watched over the conflict imposed a long trial period on him to bend the rough unruly nature to the dictates of grace: the "old man" was gradually worn down and in the end was practically subject to the will of the "new man," but never totally defeated or suppressed.

There is no doubt that Paul, on the threshold of old age, is conspicuously different from the Paul who had just been converted. The rough edges have been polished smooth, and his multiple experiences have made him more flexible and amenable, but in the last analysis he is still the same Paul. He might rather be said to have become a double Paul, for the old man and the new are working together, the former having been made subject to the latter; "Do you not know that those who run in a race, all indeed run, but one receives the prize? . . . I, therefore, so run as not without a purpose; I so fight as not beating the air; but I chastise my body and bring it into subjection, lest after preaching to others I myself should be rejected" (1 Cor. 9:24 . . . 27).

✻ ✻ ✻

With these moral endowments, Paul became a preacher of the Gospel. As a propagandist his horizons were unlimited, so much so that he aroused the doubts and even the open rebukes of others who were just as sincere but less discerning than he. To aim at the conversion of the uncircumcised pagans, excluded from the sacred enclosures of Israel, was for the majority of early Palestinian Christians indecorous audacity, almost a profanation. Paul, however, not only sets his sights on the pagans but discovers in them the chief hope of the Gospel, the particular field in which Christ will triumph. In fact, he goes even further: he, the onetime rabbi and zealous exponent of the Jewish Law, now affirms the incompatibility between the new spirit and the old letter and fights for the separation of the two, since it is no longer the time to pour new wine into old vessels. The spiritual delivery of the Church from the Synagogue was brought about principally by Paul.

This intransigent theorist is in practical matters an unequaled organizer. He pioneers without rest and spends himself, plunging ahead first and dragging the others after him by his example. By instinct, he is a centralizer, directing everything himself, trying to go everywhere himself; and where he cannot go he sends letters or his personal representatives.

His strategy is disastrous, his tactics doomed to failure. He takes no thought for financial means or for political or any other kind of support. Wearing his workman's apron, his hands calloused from the loom, he preaches to proletarians, slaves, the offscourings of society, and tells them things that must seem the most outlandish they have ever heard. In Corinth, whose people swim in lust, he preaches chastity in marriage, and even virginity. And he recommends these practices not for social, hygienic, or philosophical reasons, but only on the basis of obedience to Christ. Elsewhere and everywhere, he teaches the equality of Jew and Greek, of Greek and Barbarian and Scythian. This was the surest way to solicit the insults of Jew and Greek, Barbarian and Scythian together. Could there be any teachings more ridiculous and senseless than these, and the others which he handed them?

And Paul is completely aware of the foolishness of his teachings. It is from this very foolishness that he draws the certainty of victory. He is unshakably certain that the "foolishness of the cross" will triumph over the "wisdom of this world, because this wisdom is foolishness in the sight of God" (1 Cor. 3:19). The paradox is total and absolute but it is not new; it derives from and is an application of the paradox in the Sermon on the Mount. By virtue of the principles established in that Sermon, Paul is confident of victory.

Strong in this conviction, he reaps a more or less abundant harvest wherever he extends his labors. His efforts are almost sterile in the center of human wisdom, the Areopagus in Athens, now emptied of all true wisdom; but he achieves great success or genuine triumphs elsewhere, both among rough mountain folk like the Galatians and among city people steeped in business and vice like the Corinthians and Ephesians.

But before he triumphs he must struggle through obstacles of every kind: prisons, floggings, stonings, and even popular riots become familiar experiences. His attitude toward these difficulties is neither swaggering nor impassive; on the contrary, he fears them and feels them deeply: ". . . our flesh had no rest; we had troubles on every side, conflicts without and anxieties within" (2 Cor. 7:5). But here, too, he applies the divine paradox. In all of these occurrences, he, being but a man and weak, should be overcome, but instead his weakness will be supplemented by an external power and in the end he will triumph: "Therefore I take pleasure in infirmities, in insults, in hardships, in difficulties for the sake of Christ; for when I am weak, then I am strong" (2 Cor. 12:10).

✿   ✿   ✿

Among Paul's great loves, we find, next to his love for Christ and intimately associated with it, the love he bears his fellow Hebrews, who, on the contrary, are always and everywhere his most implacable enemies. Not only does he never forget he is a Hebrew, but rather he considers this his greatest human privilege, less useful but far superior to that of being a Roman citizen. Consequently he loves his fellow countrymen, averse to the Christ Jesus, with a love rooted in his veins and his soul and compounded of tenderness and sorrowing regret. Their obstinate rejection of Christ causes him "great sadness and continuous sorrow in [his] heart," and he would wish to become himself "anathema" and cursed by Christ in order to convert them (Rom. 9:2–3).

In addition to the Hebrews, he has several adversaries also among the Christians. His indisputable moral superiority evokes the inevitable jealousies, detractions, and calumnies. Since his daily life, filled as it is with renunciation and privations for the triumph of the Gospel, cannot be equaled, there are those who cavil over his actions, misconstrue his intentions, make fun of his methods. Sensitive as he is to friendship, he also feels deeply these enmities. That he keep silent in the face of opposition was not to be expected from either his human or his supernaturalized temperament, from the "old man" or the new. He answers with all the old fire, controlled now by his new conscience, and he chooses the most just and effective answer, appealing directly to facts. Three times he answers his adversaries by outlining his own life, past and present (1 Cor. 4:9 ff.; 2 Cor. 6:3 ff.; 11:22 ff.). His conduct past and present is known to all. Who can reproach him?

With errors he is intransigent; with the erring, patient. He is even glad of the Christians who in a spirit of rivalry had become missionaries in Rome to spite him (Phil. 1:18). He pronounces an excommunication only twice: against the incestuous man of Corinth, that his soul might be saved (1 Cor. 5:5), and against those who make a shipwreck of the faith (1 Tim. 1:19–20).

❊ ❊ ❊

Paul as an Apostle reflects the contribution of many sources combining to form a majestic whole.

First of all, there is the man himself with his natural gifts and endowments. Chronologically, the next influence is that of his family upbringing and his education in the rabbinical schools. At this point there occurs the great *hiatus* which separates the two parts of his life, namely, his acceptance of the Messias Jesus, which occasions a true spiritual rebirth. Contemporary with his conversion, there are the great mystical experiences which accompany and develop that rebirth. These in turn are supplemented by the external influence of the common Christian catechesis, from which Paul derives in large measure the concepts of his new Christian mentality. And finally, there is the contribution of Paul's own personal thinking as he meditates on the ideas he has absorbed from his Jewish education, his mystical experiences, and the Christian catechesis. All these elements, superimposed in succession on Paul's mind, form the Apostle.

Before his conversion — so far as we may gather — Paul's mentality must have been essentially dialectical. Given certain principles, he pursued them to their ultimate logical consequences. After his conversion, he is still of a dialectical turn of mind but he proves also to be intuitive. Since he has become a mystic, he applies to his mystical experiences the same processes of reasoning and logical thought development. In contemplation he seizes the great basic ideas and makes them his. Later by reflection and meditation he deepens these concepts, broadens them with speculative knowledge, and transfers them to practical life.

His contemplation loses itself in God, as his speculation embraces the whole universe. The Christian poet, after contemplating the Divinity, exclaimed in terrified awe:

"O grace abounding, whereby I presumed
to thrust my gaze through the eternal light
so long, that I consumed my sight thereon"
(*Paradiso,* 33, 82–84).

There is a similar exclamation of Paul, when, having speculated on the mysterious dispositions of Providence, he turns within himself, almost blinded, murmuring:

"Oh, the depth
of the riches and wisdom and knowledge
of God!
How inscrutable his judgments
and unsearchable his ways! . . .
For from Him and through Him and unto Him
are all things —
To Him be glory throughout the ages!
Amen"
(Rom. 11:33–36).

But this bold explorer of the Divinity, this giant whose head towers upward through celestial light, has his feet firmly planted on the ground, and the humanity in his heart responds to the life of all humanity. With characteristic boldness, therefore, he faces the most majestic problems of humanity and solves them with personal mastery. What is man? Whence does he come? Where is he going? Why is he beset from within and without with so many afflictions? Can man free himself without help? Has he need of a liberator? Has God come to meet man's efforts? What will happen one day to man and the whole universe?

Paul had perhaps already meditated on these and similar problems as a rabbi, but they undoubtedly became the perennial subject of his meditations as a Christian. His conclusions are given us only in part and incidentally, and so from the little he tells us no one may presume to explore exhaustively or sum up his thought.

After all, he considered himself spiritually in a continuous state of becoming, similar to the runner in the stadium who draws ever nearer the goal but has not yet reached it. In the year 62, though advanced in age, he could still write:

"Not that I have already obtained this [the goal] or already have been made perfect, but I press on hoping that I may lay hold of that for which Christ Jesus has laid hold of me. Brethren, I do not consider that I have laid hold of it already. But one thing I do: Forgetting what is behind, I strain forward to what is before, I press on towards the goal, to the prize . . ." (Phil. 3:12–14). While before his conversion Paul had run ever farther away from Christ, after it he does nothing but run ever toward him. He met him on the road to Damascus and was mysteriously seized by him. But he, Paul, has not succeeded in taking hold of Christ, at least completely or steadfastly. Many other times, it is true, he has had mysterious communications from Christ, but these are of such a nature as to sharpen increasingly the desire for complete and unending possession. And yet, Christ, who so often appears before him on the road of life as he did on the road to Damascus, seems to retreat constantly before him, so that he is constrained to follow, hastening his course until one day he will finally take hold of him. When will that day come? "To be with Christ [is] a lot by far the better" (1:23).

All of Paul's life after his conversion is but a running toward Christ: "for me to live is Christ" (1:21); "it is now no longer I that live, but Christ lives in me" (Gal. 2:20). But in reality this running is guided and sustained by Christ himself, whose intervention is frequent and direct. With respect to his mystical experiences, Paul feels, as it were, a sense of spiritual modesty, and he speaks of them little and reluctantly. But there is no doubt as to their frequency and power. Even from the psychological viewpoint, it would have been impossible to endure the terrifyingly difficult life Paul led for thirty years if something extraordinary had not sustained him and kept his enthusiasm constantly kindled, while safeguarding him from the intemperances of the fanatic. The roots of Paul's life, secret and public, reach deeply into his charisms and mystical experiences; without these it is unexplainable.

Paul was endowed with the ordinary charisms of early Christianity in more abundant measure than his neophytes (1 Cor. 14:18). In addition, he was assisted by repeated visions and revelations. If when he was caught up to the "third heaven" he heard things which man may not repeat (2 Cor. 12:4), on other occasions he received through mystical communications precise directions on the conduct to follow (Gal. 2:2; Acts 16:6, 7, 9; 18:9; 20:23; 22:17). Facts in the earthly life of Jesus which are of fundamental importance to the faith and the liturgy of his communities are also communicated to him through mystical means (1 Cor. 11:23). He perhaps receives also the moral criteria his neophytes are to follow (cf. 1 Cor. 7:10, 12). In any case, he has learned his particular Gospel not from men but "from a revelation of Jesus Christ" (Gal. 1:11).

The concepts Paul absorbed through these mysterious means were also subjected to reflection and inference, and from this he arrived at a broad vision of the vicissitudes of humanity in relation to the designs of God. Thus he is able to speak of his "discernment of that mystery of the Christ which in other generations was not made known to the sons of men as it has now been revealed to his holy apostles and prophets [in] the Spirit"; to him the least of all the Christians "was given this grace: to preach among the gentiles the inexplorable riches of the Christ, and to spread enlightenment as to what is the plan of the mystery hidden for ages in God the Creator of all things" (Eph. 3:4–9; cf. Col. 1:26). When these concepts are applied to the great events of human history, one arrives at broad historical syntheses like that in the epistle to the Romans.

This view of mankind is so broad, and the peak from which Paul contemplates it so high, that it cannot be dimmed by the vapors that rise from the low marshes of politics. He ignores human politics. "Our citizenship is in heaven" (Phil. 3:20), not on earth. It is true that on earth there are those who command in a tone of divinity and assume for themselves the titles of God and Lord, like the sovereign who rules over almost all the world from the Palatine in Rome. But over whom does his rule extend? At the most over the world of matter, not that of the spirit, with which alone Paul is concerned. "For even if there are what are called gods, whether in heaven or on earth (for indeed there are many gods, and many lords), yet for us there is only one God, the Father from whom are all things, and we unto him . . ." (1 Cor. 8:5–6).

It is not surprising to find in a contemplative and thinker of this kind the most clear-cut opposition to idolatry. What agreement can there be between Christ and Beliar, between the temple of God and idols (2 Cor. 6:15–16)? Paul takes care to avoid even the appearance of any similarity with idolatrous practices so that the Christian rite may not be clouded by false semblances. The devotees of the pagan mystery religions perform their dark rites in secret, but "of the things that are done by them in secret it is shameful even to speak" (Eph. 5:12). The Christians act in the light, for it is light which confounds the darkness. And even in the manifestation of their charisms, the Christians are to abstain from excesses (1 Cor. 14:23–24), so that they may not even in appearances resemble those pagans who rave in the pagan temples in a state of mantic exaltation, or the adepts of the pagan mysteries who are filled with frenzy during the performance of their rites.

Although absorbed in his Christian vision, Paul is not fanatic or intolerant. He recognizes that there may be beautiful, seemly, honorable things which do not derive directly from his principles. These he welcomes, confident that they, too, in the end will be framed within that vision and will contribute to the triumph of his idea. "For the rest, brethren, whatever things are true, whatever honorable, whatever just, whatever holy, whatever lovable, whatever of good repute, if there be any virtue, if anything worthy of praise, think upon these things" (Phil. 4:8). If for those who love God "all things work together unto good"

(Rom. 8:28), including adverse things, how much more will just and honorable things co-operate unto good?

❊   ❊   ❊

At the heart of Paul's vision stands Jesus Christ

At the name of Jesus all the beings in the universe shall bend their knees, whether "in heaven, on earth," or "under the earth" (Phil. 2:10); the three place indications here correspond to the three parts in which the Hebrews divided the universe.[1] "He is the image of the invisible God, the firstborn of every creature. For in him were created all things in the heavens and on the earth, things visible and things invisible, whether Thrones, or Dominations, or Principalities, or Powers. All things have been created through and unto him, and he is before all creatures, and in him all things hold together" (Col. 1:15–17). In Christ, therefore, the whole universe, the heavens and the earth, is summed up and "re-established" (Eph. 1:10).

> "Within its depths I saw ingathered,
>   bound by love in one volume,
>   the scattered leaves of all the universe"
>   (*Paradiso*, 33, 85–87).

The Messias Jesus, who re-established the universe, is true man. He was born of woman and is a descendant of David (Gal. 4:4; Rom. 1:3). As such he is the opposite of Adam, the first man; he is the new Adam who reverses the situation inherited from the first.

In the first place there is the intrinsic difference between the two Adams. "It is written, 'The first man, Adam, became a living soul'; the last Adam became a life-giving spirit. . . . The first man was of the earth, earthy; the second man is from heaven, heavenly"; that is, his person comes from heaven (1 Cor. 15:45–47). There is also the difference in works. The first Adam caused his descendants to be condemned to die; the new Adam brings them justification and resurrection (1 Cor. 15:20–21, 45–49; Rom. 5:12–21).

In the sin of the first Adam all his descendants sinned, therefore they were all made subject to death as he was (Rom. 5:12). And this fall affected not only all mankind but also the rest of creation, for "all creation groans and travails in pain until now. And not only it, but we ourselves also who have the first-fruits of the Spirit — we ourselves groan within ourselves, waiting for the adoption as sons, the redemption of our body" (8:22–23). Since man, the king of creation, has fallen, creation feels the effects of this fall and longs for the restoration of its royal master. But the new Adam, in contrast to the old, has reconciled God

---

[1] Cf. G. Ricciotti, *L'Apocalisse di Paolo siriaca*, Vol. II, *La Cosmologia della Bibbia*, Brescia, 1932, pp. 13–14.

with humanity offering himself on the cross in expiation of the sin committed by the first Adam. God accepted his gift of expiation, and "it
has pleased God the Father that . . . through him he should reconcile
to himself all things, whether on the earth or in the heavens, making
peace through the blood of his cross" (Col. 1:19–20).

The effects of the redemptive death of the Messias are extended without distinction to all mankind, to the Jews and to the Gentiles of whatever race, throwing down the wall of separation which rose between
these two groups, namely, the reciprocal hatred occasioned by the Jewish
Law (Eph. 2:14–15). This Law, which represented the decree of condemnation, was torn up and nailed to the cross of Christ (Col. 2:14).
Besides, the effects of Christ's redemption extend also to the invisible
spiritual beings hostile to humanity because God "disarming the Principalities and Powers . . . displayed them openly, leading them away in
triumph by the force of it [the cross]" (Col. 2:15).

The Christ, who "re-establishes" ($\dot{a}\nu a$-$\kappa\epsilon\phi a\lambda a\iota o$) the universe is also the
"head" ($\kappa\epsilon\phi a\lambda\dot{\eta}$) of the Church, which, in turn, is his "body" (Eph.
1:22–23; cf. Col. 1:18). Therefore, Christ together with his Church forms
a mystical body, composed of a head and lesser members. These are the
faithful, each with his own specific function to perform, like the various
members of the human body, but all united by virtue of charity into an
organic whole with Christ as the head (Eph. 4:15–16; 5:30; 1 Cor.
12:12 ff.).

This unifying charity is the effect of the Spirit: "one body and one
Spirit" (Eph. 4:4), just as there is "one Lord, one faith, one baptism;
one God and Father of all" (*ibid.*, 5–6). The Spirit was sent by God the
Father and is "the Spirit of his Son"; he was sent into the hearts of the
faithful that they might receive the adoption of sons of God the Father.
Hence from their innermost hearts the Spirit cries to God: "Abba! [that
is] Father!" (Gal. 4:5–6; Rom. 8:14–16.)

The intimate union between the head and members means that what
happens to one happens also to the others. What happens to the head,
who is Christ, happens also to the members, the faithful. As Christ died,
was buried, rose again from the dead, and inherited the kingdom of the
Father, so the faithful "die with" him, are "buried" with him in baptism,
rise again with him, live with his life, and are coheirs, incorporated in
him, cosharers in his kingdom. These concepts are expressed in about
thirty different Greek verbs all formed with the prefix $\sigma\upsilon\nu$.

This communion between head and members finds its clearest expression and fullest realization in the Eucharist. Paul has received the
doctrine on this rite, which he teaches his neophytes, "from the Lord"
(1 Cor. 11:23), undoubtedly to confirm and deepen the knowledge of it
he had drawn from the common catechesis. In the Eucharist, instituted
by Jesus "on the night on which he was betrayed," the eve of his death,

the faithful eat the body and drink the blood of the Lord, and through this rite they proclaim the death of the Lord until he comes in the glorious parousia (*ibid.*, 26). They also enter into union with Christ so that "whoever eats this bread or drinks the cup of the Lord unworthily, will be guilty of the body and blood of the Lord" (*ibid.*, 27). This is a union not only between the head and members, namely, between Christ and the faithful, but also among the members themselves, who by virtue of this rite are united to each other and with the head in an organic whole: "The cup of blessing that we bless, is it not the sharing of the blood of Christ? And the bread that we break, is it not the partaking of the Lord? Because the bread is one, we though many, are one body, all of us who partake of the one bread" (1 Cor. 10:16–18).

As a consequence of their union in the mystical body of Christ, a new life is infused in the faithful by the Spirit of Christ, which begins with baptism and is nourished by the Eucharist. For men who are not united with Christ, the life of the flesh sums up all their existence, but for the faithful incorporated in the mystical body of Christ, it is almost accidental. "You, however, are not carnal but spiritual, if indeed the Spirit of God dwells in you. But if anyone does not have the Spirit of Christ, he does not belong to Christ. But if Christ is in you, the body, it is true, is dead by reason of sin, but the spirit is life by reason of justification" (Rom. 8:9–10). This new life infused by the Spirit invests not only the soul of the faithful but also his body, which is therefore incorporated into the mystical body of Christ: "Do you not know that your bodies are members of Christ? Shall I then take the members of Christ and make them members of a harlot? By no means! Or do you not know that he who cleaves to a harlot, becomes one body with her? . . . but he who cleaves to the Lord is one spirit with him. . . . Or do you not know that your members are the temple of the Holy Spirit, who is in you, whom you have from God, and that you are not your own?" (1 Cor. 6:15–19.) All this is the consequence of the mutual exchange of life between the head and members, the natural effect of the spiritual symbiosis between Christ and the faithful incorporated in him: ". . . one died for all, therefore all died; and . . . Christ died for all, in order that they who are alive may live no longer for themselves, but for him who died for them and rose again" (2 Cor. 5:14–15).

Paul must have been aware of this exchange or association of life between the head and members from the day of his conversion. When he fell to the ground before the apparition on the Damascus road and asked who this was, he was answered: "I am Jesus whom thou persecutest." But was this true? It would not seem so since Paul was persecuting those heretic Christians who were chasing after the ghost of a dead man, but he was not persecuting the dead man himself in any way; being dead he was of no further interest. From the answer he received, however, Paul must have understood that in persecuting the Christians he was persecuting Jesus himself, because the one and the others formed a *quid unum,* just as the head and members form one body. He confessed this later himself, exclaiming: "I am not worthy to be called an apostle, because I persecuted the Church of God" (1 Cor. 15:9). In persecuting Jesus, he had persecuted his mystical body, namely, the "Church of God."

For Paul, the Church is the kingdom of God in its first phase, which is one of expansion and struggle and which will be followed by a second period, of manifest triumph. While, during his first imprisonment in Rome, he labors intensely despite his chains to spread the Good Tidings, he names several disciples, converts from Judaism, who are with him, saying that they are "fellow-laborers for the kingdom of God" (Col. 4:11). In working with him for the diffusion of the Church, they are working for the kingdom of God. Others, also in Rome, had limited the essence of the Gospel to mean abstaining from certain foods and drink, but Paul had admonished that the "kingdom of God does not consist in food and drink, but in justice and peace and joy in the Holy Spirit" (Rom. 14:17). Therefore, the kingdom of God corresponded to the actual Christian life which he was recommending in the communities he founded; that is, it corresponded to the living Church. This kingdom of God is not founded on long-winded, caviling disputation, but on effective and powerful example: "For the kingdom of God is not in word, but in power" (1 Cor. 4:20); these are his teachings in "Christ Jesus, even as I teach everywhere in every church" (*ibid.,* 17), for the purpose of spreading the kingdom of God throughout the earth.

This period of expansion will be very long. It will "show in the ages to come the overflowing riches of . . . grace" (Eph. 2:7). The ages to come will see the "full number of the Gentiles" enter the kingdom of God, after which the people of Israel, obstinate until then, will be converted to the Messias Jesus (Rom. 11:25–26; cf. 11:14). All these things were to be fulfilled in a far-distant future, according to Paul, because in his own day the conversion of the Gentiles was just begun and the people of Israel were increasingly obdurate in their rejection of the Christ Jesus. In addition, he foresees that the expansion of the kingdom of God will encounter tremendous opposition. Just as the heralds of the kingdom will have difficulties of every kind set in their way (2 Cor. 6:4 ff.), so will its subjects have to fight against hostile spiritual forces (Eph. 6:12).

But the Christ will triumph over all his enemies, and thus the second period of the kingdom of God will begin. On the day of the glorious parousia of Christ, when he, the head of the Church, shall triumph, then this too shall triumph, since it is the mystical body inseparably united with the head. At the final resurrection, "the first-fruits [will be] Christ, then they who are Christ's, who have believed, at his coming. Then comes the end, when he delivers the kingdom to God the Father, when he does away with all sovereignty, authority, and power [hostile to him]. For he must reign, until 'he has put all his enemies under his feet.' And the last enemy to be destroyed will be death" (1 Cor. 15:23–26). The kingdom which Christ gives to God the Father is the Church, which he loves as his bride (Rom. 8:17). The Church, having suffered with him, is now glorified with him and is therefore the joint heir with Christ (*ibid.*). On that day Christ will openly manifest that he has "re-established" the whole universe, both heaven and earth, in himself (Eph. 1:10), bringing it back and delivering it to the Father.

Paul repeatedly declares he does not know when this day will dawn, when the glorious parousia of the Messias with all the accompanying events will take place. He ardently longs for that day, and believes it can happen at any time, but he does not know whether the time is near or far distant. Did this longing become also a personal hope with Paul as with many early Christians? It would not seem so. On the contrary, he worked to restrain the feverish expectation of the parousia among the Thessalonians. Paul's own longing, in love, for the "day of the Lord" gradually diminished, and he came more and more to think of that day from the viewpoint of the perennial Church rather than his own fleeting existence. The longing remained always intense, as in the beginning, however, because in reality "that day" represented the ultimate purpose of his life, the final peak, from which he could ascend to God. A few months before his death, he says he has fought the good fight, that his race now is over. All that remains is to receive the crown awarded the winning athlete, which the Lord will give him "in that day" (2 Tim. 4:8).

This faith in "that day," namely, the faith in the invisible rather than the visible, is the secret of Paul (2 Cor. 4:18); it is also the secret of Christianity.

❀   ❀   ❀

In conclusion, what is Paul?

Taking his personality as a whole, we find he is not a typical mystic, or a man of thought, or missionary, or organizer, or ascetic, or pastor. He does not fit completely or exclusively in any one of these categories, but they are all reflected in his life as a compact whole.

He is a mystic like Catherine of Siena, who bears so many resemblances to him, but at the same time a philosopher like Thomas Aquinas, who comments with unsurpassed acumen on the epistle to the Romans. He is a missionary who opens up new regions to Christianity, like Francis Xavier, but he is also an organizer within the Church like Charles Borromeo. He is an ascetic like Thomas à Kempis, but he is also a shepherd of souls like Philip Neri. What is he not, in fact? In how many ways has not posterity interpreted various of his attitudes?

When Philip Neri daily lit a candle before the image of Savonarola, did he not believe perhaps too ingenuously that the friar of St. Mark's had imitated Paul's attitude toward Peter at Antioch? When Jerome expressed so roughly his disagreements with Ambrose, Augustine, and others, did he not think perhaps he was imitating Paul's attitude toward Barnabas?

In reality, Paul's is a many-faceted soul and in each facet he reflects, like a prism, his great ideal of the Christ Jesus. He is a man composed of many men, all in the service of Christ.

Today, the more cerebral scholars study Paul especially as a theorist, seeking out his abstract ideas. This is, perhaps, neither the most nor the best of Paul. Christianity, in every age, has conquered men not through abstract ideas alone — as any system of philosophy might — but above all through individual lives. In these, the fundamental ideas of Christianity which have won men have shown resplendent in the practical realities of daily living.

The great spirits which have had the widest influence in the spread of Christianity, especially in critical periods, taught not only with theory but with example. Benedict of Norcia set few abstract ideas in writing, but he practiced them himself and these drew after him numberless throngs in every century and in every region. Francis of Assisi wrote even less; but his ideas shone forth in his example, and his thin shoulders supported the edifice of the Church, threatening to crumble. In periods almost equally decisive, Philip Neri and John Bosco wrote little with the pen, but they wrote much with their deeds, stamping their ideas in the souls of others. Thus it was, long before, with Paul, who wrote very little in comparison with what he accomplished throughout his life. In this, too, Paul, and all those who came after him, were imitators of Jesus, who left nothing in writing and — as Luke says with calculated effect — "began to do and to teach" (Acts 1:1). For Christ, as for his disciples, teaching consists above all in doing.

Paul's one true book, therefore, is his life, in which his works are the pages and his epistles a few explanatory footnotes scattered here and there. The subject of his book is contained in his own words: "Be imitators of me as I am of Christ" (1 Cor. 11:1). It might well bear the classic title, therefore, *De imitatione Christi,* but with the name of the author written as it is at the beginning of the collected epistles: "Paul the servant of Jesus Christ" (Rom. 1:1).

General Index

The numbers in this and the following index refer to paragraphs, not to pages.

Index of Scriptural References

OLD TESTAMENT

GENESIS
2:7, 488
9:3–4, 360
Chap. 10, 223 *n*.10
14:15, 32
15:6, 508, 516
27:22, 650

EXODUS
1:15, 241
7:11, 241
7:22, 241
16:18, 240
21:1 ff, 50 *n*.7
22:28, 549
34:33–35, 240

LEVITICUS
17:10–14, 360
24:14, 256
24:16, 256

NUMBERS
6:2–21, 448
21:14, 261
22:22, 241

DEUTERONOMY
27:26, 508
30:11–14, 240

JOSUE
1:8, 232
2:15, 290

1 KINGS
17:21, 231, 527
18:17, 261
19:12, 290

2 KINGS
4:34–36, 527

PSALMS
18:5, 240
21:22, 668
119 [118], 79

ECCLESIASTES
12:11, 264 *n*.2

WISDOM
5:18 ff, 233

ECCLESIASTICUS
33:31–32, 50 *n*.7
39:1–3, 78

ISAIAS
2:2–3, 262
11:4, 441
11:5, 233
28:11 ff, 223
Chap. 53, 274
59:17, 233

JEREMIAS
1:10, 261
1:18, 261

EZECHIEL
13:10 ff, 549
34:5 ff, 410

DANIEL
7:8 ff, 442
11:38 ff, 442

MICHEAS
4:1–2, 262

2 MACHABEES
4:30 ff, 6

NEW TESTAMENT

MATTHEW
5:17, 351
9:37–38, 313
10:14, 337
10:18, 668
15:24, 311

MARK
3:11, 386
5:20, 32

6:17, 564
7:31, 32
13:9, 668
14:15, 306

LUKE
1:1, 300
1:4, 101
2:40, 295
2:52, 295

4:16–30, 331
12:37, 434
13:16, 200 *n*.4
21:12, 668
22:8, 306

JOHN
1:14 and 16, 621 *n*.7
1:15 ff, 453
3:23, 453

535